TimeOut

South West England

timeout.com/southwestengland

Penguin Books

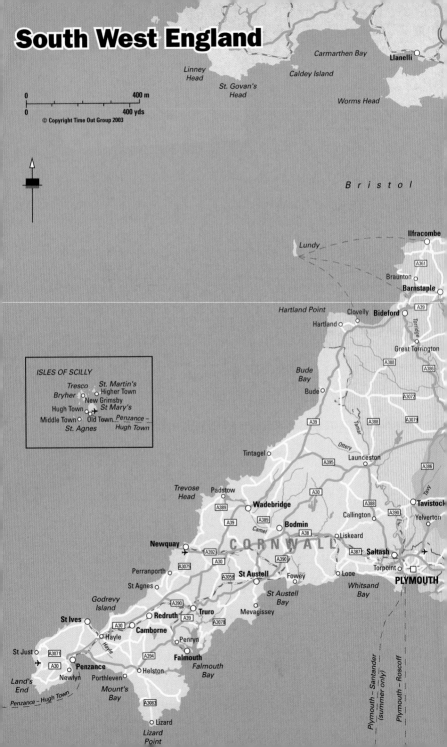

South West England

© Copyright Time Out Group 2003

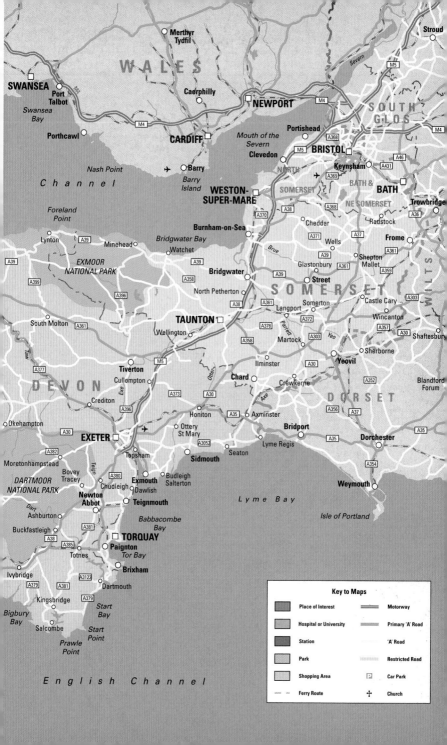

PENGUIN BOOKS

Published by the Penguin Group
Penguin Books Ltd, 80 Strand, London WC2R ORL ,England
Penguin Group (USA), Inc., 375 Hudson Street, New York, New York 10014, USA
Penguin Books Australia Ltd, 250 Camberwell Road, Camberwell, Victoria 3124, Australia
Penguin Books Canada Ltd, 10 Alcorn Avenue, Toronto, Ontario, Canada M4V 3B2
Penguin Books (NZ) Ltd, cnr Rosedale and Airborne Roads, Albany, Auckland, New Zealand

Penguin Books Ltd, Registered Offices: Harmondsworth, Middlesex, England

First published 2003
10 9 8 7 6 5 4 3 2 1

Colour reprographics by Icon, Crowne House, 56-58 Southwark Street, London SE1 1UN
Printed and bound by Cayfosa-Quebecor, Ctra. de Caldes, Km 3 08 130 Sta, Perpètua de Mogoda, Barcelona, Spain

Edited and designed by
Time Out Guides Limited
Universal House
251 Tottenham Court Road
London W1T 7AB
Tel + 44 (0)20 7813 3000
Fax + 44 (0)20 7813 6001
Email guides@timeout.com
www.timeout.com

Editorial

Editor Sophie Blacksell
Deputy Editor Lesley McCave
Listings Researchers Shane Armstrong, Eli Dryden, Holly Furneaux, Helen Gilchrist, Cathy Limb
Proofreader Tamsin Shelton
Indexer Selena Cox

Editorial Director Peter Fiennes
Series Editor Ruth Jarvis
Deputy Series Editor Jonathan Cox
Guides Co-ordinator Anna Norman

Design

Group Art Director John Oakey
Art Director Mandy Martin
Art Editor Scott Moore
Senior Designer Tracey Ridgewell
Junior Designers Astrid Kogler, Sam Lands
Digital Imager Dan Conway
Ad Make-up Glen Impey, Charlotte Blyth
Picture Editor Kerri Littlefield
Acting Picture Editor Kit Burnet
Acting Deputy Picture Editor Martha Houghton
Picture Desk Trainee Bella Wood

Advertising

Group Commercial Director Lesley Gill
Sales Director Mark Phillips
International Sales Manager Ross Canadé
Advertisement Sales (South West England) Emilie Hunter
Advertising Assistant Sabrina Ancilleri

Administration

Chairman Tony Elliott
Chief Operating Officer Kevin Ellis
Managing Director Mike Hardwick
Group Financial Director Richard Waterlow
Group Marketing Director Christine Cort
Marketing Manager Mandy Martinez
US Publicity & Marketing Associate Rosella Albanese
Group General Manager Nichola Coulthard
Guides Production Director Mark Lamond
Production Controller Samantha Furniss
Accountant Sarah Bostock

Features in this guide were written and researched by:

Introduction Sophie Blacksell. **Best of the South West** Sophie Blacksell. **History** Anna Britten (*Local heroes* Paul Newman; *Key events* Lesley McCave). **South West Today** Margaret Jones, Alex Pykett (*Long hair and ley lines* Anna Britten). **Art** Margaret Jones. **Literature** Margaret Jones (*Local heroes* Anna Britten). **Great Outdoors** Andrew Shields, Sue Viccars. **Bristol & Bath Introduction** Sophie Blacksell. **Bristol** Sophie Blacksell, Julian Owen (*Say what?* Derek Robinson). **Bath** Anna Britten (*City walk* Sophie Blacksell). **Somerset Introduction** Sophie Blacksell. **North Somerset** Andrew Shields. **Central & South Somerset** Anna Britten, Paul Gibbs (*Festival fever* Julian Owen; *Drink up* Paul Gibbs, Andrew Shields; *Say what?* Penny Blacksell). **Exmoor** Rodney Legg. **Devon Introduction** Sophie Blacksell. **North & Mid Devon** Alison Boyle, Peter Fiennes (*Surf check* Sam Le Quesne; *Tuck in* Penny Blacksell). **Exeter & East Devon** Holly Noseda (*Bend it like Uri* Paul Gibbs). **Dartmoor** Mike Hallam. **South Devon** Simon Cooke, Mike Hallam, Elly Welch. **Plymouth & Around** Simon Cooke (*Local heroes* Elly Welch). **Cornwall Introduction** Sophie Blacksell, Alex Pykett. **East Cornwall** Willa Bailey (*Tuck in* Anna Bayly; *Say what?* Ismay Atkins). **South Cornwall** Sue Smith. **From the Lizard to Land's End** Sue Smith, Amanda White (*Surf check* Sam Le Quesne). **The North Coast** Paul Newman (*Surf check* Sam Le Quesne). **Isles of Scilly** Helen Gilchrist, Lesley McCave, Amanda White. **Directory** Sophie Blacksell, Paul Gibbs.

Maps Maps by: JS Graphics (john@jsgraphics.co.uk). All maps are based on material supplied by Lovell Johns Ltd except Bristol, which was supplied by Bristol Tourism and Conference Bureau.

Photography by Héloïse Bergman Simon Cooke and Alys Tomlinson except the following: pp10, 13, 30 AKG; p17 SS Great Britain Museum; p18 Burgh Island Hotel; p19 AP; p25, 29 Courtesy of the Tate Gallery St Ives, p27(left) Courtesy of the Barbara Hepworth Museum and Sculpture Garden; p187 Westcountry Pictures; p63, 2001 Aardman Animations Ltd; p42 North Devon Marketing Bureau; p3 Jane Austen's Regency World; p136 Broomhill Sculpture Gardens; p244 Kerrier District Council; p260 Courtesy Belgrave Gallery; p163 Sidmouth Festival; p189 South Devon Railway; p288 Axiom Photographic Agency Ltd. The following pictures were courtesy of the National Trust Photographic Library, photographers listed: p99 Andrew Butler; p106 Rupert Truman; p118 Magnus Rew; p124 Joe Cornish; p267 Andrew Marshal; p170 Chris Gascoigne; p199 Derek Croucher.

The Editor would like to thank Robert Andrews, Jan Barwick, Hilary Binding, Emily Blacksell, Penny and Simon Blacksell, Simon Butler, Peterjon Cresswell, the Clifton Bookshop, Countryside Books, Christie Daugherty, Sally Davies, Anna Davis and Lucy Shrouder at the Massey Partnership, Giles Ingram and Grace Pope at Bristol Tourism, Roger Jones, the Lugger Hotel in Portloe, Claire McGaffey, James Mitchell, Cath Phillips, Ros Sales, Nige Tassell, David Taylor and Emma Charman, South West Tourism, and especially, Simon Jones.

Contents

Introduction

Beyond the reach of London's force field, a more subtle but equally potent magnetism begins to exert itself, drawing you south and west towards the setting sun.

Somerset, Devon and Cornwall have been attracting visitors for generations with the promise that here they will be one step removed from the rest of the country. If you were in any doubt that England's most south-westerly counties are – literally – out on a limb, just take a look at the shape of the peninsula: at its hip is the former merchant city of Bristol, by far the biggest urban centre in the region, while at its tip Land's End stretches a toe towards the sun-kissed Isles of Scilly. In between are landscapes of extraordinary variety and beauty that provide a natural playground for every kind of outdoor activity: wild moorland, gentle hills, luxuriant valleys and, most notably, more than 500 miles (800 kilometres) of magnificent coastline.

From the inundated flatlands of the Somerset Levels to the serrated cliffs of the North Cornish coast, this is a region whose geography and history has been shaped by the sea. The Gulf Stream conspires with varied geology to bring you some of the best beaches in the UK: rocky cliff-wrapped coves, gently shelving pine-backed bays, huge flat surfing strands and even some golden shores that will have you checking the time zone to confirm that, yes, you really are in England.

However, the British weather being what is – shall we say capricious? – you'll be wanting some alternatives to your beach towel. And the South West's got these, too – in abundance. Fancy a city break? You couldn't do better than Bath, a supermodel of a town with top-flight restaurants and shops. Somewhere a bit more metropolitan, perhaps? Try Bristol, a long-overlooked destination that's now pulling in the punters to its contemporary harbourside and funky cultural venues. Bit too urban for you? Then there's Exeter, a manageable medieval city that provides easy access to Dartmoor and the coast.

Beyond these major centres, don't be fooled into thinking you're entering some rural time warp. The South West practically invented the modern music festival in Britain, with Glastonbury in Somerset still heading the national line-up. Devon has arts centres and millionaire yachts to offset its cream teas and thatched cottages, while Cornwall shows off its rediscovered pride with the extraordinary Eden Project, an unstoppable surf culture and an effervescent art scene. What's more, all over the region you'll find historic houses, glorious gardens, ancient sites and some of the best and freshest food and drink in the UK, served straight from the sea or the field on to your plate.

But above all it's the chilled-out, easy-living atmosphere that will win you over. Crawling along the motorway at a snail's pace can be a frustrating start to your holiday. But as you jostle for position with swaying caravans, packed family hatchbacks and campervans loaded with surfboards, take comfort from the fact that you're following in the footsteps of mariners, pilgrims, artists and writers, all of whom were captivated by this region's unfailing allure. And as you venture further west you'll notice your shoulders relax, your head clear, your breathing deepen – and then you'll know you've finally arrived.

ABOUT TIME OUT GUIDES

This is the first edition of the *Time Out South West England Guide*, one of the expanding series of Time Out guides produced by the people behind London and New York's successful listings magazines. Our guides are researched and written by resident experts who have striven to provide you with all the most up-to-date information you'll need to explore the region or read up on its background, whether you're a regular visitor or a first-time tourist.

THE LOWDOWN ON THE LISTINGS

Above all, we've tried to make this book as useful as possible. Addresses, telephone numbers, websites, opening times and admission prices have all been included in the listings, checked and correct as we went to press. However, owners and managers can change their arrangements at any time, and they often do. Before you go out of your way, we'd advise you to check prices, opening times and other particulars. While every effort has been made to ensure the accuracy of the

colour maps. Please note that in the case of North Somerset and North-east Somerset, we have arranged the chapters according to the lie of the land rather than following official council boundaries (*see p94*). We hope that this structure will help you to understand the region's layout and to find its most interesting sights.

TELEPHONE NUMBERS
All telephone numbers printed in this guide include the relevant area code, which must be included if you are dialling from outside the local catchment area. Numbers that start 09 are charged at a premium rate, while those preceded by 0800 or 0808 can be called free of charge from within the UK; some of these numbers are obtainable from outside the UK, but are likely to be charged at the international rate.

ESSENTIAL INFORMATION
For all the practical information you might need when visiting South West England – including accommodation options, visa and customs information, details of transport to and around the region and a list of emergency numbers, as well as tips on books and websites for further reference, turn to the Directory chapter at the back of this guide. It starts on page 291.

MAPS
Full-colour maps are located throughout the guide. They include an overview of South West England on page ii, detailed maps of each county and street maps for the cities of Bristol, Bath, Exeter and Plymouth. Map references have been provided in the Bristol chapter, indicating the grid reference at which a specific venue can be found on the city map.

LET US KNOW WHAT YOU THINK
We hope that you enjoy the *Time Out South West England Guide*, and we'd like to know what you think of it. We welcome tips for places that you consider we should include in future editions and take note of your criticism of our choices. There's a reader's reply card at the back of this book for your feedback, or you can email us at guides@timeout.com.

information contained in this guide, the publishers cannot accept responsibility for any errors it may contain.

PRICES AND PAYMENT
We have noted where major venues such as museums, hotels and restaurants accept the following credit cards: American Express (**AmEx**), Diners Club (**DC**), MasterCard (**MC**) and Visa (**V**). Many will also accept other cards, such as Delta, Switch or JCB.

The prices we've listed in this guide should be treated as guidelines, not gospel. If prices vary wildly from those we've quoted, please write and let us know. We aim to give the best and most up-to-date advice, so we want to know if you've been badly treated or overcharged.

THE LIE OF THE LAND
In order to make the book as easy to navigate as possible, we have divided it into sections corresponding to the counties of Somerset, Devon and Cornwall, with the cities of Bristol and Bath given their own section at the start of the guide. Within each section you'll find chapters covering distinct areas of the county, plus features on subjects of particular interest, extensive travel information and detailed

There is an online version of this guide, as well as weekly events listings for 35 international cities, at www.timeout.com

FOR YOUR FREE OFFICIAL GUIDE T
WATERSPORTS CALL 0870 442 088

SWH₂O

South West Watersports

www.sw-watersports.com

SURF, SAIL, DIVE, WAKEBOARD, WATERSK
WINDSURF, COASTEER, CANOE, KAYAK...
WATERSPORT. ITS IN OUR NATURE.

EUROPEAN UNION
European Social Fund

South West
England

In Context

Salcombe Estuary

Best of the South West

The question is, where to start?

SIGHTS, SCENERY AND SEASIDE

If the seaside is the prime motivation for visiting the South West, you've got dozens of beaches to choose from, each with their own characteristics and appeal; for our pick of some of the best, *see p41*. Somerset, on the whole, can't compete with Devon and Cornwall on this score, although Exmoor's rocky coves can be great for swimming. Linking the beaches, cliffs and headlands is the **South West Coast Path** (*see p38*), a highlight of the region that you should take time to explore. Inland, the two **National Parks** have the most dramatic scenery, although it's also worth exploring some of Devon's hidden valleys and roaming through the primeval landscape of the Somerset Levels.

The region's gardens are another highlight, particularly **Hestercombe Gardens** in Somerset (*see p113*), the **Lost Gardens of Heligan in Cornwall** (*see p235*) and the **Abbey Gardens** on Tresco in the Scillies (*see p287*). Eclipsing them all, however, is the **Eden Project** (*see p233*), which takes the concept of conservation to a whole new level.

You'll find the most impressive museums in the region's cities and larger towns: check out the **British Empire & Commonwealth**

Museum (*see p57*) in Bristol; the **Royal Albert Memorial Museum** in Exeter (*see p151*) and the **Royal Cornwall Museum** in Truro (*see p237*). Bath has a particularly high-quality selection, including the **American Museum** (*see p83*), the **Building of Bath Museum** (*see p82*) and the **Museum of Costume** (*see p82*). Kids, however, are likely to prefer the gadgetry of the **@tBristol** complex (*see p50*), the underwater marvels of Plymouth's **National Marine Aquarium** (*see p204*) and the world-class boaty displays at the **National Maritime Museum Cornwall** in Falmouth (*see p240*).

Once you've ticked off the museums, there are essential historic (and prehistoric) sites demanding your attention, from **Bronze Age remains** on Dartmoor, Bodmin Moor, west Cornwall and the Scillies to the unmissable **Roman Baths** (*see p77*), **Wells Cathedral** (*see p102*) and a bevy of grand castles and estates. **Montacute House** in Somerset (*see p110*), **Saltram House** (*see p205*) and **Castle Drogo** (*see p171*) in Devon, and **Lanhydrock House** (*see p218*) and ruined **Tintagel** in Cornwall (*see p280*) are some of our favourites.

EAT, DRINK, SHOP

Bristol and **Bath** have the most varied eating and drinking venues, with Bristol winning in the style bar stakes and Bath coming up trumps for haute cuisine. Elsewhere, there's plenty of top-notch nosh to keep gourmands happy, with fresh fish and organically reared meat being particular highlights. Foodie hotspots include **Dartmouth** (*see p193*), **Penzance** (*see p250*) and **St Ives** (*see p259*), and for a real gourmet treat, there's always Rick Stein's renowned seafood empire in **Padstow** (*see p276*). Many pubs also offer an increasingly ambitious range of food, the best of which will be sourced from local suppliers. In Cornwall, a proper **pasty** (*see p219*) provides the perfect picnic food, and in Devon, be sure to indulge in a farmhouse **cream tea** (*see p148*).

If you're self-catering, don't miss the opportunity to buy fish straight from the boat in the coastal fishing ports and your groceries at the region's increasingly prevalent **farmers' markets**. Local markets are also a good place to pick up a wide range of arts and crafts, although if you're looking for the best of the region's contemporary art scene, visit one of the independent galleries in **Bath** (*see p78*), **Exeter** (*see p156*), **Dartmouth** (*see p194*), **Penzance** (*see p250*), **Falmouth** (*see p240*) and, especially, **St Ives** (*see p259*).

ACCOMMODATION

The South West has a (not entirely unjust) reputation for guesthouses with more chintz than sense and hotels that bear an uncanny resemblance to *Fawlty Towers*, but these are far from being the only options. At the top end, country-house hotels offer the chance to play at being lord or lady of the manor, with acres of private land (often with fishing rights) on the outside, acres of oak panelling on the inside, and superlative cuisine thrown in for good measure (**Gidleigh Park** on Dartmoor is a prime example; *see p172*). The equivalent on the coast are the grand resort hotels, like the **Imperial** in Torquay (*see p185*) or the **Carlyon Bay** near Mevagissey (*see p232*), while in Bath you'll find a clutch of luxury choices that make the most of the city's architecture and wealthy visitors (*see p90*).

More surprising, perhaps, are the trendy society boltholes like **Babington House** in Somerset (*see p104*) and **Hotel Tresanton** (*see p239*) in St Mawes, and a new breed of chic, contemporary hotels, including the **Lugger** in Portloe (*see p239*), **Edmund's House** in Padstow (*see p280*) and **Hotel Barcelona** in Exeter (*see p157*), which wouldn't look out of place in a modern style mag.

Look out, too, for independent guesthouses and authentic inns that offer something more than the usual bed and breakfast deals: floral-free rooms; contemporary facilities; organic breakfasts; freshly cooked local produce and welcoming but unobtrusive service; we particularly like **Pennard Hill Farm** on the edge of the Mendips (*see p96*); **Fingals Hotel** near Dartmouth (*see p197*) and the **Summer House Restaurant & Rooms** in Penzance (*see p253*).

ARTS AND ENTERTAINMENT

The South West's ancient heritage springs into action at a series of arcane rituals that offer a unique insight into the life of the region. Some of the most compelling include **tar barrelling** in Ottery St Mary (*see p166*), the **Obby Oss Festival** in Padstow (*see p276*) and the utterly bizarre **Earl of Rone procession** in Combe Martin (*see p141*). Summer sees a host of more contemporary events take pride of place on the calendar. **Glastonbury Festival** (*see p108*) is the big one, but for a more laid-back (and significantly cheaper) taste of the festival vibe, try **Ashton Court** (*see p60*) or the unexpected charisma of Sidmouth's **International Music Festival** (*see p163*). There are also high-profile, 'high culture' events in **Bath** (*see p87*) and **Fowey** (*see p228*), a fab fish festival in **Newlyn** (*see p251*) and plenty of raucous surf- and beach-based events around **Newquay** (*see p272*). Summer is also the time for various one-off outdoor concerts and theatrical performances, often staged in the grounds of country estates, but taken to the max in the seaside setting of the **Minack Theatre** (*see p255*) in Cornwall.

Bristol's vibrant cultural scene flourishes throughout the year, with nationally acclaimed theatre at both the **Old Vic** (*see p56*) and the **Tobacco Factory** (*see p70*), a host of cutting-edge performances and exhibitions at the essential **Arnolfini** (*see p50*), and a variety of DJ and live music venues catering for the city's insatiable clubbers. In contrast Bath has a rather stuffy reputation, although the **Theatre Royal** (*see p79*) hosts national touring companies of a reliably high standard, and you'll find some decent local bands in the backstreet bars and clubs (*see p86* **Going underground**).

Exeter's **Northcott Theatre** (*see p156*) is the major theatre venue in Devon but the heart of the county's cultural life is further south at **Dartington Hall** (*see p192*), which puts on an eclectic programme of arts-based performances, courses and events. Further west, experimental **Kneehigh Theatre Company** (*see p237*) is making waves in Cornwall.

Lanyon Quoit near Penzance.

History

Brave mariners, thwarted kings and revolutionary inventors: the South West has seen 'em all.

FROM CAVES TO HILL FORTS

The first proof of human existence in the area comes from as long ago as the Palaeolithic period (600,000-10,000 BC) in the form of remains found in Kent's Cavern in Torquay. However, sustained archeological evidence starts in the Neolithic period (4,000-3,000 BC), when Stone Age tribes from continental Europe settled throughout the South West and gradually began to clear ancient woodlands for farming. These tribes left behind primitive tools and weapons, and a number of burial chambers, known as quoits, which can be found on Bodmin Moor and around Land's End. A 6,000-year-old pathway of hazel and willow recently discovered on the Somerset Levels bears witness to their early attempts to master the land.

Between 2,500 BC and AD 43 the South West, including the Isles of Scilly, was occupied by Celtic tribes – mainly the Dumnonii – who arrived from France and the Netherlands. These Bronze Age people lived in small farming settlements, such as Grimspound on Dartmoor and extracted tin and copper. Their mysterious stone circles, burial mounds, menhirs and standing stones are scattered all over the region, particularly on Dartmoor and Bodmin Moor, and further west at Land's End and on

the Isles of Scilly. One of the most important sites, though, is at Stanton Drew, Somerset, where the stone circle is thought to be aligned with the rising and setting of the sun and moon.

During the subsequent Iron Age, warring Celtic tribes built hill forts, such as Brent Knoll and Cadbury Castle in Somerset and Hembury Fort in Devon, and occupied lake villages on the watery Somerset Levels. Tall, tough, blond party animals, they also introduced the drystone wall, marking out rectangular plots of land that they ploughed with oxen. These ancient field systems can still be seen on Dartmoor and around the well-preserved Iron Age village of Chysauster in west Cornwall.

ROMAN ROAMINGS

Roman merchants had traded wares in the Severn area from as early as 54 BC, so by the time of the Roman invasion in AD 43 Emperor Claudius had already had his ear bent about the favourable conditions and rich minerals of the South West. On arrival in England, the Romans seized a fertile, sheltered area named Abona around what is now Avonmouth, and developed the natural thermal waters of Bath into a major spa called Aquae Sulis.

The number of remains (especially villas) around Bristol, Bath and Somerset suggest that these areas fared particularly well under the Romans. The famous Fosse Way from Lincoln to Exeter shows the importance of smooth transport to and from the South West, with Ilchester serving as a military crossing on the route and later growing into a significant Roman town. Silver-rich lead was transported along the Fosse Way from mines in the Mendips.

In contrast, the Romans regarded the far west as a land of barbarians and left it largely alone. They certainly ventured into Cornwall to mine tin like their Bronze Age predecessors had done before them, and even travelled as far as the Isles of Scilly, but the great Roman roads ended at the military fort of Isca Dumnoniorum (present-day Exeter).

Local heroes King Arthur

Romantic legends of the Celtic King Arthur abound in Wales, Scotland and Northern England, but his dragon pennant flies highest over the West Country. Welsh scholar Geoffrey of Monmouth first promoted the association in *History of the Kings of Britain* (c1130). Arthur, he wrote, was the son of the British King Uther Pendragon, who developed a mad passion for Igerna, wife of the Duke of Cornwall. Using the wizardry of Merlin, Uther disguised himself as the duke in order to make love to Igerna at Tintagel Castle, as a result of which Arthur was conceived.

According to Geoffrey, the boy grows up to become a great warrior and king, driving out the invading Saxons from overseas. Geoffrey places Bath as the site of Arthur's famous victory at Mount Badon (AD 516), where, with the aid of a magical sword, Caliburn (Excalibur), forged in the Isle of Avalon, he defeats the Saxons. After a further series of conquests, he hears that his wicked nephew Mordred has made an alliance with the Saxons, so he proceeds to Camlann (AD 542) and fights Mordred's army. Arthur receives a deadly wound in the battle but no one sees him die, for he is spirited away to Avalon.

Geoffrey's tales, together with subsequent elaborations by men like Wace, Spenser, Malory, Tennyson and White, have bewitched generations of dreamers and grail-seekers, spreading a topography of Arthur over the West Country. If Tintagel was Arthur's birthplace, then the Iron Age hill fort of Cadbury Castle in Somerset was the palace of 'Camelot' where the king jousted and held court – although Camelford in Cornwall also vies for this honour. Slaughterbridge, near Camelford, was the site of the Battle of Camlann, and the lake into which Sir Bedivere was ordered to return Excalibur by the wounded king was either the dreary Dozmary Pool on Bodmin Moor or the weird, entrancing lagoon of Loe Pool, near Helston. Finally, the Isle of Avalon, to which the dying king returned, was Glastonbury, whose famous Tor, looming over the marshy plains of Somerset, was always regarded as sacred.

In 1190 the monks of Glastonbury Abbey dug up a coffin in the abbey grounds fashioned from a hollow log. Inside were the bones of a gigantic man and a lead cross inscribed with Arthur's name, together with the skeleton of a woman with a mass of yellow hair, thought to be Guinevere. Although this 'discovery' seems to bear out the Arthur myth, it was more likely a cynical opportunity to draw attention and funds to the abbey, which had burned down in 1184.

The Romans' occupation coincided with the spread of Christianity to the British Isles. A legend dating from the 13th century has it that under the Romans, the town of Glastonbury was twice visited by the merchant Joseph of Arimethea. On the first occasion he is said to have brought his young nephew, Jesus, along with him, returning after Christ's death to bury the chalice or Holy Grail, which had been used at the Last Supper, under Glastonbury Tor.

By the middle of the fourth century AD the Roman structure was crumbling, the legions having left England to defend Rome against barbarians at home. Soon even Bath, the jewel of Roman Britain, was deserted and falling into ruin.

'Wessex had resisted the Vikings fiercely but seemed less fussed about the next band of gatecrashers.'

ARTHUR, ALFRED AND THE ANGLO-SAXONS

In AD 300 the South West braced itself against invasions by the Angles and the Saxons from Germany. For a while Somerset provided a barrier between the invaders and the Celts, who formed an enclave of resistance in the far west. During the Dark Ages Christianity in Britain was swept away by the pagan beliefs of the Germanic invaders, but in Cornwall it survived and flourished thanks to pilgrims and saints from Wales and Ireland, who established a rich tradition of Christian Celtic culture. It is from this period that the quasi-mythical King Arthur emerged as a great Celtic leader, fighting legendary battles against the encroaching Saxons (*see p10* **Local heroes**).

By the eighth century the Christianity of the far west had spread to the Saxon newcomers, thanks to monks and missionaries like St Boniface of Crediton (680-755). Saxon King Ine (688-726) built the first stone abbey at Glastonbury and work began on draining the Somerset marshes, great stretches of which were still covered in tidal water from the Bristol Channel. By the end of the Anglo-Saxon era, the kingdom of Wessex covered most of the west of England (with the exception of Cornwall), and the monarch of Wessex was regarded as the most important ruler in the country.

From the eighth to 11th centuries, the West Country held out tenaciously against Viking incursions, with fierce skirmishes between Anglo-Saxons and Danish pirates taking place around Bridgwater Bay in Somerset.

The Wessex King Alfred the Great (849-99), whose royal palace was in Cheddar, kept the region independent of Viking occupation throughout his reign, building his army headquarters on the low hill of Athelney near Taunton from where he routed a Danish army at Southampton.

His successors continued the theme: in 918 a Danish war party led by Ohtor – whose name is believed to live on in the Somerset towns of Othery and Oath – landed secretly by night at Watchet and Porlock, but was sorely thrashed by the locals, and in 930 Vikings invaded the Isles of Scilly only to be sent packing by Alfred's grandson, King Athelstan (924-40; incredibly, the only monarch to visit the islands until Queen Victoria in 1847).

The continued threat of Viking invasion encouraged warring Anglo-Saxon factions to unite behind one leader. In 959 the Northumbrian and Mercian king, Edgar, became King of Wessex, and in 973 was crowned the first formal King of England at a ceremony in Bath Abbey. Wessex had resisted the Vikings as fiercely as it could, but seemed markedly less fussed about the next band of gatecrashers…

ROYAL WRANGLING

King Harold, Earl of Wessex, was defeated by Norman invaders led by William the Conqueror at the Battle of Hastings in 1066. William was crowned King of England shortly afterwards, and completed his domination of the country in 1068 with the fall of Exeter.

The Normans built strongholds throughout the region – at Dunster and Taunton in Somerset; Totnes, Exeter, Okehampton and Plympton in Devon, and at Launceston and Restormel in Cornwall – as bases to thwart potential local insurrection. There were certainly small pockets of rebellion in the South West – notably from the powerful Godwin family who, in 1068, launched a failed rebellion at Montacute in Yeovil – but, overall the Normans met with little resistance. In fact, when the three sons of the defeated Harold landed with forces at Avonmouth in 1069, they were seen off by locals.

From the Domesday Book it is clear that much of the West Country at this time was in the power of the churches: Glastonbury Abbey controlled an eighth of Somerset, while Cleeve Abbey owned land along the Bristol Channel from Somerset to Cornwall. In addition, a large portion of the region was made up of royal hunting forests in the Mendips, the Quantocks and on Exmoor and Dartmoor. When William's half-brother, Roger of Mortain, became the first Earl of Cornwall, his lands extended through

Cornwall, Devon, Somerset and Gloucestershire. In the 14th century this earldom became the Duchy of Cornwall and was awarded to Edward III's son, the Black Prince. The title and lands are still traditionally granted to the monarch's eldest son (currently Prince Charles), and the Duchy still exerts widespread influence in the South West.

The Norman royal succession, however, proved less easy to settle. In 1139 Bristol hosted an alternative royal court for Queen Matilda, granddaughter of William the Conqueror and heir to the English throne, who had been passed over in favour of her cousin Stephen. Matilda invaded the country from France, and ruled as queen from her Bristol throne for eight years, before Stephen wrested the crown back in 1148. He was later succeeded by Matilda's son, Henry II (1154-89), who incorporated Bristol when he became king in gratitude at the town's support of his mother.

Bristol was also unusual in siding with Henry's second son, friendless baddie King John (1199-1216). John kept Princess Eleanor of Brittany locked up in Bristol Castle for 40 years, parading her around around the battlements once a year to allay any suspicions of foul play. After the first Barons' Revolt, when John was forced to sign the 1215 Magna Carta, Bristol was one of the few places to tut sympathetically.

Amid such political in-fighting, it is perhaps surprising that the Normans had time to start on the South West's great cathedrals at Bristol, Bath, Wells and Exeter, and to rebuild the magnificent abbey at Glastonbury, which had burned down in 1184.

'The Black Death had a devastating effect on the sparsely populated, rural West Country.'

SHEEP, FISH AND TIN

While the cathedrals are the most obvious monuments of Norman achievement in the South West, Somerset's medieval parish churches are perhaps equally significant.

Bootylicious

Romanticised in the novels of Daphne du Maurier, smuggling began in the South West in the Middle Ages, when customs duties began to be levied on incoming and outgoing goods. Opportunistic locals seized the chance to supplement their fishing income, and from the 16th to the mid 19th century the illicit trade enjoyed a boom in Devon and Cornwall. Mevagissey even specialised in building fast boats for the purpose.

The variegated coastline of the far South West – its cliffs, caves and coves – provided the ideal terrain for the covert and illegal practice, which was meticulously executed. Smugglers would steal across the Channel in fishing smacks, and load up on brandy, wine, spices, silk, lace, tea and spirits in exchange for raw wool. Smugglers' wives would dilute the spirits back onshore before handing over the booty to a waiting team on land to transport by pack horse to its new owner. If the activity was threatened with discovery by the excise men, crates of waterproof goods could be hurled overboard at the last minute, to be collected at a later date – when the coast was clear, so to speak.

In 1784 the South West's favourite illegal sideline was dealt a blow. Pitt the Younger estimated that around half of all the tea drunk in England (and it was a lot, even back then) had been smuggled into the country. He therefore abolished or lowered many duties, thus reducing the demand for smuggled goods. Furthermore, as the centuries of intermittent war and coastal blockades against France, Spain and America drew to a close, the Royal Navy was free to patrol its own coasts in support of the coastguard and 'revenue' men. To the dismay of the Cornish, one in three smugglers was apprehended, and their carefully crafted boats were chopped up for firewood.

Smugglers were forced to become ever more tenacious and creative as the decades passed. During the 19th century many smuggling communities in South West England resorted to the precious loopholes of the excise-exempt Channel Islands or the French port of Roscoff. However, increasing anti-smuggling legislation, an organised coastguard and ever-tightening customs restrictions all meant that the days of small boats making midnight landings in misty coves were numbered. Modern-day smuggling is a markedly less romantic business of ferries and airports, car boots and bodily orifices. It's enough to make Daphne du Maurier weep.

The symbolic overthrow of throne and altar by Oliver Cromwell in the **Civil War**. *See p15.*

Featuring impressive Perpendicular towers and elaborately carved bench ends, they were built on the wealth of the wool trade and are striking evidence of the region's sheep-led prosperity throughout the Middle Ages.

From as early as the Iron Age, the fertile pastures of Somerset and Devon had provided an ideal habitat for sheep farming, which formed the impetus for local cloth production and trade during the Anglo-Saxon and Norman eras. Under Edward III (1327-77) the wool industry was given a boost by the immigration of Flemish weavers, dyers and fullers. (Later immigrants also introduced the art of lace-making to East Devon.) Nearly every village in Somerset and Devon had its own sheep market and wool fair, and by the end of the 14th century Somerset was producing a quarter of England's wool. Despite the Hundred Years War with France (1337-1453), cloth became the region's greatest export, resulting in prosperity for the merchant classes in Devon's market towns and south coast ports.

However, life was still very tough for the peasants. The Black Death, which is thought to have wiped out over one third of England's population between 1348 and 1350, had a particularly devastating effect on the sparsely populated, rural West Country. And in the following decades, further plagues, price rises and bad harvests ensured that the Peasants' Revolt of 1381 found widespread support throughout the region.

In coastal areas, however, other sources of income were available. From the late 13th century, fishing was supplemented by the illegal but highly profitable business of smuggling (*see p12* **Bootylicious**), while in some ports, opportunist locals engaged in out-and-out piracy. In 1403 a band of Devon part-timers ambushed France to avenge an earlier Breton attack on Plymouth, while in Cornwall, the rebellious 'Fowey Gallants' continued to raid the coasts of France and Spain long after the Hundred Years War had officially ended. When a royal messenger was sent to inform them that England was no longer at war with the French, the Gallants sent him back minus an ear, with word that, actually, Fowey still was.

Away from the coasts, Cornish prosperity was based not on wool but on tin. In the 12th century the industry had been awarded a royal charter by Richard I (1189-99); Helston, Liskeard, Lostwithiel and Truro became stannary towns (from the Latin *stannum* for tin) and were joined in the following century by the Devon towns of Tavistock, Plympton, Ashburton and Chagstock. In recognition of the metal's importance to the medieval economy, stannary towns were given special privileges with legal jurisdiction over all matters relating to tin. To test the quality of the tin, a corner – or *coign* in French – was broken off, weighed and stamped. The English word 'coin' originates from this process.

TUDOR REBELS

The Tudor period kicked off with what would be the first of many daring marine expeditions originating in the South West. In 1496, with the financial backing of Henry VII, John Cabot (1450-99) – Genoese by birth – sailed across the Atlantic from Bristol in a boat manned by local men, landing on the east coast of Canada, which he named Newfoundland.

Henry VII (1485-1509), meanwhile, was busy filling his coffers with the wealth of the Church and the taxes of common folk. Disgruntlement at the king's greed grew in the South West, particularly in Cornwall, where a 15,000-strong band of rebels assembled to march on London. The Cornish Rebellion was brutally crushed at Blackheath, but was swiftly followed by further insurrection, when Perkin Warbeck, a young Flemish pretender to the throne, landed in Cornwall with the intent of overthrowing the king. Warbeck received strong support in Cornwall and Devon from high-profile members of the clergy and the nobility, but was captured in Taunton two years later. Henry VII travelled

to the town especially to order the execution of Warbeck and his noble followers, and also instigated punitive fines against many of the towns in the South West that had assisted him.

The dissolution of the monasteries by Henry VIII (1509-47) sowed the seeds for further revolt in the South West, which had a long-established monastic tradition. The popular and aged Abbot Whiting of Glastonbury was executed on top of the Tor, and for up to 50 years afterwards, dispossessed monks wandered the countryside, unemployed and destitute. To add insult to injury, in 1549 the Act of Uniformity introduced the English Book of Common Prayer and abolished the Latin mass. Celtic hearts raged against this act of royal interference; the Prayer Book Revolt gained supporters throughout Devon and Cornwall before it was crushed at Clyst St Mary near Exeter.

'The maritime exploits of Drake, Raleigh, Hawkins and others heralded the rise of Plymouth as a naval power.'

Although his domestic policies stirred up social turmoil at home, Henry VIII also recognised the danger of foreign threats from the sea. He identified the south coasts of Devon and Cornwall as England's Achilles heel, and set about building or expanding the fortifications at Dartmouth, Fowey, St Mawes, Falmouth and St Mary's (on the Isles of Scilly).

Henry was proved right towards the end of the 16th century when the Spanish fleet seemed set to invade. The Armada was famously defeated by Francis Drake (*see p204* **Local heroes**) at Plymouth in 1588, but this victory did not deter further Spanish aggression: in 1595 the Spaniards launched raids on Cornwall from Brittany, wreaking havoc on the ports of Mousehole, Newlyn and Penzance.

EXPLORERS AND EXPLOITERS

The Elizabethan era (1558-1603) was the great age of English navigation, and, unsurprisingly, many of its greatest 'gentlemen-adventurers' were West Country born and bred. The various maritime exploits of Drake, Raleigh, Hawkins and others heralded the beginnings of British imperialism and the rise of Plymouth as a centre of naval power. However, their success was built on buccaneering, as much as exploration, and also introduced a new horrific trade to the South West.

Born near Tavistock in Devon, Francis Drake (c1540-96) took part in trading expeditions across the Atlantic, plundering Spanish ships and territories in the Caribbean and

South America, and in 1580 became the first Englishman to sail around the world, navigating both the Straits of Magellan and the Cape of Good Hope on board the *Golden Hind*. As well as defeating the Spanish Armada at home, he continued to target Spanish interests in Europe and the West Indies, until his death in Panama in 1596.

Walter Raleigh (c1552-1618), meanwhile, was trying to advance English colonialism in North America with the founding of the territory of Virginia in 1594. The son of a simple East Devon squire, he rose to prominence as one of Elizabeth's favourite courtiers and, although he never actually set foot in North America, is credited with the introduction of potatoes and tobacco to England. Raleigh became Vice-Admiral of Devon, but then fell spectacularly out of favour with James I and was ultimately beheaded for treason.

Another Devonian adventurer was Drake's cousin, Plymouth seaman John Hawkins (1532-95). Like Drake, Hawkins made his fortune raiding Spanish galleons, but he is more notorious as England's first slave trader.

During the 17th century increasing numbers of ship-owners and merchants followed Hawkins's lead, setting sail from England with trinkets, beads, pottery and firearms, which would be swapped for slaves on the coast of West Africa. The slaves were carried across the Atlantic in horrendous conditions to be sold to plantation owners in the West Indies and America, while sugar, molasses, tobacco and rum from the plantations were brought back to England. Nowhere were the merchants keener to jump aboard this lucrative trade than in Bristol.

Throughout much of the 16th century, Bristol had been a sickly town – closely built, badly drained and a hotbed for illness and plague. Despite Cabot's historic voyage, trade was down and the shipping industry was at a low ebb. By the end of the 17th century, however, the city's involvement in the slave trade had transformed it into one of the wealthiest cities in Britain. As well as African slaves, Bristol merchants also sold unlawfully kidnapped young Britons to work in Ireland, and as a result became known as the 'stepmother of all England'.

PIONEERS AND PILGRIMS
The history of English settlement in North America owes a great deal to Devon under James I (1603-25). During the early 17th century, more emigrant ships set sail from Plymouth, Bideford and Torquay than from all the other English ports put together, carrying an estimated half a million people to colonise new

territories across the Atlantic. The most famous expedition was that of the Pilgrim Fathers, who sailed from Plymouth in September 1620, bound for Massachusetts. It wasn't only Devonians, though, who joined the departing ships. A plaque in Barton St David church, Somerset, commemorates local emigrant Henry Adams, born 1583, whose descendants became the second and sixth presidents of the United States: John Adams and John Quincy Adams.

> **'Despite the bloodshed and destruction of the Civil War, the region flourished in the following years thanks to the cloth trade.'**

CIVIL WAR
The very first blood of the Civil War (1642-9) was spilt in Somerset, when a small band of Royalists met a larger Parliamentarian crowd just south of Street. The Cavaliers outnumbered six to one but sent the Roundheads packing, killing seven in the process.

It is often assumed that the West Country played a Royalist role in the war. Certainly, most of Cornwall was diehard Cavalier, provoking Charles I (1625-49) to write to the county purring '… we do hereby render our royal thanks'. But while Charles could claim many loyal supporters among the landed gentry in the rest of the region, the South West was also home to some of his fiercest opponents.

It was a Somerset man, John Pym, who led the Puritan Parliamentary opposition to Charles I, and another, Admiral Robert Blake, who held Taunton for the Roundheads in 1644. Blake, in fact, became such a close ally of Cromwell that he was buried at Westminster Abbey only to have his body exhumed during the Restoration and thrown into the streets.

As elsewhere in the country, the South West witnessed striking divisions of loyalty: Wells was extremely Royalist; Shepton Mallet just as extremely Parliamentarian; Exeter and Plymouth both swapped allegiance halfway through the Civil War; and poor Dunster Castle in Somerset withstood two sieges – first by Royalists in 1642, and then by Roundheads the following year – thanks to the fickleness of local lords, the Luttrells.

The Royalists' early successes in the South West were followed by major victories at Lansdown near Bristol in 1642 and Lostwithiel in Cornwall in 1643. However, the king's supporters ultimately succumbed to Cromwell's New Model Army under Thomas

Fairfax, which swept its way through the South West in 1645. The decisive blow was the surrender of Truro, although Royalists held out at Exeter until 1646, and St Mary's in the Isles of Scilly didn't fall to Cromwell until 1651.

REBELLION AND REPRISALS

Despite the bloodshed and destruction caused by the Civil War, the region flourished in the following years thanks to the wealth of the cloth trade. Charles II (1660-85) was sheltered by various bigwigs in the South West during his exile, twice escaping through Cornwall to the Isles of Scilly and the Continent before returning to London triumphant.

Yet, the West Country had been unsettled by the political and religious tumult of the war and its aftermath. Following on from the Puritanism of Cromwell and the Anglican settlement of Charles II, the ascension of Catholic James II in 1685 provoked Protestants in Somerset to embark on their bloodiest rebellion yet.

The threat to the crown came from the charismatic and hugely popular James, Duke of Monmouth, the illegitimate son of Charles II by his Welsh mistress Lucy Walter. Arriving in Somerset from Holland in 1680, Monmouth became such a celebrity that it was claimed he had once even cured a woman of scrofula just by touching her. In 1685 local people rallied to his cause, declaring him the rightful monarch and cheering him on with the battle cry 'Monmouth and a Protestant religion!'. In Taunton, the duke raised an army of about 3,000 disaffected farm hands, whose livelihoods he vowed to safeguard from greedy landowners.

Monmouth's ad hoc army triumphed at Norton St Philip, but on 6 July 1685 came face to face with the king's massed troops at Sedgemoor and submitted to a horrible defeat. Three hundred men died, Monmouth was captured and beheaded, and hundreds of his rebel supporters were executed by the ruthless Judge Jeffreys at the Bloody Assizes in Taunton. A further 850 people were deported as cheap slaves to Barbados, where you can still hear Somerset accents to this day.

In 1688, however, Monmouth was partially vindicated when Brixham in Devon saw the arrival of monarch-in-waiting Prince William of Orange, accompanied by his wife Mary (James II's daughter).

PARTIES, PREACHING AND PATENTS

During the early 18th century Bath took on the role of England's social capital. Its beautiful Palladian architecture, hot mineral waters and whirl of balls, concerts and tea parties drew socialites from every corner of England.

However, while high society postured and played, elsewhere in the region, John Wesley (1703-91) was spreading a zealous brand of Protestantism, known as Methodism. Wesley arrived in Bristol in 1739 from America, where he had learnt the art of open-air preaching. He set up the world's first Methodist chapel in the centre of the city and then turned his attentions towards Devon and Cornwall, where he detected a heathen land in need of a spiritual revival. Wesley initially aroused suspicion among people in the far South West, but by old age he was preaching to crowds of up to 30,000 converts at open-air amphitheatres like Gwennap Pit near Redruth.

Many of Wesley's supporters were miners and their families, whose harsh existence made them particularly open to the consolation of Methodism. During the 18th century the South West yielded various groundbreaking developments that led to the unrivalled expansion of the Cornish mining industry and to the growth of an impoverished industrial working class.

In the early days, miners had looked for minerals close to the surface by sifting streams, exploring cracks and veins, but as demand grew, they were forced to mine ever deeper shafts. These extensive underground pits were prone to flooding, which limited production and created appalling working conditions. In Devon, Thomas Newcomen (1663-1729) pioneered a steam engine for pumping water out of the pits, and his invention was developed and perfected by Cornishman Richard Trevithick (1771-1833), whose patent high-pressure engines vastly increased the efficiency and productivity of Cornish mining. Meanwhile, down the road in Penzance, Sir Humphrey Davey (1778-1829) invented the first miners' safety lamp, and in Redruth, William Murdock lit a house with coal gas for the very first time.

However, while all this was being created, something was also being irrevocably lost: in 1777 Dolly Pentreath, one of the last known monoglot speakers of Cornish, died.

A far more positive development was the abolition of the slave trade in 1807. This put paid to the profits of many Bristol merchants and signalled the start of the city's decline as a maritime power. However, as the Industrial Revolution forged ahead, trade and transport in the city were boosted by the arrival of the Kennet & Avon Canal in 1810 and by the invention of tarmac in 1815 by local man John Loudon McAdam. Bristol's newly surfaced roads were held up as an example to the rest of the country and provided fitting access to the newly developed elegant suburb of Clifton.

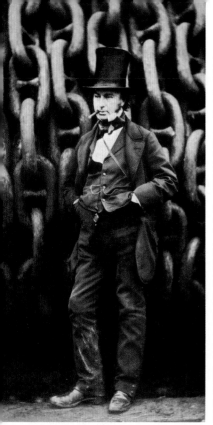

Isambard Kingdom Brunel.

McAdam's achievement, though, was soon to be overshadowed by the masterful engineering of Isambard Kingdom Brunel (*see p47* **Local heroes**). As well as endowing Bristol with its most spectacular landmark in the Clifton Suspension Bridge, his Great Western Railway and pioneering steam ships put the city firmly at the forefront of 19th-century developments in travel and transportation.

> **'The ease of rail transport allowed the burgeoning middle classes to enjoy holidays for the first time.'**

THE EFFECTS OF WAR

The Napoleonic Wars (1803-15) dealt a blow to Devon and Somerset's cloth industry and by the time peace was established textile production had moved to mills and factories in the north of England. From 1838 impoverished cloth workers in the West Country became standard-bearers for the Chartist movement. Support was particularly militant in Frome, while in conservative Bath a Chartist demonstration was halted by the twitchy authorities with police and troops.

The divide between the 'respectable' and the 'rough' widened. Even genteel Bath had its notorious slum district, Avon Street, home to beggars, thieves, prostitutes and itinerants. It's not surprising, then, that during this period many families emigrated to Australia, tempted by a free passage and promises of work.

Other mass emigrations took place from Cornwall towards the end of the 19th century, as the copper and tin mines closed in the face of competition from cheaper supplies abroad. Around St Austell, at least, the devastating effect of the mining crash was mollified by the development of the china clay industry. Deposits had first been discovered by William Cookworthy (1705-80) in the 18th century, and by the 19th century St Austell's pits were supplying ceramics manufacturers around the country.

Despite the industrial upheaval, the South West remained a fertile ground for writers: Jane Austen poked fun at Bath's pretensions, while Coleridge and Wordsworth created some of their finest verse in the Quantocks in Somerset. More significantly, war on the Continent prevented wealthy pleasure seekers from travelling abroad. Instead they flocked to the Devon towns of Exmouth, Sidmouth, Teignmouth and Torquay, and to the rugged Exmoor coast, which was romantically thought to resemble the mountainous landscapes of Austria and Switzerland.

This fledgling tourist industry received a massive boost with the arrival of the railways. In 1833 Brunel's Great Western Railway linking London and Bristol was completed; by 1841 it extended to the Somerset resort of Weston-Super-Mare and later in the decade the line reached Exeter and Torbay. The ease of rail transport allowed the burgeoning middle classes to enjoy holidays for the first time, resulting in the first serious incursions of cash-waving intruders – thenceforth half-affectionately known as 'grockles'.

As the railway network spread westwards across the Tamar, tourists also discovered the delights of Cornwall's varied coastline and quaint fishing villages. Their interest did not come a moment too soon, as by the end of the 19th century the Cornish fishing industry was in terminal decline.

For several centuries, pilchards had come to Cornwall's southern coastal waters in huge shoals to breed. They were caught in

Tourists in the 1930s enjoy seaside frolics off **Burgh Island**.

specially adapted nets called 'seines', and then salted and pressed, largely for export to France, Spain, Italy and the colonies. In the 19th century the industry shifted to the Atlantic coast, particularly around St Ives and Newquay, but the introduction of large drift nets resulted in overfishing and gradually forced the pilchards away from coastal waters.

Among the shoals of tourists who replaced the fish were artists and writers who delighted in Cornwall's rare light, beautiful scenery and rich cultural heritage. Their arrival in Newlyn and St Ives towards the end of the 19th century provided the basis for Cornwall's artistic reputation in the decades to come.

> ### 'Artists were delighted by Cornwall's light, scenery and rich cultural heritage.'

WARS OF THE WORLD

The South West welcomed in the last century of the millennium with one of the greatest technological revolutions mankind has ever seen. In 1901 the first-ever wireless message was successfully transmitted from Poldhu, Cornwall to be received by Guglielmo

Marconi in Newfoundland. A few years later in Bristol, the first flights of the box kite (a simple bi-plane) provided the impetus for the development of the city's 20th-century aviation industry. Both these innovations were to prove key in the following decades as Britain embarked on two world wars.

During World War I troops streamed in to the region, many from Canada and Australia, while recruits streamed out to be decimated in the killing fields of Northern France. Those that did return after 1918 witnessed the gradual homogenisation of West Country towns, as buildings were constructed from brick instead of local stone. England's first-ever council houses were built in Weston-Super-Mare, Somerset in 1919.

During World War II Italian prisoners of war and land girls worked on the South West's farms, and the region became an evacuation centre for London children, mainly working-class East Enders. It also attracted wealthier individuals – unofficial evacuees – who left London for the relative safety of Somerset, Devon and Cornwall. Several government departments and their staff also moved to the West Country – Bath, for instance, was virtually taken over by the Admiralty – and parts of South Devon were requisitioned by the US army.

Although Cornwall – historically never much troubled by England's enemies or invaders – and rural parts of Devon and Somerset remained relatively unscathed by the tumult of war, many of the South West's cities suffered horribly in aerial bombardments. As the home of the Royal Navy and the site of the Devonport Dockyards, Plymouth was bombed more heavily than any other British port, while the blitz of Bristol in November 1940 created an inferno that could be seen for 40 miles (65 kilometres) and destroyed the city's medieval centre forever.

'Rebuilding work saw Exeter, Plymouth and Bristol suffer at the hands of crude town planning.'

The Luftwaffe changed tactic in 1942 in response to the destruction of historic German cities by the RAF. Instead of attacking English towns of military significance, the 'Baedeker raids' – named after the famous guidebook – targeted centres of history and culture, starting with Exeter and Bath in April 1942.

Rebuilding work in the post-war years saw the centres of Exeter, Plymouth and Bristol suffer – to varying degrees – at the hands of crude town planning and brutal concrete architecture. In contrast, much of Bath's glorious Regency architecture underwent comprehensive restoration and repair.

DOOM OR BOOM?

The latter half of the 20th century saw the further decline of traditional industries in the South West to be replaced by the ineluctable rise of tourism. Dartmoor and Exmoor were both designated as National Parks during the 1950s, while the building of the M4 and M5 motorways opened up the region to motor traffic to an unprecedented degree.

The Cornish tin industry finally succumbed to the pressure of plummeting world prices in the 1980s, while fishermen faced up to the grim truth of receding stocks and the imposition of European Union quotas limiting the amount of fish they were allowed to catch. Farmers were also hard hit by European Union policies and were dealt two sucker punches by the BSE (mad cow disease) crisis in the 1990s and the national foot and mouth epidemic in 2001.

As a result of the breakdown of traditional livelihoods, Cornwall suffered from major unemployment, widespread social deprivation and the departure of vast numbers of young people from the county. All these factors contributed to a growing sense of disenchantment in the final decades of the 20th century, represented in part by the nationalist movement, Mebyon Kernow.

Tourism, too, proved a fickle mistress. In the 1970s and '80s increasing numbers of Brits chose cheap continental destinations over a traditional English seaside holiday in Devon or Cornwall, with the result that many Victorian resorts found themselves stuck in a tired rut.

However, the start of the 21st century has seen revived interest in the region's coastline, landscapes and culture result in growth and diversification for the tourism industry. Most notably, Cornwall has struggled out of its cream-teas-and-council-estates straitjacket to host two of Britain's biggest upmarket visitor attractions: in 1993 St Ives became the home of the modernist Tate art gallery, while near St Austell, the much-fêted Eden Project instantly became an economic and environmental success story on opening in 2001. With these and other attractions contributing to the South West's renewed appeal, another generation of invaders looks set to discover the delights of this ancient and fascinating region.

Churchill in Bristol in **World War II**.

Key events

PREHISTORY

4,000-3,000 BC Stone Age tribes settle in the South West.
From 2,500 BC Bronze Age tribes begin early farming and mineral extraction in the region.
From 600 BC Iron Age man establishes settlements and hill forts in the West Country.
c54 BC Romans begin to trade with Celts around the Severn estuary.

ROMAN AND ANGLO SAXON BRITAIN

AD 43-350 Roman Empire in Britain. The Fosse Way links the South West with other parts of the country.
c300-700 The Dark Ages. South West subject to raids by Angles and Saxons, but Christianity thrives in Celtic Cornwall.
700-1000 South West holds out against persistent Viking aggression
849-899 Reign of King Alfred the Great; suspension of Viking invasions.
973 Edgar crowned King of England at Bath.

THE MIDDLE AGES

1068 Exeter falls to new king, William I, signalling Norman domination of England.
1139-47 'Bristol War' – Matilda rules as queen from the city.
1180 Work begins on Wells Cathedral.
1184 Glastonbury Cathedral burns down.
From 1190 Creation of stannary towns in Cornwall and Devon.
1272 Customs duties introduced; growth of smuggling in Devon and Cornwall.
From 1300 Development of the cloth industry in Devon and Somerset.
1337 Duchy of Cornwall awarded to Edward II's son, the Black Prince.
1348-50 Black Death decimates South West's rural population.
1381 Peasants' Revolt.

TUDORS AND STUARTS

1496 John Cabot sails from Bristol and discovers Newfoundland.
1497 Cornish Rebellion.
1499 Perkin Warbeck executed in Taunton.
From 1536 Dissolution of the monasteries results in widespread social turmoil.
1542 Bristol is declared a city.
1549 Act of Uniformity sparks the Prayer Book Revolt in Devon and Cornwall.
1577 Francis Drake sets off from Plymouth on a voyage around the world.

1588 Drake defeats the Spanish Armada.
1594 Walter Raleigh claims the territory of Virginia for Elizabeth I.
1595 Spanish forces destroy the Cornish ports of Newlyn, Mousehole and Penzance.
1620 Pilgrim Fathers depart from Plymouth, heading for Massachusetts.
1642 Start of the Civil War in Somerset.
1645 Truro falls to the New Model Army under Thomas Fairfax.
1651 St Mary's, Isles of Scilly, is final place in England to fall to Cromwell.
1685 Duke of Monmouth, executed following failed rebellion against King James II.
1688 William of Orange and Mary Stuart arrive in Brixham, Devon to take up the English throne as William III and Mary II.

18TH AND 19TH CENTURIES

By 1700 Bristol is England's wealthiest city outside London, due to the slave trade.
1705 Beau Nash made Bath's Master of Ceremonies, heralding the city's Golden Age.
1739 John Wesley arrives in Bristol.
1750-1840 Expansion of Cornish mining.
1756 William Cookworthy discovers china clay in Cornwall.
1777 The last monoglot Cornish speaker, Dolly Pentreath, dies.
1803-15 Napoleonic Wars. Tourists start to visit the Devon coast.
1807 Slavery abolished.
1815 John Loudon McAdam invents tarmac.
1833 Completion of Brunel's Great Western Railway (GWR) between London and Bristol.
1838 Chartist movement .
1840s-1860s GWR extended west to Devon and Cornwall.
1880s Artists begin to visit Newlyn and St Ives in Cornwall.

20TH CENTURY

1901 First wireless message successfully transmitted from Cornwall to Newfoundland.
1914-18 World War I.
1939-45 World War II. South West becomes evacuation centre. Bristol, Bath Plymouth and Exeter are targeted in German bombing raids.
1950s Dartmoor and Exmoor designated as National Parks.
1980s Last remaining Cornish mines close.
1987 Bath is designated a World Heritage site by UNESCO.
1993 Opening of Tate gallery in St Ives.
2001 Eden Project opens near St Austell.

South West Today

While visitors flock here to relax, this holiday region is moving forward to an uncertain but exciting future.

For many people South West England is first and foremost a holiday destination: a place of rolling meadows, windswept cliffs and golden beaches; caravan sites, retirement cottages and cream teas, where the inhabitants of less-privileged locales come to breathe fresh air and the smell of the sea.

While it is to the region's credit that these images all apply to a greater or lesser extent, they are far from being the whole picture. First, they do not recognise the huge variety of landscape that the South West encompasses: urban centres, rural backwaters, fishing ports, former industrial areas, beach resorts and everything in between. And while visitors may get the impression of an untroubled pastoral idyll, for long-term residents, the reality is rather more complex, and not always so rosy.

INDUSTRIAL RELATIONS

Industry in the South West is not what it was, even 30 years ago. Bristol and Plymouth, the twin centres of seafaring in the South West, have sought to capitalise on this situation by building a tourist economy upon the relics of the past. Bristol harbour (*pictured*), which once saw

mighty ships unloading their cargoes of wine, tobacco and sugar, is now a 21st-century leisure environment, surrounded by pubs, restaurants and galleries, and dotted with tourist-friendly icons of the city's engineering heritage.

Plymouth, meanwhile, can be seen as a microcosm of the rise and decline of Britain as a naval power. Great ships once embarked on epic voyages from Sutton Harbour, but now a gleaming yacht marina and a state-of-the-art aquarium dominate the scene. In stark contrast, the Devonport dockyard is surrounded by derelict flats and an epidemic of unemployment.

In rural areas the transition from industrial to leisure economy has, perhaps, been more painful. A decline in the traditional industries of manufacturing, mining, quarrying, fishing and agriculture has created unemployment blackspots and low wages beneath the veneer of picturesque villages; a hidden, rural poverty where the difficulty of accessing services can lead to social exclusion and isolation. Cornwall is the poorest county in England and qualifies for the highest tier of aid from the European Union for regions lagging behind. Parts of Devon also qualify for extra assistance.

Long hair and ley lines

If the South West were a smell, it would be patchouli. There must be more joss sticks sold per capita in Bristol street markets alone than in any other part of the UK. From New Age travellers to old-age hippies, crusties to crustafarians, potters to pot-smokers, the South West is a mecca for the long-haired cosmic dreamer.

Take Glastonbury: drawn by Arthurian, Biblical and pagan legends (not to mention the Festival), its hippies come in various sub-genres: rainbow hippies, Celtic hippies, Gandalf-types with long grey hair and cloaks, and more. Shops heave with crystals, herbal cigarettes, essential oils and books on Celtic mythology, tantric sex and the Goddess. People talk auras, rebirthing and astrology – and how much tourists are willing to pay for a whalesong CD nowadays.

A similar breed are South Devon's artistic communities – many the product of the leftfield Dartington College of Arts – who end up in Totnes painting, drumming, working in health food shops, or setting up New Age fanzines that, even if no one buys them, are at least excellent for skinning up on.

As you pass the laybys of A roads in the South West, spare a thought for the most maligned tribe of all: New Age travellers. The Criminal Justice Act and the rising price of vintage, split-screen Volkswagen campers currently threaten these stubbly eco-nomads with extinction.

Their non-conformist lifestyle has, however, spawned its own wannabes. Cue the crusties – a little past their sell-by date but still visible in urban areas. Not to be confused with the genuinely homeless, these are people for whom grot is a DSS-funded lifestyle choice. Many are long-term, hardened 'cider punks' but dozens more merely white suburban kids who grow dreadlocks, move into central Bristol squats, get dogs-on-strings and

LIVING ON THE EDGE

Much of the history of Devon and, especially, Cornwall has been defined by these counties' peripheral location. Ignored by successions of invaders, kings and governments, the far South West has often been left to its own devices, resulting in a rich cultural identity, but also in a tendency to distrust central authority.

Although Cornwall does not fall into the A-list of Celtic nationalism, an enduring sense of being off the government's cognitive map has inspired the creation of a Cornish nationalist party, Mebyon Kernow, and a campaign for the county to have its own regional assembly. Genuine separatists are a very small, if vocal, minority but they and the rest of the county find inspiration in an ancient heritage that is lately receiving renewed attention.

On a more practical level, many are hoping that the IT revolution and the 'knowledge economy' will counter some of the problems of living 'way out west'. Throughout the region, sources of wealth lie increasingly in banking, insurance, electronics and computing. Fostering these new industries and improving the South West's infrastructure are likely to prove vital to the area's future development.

ON THE ROAD TO NOWHERE

Transport to and around the region is also a key issue. Since the closure of the vast majority of branch railways in Somerset, Devon and Cornwall during the 1960s, the main mode of transport in the South West has been the car. Devon County Council records for the 1990s show that 80 per cent of visitors to the county found their way there by car, compared with only 14 per cent by bus or train. As the South West's roads become ever-more clogged with holiday traffic and daily commuters, many rural areas still lack a frequent, reliable and cost-efficient alternative.

entertain vague anti-establishment or cosmic beliefs before winter sets in and they get a job at the Ministry of Defence.

The spiritual siblings of this set are the crustafarians. Catch any Paddington train westwards on a Friday afternoon and it'll be full of Tabithas heading home from boarding school to their country piles and coastal boltholes – all beads, bellyrings and vegetarianism. When this lot graduate (from Bristol University) they flirt with alternative, hippie lifestyles and dodgy beaus, until such time as pa threatens to pull the plug.

So what is it about the South West that inspires people to buy oil burners and spurn the nine-to-five? Any Glastonbury hippie will tell you it's the ley lines: routes of magnetic energy that run through the earth. They are detectable by the arcane skill of dowsing, and various ancient sites are aligned with them. Significantly, one of the most important in Britain is said to run right through the South West from St Michael's Mount in Cornwall through Glastonbury and on to the east coast.

Are ley lines simply a Stone Age means of navigation? Or a force of nature affecting everyone and everything in their path? Find out for yourself by sticking a joss stick on the dashboard, Fairport Convention on the Blaupunkt, and heading for the hills; your karma will thank you.

The decision whether or not to turn the A303 through Somerset and East Devon into a dual carriageway is typical of the kind of transport dilemma facing the region. Business leaders are keen to alleviate traffic jams on the single carriageway east of Honiton, but environmentalists are concerned that widening the road through the Blackdown Hills will harm an area of rare natural beauty. It seems ironic that the summer traffic chaos is caused by people flocking westwards for their holidays in search of the very landscapes that the roads are threatening to destroy.

The South West has always been at the forefront of environmental protest in the UK. In 1994 one of the earliest and most widely publicised anti-road building protests took place on the edge of Bath, against the construction of a bypass across Solsbury Hill. A few years later environmentalists at the Honiton bypass campaign in Devon developed

a technique of tunnel digging that turned a fresh-faced, dreadlocked protester by the name of Swampy into a household name.

While some dig tunnels, however, others are getting on their bikes. There is no shortage locally of dedicated cyclists, and increasingly a network of cycling routes is being developed by Sustrans (the 'sustainable transport charity') to accommodate them. One of the most ambitious routes is the Wessex Way, which on completion in 2005 will run for 74 miles (120 kilometres) from the Bristol Channel through Somerset and Devon to the coast at Lyme Bay.

CRISIS IN THE COUNTRYSIDE?

With many rural communities throughout the South West reliant on farming for their livelihood, the region was hit particularly hard by the recent crisis in agriculture, brought on by BSE, the foot and mouth epidemic, not to mention the perceived undermining of rural lifestyles by an urban-centric government.

'Blood sports divide public opinion in the South West as much as anywhere else in the country.'

Hunting, shooting and other blood sports divide public opinion in the South West as much as anywhere else in the country, with the region's conservationists and animal protection groups coming into frequent conflict with such standard bearers of rural tradition as the Devon & Somerset Staghounds (*see p127*). The pro-hunting lobby expressed its anger at government policy by taking part in the Countryside Alliance's controversial 400,000-strong 'Liberty & Livelihood' march through London in 2002.

However, while these events have caused widespread unease in the South West, they have also encouraged farmers here, as elsewhere, to experiment with new ways of making a living. A quarter of farmers surveyed by the Department for the Environment, Food & Rural Affairs (DEFRA) in February 2002 said that they were considering diversifying into non-traditional or non-farming activities.

Some of these 'activities' involve the adaptation of farming methods to meet present-day demands for organic produce. Farmers, residents and visitors have all benefited from the increasing number of farmers' markets throughout the region, while other sources of non-agricultural income have been found in the tourist sector through the provision of bed and breakfast accommodation, farm holidays or outdoor pursuits. Increasing numbers of farmers in the South West are also making the most of Environmentally Sensitive Area grants in order to restore orchards, repair farm buildings in traditional style, or other useful works. As a result, 'green' tourism as pioneered by the visionary Eden Project looks not only appropriate but desirable.

21ST-CENTURY TOURIST

Yet however much the region's economy may diversify, tourism remains a vital lifeline for the West Country, bringing around £380 million annually to Devon alone. Since Victorian times the region has attracted young families, middle-aged couples and retirees, but in recent years a whole new breed of visitor is waking up to the region's appeal. The South West's great tracts of unspoilt countryside and coastline are being rediscovered as playgrounds for the 21st century. A burgeoning surf scene attracts thousands to the north coasts of Devon and Cornwall, while other visitors enjoy improved facilities for riding, sailing, fishing, hiking, cycling and 'extreme' sports.

'Cities in the South West have rebranded themselves as perfect weekend break destinations.'

Tourist boards across the South West have – perhaps belatedly – realised that in order to compete with cheap flights and package holidays to foreign climes, they must offer something more than the traditional seaside holiday. While Bath has always been firmly on the tourist map, now the region's other cities are also entering the fray, rebranding themselves as perfect weekend break destinations and instituting a widespread rise in standards of accommodation, dining and amenities.

Improvements are not confined to the large urban centres either: seaside resorts, country house hotels, rural restaurants and provincial pubs are wising up to the needs of the 21st-century visitor – high-quality food, thoughtful service and stylish surroundings. Combined with the creation of major visitor attractions like the Eden Project and the National Maritime Museum Cornwall, these developments go some way to counter the perception of the South West as a summer-only destination.

That said, it would be a mistake to think of tourism as a panacea for the region. The unreliable British weather ensures that some parts of the South West are unlikely ever to attract significant visitor numbers year-round, and as a consequence, tourist jobs and income remain seasonal and unreliable.

HOME IS WHERE THE CASH IS

As elsewhere in southern England, property prices in the West Country have soared in recent years, with the average cost of a terraced house in rural Somerset rising from £86,143 to £109,174 by late 2002. In the South West the national phenomenon has been compounded by the region's desirability as a location for holiday homes and retirement cottages.

As Britain's population ages, more and more people are choosing to enjoy a lengthy retirement in the relatively mild and certainly beautiful surroundings of the South West. The resulting demand for housing has seen prices rise to such an extent that young, local people are squeezed out of the market altogether. And yet, in coastal regions of Devon and Cornwall, many villages are almost deserted out of season, as affluent second-home owners pack up for the winter and head back to the cities.

UNIVERSITY OF LIFE

The high cost of housing combined with the decline of traditional forms of employment has forced many younger residents away from Devon and Cornwall. Those who leave to go to university often find it impossible to return, resulting in a gradual brain drain from the region.

This exodus of younger long-term residents is far from being a one-way process, however. Bristol, Bath, Plymouth and Exeter all have substantial student populations that bring much-needed commercial bustle and a varied social scene to these cities. It is hoped that the establishment of the Combined Universities in Cornwall in 2004 (created from the Falmouth College of Art and other existing colleges) will do the same for Cornwall. The new facilities should not only encourage locals to stay in the county, but also attract students from elsewhere in the UK and abroad, with knock-on effects for the Cornish economy.

THE SOUTH WEST TOMORROW

Many would argue that the South West has reached a significant crossroads. Is it to become a land of creeping suburban sprawl and rampant road building? Does it represent the cutting-edge of sustainable living and care for the environment – the region whose example could set the standard for future conservation efforts? Or does its future lie in the revival of the area's economy through tourism, a development that, if sensitively managed, could benefit the region's magnificent countryside, rather than harm it? One thing is certain – the image of the South West as a place of timeless rural stagnation has vanished for ever.

Art

The South West's vibrant local art scene would even give London a run for its money.

One of the most impressive features of art in the South West – whether in Bath, Bristol, or St Ives – is the sheer number of pieces that have not only been created in the region in the past but that also remain accessible here in the present, instead of being carted off to London or New York. This wealth of art challenges the London-centric exclusiveness of many galleries' art policies and creates a vigorous regional scene with its own trends, standards and traditions. Much of South West art is inspired by the landscape, which calls forth an emotional response from even the most cerebral artists, and has prompted some of the most significant developments in British art.

PORTRAITS AND PASTORALS (1750-1850)

As a fashionable watering hole for the rich and famous, Bath in the 18th century offered ample opportunity for painters in search of work. Pre-eminent in his field, **Thomas Gainsborough** (1727-88) established himself as a portrait painter in the town in 1759 and worked there for 15 years. Although he is said to have

despised many of his wealthy patrons, and greatly preferred painting idealised landscapes of brooks and hay wains, Gainsborough was appreciated, then and now, for original composition, sumptuous use of colour and the astute observation with which he viewed his subjects. *Thomas Rumbold and his Son*, an elegant if stylised representation of the Governor of Madras, hangs in Bath's Victoria Art Gallery (*see p78*), while portraits of William and Ann Leyborne are on display in the Bristol City Art Gallery (*see p84*).

The leading portraitist of the day, however, was Gainsborough's contemporary, **Joshua Reynolds** (1723-92). Reynolds thought history painting to be the highest form of art, but elevated the status of portraiture by deliberate classical allusions to the great art of the past. He was born in Plympton, Devon and kept a studio in Plymouth during the early part of his career before making his fortune in London,

St Ives by Alfred Wallis (Tate St Ives).

where he became the first president of the Royal Academy. Plymouth City Museum & Art Gallery (*see p202*) still has Reynold's palette and some family portraits, while nearby Saltram House (*see p205*) displays his paintings of the Parker family, not to mention a portrait of Reynolds himself by his contemporary, Angelica Kaufman (1741-1807).

'Bristol had a reputation less for appreciation of the arts than for the money-grubbing slave trade.'

In Cornwall, meanwhile, the precociously talented **John Opie** (1761-1807) was painting rustic scenes and portraits of local people, reminiscent of Rembrandt. Opie was launched on to the London scene in 1781 by political satirist John Wolcot (aka Peter Pindar), as the 'Cornish Wonder', where he enjoyed a highly successful career, becoming professor of painting at the Royal Academy in 1805. A number of his works can be seen at the Royal Cornwall Museum in Truro (*see p237*). Other paintings by Opie and Reynolds are on display in the Royal Albert Memorial Museum & Art Gallery in Exeter (*see p151*).

In the 18th century Bristol had a reputation less for appreciation of the arts, than for money-grubbing and the slave trade, but by the 1800s a few local industrialists were beginning to take an interest in painting. Among those benefiting from this patronage was a small group of painters known as the 'Bristol School', who went on sketching expeditions together. Most prominent among them were John Eagles (1783-1855), George Cumberland (1754-1848), Edward Bird (1772-1819), EV Rippingille (1798-1859) and **Francis Danby** (1793-1861).

Danby's work in the West Country is distinguished by its loving representations of the Bristol landscape, notably the Avon Gorge and the River Frome, although he also spent time in London where he painted flamboyant biblical canvases. In later life Danby moved to Exmouth, where his landscape paintings, such as *Sunset Through Trees* – a view across the River Exe towards Dartmoor, demonstrate the influence of Turner in their representation of light effects. Danby's work, and that of other members of the Bristol School, is well represented at the Bristol City Art Gallery.

Loosely associated with the Bristol School is **Rolinda Sharples** (1793-1838), a Bristol resident from a family of artists, whose mother, Ellen, founded the Royal West of England Academy. Sharples was her own saleswoman,

who hawked her work as far afield as Cumbria. Among a few dozen of her works that survive today is *The Trial of Colonel Brereton*, a compelling courtroom scene that is an exquisite composite portrait of all the distinguished citizenry of Bristol.

THE NEWLYN SCHOOL (1882-1900)
Later in the 19th century the newly extended railway took artists further west to Cornwall. Attracted by the clear light and mild climate, they arrived in the little harbour of Newlyn in the 1880s and, influenced by artists in Paris and Antwerp, proceeded to record the life of the fishing community there. **Walter Langley** (1852-1922) and **Edwin Harris** (1855-1906) were among the first to arrive in 1882, followed two years later by **Stanhope Forbes** (1857-1947), the most influential member of the group. The Newlyn School of artists are regarded as the pioneers of *plein air* painting in Britain. Their paintings are characterised by an absorbed portrayal of the lives of ordinary Cornish people and by the representation of natural light effects.

The results at their best include realistic narrative paintings like Forbes' unpretentious wedding party scene *The Health of the Bride* (1889) or *A Hopeless Dawn* (1888) by Frank Bramley (1857-1915), in which two women comfort each other, certain their husbands have drowned at sea. Later work tended to degenerate into sentimentalised costume drama, although *Home-Along: Evening* by Forbes evokes a whole way of life in its tender portrayal of facial expressions bathed in the light of sunset-to-dusk by water.

Other painters associated with the Newlyn School included Forbes' wife Elizabeth (1859-1912), HS Tuke (1858-1929), TC Gotch (1854-1931), and the Irish painter **Norman Garstin** (1847-1926), who arrived in Newlyn in 1886. Garstin was regarded as the most intellectual painter in the group, and was deeply influenced by the French impressionists. His most famous painting, *The Rain It Raineth Every Day* (1889), is on show in the Penlee House Gallery in Penzance (*see p250*). This gallery has the most significant collection of Newlyn School paintings, although there are also examples in the Bristol City Art Gallery, the Royal Cornwall Museum and the Plymouth City Museum & Art Gallery.

THE LIGHT OF ST IVES
As the Newyln School's influence waned at the beginning of the 20th century, so artistic interest turned to another small fishing harbour on the opposite side of the peninsula. **JMW Turner** (1775-1851) had painted a panorama

of St Ives Bay as early as 1811, but it was the visit of **James McNeill Whistler** (1834-1903) and his disciple **Walter Sickert** (1860-1942) in 1883 that signalled the earliest stirrings of an artists' community in the town. Sickert and Whistler worked with frenetic energy, painting the Cornish landscape as if it might melt, and produced a handful of oil studies – including Sickert's *On The Sand*, which is displayed in the Tate, St Ives (*see p260*). Their free appropriation of the lessons of impressionism and Japanese art opened new directions in painting for others to follow.

From the 1890s a fledgling artists' colony developed in St Ives, as increasing numbers of painters flocked to the town, attracted by its famously luminous light. Studios were created in former sail lofts and pilchard cellars on Back Road West – many are still in use to this day – and paintings were sent to London once a year for the Royal Academy Summer Exhibition. During the 1920s prominent visitors included the pioneering abstract artist **Ben Nicholson** (1894-1982), the primitive painter **Christopher Wood** (1901-30) and the Hong Kong-born potter **Bernard Leach** (1887-1979).

Leach arrived in 1920, accompanied by his Japanese associate Shoji Hamada, to set up the St Ives Pottery. Hamada left St Ives in 1923, but Leach remained in the town for the rest of his life, producing 25,000 pieces that successfully combined the eastern and western traditions of ceramic art and established his reputation as the father of modern British pottery.

It was not only newcomers that put St Ives on the art map, however. The self-taught artist **Alfred Wallis** (1855-1942) was a retired Cornish fisherman who settled in St Ives in 1890 and made a living as a rag-and-bone trader and ice-cream seller. After the death of his wife, Wallis started painting seascapes and harbour scenes, using ship's paint and pieces of driftwood he had found on the beach. Discovered by Nicholson and Wood in 1928, Wallis became one of the country's most important naïve artists, but nevertheless ended his days in a workhouse. His grave is decorated with tiles by Leach and lies close to the Tate, where many of his paintings are displayed.

In 1939 Nicholson moved to Cornwall, first to Carbis Bay, then to St Ives, with his wife, the sculptor **Barbara Hepworth** (1903-1975). From this seemingly remote corner of the world, they became the undisputed leaders of a formalist and abstract tendency that united them with the international mainstream of contemporary art. Nicholson and Hepworth were joined by the Russian constructivist sculptor **Naum Gabo** (1890-1977), who greatly influenced the wave of artists that was to follow.

The so-called St Ives School flourished between the 1940s and the 1960s and made the town a globally recognised centre of abstract art. Although not united by a common style or philosophy, the artists did share an interest in portraying the local landscape in abstract terms, exemplified in the organic sculptures of Barbara Hepworth.

The **Barbara Hepworth Museum** contains over 40 pieces of the sculptor's work.

It was during the 1940s that Hepworth first experimented with the opening of form to the play of light on curved interiors, which was to become her signature style. The inspiration of the Cornish coastline – its cliffs, rocks and prehistoric standing stones – is nowhere more apparent than in the sculpture garden of her former home, Trewyn Studio. Hepworth died in a fire here in 1975, but the house and garden have since been restored as the unmissable Barbara Hepworth Museum (*see p261*), and display over 40 examples of her work.

'St Ives School artists shared an interest in portraying the landscape in abstract terms.'

Peter Lanyon (1918-64) broke free from the severe abstraction of Nicholson in order to evoke more explicitly the landscapes of his native Cornwall. *Harvest Rain* (1964) is a work in primary hues that has the economy and purity of the formalist aesthetic, but also a suggestion of the contours of sea cliffs, with a glimpse of brown hinting at a rain-sodden harvest field. Many of Lanyon's images were inspired by glider flights over the land he loved. Ultimately, though, this unusual method of observation was to cost him his life when his glider crashed in 1964.

Although he inherited Nicholson's studio on Back Road West, **Patrick Heron** (1920-99) represents the middle generation of St Ives painters – including Lanyon, Brian Wynter (1913-75) and Roger Hilton (1911-75) – who overcame the dominant influence of Hepworth and Nicholson. Heron developed his own varied, semi-abstract style, influenced by Matisse and notable for its vibrancy of colour. One of his most striking pieces is the vast stained glass window in the entrance of the Tate, St Ives.

Heron's contemporary **Terry Frost** (b.1915) worked as an assistant to Barbara Hepworth in the 1950s but has been based in Newlyn since 1974. Recognised as a major figure in the post-war British abstract movement, Frost produces drawings, paintings and collages that use bold colours and shapes – stripes, circles and ovals – to evoke direct visual experiences. He is regarded with veneration as the granddad of the current Penwith art scene. Another surviving member of the St Ives School is **Wilhelmina Barns-Graham** (b.1912), now in her nineties, who came to the town in 1940. The influence of her widespread travels in Spain, France and Italy is apparent in rich abstract paintings of great depth and feeling.

FROM RURAL NOSTALGIA TO 'WALKING AS ART' (1975-2002)

In 1975 a group of seven West Country-based artists founded the Brotherhood of Ruralists. Defining a Ruralist as 'someone who is from the city who moves to the country', the group shared ideals and sources of inspiration from nature rather than a common style, although in much of their work, representations of the countryside are combined with literary and musical references.

Among the founding members were **Sir Peter Blake** (b.1932) and **Jann Haworth** (b.1942), who had established their reputations as Pop artists in London in the 1960s. They moved to Somerset in 1969, carrying out much of their work in Bath. **David Inshaw** (b.1943) taught in Bristol in the late 1960s, where he was first inspired by the work of Thomas Hardy; **Annie Ovenden** (b.1945) and her husband **Graham** (b.1943) moved to live near Bodmin, while **Graham Arnold** (b.1932) and his wife **Ann** (b.1936) based themselves in Wiltshire. The group took annual working holidays to Coombe in Cornwall and first exhibited together in the Royal Academy Summer Exhibition in 1976; this was followed by a joint commission to design book covers for the New Arden Shakespeare series, and in 1981 by a major touring exhibition, starting at the Arnolfini Gallery in Bristol (*see p50*).

Art critics have accused the Ruralists of being hopelessly nostalgic and even unbearably twee – Blake's work from this period includes a series of fairy paintings – but the artists themselves claim they aspire to a 'visionary realism'. These values are evident in David Inshaw's photographs of Morwenstow, Cornwall, and in Ann Arnold's *Rebecca Dreaming at Coombe* (1977), in which the sky looms wild and enormous over the house and a child's face at the window.

Blake, Inshaw and Hawarth left the Brotherhood in the early 1980s, but work by the remaining Ruralists is still exhibited regularly at galleries throughout the South West. Paintings by David Inshaw and Graham Arnold are also on display at the Bristol City Museum & Art Gallery.

Since the 1960s Plymouth has also laid claim to a significant place on the art map of the South West. **Beryl Cook** (b.1926), now resident in Bristol, spent several years in the city as the landlady of a seafront guesthouse. These experiences inform her humorous depictions of blowsy women, which combine elements of naïve art with the sensibility of saucy seaside postcards, and have made her one of the most popular artists in the UK.

Rather less accessible is the work of the celebrated but controversial artist **Robert O Lenkiewicz** (b.1941), who died in Plymouth in 2002. Lenkiewicz spent 30 years on a series of deeply thoughtful but frequently disturbing 'projects' depicting and exploring the human condition, and often using people on the very margins of society as models. A small selection of his prolific output is exhibited in the Annexe Gallery in Plymouth (*see p204*), but the studio of this great artist remains closed to visitors.

In the 21st century St Ives continues to be a mecca for amateur and professional artists following in the prestigious footsteps of Hepworth et al. As well as the old-timers, younger artists animate the scene with new styles and methods, although a preoccupation with the West Penwith landscape remains a dominant theme in their work. The converted sail lofts that once housed the paintings of Nicholson and Heron now contain the elemental seascapes of **Margo Maeckelberghe**, the preeminent naïve art of **Bryan Pearce** and the still lifes of **Terry Whybrow**. For other significant artists working in the area, *see p264* **Ones to watch**.

This part of Cornwall does not hold the sole rights to contemporary art in the region, however. Some of the most successful artists in the South West today have chosen not to work in the shadow of such an overwhelming artistic heritage. The highly acclaimed op-artist **Bridget Riley** (b.1931), for example, is based in St Merryn, near Padstow, while the renowned environmental artist **Richard Long** (b.1945) chooses to live and work in Bristol, with Dartmoor and the River Avon featuring prominently in his work.

Long has created a unique form of landscape art that combines elemental natural materials, like stones and grass, with explorations of the countryside on foot – 'walking as art' recorded as photographs, maps or text. *Dartmoor Time* (1995), for example, portrays a 24-hour walk on the moor through representations of natural time encountered along the way, such as 'The split-second chirrup of a skylark'. Inextricably linked to nature, Long's graphic walks and stone circles can be seen as the apotheosis of a long tradition of West County art that has aspired to record and capture the region's varied and absorbing landscapes.

R B and W Spiral for A by Terry Frost and **Thermal** by Peter Lanyon (Tate St Ives).

John Keats.

Literature

Coleridge, Austen, Tennyson, Thackeray… and many more.

It would be presumptuous – but tempting all the same – to claim for the South West the title of cradle of English literature. The beauty of a landscape interwoven with deeply rooted legends, not to mention the allure of foreign parts conjured by seaports open to a vast ocean, have awoken the literary impulse in every generation in the area.

Bristol, at least, can claim to have been instrumental in the birth of the English novel – it was here in about 1709 that Alexander Selkirk intrigued **Daniel Defoe** (1660-1731) with the wild tale of shipwreck and redemption that became *Robinson Crusoe* (1719).

ROMANTIC RAMBLES

Towards the end of the 18th century, the South West provided the setting for a momentous meeting of literary minds. In 1795 **Samuel Taylor Coleridge** (1772-1834; *see p32* **Local heroes**) was giving lectures in Bristol with his friend, the Bristolian **Robert Southey** (1774-1843). Southey was later to become Poet

Laureate, but in 1795 he was still an ardent young liberal, producing political plays and ballads. Southey and Coleridge's friendship was short-lived, but it prefigured the much more prestigious and fruitful working relationship between Coleridge and **William Wordsworth** (1770-1850), who met for the first time in 1796.

Coleridge and Wordsworth were united by a mutual love of poetry, philosophy, politics and hill-walking, and when the Coleridge family settled in Nether Stowey near Bridgwater in 1797, Wordsworth and his sister Dorothy moved to nearby Alfoxden Manor in Holford to have the pleasure of Coleridge's company. The Somerset years saw the genesis of the *Lyrical Ballads* (1798), the cornerstone of the Romantic movement, which included 'The Rime of the Ancient Mariner', 'The Nightingale' and 'Tintern Abbey'.

Not everyone appreciated having poets on their doorstep. Some of the neighbours mistook the nature-lovers' midnight outings for trysts with Napoleonic spies and they were asked to leave after a year. Similar suspicions were to fall upon the younger Romantic poet **Percy Bysshe Shelley** (1792-1822). During a stay in Lynmouth in June 1812, when he wrote the polemical vision poem 'Queen Mab', he was observed floating messages in bottles out to sea; a bit of innocent fun that the literal-minded locals didn't grasp at all.

'A splashy, rainy, misty, snowy, foggy, haily, floody, muddy, slipshod county.'

The Romantics in general had an ambivalent relationship with the West Country. They cherished the green spaces and untrodden ways, but Coleridge suffered from recurrent periods of melancholia at Nether Stowey, and **John Keats** (1795-1821), writing 22 years later, from Teignmouth, had nothing good to say about the place. Devon, he wrote, was 'a splashy, rainy, misty, snowy, foggy, haily, floody, muddy, slipshod county'.

BATH TIME
Geoffrey Chaucer's (c.1343-1400) saucy Wife of Bath put the spa city on the literary map in the 14th century, but it was from the 18th century onwards that Bath became firmly cemented on the high road of fashion – a playground for the rich and famous to see and be seen, while nursing their ailments. As early as 1668 **Samuel Pepys** (1633-1703) was praising the place for its architecture. He was followed by the playwrights **William Congreve** (1670-1729) and Barnstaple-born **John Gay** (1685-1732), the novelists **Fanny Burney** (1752-1840) and **Samuel Richardson** (1689-1761), and the essayist **Dr Johnson** (1709-84), with Boswell in tow.

Henry Fielding (1707-54), who was born at Sharpham Park near Glastonbury, based the character of Squire Allworthy in *Tom Jones* (1749) on his friend, the Bath bigwig Ralph Allen, while **Richard Brinsley Sheridan** (1751-1816) dramatised some of his experiences of Bath's licentious society in the comic masterpiece *The School for Scandal* (1777). Sheridan had started writing *The Rivals* (1775) during his three-year stay in Bath in the early 1770s.

Less celebrated by the city's tourism industry, not surprisingly, is **Tobias Smollett** (1721-71), who in *Humphrey Clinker* (1771) penned a disgusting account of the water at the famous spa: 'What a delicate beveridge is every day quaffed by the drinkers; medicated with the sweat and dirt, and dandruff; and the abominable

discharges of various kinds, from twenty different diseased bodies, parboiling in the kettle below.'

Bath's most famous literary resident is **Jane Austen** (1775-1817; *pictured p33*) who lived here from 1801 to 1805. Much of *Persuasion*, and *Northanger Abbey*, both published in 1818, have their settings in Bath. However, although the city makes much of its Austen credentials, the novelist was not fond of life here, and her novels are often subtly scathing of the society rounds.

VICTORIAN VALUES
During the 19th century the West Country was awash with novelists. **William Makepeace Thackeray** (1811-63) stayed in the seaside village of Clevedon to write part of *Vanity Fair* (1847-8), and later used it as the setting for *Henry Esmond* (1852). He also spent three years at Larkbeare, near Ottery St Mary, which became the Clavering St Mary of his autobiographical novel *Pendennis* (1848).

Charles Kingsley (1819-75), Christian social reformer and author of the well-loved moral tale for children, *The Water Babies* (1863), was vicar of Holne in Devon and lived in Bideford from 1854. The Devon town of Westward Ho! takes its name (and exclamation mark) from Kingsley's novel of 1855, and later become the setting for the school adventures of *Stalky and Co* (1899), based on experiences of **Rudyard Kipling** (1865-1936) as a boarder there from 1878 to 1882.

Arthur Conan Doyle (1859-1930) lived in Plymouth in the 1880s, where he practised medicine, and wrote his first major work featuring Sherlock Holmes, *A Study in Scarlet* (1887). His most famous evocation of the South West, however, is in the *Hound of the Baskervilles* (1902), set on Dartmoor. Doyle wrote the novel during a stay at Princetown, and the moor's eerie gloom permeates every aspect of the novel.

Devon's other great tract of moorland is immortalised in *Lorna Doone* (1869) by **RD Blackmore** (1825-1900). The novel follows the love story of Lorna Doone and John Ridd, against a background of banditry and murder in the hidden valleys around the Somerset/Devon border in the late 17th century (*see also p122* **Country walk**).

The South West attracted its fair share of Victorian poets too. **Alfred Lord Tennyson** (1809-92) was deeply attached to the Somerset town of Clevedon, not least for its associations with his beloved friend Arthur Hallam, who is buried there. On Hallam's death, Tennyson had a memorial stone placed in the church, and his poem 'Break, break, break' is thought to have been composed on the coast nearby. Tennyson

Local heroes
Samuel Taylor Coleridge

The South West's most famous drug addict was undoubtedly the poet Samuel Taylor Coleridge, who was born in Ottery St Mary, Devon, in 1772, as the youngest son of the local vicar. After his father's early death, Samuel was sent away to school in London, where he made friends with Leigh Hunt and Charles Lamb, who later described him as 'an archangel slightly damaged'. Coleridge attended Jesus College, Cambridge, but a heady concoction of love, alcohol and French revolutionary politics proved too potent for his academic studies, and he never completed his degree.

In 1794 Coleridge met the Bristol-born poet Robert Southey. Together they planned to found a Utopian colony in New England and undertook a lecture tour around Bristol in order to fund the project. All that came of their grand scheme, however, was a double wedding to the sisters Sara and Edith Fricker at St Mary Redcliffe church in 1795. Southey and Coleridge subsequently quarrelled over money and politics, and the latter moved to Clevedon with Sara, where he published *Poems on Various Subjects* (1796).

A year later the young family settled at Nether Stowey near Bridgwater, where Coleridge was to produce some of his most successful poetry. During his time in Somerset he collaborated with Wordsworth on the seminal *Lyrical Ballads* (1798), contributing, among other poems, 'The Rime of the Ancient Mariner', which was inspired by walks with Wordsworth along the Exmoor coast. He also wrote moving conversation pieces, such as 'The Nightingale' and 'Frost at Midnight', which recalls his childhood happiness in Ottery St Mary. Yet Coleridge's time at Nether Stowey was far from an idyll of hearty walks and endless romantic outpourings. The poet increasingly relied on opium to combat moments of sickness and depression, evident in the agonising 'Fears in Solitude' and his incomplete, opium-induced vision poem, 'Kubla Khan'.

In 1798 Coleridge left the West Country for good, but his opium addiction stayed with him, resulting in ill-health and near-suicidal bouts of depression. 'Dejection: An Ode' (1802) is a brilliant, emotional response to his own predicament. He travelled widely in the early 19th century in an attempt to restore his health and escape his troubled marriage, but returned to the UK in 1807, and despite continued illness, began a series of lectures on poetry and drama.

By 1811, Coleridge had been rejected by many of his friends, including Wordsworth, most of whom were fed up with his opium habit and unpredictable temperament. However, the resurgence of his Christian beliefs and a strict medical regime saved him from suicide and in 1816 he moved to the Highgate home of Dr James Gillman.

Christabel and Other Poems, which included 'Kubla Khan' and The Pains of Sleep', was published in the same year and cemented Coleridge's reputation among the younger Romantics, and although he concentrated on critical prose works in his final years, often with a radical Christian bias, he also wrote some moving late poems.

was also inspired by Salcombe in Devon; the 'surfy, slow, deep, mellow voice' of the harbour when the tide runs high is recreated in his poem 'Crossing the Bar'.

Elizabeth Barrett (1806-61) lived in Sidmouth for three years in the early 1830s, and spent an extended period in Torquay for her health from 1838. *The Seraphim, and Other Poems* – the first of her works to gain attention – was published in the same year. However, the trauma of her brother's death in a sailing accident in 1840 put paid to any benefits she might have derived from the sea cure, and she had to be carried back to London.

Grief and loss are a recurrent theme for Victorian poets in the South West. It was in 1871, while working as an architect in St Juliot, Cornwall, that **Thomas Hardy** (1840-1928) met Emma Gifford, his Plymouth-born 'West-of-Wessex girl'. Their courtship is recorded in *A Pair of Blue Eyes* (1873) and, after her death, in a series of moving late poems.

20TH CENTURY
DH Lawrence (1885-1930) settled in Zennor, Cornwall, with his German wife, Frieda, completing *Women in Love* there between 1916 and 1917. Lawrence and Frieda showed

a lively interest in Cornish culture, even though an acquaintance described their singing in Cornish as 'howling in what [was] ingenuously supposed to be the Gaelic, at the same time endeavouring to imitate the noise made by a seal'. Following the time-honoured West Country tradition of regarding eccentric literati as spies, the police searched the Lawrences' cottage, and issued them with an expulsion order. Lawrence got his revenge by writing it all up in *Kangaroo* (1923).

'There was a time-honoured West Country tradition of regarding eccentric literati as spies.'

Perhaps the local police in North Devon should have been more concerned by the Nazi sympathies of **Henry Williamson** (1895-1977), who enjoyed a serene country life at Georgham from 1922. But in the early years his dodgy politics were masked by beautiful depictions of the landscapes of the Taw and the Torridge in *Tarka the Otter* (1927) and other countryside novels.

To a conservative traditionalist like **Evelyn Waugh** (1903-66), a rural setting was more appealing for its sense of ancestral roots than for its picturesque qualities. Waugh wrote *Brideshead Revisited* (1944), the quintessential lament for aristocratic Britain, while staying in Chagford, Devon, and *Unconditional Surrender* (1961) during his time at Combe Florey in Somerset in the 1950s. Somerset also provided inspiration for **John Cowper Powys** (1872-1963), even though he spent much of his life in the United States. His most famous work is *A Glastonbury Romance* (1933), in which the legends of Glastonbury exert a mystical influence on events and residents in the town.

On the whole, the literary modernists are associated more with the city life than with the rural West Country. An exception is **Virginia Woolf** (1882-1941), who in *To the Lighthouse* (1927) evokes the scene of her childhood

summers near St Ives. Although ostensibly set on a Scottish island, the novel is dominated by the unmistakable presence of Godrevy Lighthouse. **TS Eliot** (1888-1965) also had his own little patch of the South West. The second of the *Four Quartets* (1944) is named after the village of East Coker, near Yeovil, from where Eliot's ancestors set out for America in 1669. The poet's ashes are buried in the village churchyard.

Cornwall's history and landscape was romanticised in the mid century by the popular novels of **Daphne du Maurier** (1907-89; *see p229* **Local heroes**) and **Winston Graham** (b.1910), whose pop-historical *Poldark* (from 1945) later became a cult television series. The county also captured the imagination of the Poet Laureate **Sir John Betjeman** (1906-84), who maintained a life-long love affair with Cornwall after childhood holidays on the Camel Estuary, as recalled in his verse autobiography *Summoned by Bells* (1960). Many of his musings in poetry and prose on the Cornish countryside, coastline and churches are collected in *Betjeman's Cornwall* (1988). The poet died in 1984 at Trebetherick near Polzeath and is buried in St Enodoc churchyard. And then of course there's **Agatha Christie** (1890-1976), who was born in Torquay and spent much of her writing career in the area, settling finally at Greenaways on the River Dart. Although critics may quibble about her literary credentials, no one can argue with her prolific output and the success of her 'whodunnit' novels, recreated in numerous films and TV series. The respectable holiday atmosphere of South Devon in the 1930s and '40s provides the perfect curtain-twitching setting for many of her mysteries, including *Evil Under The Sun* (1941) and *And Then There Were None* (1939), both of which feature Burgh Island (*see p200* **Island retreat**).

▶ For further details of books about the South West, including those by present-day writers, *see chapter* **Further Reference**.

South West Coast Path, between Polperro and Polruan. *See p38.*

In Context

Great Outdoors

Bike, climb, fish, swim or simply soak up the scenery.

Landscapes & Wildlife

In terms of landscapes, the South West of England just about has it all. OK, so there are no mountains and no deserts, but you'll find pretty much everything else: sweeping moorland, wooded valleys, patchwork fields, wildfowl-rich wetlands, broad estuaries, sparkling rivers, a uniquely varied coastline – and even a rainforest, courtesy of the world-famous **Eden Project**.

Man has been influencing the look and shape of the land here since neolithic times, when the process of clearing the indigenous woodland began. Until then, much of the South West had been forested, but now only a few patches of ancient oak woodland remain in sheltered spots on Dartmoor: the best-known being **Wistman's Wood** in the valley of the upper West Dart.

Another factor affecting the South West's landscape – and assuring its particular appeal – is the climate. The region lies in the path of the Gulf Stream, resulting in mild, wet winters, warm, sunny summers, and a growing season that lasts for longer than in the rest of the country. As a result, subtropical vegetation thrives in sheltered areas of the South West. There are superb gardens along the river estuaries of the south coast and, most famously, on the Isles of Scilly, where a visit to the exotic **Tresco Abbey Gardens** will make you feel like you're thousands of miles from the British mainland.

THE MOORS
The three great upland areas of the South West – **Dartmoor** in Devon, **Exmoor**, straddling the northern Devon and Somerset border, and **Bodmin Moor** in Cornwall – all have their particular attractions for lovers of the outdoors. Dartmoor and Exmoor were given formal recognition in

the early 1950s when National Parks were established to help conserve their natural beauty and wildlife.

Dartmoor and Bodmin Moor are both raised granite plateaux, part of the same huge belt of ancient rock that finally forms the Isles of Scilly off Land's End. Both are characterised by the presence of tors, heavily weathered granite outcrops that have split into blocks to form fantastic shapes, such as **Haytor** on Dartmoor and the **Cheesewring** on Bodmin Moor.

Dartmoor rises to 2,037 feet (621 metres) at **High Willhays** in the north-west, the highest point in the South West peninsula. The high moor receives around 82 inches (2,160 millimetres) of rainfall a year, which runs south off the tilted granite plateau, cutting deep valleys through the softer rocks at the moor's edge. Dartmoor's rivers tumble through beautiful steep-sided wooded valleys, along the Teign gorge and the valleys of the Dart, Avon and Erme to create the undulating landscape of the **South Hams**.

Exmoor has a different feel. Here sedimentary sandstone underlies sweeping areas of heather, wooded combes (valleys) and a patchwork of small hedged fields, ancient farms and sheltered villages to create a kinder landscape than the granite grandeur of Dartmoor. That said, the notoriously boggy **Chains** at the heart of Exmoor are an area of unique wilderness, rising 1,500 feet (457.5 metres) above sea level and soaking up an annual rainfall of 80 inches (2,032 millimetres). Further north, the boundary of the National Park runs along a stunning coastline, where the soaring 'hog-back' cliffs rise to almost 1,000 feet (300 metres) in places, interspersed with inaccessible rocky coves.

The South West's third area of moorland, Bodmin Moor, is smaller and lower than either Dartmoor or Exmoor, reaching 1,368 feet (417 metres) at **Brown Willy**, with the source of the River Fowey just below. Many of Cornwall's rivers rise on the boggy moorland heights before running down to the lush inlets and estuaries of the south coast.

Wildlife is plentiful on all three moors. Expect to see a variety of birds, including skylarks, meadow pipits and wheatears, and rarer curlews, snipe, lapwings and golden plovers, plus redstarts on Bodmin Moor. In the wooded valleys you may spot woodpeckers, tits, thrushes, nuthatches and dippers flitting above the streams. Keep an eye out too for adders basking on warm rocks in summer, and badgers, foxes and deer (especially on Exmoor) lurking among the trees.

You'll also come across plenty of ponies. The mealy-muzzled Exmoor ponies, now an endangered species, are the native breed that most closely resembles the indigenous British prehistoric horse. Dartmoor ponies, on the other hand, have been crossed with small, tough species such as Shetlands to produce the breed that you'll see on the moor today.

THE HILLS

The South West has four distinct ranges of hills, all in Somerset: the Brendon Hills and the Quantocks to the west, the Mendips to the north-east, and the Blackdown Hills on the border with Devon. The hills are home to foxes, badgers, red deer, owls, woodpeckers, nightjars, Dartford warblers and stonechats, with yellowhammers, swallows, house martins, rooks and swifts a common sight over more open farmland.

Rising to 1,391 feet (424 metres) at **Lype Hill**, the **Brendon Hills** form the eastern part of Exmoor and share the moor's sandstone geology. However, despite areas of open moorland, such as Withycombe Common, the landscape here is generally gentler, greener, more wooded and more enclosed, with a certain amount of coniferous plantation. The underlying sandstone is rich in iron, which was mined from Roman times until the end of the 19th century.

Across a low-lying vale to the east lie the **Quantock Hills**, a self-contained little range of sandstone hills that reach 1,250 feet (380 metres) at their highest point. Typified by wooded slopes, deep combes, small, hedged fields and sheltered farms, this pretty landscape was designated as one of the first Areas of Outstanding Natural Beauty (AONB) in the country in 1957.

Running for about 25 miles (40 kilometres) west–east from the Bristol Channel to the valley of the River Frome, the limestone ridge of the **Mendip Hills** forms the largest range in Somerset, rising to 1,000 feet (305 metres) in some parts. The landscape is characterised by bleak uplands, heavily incised by the effects of water weathering the porous limestone, and undermined by a honeycomb of caves and underground channels, most famously at **Cheddar Gorge** and **Wookey Hole**. Lead, running in veins through the limestone, was mined here from Roman times, and the few settlements that survive on the windswept Mendip plateau have their origins in lead mining and sheep farming.

Finally, the chalk, greensand and clay **Blackdown Hills** straddle the border between Somerset and Devon, overlooking the Vale of Taunton to the north-west, and rising through beechwoods and pastureland to the remains of the ancient royal forest of Neroche. Although the area is now sparsely populated, back in the 18th and 19th centuries it was the site of a flourishing whetstone industry, used for the sharpening of sickles.

THE LOWLANDS

There are extensive tracts of undulating farmland, low wooded hills and meandering river valleys in the South West, but only one significant area of low-lying wetland – and it's one of the largest in England. The **Somerset Levels** are an extraordinary 250-square mile (648-square kilometre) stretch of atmospheric marshy meadows and moors, studded with the stark outlines of pollarded willows.

This area of central Somerset was originally covered by the waters of the Bristol Channel, with pockets of high ground forming 'islands' in the flooded landscape: **Brent Knoll** and conical **Glastonbury Tor** are two of the best known, and both command excellent views over the surrounding countryside. The Levels are still subject to frequent flooding today, with many of Somerset's rivers – the Axe, Brue, Cary, Parrett and Tone – running west through this unique landscape to the sea, interlinked by a system of man-made canals ('rhynes'), which were created when the wetlands were drained and reclaimed for agriculture.

Today the remaining marshes are threatened by intensive farming that makes the most of the Levels' very rich peaty soil, although recent initiatives have gone some way to protect the environment and wildlife of this watery habitat. The otter is making a comeback here, and the wetlands are home to many kinds of waterfowl, such as lapwing, teal, wigeon, snipe, redwing, fieldfare, heron and Bewick's swan.

THE COAST

The influence of the sea on the landscape, the people and their way of life, and even the quality of the light, becomes increasingly apparent the further south-west you travel until, in West Penwith, you feel that you have reached the end of the world. Trees and shrubs curve away from the coast, forced into weird shapes by the prevailing winds; small villages are found only where a cleft in the cliffs affords some shelter; and, depending on the resistance of the underlying rock, cliffs are continually undermined by the constant hammering of the waves.

The nature of the coast changes constantly as you move around the South West peninsula. In the north the **Bristol Channel** is characterised by huge tides, including the famous Severn Bore, when a huge wall of water surges up

Bodmin Moor. See p34.

the channel. Beyond, the open waters of the Atlantic hammer an unforgiving coast that faces the full force of the westerly gales. **Hartland Point**, the outer tip of one of the remotest areas in North Devon, is particularly magnificent, with jagged ridges of rock disappearing menacingly into the sea. The original muds and sands here, dating back more than 300 million years, have been buckled and forced into a series of twisted, tortured cliffs, split by steep-sided coombes, where waterfalls tumble on to rocky beaches far below.

The southern coast is, on the whole, different: this is a 'ria' coastline, where drowned river valleys provide sheltered sites for picturesquely situated villages and towns, such as those along the Fal, Fowey and Dart. But there are wonderful cliff landscapes here too. Around the **Penwith peninsula** granite rocks have been weathered into stacked blocks, reminiscent of the Dartmoor tors. Further east the serpentine rocks of the **Lizard peninsula** reach out towards the European mainland from which they were severed thousands of years ago, while in Devon coarse-grained gneisses and crystalline schists cluster around the county's most southerly headland at **Prawle Point**.

Moving east, the coastal landscape changes yet again, as the red sandstone cliffs of Devon run into the chalk cliffs of Dorset. A 95-mile (153-kilometre) stretch from Exmouth to Poole, known as the **Jurassic Coast**, became the UK's first UNESCO World Heritage Site in 2001, partly due to the wealth of fossils found in the chalk here. On the North Devon coast the high, shifting dunes of **Braunton Burrows** are also recognised as an internationally important environment and were granted UNESCO Biosphere Reserve status in 2002.

It's worth the climb up to **Glastonbury Tor**. See p36.

Elsewhere, the South West's varied coastline is interspersed with hundreds of superb beaches, ranging from magnificent stretches of golden sand to tiny, rock-girt coves. Many of the prettiest and quietest beaches can only be reached by walking along the South West Coast Path (*see p38*), which runs right around the coast from Dorset to Somerset.

In addition to glorious scenery, from the path you may spot grey seals and a wealth of sea birds: gannets, kittiwakes, shags, cormorants, grebes and gulls – and, on the Lizard peninsula, spectacular red-legged choughs, back after an absence of 50 years.

THE ISLANDS

From Land's End, on a good day, the jagged outlines of the **Isles of Scilly** can be seen 28 miles (45 kilometres) away to the west. Submerged beneath the waters of the Atlantic between Land's End and the islands is said to lie the legendary Lost Land of Lyonesse, and when you visit the Scillies it's not hard to believe; England's smallest AONB feels wonderfully isolated and almost unreal.

Six inhabited and 50 uninhabited low-lying granite islands make up the Isles of Scilly, divided by shallow turquoise seas, with long sandy beaches and, in places, subtropical vegetation. The islands are home to a wealth of wildflowers, butterflies and moths, and attract hundreds of birdwatchers every year, keen to spot rare migrants, including the only breeding colony of storm petrels in England. There are also manx shearwater; nationally important colonies of shag, rock pipit and great black-backed gulls; gadwall, shelduck, common tern and razorbill, not to mention significant numbers of grey seals and dolphins.

Although it's also a haven for wildlife, **Lundy**, the other notable island in this region, couldn't be more different from the Isles of Scilly. This steep-sided granite outcrop lies 12 miles (19 kilometres) off the North Devon coast, where the Bristol Channel meets the Atlantic, and is only three miles (five kilometres) long and one mile (1.6 kilometres) wide. Owned by the National Trust and managed by the Landmark Trust, Lundy (also known as Puffin Island – 'lundy' is Norse for puffin) is an exceptional place for those who want to get away from it all. Puffins can only be seen in breeding season but you'll find plenty of other birdlife, plus plenty of rabbits, Soay sheep (introduced in 1944), sika deer (since the 1920s), feral goats and Lundy ponies. The waters around the island are one of only two Marine Nature Reserves in Britain, hosting a fantastic range of marine life, including all five native species of British coral. Grey seals are also commonly seen here.

Sports & Activities

Once regarded as a destination for sedate family holidays, the South West has begun to exploit its superb natural resources as a destination for lovers of the great outdoors. Environmental issues in areas such as the Dartmoor and Exmoor National Parks have been sensitively handled, with strategies enabling mountain bikers, climbers, walkers and lovers of simple peace and quiet to co-exist amicably. On the coast, too, potential tensions between surfers, watersports fans and swimmers have – on the whole – been defused by skilful planning and beach management.

Whether you're already into adventure sports or fancy trying something new, there's no shortage of opportunities in the region. However, don't let enthusiasm for your new hobby cloud your critical judgment; there's a risk attached to every outdoor activity and it's the job of any training centre to minimise it. When seeking tuition, always ask for proof that instructors are appropriately qualified, and that insurance adequately covers both them and you. Details of courses should be available in advance to ensure that nothing is left to chance.

The website for South West Tourism (www.westcountrynow.com) has a section devoted to outdoor activities, with links to many training schools and activity centres in the region. Extensive links for riding,

angling, walking, cycling, surfing and golf in North Devon are available on www.country-ways.net. For Cornwall, www.cornishlight.co.uk is an excellent resource for those that want to walk, cycle, fish, swim or surf their way around the county.

ANGLING

You can buy bait and dangle a line over a harbour wall almost anywhere – indeed, a morning's crabbing is usually a holiday highlight for kids. Sea fishing from a boat requires greater preparation. Most ports have a flotilla of small craft offering four-hour or day trips to catch mackerel, while some (**Looe** in Cornwall is the most notable example) can also offer deep-sea fishing trips for big-game species including sharks.

South West Coast Path

Britain's longest waymarked trail runs for an incredible 630 miles (1,013 kilometres), from Minehead in North Somerset to South Haven Point in South Dorset. The origins of this continuous coastal route date back to the 18th century, when customs and excise officers roamed the cliff tops on the look-out for smugglers (*see also p12* **Bootylicious**), and 'huers' watched the sea for shoals of fish swimming off the coast. Over the years the role of the various paths changed, and today the South West Coast Path is used almost exclusively for leisure activities. It is managed by the National Trust and other conservation organisations.

The South West Coast Path is fantastically varied, and can be enjoyed by all levels of walker, although it's worth noting that cyclists and horse riders are not allowed on the path. In its early stages the route runs along the edge of Exmoor National Park, crossing the highest point on the whole path at **Great Hangman**, where the land rises to 1,043 feet (318 metres). For most of the North Devon and north Cornwall coasts the path runs along stunning clifftops, dropping down steep-sided combes. By contrast, on the southern side walkers have to rely on ferries to cross river estuaries, or else face a long detour inland to find the first bridge upriver.

Experienced hikers or those who like a challenge should try the section of the path around **Hartland Point** in North Devon. There is virtually no sign of human habitation along the stretch between Clovelly and Bude, and the exhausting rollercoaster route crosses

spectacular cliffs. Less intrepid walkers might prefer to explore the **Lizard** peninsula, with its succession of sandy coves, tucked-away fishing villages and gentle paths through springy, flower-covered turf. Even easier sections run through sandy **Braunton Burrows** in North Devon, or along the beach at **Loe Bar** in Cornwall.

More information can be obtained from local tourist offices or from the **South West Coast Path Association** (Windlestraw, Penquit, Ermington, Devon PL21 0LU, 01752 896237, www.swcp.org.uk).

Inland, the long, canal-like drainage ditches that criss-cross the **Somerset Levels** offer excellent coarse fishing, with tench, perch, carp, orfe, bream and chub among the species to be found. You'll need a permit to fish from a designated site along the bank, but there's usually a notice stating where to get one.

Freshwater game fishing comes into its own further west, promising wild brown trout on the moors, spring salmon in North Devon and winter salmon in Cornwall. The river trout season runs from mid March to mid October, though the growth of fisheries stocked with rainbow trout means that you can cast a fly every month of the year. Many hotels and fishery owners in the area can provide day permits.

Whichever type of freshwater rod fishing you want to try, you must obtain an Environment Agency licence (if you're aged over 12) – or risk a fine of up to £2,500. A single-day licence costs as little as £2.75 and can be purchased at any post office, by phone on 0870 1662 662 or online at www.environment-agency.gov.uk.

Get Hooked! Angling in South-West England (£2.99) is the essential guide to more than 600 venues and is available from tackle shops, newsagents or direct from Diamond Publications, PO Box 59, Bideford, Devon EX39 4YN (add £1 p&p). Some of the contents are available online at www.gethooked.co.uk. Another good general contact for fishing in the area is the Southwest Lakes Trust (call 01837 871565 for information).

CAVING

If you've ever spent a half-hour wedged in the corner of a rush-hour tube carriage, you'll have a good idea of what caving's all about. It can be damp and claustrophobic – but it also offers the extraordinary thrill of exploring a world unseen by the vast majority of surface-dwellers.

The action of water on the limestone Mendip Hills has, over millions of years, created spectacular showcaves at **Cheddar** and **Wookey Hole**, and also gouged out less-accessible caverns that are just as thrilling to see – as long as you have the required training and equipment.

Caving is a relatively exclusive activity in that it is deeply unwise even to think of heading down a hole on your own. Instead, get a feel for life beneath the surface by joining an introductory session run by an organisation registered with the **National Caving Association** (0114 230 3575, www.nca.org.uk), which has strict safety regulations. In the West Country, speleologists – that's cavers to you and me – head for the Somerset village of **Priddy**, which is a good place to find out

about training courses. After an initial trip, you can hook up with a local club, as listed on www.caving.uk.com.

CLIMBING

The sheer range of geology across the South West is what keeps climbers coming back for more. In South Devon alone you could climb steep limestone in the morning, sandstone sea stacks in the afternoon and then finish off with some bouldering on one of the tors on Dartmoor – all within a radius of 20 miles (32 kilometres). In North Devon and Cornwall, the coast right down to St Ives offers a wide variety of crags, while the cliffs around Land's End and the Lizard rival any in the country.

The best way to learn the basic skills is on a course run by an outdoor activity centre. A two-day introduction to climbing will teach you how to move on rock, manage ropes, choose your equipment and belay (limiting the impact of a fall) – at the end of which you should be able to decide whether climbing is the lifetime obsession you've been looking for. A head for heights and basic all-round fitness are essential.

The **British Mountaineering Council** (0870 010 4878, www.thebmc.co.uk), promotes the interests of climbers, hillwalkers and mountaineers, and can provide details of local clubs. A superb source of information for more experienced climbers is www.javu.co.uk, which includes details of all the major climbing areas, accommodation and essential guidebooks.

CYCLING

As well as local initiatives throughout the region, there are also plenty of longer-distance cycling routes in the South West along traffic-free paths and traffic-calmed roads that are part of the National Cycle Network. National Cycle Route No.3 ('the West Country Way') run by Sustrans (0117 929 0888, www.sustrans.org.uk) covers 250 miles (402 kilometres) from Bristol down to Padstow. There's also the **Devon Coast to Coast** route (Plymouth to Ilfracombe; 102 miles/164 kilometres) and the **Cornish Way** (Land's End to Bude; 180 miles/289 kilometres).

The flat landscape of south Somerset is best suited to families with young children or those who just want a leisurely pedal. The 'Somerset Cycle Guide' includes all routes throughout the county and is available from tourist information centres. For tougher challenges head further south-west. **Exmoor** has hilly but quiet country lanes leading to tiny hamlets, as well as a network of bridleways and trails for mountain bikers. In addition, rangers offer summer 'bike hikes' over the moor, with details available on the National Park website (www.exmoor-nationalpark.gov.uk).

Life's a beach at **St Ives**.

Cycling is forbidden on **Dartmoor**'s high open moorland and National Park footpaths, but the Devon Coast to Coast route traverses the north-west side of the moor and is ideal for mountain bikers. For further information, get hold of the National Park Authority's map, 'Dartmoor for Off-Road Cyclists', which shows all the legal and rideable routes.

Gentler riding in Devon can be had along the Tarka Trail cycle/walkway, which extends from Barnstaple to Petrockstowe (*see p135* **Tarka territory**), while in Cornwall various routes give a taster of the county's scenery and heritage. The industrial past can be explored on the 15-mile (24-kilometre) **Coast to Coast** route from Portreath to Devoran (*see p269*), or there's the **Camel Trail**, which follows a disused railway along the estuary from Padstow to Wadebridge and Bodmin (*see p279*). The **Pentewan Valley Cycle Trail** (*see p234*) near Mevagissey is a shorter, traffic-free route ideal for families.

GOLF

The South West is an underrated area for golfers: **Saunton** in Devon, **St Mellion** and **St Enodoc** in Cornwall and the links at **Burnham** and **Berrow** in Somerset are among the finest courses in the country. These three counties also boast more than 100 other courses of varying attractiveness and difficulty. The best source of information is the *Sunday Telegraph Golf Course Guide to Britain and Ireland* (Collins Willow, £9.99).

However, your chances of playing at such prestigious venues are nil unless you turn up in respectable clothing (no shorts, jeans or loud shirts) and can produce a handicap certificate. Almost all private clubs will demand you flourish a certificate before you set foot on their kempt greens.

Wannabe golfers without a certificate should contact the **English Golf Union** (01526 354500, www.englishgolfunion.org), which can offer advice on getting started and provide free taster sessions in partnership with a number of clubs. Alternatively, just head for one of the region's public courses. These are not so fussy about handicaps and, at off-peak times, you'll be able to hire a set of clubs and hack away to your heart's content. For a more elegant introduction to the sport, book a course of lessons with a PGA-qualified professional; details are usually available from the club shop.

Golfers in possession of a handicap certificate, who are looking for a golf holiday should log on to www.britishgolfonline.com, which has links to around 30 courses across the region offering discounts on green fees, as well as 'stay and play' accommodation. Great Golf Holidays (01637 859965, www.greatgolf holidays.com) provides a selection of short breaks that include rounds on some of the best courses. Also useful are the free brochures 'Golf in Cornwall' and 'Golf in Devon', available by sending an A5 SAE to the Nook, Egloskerry, Launceston, Cornwall PL15 8ST (01566 785628).

RIDING AND PONY TREKKING

Exploring the countryside from the saddle of a horse is popular with all ages – and you don't need any training or much special clothing.

A gentle half-day trek into the countryside may be enough if you have small children to entertain, while equestrian devotees might prefer a week of tougher – and faster – riding.

There are schools and centres throughout the South West, so it pays to choose carefully. Look for a facility that is approved by the **British Horse Society** (08701 202244, www.bhs. org.uk) and has staff holding the minimum BHS qualification of assistant instructor. Most centres will supply British Safety Standard hats, which are compulsory; you will also need stout shoes with a heel.

The BHS publishes 'Where to Ride' (£2), a booklet listing more than 700 schools, which are inspected at least annually. Its website also has a comprehensive directory of approved holiday centres offering escorted or independent rides. If you want to arrange your own route and accommodation, the BHS guide *Bed and Breakfast for Horses* (£5.95) lists around 400 places where both animal and rider can eat and rest.

The best Beaches

For catching a wave
Fistral (*see p272*), **Widemouth Bay** (*see p284*) and **Woolacombe** (*see p138*).

For hardcore surfers
Porthleven (*see p245*), **Croyde** (*see p138*) and **Constantine Bay** (*see p276*).

For families
Dawlish Warren (*see p181*), **Blackpool Sands** (*see p195*) and **Bigbury-on-Sea** (*see p198*).

For golden sands
Bantham (*see p198*), **North Sands** (*see p198*) and **St Ives Bay** (*see p259*).

For a lazy-day picnic
Mill Bay (*see p198*) and **Watermouth Cove** (*see p141*).

For stunning scenery
Kynance Cove (*see p246*), **Porthcurno** (*see p254*) and **Bedruthan Steps** (*see p273*).

For getting away from it all
Rushy Bay (*see p288*) and **Pentle Bay** (*see p287*).

For shell seekers
Barricane (*see p138*) and **Lawrence's Bay** (*see p288*).

SURFING AND WATERSPORTS
Cornwall is Britain's surfing epicentre, with dozens of beaches along the north coast from Widemouth Bay right down to St Ives. Among these is **Fistral**, near Newquay, which is home to all major UK competitions and can get very crowded in summer. There are fewer spots along the south and west coasts, though Gwenvor and Sennen Cove – Britain's most westerly beach – are also highly rated. North Devon surfing is centred around Croyde, although some of the best spots are found outside this limited area, with sheltered bays providing surprising variety. For further information refer to our **Surf check** features on pages 140, 253 and 268.

The **British Surfing Association** (01736 360250, www.britsurf.co.uk) is the sport's governing body and includes third-party public liability insurance among its services. Daily Surf Call reports are available around the clock by calling 09068 360360 (calls 60p per minute).

You'll also find every other type of watersport on offer around the South West's coastline, along with training schools offering day, weekend and week-long courses suitable for all standards. The **Royal Yachting Association** (02380 627400, www.rya.org.uk) is the governing body for sailing, windsurfing, powerboating and aquabiking. Most would-be sailors begin in a one-person dinghy, such as a Topper, and succeed in completing an RYA beginners' course in two days. The basics of windsurfing are equally easy to master, so long as you're happy to spend your first few hours falling into the water'. Powerboating and aquabiking, meanwhile, are much faster, considerably more noisy and not universally welcomed by seekers of peace and tranquility.

For comprehensive information, check out South West Tourism's dedicated watersports website (www.sw-watersports.com).

SWIMMING
The European-wide **Blue Flag** system judges the standard of resort beaches, with a blue flag awarded to those that meet EC guidelines for water quality and provide approved sanitary and safety facilities. In 2002 South West beaches awarded a Blue Flag included Brixham, Woolacombe, Torquay, Blackpool Sands, Dawlish Warren, Bigbury-on-Sea, Croyde and Polzeath. The complete list along with judging criteria are detailed on the ENCAMS website (www.seasideawards.org.uk).

Bear in mind, however, that rural beaches are not currently included in the Blue Flag scheme; for a comprehensive guide to the quality of the region's beaches – based on stricter environmental criteria – refer instead

In Context

North Devon surfing:
'proper job'.

to the **Marine Conservation Society**'s 'Good Beach Guide' (www.goodbeachguide.co.uk). In 2002 the MCS recommended 125 beaches in the South West based on stringent water-quality standards. However, although this tally was higher than any other part of Britain, there remain a number of beaches in the region where the water has unacceptable levels of bacterial pollution, and swimming or watersports are not recommended.

Most resort beaches are patrolled by lifeguards from May to September and employ a flag system to indicate when and where the water is safe for bathing. Designated supervised bathing and body-boarding areas are marked by red and yellow flags, while canoes, windsurfers and other craft over five feet (1.52 metres) long must keep within the black-and-white chequered flags. A red flag means that sea conditions are dangerous, in which case lifeguards will prevent you from entering the water

On more isolated beaches, whether you choose to swim is up to you, so exercise caution before venturing in for a dip. Even strong swimmers can get into trouble: there are strong currents around piers, rocks, groynes and headlands; flat beaches are susceptible to fast-moving tides; and a number of spinal injuries occur each year due to people diving into shallow water. Always seek local advice rather than trusting your intuition.

It's legal to bathe in rivers and lakes unless signs indicate otherwise; however, the same warnings about safety apply. What's more, an Environment Agency report found that, in 2000, 55 per cent of British rivers had high phosphate concentrations, making them unsafe for swimming. By all means dip your feet in a fast-moving Dartmoor stream, but be more circumspect about going in up to your neck.

WALKING

Serious walkers head for the 368 square miles (953 square kilometres) of **Dartmoor National Park**. With its extraordinary beauty and unpredictable weather, it can present a challenge even for experienced outdoor enthusiasts. An excellent – and safe – way to explore Dartmoor is to join one of the guided walks that take place almost daily in summer and at least weekly in winter. A full programme is available on the National Park website. A similar though briefer programme is arranged by **Exmoor National Park Authority**.

If you prefer to take off on your own, there are excellent long-distance walks throughout Devon, Cornwall and Somerset, including the Tarka Trail (*see p135* **Tarka territory**). And, finally, if you're staying by the seaside, make sure you take at least one day out from your sunbathing schedule to explore the stunningly varied **South West Coast Path** (*see p38*).

Bristol & Bath

Introduction

Between them, these contrasting cities can offer pretty much everything the visitor could desire.

Although they are separated by a distance of only 13 miles (21 kilometres), the cities of Bath and Bristol make much of their differences, eyeing each other suspiciously along the Avon valley like rival siblings.

Far the bigger of the two, **Bristol** has a reputation as a hard-working merchant city with little time for the trappings of tourism. More recently, however, the regeneration of the harbour area and a flourishing cultural scene have put it firmly on the tourist map as an ideal weekend break destination. The city's fascinating past is brought to life by a number of engrossing historic sights and museums, while stylish restaurants and cafés provide a welcome refuelling stop between photo opportunities. In summer, make the most of Bristol's wide open spaces and outdoor

festivals, and after dark head for some of the best music, clubbing and theatre venues in the South West.

While Bristol is a relative newcomer on the tourist circuit, **Bath** is a seasoned campaigner. A Roman spa and an 18th-century party town, this compact city is one of the most beautiful destinations in the country, exuding an air of cultured elegance that still has enormous appeal. Bath's Georgian architecture, Roman remains and high-class museums are likely to keep you busy, but you should also take time out from the sightseeing rounds to simply stroll the streets, where excellent shops and restaurants are set against an exquisite 18th-century backdrop. By night seek out eclectic bars and pubs for a taste of the city's more alternative side.

Don't miss **Bristol & Bath**

@t Bristol
Kid-friendly gadgetry, wonderful wildlife exhibits and an IMAX cinema – the answer to a parent's prayers. *See p50.*

Clifton
This Bristol suburb boasts elegant architecture, chi-chi boutiques, cosy pubs, not to mention Brunel's iconic suspension bridge. *See p58.*

Ferry ride around Bristol docks
Explore the city's maritime heritage from the water and get a tantalising smell of the sea. *See p72.*

The Circus and the Royal Crescent
Check out Bath's most famous architectural show-stoppers. *See p81-2.*

Roman Baths
This is an utterly engrossing historic site – if you can avoid the tourist hordes. *See p77.*

Thermae Bath Spa
At last, a chance to enjoy Bath in your swimming cossie. *See p81.*

Bristol

Welcome to a vibrant city with a fascinating past and a ship-shape future.

Clifton Suspension Bridge.
See p59.

Bristol's reputation has waxed and waned to a dizzying degree over the centuries. The city has been praised for its mercantile prosperity yet despised for its involvement in the slave trade. In the 1980s it became infamous as the site of the St Paul's riots, only to emerge in the 1990s as a byword for innovation at the forefront of the UK music scene (*see p65* **Sound effects**).

What's more, since the 18th century, the city has lived in the shadow of its elegant little sister upriver. Bath, with its gorgeous Georgian architecture, has always been the tourist honeypot in this area, leaving Bristol's charms to pass largely unnoticed – even by its own residents.

Currently, though, Bristol is riding high on a wave of confidence that has transformed it into one of the most appealing cities in the UK and a contender for European Capital of Culture in 2008. Thanks to its proximity to both coast and countryside, the city combines a contemporary urban vibe with the promise of more rural pleasures on its doorstep. Culturally, ethnically and economically diverse, it's a city where the maritime and industrial achievements of the past provide a context for artistic and cultural success in the present. And where ambitious self-promotion is tempered by a laid-back, easy-living attitude.

HISTORY

Bristol's status as a port at the confluence of the Avon and Frome rivers was already well-established when Bristol-based explorer John Cabot discovered Newfoundland in 1497. This event, however, presaged a whole new era in the city's fortunes, firmly cementing it on the world's sea-bound trading routes. From the Middle Ages until the 20th century, merchant ships importing wine, cotton, sugar and tobacco sailed right into the city centre – as Alexander Pope commented in 1739, 'in the middle of the street, as far as you can see, are hundreds of ships, their masts as thick as they can stand by one another…'.

By the 18th century Bristol was the richest English city outside London. Much of its wealth came from the so-called 'triangular trade', which exported cloth and cheap jewellery from Bristol to West Africa, slaves from West Africa to work on plantations in the Caribbean, and cotton, sugar and tobacco from the plantations back to Bristol. Most successful shipowners and merchants were also slave-traders or plantation owners, whose interests were intimately bound up in the continuance of this barbaric but highly lucrative business. Most controversially, Edward Colston, Bristol's great benefactor, whose name graces a street, a concert venue and several schools in the city, played a key role in the planning and financing of slaving ventures to Africa in the late 17th century. The slave trade was, until recently, largely excised from any telling of Bristol's history, but is now

increasingly being discussed as an inescapable and enduring part of the city's heritage.

The abolition of the trade in 1807 coincided with Bristol's gradual decline as a maritime city. As ships became larger, the infamous 40-foot (12-metre) tides in the Bristol Channel became an obstacle to the port's development, and despite the creation of the Floating Harbour, with locks at either end to control water levels, Liverpool usurped Bristol as the country's main port outside London.

Local heroes
Isambard Kingdom Brunel

Though he was born in Portsmouth and lived most of his life in London, Isambard Kingdom Brunel (1806-1859) is regarded as a true Bristolian by those who live in the city. Designer, engineer and inventor, Brunel exemplified the Victorian ideal of innovation and progress, and nowhere did he leave his mark more indelibly than in Bristol.

Isambard was the son of a successful French engineer, Marc Brunel, who had settled in England at the turn of the 18th century. The young Brunel was trained in Paris and subsequently worked with his father on the Rotherhithe–Wapping tunnel under the Thames in London. During construction, the tunnel flooded and Isambard was almost drowned. He was sent to Clifton to recuperate and there heard of a competition to design a bridge over the Avon Gorge.

Brunel submitted four designs, all of which were initially rejected by the judging panel led by Thomas Telford. However, in a second competition in 1831, Brunel's 'Egyptian' design was declared the winning entry and the young designer was appointed as the project's chief engineer. Construction of **Clifton Suspension Bridge** (*see p59*) was dogged by financial and practical difficulties from the outset, not least the outbreak of the Bristol riots in October 1831, but by 1833 its architect had another important commission to occupy him.

Aged just 26, Brunel became chief engineer for the new **Great Western Railway** between London and Bristol, nicknamed God's Wonderful Railway. Brunel introduced broad-gauge track to maximise the speed and efficiency of the line, and when it opened in 1841 it reduced the 118-mile (190-kilometre)

journey from 24 hours by horse-drawn carriage to just four hours by train. The engineering highlight is **Box Tunnel** in Wiltshire, a two-mile (three-kilometre) stretch through the limestone hills, whose construction cost the lives of more than 100 navvies.

At the terminus of the railway Brunel built **Temple Meads**, a grand, turretted station that is the oldest in the world (*see p57*). Brunel did not regard this as the end of the line, however. In his vision, passengers from London would continue from Bristol to New York on board his **SS Great Western**, the biggest paddlesteamer of the age. Launched in Bristol in 1837, it was the first liner to cross the Atlantic and completed the journey in just 15 days.

The *Great Western* was followed by the **SS Great Britain** in 1843, a six-masted, propellor-driven steamship that revolutionised ship design (*see p51*). Sixteen years later the **SS Great Eastern** was launched. This monster boat was 693 feet (211 metres) long, carried 2,996 passengers, and was driven by the combined force of a screw propellor, two paddle wheels and sails. Yet, despite its impressive size, it was a technical and financial failure.

Brunel died in 1859 from an excess of hard work and cigars. He never saw the opening of his **Tamar Bridge** at Saltash, which still carries trains over the border between Devon and Cornwall. Nor did he witness the completion of his architectural masterpiece, the Clifton Suspension Bridge, which was not officially opened until 1869. Brunel referred to the bridge in his diary as 'My first love, my darling', and it remains, perhaps, the engineer's most enduring memorial.

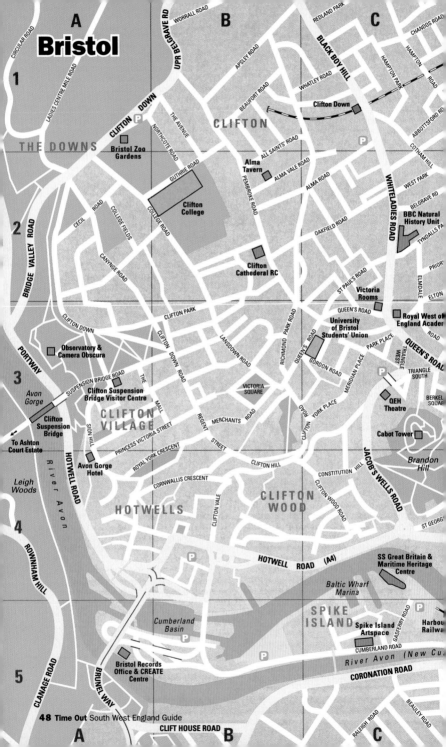

Bristol

A
B
C

CIRCULAR ROAD
LADIES CENTRE MILE ROAD
UPR BELGRAVE RD
WORRALL ROAD
REDLAND PARK
CHANDOS ROAD
BLACK BOY HILL
HAMPTON PARK
HAMPTON ROAD
APSLEY ROAD
WHATLEY ROAD
BEAUFORT ROAD
ABBOTTSFORD RD
COTHAM HILL

THE DOWNS

CLIFTON DOWN

Bristol Zoo Gardens

CLIFTON

Clifton Down

NORTHCOTE ROAD
THE AVENUE
GUTHRIE ROAD

ALL SAINTS' ROAD

Alma Tavern
ALMA VALE ROAD
Alma Road

WEST PARK

CECIL ROAD
COLLEGE FIELDS
ROAD
COLLEGE ROAD

Clifton College

PEMBROKE ROAD

OAKFIELD ROAD

BELGRAVE RD

WHITELADIES ROAD

BBC Natural History Unit
TYNDALLS PA

CANYNGE ROAD

PRIOR

ELMDALE

ELTON

Clifton Cathedral RC

ST PAUL'S ROAD

Victoria Rooms

QUEEN'S ROAD

Royal West of England Acader

CLIFTON DOWN

CLIFTON PARK

LANSDOWN ROAD

RICHMOND PARK ROAD

University of Bristol Students' Union

PARK PLACE

QUEEN'S ROAD

ROAD

Observatory & Camera Obscura

PORTWAY

CLIFTON DOWN ROAD

QUEEN'S ROAD
GORDON ROAD

MERIDIAN PLACE

TRIANGLE WEST
TRIANGLE SOUTH
BERKEL SQUAR

SUSPENSION BRIDGE ROAD

Clifton Suspension Bridge Visitor Centre

THE MALL

VICTORIA SQUARE

YORK PLACE

QEH Theatre

Avon Gorge

Clifton Suspension Bridge

CLIFTON VILLAGE

SION HILL
PRINCESS VICTORIA STREET
ROYAL YORK CRESCENT

REGENT STREET

MERCHANTS ROAD

CLIFTON ROAD

Cabot Tower

Brandon Hill

To Ashton Court Estate

Avon Gorge Hotel

CLIFTON HILL

JACOB'S WELLS ROAD

Leigh Woods

River Avon

HOTWELL ROAD

CORNWALLIS CRESCENT

CONSTITUTION HILL

CLIFTON WOOD ROAD

CLIFTON WOOD

ST GEORG'

CLIFTON VALE

ROWNHAM HILL

HOTWELLS

HOTWELL ROAD (A4)

SS Great Britain & Maritime Heritage Centre

Baltic Wharf Marina

SPIKE ISLAND

Spike Island Artspace

GASFERRY ROAD

Harbou Railwa

Cumberland Basin

CUMBERLAND ROAD

River Avon (New Cu

CLANAGE ROAD

BRUNEL WAY

Bristol Records Office & CREATE Centre

CORONATION ROAD

CLIFT HOUSE ROAD

A
B
C

By the 19th century wealthy merchants were moving away from the centre of Bristol to the exclusive Georgian suburb of Clifton. Isambard Kingdom Brunel (*see p47* **Local heroes**) bequeathed the city – among other gems – the graceful Clifton Suspension Bridge and a rail link to London Paddington, while maritime trade was supplemented by the tobacco and brewing industries – both largely gone today. In the 20th century, aviation took over from seafaring as the city's chief industry; the last section of the River Frome (under the Centre) was covered over in 1938 and the City Docks were closed to commercial traffic in 1976.

Badly damaged in German bombing raids in 1942, Bristol was further blighted by crude 1960s planners. Much of the centre of the city is still dominated by the soulless Broadmead shopping centre and a surrounding jumble of concrete-clad streets. In recent years, however, the city's ebullience has manifested itself in a radical transformation of the urban landscape. Bristol's focus has shifted back to the river, and the source of the city's prosperity for many centuries is now at the vanguard of its regeneration. The redevelopment is not all about fancy al fresco eateries and luxury warehouse apartments either; the Floating Harbour is now one of the most worthwhile areas of the city to visit, with numerous contemporary waterside attractions that are rooted firmly in the city's maritime past.

Sightseeing

It is relatively easy to explore the city on foot; a network of blue pedestrian signposts helps to point you in the direction of the main sights and there are pleasant footpaths alongside the Floating Harbour. Bear in mind, though, that away from the river, Bristol is a hilly city and you may want to use local buses (*see p72*) to reach Clifton or other suburbs.

Harbourside

The most obvious place to start an exploration of Bristol's waterfront is at the **Centre**, the large traffic island covering the River Frome. From here a series of waterjets flows in the direction of the dock at **Augustine's Reach**, where a converted red-brick Victorian wine warehouse shelters a series of bars and the much-loved **Watershed** media centre, which runs an extensive programme of events associated with digital media, photography and film (*see p68*). It has an airy bar-cum-café with extensive views over the waterside.

Beyond the Watershed, **Canon's Marsh** is the site of the Harbourside's most obvious and ambitious regeneration programme. With the

help of £42-million lottery grant, it has been transformed into an area of wide piazzas surrounded by lively bars and waterside restaurants. It is also the setting for the city tourist office (*see p72*) and for the award-winning **@tBristol** complex.

Unaccompanied adults may find the superabundance of levers, buttons, screens and pulleys at **Explore@tBristol** somewhat overwhelming, but for families this place is a rainy-day godsend. In-yer-face corporate sponsorship detracts from the educational appeal of some exhibits, but there's some serious science here too among all the gadgetry, and the Orange Imaginarium (actually a planetarium) offers an exploration of the night sky.

Cross the piazza to reach Explore's partner attraction, **Wildwalk@tBristol**. This is a truly impressive exhibition devoted to the natural world. The visitor is led through the history of life on earth, with sections devoted to different life forms. Interactive screens and film footage are complemented by live exhibits – fish, insects, spiders, reptiles and two walk-through botanical habitats – to create an informative and thought-provoking attraction. You'll need at least two hours to explore it thoroughly, but it will be time well spent. An **IMAX** cinema is housed in the same building.

After the exhaustion-inducing entertainment of @tBristol, spend some time relaxing among the water features, skateboarders and statues in **Millennium Square** – can you spot Bristol-born Archie Leach, aka Cary Grant? Returning to the waterfront, Narrow Quay is reached via **Pero's Bridge**, named after a slave owned by the 18th-century merchant John Pinney (*see p54*). The bridge has distinctive funnel-like horns that act as weights, allowing it to open for larger boats to pass through.

On Narrow Quay, the **Architecture Centre** is an independent organisation devoted to design and the built environment, with excellent temporary exhibitions and a good gift shop. Nearby, the **Arnolfini** is a leading arts centre housed in a refurbished 1830s tea warehouse. It presents innovative visual art exhibitions, plus contempory performances (*see p70*) and arthouse films (*see p68*), and the café-bar is a popular haunt of the city's culturati. Thanks to lottery funding, the Arnolfini is due to expand its gallery space and facilities in 2003 and beyond, and may be closed for extended periods as a result.

Outside, a pensive-looking statue of John Cabot by Stephen Joyce stares out across the harbour. The Italian explorer set out from Bristol in 1497 under licence from King Henry VII to try to find a westward sea route to the Orient. Instead he discovered Newfoundland.

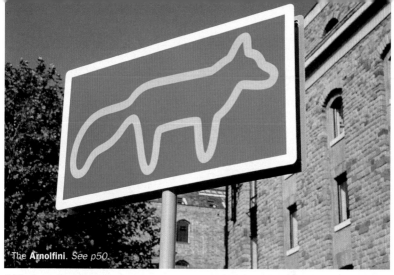
The **Arnolfini**. *See p50.*

A life-size replica of his boat, the *Matthew*, is docked further downstream (*see p51*).

From the Arnolfini, it's a short walk across the narrow swing bridge to the red and white hulk of the **Bristol Industrial Museum**, fronted by sentinel-like electric cranes. The large ground-floor gallery is devoted to road and rail hardware built in the city, while upstairs are sections on printing, packaging, the port and the aerospace industry. While these examples of the city's engineering heritage are certain to excite car-, train- and plane-spotters, the highlight of the museum for many other visitors is the in-depth – and disturbing – display devoted to the slave trade and its continuing legacy in the city.

In summer the museum's vintage boats tour the harbour and a steam railway carries passengers along the docks. You can follow the tracks on foot for about half a mile, past new designer apartment complexes, to the **Maritime Heritage Centre**, which tells the story of shipbuilding in Bristol from medieval times to the present day. Just outside is the **SS Great Britain**, high and dry in the Great Western Dockyard where she was first constructed.

This grand old lady was the first ocean-going ship to be constructed of iron and driven by a propellor (rather than paddles) and is regarded as the grandmother of modern shipbuilding. Designed by Isambard Kingdom Brunel (*see p47* **Local heroes**) and launched in 1843 by Prince Albert, the *SS Great Britain* served as a luxury transatlantic cruiseliner before ignominiously running aground on the Irish coast in 1846. On recovery she served as passenger liner carrying emigrants to Australia, a troop carrier taking soldiers to the Crimean War and a cargo ship transporting coal to San Francisco. Eventually, in 1937, after one million ocean miles, she was beached in the Falkland Islands and left to rust. In 1970 the rotting hull was towed 9,000 miles (14,500 kilometres) back to the Great Western Dockyard in Bristol, arriving on 19 July – 127 years to the day after her launch.

Restoration of the ship and the dockyards has been under way since the 1970s and is still very much a work in progress, so don't expect Disneyesque perfection from this unique site. The hull itself has been substantially reconstructed, but the interior, including the massive engine, is yet to be restored, although contemporary sketches and plans give clues to the ship's original style and opulence.

Moored in the Floating Harbour next to the *SS Great Britain* is the touchingly small and fragile-looking **Matthew**, a life-size replica of the boat sailed by John Cabot (*see p50*). The ship was built to commemorate the 500-year anniversary of Cabot's Atlantic crossing and completed a seven-week replica voyage from Bristol to Newfoundland in the summer of 1997. For information on cruises and the *Matthew*'s residential sailing programme, *see p61*.

Also in the Great Western Dockyard is the **Bristol Blue Glass Studio** (0117 902 7888, www.stclairglass.co.uk) where glass-blowing demonstrations are held every hour, while at the other end of Gas Ferry Road is **Spike Island Artspace** (133 Cumberland Road, 0117 929 2266), a gallery complex that offers affordable studios for emerging artists and hosts innovative art installations and exhibitions.

West of the *Great Britain*, **Baltic Wharf** is where wood from Scandinavia was unloaded. It is now occupied by new housing, a marina, a sailing school and a couple of waterside pubs.

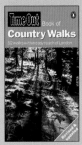

Bristol Industrial Museum.
See p51.

Beyond, the far western end of the Floating Harbour is dominated by two Edwardian red-brick tobacco warehouses. One of these houses the **CREATE Centre**, which showcases and provides support for environmental initiatives. It is not primarily a sightseeing attraction, but ecologically minded visitors may be interested in the Ecohome, a sustainable house of the future, and in the recycling exhibition. There's also a small art gallery and a café on site.

Architecture Centre

Narrow Quay (0117 922 1540/www.arch-centre. demon.co.uk). **Open** 11am-5pm Tue-Fri; noon-5pm Sat, Sun. **Admission** free. **Credit** *shop* MC, V. **Map** p49 D4.

Arnolfini

16 Narrow Quay (box office 0117 929 9191/bar 927 9330/www.arnolfini.demon.co.uk). **Open** (until Aug 2003) *Bar* 10am-11pm Mon-Sat; noon-10.30pm Sun. *Cinema* times vary; phone for details. *Gallery* 10am-7pm Mon-Wed, Fri, Sat; 10am-9pm Thur; noon-7pm Sun. **Admission** *Cinema* £4.40; £3 concessions. *Gallery* free. **Credit** MC, V. **Map** p49 D4.

@tBristol

Anchor Road, Harbourside (0845 345 1235/www.at-bristol.org.uk). **Open** *Explore & Wildwalk* 10am-6pm daily. *IMAX* (shows every 75mins) 10am-4.30pm Mon-Wed; 10am-8.30pm Thur, Fri; 12.30-8.30pm Sat, Sun. **Admission** *Explore* £7.50; £4.95-£5.95 concessions; £21 family; free under-3s. *Wildwalk* £6.50; £4.50-£5.50 concessions; £19 family; free

under-3s. *IMAX* £6.50; £4.50-£5.50 concessions; £19 family; free under-3s. *Combined tickets* phone for details. **Credit** MC, V. **Map** p49 D4.

Bristol Industrial Museum

Princes Wharf, Wapping Road (0117 925 1470/ www.bristol-city.gov.uk/museums). **Open** *Apr-Oct* 10am-5pm Mon-Wed, Sat, Sun. *Nov-Mar* 10am-5pm Sat, Sun. **Admission** free. *Weekend boat trip* (Apr-Oct only) £3; £1.50 concessions. *Bristol harbour railway* (Mar-Oct only) £1; 60p concessions; £3.50 family; free under-6s. **Credit** MC, V. **Map** p49 D5.

CREATE Centre

Smeaton Road, Cumberland Basin (0117 925 0505/ www.createcentre.co.uk). **Open** *Ecohome* noon-3pm Mon-Fri. *Recycling exhibition & art gallery* 9am-5pm Mon-Fri. **Admission** free. **Map** p48 A5.

SS Great Britain & the Maritime Heritage Centre

Great Western Dockyard, Gas Ferry Road (0117 926 0680/www.ss-great-britain.com). **Open** *Apr-Oct* 10am-5.30pm daily. *Nov-Mar* 10am-4.30pm daily. **Admission** £6.25; £3.75-£5.25 concessions; £16.50 family. **Credit** MC, V. **Map** p48 C4.

West End

West of the Centre, **College Green** is a favourite haunt of the city's skateboarders, flanked on one side by the uninspiring red-brick curve of the Council House (1935-56) and on the other by the façade of **Bristol Cathedral**.

The cathedral began life as an abbey church serving the Augustinian community that was founded here in 1140. It was modified and developed over the following centuries, particularly under Abbot Knowle, and on the dissolution of the monasteries in 1539 was granted cathedral status by Henry VIII; the adjoining abbey buildings became the cathedral choir school, a role they retain to this day. It was not until the late 19th century under the neo-Gothic architect George Edmund Street that the nave and west front of the cathedral were completed, following Abbot Knowle's medieval plan.

Although Bristol Cathedral is not as instantly awe-inspiring as the cathedrals of Wells (*see p102*) and Salisbury, it retains a unique place in the development of Christian architecture as one of the finest 'hall churches' in Europe. The uniform height of its interior creates an open, democratic space in which no single area is given undue prominence. Points of interest include the brightly coloured 13th-century Lady Chapel, with its unusual star-shaped recesses, and the 14th-century Berkeley Chapel. The highlight, though, is the Chapter House, a late Norman masterpiece from 1165 featuring dazzling geometric stone work.

Squashed in among the shop fronts on the edge of College Green, the **Lord Mayor's Chapel** (aka St Mark's; 0117 929 4350) was built in 1230 as part of a medieval poor hospital. It became the property of the city when the hospital was dissolved in the 16th century and remains the only church in Britain owned by a government authority. Look out for the two ornately carved wooden chairs used by the Lord Mayor and Lady Mayoress.

Stretching up the hill to the north, **Park Street** is lined with some of the city's hippest shops (*see p67*), while off to the west, the 18th-century terraces on Great George Street and Charlotte Street give a foretaste of Clifton's elegant architecture. At No.7 Great George Street, the **Georgian House** was built between 1788 and 1791 by the Bristol architect William Paty for the successful sugar merchant John Pinney; it is a prime example of a merchant's house from the city's heyday. A number of rooms, decorated and furnished in Georgian style, are open to the public, including the unusual cold plunge bath in the basement. On the second floor is a small display examining John Pinney's association with the slave trade.

Looking down on the house from the other side of the street is **St George's** church, built in 1823 in the style of a doric temple by Greek revivalist Robert Smirke, and now a well-known venue for jazz and chamber concerts (*see p69*).

Bristol Cathedral: a fine 'hall church'.

At the end of Great George Street, the steep-sided, grassy park at **Brandon Hill** is crowned by **Cabot's Tower**, built in 1897 to mark the 400th anniversary of the discovery of Newfoundland. Climb the stairs to the viewing platform at the top for fabulous views of the city, harbour and surrounding hills.

Another tower stands at the top of Park Street, marking the entrance to the Wills Memorial Library and the School of Law. Endowed by the wealthy local tobacco family, the neo-Gothic **Wills Memorial Tower** was completed in 1925 and is a distinctive symbol of the University of Bristol. The Wills family were also responsible for the **City Museum & Art Gallery** next door, which opened in 1905. Built in grand municipal style, the museum combines displays of local natural history, geology and archaeology with unexpectedly impressive examples of European and oriental decorative arts; paintings by British, French and Dutch masters; Egyptian and Assyrian artefacts; plus temporary art and science exhibitions. There's an attractive café at the back.

Heading east along **Park Row**, you'll come to a red door, which marks the modest entrance to **Red Lodge**. Built in 1590, this red stone Elizabethan lodge is the only surviving remnant of the Great House estate where Queen

Elizabeth I once stayed. (The Great House itself stood on the site of the present Colston Hall.) Much of the Lodge was substantially remodelled in the 1730s, but a couple of original Elizabethan rooms remain intact, including the first-floor Oak Room, the undisputed highlight of the house. Entered through an elaborately carved wooden doorway, it features intricate wood panelling, a plaster ceiling and a huge, ornate stone fireplace. Outside, the south-facing garden has been redesigned in Elizabethan style as a knot garden with herbaceous borders.

Bristol Cathedral

College Green (0117 926 4879/www.bristol-cathedral.co.uk). **Open** 8.30am-6pm daily. **Admission** free. **Credit** *Shop* MC, V. **Map** p49 D4.

City Museum & Art Gallery

Queen's Road (0117 922 3571/www.bristol-city.gov.uk/museums). **Open** 10am-5pm daily. **Admission** free. **Credit** *Shop* MC, V. **Map** p49 D3.

Georgian House

7 Great George Street (0117 921 1362/www.bristol-city.gov.uk/museums). **Open** *Apr-Oct* 10am-5pm Mon-Wed, Sat, Sun. Closed Nov-Mar. **Admission** free. **Map** p49 D3.

Red Lodge

Park Row (0117 921 1360/www.bristol-city.gov.uk/museums). **Open** *Apr-Oct* 10am-5pm Mon-Wed, Sat, Sun. Closed Nov-Mar. **Admission** free. **Map** p49 D3.

The Old City & Broadmead

East of Narrow Quay lie Princes Street and Queen Square, where the city's merchants made their homes in the early 18th century. Designed in 1699, **Queen Square** occupied a prime position on the horseshoe bend between the Frome and Avon rivers. The merchants' brick townhouses fronted the square, while their warehouses overlooked the quays at the back.

Queen Square has suffered numerous indignities over the years. In 1831 it was badly damaged by rioters, who took to the streets in support of the Reform Act. The square was restored, but replacement houses were constructed in stone instead of brick, resulting in the square's uneven architecture. In 1935 town planners allowed a dual-carriageway to be constructed diagonally across the square, leaving Rysbrack's bronze statue of William III (1732-36) marooned on a traffic island, and a few years later the square was badly bombed by German planes targeting the port.

Recent welcome developments have seen Queen Square returned to something like its former glory: the road has been removed to create a grassy park, crossed by gravel paths where boules matches are played during the

Cabot's Tower... and the view from the top. *See p54.*

summer. Of the remaining brick houses, No.29 on the south side is the finest and is now the regional headquarters of English Heritage.

Immediately north is cobblestoned **King Street**, laid out in 1633 and still lined with some impressive 17th- and 18th-century buildings, including two sets of almshouses. The most important building on the street, though, is the **Theatre Royal**, home of the Bristol Old Vic repertory company (*see p69*). Built in 1766, it is the longest continually running theatre in England and has an ornate Georgian interior.

Near the water is the distinctive 17th-century half-timbered **Llandoger Trow** pub (King Street, 0117 926 0783), named after the flat-bottomed Welsh trading boats that used to moor around the corner on Welsh Back. The pub is supposedly the model for the Admiral Benbow in RL Stephenson's *Treasure Island*, and is also credited as the meeting place of Daniel Defoe and Alexander Selkirk, the rescued seaman on whom Defoe based Robinson Crusoe. Opposite, the **Old Duke** pub is a renowned trad jazz venue (*see p69*).

North of King Street is the business heart of the Old City, where local traders would buy and sell shares in the Italianate **Stock Exchange** on St Nicholas Street – now an upmarket Indian restaurant (*see p62*). Backing on to the street, **St Nicholas Markets** (*see p67*) were established in 1743 and now incorporate three covered markets selling arts, crafts, bric-a-brac, books, clothing and food. Many of the stalls are housed in the former **Corn Exchange** built in 1741-3 by John Wood the Elder and regarded as the city's finest 18th-century public building. Outside on Corn Street are four brass pillars, known as 'nails', where 17th-century tradesmen would make their payments in the days before the Exchange was built – hence the expression 'to pay on the nail'.

Further down Corn Street are the **Commercial Rooms** (now a beautifully converted Wetherspoons pub; 0117 927 9681), where Bristol's businessmen met in the 19th century; John McAdam (of tarmac fame) was the first president in 1811. The top of the street, meanwhile, is graced by the Georgian tower and cupola of **All Saint's Church**, which houses a memorial to Edward Colston by Rysbrack. Opposite, on the corner of Broad and Wine Streets, **Christchurch** was built in 1740 by William Paty and has striking quarterjacks on its tower that mark each quarter of an hour. Further down Broad Street, look out for the art nouveau tile façade of the **Edward Everard** printshop.

St John's Arch at the end of the street is the only surviving medieval city gate, and once overlooked the River Frome at what is now Quay Street. The gateway consists of a central vaulted arch for wagons, flanked by two pedestrian walkways, and is topped by the tiny 14th-century church of St John the Baptist, commonly known as **St John-on-the-Wall**.

On the other side of Wine Street is **Castle Park**, a pleasant grassy enclave overlooking the water. This was the heart of the medieval city, occupied, until Cromwell's time, by a fortress that guarded the bridge over the Avon. The ruins of **St Peter's Church** at the centre of the park are a reminder of the destruction wreaked on the city by German bombs in November 1940.

Also destroyed in the bombing campaign were the old workshops and businesses that occupied Broadmead immediately to the north. Redeveloped in the 1950s as a pedestrian shopping zone, **Broadmead** is now a prime example of the uninspiring post-war architecture that blights many British cities, although the Galleries shopping centre (*see p67*), built in 1991 and entered through

Red Lodge: a hidden haven of Elizabethan style. *See p54.*

18th-century almshouses, does a little to improve the area's appeal. Having said that, shoppers will find all the high-street favourites here, plus a couple of decent department stores, and a lovely shopping arcade, built in 1825.

Amid the banality of modern-day Broadmead, it is a surprise and a delight to find **John Wesley's New Room**, tucked away next door to the Arcade. Built in 1739 by John Wesley himself, this was the first Methodist chapel in the world. The peaceful interior has changed little since Wesley's day and it's easy to conjure an image of the preacher holding forth from the double-tiered pulpit. Above the chapel are a series of rooms used by Wesley and his associates, including his brother, the hymn-writer Charles Wesley.

John Wesley's New Room

36 The Horsefair (0117 926 4740/ www.methodist.org.uk/new.room). **Open** 10am-4pm Mon-Sat. **Admission** free. *Guided tours incl Charles Wesley's house* (by appointment only) *£4.50; £2.25 concessions; free under-5s.* **Credit** MC, V. **Map** p49 E3.

Redcliffe & further east

From Queen Square it's a short hop across Redcliffe Bridge to **St Mary Redcliffe**, called 'the fairest, goodliest, and most famous parish church in England' by Elizabeth I in 1574.

First recorded in 1115, the church is a monument to the wealth of local merchants who lived in this suburb outside the city walls. Its neo-Gothic spire, completed in 1872, rises 292 feet (89 metres) above the red sandstone cliffs on the south bank of the Avon, from which the church takes its name.

Most visitors enter the church through the ornately carved, hexagonal north porch, built in the early 14th century. It is one of the most attractive parts of the whole building and leads through to an early English inner porch, built in 1185. Once in the main body of the church, stand at the west door to admire the consistent perpendicular architecture and stone vaulting of the interior, which dates from the 14th and 15th centuries. The ceiling displays over 1,000 bosses decorated in gold leaf.

Points of interest include St John's Chapel, which contains the only surviving medieval stained glass in the church and a whale bone, believed to have been brought back from Newfoundland by John Cabot. Elsewhere, look out for the Chaotic Pendulum in the north transept, the modern stained glass in the Lady Chapel and the distinctive 14th-century star-shaped tomb recesses in the south aisle.

The church has an illustrious cultural heritage: Handel played the organ here; Hogarth painted a Resurrection triptych for the altar (now hidden away from public view in St Nicholas church in the Old City); and the Romantic poets Samuel Taylor Coleridge and Robert Southey got married to sisters Sara and Edith Fricker here in 1795. Most famously, in the 1760s the precociously talented Thomas Chatterton claimed to have discovered poetic manuscripts written by a 15th-century monk in the muniment room above the north porch. In fact, the manuscripts were skillful forgeries created by Chatterton himself. The poet killed himself with arsenic in 1770 aged just 18, but was immortalised as a Romantic martyr ('the marvellous boy') by Wordsworth and others.

During the 18th century the cliffs west of the church were quarried for sand for use in the glassmaking and pottery trades, resulting in a network of underground caverns known as the **Redcliffe Caves**. Local lore suggests that slaves were once incarcerated underground here, although there is no actual evidence for this. You can catch a glimpse of one of the caves inside the Ostrich pub on Bathurst Basin (*see p64*). To the north, immense Victorian brick warehouses line **Redcliffe Backs** along the eastern bank of the Floating Harbour. Most have now been renovated and converted into sought-after city-centre apartments, although Courage Brewery still operates from its site near Bristol Bridge.

Further east, just off Victoria Street is the leaning tower and ruins of **Temple Church**. The main body of the 14th-century church was a victim of German incendiary bombs, but its tower has always been at an angle due to the soft soil around the foundations; it currently leans more than five feet (1.60 metres) off the vertical on the west face. North of here it is possible to follow a path along the Floating Harbour to redeveloped **Temple Quay**, Bristol's newest business district, where the waterside is dominated by large, modern office buildings. Ferry passengers disembark here for **Temple Meads** station.

Built on land once owned by the Knights Templar, the original turretted station building (which ceased operation in 1966) was constructed in 1840 by Isambard Kingdom Brunel (*see p47* **Local heroes**), making it the oldest railway station in the world. In autumn 2002 the former engine shed became the clumsily named **British Empire & Commonwealth Museum**, the first museum of its kind in the world. Tracing the history of the Empire and Commonwealth from the early European explorers to the multiracial communities of today, it offers an international perspective on the motives, achievements, exploitation and impact of British imperialism.

The rugged cliffs of the **Avon Gorge** once inspired poets and painters. *See p59.*

The museum handles this controversial subject with a degree of imagination, using interactive displays, artefacts sourced from other major museum collections and some fascinating early photos, films and oral history exhibits.

British Empire & Commonwealth Museum

Station Approach, Temple Meads (0117 925 4980/ www.empiremuseum.co.uk). **Open** 10am-5pm daily. **Admission** £4.95; £2.95-£4.35 concessions; £12 family; free under-5s. **Credit** MC, V. **Map** p49 F4.

St Mary Redcliffe

Redcliffe Way (0117 929 1487/www.stmary redcliffe.co.uk). **Open** *May-Oct* 9am-5pm Mon-Sat; 8am-8pm Sun. *Nov-Apr* 9am-4pm Mon-Sat; 8am-8pm Sun. *Services* 9.15am, 5pm Mon-Sat; 8am, 9.30am, 11.15am, 6.30pm Sun. **Admission** free; donations welcome. **Credit** *Café* MC, V. **Map** p49 E5.

Clifton & Hotwells

Hotwells lies on the north side of Cumberland Basin, where the Floating Harbour rejoins the River Avon as it enters the cliffs of the Avon Gorge. Although it is now dominated by the very busy A4 (dangerous for pedestrians), this area was once the site of a health resort, centred around a natural spring. A pump room was built in 1696, and by 1760 Hotwells had become a fashionable spa, attracting the great and good

of society during the 'season' from May to October. (Many visitors then moved on to spend the winter in the more formal surroundings of Bath.) However, Hotwells never achieved the social style of Bath and by the end of the 18th century it had gained the dubious reputation of being the last resort of the incurable. The spa buildings were finally demolished in 1867, and all that now remains is a small cave where the pump once stood.

The decline of Hotwells was countered by the rise of **Clifton** as a desirable residential suburb on the hill above the gorge. Developed during the late 18th and early 19th centuries with grand crescents and elegant Georgian architecture, Clifton did not become part of the city until 1835 and has managed to retain its exclusive (not to say snobbish) character to this day, looking down on the rest of Bristol from its imperious perch to the north-west.

Clifton's Georgian crescents do not have the architectural panache of those in Bath but their position on the hillside above the River Avon is more dramatic. The façade of **Royal York Crescent**, which was built between 1791 and 1820, consists of 46 houses and stretches in a wide arc for a quarter of a mile (390 metres), making it the longest Georgian crescent in the world. Just as fine, though less enormous, are Cornwallis Crescent and Windsor Terrace to the south. Other architectural highlights include grandiose **Victoria Square**, which was laid out in the 1830s and '40s. (The cricketer WG Grace later lived at No.16.)

At the heart of the district, **Clifton Village** is a picturesque amalgam of bijou boutiques, traditional shops, pastel-coloured terraces and Georgian splendour, centred around Regent Street, Princess Victoria Street and the Mall. The latter is dominated by the **Clifton Assembly Rooms**, which were designed by the architect Francis Greenway in 1806, and originally incorporated the Royal Clifton Hotel, where the young Princess Victoria stayed in 1830. Greenway was deported to Australia for fraud in 1813, and went on to became one of the country's most celebrated colonial architects.

Despite the beautiful architecture and appealing atmosphere, the highlight of Clifton remains Brunel's magnificent **Suspension Bridge**, which spans the chasm of the Avon Gorge. In the 17th and 18th centuries, the Gorge was considered one of the country's natural wonders, with poets and travellers waxing lyrical about its wild, romantic scenery. Its appearance has been substantially altered over the years by quarrying and road building, but it remains an impressive sight.

The project to bridge the Gorge between Clifton and Leigh Woods was initiated in 1754 by the merchant William Vick, who left £1,000 in his will as a foundation for construction, and in 1829 the trustees announced a competition to design an iron suspension bridge. Isambard Kingdom Brunel (*see p47* **Local heroes**) submitted four designs for the competition, all of which were rejected by the judge, Thomas Telford, who instead produced his own plan. However, Telford's design failed to gain public support; in the following year another competition was held, and Brunel's Egyptian-style bridge emerged as the winner.

During the bridge's long and problematic construction, Brunel's elaborate design had to be scaled back, but eventually in 1864 the bridge was officially opened as a memorial to its architect, who had died five years previously. It measures 702 feet (214 metres) across and spans the gorge at a dizzying 245 feet (75 metres) above the river. Each year over four million vehicles cross the bridge, with 3,000 Bristol commuters an hour using it every weekday morning (20p cars, free pedestrians and bicycles). Unfortunately, its height also makes it a popular suicide spot.

To learn more about the history and engineering of the bridge, pop into the **Visitor Centre**, currently on Sion Place, but due to move to a purpose-built location on Suspension Bridge Road in early 2004.

One of the best views of the suspension bridge can be had from the large terrace of the **Avon Gorge Hotel** to the south. Originally known as the the Clifton Grand Spa & Hydropathic Institution, the hotel was opened in 1890 as a last – and unsuccessful – attempt to revive the spa, using water piped up from the Hotwells spring. The **Clifton Rocks Railway**, a hydraulic transport system, travelled in a tunnel through the cliffs between the hotel and Hotwells from 1893 to 1934.

Just above the bridge is the **Clifton Observatory** (0117 974 1242), a small, squat tower that was converted from a burnt-out windmill by the artist William West in 1829. Inside is the only surviving example of a 'camera obscura' in England – a Victorian contraption of lenses that projects an image of the surrounding land on to the interior of the tower. From the observatory visitors can also descend through a claustrophobia-inducing tunnel to the Giant's Cave viewing platform overlooking the gorge. Note that Observatory opening times are erratic, particularly in winter.

The Observatory sits on the edge of **Clifton and Durdham Downs**. Stretching for 400 acres (1.6 square kilometres) east from the Avon Gorge, the Downs act as the city's green lungs, and at weekends provide a vast, grassy, breezy playground for scores of dog-walkers, Sunday footballers, joggers and kite-flyers.

Adjoining the Downs is **Bristol Zoo**, the second oldest zoo in the country, opened in 1836. Its most famous resident was George the Gorilla, who became one of the first animal celebrities in the 1930s. His stuffed form now graces the City Museum & Art Gallery (*see p54*). Bristol Zoo prides itself on its conservation and education work; as well as caring for 300 species of wildlife, it runs breeding programmes and supports international projects in the wild. Highlights of this appealing and informative zoo include the underwater seal and penguin enclosure and the Brazilian rainforest habitat.

Opposite the zoo, examples of the human species at work and play can be observed at **Clifton College**, a prestigious Victorian public school opened in 1862. Among the college's famous alumni is John Cleese, who is supposed to have first developed his famous silly walks by pacing the cricket boundary in imitation of his teachers.

The eastern boundary of Clifton is marked by **Whiteladies Road**, a one-and-a-half mile (two-kilometre) stretch of shops, restaurants and bars, locally known as the 'Strip'. A popular haunt of students and the shiny-shirt brigade, it teeters on the brink of brash overkill at weekends, but for the moment remains one of the city's top destinations for a 'good night out'.

At the foot of Whiteladies Road, beyond the BBC's Natural History unit, is the **Royal West of England Academy** (RWA), established in 1858 as a centre for fine art. The Academy holds at least six exhibitions each year covering a diverse range of themes and media; artists featured in 2002 included Damien Hirst, Tracey Emin and David Inshaw. Consult the website for details of current exhibitions.

Opposite the RWA are the **Victoria Rooms** (*see p69*), fronted by an ornate fountain and a statue of Edward VII. The Rooms were established in 1841 as an entertainment venue for Clifton society and attracted some famous performers including Charles Dickens and Oscar Wilde. Today the Rooms are home to the University's music department and host frequent concerts.

Bristol Zoo

Clifton Down Road (0117 974 7300/ www.bristolzoo.org.uk). **Open** *Summer* 9am-5pm daily. *Winter* 9am-4pm daily. **Admission** £8.60; £3.85-£7.70 concessions; free under-3s. **Credit** MC, V. **Map** p48 A1.

Clifton Suspension Bridge Visitor Centre

Bridge House, Sion Place (0117 974 4664/ www.clifton-suspension-bridge.org.uk). **Open** *Summer* 10am-5pm daily. *Winter* 11am-4pm Mon-Fri; 10.40am-4.30pm Sat, Sun. **Admission** £1.90; £1.30-£1.70 concessions; £5 family; free under-5s. **No credit cards**. **Map** p48 A3.

Royal West of England Academy

Queens Road (0117 973 5129/www.rwa.org.uk). **Open** (during exhibitions only) 10am-5.30pm Mon-Sat; 2-5pm Sun. **Admission** £2.50; £1.25 concessions; free under-16s. **No credit cards**. **Map** p48 C3.

Further afield

Across the Suspension Bridge from Clifton are **Leigh Woods**, an area of steep, overgrown semi-wilderness on the western side of the Avon. Also here is **Ashton Court**, originally the stately home of the merchanting Smyth family, but owned by Bristol City Council since 1959. The estate incorporates woodland, parkland and a golf course, and plays host to many of the city's major festivals (*see p68* **Summer in the city**). The manor house is closed to visitors, but Ashton Court's sweeping, scenic grounds are beloved of sporty types – mountain bikers, kite-boarders, joggers – as well as those simply looking to enjoy a relaxed walk and stunning views (particularly at sunset) over the city.

Royal York Crescent. *See p58.*

More good yomping territory can be found in the village suburb of Henbury to the north of the city. **Blaise Castle Estate** is an atmospheric park of wooded glens, rocky outcrops and winding paths around the steep gorge of the River Trym. Once the site of an Iron Age settlement and Roman garrison, the estate takes its name from the castellated 18th-century folly at its summit, which offers far-reaching views towards the industrial landscapes of the Bristol Channel at Portishead.

At the foot of the hill, **Blaise Castle House** was designed by Thomas Paty in 1790 for John Scandrett Harford, a wealthy merchant and banker. Since 1949 it has housed social history exhibits from the Bristol City Museum & Art Gallery, including children's toys, Victorian gowns, kitchen and laundry equipment, and displays on the history of the estate. At the back of the house is a thatched dairy designed by John Nash.

Nash was also responsible for the idealised fairytale cottages at **Blaise Hamlet** nearby.

Built in 1811 to house Harford's pensioned-off servants, this cluster of nine dwellings around a green typifies the *cottage-orné* style, with thatched roofs, Jacobean chimneys and an overriding air of story-book perfection – you half expect to see the Three Bears sipping porridge through the mullioned windows.

Ashton Court Visitor Centre

Stable Block, Ashton Court Estate, Long Ashton (0117 963 9174). **Open** *July, Aug* 1-5pm Mon-Fri; 10am-5.30pm Sat, Sun. *Apr-June, Sept* 10am-5.30pm Sat, Sun. *Oct-Mar* 11am-4pm Sun. **Admission** free.

Blaise Castle House Museum

Henbury Road, Henbury (0117 903 9818). **Open** *Apr-Oct* 10am-5pm Mon-Wed, Sat, Sun. Closed Nov-Mar. **Admission** free.

Activities

Ballooning

Bristol is a major ballooning centre; for an aerial view of the city, contact **Bailey Balloons** (44 Ham Green, 01275 375300, www.baileyballoons.co.uk) or **Bristol Balloons** (73 Winterstoke Road, 0117 947 1050, www.bristolballoons.co.uk). Both offer champagne flights Apr-Sept for £135 per person.

Boating

The **Bristol Packet** (Wapping Wharf, Gas Ferry Road, Harbourside, 0117 926 8157, www.bristol packet.co.uk) offers river trips around the docks, to Bath or through the Avon Gorge, with stops at waterside pubs. The **Matthew** (*see p51*; 0117 922 0441, www.matthew.co.uk) cruises the Floating Harbour on summer evenings (£12) and also runs a residential sailing programme of short voyages to British and continental destinations.

Cycling

Bristol Bike Hire (Smeaton Road, Cumberland Basin, Harbourside, 07803 651945) rents out all kinds of bicycles, plus locks, helmets and other accessories. Easy cycling is on offer along the **Bristol & Bath Railway Path**, which follows the former Midland Railway for over 12 miles (20km) between the two cities. The Tourist Information Centre has details of this and other routes.

Where to eat & drink

For late-night bars and clubs, *see p70*; for pubs that double as live music venues, *see p69*.

Harbourside

The city's arts-based movers and shakers congregate at the bars in the **Arnolfini** (*see p50*) and the **Watershed** (*see p68*). Nearby is **The River** (1 Canons Road, 0117 930 0498, main courses £5-£6.50), a recent addition to the Harbourside scene that looks set to do well, with cocktails for the boozers and a fab

sausage-and-mash menu for the gorgers. Among the flashest of the waterfront imbiberies is **Bar Room Bar** (Waterfront, Canon's Road, 0117 929 4276, main courses £3.50-£7.25), with its funky lighting and stylish pods, although it gets packed at the weekends. A different vibe is offered by the **Cottage** (Baltic Wharf, Cumberland Road, 0117 921 5256, main courses £5.30-£6.45), where you can laugh at the capsizing efforts of the sailing school while tucking into pub grub.

Firehouse Rotisserie

The Leadworks, Anchor Square (0117 915 7323/ www.firehouserotisserie.co.uk). **Open** noon-11pm daily. **Main courses** £8.95-£14. **Credit** AmEx, DC, MC, V. **Map** p49 D4.

A winning combination of spit-roasted chicken, tasty-topped pizzas and southwestern specialities (the American south-west, that is) is served in the airy, open-plan interior, supplemented by plenty of outdoor tables next to the @tBristol complex.

Mud Dock Cycleworks & Café

40 The Grove (0117 934 9734/www.muddock.com). **Open** noon-3pm, 7-10pm Mon-Fri; 10am-3pm, 7-10pm Sat; 10am-3pm, 7-9pm Sun. **Main courses** £6.95-£16.95. **Credit** AmEx, MC, V. **Map** p49 E4.

Atop a fab cycle shop, Mud Dock is a long-standing Bristol favourite, with a compact south-facing sun deck, a confident Mediterranean menu and an interior decorated with bits of cycling paraphernalia. Trendy, but without an ounce of pretension.

Olive Shed

Princes Wharf (0117 929 1960/www.therealolive company.co.uk). **Open** 10.30am-10.30pm Tue-Sat; noon-6pm Sun. **Main courses** £9.50-£14.50. **Credit** MC, V. **Map** p49 D5.

A taste of the Mediterranean in the middle of Bristol docks. The outside terrace is just the place to tuck into tapas from the ground-floor delicatessen, and the bright dining room offers broadly Mediterranean cuisine with seafood and vegetarian highlights.

riverstation

The Grove (0117 914 4434/www.riverstation.co.uk). **Open** noon-2.30pm, 6-10.30pm Mon-Fri; 10.30am-2.30pm, 6-11pm Sat; noon-3pm, 6-9pm Sun. **Main courses** £10-£16. **Credit** DC, MC, V. **Map** p49 E4.

The old headquarters of the city's river police, riverstation remains at the vanguard of Bristol's increasingly hip dining scene due to its bold architecture and creative cuisine. 'Deck one' incorporates a deli and a bar, while the upstairs restaurant caters for an urbane crowd of business lunchers, leisured ladies and trendy twentysomethings.

Severnshed

The Grove, Harbourside (0117 925 1212/ www.severnshed.co.uk). **Open** noon-midnight Mon-Wed, Sun; noon-2am Thur-Sat. **Main courses** £8.95-£14.75. **Credit** AmEx, MC, V. **Map** p49 E4.

Bristol & Bath

This former boathouse has a long riverside terrace complete with glorious views of St Mary Redcliffe, where you can tuck into a selection of light, summer dishes that are big on flavour. Inside, you'll find Modern British cuisine served in an airy dining area, as well as a moveable bar where stylish staff mix some of the meanest cocktails in the city of Bristol for a work-and-play crowd.

West End

During the day, tired shoppers and work-shy students hang out at the **Boston Tea Party** (75 Park Street, 0117 929 8601). It serves what is arguably the city's finest coffee, along with a good selection of light bites, and has a terrace garden out back. Further up the hill, the **HaHa Bar** (Berkeley Square, 0117 927 7333, main courses £6.30-£9.50) is a popular lunch stop, due to its secluded courtyard and pleasing interior. For a trad pub experience, head for the unfussy, gaslit atmosphere of the **Bag O'Nails** (141 St George's Road, 0117 940 6776), a former CAMRA pub of the year that's famed for its port and stilton nights.

Bocanova

90 Colston Street (0117 929 1538). **Open** 9.30am-10.30pm Mon-Thur; 9.30am-11pm Fri, Sat. **Main courses** £7.95 lunch. *Set dinner* £16.50 2 courses; £19.50 3 courses. **Credit** MC, V. **Map** p49 D/E3.
Citrus-coloured decor and funky prints provide the perfect sun-infused setting for a Mediterranean and Brazilian fusion menu that may occasionally be over-complicated but is certainly never boring. There's live bossanova music to be enjoyed on Monday evening, or try the Brazilian evening on Wednesdays. Wicked Caipirinhas.

Budokan

31 Colston Street (0117 914 1488/www.budokan. co.uk). **Open** noon-2.30pm, 5.30-11pm Mon-Sat. **Main courses** £8-£9. **Set menu** £6.50 3 courses. **Credit** AmEx, DC, MC, V. **Map** p49 D3.
A classy noodle kitchen, whose sleek modern interior is bathed in a soft, reddish light. You'll find plenty to occupy your chopsticks on the pan-Asian menu, and although the quality can sometimes falter for the Rapid Refuel menu (lunchtime and early evening), you can't argue with the price.

Coccobello

Colston Tower, Colston Street (0117 929 4455). **Open** noon-2.30pm, 6-10.30pm Mon-Sat. **Main courses** £6.95-£12.50. **Credit** AmEx, MC, V. **Map** p49 D3.
This Italian oozes retro 1980s chic: granite floor, dark woodwork and sumptuous suede seating. The wide-ranging menu takes in all sorts, from strawberry risotto to hearty meat dishes, as well as deftly executed pasta favourites and thin, crisp pizzas with generous toppings.

Harvey's Restaurant & Wine Cellars

12 Denmark Street (0117 927 5034/www.harveys resaurant.co.uk). **Open** noon-2pm, 7-9.45pm Mon-Fri; 7-9.30pm Sun. **Main courses** £13-£26. **Credit** AmEx, DC, MC, V. **Map** p49 D4.
Bristol's only Michelin-starred eaterie is located in 13th-century wine cellars, redesigned by a youthful Terence Conran in the 1960s. The pink banquettes and wood cladding are beginning to look rather outdated, but there's nothing old fashioned about the classic French food, which is brought bang up to date by sassy modern flavours. An exemplary wine list is supplemented by vintage wines for the serious (and seriously rich) oenophile.

Thomas Urch began a wine business here in 1796, and his nephew, John Harvey, established the company we know today – purveyors of the world-famous Harvey's Bristol Cream. The cellars house displays on the history of wine making and an impressive collection of wine ephemera. Phone for details of the group guided tours and tastings.

Old City

For a global range of lunchtime snacks, check out the food stalls in **St Nicholas Markets** (*see p67*). Nearby, **Revolution** (Old Fishmarket, St Nicholas Street, 0117 930 4335) serves a befuddling array of vodkas in airy, Soviet-chic surroundings. In King Street, theatre luvvies tuck into authentic northern Italian cuisine at **Renato's** (No.19, 0117 929 8291, main courses £9.95-£14.95) before crossing the road to the shabby but friendly **Taverna dell'Artista** (No.33, 0117 929 7712, closed Aug, main courses £7-£14) for late-night drinking and conversation.

Hotel du Vin & Bistro

The Sugar House, Narrow Lewins Mead (0117 925 5577/www.hotelduvin.com). **Open** noon-2pm, 6.30-9.45pm daily. **Main courses** £14.50. **Credit** AmEx, DC, MC, V. **Map** p49 E3.
Classic bistro cuisine is the order of the day here: unfussy dishes created from the freshest local ingredients. Wine is a strong point: the varied list includes unusual regional wines at reasonable prices as well as serious French vintages. The setting is chic but relaxed – perfect for a special occasion. For the hotel, *see p72*.

Old India

34 St Nicholas Street (0117 922 1136/www.old india.co.uk). **Open** noon-2pm, 6pm-midnight daily. **Main courses** £6.50-£14. **Credit** MC, V. **Map** p49 E3.
Housed in the former Stock Exchange and making full use of the building's inate grandeur, this Indian restaurant is a real eye-opener. Traditional dishes are given an avant-garde makeover to create delicious contemporary flavours that are a far cry from your average chicken tikka masala.

Model behaviour

Not too long ago, the height of animated sophistication was a tiny plasticine character called Morph, painstakingly brought to life by a couple of guys in a flat in Clifton. Morph proved popular enough to outgrow his slot on an earnest BBC children's television art programme and be given his own stand-alone five minute show – success indeed.

Times change. 2000 saw the release of *Chicken Run*, a feature-length film starring animated plasticine chickens planning a daring escape from a battery farm. Three years in the making, it proved to be a massive box office draw. *Chicken Run* was the first part of a five-film, £157-million deal between the Steven Spielberg-backed DreamWorks SKG studio and the Bristol-based company **Aardman Animation**, co-founded way-back-when by those same two guys from Clifton. By this time, though, David Sproxton and Peter Lord had moved their operation from a residential flat to an edge-of-town warehouse, and were employing a workforce of 180 staff.

The rise of Aardman – now widely regarded as the world's leading model animation studio – has a great deal to do with an eccentric, cheese-munching inventor called Wallace and his long-suffering dog Gromit. Created by the director and animator Nick Park, who joined Aardman in 1986, these two characters were the stars of

A Grand Day Out, which was nominated for an Academy Award in 1989. The undisputed Posh and Becks of the animated world, Wallace and Gromit (with a little bit of assistance from Park et al) went on to win further Oscars, for *The Wrong Trousers* in 1994 and then for *A Close Shave* the following year.

Aardman is the most compelling of Bristol's animation success stories – but it's not the only one. The city is now reckoned to be the brightest animation hotspot in the UK outside London, with the industry adding £60 million to the city's annual economy. Aardman's high profile success has led to contracted work for other local outfits, such as the wonderful **John Wright Modelmaking**, responsible for such key models as Wallace's motorbike and Preston the cyberdog in *A Close Shave*.

Intelligent and subversive animated film-making – such as the surreal, award-winning fare of the **Bolex Brothers** – is now also attracting responsive adult audiences. Neatly summised by one local journalist as 'Aardman's dark side', Bolex's work includes a sinister update of the Tom Thumb tale that was shown by the BBC at Christmas to critical acclaim, although it was later described as a 'little too grotesque' for its family slot.

Successes such as these, along with other such notables as **Fictitious Egg Ltd** and **Peter Peake** (a former Aardman animator who won his own Oscar nomination for *Hum Drum*) have made Bristol the ideal home for the estimable **Animated Encounters** (www.animated-encounters.org.uk) film festival at the Watershed in April. Firmly rooted in the local scene, this annual event is a paragon of fine programming, with the most obscure films and names sharing the billing with such illustrious speakers as *The Simpsons'* creator Matt Groening and Richard 'Who Framed Roger Rabbit?' Williams.

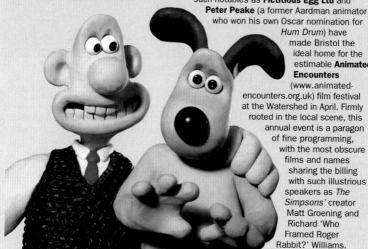

San Carlo

44 Corn Street (0117 922 6586). **Open** noon-11pm
daily. **Main courses** £6.75-£24.95. **Credit** AmEx,
DC, MC, V. **Map** p49 E3.
This glitzy Italian restaurant has a glamorous
atmosphere and a huge menu, incorporating authentic Italian favourites and impressive fish dishes.

Redcliffe & Temple

Tucked surreptitiously away in a concrete-laden
side street, **Cornubia** (142 Temple Street,
0117 925 4415) is an old-fashioned gem and
a CAMRA fave. It's filled with local workers
by day and pub-lovers in the know come
sundown. In summer, though, you may prefer
the dockside **Ostrich** (Lower Guinea Street,
0117 927 3774, main courses £3.95-£5.95),
which has loads of outdoor seating. It serves a
wide range of draught beers and an extensive
menu, making it a popular stop-off on harbour
booze-cruises. Check out the peculiar cave at
the back of the bar.

Byzantium

2 Portwall Lane (0117 922 1883/
www.byzantium.co.uk). **Open** noon-2pm, 6.30-10pm
Mon-Fri; 6-10pm Sat. **Main courses** £6.50-£19.
Credit AmEx, DC, MC, V. **Map** p49 E4.
Prepare yourself for an utterly decadent night out at
this Moorish- and Middle Eastern-themed bar and
restaurant. Belly dancers, magicians and DJs provide the entertainment while up-for-it diners tuck
into fresh and flavourful modern European dishes.

Clifton & Hotwells

Pubs in Clifton Village tend to be overrun with
students in term time – but don't let that put
you off. The **Lansdowne** (8 Clifton Road,
0117 973 4949, main courses £4-£8) is a
particular favourite, thanks to its cosy interior,
good grub and a big screen out back for sports.
The Mall (The Mall, 0117 974 5318, main
courses £4.50-£10.90), meanwhile, is just the
place to relax after a yomp across the Downs.
Kick back into the comfort-worn seating to
enjoy a coffee, a pint or some decent bar food.
Nearby is **Bar Chocolat** (19 The Mall, 0117
974 7000), a café devoted entirely to the sweet
stuff: artful piles of sweets, cake and biscuits
plus mugs of wickedly decadent hot chocolate.
For a more earthy experience, try the
Coronation Tap, a near-legendary cider
pub (*see p114* **Drink up**).
There are dozens of bars and restaurants
lining the Whiteladies Strip; many become
unbearably crowded at the weekends, but offer
a good time during the week. **Bar Humbug**
(No.89 , 0117 904 0061, main courses £6.50-
£8.50) is one of the most appealing hangouts,

The Matthew. *See p51.*

thanks to platters of Morrocan-inspired food,
quality cocktails and a hip but relaxed
atmosphere. Further up, the **Z Bar** (No.96,
0117 973 7225, main courses £4.95-£6.95) is
big, loud and usually full of the young and
beautiful. It serves killer cocktails and
Mediterranean-style munchies.

Deason's

43 Whiteladies Road (0117 973 6230/
www.deasons.co.uk). **Open** noon-2.30pm, 6.30-
9.30pm Mon-Thur; noon-2.30pm, 6.30-10.30pm Fri,
Sat; noon-3pm Sun. **Main courses** £12.50-£19.50.
Credit AmEx, DC, MC, V. **Map** p48 C2.
Shiny floors and fresh flowers combine to create an
appealing atmosphere at this ambitious restaurant,
which serves beautifully presented international
dishes, displaying influences from France to Japan.

Fishworks Seafood Café

128-130 Whiteladies Road (0117 974 4433/
www.fishworks.co.uk). **Open** noon-2.30pm, 6-10pm
Tue-Fri; noon-3pm, 6-10pm Sat; noon-3pm Sun.
Main courses £7-£20. **Credit** AmEx, MC, V.
Map p48 C1.
Utter freshness of ingredients and simplicity of
presentation are key to the deserved success of this
fish restaurant-cum-fishmonger, where the seafood
counter positively glitters with the day's catch;
a buzzy atmosphere, well-informed staff and good-
value wine list are the final touches that go to ensure
a winning formula.

Quartier Vert

85 Whiteladies Road (0117 973 4482/
www.quartiervert.co.uk). **Open** 10am-11pm Mon-
Sat; 11am-6pm Sun. **Set lunch** £14.50-£17.50.
Dinner main courses £10.50-£18.50. **Credit** MC, V.
Map p48 C2.
A good-looking bar and restaurant, Quartier Vert
offers well-executed Spanish-inspired dishes that are
made using local organic produce. The calming

white decor and bare wooden floors provide an
appealing backdrop for the crowds of weekend
drinkers and diners.

Sands

95 Queen's Road (0117 973 9734). **Open** noon-
2.30pm, 6-11pm daily. **Main courses** £8.50-£11.50.
Set menus £14.95-£16.50. **Credit** AmEx, DC, MC,
V. **Map** p48 C3.
The basement of a Clifton villa has been converted
into a vaulted Lebanese restaurant. Order the
Special Mezze for a feast of Middle Eastern flavours,
and round the meal off with a sweet Arabic coffee,
or a puff on a traditional sheesha.

Wagamama

63 Queen's Road (0117 922 1188/www.wagamama.
com). **Open** noon-11pm Mon-Sat; 12.30-10pm Sun.
Main courses £3.95-£7.75. **Credit** MC, V.
Map p48 C3.
The Bristol branch of the hugely successful London
noodle chain draws in the hordes with its cheap 'n'
tasty Asian food and communal dining experience.

Sound effects

The first thing to say about the so-called
'Bristol Sound' is that, as far as most locals
are concerned, the term shouldn't actually
exist. Coined by London-based journos from
the national weekly music papers to
pigeonhole the work of **Portishead**, **Tricky**,
Massive Attack and their bass 'n' beats-
heavy, spliff-loving ilk, it is regarded more
as a curse than a blessing by many in
Bristol's music business. OK, so these
groups were the first chart acts from the city to
enjoy sustained chart success since the
late Russ 'Sidesaddle' Conway in the late
'50s, but rather than being a one-off
phenomenon, their sound grew out of the
city's diverse musical roots.

Punk, for example. Though the thriving
Bristol scene barely registered beyond the city
limits, it marked the first time that the guitar-
loving white boys and girls from Clifton,
Cotham and other middle-class districts truly
mixed freely with the black reggae lovers from
St Paul's. Familiarity bred respect. Musical
ideas cross-pollinated, and the seeds of the
(if we must) Bristol Sound – dub-based
rhythm with a pop sensibility – were planted.

The first signs of shoots came with **The
Wild Bunch**, whose alumni include Massive
Attack producer Nellee Hooper, later to work
with the likes of Björk and Madonna. Perhaps
more importantly, Hooper later combined with
local sound-system operator Jazzy B to form

Soul II Soul, whose shuffle beat-backed
Club Classics Volume 1 album became the
template for countless artists declaring that
there'd 'always been a dance element' to
their music. Worth a mention, too, are **Rip,
Rig & Panic**, a riotous ensemble fronted
by the then-unknown Neneh Cherry. Any
discerning music lover will also recall the
likes of The Moonflowers, Pigbag, The
Brilliant Corners, The Pop Group, Strangelove
and Experimental Pop Band. Later, the
crossover scene brought drum 'n' bass to
the masses, first in the Mercury Prize-winning
guise of **Roni Size** and **Reprazent** and, most
recently, **Kosheen**.

Despite constant berating in the local
press, Bristol's lack of mid-size and large
music arenas has been an advantage for the
city's musical insiders. Without a constant
influx of national touring bands, keen gig-
goers have had little choice but to attend the
city's thriving smaller venues, and local
artists have been able to hone their sound
away from the national glare.

Today? Well, Bristol still suffers the post-
Sound effect of a few too many bands with
DJs bolted gratuitously on to their line-ups.
But the same willingness to experiment that
pushed Massive Attack and Tricky into the
spotlight can still be witnessed in the guise
of local favourites **Minotaur Shock**, **The
Heads** and **Madnomad**.

North of the centre

If you stray north of Broadmead during the day, make straight for the **Bristolian** (2 Picton Street, Montpelier, 0117 924 4419, closed late Dec-early Jan, main courses £3.50-£5.95), a hip, laid-back café that's a great place to ponder the morning papers. There are also a number of good pubs in this area, including the delightful **Hare on the Hill** (St Thomas Street North, Kingsdown, 0117 908 1982, main courses £2.95-£5.95), which serves delicous local Bath Ales and simple food to a mix of regulars.

Bell's Diner

1-3 York Road, Montpelier (0117 924 0357/ www.bellsdiner.co.uk). **Open** noon-2pm, 7-10.30pm Tue-Fri; 7-10.30pm Mon, Sat. **Main courses** £10.50-£18. **Credit** AmEx, MC, V. **Map** p49 F1.

A 1950s grocer shop in the bohemian Montpelier district has been transformed into one of Bristol's most highly acclaimed restaurants. A thoroughly modern British menu combines wild foods with local delicacies and carefully sourced organic produce. The superlative cooking is complemented by a well-chosen wine list and a convivial atmosphere. This place is highly recommended.

Okra

6 Chandos Road, Redland (0117 970 6078/ www.okra-restaurant.com). **Open** noon-2.30pm, 6-11pm daily. **Main courses** £10.50-£16.95. **Credit** MC, V. **Map** p48 C1.

This clean-cut restaurant has garnered rave reviews from the local press. The menu combines Spanish, Sicilian, Moorish and Berber flavours to create dishes that are paragons of subtle spicing, balanced flavours and beautiful presentation.

One Stop Thali Café

12A York Road, Montpelier (0117 942 6687). **Open** 11am-4pm, 6-11pm Tue-Sat. **Set menu** £6.50. **No credit cards**. **Map** p49 F1.

This tiny but legendary restaurant serves Asian street food in a laid-back, Bohemian-kitsch setting. Diners tuck into six beautifully spiced, all-vegetarian dishes that are served with chapatis on a specially divided steel plate. And, on a good night, you may catch some local musicians jamming unobtrusively in the corner.

Red Snapper

1-3 Chandos Road, Redland (0117 973 7999). **Open** 7.30-10pm Mon; noon-2pm, 7.30-10pm Tue-Sat. **Main courses** £10.50-£18.50. **Set lunch** £12.50 2 courses. **Credit** AmEx, MC, V. **Map** p48 C1.

One of Bristol's most highly regarded restaurants, and rightly so – just don't let the formica tables and dodgy '80s seating put you off. The fish-dominated menu offers superlative but unpretentious modern European cuisine and is constantly evolving to ensure fresh, seasonal produce.

Millennium Square and **Pero's Bridge**. *See p50.*

Say what? Bristle

The origins of the Bristol accent are lost in the mists of time, or perhaps in the city's one-way traffic system, both of which were designed to baffle foreigners. Take the city's name. Originally *Brig-stowe*, meaning 'Bridge place', it became *Bristow*, so the natives put an L on the end to keep out the Welsh. That final 'L' became an icon, sacred to Bristle-speaking folk. Nowhere else in the English-speaking world is an 'L' tacked on to words ending with an 'A' or 'O'. Thus area becomes *aerial*, idea becomes *ideal*, tourists fly to the *Costal Braval*, a motorist drives an *Alfal-Romeol*, etceteral, etceteral. It's all part the aerial's charismal.

But this is only the most obvious of the region's idiomatic idiosyncracies. Bristle packs huge meaning into very few words. English needs four words to say: 'Where have you been?'; Bristle does it in two:

'*Worse bin?*'. Outsiders enquire: 'What is your opinion?'; Bristle asks: '*Woss sink?*'. This is brevity as an art form. The Bristle exclamation, '*Bleed nell!*' wastes no words. And, as an economical denial, '*snot*' cannot be beaten, and '*nose snot*' adds a terse passion.

Yet Bristle can open its shoulders, when it must. '*Stain a payment!*' is the warning shouted by Bristle mums to keep their kids out of the traffic. Bristle sceptics ask: '*jew asbestos bleev that?*', and, when faced with a problem, Bristle optimists claim that '*seizure knit looks*'. Finally, remember that Bristolians never say 'goodbye'; instead they say '*gob less*'.

For further exploration of the eccentricities and hilarities of the Bristol dialect, read *A Load of Ole Bristle* by Derek Robinson and Vic Wiltshire (*see p307*) – '*sink ready bull!*'.

South of the river

Tobacco Factory Café & Bar
corner of Raleigh Road & North Street, Southville (0117 902 0060/www.tobaccofactory.com). **Open** noon-11pm Mon-Sat; noon-10.30pm Sun. **Main courses** £5-£9. **Credit** AmEx, MC, V. **Map** p48 C5. This airy, industrial-style space has got warehouse chic off to a tee and has been a major player in the hip regeneration of Southville. Arty types chow down on restaurant-standard food or lounge around on the benches and beanbags.

Shopping

If you're after the regular high-street stores – Boots, Marks & Spencer, Top Shop and the like – then you should either head north from the city to the huge American-style out-of-town mall at **Cribbs Causeway** (0117 903 0303, www.mallcribbs.com), or stick with **Broadmead** in the city centre. The latter is also where you'll find the **Galleries** mall, which has a few independent shops worth browsing through.

In the Old City, the absolute must-visit is **St Nicholas Markets** (Corn Street, 0117 922 4017) a wonderfully old-fashioned market dating back to 1743, and due to undergo extensive refurbishment during 2003. Sixty traders currently reside here, with some fine bargains to be had in clothing, music, crafts, deli goodies, homewares and all the other usual market offerings. Don't miss the excellent

global food stalls lining the Glass Arcade and the **farmers' market**, which is held on Corn Street every Wednesday.

Park Street is the place for street fashions. Labels such as Diesel, Miss Sixty, Camper and Red or Dead are sold by **Cooshti Clothing** (No.57, 0117 929 0850), **Mapatasi** (No.71, 0117 934 9444) and **Westworld** (WRC; No.37, 0117 945 7783); there's classy men's clobber at **Wired** (No.30, 0117 903 0942), while edgier clubwear is on offer at **BS8** (No.34, 0117 949 3549). There are also some decent music shops here – try the great-value **Fopp** (No.43, 0117 945 0685) or **Replay Records** (No.73, 0117 904 1134). At the bottom of Park Street, **Avery's** (9 Culver Street, 0117 921 4146) has extraordinary wine cellars, while halfway up, the **Bristol Guild of Applied Art** (Nos.68 & 70, 0117 926 5548) has labyrinthine rooms stuffed with beautiful homewares, kitchen stuff, prints and crafts. There's a pleasant café on site too. Rather more offbeat goodies can be discovered at **Ripe** (6 Perry Road, West End, 0117 909 4415), with its eye-catching indigo frontage and range of kitsch gifts and at **Point Blank** (75 Queen's Road, Clifton, 0117 904 6690). Also try the **Ginger Gallery** down the hill in Hotwells (84-86 Hotwell Road, 0117 929 2527) for a massive selection of arts and crafts.

Clifton Village is dominated by upmarket independent shops selling jewellery, art, wine, fine foods, antiques and clothes. **Focus On The Past** (25 Waterloo Street, 0117 973 8080) has plenty of smaller collectibles, while the Victorian **Clifton Arcade** on Boyces Avenue incorporates several retailers selling books, glassware, ceramics, jewellery, rugs, paintings and so on. There are also Moroccan homewares – plus tasty coffee and food – at **Saha** (12-13 Waterloo Street, 0117 317 9696).

Gloucester Road, North Bristol has a selection of altogether more downbeat stores, including **Re-Psycho** (No.85, 0117 983 0007), stocked with everything the retro-conscious could desire: excellent vintage clothing; a sizeable second-hand vinyl collection and eclectic '60s and '70s homewares.

Arts & entertainment

For up-to-date information about what's on in the city, buy a copy of the weekly listings magazine *Venue*. Tickets for many local and national events are available from the **Bristol Ticket Shop** (12 The Arcade, Broadmead, 0870 4444 400, www.bristolticketshop.co.uk).

Film

For arthouse offerings and first-runs of the latest in off-beat movie-making, head for the **Watershed** (1 Canons Road, Harbourside, 0117 925 3845, www.watershed.co.uk, closed late Dec), which also hosts a number of prestigious festivals including April's Animated Encounters shindig (*see p63* **Model behaviour**), the short-flick-based Brief Encounters in November, and the bi-annual Wildscreen International Festival (www.wildscreen.org.uk), the world's largest festival of natural history filming. Arthouse fare is also on the bill at the **Arnolfini** (*see p50*). It's not the most comfortable venue,

Summer in the city

Bristol hosts festivals in the same way that lesser cities host estate agents and shoe shops, with a plethora of appealing outdoor events taking place throughout the summer. Here are some of the best:

St Paul's Carnival

St Paul's, North Bristol (0117 944 4176). **Date** early July.

The city's equivalent to Notting Hill Carnival offers similar entertainment, large crowds, but mercifully lacks the attendant glare of publicity. Schoolchildren work with organisers weeks in advance to produce costumes and floats for the procession, while the music stages lay on an aural feast of reggae, garage and drum 'n' bass. The carnival is a chance for the area's largely black community to lay waste to St Paul's (often unfairly) troubled reputation, and after a rest year in 2002, is likely to return bigger and brighter than ever in 2003 and beyond.

Orange Ashton Court Festival

Ashton Court (0117 904 2275/www.ashton courtfestival.com). **Date** late July.

This is the festival of the year for many city dwellers, and has often been likened to Glastonbury without the camping. Since its inception in 1974 it has certainly grown along similar lines, with theatre, dance, cabaret, classical and film areas being added to the original musical arenas, although many of the 100,000 people it attracts are content to just sit and sample the atmosphere. Indeed, if you're looking to experience Bristol's distinct laid-back hedonism in concentrated form, this is probably your best bet.

Bristol Harbour Festival

Harbourside (0117 922 3719/www.bristol-city.gov.uk/harbourfestival). **Date** late July/early Aug.

This weekend fiesta celebrates the city's strong maritime heritage with raft races, trapeze acts, live music acts, some spectacular fireworks and, of course, a huge flotilla of boats.

Bristol Balloon Fiesta

Ashton Court (0117 953 5884/www.bristolfiesta.co.uk). **Date** early Aug.

Testament to Bristol's close ties to the ballooning industry, this is the largest balloon gathering in Europe, with spectacular group ascents of up to 150 fliers, and peripheral entertainments, including a full-on funfair. The Thursday evening 'nightglow' – a mass of tethered balloons illuminated by their burners – is well worth a look.

Bristol International Kite Festival

Ashton Court (0117 977 2002/www.kite-festival.org). **Date** late Aug/early Sept.

Far more than a gathering of impatient kids urging their dads to run faster, this increasingly popular festival features Japanese fighting kites, giant soft kites and massed aerial acrobatics. A great way to round off the summer.

but more than makes up for it with smartly themed double-bill screenings. North of the centre, the **Cube** (Dove Street South, King Square, 0117 907 4190, closed late Dec) is a self-styled 'microplex' run by a team of volunteers. It screens a truly esoteric selection of films, often by local directors and accompanied by live music or talks.

There are a number of mainstream cinemas in town, plus a clutch of suburban multiplexes, notably the vast **Warner Village** (08702 406020) at Cribbs Causeway. In a genre all of its own, the **IMAX** (*see p50*) offers the usual wow-factor footage, plus some classic films shown in extra-large format.

Music

Bristol's impressive live music scene (*see also p65* **Sound effects**) caters to all tastes and is spread over a wide variety of venues, but none of them are particularly large. **Bristol Academy** (Frogmore Street, West End, 0117 927 9227, www.bristol-academy.co.uk) is one of the biggest in town, and plays host to nationally touring rock, indie and dance names who haven't quite graduated to the arena circuit. Bristol University's **Anson Rooms** (Queens Road, Clifton, information 0117 954 5810, tickets 0870 444 4400, closed May, June) is the Academy's chief rival, and, despite constricted acoustics, it has established a tradition of bringing critically acclaimed bands – the White Stripes, Mercury Rev and the Coral, for example – to a grateful, mainly student crowd.

The one place with real potential to stage genuinely large gigs is the **Colston Hall** (Colston Street, West End, 0117 922 3682, closed Aug). However, this remains a largely seated venue, and though it hosts credible classical and world music events, its rock and pop programming leaves a lot to be desired.

The **Fleece** (12 St Thomas Street, Redcliffe, tickets 0117 929 9008) provides a welcome forum for local talent and a key player on the up-and-coming band circuit, with famous names (the Strokes, for example) passing through on their way to bigger and brighter things. **The Louisiana** (Bathurst Terrace, Wapping Road, Harbourside, 0117 926 5978) offers similar fare.

Other pop and indie venues include the **Fiddlers** (Willway Street, Bedminster, 0117 987 3403, www.fiddlers.co.uk), and the **Bierkeller** (All Saints Street, The Pithay, Broadmead, 0117 926 8514), the sweaty, cavernous haunt of the metal and punk brigade.

For folk and roots, check out the intimate **Folk House** (40A Park Street, West End,

0117 926 2987) and for jazz, don't miss the much-loved **Old Duke** (45 King Street, Old City, 0117 927 7137); it even puts on its own jazz festival come summertime, when the living is easy indeed.

In addition to the Colston Hall's offerings, classical and jazz fans are well served by the high-quality chamber, world music and jazz concerts at **St George's** (Great George Street, West End, 0117 923 0359, closed Aug) – often featured on BBC Radio 3. There are also free lunchtime concerts by University musicians at the **Victoria Rooms** (Queens Road, Clifton, 0117 954 5032, closed late Dec), and choral and organ recitals in the **cathedral** (*see p54*).

Sport

Football fans in Bristol are often tagged 'unfailingly loyal', although 'masochistic' serves equally well. **Bristol City** (Ashton Gate Stadium, South Bristol, 0117 963 0630, www.bcfc.co.uk) languishes in Division Two, despite seasonal flirtations with Divison One and the odd dream-making cup run. The city's other team, **Bristol Rovers** (Memorial Ground, Filton, North Bristol, 0117 924 7474, www.bristolrovers.co.uk). nearly dropped out of the league altogether in 2002.

Time was when at least some solace could be sought in cricket. However, **Gloucestershire** (County Ground, Nevil Road, 0117 910 8000, www.gloucestershire.cricinfo.com) has become increasingly reliant on success in one-day cricket to cover its glaring ineptitude in the long form of the game, concluding the 2002 county season just off the bottom of Division Two.

Fortunately, it's a less depressing tale on the rugby field. The **Bristol Shoguns** (Memorial Ground, Filton, North Bristol, 0117 311 1461, www.bristolrugby.co.uk) are well established in the premiership and even reached the European Championships in 2002. The team's erratic moments of glory are made all the sweeter by the relative decline of near-neighbours and bitter rivals, Bath.

Theatre & dance

The Edwardian **Bristol Hippodrome** (St Augustine's Parade, Centre, information 0117 929 9758, tickets 0870 607 7500) is one of the largest provincial stages in the country and host to a steady stream of West End musicals, celebrity-festooned pantomimes and other crowd-pleasers. Cary Grant was a callboy here before he went to make his fortune in Hollywood. However, it's the **Bristol Old Vic** (Theatre Royal, King Street, Old City, 0117 987 7877, closed mid July-end

Bristol & Bath

Aug) that is the real jewel in the city's theatre crown. Esteemed as the foremost production company in the South West, the Old Vic boasts such alumni as Pete Postlethwaite, Miranda Richardson, Patrick Stewart and Gene Wilder. The Theatre Royal is also home to the **New Vic**, a company that stages in-house work and touring productions, along with the excellent **Basement Theatre**, a forum for new writers.

The Old Vic does not, however, hold the monopoly on quality theatre or imaginative use of space. The **Tobacco Factory** (Raleigh Road, Southville, 0117 902 0344), a studio theatre housed in a former warehouse, is the scene of some of the city's most innovative productions, including the award-winning 'Shakespeare at the Tobacco Factory' series.

Less well-known, the **QEH** (Jacob's Wells Road, Hotwells, 0117 925 0551) offers a nicely judged selection of fringe drama, dance shows and improv work, while the pub theatre at the **Alma Tavern** (18-20 Alma Vale Road, Clifton, 0117 946 7899), home to Theatre West, offers intimate, and often visceral, productions. Finally, the **Arnolfini** (*see p50*) is the place for decidedly left-field theatre and dance.

Nightlife

Bristol's reputation as the nightlife capital of the region is well founded, with a scene that takes in every type of music – breakbeat and drum 'n' bass nights are particularly popular – and a wide variety of venues. Increasingly, DJ bars and intimate dance clubs are replacing super-clubs as the hangouts of choice for the city's nightbirds.

Late-night bars

On the waterfront, the bright red **E-Shed** (Canons Road, Harbourside, 0117 907 4287, free) is a regular bar by day, but, as night falls, the volume and the thronging crowds turn up (so it's best avoided at the weekends). Music ranges from garage to funk and soul to drum 'n' bass. In the Old City, the **Arc Bar** (27 Broad Street, 0117 922 6456, free) is an excellent all-rounder, with music that's often deliberately experimental and ample seating for those just wanting to chat. A similar vibe is offered by **Bar Ether** (2 Trenchard Street, West End, 0117 922 6464, free-£2), with its '60s space-age decor and potent cocktails. Up the hill from here is **The Park** (37 Triangle West, West End, 0117 940 6101, free-£2), a small, loungy bar, with a cool, classy vibe and a fair share of top-line DJs wowing the crammed-in clientele who come here to see and be seen. **Nocturne**

St Nicholas Markets. *See p67*.

(1 Unity Street, West End, 0117 929 2555), meanwhile, is a secretive bar-club co-owned by Massive Attack. It's usually members only, but lesser mortals can enjoy the exclusive vibe at Tuesday night's Storm.

Clubs

Lakota (6 Upper York Street, off Stokes Croft, North Bristol, 0117 942 6208, £5-£10) is a stalwart of the scene, with a 1,500 capacity helping to sustain one of the best atmospheres in town. Turn up for Freefall (Fri monthly) for top-drawer drum 'n' bass. Nearby, the revamped **Blue Mountain** (Stokes Croft, North Bristol, 0117 942 0341, £7-£10) is another cavernous club, which has a hedonistic reputation and a far-reaching music policy.

At the cosier end of the market, **The Cooler** (48 Park Street, West End, 0117 945 0999, £3-£5) is a relaxed student destination, featuring soul, indie and alternative nights.

The **Elbow Room** (64 Park Street, West End, 0117 930 0242, free), meanwhile, combines full-size pool tables with music from Cream regular Paul Myers and headliners such as Utah Saints. Around the corner on Park Row, the **Dojo Bar** (12-16 Park Row, West End, 0117 925 1177, £1-£5) is another intimate party den, thanks to a music policy that incorporates everything from soul to funk to hip hop. Further along the same stretch, the **Level** (Park Row, West End, 0117 373 0473, £4-£10) is a favourite on Bristol's drum 'n' bass scene (Roni Size turns up on a regular basis), but is equally adept at R&B, funky electronica and UK hip hop. It also offers a great night view of Bristol from its groovy, airport-style upstairs lounge.

At the bottom of Park Street, you're back in major venue land at the **Bristol Academy** (*see p69*), which caters for all tastes with school disco-themed nights, big-name house DJs and funky breakbeats from local supremos, Blowpop. Nearby **Q/-** (9 Frogmore Street, West End, 0117 926 4342, usually free) is the city's most popular gay club, with a mirrored interior that attracts a good-looking crowd.

Creation (13-21 Baldwin Street, Old City, 0117 922 7177, £3-£10) is the big boy in the centre, with a large chrome-laden interior woven together by an assault course of staircases and walkways. Slinky (Sat) is probably the best night to drop by, featuring house, trance and garage. Scream (Fri) at **The Station** (Silver Street, Broadmead, 0117 840 5626, £2-£10) is its main contender as the city's biggest house night. The good-looking Moroccan-styled **Fez Club** (26-28 St Nicholas Street, 0117 925 9200, £3-£5), meanwhile, attracts a well-dressed crowd with the very latest in house, R'n'B and disco.

Finally, moored in the docks you'll find the inimitable **Thekla** (East Mud Dock, The Grove, Harbourside, 0117 929 3301, £4-£8). This club-on-a-boat plays host to 'Espionage' (Sat), focusing on '60s freakbeat, garage punk, northern soul and lounge, but also throwing in such concessions to modernity as Beck and, er, Motörhead. It's reckoned by many to enjoy the best atmosphere in town.

Where to stay

For further accommodation options and reservations, contact the Tourist Information Centre (*see p72*).

Berkeley Square Hotel

15 Berkeley Square, West End, BS8 1HB (0117 925 4000/www.cliftonhotels.com). **Rates** (B&B) £54-£106 single; £85-£127 double. **Credit** AmEx, DC, MC, V. **Map** p48 C3.

Standard hotel decor and furnishings predominate here, but the so-called executive rooms have a more stylish contemporary vibe, with CD players and minibars – the complimentary decanter of sherry is a nice touch. Respectable modern British cuisine is served in the Square Restaurant (mains £7-£14) and there's a members-only bar in the basement.

Brigstow Hotel

Welsh Back, Old City, BS1 4SP (0117 929 1030/www.brigstowhotel.com). **Rates** *Mon-Thur* (room only) £140-£165 single/double. *Fri-Sun* (B&B) £89-£119 single/double; £175-£250 suite. **Credit** AmEx, DC, MC, V. **Map** p49 E4.

One of Bristol's newest hotels, the harbourside Brigstow has 120 rooms – you'll pay extra for a river view – all stylishly kitted out in a subtle palette of beige, red and green, and sporting up-to-the-minute facilites, including a plasma TV screen in the bathroom. Facilites include extensive business resources, a restaurant, bar and 24-hour room service.

Bristol Marriott Royal Hotel

College Green, West End, BS1 5TA (0117 925 5100/www.marriotthotels.com). **Rates** *Mon-Thur, Sun* (room only) £149-£159 double; £189-£305 suite. Breakfast £11.95-£13.95. *Fri, Sat* (B&B) £98-£118 double; £138-£249 suite. **Credit** AmEx, DC, MC, V. **Map** p49 D4.

Recarpeted, decorated and upholstered in early 2003, this Victorian hotel, next to Bristol Cathedral, is looking spick and span but maintains its classic ambience, with rich reds, greens and creams dominating the decor. Enjoy afternoon tea in the lounge; dinner in the high-ceilinged splendour of the Palm Court or a swim in the stunning mock-Roman baths.

City Inn Hotel

Temple Way, Temple, BS1 6BF (0117 925 1001/www.cityinn.com). **Rates** *Mon-Thur* (room only) £99 single/double. *Fri-Sun* (B&B) £80 double. **Credit** AmEx, MC , V. **Map** p49 F4.

This sleek urban hotel is close to Temple Meads station but backs on to the leafier surroundings of Temple churchyard. The contemporary rooms are light, bright and well-equipped with CD players, power showers and satellite TVs. They're also thankfully well soundproofed against noise from the busy main road. Classy modern British cuisine is served in the City Café (set menu £17.50).

Clifton Hotel

St Paul's Road, Clifton, BS8 1LX (0117 973 6882/www.cliftonhotels.com). **Rates** (B&B) *Mon-Thur, Sun* £69-£79 single; £79-£89 double/twin. *Fri, Sat* £44 single; £65 double/twin. **Credit** AmEx, DC, MC, V. **Map** p48 C2.

This decent two-star choice is probably the most appealing of several hotels on St Paul's Road. The decor's nothing special but is unlikely to offend all but the most style-conscious visitor. The best feature, though, is undoubtedly Racks restaurant and wine bar in the basement.

Branch: **Rodney Hotel** 4 Rodney Place, Clifton Village, BS8 4HY (0117 973 5422).

Hotel du Vin & Bistro

The Sugar House, Narrow Lewins Mead, Old City, BS1 2NU (0117 925 5577/www.hotelduvin.com). **Rates** £120-£125 double/twin; £170-£295 suite. *Breakfast* £9.50-£13.50. **Credit** AmEx, DC, MC, V. **Map** p49 E3.

Converted from an 18th-century sugar warehouse, this is a welcome change from the city's usual identikit accommodation. Exposed brickwork, wooden floors and metal joists provide a soft industrial-chic setting for spacious bedrooms and loft suites, with Egyptian linen bedclothes, stand-alone baths and walk-in showers. Communal areas include a snooker room, comfy lounge bar with cigar humidor, and an excellent bistro-style restaurant (*see p62*).

Naseby House Hotel

105 Pembroke Road, Clifton, BS8 3EF (0117 973 7859/www.nasebyhousehotel.co.uk). **Rates** (B&B) £40-£55 single; £67-£70 double. **Credit** MC, V. **Map** p48 B2.

This Victorian villa offers a taste of Clifton elegance and a home-from-home ambience. Standards vary among the 15 en suite guest rooms, but they were all being upgraded as this guide went to press, with individual furnishings and soothing decor. The best is on the ground floor, with a draped double bed and french windows leading to the beautiful garden.

Rosebery House

14 Camden Terrace, Clifton Vale, BS8 4PU (0117 914 9508/www.roseberyhouse.net). **Rates** (B&B) from £45 single; £65 double/twin. **Credit** MC, V. **Map** p48 B4.

Perfectly poised between Clifton and Hotwells, this utterly delightful B&B has three spotless, inviting rooms, with crisp white linen on the brass beds and carefully chosen artwork on the walls. Breakfast is served in a candlelit dining room by the smiley, welcoming hosts. Book well in advance.

Washington Hotel

St Paul's Road, Clifton, BS8 1LX (0117 973 3980/www.cliftonhotels.com). **Rates** (B&B) *Mon-Thur, Sun* £49 single; £64 double/twin. *Fri, Sat* £39.50 single; £52 double. **Credit** AmEx, MC, V. **Map** p48 C2.

The Washington won't set the world on fire in the style stakes, but it is clean, spacious and has decent basic facilities: most rooms are en suite and all have TVs, kettles and direct-dial phones. The breakfast room is bright and airy, and guests have full use of the restaurant and bar at the nearby Clifton Hotel.

Resources

Hospitals

Bristol Royal Infirmary *Marlborough Street, West End (0117 923 0000).* **Map** p49 E2.

Internet

Easycaf *108 Stokes Croft, North Bristol (0117 924 1999).* **Open** 10am-9pm Mon-Sat; 11am-7pm Sun. **Map** p49 E1.

Internet Exchange *23-25 Queen's Road, Clifton (0117 929 8026).* **Open** 9am-9pm Mon-Thur; 9am-8pm Fri; 9am-7pm Sat; 11am-6pm Sun. **Map** p48 C3.

Police

Bridewell Police Station *Nelson Street, Broadmead (01275 818181).* **Map** p49 E3.

Post office

13 Castle Gallery, The Galleries, Broadmead (0845 722 3344). **Open** 9am-5.30pm Mon-Sat. **Map** p49 E3.

Tourist information

Bristol Tourist Information Centre *The Annexe, Wildscreen Walk, Harbourside, BS1 5DB (0117 926 0767/hotel reservations 0117 946 2222/www.visitbristol.co.uk).* **Open** *Mar-Oct* 10am-6pm daily. *Nov-Feb* 10am-5pm Mon-Sat; 11am-4pm Sun. **Map** p49 D4.

In addition to the tourist information offices, look out for the touch-screen information kiosks dotted around town, providing free email and access to the visitbristol website.

Getting there & around

By air

Bristol International Airport (0870 121 2747, www.bristolairport.co.uk) is 8 miles (12.5km) south-west of the city centre on the A38. The Bristol International Flyer coach service connects the airport with the bus station and Temple Meads (£3-£4 single, £5-£6 return). *See also p292.*

By bus

The bus station on Marlborough Street is served by **National Express** services from all over the UK (08705 808080, www.gobycoach.com). **First** (0117 955 8211, www.firstcityline.co.uk) operates buses in and around Bristol, with many routes stopping at the Centre. Useful routes include Rail Link 180 and bus No.8 from Temple Meads to Clifton Village via Broadmead and the Centre, and circular route 500 (Temple Meads, Broadmead, the Centre, Clifton Triangle and Spike Island). For timetable information phone Traveline (0870 608 2608) or visit the Central Booking Office on Colston Street.

By ferry

The **Bristol Ferry Boat Company** (0117 927 3416, www.bristolferryboat.co.uk) operates daily services in the Floating Harbour between Temple Meads and Brunel Lock, Hotwells, with stops at Castle Park, Welsh Back, the Centre and the *SS Great Britain*. A 40-minute round-trip is also available.

By train

Bristol's main station, **Temple Meads**, connects the city to destinations throughout the country including Bath, Paddington, Birmingham, Cardiff, Exeter and Penzance. Another station, **Bristol Parkway**, is located in the north of the city, with connections to Paddington and South Wales.

Bath

Relax, shop, eat and bathe in this glorious Georgian spa town.

The sweep of the **Royal Crescent**. *See p82.*

To the approaching visitor, Bath is a veritable sight for sore eyes – a fantasy in golden limestone, sprawled elegantly in a river valley and surrounded, like Rome, by seven hills. 'Take Bath and 20 miles round it and there is not anything in the world superior to it', exclaimed the painter Benjamin West, just one of innumerable visitors to be captivated by the city's unfailing allure.

Celtic legend has it the city was founded in 863 BC by prince-turned-leper-turned-swineherd Bladud, who noticed that his pigs were cured of leprosy after a roll in the naturally hot water here. He eventually lured them out with acorns, plunged in himself, was healed, and bingo, Bath was born.

Since then, Bath's legendary ability to restore and revive – its 'holiday' vibe – has been exploited and enjoyed by successive

generations. It was the arrival of the Romans in AD 43 that spelt the beginning of Bath's transformation into a major spa, but there is evidence that our Stone Age and Bronze Age ancestors also paddled their feet here. In fact, the Roman name for Bath, Aquae Sulis, means 'the waters of Sul', the Celtic goddess of springs. Medieval times saw swarms of pilgrims and monks transform the town into an ecclesiastical centre, while their less holy contemporaries revelled in nude mixed bathing in the hot springs. In the early 18th century Bath's reputation grew, and it became a fashionable Mecca for high society – all balls, bathing, banter and powdered hair.

A housing boom in the 18th century signalled the rise of Georgian Bath. About 7,000 new houses were built from 1714 to 1830 of which 200 were designed by the visionary architect John Wood the Elder (1704-54), who dreamt of a creating a new Rome, and his son John Wood the Younger (1728-82). Although much of the building was speculative, it created an extraordinary unity of architecture – an English Palladianism that remains the epitome of elegance. Economic imperatives meant houses were built in terraces, with minimal external decoration. The city's famously golden stone – much of it supplied by the quarries of the Woods' patron, Ralph Allen – was only used as a veneer, resulting in the motley appearance of many Bath buildings from the rear.

Although the Woods and Allen provided the glorious setting, the mastermind behind Bath's Golden Age was Richard 'Beau' Nash (1674-1762), the self-styled 'Uncrowned King of Bath', 'Arbiter of Elegance' and 'Dictator of the Manners of Polite Society'. A bon viveur with enormous social influence, Beau Nash was made Master of Ceremonies in the city in 1705. He ran Bath society with a rod of iron and would severely reprimand any gentleman who dared to turn up to functions wearing riding boots.

Bath's heyday lasted almost a century, until Jane Austen's time (she lived here from 1800 to 1805), when Bath began gradually to lose its air of glamour. The middle classes limped in the footsteps of Beau Nash's trendy crowd, and the city became a final resting place for retired dignitaries and their bath-chairs.

Bath Abbey overlooks the
Roman Baths. *See p77.*

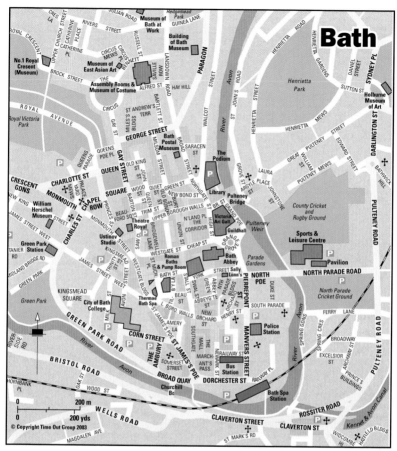

Bath

The decline continued into the 20th century when wartime bombing in 1942 destroyed much of the working-class district around the station and river. Miraculously, the Royal Crescent, the Circus and many other architectural gems survived virtually unscathed, and in 1987 the UN declared Bath a World Heritage city – the only one in Britain – for the quality of its Roman remains and Georgian splendours.

Bath can be stiflingly crowded in summer, with most of its three million visitors per year passing through at this time. Fierce debate rages eternal in the pages of the local press and on the streets between the conflicting needs of residents and tourists. You, however, will probably find it difficult to muster the energy to adjust your sunglasses. It's just that kind of place. Tranquil, compact and with barely an

unsightly square inch to be found, Bath lends itself perfectly to a luxury break. Relax. Drink it in. Just remember to take off your riding boots.

TOURS

Regular free guided walks, starting from the Pump Room, are offered by the **Mayor's Honorary Guides** (01225 477408), unpaid volunteers, who are genuinely passionate about the city. As an alternative, **Bizarre Bath** (01225 335124, www.bizarrebath.co.uk, £5, £4.50 concessions) is a well-established comedy tour, departing from outside the Huntsman pub, Bog Island at 8pm daily. For the techno-savvy visitor there's **Texting Trails** (£5.99) – a guide texted to your mobile phone with clues leading you to various sights. Get connected at the Tourist Information Centre (see p91).

Better than the smelly water? Time for tea at the **Pump Room**.

Sightseeing

Ideal for committed sightseers, the **Bath Pass** (0870 242 9988, www.bathpass.com) allows free admission to over 30 of Bath's attractions, as well as some in Bristol, and is available for one, two, three or seven days.

The Abbey & around

At the heart of the city is **Bath Abbey**, technically a parish church, but called an 'abbey' because it was part of Bath monastery from the eighth century until the dissolution in 1539. The Anglo-Saxon church on this site – where the coronation of the first English monarch, Edgar, took place in AD 973 – was replaced by a massive Norman cathedral, but by the end of the 15th century this had fallen into ruins.

The present structure was built in the early 16th century by Bishop Oliver King. The bishop claimed that angels had appeared to him in a dream, descending from heaven on ladders, and instructing him to rebuild the Abbey church. Loiter awhile in front of the magnificent West Front, where Bishop King's dream is realised in stone, with angels climbing up and down the turrets on carved ladders.

The Abbey is often dubbed the 'Lantern of the West' due to its huge and plentiful stained glass windows. These illuminate the incredible fan-vaulted ceiling that stretches the full length of the interior. Below, in the former cellars of surrounding houses, are the **Heritage Vaults**, with displays on the history of the monastery, Saxon and Norman sculptures, a reconstruction of the medieval abbey and documentation from the Bath Blitz and post-war restoration project.

In summer Abbey Churchyard is a popular spot for street performers who entertain the throngs of tourists visiting the Abbey and the **Roman Baths** on the other side of the square. The Baths are the most-visited attraction in the city and their popularity is well deserved.

The Romans constructed a spa complex here in about AD 54 dedicated to the goddess Sulis Minerva and incorporating a temple, and a number of hot and cold baths, serviced by underground heating and a sophisticated plumbing and drainage system. Bathers would swim, socialise or do business in the Great Bath, and use other areas of the complex for exercise, saunas, massage and cleansing. Aquae Sulis was abandoned when the Romans left Britain and was not rediscovered until the 18th century.

A handset takes you on a guided tour around the peaceful Great Bath – overlooked over by a relief of Bladud – to the indoor baths, Minerva temple and King's Bath source, where over a million litres of water rise per day, at a scorching temperature of 46.5°C. The complex is remarkably intact and is supplemented by fascinating displays of artefacts found on site. Don't make the mistake of some tourists and turn up with your cossie; the water has not been used for bathing since the late 1970s. Instead, for the full Bath aquatic experience you now have to head west along colonnaded Bath Street to the new Thermae Bath Spa (*see p81* **Spa attraction**).

Next door to the Roman Baths, the wonderfully elegant **Pump Room** was founded by Beau Nash as the social heart of the Georgian spa town (the present neo-classical building dates from 1786). Here Bath society met to 'take the water', to see and be seen. You can still sup

Bath Abbey's heavenly ladder. *See p77.*

the mineral-rich and decidedly smelly H_2O here today, although you may prefer to opt for a pot of tea, accompanied by music from the Pump Room Trio.

South of the Abbey is **Sally Lunn's Refreshment House & Museum**, once a bakery serving the monastery, and widely regarded as the oldest house in the city; excavations here have revealed Roman, Saxon and medieval remains. It was taken over in 1680 by a French baker called Sally Lunn, who specialised in making *brioche*. The café still does a roaring trade in the sweet bread rolls today, now known here as Sally Lunn Buns. A tiny museum occupies the former kitchens in the basement, and shows the ancient foundations, plus Roman and medieval objects and period kitchen equipment.

Bath Abbey & Heritage Vaults

Abbey Churchyard (01225 422462/www.bath abbey.org). **Open** *Abbey* Easter-end Oct 9am-6pm Mon-Sat; end Oct-Easter 9am-4.30pm Mon-Sat. *Heritage Vaults* 10am-4pm Mon-Sat. **Admission** *Abbey* (suggested donation) £2. *Heritage Vaults* £2.50; £2 concessions; free under-16s. **Credit** (shop only) MC, V.

Roman Baths & Pump Room

Abbey Churchyard (01225 477785/www.roman baths.co.uk). **Open** *Apr-June, Sept, Oct* 9am-5pm daily. *Nov-Mar* 9.30am-4.30pm daily. *July, Aug* 9am-9pm daily. **Admission** *Roman Baths* £8; £7 concessions; £20.50 family; free under-5s. *Pump Room* free. *Combined ticket with Museum of Costume* £10.50; £5.90-£9 concessions; £27 family. **Credit** MC, V.

Sally Lunn's Refreshment House & Museum

4 North Parade Passage (01225 461634/www.sally lunns.co.uk). **Open** 10am-10pm Mon-Sat; 11am-10pm Sun. **Admission** free. **Credit** MC, V.

Pulteney Bridge & around

North of the Abbey on the High Street is the entrance to the **Guildhall** (01225 477793, closed Sat & Sun, free), constructed in 1777 on the site of the city's medieval meat market. The municipal building is used for civic functions and is worth a snoop for its magnificent green-and-gold banqueting room – the grandest Georgian interior in the city, with fine art and three awesome chandeliers. Next door is the traditional market hall, a good place to pick up a bargain.

Leaving the market by the eastern door you'll be greeted by the picture-postcard sight of three-arched **Pulteney Bridge** spanning the River Avon. This neo-classical structure was built in 1770 to a design by Robert Adam and is one of only three shop-lined bridges in the world. The U-shaped weir below was added later to safeguard the city from frequent floods: check out the alarmingly high water mark, almost at pavement level, along the pillared walkway on the west bank. There are lovely views of the river from the **Parade Gardens** (Grand Parade, £1.20, 60p concessions) just to the south.

West of Pulteney Bridge, a splendid two-floor Georgian building houses the **Victoria Art Gallery**, which opened in 1900. The gallery is home to a one-room permanent collection of paintings by artists including Sickert, Gainsborough, Leighton and Nash, many depicting Bath and environs, plus display cases crammed with glassware, porcelain and miniatures. Exhibitions of a more contemporary nature – everything from African sculpture to the annual exhibition of the Bath Society of Artists – can be viewed in the Lower Gallery on the ground floor.

A few minutes' walk north of here, beyond Northgate Street, Broad Street is home to philatelist's favourite the **Bath Postal Museum**, from where the first-ever stamped letter – using the Penny Black – was posted in

1840. The museum follows the history of mail from 2000 BC to the present day, with a reconstruction of a Victorian post office and a special nod to local bigwig Ralph Allen, who streamlined the national mail system in the 18th century.

East of the river, meanwhile, **Great Pulteney Street** stretches a long, elegant arm. Begun by Thomas Baldwin in 1789, this 100-foot (30-metre) wide thoroughfare is a consummate exercise in Georgian symmetry, concluding at the classical façade of the **Holburne Museum of Art**. In Jane Austen's day this was a hotel for the glitterati of Georgian Bath, but today it houses the fine and decorative art collection of the 19th-century enthusiast Sir William Holburne. Paintings by Turner, Gainsborough and Stubbs, plus gleaming displays of silverware, porcelain, majolica, glass and bronze, are supplemented by regular temporary exhibitions. Behind the museum, the 12-acre **Sydney Pleasure Gardens** were a favourite haunt of Jane Austen, when she lived at nearby Sydney Place. Explore the park's Chinese-style footbridges, discover the replica Temple of Sulis Minerva, and ponder the elegance of it all over a slab of delicious homemade cake in the tea shop.

Bath Postal Museum

8 Broad Street (01225 460333/www.bathpostal museum.org). **Open** *Nov-Mar* 10.30am-4.30pm Mon-Sat. *Apr-Oct* 11am-5pm Mon-Sat. **Admission** £2.90; £2.40-£1.50 concessions; £6.90 family; free under-5s. **Credit** MC, V.

Holburne Museum of Art

Great Pulteney Street (01225 466669/ www.bath.ac.uk/holburne). **Open** *Mid Feb-mid Dec* 10am-5pm Tue-Sat; 2.30-5.30pm Sun. Closed mid Dec-mid Feb. **Admission** £3.50; £1.50-£3 concessions; £9 family. **Credit** MC, V.

Victoria Art Gallery

Bridge Street (01225 477233/www.victoriagal.org.uk). **Open** 10am-5.30pm Tue-Fri; 10am-5pm Sat; 2-5pm Sun. **Admission** free. **Credit** *Shop* MC, V.

Upper town

The **Theatre Royal** (*see p89*) on Sawclose opened in 1805 and remains one of the finest Georgian theatres in the country. Next door, Popjoy's restaurant is housed in Beau Nash's former home and is named after his mistress Julianna Popjoy.

North of here, stately **Queen Square** was the first Bath commission for John Wood the Elder in 1729, while to the west, the **William**

Pulteney Bridge: one of only three shop-lined bridges in the world. *See p78*.

Herschel Museum recreates the home of the 18th-century astronomer. Among the contemporary furnishings and personal effects is a replica of the telescope through which Herschel discovered the planet Uranus in 1781.

Heading uphill from Queen Square, you are likely to be leafleted by someone dressed like an extra from *Pride And Prejudice*. Jane Austen may have despised what she considered Bath's snooty claustrophobia, but the town has claimed her as one of its own. Austen lived for a time at 25 Gay Street, and a nearby house is now the Jane Austen Centre with displays, reproduction costumes and facsimile documents celebrating the author's connection with the city; the highlight is the amusing talk that dispels the twee Jane of popular thought and reveals the witty young miss so loved by Austenophiles. True disciples can buy lace toilet-roll holders and other keepsakes in the crammed gift shop.

Traditionally the highbrow end of town, and still the priciest in terms of housing, the tidy area north of Gay Street is a honey-coloured architectural marvel. At its heart is the Circus, a perfectly circular street of Georgian townhouses, whose diameter matches that of Stonehenge. Designed by John Wood the Elder and realised by his son, it was once entirely cobbled, with a watchman's hut in the middle protecting the residents from the hoi polloi. The portrait painter Thomas Gainsborough once lived at No.17.

Spa attraction

'Wonderful and most excellent against... rhumes, agues, lethargies, apoplexies, the scratch, inflammation of the fits, hectic flushes, pocks, deafness, forgetfullness, shakings and weakness of any member.' Thus was the water of Bath described in Georgian times. Blue-green, hot, mineral-rich, slightly opaque and sulphur-scented, it is the result of rain that fell on the Mendip Hills thousands of years ago, filtering through the limestone and heated by volcanic strata to around 46°C before emerging into the heart of the city. Touch one of the manhole covers in the Bath Street area and you can feel the heat as the water flows under your feet.

The waters are Bath's *raison d'être*. Without them the city is like Rome without its amphitheatre, Vienna without its waltz. However, since the closure of the Roman Baths to bathers following a public health scare in the late '70s, a million litres a day of this precious resource has been gushing – unused – straight into the River Avon.

An astonishing waste? That's what the brains behind the Thermae Bath Spa thought, so they decided to build a brand new spa to tend to the rhumes and agues of modern Britain. The keenly awaited venture aims to rejuvenate spa culture in the city by harnessing Bath's hot 'n' wholesome H_2O and promoting it as the only natural thermal spa in the UK (other springs, like Buxton, are cold).

It's to the credit of all concerned that the spa isn't a corny Roman or Georgian pastiche. Instead, the main building is a brand new vision in glass and Bath stone by renowned architect Nicholas Grimshaw, and its *pièce de résistance* is a rooftop, open-air swimming pool with views across the city.

The complex also lovingly incorporates existing spa buildings that have lain neglected for decades. The Cross Bath, a Grade I-listed Georgian building erected on the site of an earlier medieval bath has been restored as a open-air thermal pool, while the nearby Hot Bath, designed by John Wood the Younger in 1773, houses a variety of treatment rooms for everything from acupuncture to mud wraps. The 18th-century Hetling Pump Room serves as the Spa Visitor Centre.

With no membership fees and reasonable entrance prices, the aim here is to create a venue that is inclusive and unpretentious – after all, pigs, beggars and royalty alike have all swilled their aching bodies in Bath's famous waters. A two-hour session includes use of the roof-top pool, main spa, whirlpool, steam rooms – in the shape of space-age circular glass pods– footbaths, relaxation areas and yoga and meditation classes. Complementary treatments, massages and solarium cost extra. The only proviso is that you bring your costume: Bath isn't quite ready for a return to public displays of nudity just yet...

Thermae Bath Spa

Hot Bath Street (01225 338175/ www.thermaebathspa.com). **Open** 9am-10pm daily. **Admission** *2hr session £17. 4hr session £23. All day £35; £17.50 concessions.* **Credit** MC, V.

Bristol & Bath

From the Circus, elegant but understated Brock Street leads west to the Royal Crescent. En route stop off at **Margaret's Buildings**, a pedestrianised parade of high-quality shops selling antiques, second-hand books, designer clothes and fine art. The **Anthony Hepworth Fine Art Gallery** (1 Margaret's Buildings, Brock Street, 01225 447480, phone for opening times) specialises in work by the St Ives School.

The **Royal Crescent** is the most imposing and historically significant crescent in Bath. Built in 1767-74 by John Wood the Younger, this sweeping Palladian landmark stretches for 605 feet (184 metres) in a single, curved façade, lined with more than 100 Ionic columns, and has breathtaking views across the city.

No.1 Royal Crescent – the end house nearest to the town centre – was one of the first to be built and has been lovingly restored to its former elegance, with authentic 18th-century furniture and decoration. A team of guides – largely brisk, redoubtable pensioners – talk you through each room, successfully recreating the atmosphere of life in Beau Nash's time.

Below the crescent an expanse of kempt lawn leads down to **Royal Victoria Park**, formally opened in 1830. Take a break from the rigours of sightseeing here to join the masses lolling around, playing frisbee or watching hot air balloons ascend. The park also has botanical gardens, a huge children's playground, tennis courts, putting green, golf course and an aviary.

On the other side of the Circus is the **Museum of East Asian Art**, a discreet Georgian townhouse with 7,000 years' worth of Chinese, Japanese, Korean and South-east Asian art. Rarities include over 100 examples of ancient Chinese jade – some dating back to the neolithic period – and 'Ordos' bronzes created for nomadic horsemen on the borders of China. Another gallery houses exhibitions by contemporary Asian artists.

Almost opposite are the **Assembly Rooms**, a set of public rooms designed by John Wood the Younger in 1771 as a playground for polite society to hobnob, dance, drink tea, play cards, listen to music and flirt. The rooms have been painstakingly restored – it's hard to believe they were badly damaged in the Bath Blitz – and are still used for weddings and parties.

Downstairs is the **Museum of Costume**, dimly lit to preserve its treasures, which include over 150 male and female outfits from the 16th century right up to the diaphanous green Donatella Versace creation worn by Jennifer Lopez. An audio guide takes you through the collection, which also includes historical underwear and more embroidery than you can shake a bodkin at; the **Card Room Café** offers a dignified cuppa in Regency surroundings.

Parade Gardens. *See p78.*

In sharp contrast, the life of working folk is explored a couple of streets away in the **Museum of Bath at Work**. The exhibition is based on the life and toil of one Mr Bowler – engineer, gas-fitter, locksmith, bell-hanger, maker of soda-water machinery and producer of fizzy drinks. His family-run business lasted 97 years and is reconstructed here in all its chaos.

Back towards the centre of town, the absorbing **Building of Bath Museum** is set in a unique 18th-century Gothic chapel. It describes how Georgian Bath was built, decorated and lived in, with displays ranging from architectural drawings and scale models to fragments of flock wallpaper.

Assembly Rooms & Museum of Costume

Bennett Street (01225 477789/www.museum ofcostume.co.uk). **Open** *10am-4.30pm daily.* **Admission** *Museum of Costume* £5; £3.50-£4 concessions; £14 family. *Combined ticket with Roman Baths* £10.50; £5.90-£9 concessions; £27 family. **Credit** MC, V.

Building of Bath Museum

Countess of Huntingdon's Chapel, The Vineyards, Paragon (01225 333895/www.bath-preservation-trust.org.co.uk). **Open** *Mid Feb-Nov 10.30am-5pm Tue-Sun. Closed Dec-mid Feb.* **Admission** £4; £3 concessions; £10 family. **Credit** AmEx, MC, V.

Jane Austen Centre
*40 Gay Street (01225 443000/www.janeausten.
co.uk).* **Open** 10am-5.30pm Mon-Sat; 10.30am-5.30pm
Sun. **Admission** £4.45; £2.45-£3.65 concessions;
£11.95 family; free under-6s. **Credit** MC, V.

Museum of Bath at Work
*Bath Industrial Heritage Centre, Camden Works,
Julian Road (01225 318348/www.bath-at-
work.org.uk).* **Open** *Apr-Oct* 10.30am-4.30pm daily.
Nov-Mar 10.30am-4.30pm Sat, Sun. **Admission**
£3.50; £2.50 concessions; £10 family.

Museum of East Asian Art
12 Bennett Street (01225 464640). **Open** 10am-5pm
Tue-Sat; noon-5pm Sun. Closed late Dec. **Admission**
£3.50; £1-£3 concessions; £8 family; free under-6s.
Credit MC, V.

No.1 Royal Crescent
*1 Royal Crescent (01225 428126/www.bath-
preservation-trust.org.uk).* **Open** *Mid Feb-Oct*
10.30am-4.30pm Tue-Sun. Closed Dec-mid Feb. **Admission** £4;
£3.50 concessions; £10 family. **Credit** (shop only)
MC, V.

William Herschel Museum
*19 New King Street (01225 311342/www.bath-
preservation-trust.org.uk).* **Open** *Dec-mid Feb* 11am-
5pm Sat, Sun. *Mid Feb-Nov* 2-5pm Mon, Tue, Thur,
Fri; 11am-5pm Sat, Sun. **Admission** £3.50; £2
concessions; £7.50 family. **Credit** MC, V.

Beyond the city centre

Without straying too far from the hubbub, a
trip by bus or cab a mile or two out of town
allows you to take better advantage of the
panoramic views from Bath's surrounding hills.

Two miles (three kilometres) south-east of the
city centre (buses run regularly from the bus
station) is the fascinating **American Museum
in Britain**, an 1820 manor house converted
into a museum in 1961 by two Americans in the
noble pursuit of improving transatlantic
relations. It paints a picture of the lives of 17th-
to 19th-century Americans through a series of
reconstructed rooms, including a New Orleans
bedroom and a village shop. In addition, there
are lovely displays of Shaker furniture, plus an
arboretum of American trees and a replica of
the flower garden at Mount Vernon, where
George Washington lived in retirement. The
café serves authentic American munchies.

Not far away sits the idyllic 18th-century
Prior Park Landscape Garden, designed
in part by the poet Alexander Pope and later
landscaped by Capability Brown. The mansion
house, built by John Wood the Elder for Ralph
Allen, is now a school, but the grounds are open
to the public and include a Palladian bridge,
three lakes and numerous wooded paths.

On the north side of Bath, meanwhile, is
the Grade I-listed, 154-foot (47-metre) neo-
classical **Beckford's Tower**. Designed as
the home of eccentric 18th-century traveller,
scholar and novelist William Beckford, it is
now a museum devoted to its owner's life
and interests; it also has fantastic views. Not
for vertigo sufferers.

The American Museum in Britain
*Claverton Manor (01225 460503/www.american
museum.org).* **Open** *Museum, galleries & grounds*
end Mar-early Nov 1-6pm Tue-Sun. Grounds closed
early Nov-Mar. *Museum* 2-5pm Tue-Sun. **Admission**
Museum, grounds & galleries £6; £3.50-£5.50
concessions. *Grounds, folk art & new galleries* £3.50;
£2.50-£3 concessions. **Credit** MC, V.

Beckford's Tower
*Lansdown Road (01225 422212/www.bath-
preservation-trust.org.uk).* **Open** *Easter-Oct*
10.30am-5pm Sat, Sun. Closed Nov-Mar.
Admission £2.50; £2 concessions; £6 family.
No credit cards.

Prior Park Landscape Garden
*Ralph Allen Drive (01225 833422/www.national
trust.org.uk).* **Open** *Feb-Nov* 11am-dusk Mon, Wed-
Sun. *Dec, Jan* 11am-dusk Fri-Sun. **Admission** £4;
£2 concessions. **Credit** MC, V.

Activities

Ballooning
On clear, sunny evenings the skies over Bath are
dotted with hot air balloons. Champagne flights
are available from **Bath Balloon Flights** (01225
466888), which launch from Royal Victoria Park
and charge up to £135 per person.

Boating
Few of Bath's sights are on the river but a relaxed
upstream cruise on board the **Pulteney Princess**
(07816 530247) is a delight nonetheless. The boat
leaves from Pulteney Weir for a 25min ride to the
photogenic village of Bathhampton. A more *Swallows
and Amazons* kind of afternoon can be enjoyed at
Bath Boating Station (Forester Road, Bathwick,
01225 466407, closed Oct-Easter), which has rowing
boats, punts and canoes for hire.

Cycling
To escape the traffic, hire a bike from the **Avon
Valley Cyclery** (Bath Spa Railway Station, 01225
461880). The Bristol to Bath Railway offers a flat
ride through countryside between the two cities,
and there are also interesting routes along the
Kennet & Avon canal. For details, pick up the free
leaflet 'Cycling in Bath and Beyond' from the
Tourist Information Centre.

Golf
Golfers are spoilt for choice with ten greens in the
area, including the public pay-and-play **Approach
Course** (Royal Victoria Park, 01225 331162).

Where to eat & drink

Cafés & tearooms

If the likes of the Pump Room (see p77), Sally Lunn's (see p78) and the Card Room Café (see p82) are not your cup of tea, you'll be glad to know that coffee culture has flooded Bath as much as any other UK city, and happily there are finer spots to sip your skinny latte than the ubiquitous Starbucks.

As well as the ever-popular **Café Retro** (see p85) or the excellent **Boston Tea Party** (1 Kingsmead Square, 01225 313901), try the colourful coffee lounge **Doolallys** (51 Walcot Street, 01225 444122) for coffee, chai, herbal tea, lassi and snacks, plus alcohol and entertainment in the evening. The **Jazz Café** (1 Kingsmead Square, 01225 329002, main courses £2.60-£6.50) is a great spot to grab a bite before a show at the nearby Theatre Royal.

People-watchers should make a beeline for the **Adventure Café** (5 Princes Buildings, George Street, 01225 462038, main courses £3.85-£4.95), a trendy spot for lounging outside in summer. Salads, sandwiches and snacks are available, and the premises are licensed.

Pubs & bars

Although some of Bath's top pub locations have been snaffled up by the chain gang, there are still numerous authentic watering holes. For unpretentious town-centre fun the **Pig & Fiddle** (2 Saracen Street, 01225 460868, main courses £2-£7) rarely fails; other city-centre options include the tiny, intimate **Old Green Tree** (Green Street, 01225 448259, main courses £5.50-£6.50), and the historic **Crystal Palace** (10-12 Abbey Green, 01225 482666, main courses £3.95-£8.25) – this pub is nearly 300 years old and Nelson once convalesced there. A walled back garden makes it a popular summer choice. For live music, a bohemian throng and a heated garden try the **Bell Inn** (103 Walcot Street, 01225 460426), or head for the lively, ramshackle **Hat & Feather** (14 London Street, 01225 425672)

Festival fever Take a dip

Beer, books or the Bard, the spirit of Beau Nash lives on, with barely a week passing in Bath without some sort of festival. For more details on all of these, and to book tickets, contact **Bath Festivals** box office (01225 463362, www.bathfestivals.org.uk).

Spring

Bath International Literature Festival (Feb/Mar, www.bathlitfest.org.uk). Talks, discussions and performances of world literature, with prominent guest authors.
Bath Shakespeare Festival (Mar, www.bathshakespeare.org.uk). The Theatre Royal and Ustinov Studio set the scene for international interpretations of the Bard using drama, puppetry and comedy.
Spring Flower Festival (May). With so many herbaceous delights in Royal Victoria Park, who needs Chelsea?
Bath Balloon Fiesta (May). A real spectacle, with hot air balloons of all shapes and sizes taking to the skies above Royal Victoria Park.

Summer

Bath International Music Festival (May/June, www.bathmusicfest.org.uk). Venues such as the Assembly Rooms, Abbey and Guildhall ring to the sounds of top world music, jazz, classical and pop.

Bath Fringe Festival (May/June). The biggest British fringe festival after Edinburgh, this is a mixed bag of street theatre, comedy, music and parades, including Walcot Nation Day, when the city's hippy end shakes its thing in a giant street party.
Bath International Guitar Festival (July/ Aug). Concerts, workshops and seminars for all levels from experts to children take place all over the city with appearances from guitar legends.

Autumn

Jane Austen Festival (Sept). Nine days of Austen-centred plays, films, readings, talks, walks, picnics and tours organised by the Jane Austen Centre.
Bath Beer Festival (Oct). An orgy of brews, organised by the Campaign for Real Ale and held at the Royal Pavilion on North Parade Road.
Bath Film Festival (Oct/Nov). Local cinemas screen the sort of cutting-edge films that otherwise are rarely shown in the city.
Bath Mozartfest (Nov). Ten days of top-notch classical concerts (not just Mozart) at various venues around the city, featuring world-class artists and orchestras.

Building of Bath Museum: the story of a Georgian city. *See p82.*

up the road. Quiet, wood-panelled ambience can be found at the more civilised **Curfew** (11 Cleveland Place West, 01225 424210, main courses £3.50-£4.95).

Uptown, try **St James' Wine Vaults** (10 St James Street, 01225 310335), a small local covered in framed Russian posters, where the eclectic clientele once included Brad Pitt and Johnny Depp, who were filming nearby. Those in search of a swankier tipple can strike a pose in bars such as the art deco-styled **Delfter Krug** (Saw Close, 01225 443352, main courses £4-£8), the mellow **Raincheck Bar** (Monmouth Street, 01225 444770, main courses £5.90-£7.90) and, particularly, the excellent **Central Wine Bar** (Upper Borough Walls, 01225 333939, main courses £4-£8), whose relaxed mood, friendly staff and larger-than-standard spirit measures pack them in.

Restaurants

Bath has a formidable gourmet reputation, with far more high-class dining establishments than you might expect for a town this size. Some of the most exclusive dining is to be had at the city's hotels, including the **Bath Priory** (*see p90*), the **Queensberry** (*see p91*) and the **Royal Crescent** (*see p91*), but there are also plenty of informal eateries, offering good grub at a fair price.

Le Beaujolais

5 Chapel Row, off Queen Square (01225 423417). **Open** noon-2.30pm, 6-10pm Tue-Sat; 6-10pm Mon, Sun. **Main courses** £4.80-£24. **Credit** AmEx, MC, V.
Le Beaujolais has been serving classic French food in jolly surroundings for more than 30 years. Tongue-in-cheek postcards cover the walls, and

rather risqué knick-knacks peek out of every alcove. The menu is distinctly traditional: the likes of foie gras terrine with toasted brioche, followed by steak tournedos or monkfish medallions. Expect a long wait if you don't book.

Bistro Papillon

2 Margaret's Buildings, Brock Street (01225 310064). **Open** noon-10pm Tue-Sat. **Main courses** £9.95-£13.25. **Set lunch** £7.50 2 courses. **Credit** AmEx, MC, V.
This place has an understated, sophisticated air, with chequered tablecloths, country-house kitsch and an efficient kitchen. The à la carte dinner menu features bistro staples such as leg of duck confit with Puy lentils, and the set lunch is a steal.

Café Retro

18 York Street (01225 339347). **Open** *Restaurant* 9am-10pm Mon-Sat; 10am-10pm Sun. *Café* 9am-6pm Mon-Sat; 10am-6pm Sun. **Main courses** £8-£12 **Credit** AmEx, MC, V.
Hordes of trendy young things pack the tables at this boho café and restaurant to enjoy anything from a luxurious hot chocolate to a full fried breakfast or an international dinner. The eclectic menu draws on Asian and North African cuisine plus French and British classics. There's a licensed bar, but you can also bring your own.

Demuths

2 North Parade Passage, off Abbey Green (01225 446059/www.demuths.co.uk). **Open** 10am-9.30pm Mon-Thur; 10am-10pm Fri; 9.30am-10pm Sat; 9.30am-5pm Sun. **Main courses** £5.75-£11.50. **Credit** AmEx, DC, MC, V.
A vegetarian and vegan restaurant, with bold and clashing decor, Demuths has been serving cruelty-free meals to the inhabitants of Bath for 16 years. The inventive menu takes its inspiration from all around the globe, and includes such local delicacies as Somerset goat's cheese wrap alongside the likes of Malaysian curry.

Firehouse Rotisserie

2 John Street (01225 482070/www.firehouse
rotisserie.co.uk). **Open** noon-11pm Mon-Sat; noon-
4pm Sun. **Main courses** £8.95-£13.95. **Credit**
AmEx, DC, MC, V.

Spit-roasted chicken, Southwestern US classics and
excellent luxury pizzas – plus friendly staff and a
stylish, relaxed atmosphere – make this place one of
Bath's most popular restaurants.

Fishworks

6 Green Street (01225 448707/www.fishworks.co.uk).
Open noon-10pm Tue-Sat. **Main courses** £10-£18.
Credit AmEx, MC, V.

This award-winning restaurant is the best place
in Bath to eat fish. Chef Gary Rosser combines
superlative cooking with delicate seasoning and
fresh ingredients to create flavourful and fairly
priced dishes. A complete refurbishment in 2002

Going underground

Tucked away under the raised pavement on
George Street there's a small door that, but
for the sign outside, might be mistaken for
a store room. Get a little closer though and
the board inside will reveal the names of
virtually every notable rock and pop band
from the '80s and '90s: Radiohead, Oasis,
Blur, Massive Attack, Pulp, Primal Scream.
Heck, even T'Pau.

Moles is – literally – an underground club
and live music venue that has been lending
the World Heritage City some much-needed
street cred for almost a quarter of a century.
It has the rare distinction among provincial
music venues of being well known far beyond
the boundaries of the city. The walls drip
history, and this adds to the special
atmosphere that both customers and bands
rave about.

Jane Mountain of The Lollies is typical:
'It's almost too small to imagine all those
rock star egos squeezing in', she says
'But there's some sort of electrical charge.
As soon as you get on stage, the close,
cramped quarters come alive. Before you
know it, the band is sweating, the audience
is sweating, the ceiling is sweating,
everybody's dancing and shouting and
glowing. Only then do you understand why
Moles is such a special venue.'

After spells as a strip joint and gay
nightclub in the '60s and '70s, the empty
venue was bought in 1978 by local jazz
trumpeter Phil Andrews. He named it Moles,
because of the murky, underground location,
although the name had extra significance for
him as his father had been posthumously
revealed as an MI5 spy.

Moles was ahead of its time in being a
vegetarian café by day and a hotspot for jazz,
folk and blues by night. There was no PA
system so the music was usually drowned
out by conversation, but the venue was still
considered a welcome alternative to the
glittery, disco-mad nightclubs of the 1970s.

Eventually Andrews borrowed the money for
a small PA system and the modern Moles
was born. The first night performance by
rock band The Spoons was a packed-to-the-
rafters success and unleashed a hitherto
unimagined rocklust in Bath folk. A gig by
The Smiths – then unknown – followed
shortly afterwards.

During the '80s a steady stream of top
bands, such as The Cure, stormed this tiny
venue, playing in the middle of the floor,
because of the lack of a stage. Moles
remains sorely lacking in creature comforts
even today – the cramped backstage area
has barely enough room to swing a drumstick
– but that doesn't prevent a host of stars
from loving the place: Gabrielle has sung
here three times; Peter Gabriel and The
Stranglers' Hugh Cornwell have propped
up the bar on innumerable occasions, and
many artists have used the recording
studios above the club. The Britpop
phenomenon of the mid '90s saw Blur,
Radiohead, Supergrass, Pulp, Ocean Colour
Scene, Suede and Oasis all take early steps
at Moles; Oasis's performance turned out to
be one of the most exciting nights the venue
had ever seen.

Today, with UK 'tours' confined to four or
five major cities, big names are few and far
between at Moles. Yet the club remains one
of the region's most important music venues
for nurturing new talent, both local and
international. Intimate, friendly and agreeably
scruffy, it's a venue that lives and breathes
music. Even after hours the place doesn't
sleep – according to staff there's a
poltergeist in the cellar that shifts barrels
around late at night.

Moles

14 George Street (01225 404445/
www.moles.co.uk). **Open** *Club* 9pm-2am Mon-
Thur; 9pm-4am Fri, Sat. **Admission** £2-£5.
Credit MC, V.

The Georgian **Theatre Royal**. See p89.

has added a new dining room, terrace and an express bar, where diners can enjoy a glass of wine and a seafood nibble.

Green Park Brasserie & Bar

Green Park Station, Green Park Road (01225 338565/www.greenparkbrasserie.com). **Open** 7am-11pm Mon; 11am-11pm Tue-Sat; 10am-11pm Sat; 11am-3pm Sun. **Main courses** £11.95-£15.95. **Set meals** £13.95 2 courses; £15.95 3 courses. **Credit** AmEx, DC, MC, V.

Visit this rambling brasserie for a tasty meal accompanied by some good local jazz. Food is French with a twist (lamb and mint triangles with sweet chilli marmalade). Outside tables are popular in summer.

Martini

8-9 George Street (01225 460818/www.martini restaurantbath.co.uk). **Open** noon-10.30pm daily. **Main courses** £7.95-£39. **Set lunch** £8.95 2 courses, £9.95 3 courses. **Credit** MC, V.

Situated in two adjoining Georgian houses on one of Bath's smartest streets, this Italian lives up to its address: the service is professional, the presentation superb, and the food fine: pasta and pizzas supplemented by daily fresh fish, risotto and soup specials.

Moody Goose

7A Kingsmead Square (01225 466688/www.moody-goose.com). **Open** noon-9.30pm Mon-Sat. **Main courses** £15-£19.50. **Set meal** £25 3 courses. **Credit** AmEx, DC, MC, V.

The Goose is one of Bath's best restaurants, and dining here means being pampered. Beautifully presented modern British cuisine – with a hint of French *je ne sais quoi* – is served by discreetly attentive waiting staff. Leave room for seductive desserts like vanilla and pear bavarois with star anise sorbet.

No.5 Bistro

5 Argyle Street (01225 444499/www.no-5-bistro. fsbusiness.co.uk). **Open** noon-2.30pm, 6.30-10pm Mon-Fri; noon-2.30pm, 6.30-11.30pm Sat. **Main courses** £12.50-£15.75. **Credit** AmEx, MC, V.

There's little to fault at this adorable bistro. It's small, but snug tables and candlelight create a charmingly intimate atmosphere, in which friendly staff serve the likes of paupiette of veal with sautéd morels.

Rajpoot

Rajpoot House, 4 Argyle Street (01225 466833/ www.rajpoot.com). **Open** 11am-3.30pm, 6-11pm Mon-Thur, Sun; 11am-3.30pm, 6-11.30pm Fri, Sat. **Main courses** £7.95-£13.50. **Set meals** £16.95-£25 4 courses. **Credit** AmEx, DC, MC, V.

Rajpoot is renowned around the country for its top-drawer Indian cuisine. The place has a dark, cavernous feel, with luxurious fabrics draping intimate alcoves. Standard curry faves are supported by more unusual ceremonial dishes, such as rezala lamb. There's also a wide vegetarian selection.

Sukhothai

90A Walcot Street (01225 462463). **Open** noon-11pm daily. **Main courses** £4.50-£7. **Set meals** £16-£25 3 courses. **Credit** MC, V.

Arguably Bath's best Thai restaurant. Everything here is as authentic as can be, from the rather brusque service to the kitsch decor and the fish tank against the wall. Try the mixed starter of satay, fish cakes and prawns, followed by one of the large array of meat, fish and vegetarian dishes, and a dessert of banana fritters in sesame seeds.

Arts & entertainment

Timing your trip around one of Bath's innumerable festivals is a good way to enjoy the best of the city's rich cultural life (*see p84* **Festival fever**).

Film

Mainstream blockbusters occupy the screens at the **ABC** (22-23 Westgate Street, 01225 461730) and **Robins Cinema** (St John's Place, off Monmouth Street, 01225 461506). For arthouse, foreign and independent films make your way to the bijou **Little Theatre** (St Michael's Place, 01225 466822), but be aware that the runs here are often very short and seats sell out quickly.

Music

There are frequent classical and world music concerts at the **Assembly Rooms** (*see p82*), **Pump Room** (*see p77*), the **Guildhall** (*see p78*) and the **Michael Tippett Centre** (Bath College, Newton St Loe, 01225 875875), plus free organ recitals every Wednesday lunchtime in the Abbey (*see p77*).

For pop and rock with an indie bias head for **Moles** (*see p86* **Going underground**) or the **Window Arts Centre** (St James Memorial Hall, Lower Borough Walls, 01225 421700). The **Porter Butt** (York Place, London Road, 01225 425084) is the hub of a burgeoning punk scene, while free shows of up-and-coming acoustic singer-songwriters are held in the comfortable

City walk Shop 'n' stroll

Distance approx 1 mile (1.5 kilometres).
Time anything from 30 minutes to several
hours, depending how many shops you visit.
Difficulty Easy; pavements all the way.

Start at the top of Milsom Street, designed
by the elder John Wood as one of Georgian
Bath's main thoroughfares. This is where
Isabella and Henry Tilney lodged in
Northanger Abbey, and it remains the 'posh'
end of town when it comes to shopping.
On the west side is **Jolly's** (Nos.7-13,
01225 462811), a traditional and rather
snooty department store, while opposite
is Shires Yard, an upmarket arcade for
retailers of haute couture, handmade
choccies and the like.

Nearing the bottom of the street, turn right
into Quiet Street to take in the spread of deli
goodies at **Paxton & Whitfield** (1 John Street,
01225 466403, closed late Dec-early Jan)
– including the local, brie-like Bath Soft
Cheese. Fashionistas may also want to make
a special detour to **Mrs Simpson** (Kingsmead
Square, 01225 461518), where they'll find
cast-off Gucci pumps, MaxMara gowns and
Lulu Guinness bags – all sold for peanuts.

Returning to Milsom Street, follow the
road as it curves left into New Bond Street.
There's upmarket gifts – and a lovely first-
floor café – at **Bloomsbury** (No.15, 01225
461049) and delectable luxury cosmetics at
Space NK (No.10, 01225 482804). Next door

is New Bond Street Place, the beginning of a
network of shop-lined pedestrian alleyways.
Cross over Upper Borough Walls into Union
Passage and then left into picturesque
Northumberland Place, with **Neal's Yard
Remedies** (No.7, 01225 466944) on the
right and a clutch of contemporary jewellers
on the left. At the far end, turn right and then
right again into the covered shopping arcade
known as the Corridor. Built in 1825 by the
Henry Goodridge – who also designed
Beckford's tower in Lansdowne (*see p83*)
– it was extensively rebuilt after an IRA bomb
attack in 1974. At the end of the Corridor,
continue down Union Passage and cross
over Cheap Street into Abbey Churchyard.
Try to ignore the watchful gaze of the Abbey
as you indulge in the sinful delights on offer
at **Jim Garrahy's Fudge Kitchen** (10 Abbey
Churchyard, 01225 462277). Dedicated
souvenir hunters may also want to check
out the **Roman Baths Shop** (The Pump
Room, 01225 477798), around the corner
on Stall Street. Otherwise dodge the tourists
and buskers and make your way to exquisite,
cobbled Abbey Green. **Eric Snook's The
Golden Cot** (Abbey Gate Street, 01225
464914) is stuffed with upmarket togs
and toys for babies and children, while
the **Sweet Shop** (8 North Parade Passage,
01225 428040) has huge jars of barley
sugars, liquorice comfits and humbugs
served in traditional paper bags.

---

pub surroundings of the **Porter Cellar
Bar** (15 George Street, 01225 424104).

For jazz, try the **Farmhouse** (1 Lansdown
Road, 01225 316162), **Green Park Brasserie
& Bar** (*see p87*) or the **Bell** (*see p84*), which
also hosts blues, country and folk performers.

Nightlife

One doesn't really 'large it' in Aquae Sulis, and
serious nightowls are advised to head straight
to distinctly more bassline-friendly Bristol.
However, if all you want is a quick post-pub
shuffle and aren't concerned with hipness,
try **Cadillacs** (90B Walcot Street, 01225
464241, admission £2.50-£6) or the natty,
Moroccan-styled **Po Na Na** (North Parade,
01225 401115) and its sister club, the **Fez** (7A
Bladud Buildings, The Paragon, 01225 444162).
'Drive By' at Po Na Na shakes the foundations
with drum 'n' bass.

Sport

Hugely successful in 1980s and '90s, but
currently experiencing something of a slump,
Bath Rugby Club (Bath Recreation Ground,
information 01225 325200/09068 884554,
tickets 01225 460588) still packs in loyal
supporters for premiership and European Cup
rugby throughout the season. Tickets go on
sale five weeks in advance and popular fixtures
sell out fast. Heroes of the – ahem – Dr Martens
League Premier Division, **Bath City FC** (also
known as the Romans) play in Twerton Park
(01225 423087) and seats are almost guaranteed.

Bath Cricket Club (North Parade Road,
01225 336255) is a lovely venue overlooking
the river and plays host to the Somerset
County Cricket festival in June. Finally, horse
racing has been enjoyed since 1874 at **Bath
Racecourse** (Lansdowne, 01225 424609) just
outside the city. It's the highest track in the UK.

From here, head east along York Street – where the **Beaux Arts Gallery** (12-13 York Street, 01225 464850) displays modern British painting, sculpture and ceramics – to emerge at delightfully named Bog Island and a glorious view over the Parade Gardens to Bathwick Hill. Make your way north into Orange Grove, characterised by its scallop-shaped window canopies, and into the High Street to reach the **Guildhall Market** (01225 477000) for hardware, books, food and gifts.

On the corner of Bridge Street, the **Square** (16 Northgate Street, 01225 334421) has shoes, clothes and handbags by the likes of Gucci and Prada, while next door, the **White Company** (15 Northgate Street, 01225 445284) lives up to its name with a gorgeous array of monochrome goodies. Ignore the Podium shopping centre on your right and head north, past the post office, into Broad Street. There's an impressive range of handmade bangers at the **Sausage Shop** (7 Green Street, 01225 318300) and oodles of classy homewares at **Rossiters** (38-39 Broad Street, 01225 462227). Hang a right along Saracen Street to reach Walcot Street and the wonderful **Fine Cheese Company** (29-31 Walcot Street, 01225 483407), purveyor of cheese, coffee and high-class deli delights.

Walcot Street is an enclave of bohemian scruffiness in the heart of the chi-chi city, particularly during Saturday's **flea market** (01225 852773, 8am-4pm), which offers antiques, arts and crafts, vintage clothing and fresh food. At other times, check out the second-hand clobber at **Billie Jean** (No.49, 01225 464946), contemporary interiors at **Shannon** (No.68-70, 01225 424222) and a plethora of antiques ranging from Oriental art at **Indigo** (No.59, 01225 311795) to architectural cast-offs at **Walcot Reclamation Yard** (108 Walcot Street, 01225 444404). Also, don't miss the **Bath Aqua Theatre of Glass** (105-107 Walcot Street, 01225 428146, admission £1.50-£3), an absorbing glass-blowing centre, specialising in pretty aquamarine-coloured glass, with a museum, children's activities and hand-crafted pieces for sale.

At the far end of the street, cross over to St Swithan's church and head south along the glorious curved sweep of the Paragon. You'll pass No.33 on your left, where the 18th-century actress Sarah Siddons resided during numerous visits to Bath, and the Countess of Huntingdon's Chapel on your right, which houses the Building of Bath Museum. At the end of the Paragon, antique-lovers should head straight for the cluster of dealers north of George Street, specifically the **Bartlett Street Antiques Centre** (5-10 Bartlett Street, 01225 345610/763054, www.antiques-centre.co.uk), which has a huge array of collectables. Wearier shoppers, however, will be glad to regain the top of Milsom Street.

Theatre

The **Theatre Royal** (Sawclose, 01225 448815) hosts previews of many West End shows, performances by renowned companies like the Almeida and the National Theatre, plus some opera and jazz, and '60s artists. Tastes tend towards the middlebrow – lots of Noel Coward and Alan Aykbourn for the blue rinse brigade – but there's occasionally the odd controversial piece: *Shopping and Fucking* played here a few years ago. For smaller-scale, cutting-edge drama and improv, including shows returning from the Edinburgh festival, try the **Ustinov Studio** (Monmouth Street, 01225 448844) around the back. The small but atmospheric **Rondo Theatre** (St Saviour's Road, Larkhall, 01225 463362, closed late Dec), meanwhile, is a former church hall that stages amateur and professional productions of everything from Shakespeare to Pinter.

Shop & services

Why bother with museums and architecture when there's so much shopping to do? Bath is a shopaholics delight, with high-street faves cosying up to stylish boutiques and tempting delicatessens throughout the city centre. A crowded half-mile or so of shops – much of it pedestrianised – runs from the top of Milsom Street down through Old Bond Street, Union Street, Stall Street to Southgate Street. The streets and alleys east and west of the main drag – Quiet Street, Trim Street, Green Street, New Bond Street and Queen Street, for example – shelter smaller, unique retailers and provide some of the most enjoyable shopping in the city (*see p88* **Shop 'n' stroll**).

For fruit and veg, meat, dairy produce and preserves, check out Bath's **farmers' market**, which is held every Saturday morning in Old Green Park Station, Green Park Road.

Where to stay

If you can afford it, Bath's smartest hotels offer a luxury stay to remember. Happily, though, epicureans on a budget can still bed down in comfort and elegance at one of the city's guesthouses or B&Bs. Situated in residential areas of town, usually less than ten minutes' walk from the centre, the best are charming and reasonably priced, with hotel-standard facilities and large, beautifully furnished rooms.

In the summer months you'd be advised to book up as far in advance as you can. And note that many establishments require a two-night minimum stay in high season.

Albany Guest House

24 Crescent Gardens, BA1 2NB (01225 313339/ www.bath.org/hotel/albany). Closed late Dec. **Rates** (B&B) £30-£40 single; £36-£55 double/twin. **No credit cards**.

This small Victorian B&B offers excellent value for such a handy location, close to the Royal Crescent, and double-glazing ensures peace and quiet despite the busy road outside. Only one of the four snug bedrooms is en suite, but all the rooms benefit from extra touches like sweets and flowers. A cottagey breakfast room and pretty hanging baskets complete the picture.

Athole Guest House

33 Upper Oldfield Park (01225 334307/www.athole house.co.uk). **Rates** (B&B) £48 single; £65 double. **Credit** AmEx, MC, V.

Athole Guest House prides itself on being one of the few Bath guesthouses to be Laura Ashley free. Instead, the spotless, yellow, modern bedrooms come with contemporary furniture, along with laptop connections, minibars and satellite TV. Communal areas include a glass conservatory and a cosy, red breakfast room.

Bath Priory Hotel

Weston Road (01225 331922/www.thebath priory.co.uk). **Rates** (B&B) £145 single; £260-£320 double; £400 suite. **Set lunch** £20 2 courses, £25 3 courses, £30 Sunday. **Set dinner** £47.50 3 courses. **Credit** AmEx, DC, MC, V.

This discreet Gothic manor house (plus new annexes) is approached via a grand, circular, gravel drive. Yet, despite the imposing entrance, there are homely touches: chopped logs in the porch and squashy sofas in front of enormous fireplaces. Bedrooms and apartments are decorated in a modern English country-house style. The indoor spa is supplemented by a heated outdoor pool and the four-acre, sunken walled garden contains an organic vegetable plot to supply the highly acclaimed restaurant. Here, fine modern French cuisine – with dishes such as local organic lamb with aubergine, sweet pepper, caviar and claret sauce – is created from the very best ingredients and served with panache by the charming French staff.

Anyone for rugger? *See p88.*

Bath Spa Hotel

Sydney Road (01225 400 8222/www.bathspa hotel.com). **Rates** (B&B) £125-£135 single; £210-£280 double; £400-£450 suite. **Credit** AmEx, DC, MC, V.

This palatial, five-star, 102-bedroom Regency pile (it was once a hospital) stands in seven acres of gardens overlooking the city. Opulence is the key note here: chandeliers, pillars, heavy swagged curtains, huge mirrors and four posters. However, guests with children are catered for too: there's a baby-monitoring service and a nursery, so parents can pamper themselves in the spa without having to worry about the kids.

Dorian House

1 Upper Oldfield Park (01225 426336/www.dorian house.co.uk). **Rates** (B&B) £60 single; £78-£140 double. **Credit** AmEx, MC, V.

Tasteful, and soothing, with stained glass, old prints, antiques, and a handsome tiled hallway, Dorian House is owned by cellist Tim Hugh, whose classical sensibilities have extended as far as the room names: Du Pré, Casals and Stradivari are particularly resplendent. The refurbished basement rooms have tiled floors, a clean design and a Mediterranean vibe.

Haringtons's Hotel

8-10 Queen Street (01225 461728/www. haringtonshotel.co.uk). **Rates** (B&B) £68-£98 single; £88-£118 double. **Credit** AmEx, DC, MC, V.

Slap bang in the centre of town, Harington's Hotel is located in one of the city's most-photographed streets. The rooms are modern, if slightly motel-ish, and the service is smiley and informal. Drivers will be pleased to learn that there are reserved spaces for guests in the Charlotte Street car park.

Laura Place

3 Laura Place, Great Pulteney Street (01225 463815). Closed late Dec-end Feb. **Rates** (B&B) £70-£92 double; £115 suite. **Credit** AmEx, MC, V.

Handsome and terrific value, this 18th-century cornerhouse overlooking Laura Place is a dropkick away from Bath Rugby Club. Its romantic bedrooms are crammed with antiques (some four-poster beds) and remain just on the elegant side of chintzy. The overall atmosphere is stylish and homely.

Paradise House Hotel

86-88 Holloway (01225 317723/www.paradise-house.co.uk). **Rates** (B&B) £70-£90 single; £75-£120 double; £110-£150 deluxe. **Credit** AmEx, DC, MC, V.

Popular with honeymooners, Paradise House is an impossibly romantic hideaway set on a leafy lane next to a tiny chapel about seven minutes' walk from the centre of town. The grand 18th-century front is upstaged by a palatial rear end, whose columns and tranquil gardens resemble a mini-palace. The standard rooms, though luxurious, are on the small side. For a real treat choose deluxe room 12, set in its own annex, with French doors on to the garden, and a jacuzzi.

Queensberry Hotel

Russell Street (01225 447928/www.bathqueens berry.com). Closed late Dec. **Rates** (B&B) £120-£185 double; £210-£225 deluxe. **Main courses** £15-£18. **Set lunch** £13.50 2 courses, £15.50 3 courses. **Set dinner** £26 3 courses. **Credit** Am Ex, MC, V.

Guests return time and again to this charming, award-winning retreat made up of four Regency townhouses close to the Royal Crescent. It's full of comfy nooks and crannies such as the intimate bar area and the rear walled courtyard, and crammed with period features. Of the 29 rooms, the grandest are at the front, but the best views are at the back.

The Olive Tree restaurant in the basement is one of the finest in Bath, serving a blend of traditional and contemporary Anglo-French cuisine – typical dishes could include Provencal fish soup and partridge with lentils and ceps – accompanied by a Francophile wine list.

Royal Crescent Hotel

16 Royal Crescent (01225 823333/www.royal crescent.co.uk). **Rates** £170-£240 double; £340-£800 suite. **Set lunch** £15.50 2 courses, £18 3 courses. **Set dinner** £45 3 courses. **Credit** AmEx, DC, MC, V.

Bang in the centre of the crescent, and identifiable from the outside only by the foliage surrounding the doorway, this elegant five-star hotel is home from home for visiting celebrities. Yet with just 45 Georgian-style rooms and suites, it manages not to feel haughty. The former stable block houses a dreamy spa complete with pool, steam room, sauna and a range of beauty treatments, while Pimpernel's restaurant – despite its period setting – serves modern fusion cooking that's lively and technically assured, if a little over-priced. The restaurant is named after the Scarlet Pimpernel, a former owner of the property.

Resources

Hospital

Royal United Hospital *Combe Park (01225 428331).*
NHS Walk-In Centre *Henry Street (01225 447695).* **Open** 7am-10pm daily.

Internet

Mail Boxes Etc *3 Edgar Buildings, George Street, (01225 482777/www.mbebath.co.uk).* **Open** 8.30am-6pm Mon-Fri; 9am-4pm Sat.

Police station

Manvers Street (01275 818181).

Post office

25 New Bond Street (0845 722 3344). **Open** 9am-5.30pm Mon-Sat.

Tourist information

Bath Tourist Information Centre *Abbey Chambers, Abbey Churchyard, BA1 1LY (01225 477101/www.visitbath.co.uk).* **Open** 9.30am-5.30pm daily.

Getting there & around

Bath city centre is very pedestrian friendly but positively contemptuous of cars. Leave your vehicle at home, or park it at your hotel and don't return to it for the duration of your visit.

By bus

National Express (08705 808080, www. gobycoach.co.uk) serves Bath bus station on Manvers Street. For local routes contact **Bath Bus Company** (01225 330444, www. bathbuscompany.com) or **First Badgerline** (0845 606 4446, www.firstbadgerline.co.uk). **Guide Friday** (01225 444102, www.guidefriday. com) provides open-topped bus tours (£8.50; £6.50 concessions) around town, which can be picked up at various points including the bus station, Grand Parade and the Royal Crescent.

By train

Bath Spa is on the main line from London Paddington to Bristol Temple Meads. Regular trains leave London for Bath approximately every 30mins (journey time 1hr 20mins). For further information, *see p293.*

What
Londoners
take when
they
go out.

Somerset

Introduction

Welcome to cider country.

At the heart of the Anglo-Saxon kingdom of Wessex, Somerset historically formed a buffer zone between the Celtic heartlands of the far west and the rest of England. Today it's a largely rural area where tourism often takes a back seat to the demands of agriculture. That said, there's still plenty here to entice the visitor, with the added bonus that few destinations in Somerset attract the kind of crowds you may find in parts of Devon and Cornwall.

The coast of **North Somerset** cannot compete with the lovely strands further west, but the sunsets here can be spectacular. Inland, the limestone of the **Mendip Hills** has been gouged out over millions of years to form the famous caves at **Wookey Hole** and **Cheddar** – where you should take the opportunity to taste some local cheese. In fact, Somerset is one of the best places in the UK to sample all kinds of local produce, with farmers' markets (01460 78223, www.somersetfarmersmarkets.co.uk), cider orchards and organic suppliers dotted all over the county.

On the southern slopes of the Mendips, the splendid Gothic cathedral at **Wells** is surrounded by a mini medieval 'city', while just to the south the unmistakable form of the tor draws tourists and pilgrims to the intriguing religious and New Age town of **Glastonbury** – accompanied in June by music fans en route to the festival. All around, the heart of the county is dominated by the **Somerset Levels**, an evocative landscape of moor and marsh, with a history stretching back thousands of years. The Levels are edged to the south-east by picturesque villages built from golden Ham stone, and to the west by the rolling **Quantock Hills**.

West again is **Exmoor**, where tracts of heather- and gorse-clad moorland and deep, wooded valleys culminate at a stunning but inaccessible coastline. Although some of the National Park officially lies in Devon, Somerset claims the lion's share, including Dunster, Porlock and Dunkery Beacon.

Note: In 1996 the county of Avon was abolished and its territory carved up to form the new counties of South Gloucestershire, Bristol, Bath & North-east Somerset and North Somerset. For the purposes of this guide the latter two counties have been included as part of Somerset, although the official county boundaries are shown on the map opposite.

Don't miss > Somerset

A glass of scrumpy
Get a real insight into the Somerset way of life. *See p114.*

Cheddar Gorge
A limestone chasm that's impressive both above and below the surface. *See p98.*

Dunster
This picturesque market town is the gateway to Exmoor. *See p117.*

Exmoor coast
Hog-backed hills lunge precipitously towards the sea. *See 117.*

Glastonbury
Abbey ruins, Arthurian legends, a dramatic tor and an unrivalled music festival. *See p105.*

Hestercombe Gardens
If you thought landscape gardening meant some dodgy decking and a faux rockery, think again. *See p113.*

Wells
England's smallest city has an awesome cathedral at its heart. *See p102.*

Somerset

North Somerset & the Mendips

Spectacular caves, gorgeous cheese and a stunning cathedral at Wells.

Somerset

Driving along the M5 towards Taunton or Bristol, it's easy to miss north Somerset. Apart from the tourist traps of Cheddar, Wookey Hole and Wells, it's an area that is often ignored – a fact that helps to explain how it has retained its bucolic, unassuming charm. There are contrasts aplenty – the Mendip plateau, with its limestone landscape and lead-working remains, is totally different to the lush pastures around Wells and Shepton Mallet just a few miles away – but there's none of the wildness and weirdness of the Levels, nor Glastonbury's bizarre mingling of fact and fantasy. Despite its proximity to two cities, north Somerset is still a largely rural part of the county – famous for its cheese, its cider and its strawberries.

For a hint of its character, seek out the CD *The Finest 'Arvest of the Wurzels* (EMI Gold). No, seriously. Skip the late-'70s hammed-up yokel-pop like *I've Got A Brand New Combine Harvester* and listen to the early material recorded live at the Royal Oak in Nailsea more than a decade earlier. *Drink Up Thy Zider*, *The Champion Dung Spreader* and *All Over Mendip* were written by the group's founder Adge Cutler, who has always been revered as the authentic voice of Zummerzet.

The coast

Don't arrive at Clevedon, Weston-super-Mare or Burnham-on-Sea expecting crystal blue waters and foaming surf. This is the Bristol Channel, after all, and is better enjoyed for its pleasant strolls and glorious sunsets than for its bathing.

Fans of **Portishead** may want to visit the town that spawned the band, but there's little else of interest here beyond glimpses of the Severn Crossings. Head instead for **Clevedon** a couple of miles south, described by Sir John Betjeman as 'a beautiful haven of quiet' and still holding much Victorian charm. Its **pier** (run by Clevedon Pier Trust, 01275 878846) opened in 1869 and is considered the finest of its era. The pleasure steamer, *Balmoral*, runs day trips from here to Ilfracombe, Minehead and Barry (0845 130 4647, www.waverleyexcursions.co.uk).

At the opposite end of Clevedon's late Georgian and Regency seafront (where a miniature railway runs in summer), the **Poet's Walk** offers views across to the Welsh mountains and the islands of Flat Holm and Steep Holm (*see p97*). Coleridge, Thackeray and Tennyson are said to have been inspired by this gentle amble; St Andrew's Church on the headland serves as the final resting place of Tennyson's friend Arthur Hallam (1811-33), who he immortalised in the poem 'In Memoriam'.

Hallam's mother was a member of the Elton family, owners, since 1709, of **Clevedon Court**, located just outside the town. Altered and added to by the Elizabethans, this 14th-century manor house, incorporates a 12th-century tower and 13th-century great hall, and is now owned by the National Trust. The house contains many pieces of the highly collectable pottery known as Eltonware, along with examples of Nailsea glass, made nearby in the 19th century. The house is surrounded by a small but charming terraced garden.

The town's pottery connection continues today at the **Clevedon Craft Centre** (Moor Lane, 01275 342114, closed Mon), where ten studios are housed in the outbuildings of a 17th-century farm. In addition to pots, you'll find beautiful jewellery and unusual hand-carved leather goods here – not to mention ducks, chickens and geese for children to feed.

Weston-super-Mare was just plain old Weston until the early 19th century, when the craze for the 'sea cure' drove the fashionable residents of Bristol and Bath to their nearest coastal village. The first spa baths opened in 1820, and the Latin suffixes to the name (meaning 'on sea') were added in a pretentious attempt to rival the resorts on the continent. The arrival of Brunel's railway in 1841 turned Weston into a thriving seaside resort for all social classes; a number of typical Victorian parks and pleasure gardens from this time survive to this day.

The town's once-genteel atmosphere is, however, harder to detect now. With John Cleese as its most famous former resident and disgraced Tory peer Jeffrey Archer as the local lord, Weston is having to battle against a somewhat comic image. The situation is not helped by the nickname Weston-super-Mud, a reference to the huge expanse of gloopy brown sand that is left when the tide goes out. (The tidal range here is the second largest in the world, peaking at around 48 feet/14.5 metres on the highest spring tides.) The sandy beach may be raked clean every morning, but most of the attendant attractions are banal. **Seaquarium** on Marine Parade has the usual assortment of underwater beasties, while the **Grand Pier** (www.grandpierwsm.co.uk), completed in 1906, is given over to a covered amusement arcade.

On the north side of the beach, **Birnbeck Pier** (01793 618566, www.birnbeck.co.uk) is Weston's original pier and was completed in 1867. It is Grade II listed, but remains on English Heritage's list of buildings at risk despite ambitious plans for restoration. Just to the south, **Knightstone Harbour** is perhaps the most picturesque section of the seafront and, when the tide is right, serves as the departure point for summer boat trips (01934 632307, £14, £7 concessions) to **Steep Holm** island. This 50-acre island rises 256 feet (78 metres) from the Bristol Channel and offers superb views up to the Severn Crossings and across to the Welsh coast. It is also a nature

reserve, supporting lush vegetation, timid Muntjac deer and an abundance of gulls and cormorants during the spring breeding season.

Among the town's other limited attractions are the **North Somerset Museum**, a local history musem that features reconstructed shops, houses and seaside ephemera from Weston's heyday; and the surprisingly interesting **Helicopter Museum** on the A371 at Locking, which houses some 50 choppers from all over the world, including Russian and Vietnam veterans. 'Open cockpit' days are held roughly once a month, and allow visitors to sit inside many of the aircraft and then enjoy a short flight (at a price, of course).

Heading south from Weston, the seven miles (11 kilometres) of flat, wide and breezy beaches stretching from Brean to Burnham-on-Sea are a mecca for sand-yachting, sea-fishing and cheap family holidays in the numerous caravan and chalet parks. **Brean Down** itself is a peculiar outcrop of the Mendip Hills – a National Trust-managed headland, which was the site of a Roman temple and Iron Age hill-fort. These days it's ideal for a bracing walk and great views.

If you have kids to entertain, **Brean Leisure Park** will keep them amused with pools, flumes and white-knuckle rides, or there's the **Brean Down Tropical Bird Garden**, only a few metres from the beach.

Burnham is another failed 19th-century spa town, an inoffensive little place with the usual donkeys and amusements, views across to Bridgwater Bay and a remarkable surprise in the plain-looking **St Andrew's** church. The medieval interior contains superb 17th-century carvings by Grinling Gibbons taken from an altarpiece intended for the chapel at the long-demolished Palace of Whitehall, and later installed at Westminster Abbey by Christopher Wren. Inland is the landmark Iron-Age hill fort of **Brent Knoll**, while at the mouth of the River Parrett, **Steart Point** is a great spot for bird-watching.

Brean Down Tropical Bird Garden

Brean Down, Brean (01278 751209/www.burnham-on-sea.co.uk/brean_bird_garden). **Open** *Apr-Oct* 10am-dusk daily. Closed Nov-Mar. **Admission** £1.95; 95p concessions. **No credit cards.**

Brean Leisure Park

Coast Road, Brean Sands (01278 751595/ www.brean.com). **Open** *July, Aug* 11am-10pm daily. *Sept, Oct, Easter-June* hours vary; phone for details. Closed Nov-Easter. **Admission** free; charges for rides vary; phone for details.

Clevedon Court

Tickenham Road (B3130), Clevedon (01275 872257). **Open** *Easter-Sept* 2-5pm Wed, Thur, Sun. Closed Oct-Easter. **Admission** £4.50. **No credit cards.**

Have buckets of fun at **Weston-super-Mare**.

Helicopter Museum

Weston Heliport, Locking Moor Road, Weston-super-Mare (01934 635227/www.helicoptermuseum.co.uk). **Open** *Easter, July, Aug* 10am-6pm daily. *Apr-June, Sept, Oct* 10am-6pm Wed-Sun. *Nov-Mar* 10am-4pm Wed-Sun. **Admission** £3.95; £2.75-£3.25 concessions; £11 family; free under-5s. **Credit** (over £5) MC, V.

North Somerset Museum

Burlington Street, Weston-super-Mare (01934 621028/www.n-somerset.gov.uk/museum). **Open** 10am-4.30pm Mon-Sat. **Admission** £3.50; £2.50 concessions; £8 family. **Credit** AmEx, MC, V.

Seaquarium

Marine Parade, Weston-super-Mare (01834 613361/ www.seaquarium.co.uk). **Open** 10am-4pm daily. **Admission** £4.75; £3.75 concessions; £17 family. **Credit** AmEx, MC,V.

Where to eat & drink

Café society has yet to make an impact in this part of the world, so pubs represent the most reliable eating option. The **Moon in Sixpence** on Clevedon seafront (15 The Beach, 01275 872443, main courses £4-£12) is a substantial Victorian family diner, while Weston's best is the **Claremont Vaults** (1-3 Birnbeck Road, 01934 629503, main courses £3-£15), which usually has decent fish dishes. The **Red Cow** (Brent Street, Brent Knoll, 01278 760234, main courses £5-£14) is a good choice for Sunday lunch, or there's the atmospheric **Black Horse** (Clapton-in-Gordano, 01275 842105), near Portishead, a flagstoned inn that once doubled as the petty-sessions jail.

Where to stay

The coastal towns have an abundance of B&Bs, guesthouses and family-run hotels with sea views and limited ambitions. More appealing, however, is **Church House** (27 Kewstoke Road, Kewstoke, 01934 633185, double B&B £65), located just outside Weston to the north, a Georgian rectory with five immaculately tasteful rooms.

Other options include the **Old Rectory** (Church Road, Brean, 01278 751447, double B&B £20-£25), a five-minute walk from the beach, where rooms are offered in a converted schoolroom, stables and carriage house, or, further afield still, **Woodlands Country House Hotel** (Hill Lane, Brent Knoll, 01278 760232, main courses £11.25-£17.95, double B&B £79-£115) near Burnham, a peaceful Victorian farmhouse with nine attractive rooms beneath the ancient hill fort, whose restaurant serves more imaginative food than is the norm around these parts.

Resources

Hospital

Weston-super-Mare *Weston General Hospital, Grange Road, Uphill (01934 636363).*

Police station

Weston-super-Mare *Walliscote Road (01275 818181).*

Post offices

Burnham *6 Victoria Street (01278 782013).* **Open** 9am-5pm Mon-Fri; 9am-12.30pm Sat.
Clevedon *13 The Triangle (01275 873081).* **Open** 9am-5pm Mon-Fri; 9am-12.30pm Sat.
Weston-super-Mare *9 Aller Parade (01934 812103).* **Open** 9am-5pm Mon-Fri; 9am-12.30pm Sat.

Tourist information

Burnham *Tourist Office, South Esplanade (01278 787852/www.burnham-on-sea.co.uk).* **Open** *Easter-mid Nov* 9.30am-5pm daily. *Mid Nov-Easter* 9.30am-1pm, 2-4.30pm Mon-Sat.
Weston-super-Mare *Tourist Office, Centre Beach Lawns (01934 888800).* **Open** *Apr-Oct* 9.30am-5.30pm daily. *Nov-Mar* 9.30am-5pm Mon-Fri; 9.30am-1pm, 1.45-4pm Sat.

The Mendip Hills & around

Stretching from the coast at Weston-super-Mare to Frome in the east, the limestone ranges of the Mendip Hills are on a modest scale, seldom scaling 1,000 feet (305 metres). However, because they rise steeply both from sea level and from Wiltshire's chalk plains, they offer panoramic views of surprising grandeur and were deservedly designated an Area of Outstanding Natural Beauty in 1972. The hills are best known for the honeycomb of caves that have made this area a mecca for lovers of life beneath the surface.

Cheddar can become insufferably busy at holiday times, but even the throng of visitors and some tacky attractions can't disguise the sheer majesty of **Cheddar Gorge**: 400 feet (122 metres) deep, three miles (five kilometres) long and scoured out of the carboniferous limestone during the Ice Age.

An Explorer ticket allows access to the gorge, caves and other attractions, starting with the quarter mile-long Gough's Cave, a series of vast caverns named after the retired sea captain who discovered them in 1890. It was here that 'Cheddar Man', Britain's oldest complete skeleton, was buried 9,000 years ago – details are provided in the Cheddar Man Museum further down the road. According to DNA tests, his descendants still live in Cheddar. Cox's Cave is smaller than Gough's but even more intensely coloured and crammed with stalactites and stalagmites.

Adults may wish to steer clear of the Crystal Quest, a cave decked out as the 'Halls of Mordon, Lord of Darkness', but you try not to miss the climb up the 274 steps of Jacob's Ladder to the top of the Mendip plateau, where there's a lookout tower that offers fabulous views of the gorge, the coast and Glastonbury Tor.

This is also the starting point for a three-mile (five-kilometre), waymarked clifftop walk through the Cheddar Caves Nature Reserve, where you may spot peregrine falcons, the rare Cheddar Pink flower, and Soay sheep keeping the scrub in check. If that sounds too strenuous, an open-top bus tour runs through the gorge from March to September.

The house that time forgot

In an age when secrecy is frowned on, it seems almost inconceivable that a major country house could survive hidden from public view and largely ignored for the best part of a century. However, when the second Lord Wraxall died in 2001, the bizarre tale of **Tyntesfield** began to unfold. With none of the lord's 18 beneficiaries interested in taking on such a vast pile, the house and its 1,870 acres of land near Nailsea in North Somerset were placed on the market with a guide price of £14.55 million. (Kylie Minogue was reported to be a potential buyer.)

At this point the National Trust discovered the architectural and historic merit of Tyntesfield and launched a campaign to prevent its idiosyncratic contents being dispersed. The National Heritage Memorial Fund gave its biggest ever grant of £17.5 million, two anonymous donors chipped in £5 million between them, and 60,000 individuals contributed a further £1.5 million. In just 50 days, this remarkably untouched estate was secured intact.

The house was built between 1863 and 1882 by William Gibbs and his son Anthony, who made their fortunes importing guano, used as agricultural fertiliser, from South America. Designed by little-known Bristol architect John Norton, Tyntesfield exemplifies the muscular pomp of the Gothic Revival, and its roofline, with spires, turrets and an array of chimney pots, is spectacular. Yet, what makes Tyntesfield so worthy of preservation is its contents list. Lord Wraxall was an eccentric bachelor, quite content to live among the trappings of a bygone age with nothing modernised or discarded. The National Trust discovered prototype fire

extinguishers and 'douche' showers, a cast-iron chair with crystal decoration, and a billiard table with plumbed-in hot water to heat the baize and make the balls run more smoothly. The jewel-encrusted chapel was inspired by the Sainte Chapelle in Paris, and the children's nurseries are a turn-of-the-19th-century time capsule. Outside, the estate buildings include a sawmill and a perfectly preserved gasworks.

The challenge facing the National Trust has been to open Tyntesfield to the public without destroying its unique and fragile atmosphere. Just as it took hundreds of local workers to keep this massive estate functioning in the 19th century, so it may again require a small army to do so in the 21st.

The National Trust runs pre-booked guided tours of Tyntesfield house, chapel and formal gardens on Mondays and Sundays (£10), with additional tours of the chapel and gardens only on Wednesdays and Thursdays (£6). Refer to www.nationaltrust.org.uk/tyntesfield for further information and phone 0870 241 4500 to make a reservation.

Somerset

Cheddar's other claim to fame is, of course, its cheese. Local legend has it that a village milkmaid left a pail of milk in the caves for safe-keeping and on returning found it had changed into a tasty new substance. What's certain is that the industry was already well established more than 800 years ago. Henry II declared Cheddar cheese to be the finest in Britain and in 1170 bought 10,240 pounds of it, at a cost of a farthing a pound. Today you can watch it being made at the award-winning **Cheddar Gorge Cheese Company**.

An easy two-mile (three-kilometre) stroll skirts past Cheddar Reservoir on to the small town of **Axbridge**, with its medieval square and **King John's Hunting Lodge**, an early Tudor merchant's house with no connection to King John or, indeed, hunting. Now owned by the National Trust and housing the local history museum, this half-timbered building reflects the wealth of the town in Somerset's wool-producing heyday during the 14th century. Also worth a look is **St John the Baptist** church, an archetypal Somerset wool church with a magnificent tower and a Jacobean plastered, barrel vaulted ceiling.

For further subterranean delights, visit **Wookey Hole**, a complex of tunnels and caverns carved out by the River Axe, and now run by Madame Tussaud's. Special lighting picks out the main geological features, while the guided tour tells the true story of how Alexander Pope raided the place for his grotto at Twickenham, and the rather more fantastical account of how a local hag was turned to stone by a monk from Glastonbury Abbey.

Wookey Hole is considered the birthplace of British cave diving. In 1935 two divers, using cumbersome deep-sea gear, penetrated four previously inaccessible caves, and in 1948 reached the 100-foot (30-metre)-high chamber nine, now known as the Cathedral Cave. Although modern technology has since enabled divers to explore a total of 25 chambers, others still remain tantalisingly unvisited.

In 1857 a canal was dug to bring water from the River Axe to a papermill at Wookey Hole. The river emerges and cascades down a series of waterfalls into a lovely ravine, with a number of small caves where prehistoric remains and flint tools have been discovered. You can watch paper being made here, though the other attractions on the site – the Magical Mirror Maze and Edwardian Penny Arcade – will not be to everyone's taste.

Just outside Wookey on the B3139, **Burcott Mill** is the only remaining water-powered flour mill of the 11 once located along the river. After a tour, sample Burcott bread in the tearoom while kids enjoy the playground and pet corner.

Wells Cathedral: the city's jewel. *See p102.*

If you want to escape the tourist traps, take the road from Wookey towards Priddy on to the Mendip plateau. East of the road, **Ebbor Gorge** (01749 679546) is a National Nature Reserve run by English Nature, with views over the Somerset Levels. Continue up the hill past the car park, to reach Deer Leap Reserve, a great place for a picnic. **Priddy** itself is the highest village in Mendip, with extensive lead-working remains and evidence of mineral extraction dating back to the Roman period. It's also known for its annual folk fair in July (01749 675562, www.priddy.inuk.com).

On the north side of the Mendips, the Chew Valley's gentle, rolling scenery is a complete contrast to the upland landscape of the plateau, with lovely, tucked-away villages, such as Nempnett Thrubwell and Hinton Blewitt, now serving as dormitories for affluent commuters to Bristol and Bath. At the heart of the area are two reservoirs: **Blagdon Lake** and **Chew Valley Lake**, the largest artificial freshwater reservoir in the South West. There are picnic areas here, plus nature trails, an information centre and a number of hides giving good views of the waterfowl. (Note that only one hide is open to allcomers; dedicated twitchers should buy a permit from Woodford Lodge; *see p101.*)

Head south from the lake to reach the attractive wooded gorge of **Burrington Combe** (off the B3134).There's a lovely walk through the gorge or you can park at the top end to climb up to **Black Down**, the highest point on the Mendips at 1,065 feet (325 metres). East of the lake, meanwhile, the three stone circles at **Stanton Drew** date from around 2000 BC and are believed to be a key neolithic site of pagan worship.

Burcott Mill

Wookey, nr Wells (01749 673118/ www.burcottmill.com). **Open** *Easter-Oct* 11am-5pm Tue-Sun. Closed Nov-Easter. **Admission** £2; £1 concessions; £5 family. **Credit** MC, V.

Cheddar Caves & Gorge

Cheddar (01934 742343/www.cheddarcaves.co.uk). **Open** *May-mid Sept* 10am-5pm daily. *Mid Sept-Apr* 10.30am-4.30pm daily. **Admission** £8.90; £5.90 concessions; £24 family; free under-5s. **Credit** AmEx, MC, V.

Cheddar Gorge Cheese Company

The Cliffs, Cheddar Gorge (01934 742810/ www.cheddargorgecheeseco.co.uk). **Open** 10am-5pm daily. **Admission** £1.50; £1-£1.25 concessions; free under-5s. **Credit** MC, V.

King John's Hunting Lodge

The Square, Axbridge (01934 732012/ www.nationaltrust.org.uk). **Open** *Easter-Sept* 1-4pm daily. Closed Oct-Easter. **Admission** free.

Wookey Hole Caves & Papermill

Wookey Hole, near Wells (01749 672243/ www.wookey.co.uk). **Open** *Apr-Oct* 10am-5pm daily. *Nov-Mar* 10.30am-4.30pm daily. **Admission** £8; £5 concessions; free under-4s. **Credit** MC, V.

Activities

Caving & climbing

Rock Sport at the top end of Cheddar Gorge offers introductory climbing, caving and abseiling sessions (01934 742343) for £12.50 per person.

Fishing

Woodford Lodge (off Harptree Road, Chew Stoke, 01275 332339, www.chewvalleylake.org.uk) has good facilities for anglers: buy day permits for fishing on Chew Valley Lake (£13 bankside, £28.50 boat), book lessons or stock up on necessities in the tackle shop.

Walking & cycling

The former Whitham to Yatton Railway, known as the 'Strawberry Line', carried local dairy produce and strawberries for almost a century until 1965. A 10-mile (16km) section is now open to walkers and cyclists using maps available from the Cheddar Tourist Information Centre (*see also p102*). For other local walking information, consult the website of **The Gorge Outdoors** (Hanliff House,

The Cliffs, Cheddar, 01934 742688, www.thegorge outdoors.co.uk), a well-stocked outdoor clothing and equipment store.

Where to eat & drink

The **Bath Arms Hotel** (Bath Street, Cheddar, 01934 742425, www.batharmshotel.co.uk, main courses £3-£14, double B&B £30-£40) offers good B&B deals as well as a restaurant with a rare British Cheese Board recommendation. The **Lamb** (01934 732253, main courses £5-£10.95) on the corner of the square in Axbridge serves local Butcombe bitter, Thatcher's cider and good-value food, while the wonderfully unmodernised **Hunter's Lodge** (01749 672275, main courses £2.50), east of Priddy, is loved by local cavers thanks to beer served straight from the cask. Further north, try the back garden of the **New Inn** (Church Street, Blagdon, 01761 462475, main courses £5.95-£7.95) for lunch overlooking the lake, or the **Pony & Trap** (Chew Magna, 01275 332627) for an amiable atmosphere and Ushers beer.

Where to stay

On a steep hill north of Cheddar, **Daneswood House** (Cuck Hill, Shipham, 01934 843145, www.daneswoodhotel.co.uk, set meal £25, double B&B £90-£150) offers splendid views from its 17 guestrooms. Originally an Edwardian homeopathic spa, it's now a destination for local foodies who relish its eccentric atmosphere and local ingredients.

The luxury choice in Wookey is **Glencot House** (Glencot Lane, 01749 677160, www.glencothouse.co.uk, set meal £26, double £88), a 19th-century, mock-Jacobean house set in 18 acres of parkland. It's furnished with taste, charm and plenty of four-poster beds, and the opulent dining room overlooking the Axe has a menu that rises to the setting. A funkier vibe is offered at the **Wookey Hole Inn** (01749 676677, www.wookeyholeinn.com, main courses £11.50-£17, double B&B £70-£90), which has five rooms with low-slung, king-size beds, Santa Fe styling and widescreen TVs. (There's a cult video library for guest use.) Downstairs, guests are kept happy with draught Belgian beers, fusion cooking and live bands.

Resources

Police station

Cliff Street, Cheddar (01823 337911).

Post office

Bath Street, Cheddar (0845 722 3344). **Open** 9am-5pm Mon-Fri; 9am-12.30pm Sat.

Tourist information

Cheddar Tourist Information Centre
*The Gorge, Cheddar (01934 744071/
www.sedgemoor.gov.uk/tourism).* **Open** *Mid
Mar-mid Sept* 10am-5pm daily. *Mid Sept-mid
Oct* 10.30am-4.30pm daily. *Mid Oct-mid Mar*
11am-1pm, 1.30-4pm Sun.

Wells

On the southern slopes of the Mendips,
Milton Lodge is a mature Grade II-listed
terrace garden, with mixed borders, roses
and a seven-acre arboretum. As well as
delightful horticultual surroundings, it
offers panoramic views south towards Wells
and the Vale of Avalon.

Wells is England's smallest city, but boasts
one of the country's finest cathedrals, whose
distinctive form is clearly visible from the
gardens at Milton Lodge. The cathedral lies
at the heart of a skilfully preserved medieval
town that despite ancient architecture and a
picturesque setting has successfully avoided
becoming a historical theme park.

Wells Cathedral was the first completely
Gothic edifice to be built in England. Although
there had been a church here since AD 700 and
a bishop since 909, the cathedral we now see
was begun around 1180 and took 250 years
to complete. Particular impetus came from
the election of Bishop Jocelin in 1206, who
was responsible for two of the cathedral's
Early English masterpieces: the nave, with
its unique monumental 'scissor arches' –
an ingenious way of holding the weight of
the Crossing Tower above – and the
magnificent west front.

The latter is the highlight of the cathedral
and can be viewed in all its glory from the
expanse of lawn outside. It incorporates the
largest gallery of medieval sculpture in the
world, a panorama of the Last Judgement now
fully restored after surviving Puritan assault in
the 17th century and atmospheric pollution in
the 20th. Beginning in the lower niches with
Biblical scenes, it rises through kings, bishops
and orders of angels to the 12 apostles topped
by the risen Christ – the last a replacement
statue unveiled in 1986. Originally, all would
have been painted in vivid colours as a
spectacular declaration of the Christian faith.

Inside, the astronomical clock in the north
transept was made in 1392 and is among
the oldest working clocks in the world. On
the quarter-hour, four mounted knights
emerge from a castle to stage a jousting
contest; they are joined on the hour by a man
in red, who hammers the bells with his hands
and feet. Opposite, climb an elegant, timeworn

staircase to reach the beautiful octagonal
Chapter House with its ribbed fan ceiling.
Across in the south transept, seek out the
carvings of a toothache victim and an old man
stealing fruit and getting his comeuppance.
The famous choir sings at services throughout
the week, and the cloister restaurant is an
excellent stop for lunch.

At one side of the cathedral, **Vicars' Close**
was constructed in 1348, making it the oldest
complete medieval street in Europe, and is still
occupied by members of the cathedral clergy.
Particularly astonishing, given its date, is the
understanding of perspective, with the two
rows of one-up, one-down cottages nine feet
(2.74 metres) closer together at the north end
than they are at the south.

On the other side is the **Bishop's Palace**,
reached from the Market Place through a
gateway called the Bishop's Eye. Home of
the Bishop of Bath & Wells, the palace
developed from a residence built by Bishop
Jocelin and was fortified in the 14th century
due to disputes between the church and the
borough. Portcullis grooves and a chute for
dispensing oil and molten lead on to would-
be intruders are still visible on the gatehouse.
The moat, however, is now the preserve of the
bishop's mute swans.

In the palace grounds are the ruins of 13th-
century Bishop Burnell's Hall and the springs
from which the city takes its name; you can see
water bubbling up through the silt, before being
sluiced into channels to run down the High
Street into the River Sheppey.

Located in the former chancellor's house on
Cathedral Green, **Wells Museum** tells the
story of the city and the Mendips past and
present, and also houses some of the stone
figures from the cathedral's west front that
are too fragile to be restored.

Once you've had your fill of history, pick
up a tourist leaflet to guide you around the
town's art and antique emporia. Local artists
often show at the **Sadler Street Gallery**
(7A Sadler Street, 01749 670220) while, in
Market Street, **Erica Sharpe** (01749 670926)
is the place for unusual jewellery. Food
lovers should head for Wednesday's
farmers' market (01460 78223,
www.somersetfarmersmarkets.co.uk).

Bishop's Palace

Wells (01749 678691). **Open** *Apr-Oct* 10.30am-
6pm Tue-Fri; 1-6pm Sun. Closed Nov-Mar.
Admission £3.50; £1-£2.50 concessions;
free under-12s. **Credit** MC, V.

Milton Lodge

Old Bristol Road, Wells (01749 672168). **Open**
Easter-Oct 2-5pm Wed, Sun. Closed Nov-Easter.
Admission £2.50. **No credit cards**.

Bowling by the **Bishop's Palace**. *See p102*.

Wells Cathedral

Chain Gate, Cathedral Green (01749 674483/ www.wellscathedral.org.uk). **Open** *Apr-Oct* 7am-7pm daily. *Nov-Mar* 7am-6pm daily. **Admission** (suggested donation) £4.50; £1.50-£3 concessions. **Credit** AmEx, MC, V.

Wells Museum

8 Cathedral Green (01749 673477). **Open** *Apr-Oct* 10am-5pm daily. *Nov-Mar* 11am-4pm Mon, Wed-Sun. **Admission** £2.50; £1-£2 concessions; free under-5s. **No credit cards**.

Where to eat, drink & stay

You can eat and sleep history in the cathedral city. The **Crown at Wells** (Market Place, 01749 673457, www.crownatwells.co.uk, main courses £9.50-£14.95, double £60-£90) is a 15th-century coaching inn with a bar named after Quaker William Penn, who preached to a crowd in the Market Place in 1695, before going on to found Pennsylvania. Or there's the family-friendly **City Arms** (High Street, 01749 673916, main courses £4.95-£9.95), a 16th-century pub that was once the city jail. Its cobbled courtyard is the perfect place to sample superb local beer and imaginative pub food. For location, though, it's hard to beat the 14th-century **Ancient Gate House Hotel** (20 Sadler Street, 01749 672029, www.ancientgatehouse.co.uk, main courses 6.90-£16.50, double £78.50), which incorporates the former keep of Browne's Gate and overlooks the cathedral's west front. It has nine bedrooms

(six with four-posters) reached via a worn spiral stone staircase, and a restaurant offering an Italian-influenced dinner menu.

Ritcher's (5 Sadler Street, 01749 679085, set dinner £23) offers a British-with-a-twist menu, decent prices and prompt service, while the friendly **Fountain Inn & Boxer's Restaurant** (1 Saint Thomas Street, 01749 672317, main courses £6.50-£14) is particularly commended for its interesting local cheeses. A bit funkier, **Le Café Bleu** (9 Heritage Courtyard, Sadler Street, 01749 677772, main courses from £4) boasts casual lunches, 'serious fish' in the evening, and jazz on Sundays.

Resources

Hospital

Wells & District Hospital *Bath Road, Wells (01749 683200).*

Police station

18 Glastonbury Road, Wells (01823 337911).

Post office

Market Place, Wells (01749 673311). **Open** 9am-5pm Mon-Fri; 9am-12.30pm Sat.

Tourist information

Town Hall, Market Place, Wells (01749 672552/ www.wells.gov.uk). **Open** *Apr-Oct* 9.30am-5.30pm daily. *Nov-Mar* 10am-4pm Mon-Sat; 10am-3pm Sun.

Frome & around

East of Wells, **Shepton Mallet** grew rich on the wool industry, with fine examples of 17th-century cloth merchants' houses still to be seen around town. The main point of interest, though, is the church of **St Peter & St Paul**, whose wool tower, built around 1380, is one of the oldest in Somerset. Also check out the spectacular barrel-vaulted wagon roof inside. From Shepton Mallet, steam locomotives run along the restored **East Somerset Railway** to Cranborne station, where there's a busy engine shed and a gallery of art by the line's founder.

Frome is both the largest and the most easterly of Mendip's wool towns, and makes a good base for exploring the quiet, rural villages of North-east Somerset. It's a characterful place built on steep hills with cobbled streets and more listed buildings than anywhere else in the county – it frequently doubles as 19th-century London in period TV dramas. Like the more celebrated Pulteney Bridge in Bath, Frome Bridge has the architectural rarity of buildings along its length. Cheap Street preserves the medieval street pattern and has a leet (water channel) running down its middle, while Sheppard's Barton (just off the pedestrianised Catherine Hill) is a superbly preserved row of 18th-century workers'

Somerset

cottages. You'll find specialist shops, booksellers and antique dealers to nose around on both Cheap Street and Catherine Hill.

Frome's cultural reputation has been enhanced by the **Merlin Theatre** (Bath Road, 01373 465 949, www.merlintheatre.co.uk), and by **Black Swan Arts** (2 Bridge Street, 01373 473980, www.blackswan.org.uk), which houses galleries, craft studios and a veggie restaurant. Also check out the local arts and crafts at **Enigma** (15 Vicarage Street, 01373 452079, www.enigma-gallery.com). The town also hosts an arts and music festival in July, a medieval fair in August, and a cheese show in September.

East Somerset Railway

Cranmore Railway Station, Cranmore, nr Shepton Mallet (01749 880417/www.eastsomersetrailway.org). **Open** phone for details. **Admission** £5.75; £3.75-£4.75 concessions; free under-2s. **Credit** MC, V.

Where to eat, drink & stay

For a treat visit **Bowlish House** (Coombe Lane, off Wells Road, Shepton Mallet, 01749 342022, set meal £29.95, double B&B £75), an immaculate Palladian mansion, with a high-class menu that ranges from local organic lamb to sashimi. Even more upmarket is **Charlton House** (Shepton Mallet, 01749 342008, www.charltonhouse.com, set meal £42, double £155), set in gorgeous grounds, with croquet, trout fishing and plans for a full-on spa. This place is a showcase for Mulberry and its 16 bedrooms use the full range of furnishings, fabrics and curios. The fabulous Michelin-starred restaurant has an ambitious, wide-ranging menu to suit the stylish setting.

South of Shepton Mallet, enjoy the very special, award-winning surroundings at **Pennard Hill Farm** (Stickleball Hill, East Pennard, 01749 890221, www.pennardhill farm.co.uk, double B&B £100-£200). Rooms in the main house are decorated in warm tones with a host of quirky but perfectly poised furnishings, and the highlight is a private luxury suite in the barn incorporating an indoor swimming pool with gobsmacking views. Self-caterers will be equally delighted by two exquisitely designed cottages on the estate.

For food, try **Blostin's** (29-33 Waterloo Road, Shepton Mallet, 01749 343648, closed Mon & Sun, main courses £8.95-£14.50), popular for its vegetarian food, or the **Strode Arms** in West Cranmore (01749 880450, main courses £7.50-£15), a 15th-century former farmhouse with imaginative food and well-kept ale. In Frome, don't miss the cheery **Old Bake House** (15 Cheap Street, 01373 455456), which sells the local delicacy, Frome bobbins (fruit soaked in cider and wrapped in pastry), or the tiny **Farmer's Arms** (Spring Gardens, 01373 453477, main courses £7.95-£15.90), which has built a reputation for New World-inspired food.

London's media and music glitterati flock to **Babington House** (Babington, nr Frome, 01373 812266, www.babingtonhouse.co.uk, main courses £10-£16, double £195-£290), *the* place to splash your cash in this neck of the woods. The atmosphere's laid-back and family-friendly, with loads of outdoor activities, kids' facilities, an informal Italian restaurant and the Cowshed spa to soothe away your cares. Luxury minimalist rooms come with clawfoot baths, huge plasma TVs and DVD players.

Finally, the wonderful, half-timbered **George Inn** (High Street, Norton St Philip, 01373 834224, www.thegeorgeinn-nsp.co.uk, main courses £7.95-£14.95, double B&B £80-£110) has been catering for travellers since the 12th century and once hosted the diarist Samuel Pepys. Its ancient beams, flagstoned floors and antique wall paintings create a uniquely historic setting – although, thankfully, there's all mod cons in the bathrooms and decent restaurant-style food in the dining room.

Resources

Police stations

Frome *Oakfield Road (01225 444343).* **Shepton Mallet** *23 Commercial Road (01225 444343).*

Post offices

Frome *9 Market Place (0845 722 3344).* **Shepton Mallet** *8 Town Street (01749 342762).*

Tourist information

Frome *2 Bridge Street (01373 467271/frome.tic @ukonline.co.uk).* **Open** *Easter-mid Oct* 10am-5pm Mon-Sat. *Mid Oct-Easter* 10am-4.30pm Mon-Sat. **Shepton Mallet** *48 High Street (01749 345258/ sheptonmallet.tic@ukonline.co.uk).* **Open** *Apr-Sept* 10am-4pm Mon-Fri, 10am-2pm Sat. *Oct-Mar* 10am-2pm Mon-Sat.

Getting there & around

By train

Weston-Super-Mare station is served by trains from Bristol Temple Meads (30mins) and London Paddington (2hrs 15mins). Paddington–Penzance services stop at Westbury for connections to Frome.

By bus

National Express (08705 808080, www.gobycoach. com) runs daily coach services to Frome, Shepton Mallet, Wells and Weston-super-Mare. Local bus services are mostly operated by **First Badgerline** (Wells 01749 673084, Weston-super-Mare 01934 429336, www.firstbadgerline.co.uk).

Central & South Somerset

So much more than just a festival.

Ruins of **Glastonbury Abbey**. *See p106.*

Located midway between the Bristol and English Channel coasts, this area of Somerset is rich in wildlife and ancient history. Iron Age tribes built hill forts around the county, while the Romans left a permanent mark in the form of the Fosse Way (now the A37 and A303), which slices through Somerset en route to Exeter. However, it is perhaps the pagan, Christian and Arthurian legends that surround **Glastonbury** that prove most engrossing for visitors. Myth and mysticism collide in this ancient town, resulting in some evocative historic sites – not to mention more New Age garnishing than is strictly healthy.

Surrounding Glastonbury on all sides are the **Somerset Levels**, a large expanse of flat marsh and moorland that spreads from central Somerset to the coast at Bridgwater

Bay. Recognised as one of the most important wetlands of its type in the world, the 140,000-acre floodplain was once covered by the high tides of the Bristol Channel and, to this day, remains no more than 25 feet (seven metres) above sea level. At the centre of the Levels, peat moors are protected from sea flooding only by a slightly higher clay ridge at the coast and by man-made channels, known as 'rhynes' (pronounced 'reens'), which were first dug in the Middle Ages in an attempt to drain and enclose the land. Until this time the Levels' inhabitants had lived in raised villages, catching eels for food and laying tracks of wood and willow in order to get across the marshes.

The medieval rhynes and 'droves' (lanes) are still used today instead of hedges and fences to divide the reclaimed marshland into pastures, and are interspersed with pollarded willows, which contribute to the Levels' distinctive appearance. Recent restrictions on drainage mean that during the winter the pastures are once again inundated with floodwater, making for a uniquely atmospheric landscape.

Edging the endless horizons of the Levels are pretty villages, market towns, grand country houses and gentle countryside that will draw you into a rural time warp. To the south, the border with Devon is straddled by the little-visited **Blackdown Hills**, while to the east, the county town of **Taunton** affords access to the unexpected beauty of the **Quantock Hills**.

Glastonbury & around

Tourist boards up and down the country must surely be bitterly jealous of the interest generated by the small town of **Glastonbury**. Meandering A-roads from the Mendips and further east succumb eventually to the magnetism of Glastonbury Tor, a cone-shaped hill that forms an unmissable landmark amid the flat landscape of the Levels. The Tor is synonymous in many minds with the legendary Isle of Avalon and is an enduring symbol of the magic and mystery that surrounds the town.

Montacute House, dating from the 16th century. *See p110.*

Although the world-famous music festival has put Glastonbury on the map for the present generation (*see p108* **Festival fever**), it is the powerful trinity of history, legend and religion that first established this Somerset town as a mecca for pilgrims, grail seekers and dreamers.

On arrival you could be forgiven for driving straight through the centre, mistaking it for an off-shoot of the main attraction. Size is certainly not everything when it comes to Glastonbury. However, even the high street is the site of some memorable juxtapositions, with Sufi charity shops next to kebab houses and crystal sellers rubbing shoulders with estate agents.

Number one on most visitors' itinerary, however, will be world-famous **Glastonbury Abbey**, an unmissable assembly of ruins surrounded by tranquil parkland in the centre of the town. According to legend, the abbey was founded in AD 63 by the merchant Joseph of Arimathea, who came here after Christ's death to bury the Holy Grail. The grail was the chalice from which Jesus drank at the Last Supper, and in which Joseph caught drops of Christ's blood at the crucifixion.

More prosaically, the first stone church was built on this site in the eighth century by Saxon King Ine of Wessex, who boosted the status and income of Christian foundations in the region. His church was enlarged in the tenth century by the Abbot, St Dunstan, who went on to become the Archbishop of Canterbury. More extensive developments took place under the Normans, who added magnificent buildings to the east of the original Saxon church and extended the nave to 580 feet (177 metres), making it the longest in Britain.

In 1184 many of the monastic buildings, including the abbey church, were destroyed by fire. A new Great Church was reconsecrated on Christmas Day 1213 and by the 14th century

Glastonbury was the second wealthiest abbey in Britain. However, its riches made it a prime target for Henry VIII's greed and reforming zeal: during the Dissolution, Glastonbury was ransacked, and the incumbent Abbot Whiting was executed on Glastonbury Tor.

The only monastic building to survive the Dissolution is the 14th-century Abbot's Kitchen, which provides compelling evidence of the considerable wealth and power enjoyed by the Abbot of Glastonbury. Elsewhere, the abbey is reduced to foundation stones and crumbling shells that cannot begin to evoke the scale and grandeur of the original structure. The most conspicuous remains are the 12th-century Lady Chapel and the area around the choir and high altar.

The majority of visitors, however, head straight for a small sign behind the Lady Chapel indicating the supposed burial place of King Arthur. Two skeletons believed to be the king and his wife Guinevere were discovered by monks here in 1191. The bodies were later reburied in state close to the high altar, but no traces of their tomb remain (*See also p10* **Local heroes**). Legends aside, the Abbey was undoubtedly the final resting place of three Saxons kings: Edmund I, Edgar and Edmund Ironside.

Surrounding the ruins, the beautiful grassy park extends over 36 acres, providing ample room for exploration. It is also the setting for numerous summer events including an annual concert arranged by Michael Eavis, of Glastonbury Festival fame (phone 01458 831631 for further information). On the edge of the grounds, the 14th-century Abbey Barn houses the **Rural Life Museum**, with displays relating to Victorian Somerset, including the life story of a farm worker, as well as regularly changing exhibitions.

Onwards and upwards, and the ever-looming **Tor** demands a visit. Two thousand years ago, the foot of the Tor was washed by the tides of the Bristol Channel, creating the enchanted Isle of Avalon, named after the Celtic god Avalloc who ruled the underworld. Today it rises 518 feet (158 metres) above the Levels, but it's worth the strenuous climb for the views, which can take in the three counties of Somerset, Dorset and Wiltshire on a clear day. At its summit is **St Michael's Tower**, part of a 14th-century church, built to replace a previous structure that was destroyed by an earthquake in 1275. As the supposed crossing point of myriad ley lines and energy sources, the Tor is an important destination for New Age pilgrims, who come here to celebrate the summer solstice.

The Tor is also a good vantage point from which to see **Wearyall Hill**, a low-lying hillock on the south-west edge of town, where Joseph of Arimathea is supposed to have inadvertently planted the original Glastonbury Thorn. Descendants of the bush now grow in Glastonbury Abbey grounds and two sprigs are sent up to adorn the Queen's breakfast table every Christmas.

Joseph supposedly buried the Holy Grail just below the Tor, thus providing both the impetus for the questing legends of the Knights of the Round Table and the foundation for Glastonbury's peculiar blend of religious and secular mythology.

Descending back in to town, stop off at the **Chalice Well**, actually a spring, that produces 25,000 gallons of water daily. It is here that the Holy Grail was meant to have been secreted, hence the water's fabled healing properties. Some people claim that the red deposits left by the water are the marks of Christ's blood, but geologists will tell you that it's naturally occurring iron oxide. The well is surrounded by a beautiful garden that combines New Age mysticism with good ol' herbaceous borders.

If all this myth and mystery is proving too much, explore the more material history of the town on the **Millennium Trail**, an hour-long circular walk that follows 20 numbered paving stones, starting from the Town Hall opposite the abbey entrance. For a bit of background reading, the atmospheric **Book Barn** (17-18 Market Place, 01458 835698) is also worth a stop. This is the West Country's largest used bookshop, with never-ending corridors of books, and no electronic cataloguing system.

Further along the high street, the 15th-century Glastonbury Tribunal houses the tourist office and **Glastonbury Lake Village Museum**. In 1892 Arthur Bulleid, a local man, discovered and began the excavation of a 2,000-year-old settlement, constructed upon a man-made island close to present-day Glastonbury. The Levels' peaty wetland soil had preserved a huge number of significant archaeological remains, now displayed in the museum.

Reconstructions of the lake village dwellings can be seen not far from Glastonbury at the **Peat Moors Visitor Centre**, which provides information on the unique landscape and varied history of the Levels. There are also re-creations of the wooden causeways built by Stone Age man to cross the marshes, plus displays and demonstrations of peat cutting, which has taken place on the Levels since prehistoric times.

For something completely different, venture south of Glastonbury to **Street**, where Cyrus Clark and his brother James started a shoe business in 1825. The **Shoe Museum** details the history of footwear from Roman times to the present day, while **Clark's Outlet Village** (Farm Road, 01458 840064) sells plenty of Clark's samples, along with other well-known brands of footwear.

Holy water in the gardens of **Chalice Well**.

Chalice Well

Chilkwell Street, Glastonbury (01458 831154/ www.chalicewell.org.uk). **Open** *Apr-Oct* 10am-6pm daily. *Nov* 10am-5pm daily. *Dec, Jan* 11am-4pm daily. *Feb, Mar* 11am-5pm daily. **Admission** £2.50; £1.20-£1.80 concessions. **Credit** AmEx, MC, V.

Festival fever Glastonbury

If the word 'Glastonbury' has become synonymous with the summer festival rather than the town, then it's not been by design. When Michael Eavis organised the first Worthy Farm Festival back in 1970, highlights included Keith Christmas, free milk and Marc Bolan complaining about bumpy roads ruining his Cadillac. It cost £1 to get in and around 1,500 people turned up. Fast forward to today and you can multiply both those figures by 100, substitute helicopters for cars, and bet that, for whoever's bagged the main headline slots, subsequent record sales will be like Christmas come early.

For the clearest idea of how Glastonbury Festival's image has changed, look back to the TV news footage from the time. Back in the mid '80s, organiser Michael Eavis was portrayed in the local media as a West Country version of Arthur Scargill at the time of the miners' strike – as a man whose actions were bringing decent society to the very brink of implosion. Who was this lunatic encouraging hippies to converge in rural Somerset to practise their weird vegetarian ways at his so-called Pilton Pop Festival?

He was, of course, the same man who today welcomes the world's media on to the site as they prepare for hour upon hour of live festival coverage, and smiles indulgently in the background as those same local reporters exchange feeble jokes with desk-bound presenters about having to sleep in a tent.

The travellers are still there too, albeit in somewhat annexed form over by the tipi field, and year upon year have watched the festival grow around them. One main stage has become two, supplemented by the Dance Tent, the New Bands Tent, the Theatre and Circus areas, the Green Fields and a whole lot more besides. Such expansion has brought with it the widely documented problems of fence jumping, overcrowding and the introduction in 2002 of a supposedly impregnable fence.

Gone, however, is the floodlit cross on an adjacent hillside, erected by a God- (and hippy-) fearing woman to offer hope to all those innocent, virginal young things drowning in a sea of immoral pagan ritual, free love and, in inclement years, mud. The promise of free love was, of course, the reason why so many innocent, virginal young things turned up in the first place, but whether such an atmosphere ever really existed remains a moot point.

Nevertheless, Glastonbury is still a one-off – a festival able to sell out by reputation alone. A large proportion of punters give the bands a miss and simply go to 'live in a medieval city for a few days', as *NME* editor Steve Sutherland once put it. Indeed, as he explained, 'the thing with Glastonbury is that it's uniquely a festival. Almost everything else that happens in Britain is, in fact, just a gig in a field.'

Glastonbury Abbey

Abbey Gatehouse, Magdalene Street, Glastonbury (01458 832267/www.glastonburyabbey.com). **Open** *Feb* 10am-5pm daily. *Apr, May, Sept* 9.30am-6pm daily. *June-Aug* 9am-6pm daily. *Oct* 9.30am-5pm daily. *Nov* 9.30am-4.30pm daily. Dec, Jan 10am-4.30pm. **Admission** £3.50; £1.50 concessions; free under-5s; £8 family. **Credit** MC, V.

Glastonbury Lake Village Museum

9 High Street, Glastonbury (01458 832954/832949). **Open** *Apr-Sept* 10am-5pm Mon-Thur, Sun; 10am-5.30pm Fri, Sat. *Oct-Mar* 10am-4pm Mon-Thur, Sun; 10am-4.30pm Fri, Sat. **Admission** £2; £1-£1.50 concessions. **Credit** MC, V.

Peat Moors Visitor Centre

Shapwick Road, Westhay, nr Glastonbury (01458 860697). **Open** *Apr-Oct* 10am-4.30pm daily. Closed Nov-Mar. **Admission** £2.50; £1.95 concessions; £8 family. **No credit cards**.

Rural Life Museum

Abbey Farm, Chilkwell Street, Glastonbury (01458 831197/www.somerset.gov.uk/museums). **Open** 10am-5pm Tue-Sat. **Admission** free.

Shoe Museum

C&J Clark, 40 High Street, Street (01458 842243). **Open** 10am-4.15pm Mon-Fri; 10am-5pm Sat; 11am-5pm Sun. **Admission** free.

Where to eat, drink & stay

The small entrance to **Rainbow's End Café** (17A High Street, Glastonbury, 01458 833896, main courses £4.50-£6.75) could easily be overlooked, but its tasty vegetarian and vegan dishes and relaxed atmosphere should entice you inside. In fine weather enjoy lunch in the garden courtyard at the **Brasserie** (Hawthorns Hotel, Northload Street, Glastonbury, 01458 831255, main courses £6.50-£13.50), which

Somerset

specialises in fresh fish with plenty of vegetarian options. For supper on the run, don't miss classic fish and chips from **Knight's** (5 Northload Street, 01458 831882), a family-run business established in 1909 that serves up excellent cod, chips and mushy peas.

The 14th-century **George & Pilgrims Hotel** (1 High Street, Glastonbury, 01458 831146, www.georgeandpilgrims.active hotels.com, set menu £11.95/£15, double B&B £50-£95) is a popular choice for those seeking to immerse themselves in the town's history. It has plenty of oak beams, a few four-posters and decent pub food. A more intimate vibe is offered by **No.3** (3 Magdalene Street, 01458 832129, www.numberthree.co.uk, double B&B £90-£100), a beautiful Georgian house adjoining Glastonbury Abbey. Five rooms with sumptuous furnishings overlook a lovely floodlit garden.

If you want to experience the essence of New Age Glastonbury, stay at **Shambhala** (Coursing Blatch, Glastonbury, 01458 831797, www.shambhala.co.uk, B&B £35 per person plus treatments), a retreat at the foot of the Tor. It is run by the energising figure of Isis, an ex-City worker, and is a place to relax and recharge. Five treatment and therapy rooms are supplemented by a sauna and jacuzzi.

Resources

Internet
Glastonbury *Café Galatea, 5A High Street (01458 834284).* **Open** 11am-4pm Mon; 11am-9pm Wed, Thur; 11am-10pm Fri, Sat.

Police station
Street *1 West End (01823 337911).*

Post office
Glastonbury *35 High Street (01458 831536).* **Open** 9am-5.30pm Mon-Fri; 9am-1pm Sat.

Tourist information
Glastonbury *Tourist Information Centre, The Tribunal, 9 High Street (01458 832954/ www.glastonburytic.co.uk).* **Open** Oct-Mar 10am-4pm Mon-Thur, Sun; 10am-4.30pm Fri, Sat. *Apr-Sept* 10am-5pm Mon-Thur, Sun; 10am-5.30pm Fri, Sat.

South-eastern Somerset

In the south-eastern corner of the county the flatland of the Levels takes on a less austere aspect, dotted with ancient towns and picturesque villages that are linked by a network of pleasant country lanes.

During the 19th century, the main industry in this area was the growing of willows ('withies') for baskets and hurdles. Stoke St Gregory lies at the centre of the willow

beds and its **Willows & Wetlands Visitor Centre** provides details of the local basketweaving industry and gives visitors the chance to buy current work from craftspeople based at the centre. Production has dramatically fallen off over the last 30 years, but the traditional skills are preserved in the making of baskets – and cricket bats.

In the Middle Ages, towns and religious settlements on the Levels were confined to islands of higher ground that provided some protection from the encroaching water. One of these is the wonderfully named **Burrow Mump**, just north of the Wetlands centre, which rises audaciously from the flat land topped by the remains of **St Michael's Church**. Come up here after heavy rain to see the surrounding countryside returned to its primeval, watery state.

There was another island settlement up the road at **Athelney**, where Alfred the Great set up his headquarters after fleeing a surprise Viking attack. Down, but definitely not out, he proceeded to wage war on all things Danish and eventually oversaw the baptism of defeated King Guthrum in AD 878 in the nearby village of Aller. Unfortunately, Alfred's culinary skills did not live up to his military abilities: it is in this area that the story of the king burning the cakes originates.

Built on a bend in the River Parrett, the ancient market town of **Langport** was developed by the Romans, who erected a causeway along present-day Bow Street. The houses along the street tilt gently backwards, probably because the causeway only supports

Market time in **Glastonbury**. *See p105.*

their fronts. The town centre is somewhat spoiled by main road traffic today but it's worth seeking out the gatehouse topped by a chapel in the old town walls, and the **Langport & River Parrett Visitor Centre** at Bow Bridge, which has exhibits about the history and landscape of the Levels, plus displays about the River Parrett Trail (*see p112*). There are also plenty of leaflets detailing walking and cycle routes in the area, and bicycles for hire (*see p112*).

South of Langport, the village of **Muchelney** was known during medieval times as the 'great island' for its elevated position above the wetlands. A Benedictine abbey was founded here in the tenth century, but was already on the brink of financial ruin by the time of the Dissolution. The complex was ransacked for building materials in succeeding centuries, and all that remains now is the **Abbot's House** (01458 250664, closed Nov-Mar, admission £2.50, £1.30 concessions, free under-5s) and excavated stones marking the ground plan of the former buildings.

Next to the ruins, the parish church of **St Peter & St Paul** merits a look for its 12th-century floor tiles and painted ceiling, while across the lane, the immaculate **Priest's House** (01985 843600; phone for details of irregular opening times) is a 14th-century thatched building with large Gothic windows where the parish priests once lived.

On the edge of the village a 16th-century thatched farm building houses the **Muchelney Pottery** (01458 250324., www.johnleach pottery.com, closed Sun) where John Leach – grandson of the pioneering potter, Bernard Leach – continues the family tradition. His pots are on sale here, and are also displayed in the Abbot's House during the summer.

A little further east, **Somerton** was the ancient capital of Wessex and provides the county of Somerset with its name (taken from the Old English for an enclosure used in summer). It's a well-ordered, picturesque town, with a beautiful 17th-century market square, and is something of a honeypot for antique-hunters, with plenty of shops and markets to explore, including **Somerton Antique Centre** (Old Court House, Market Place, 01458 274423) and **Westville House Antiques** (Westville House, Littleton, 01458 273376).

Further east, the small town of **Ilchester** was once an important Roman settlement at a river crossing on the Fosse Way. A medieval bridge still straddles the Yeo in the centre of Ilchester, but the main A303 now skirts the town to the north-west, passing close to RNAS Yeovilton, where the **Fleet Air Museum** displays more than 40 aircrafts. Nearby, there are more treats for transport

enthusiasts at the **Haynes Motor Museum**, which has a 300-strong collection of vehicles dating from 1885 to the present day.

Further east, however, the technological age gives away once again to the lure of the Dark Ages at **Cadbury Hill**, a possible contender for the site of Arthur's Camelot. Steaming along the A303 towards Dorset and Wiltshire, it's quite possible not to notice this wooded hump south of the main road. The hill was the site of an important Iron Age fort and was reoccupied and massively extended during the sixth century by a powerful leader, who many claim was the legendary King Arthur.

To the south, **Yeovil** is by far the biggest town in this area. There's not much to entice you into the centre, unless you're desperate for a high-street shop, but the **Museum of South Somerset** has some interesting displays on rural life in the region, including original mosaics excavated from local Roman villas. It's also worth checking out the forthcoming programme at the town's **Octagon Theatre** (01935 422884, www.octagon-theatre.co.uk).

West of Yeovil many of the pretty villages and hamlets are built from the distinctive, honey-coloured stone that has been quarried from **Ham Hill** since Roman times. The hill is now part of a country park (01935 823617), but you can still see the network of ramparts, ridges and terraces that formed the original Iron Age hill fort.

Not far away, **Montacute House** is by far the most impressive building to have been constructed from the local stone. Built by Sir Edward Phelips in 1588, this is an exemplary Elizabethan manor, designed on an H-shaped ground plan with Flemish gables, large windows and tall, rounded chimneys. A showcase home, Montacute cemented the social standing of the Phelips family, who had risen to wealth and prominence following the Dissolution; Sir Edward later became Speaker in the House of Commons and presided over the trial of Guy Fawkes in 1605.

The magnificent state rooms include the Long Gallery, which stretches 172 feet (52 metres) along the entire length of the house. Its walls are lined with Elizabethan and Jacobean portraits on loan from the National Portrait Gallery. Elsewhere, the house is full of fine furniture, tapestries and textiles, while outside the formal gardens include mixed borders, old roses and ancient yew trees, surrounded by a landscaped park. Montacute featured in the film version of *Sense & Sensibility*, and provides an idyllic setting for theatrical and musical events during the summer.

Barrington Court is another enticing property in the area, owned by the National Trust. The Tudor manor was restored in the

1920s by the Lyle family (of Tate & Lyle sugar fame) and now acts as a showroom for the sale of antique and reproduction furniture. The kempt, formal gardens are the real draw, however: laid out in a series of 'rooms', they incorporate a rose garden, a white garden and a fabulous kitchen garden that groans with vegetables and fruit trees.

The nearby village of **Martock** has a disproportionally large and elaborate 15th-century parish church with a wonderful carved tie-beam roof. Outside, look out for the foot-holds on the north wall, which were originally used in the old game of Fives. Opposite the church is the 13th-century **Treasurer's House** (01935 825801, closed Oct-Mar & Mon in summer), which was inhabited by the treasurer of Wells Cathedral. It has a medieval hall and kitchen and is presently being renovated by the National Trust.

After so much history, younger visitors will be glad to hang out with the animals at **Cricket St Thomas Wildlife Park**, located in the very south of the county, close to the town of Chard. This conservation-conscious zoo keeps dozens of birds, reptiles (including iguanas) and mammals in spacious, sensitively designed habitats on the edge of the **Blackdown Hills**.

Barrington Court
Barrington, nr Ilminster (01460 241938). **Open** *Mar* 11am-4.30pm Thur-Sun. *Apr-Sept* 11am-5.30pm daily. *Oct* 11am-4.30pm Thur-Sun. Closed Nov-Feb. **Admission** £5.20; £2.50 concessions; £13 family. **Credit** *Shop* MC, V.

Cricket St Thomas Wildlife Park
off A30, nr Chard (01460 30111/www.cstwp.co.uk). **Open** *Oct-Mar* 10am-4pm daily. *Apr-Sept* 10am-6pm daily. **Admission** £6.95; £4.95 concessions; free under-3s. **Credit** MC, V.

Fleet Air Museum
RNAS Yeovilton, nr Yeovil (01935 840565/ www.fleetairarm.com). **Open** *Nov-Mar* 10am-4.30pm daily. *Apr-Oct* 10am-5.30pm daily. **Admission** £8.50; £5.75 concessions; free under-5s. **Credit** MC, V.

Haynes Motor Museum
Sparkford, nr Yeovil (01963 440804/www.haynes motormuseum.co.uk). **Open** *Mar-Oct* 9.30am-5.30pm daily. *Nov-Feb* 10am-4.30pm daily. **Admission** £6; £3.50-£5 concessions. **Credit** AmEx, MC, V.

Somerset

Say what? Zummerzet

According to a paper written for the Somerset Archaeological Society in 1865, the area's dialect 'has done very heavy duty as the representative of the clownish element in literature'. It is still true that something approximating the dialect of this area is often used in television and radio dramas to represent some generalised West Country bumpkin. However, linguistic connoisseurs will argue that, far from being poor or risible English, the Somerset dialect is actually the language of King Alfred and was the standard English of its day.

Local Somerset speech retains much that is traceably West Saxon, a Germanic dialect that permeated much of south and south-west England from roughly the sixth to the 12th centuries (but stopped short at Celtic-held Cornwall).

Today, modern county boundaries rarely coincide with variations in dialect: Somerset blurs into Devonshire on Exmoor, and blends with the Bristol accent (complete with extra 'l' in the north-west of the county (*see p67*). There does, however, seem to be some agreement that the River Parret forms a natural boundary between the dialect of West Somerset and the rest.

If you get into conversation with a real Somerset local (or eavesdrop in the pub), you'll notice the ubiquitous 'z' sound and the use of 'un' instead of him/her (a hold-over from West Saxon), in such phrases as '*I zee'd 'un on Zunday*' (I saw him on Sunday). 'F' changes to 'v' as in '*I do like a vew vlowers in my gardin'*, with 'afraid' becoming '*aveard*' and 'farm' sounding more like '*varm*'.

Still commonly heard is '*thik*' for 'the', '*twern't*' for 'it wasn't' and '*we'm*' for 'we are' – not to mention '*lebm*' for eleven and '*zebm*' for seven. There are also intriguing inversions like '*wopse*' for 'wasp', short forms like '*empt*' for 'empty', and reminders of Germanic links in '*thee bisst*' for 'you are'. '*Maze*' is the Somerset word for 'mad' or 'confused', so listen out for wonderfully inventive similes such as '*as mazed as a sheep*'.

Children were often beaten for speaking in dialect in the old dame schools, but now linguistic traditions should be cherished. If you find yourself barely able to understand the response when you stop and ask for directions in a Somerset lane, just listen carefully and rejoice.

Langport & River Parrett Visitor Centre
Westover, Langport (01458 250350/www.river parrett-trail.org.uk). **Open** *Easter, July, Aug* 10am-6pm daily. *Apr-June, Sept* 10am-6pm Tue-Sun. *Oct-Mar* 10am-4pm Tue-Sun. **Admission** free. Credit MC, V.

Montacute House
Montacute, nr Stoke-sub-Hampden (01935 823289). **Open** *House* Apr-Oct 11am-5pm Mon, Wed-Sun; closed Nov-Mar. *Gardens* Apr-Oct 11am-5pm Mon, Wed-Sun; Nov-Mar 11am-4pm Tue-Sun. **Admission** £6.50; £3 concessions; free under-5s; £16 family. **No credit cards**.

Museum of South Somerset
Hendford, Yeovil (01935 424774). **Open** *Apr-Sept* 10am-4pm Tue-Sat. *Oct-Mar* 10am-4pm Tue-Fri. **Admission** free.

Willows & Wetlands Visitor Centre
Meare Green Court, Stoke St Gregory (01823 490249). **Open** 9am-5pm Mon-Sat. *Guided tours* 10am-noon, 2-4pm Mon-Fri. **Admission** free. *Guided tours* £3.50; £1.75 concessions. Credit MC, V.

Activities

Cycling
With a landscape as flat as the Netherlands in places, this part of Somerset makes perfect cycling country. The 80-mile (129km) **South Somerset Cycle Route** takes in many local attractions and has links to the National Cycle Network. For details of this and other cycle tours contact **Cycle Dorset & South Somerset** (01935 881166, www.cycledorset.com). Bikes can be hired from **Bow Bridge Cycle Hire** at the Langport & River Parrett Visitor Centre (01458 250350).

Fishing
The **Chard Reservoir** (01460 64000) and **Sutton Bingham Reservoir** (01935 872389) both provide ample opportunity to flex your rod. Coarse fishing is also allowed on the Rivers Yeo, Isle and Parrett. For further information contact the Environment Agency (0845 933 3111, www.environment-agency.gov.uk). To obtain a licence, phone 0870 166 2622.

Golf
There are 18-hole courses at **Long Sutton** (01458 241017), **Wheathill** (01963 240667), **Windwhistle** (01460 30231) and **Yeovil** (01935 422965), plus a nine-hole pitch-and-putt course at **Yeovil Recreation Centre** (01935 411120).

Walking
The **River Parrett Trail** is a 50-mile (80km) route that follows the River Parrett from its source in Dorset, passing through South Somerset and across the Levels to the mouth of the river on Bridgwater Bay. Other routes include the **Leland Trail** (28 miles/45km) from Penselwood on the Dorset

border to Ham Hill Country Park; and the **Liberty Trail** (28 miles/45km), which continues south from Ham as far as the south coast at Lyme Regis. The latter follows the route taken by supporters of the Duke of Monmouth, who joined in his ill-fated rebellion in 1685 (*see p16*).

Where to eat, drink & stay
The **Old Pound Inn** (Aller, near Langport, 01458 250469, main courses £8.95-£14.95, double B&B £55) was built in 1571 as a cider house, and offers hearty pub lunches and comfortable en suite accommodation. The **Langport Arms Hotel & Carvery** (Cheapside, Langport, 01458 250530, main courses £6-£10.75, double B&B £40) is a convenient and comfortable alternative.

In Somerton, try the beautiful **Lynch Country House Hotel** (01458 272316, www.thelynchcountryhouse.co.uk, double B&B £49-85), which offers bed and breakfast in eight spacious, comfortable rooms. The ebullient host was a member of some notable 1950s big bands, so expect a classy jazz soundtrack to accompany your breakfast. The house is fronted by expansive lawns, a lake and woodlands.

The award-winning **Little Barwick House** (Barwick, Yeovil, 01935 423902, www.littlebarwickhouse.co.uk, closed two weeks early Jan, set dinner £26.50/£29.50, double B&B £93-£103) is a delightful place to stay or eat. The chef prides himself on serving fresh, specialist West Country ingredients, including Somerset smoked eel. The **Walnut Tree** (West Camel, near Yeovil, 01935 851292, www.thewalnut treehotel.com, main courses £8.95-£13.95, double B&B £85-£95) has two restaurants: one serves traditional dishes, while the brasserie specialises in Mediterranean and Asian foods.

Resources

Hospital
Yeovil *District Hospital, Higher Kingston (01935 475122).*

Internet
Yeovil *Library, King George Street (01935 423144/www.foursite.somerset.gov.uk).* **Open** 9.30am-5.30pm Mon-Thur; 9.30am-6.30pm Fri; 9.30am-4pm Sat.

Police stations
Somerton *Kirkham Street (01823 337911).* **Yeovil** *Horsey Lane (01823 337911).*

Post office
Yeovil *King George Street (08457 223344).* **Open** 9am-5.30pm Mon-Sat.

Tourist information

Somerton *Parish Rooms, Market Place (01458 274070/www.southsomerset.gov.uk).* **Open** 9am-1pm, 2-5.15pm Mon-Thur; 9am-1pm, 2-4.45pm Fri. **Yeovil** *Tourist Information Centre, Petter's House, Petter's Way (01935 462991/www.southsomerset. gov.uk).* **Open** *Mar-Oct* 9am-5pm Mon-Sat. *Nov-Feb* 9am-5pm Mon-Fri.

Taunton & the Quantocks

Taunton – the County Town of Somerset – is no oil painting. Most of its medieval and Tudor buildings were destroyed by fire, and charity shops and 'To Let' signs now crowd the streets – a far cry from the bustling market town of yore. Believed to have been founded by the Saxon king Ine in the seventh century, Taunton's most famous moment in history came in 1685, when the Duke of Monmouth, the illegitimate son of Charles II, rallied troops here against James II. Monmouth was captured and executed, and his rebels were severely punished at the castle by the infamous Judge Jeffreys (*see also p16*).

A Heritage Trail around Taunton (in the form of brass plaques in the pavement) begins at the red sandstone **Church of St Mary Magdalene**, founded in 1488, whose 163-foot (50-metre) tower is one of the finest in the country. The stone **Castle Bow**, at the entrance to Castle Green, is all that survives of the outer town walls and Norman-built castle, which saw action during the English Civil War, and again in 1685 during Judge Jeffreys' 'Bloody Assize'. The **County Museum** is based in and around the castle's Great Hall, and is the sort of musty-smelling, municipal museum familiar from school trips, with incongruous displays of everything from gargoyles to spooky skeletal remains dating from around 2,300 BC.

It is the countryside around Taunton that provides the most persuasive reason to stop the car between Glastonbury and Exmoor: namely the **Quantock Hills**, which stretch northwards from the town to the coast at Watchet. There's tremendous variety within this lush 23,500-acre landscape: rolling heathlands burnished brown, red and purple by heather and bracken; bracing open hill tops; deep combes ribboned with streams; and misty woodlands. Little wonder Coleridge and Wordsworth fell in love with it.

In 1957 the Quantocks were designated Britain's first ever Area of Outstanding Natural Beauty. They are the habitat of sheep, ponies, pheasants and rare birds, and a haven for over 700 red deer (the largest surviving native mammal in the British Isles) – when they're not being chased by staghounds.

Four miles (six kilometres) north of Taunton, lie beautiful **Hestercombe Gardens**, first laid out in the 18th century by the lavishly named soldier, artist and landowner Coplestone Warre Bampfylde, with adjacent formal gardens designed by Sir Edwin Lutyens and Gertrude Jekyll in 1904. Four different walks (the one-hour 'orange' walk is the best) take you through sylvan scenery, past cascading waterfalls and up steep banks to marvel at perfectly composed panoramas from special vantage points. More romantically still, much of Hestercombe lay hidden and overgrown for 125 years until enterprising dairy farmer Philip White restored and reopened the gardens in the 1990s.

Slightly further north, the air is thick with bird song at the headquarters of the Somerset Wildlife Trust at **Fyne Court**. The house was built in the 1600s by the Crosse family, but its most famous inhabitant was Andrew Crosse (1784-1855), aka 'the wizard of Fyne Court', who was believed to have magic powers due to his spectacular electrical experiments involving violent flashes and bangs. Most of the house was destroyed by fire in 1894, although the Visitor Centre is based in Crosse's old laboratory and houses displays on Quantock wildlife and conservation. Surrounding the house, 26 acres of woodland contain a network of educational nature trails.

Five miles (eight kilometres) north in Nether Stowey, magic of a different sort was created by the Romantic poet Samuel Taylor Coleridge (*see p32* **Local heroes**). **Coleridge Cottage** (35 Lime Street, 01278 732662) is where he lived with his wife Sara and baby son Hartley for three years in the late 1700s. Only four of the original rooms remain, and the interior is no longer authentic, but exhibits include the poet's ink stand, locks of hair and letters. It's easy to picture him here writing 'Frost At Midnight', 'The Rime of the Ancient Mariner' and 'Kubla Khan', supping laudanum; and talking iambic pentameters with neighbours William and Dorothy Wordsworth, who dwelt for a while at Alfoxden House nearby.

For a delightful overview of the Quantocks' scenery, visitors can take a nostalgic ride on the **West Somerset Steam Railway** (01643 707650, www.west-somerset-railway.co.uk) from Bishops Lydeard to Minehead, staffed by retired gents. The journey takes just over an hour and passes through some beautiful old stations, including Crowcombe, which was used in the Beatles film *A Hard Day's Night* and more recently in *The Land Girls*.

On reaching the coast, stop off at the historic harbour town of **Watchet**, whose maritime heritage stretches back over 1,000 years. Its weathered fishermen, who heaved 'flattie' boats

Somerset

Drink up Somerset cider

Cider has an image problem. On a recent visit to the House of Commons with numerous industry colleagues, Julian Temperley, proprietor of Burrow Hill Cider in Somerset, was surprised to find that the atmosphere in the members' bar was one of mild hysteria. 'The cider has entered the building, right?', the MPs asked excitedly; even the stony-faced security guards softened around the edges. The country boys had come to town and they had brought with them a drop of the good stuff. Bring on the wenches and let the good times roll!

Cider was originally a drink for workers on the land: cheap, energy-giving and plentiful, it was made by and for local people. It is with some difficulty, then, that companies have attempted to market the product to a larger, alcopop-drinking audience. Cider that has filtered through to the mass market tends to be a rather tasteless version of the real thing; you'll have to go to the smaller producers if you want to sample the genuine article.

Cider-making is relatively simple: apples are washed, pulped and pressed, and the pure apple juice is allowed to ferment in wooden barrels for up to two years. When the waiting's over you have quite a choice on your hands, with drys, mediums and sweets to be sampled, the output depending primarily on the apples that went into the mix. If the cider is distilled, then the delights of cider brandy make themselves known – a drink that would sit proudly on any discerning table. In fact, Mr Temperley's ten-year-old vintage cider brandy has now been taken under the wing of the Malt Whiskey Society, and is promoted worldwide to its members.

Of course, the strength of some cider means it will always be regarded as a quick way of getting from A to B(lottoed), with scrumpy (an unfiltered cider produced with

natural yeasts) perhaps the best exponent of that mode of transport. However, with the French, Italians, Japanese, Kiwis and many others starting to pay it serious signs of respect, it seems that cider is destined to outgrow its rather humble roots.

CIDER PRODUCERS

The handy leaflet 'Somerset Cider & Apple Juice: A Guide to Orchards and Cider Makers' is available from tourist information centres in the county. The majority of traditional cider producers welcome visitors, but you should always phone ahead before pitching up at a busy working farm expecting a guided tour.

Thatcher's (Myrtle Farm, Station Road, Sandford, Winscombe, 01934 822862, www.thatcherscider.co.uk) is a well-known producer; it supplies refined bottled cider to some UK supermarkets, but you can try the scrumpy if you visit the farm. An alternative is **Broadoak Cider** (Clutton Hill Farm, Clutton, 01275 333154), which produces more than a dozen varieties, including Rustic Gold, Mega White and the splendidly named Black Out.

out on to the channel mud to fish for eels, inspired Coleridge to write 'The Rime of the Ancient Mariner'. The docks are no longer operational, but a smart new marina provides facilities for leisure boats and deep-sea fishing. Nearby, **Watchet Museum** (Old Market House, Market Street, closed Nov-Mar) is devoted to the town's seafaring past.

Set alongside a stream in a tranquil valley just to the south of Watchet are the remains of **Cleeve Abbey**, a Cistercian monastery founded in 1198. All that survives of the church itself are grass-level ruins, but the domestic quarters have been well preserved, most notably the former monks' dormitory. The property is conserved by English Heritage.

Cleeve Abbey

Cleeve Abbey, Washford (01984 640377/ www.english-heritage.org.uk). **Open** *Apr-Sept* 10am-6pm daily. *Oct* 10am-5pm daily. *Nov-Mar* 10am-1pm, 2-4pm daily. **Admission** £2.80; £1.40-£2.10 concessions. **Credit** MC, V.

Somerset

Just outside Burnham-on-Sea, **Coombes** (Japonica Farm, Mark Causeway, near Highbridge, 01278 641265) is a third-generation cider producer of dry, medium and sweet cider, plus sparkling perry (made from pears). The farm shop sells local cheese and country wines, and a small museum includes a 20-minute video on the manufacturing process. Further east, **Wilkins** (Land's End Farm, Mudgley, near Wedmore, 01934 712385) has been producing strong dry, medium and sweet farmhouse cider since 1917. Cheese, chutneys and fresh vegetables are on sale as well.

In the south of the county is **Burrow Hill Cider** (Pass Vale Farm, Burrow Hill, Kingsbury Episcopi, Martock, 01460 240782, www.cider brandy.co.uk), producer of the famous vintage cider brandy, and **Perry's Cider Mills** (Dowlish Wake, Ilminster, 01460 52681, www.perryscider.co.uk). The latter has cider industry paraphernalia dating back over the years and engrossing early photos of farm and village life at the turn of 19th century. The specialities here include Redstreak and Morgan Sweet.

Near Taunton, the Sheppy family has been scrunching down apples for more than two centuries. Visits to **Sheppy's Cider Farm & Museum** (Three Bridges, Bradford-on-Tone, 01823 461233, www.sheppyscider.com) include a tour of the orchards and cellars and the chance to examine antique agricultural and cider-making equipment before sampling single-variety cider, scrumpy and apple juice.

CIDER PUBS
Another way of tasting the local brew is to visit one of Somerset's cider pubs, where locally produced varieties are served straight from the barrel. The **Rose & Crown Inn** (aka Eli's; Huish Episcopi, near Langport, 01458 250494; *pictured*) is one of the best spots to get stuck in, with plentiful Burrow Hill cider and an authentic local atmosphere. Burrow Hill is also on the menu at the **Wyndham Arms** (Kingsbury Episcopi, near Martock, 01935 823239, www.wyndhamarms.com), a traditional village pub dating back four centuries; while Thatcher's and Addlestone's Clear (Matthew Clark cider) is served in the cathedral city of Wells at the **City Arms** (69 High Street, 01749 673916). This child-friendly local also has a pretty courtyard and a well-regarded restaurant. Further north, the **Coronation Tap**, or Cori Tap (Sion Place, Clifton, Bristol, 0117 973 9617, www.thecoronationtap.com) is a powerful reminder that Bristol was once a Somerset city. This is a near-legendary pub (and the only remaining cider house in Bristol), selling, among others, a cider so strong (Exhibition) that it's only served by the half pint. The pub's traditional interior is usually full of rustic charm and pissed locals, including the odd celebrity.

Another one-off is the **Tucker's Grave Inn** (A366, Faulkland, near Radstock, 01373 834230), an unmodernised cottage with no real bar, serving traditional cider and real ale from barrels out back. Just make sure you arrange a ride home.

Somerset

County Museum & Castle
Castle Green, Taunton (01823 320201).
Open 10am-5pm Tue-Sat. **Admission** free.

Hestercombe Gardens
Cheddon Fitzpaine (01823 413923/www.hestercombe gardens.com). **Open** 10am-5pm daily. **Admission** £5; £1.20-£4.70 concessions. **Credit** MC, V.

Somerset Wildlife Trust
Fyne Court, Broomfield (01823 451587/ www.wildlifetrust.org.uk/somerset). **Open** 9am-5pm daily. **Admission** free (50p car park charge).

What to do

Cycling
This area has miles of cycle routes, from leisurely glides along the canal towpath to rough 'n' tough mountain bike scrambles. It also boasts the country's first-ever **Bike Park** (St James Street, Taunton, 01823 365917, closed Sun), with hire, repair, parking and shower facilities. Taunton Tourist Information Centre can advise on routes, while **Fasttrack SMTB** (01823 433139) organises all-inclusive bike weekends and evening rides.

Riding

Racehorse trainers at **Manor Farm** (Water Pitts, Broomfield, 01823 451266) will take you the length and breadth of the Quantocks, whatever your ability.

Walking

The 50-mile (80km) **West Deane Way** begins and ends in Taunton, leading along the River Tone to the slopes of the Quantocks, and through several untouched villages where you can hang up your boots for the night. Useful leaflets are available from the Taunton Tourist Information Centre.

Where to eat, drink & stay

The **Castle Hotel** (Castle Green, 01823 272671, www.the-castle-hotel.com, set dinner £33/£39, double B&B £165-£245) has been welcoming travellers since the 12th century. The 44 rooms are all luxuriously furnished in old-English style with heavy curtains and Persian rugs, while the seven suites border on the Trumpesque. The hotel restaurant has won a Michelin star for its modern British cuisine, and uses local produce for specialities such as home-cured beef. An alternative eating spot is the sleek, cosmopolitan **Brazz** (Castle Bow, 01823 252000, main courses £5.95-£15.95), which lies in a coveted spot under the ancient castle wall.

Bindon Country House (Langford Budville, Wellington, 01823 400070, www.bindon.com, set dinner £29.95-£36, double B&B £95-205) is a cream coloured, Gothic-style, 12-bedroom hotel, built around the time of the English Civil War. Nibble petit-fours over a game of chess in the handsome, wood-panelled bar before heading to your spacious, floral bedroom. If you prefer cosy cottage accommodation, snuggly thatched **Gatchells** (Angersleigh, 01823 421580, www.gatchells.org.uk, double B&B £46-£60) is tucked away on the edge of the Blackdown Hills and dates back to 1420. The well-tended flower garden has a pool for the summer months, while inside there are low, sloping ceilings, heavy beams and an inglenook fireplace.

Heading through the Quantocks, several quaint and authentic timber-beamed taverns vie for custom. Try the unspoiled, flagstoned **Carew Arms** (Crowcombe, 01984 618631, www.carewarms.co.uk, main courses £5.50-£12.50) for real ale and good food, or the **Lethbridge Arms** (Bishops Lydeard, 01823 432234, main courses £3.50-£9.95), a 16th-century former coaching inn serving home-cooked fare. Book in advance for elbow room at the cosy **Rising Sun Inn** (West Bagborough, 01823 432575, closed Mon, main courses £9.99-£14.50), which, despite a devastating fire in January 2002, is open for business with a classy menu of traditional comfort food, gastropub dishes and an excellent wine list. Finally, join

the locals at pretty village hostelry the **Rose & Crown** (Nether Stowey, 01278 732265, main courses £2.50-£9.95), where specials include such heart-warming treats as beef stuffed with stilton and venison sausages in red wine.

Resources

Hospital

Musgrove Park Hospital *Taunton (01823 333444).*

Internet

Taunton Library *Paul Street, Taunton (01823 336334).* **Open** 9.30am-5.30pm Mon, Tue, Thur; 9.30am-7pm Wed, Fri; 9.30am-4pm Sat.

Police station

Upper High Street, Taunton (01823 337911).

Post office

38 North Street, Taunton (08457 223344). **Open** 9am-5.30pm Mon-Fri; 9am-12.30pm Sat.

Tourist Information

Taunton Tourist Information Centre *Paul Street, Taunton (01823 336344/ www.heartofsomerset.com).* **Open** 9.30am-5.30pm Mon-Fri; 9.30am-5pm Sat.

Getting there & around

By train

First Great Western runs services from London Paddington to Taunton approximately every hour (journey time up to 2hrs). The nearest stations to Glastonbury are at **Bridgwater** and **Castle Cary** (both served by Wessex Trains from Bristol Temple Meads), but there are also bus links from Bristol, Taunton and Bath. **South West Trains** from Waterloo serve Yeovil Junction and Crewkerne. For details, call National Rail Enquiries (08457 484950).

By bus

Local services around Glastonbury (01749 673084) and Taunton (01823 272033, 0870 6082608) are run by **First Group**. For general information about bus services throughout the county, phone **ATMOS** (01823 251151).

Exmoor

Despite acres of beautiful scenery and a spectacular coastline, England's least-visited national park remains a well-kept secret.

With its combination of extensive wilderness and dramatic coast, Exmoor stands out from other English national parks. The landscape, criss-crossed by flashing rivers, varies between wooded glens and open moorland, both extending to a shoreline that is wonderfully but frustratingly remote. Along Exmoor's coast, densely wooded, precipitous cliffs ensure that in many places there is no landward access to the sea at all and very few places where you could safely land a boat.

Exmoor National Park, which covers 267 square miles (692 square kilometres) straddling the Somerset–Devon border, was designated in 1954. It abounds with native livestock – not only the famous wild red deer and sturdy Exmoor ponies (which were granted rare breed status in 1981) – but animals such as Exmoor horn sheep and red ruby cattle, which were taken to North America by the Pilgrim Fathers.

Oddly, this startling variety of scenery and wildlife is still largely undiscovered. Maybe 1.4 million annual visitors sounds like a lot, but this is the lowest number for any English national park. Many of the park's visitors come for country pursuits such as fly-fishing, riding and, notably, hunting, which remains an integral if controversial part of Exmoor life (*see p127*).

Others come to exploit the 620-odd miles (1,000 kilometres) of scenic footpaths and bridleways. The **South West Coast Path** runs along Exmoor's coastline from Minehead to Combe Martin. It takes two or three days to complete this section of the route, which includes the highest and remotest stretches, with ascents totalling more than the height of Ben Nevis. Another long-distance trail, the **Two Moors Way** from Lynmouth, passes through some of Exmoor's remotest tracts around Simonsbath and the Barle valley en route to Ivybridge on the southern edge of Dartmoor.

FURTHER INFORMATION

For detailed information about the National Park, contact the headquarters of the **Exmoor National Park Authority** (Exmoor House, Dulverton, Somerset, TA22 9HL, 01398 323665, www.exmoor-nationalpark.gov.uk). If you are planning exploration of the area in the car or on foot, the OS Outdoor Leisure Map (No.9: Exmoor) is essential.

Exmoor Coast

As far as the Exmoor coast is concerned, west is best. Not only do the hills gather in size and profile the further west you go, but the water changes colour too. Beyond Porlock, the sea becomes bluer by the mile, as you approach the Atlantic Ocean, and between Lynmouth and Combe Martin the water even has a touch of Mediterranean colour, with a ribbon of turquoise along the rocks and bays. The problem for sun-seekers, though, is that the Exmoor coast faces the wrong way, looking north across the Bristol Channel, and so cannot compete with the south-facing bays and sands of the English Channel.

Those exploring the Exmoor coast should note that few points are accessible by car, and even the coast path doesn't hug the shore, but drifts towards higher hills inland.

From Dunster to Doone Valley

On the north-eastern edge of the National Park, the village of **Dunster** oozes history and picturesque charm. The poet and essayist William Hazlitt, looking down on the village in the 1820s, recalls 'eyeing it wistfully as it lay below us, contrasted with the woody scene around, it looked as clear, as pure, as embrowned and ideal as any landscape I have seen since.' Hordes of visitors seem to agree, making this village one of the most popular destinations on Exmoor.

Dunster Castle began life as a Saxon outpost and was later a Norman fort, before being inherited by the Luttrell family in 1376, who held on to it for 600 years. Much of the original structure was wiped out during the Civil War, and the castle was redesigned as a Jacobean manor house. The interior dates largely from this period and includes a splendidly ornate oak-carved staircase, and some fine artwork and furniture. A final reincarnation came in the 1870s, when the building was remodelled as a grand, castellated pile by architect Antony Salvin, resulting in its current irregular appearance. It was donated to the National Trust in 1976.

The imposing Jacobean form of **Dunster Castle**. *See p117.*

Terraced gardens, planted with citrus fruits, palms and mimosas, characterise the castle grounds, where outdoor theatre performances are held in summer. Beyond is the River Avill and a couple of graceful bridges, with the restored and active 18th-century **Dunster Castle Mill** further upstream.

Dunster High Street stretches north from the castle through the centre of the village. The octagonal covered **Yarn Market** (1609) is the most prominent reminder of the village's once-prosperous wool trade. Look out for a hole in one of the oak beams, which was caused by a cannonball in the long siege of Dunster Castle during the Civil War.

Souvenir-shopping opportunities abound in the centre of Dunster, some a notch or two above tourist-fodder level. Check out the prints and paintings at the **Studio Gallery** (Castle Gate, 01643 821052), and the handiwork of the Somerset Guild of Craftsmen at **Dunster Craft Shop** (Dunster Steep, 01643 821235). Opposite is the **Exmoor National Park Visitor Centre** (*see p121*), which has a permanent exhibition about the moor.

In Church Street are the remains of 12th-century **Dunster Priory**, including an atmospheric B&B (*see p120*), a tithe barn and a beautifully preserved dovecote. Adjoining the priory garden, **St George's** church has an elaborately carved rood-screen and a 15th-century bell-tower.

Dunster is surrounded by some idyllic countryside. North of the High Street, **Conygar Tower** is an 18th-century folly with views to Dunster Beach and the Bristol Channel, while to the south of town, across the River Avill, lies historic **Dunster Park**. The slopes here are covered with ancient trees and clumps of heather sheltering the rare heath fritillary butterfly, while at the top, the Iron Age fort of **Bat's Castle** affords fabulous long-range views across the surrounding countryside.

A short hop along the A39 is the seaside town of **Minehead**. It's an unremarkable resort, but nevertheless makes an accessible spot from which to explore west Somerset and the Exmoor coast. Until the late 18th century Minehead was an important port for herring fishing and the wool and coal trades, but a couple of disastrous fires and the silting up of its harbour caused a slump in the town's fortunes. It revived as a seaside resort in the 19th century with the arrival of tourists and the completion of the scenic **West Somerset Railway** from Bishop's Lydeard (*see p126*).

Today, a Butlins holiday camp, fronted by a wide sandy beach, dominates the eastern side of Minehead Bay, while to the west, cobbled slopes rise to Higher Town, a pretty villagey district with great views over the Bristol Channel. Here, archetypal thatched cottages cluster around 15th-century **St Michael's Church**, which houses the beautiful illuminated Fitzjames Missal, a hand-written Gothic script dating from the 14th century.

From Higher Town, steep lanes lead down to Minehead's stone-walled **harbour**, built by the Luttrell family in the 17th and 18th centuries, but now often deep in silt and left dry by the receding tide. Boat trips on board the *Balmoral* depart from here to Ilfracombe, Clevedon and Barry Island (0845 130 4647, www.waverley excursions.co.uk). Nearby Quay Street is the starting point for the South West Coast Path, which heads west up North Hill and on to the cliffs, but cuts inland soon afterwards to **Selworthy Beacon** (1,012 feet/348 metres).

A mile's walk out of Minehead, a lower path ends in the middle of a wood at the medieval ruins of **Burgundy Chapel**. The surviving structure has a single wall with a finely carved door, and is said to have been built by a member of the Luttrell family as thanks for his safe return to Dunster Castle from the Burgundian War in the 14th century.

Covering a huge tract of land west and south of Minehead, the **Holnicote Estate** was given to the National Trust by Sir Richard Acland in 1944. As well as the high tors of Dunkery and Selworthy Beacons, it incorporates several picturesque thatched villages. Particularly idyllic (or twee, perhaps) is **Selworthy Green**, whose perfect rustic cottages were built in the mid 19th century by Sir Thomas Dyke Acland as retirement homes for his estate workers. In nearby **Allerford** is a 15th-century packhorse bridge and a former schoolhouse that now houses the **West Somerset Rural Life Museum**, with local photos and artefacts, and a recreated Victorian schoolroom. More appealing for children, though, is the **Exmoor Falconry & Animal Farm**, where you can watch flying displays, learn aspects of falconry, pet wee beasties or take off on a pony ride across the moor.

Porlock is a quaint, semi-coastal town nestling in a hollow between hog-backed Exmoor hills, and protected from the sea a mile away by a shingle breakwater. On 28 October 1996 the sea broke through the shingle in the tail-end swish of Hurricane Lily, flooding the meadows behind to create a brackish marsh, which attracts a fascinating variety of bird life. The lengthy High Street is crammed with hotels, antique shops, outdoor suppliers and a couple of historic pubs. Most notable of these is the **Ship Inn**, which is said to have been

frequented by poets Samuel Taylor Coleridge and Robert Southey in the late 18th century. It was later immortalised by RD Blackmore in his 1869 novel, *Lorna Doone*. The town's other literary connection is less auspicious: Samuel Taylor Coleridge claimed that it was an unidentified 'person from Porlock' who spoilt his recall of the dream-poem *Kubla Khan*.

Near the centre of Porlock, Doverhay Court, dating from 1450, was rebuilt in Victorian times and now houses **Doverhay Manor Museum**, with a small collection of photos and paintings detailing Porlock's history. The **Doverhay Forge Studios** (01643 862444) produce wrought-iron chandeliers and screens. Porlock's parish church is dedicated to **St Dubricius**, a post-Roman archbishop who, according to legend, conducted the marriage of King Arthur and Guinevere. The church is crowned by an apparently unfinished oak-shingle spire. Local lore claims that its top was blown off in a gale and ended up on the roof of Culbone church (*see below*).

One mile (1.5 kilometres) west across reclaimed marshland is the ancient harbour of **Porlock Weir**. It's a peaceful spot, with thatched cottages overlooking the stony coast. Distinctive hand-blown cranberry-coloured glass is made by **Exmoor Glass** at the Harbour Studios (01643 863141).

Southey commented that 'Porlock is called in the neighbourhood the "End of the World". All beyond is inaccessible to carriage or even cart.' Even today vehicles heading west must either use the scenic toll road or take the zig-zagging A39 up fearsome **Porlock Hill** at a one-in-four gradient.

On top of the hill are several prehistoric standing stones, including the enigmatic **Culbone Stone**, which combines a Celtic cartwheel design with a Dark Age tail to make a Christian cross. Further north is miniscule and idyllic **St Culbone**, a medieval church that's said to be the smallest in England. Note the 'leper-squint' window in the church wall, which enabled sufferers from the local leper colony to watch services from the churchyard.

Equally isolated is the hamlet of **Oare** to the south of the A39. There's another tiny church here, famed as the fictional location of Lorna Doone's marriage and shooting. Although not many people read the novel today, its tale of 17th-century brigands along the Somerset–Devon border has perhaps as strong a claim on the romantic imagination as Wordsworth and his Lakeland daffodils. The real-life valleys of Lank Combe, Hoccombe Combe and Badgworthy Water are among the wildest and most isolated on Exmoor and still resonate with the fictional characteristics of **Doone Valley**.

Somerset

At the heart of Doone country, a single stony cart-track leads to the lost village of **Badgworthy** (*see p122* **Country walk**), the fictional home of the Doone family. This is one of the wettest spots in the West Country, where the humid micro-climate creates a landscape dominated by stunted oaks, festooned with ferns.

Doverhay Manor Museum

Porlock (01643 862420). **Open** *Easter-Sept* 10am-1pm, 2-5pm Mon-Fri; 10am-noon Sat. Closed Oct-Mar. **Admission** free.

Dunster Castle

Dunster, nr Minehead (01643 821314/ www.nationaltrust.org.uk). **Open** *Castle* late Mar-late Sept 11am-5pm Mon-Wed, Sat, Sun; late Sept-Nov 11am-4pm Mon-Wed, Sat, Sun; closed Dec-late Mar. *Garden & park* late Mar-late Sept 11am-5pm Mon-Wed, Sat, Sun; late Sept-late Mar 11am-4pm Mon-Wed, Sat, Sun. **Admission** *Castle, garden & park* £6.20; £3.10 concessions; £15.50 family. *Garden & park* £3; £1.50 concessions; £7.50 family. **Credit** MC, V.

Dunster Castle Mill

Mill Lane, Dunster, nr Minehead (01643 821759). **Open** *Mar-early Nov* 10.30am-5pm daily. Closed early Nov-Feb. **Admission** £2.30; £1.30 concessions; £5.60 family. **No credit cards**.

Exmoor Falconry & Animal Farm

Allerford, nr Porlock (01643 862816/ www.exmoorfalconry.co.uk). **Open** *Mar-Oct* 10.30am-5pm daily. *Nov-Feb* 10.30am-4.30pm Mon, Fri-Sun. **Admission** £5.50; £4.50 concessions; £17.50 family. **Credit** MC, V.

West Somerset Rural Life Museum

The Old School, Allerford, nr Porlock (01643 862529). **Open** *Easter, May-Oct* 10.30am-1pm, 2-4.30pm Mon-Sat; 2-4.30pm Sun. Closed Nov-Mar. **Admission** £1.50; 50p-£1.20 concessions. **No credit cards**.

Activities

Fishing

Numerous outfits advertise sea fishing trips (and other excursions) from the harbours at Minehead and Porlock Weir. Try **Atlantic Blue** (7 South Park, Minehead, 01643 705361).

Riding

Explore Doone Country on horseback from **Cloud Farm** (Malmsmead, 01598 741278, www.doonevalleyholidays.co.uk). More serious equestrians should attend the riding stables at **Porlock Vale House** (*see p121*).

Where to eat, drink & stay

Hathaway's in West Street at Dunster (01643 821725, closed Mon in winter, main courses £8-£14) specialises in lunches and cream teas with

The topless church of **St Dubricius**. See p119.

old-fashioned service under 16th-century beams. If it's full, there are plenty of teashops and historic inns within walking distance. The **Restaurant in the High Street** (Dunster, 01643 821304, closed Jan, main courses £7.50-£13.50) has a centre-stage setting to die for, while the **Luttrell Arms** (Dunster, 01643 821555, double B&B £95-£105) incorporates both the elegant Luttrell Restaurant (set menus £22/£28) and less formal Old Kitchen (main courses £3.95-£10.95), with its own garden looking across to Dunster Castle. For atmospheric accommodation, it's hard to beat the medieval **Old Priory** (Priory Green, 01643 821540, closed late Dec, double B&B £60-£75), with its artistically decorated rooms and walled garden adjoining St George's church. There's a self-catering cottage here too.

Minehead has plenty of cheapish B&Bs, but nowhere that particularly stands out from the crowd. Near the old harbour, the **Old Ship Aground** (Quay Street, 01643 702087, main courses £4.45-£8.95, double B&B £40-£45) offers quiet rooms and reasonable bar food.

Just off the A39, the most scenic of pit-stops is **Periwinkle Tea Room** on Selworthy Green (01643 862769, closed winter). For accommodation, you can enjoy simple farmhouse B&B with a menagerie of wildlife at the **Exmoor Falconry & Animal Farm** (*see p119*; double B&B £50-£60).

Pubs abound in Porlock, many offering reasonable grub and basic accommodation. When the poet Robert Southey visited, he stayed at the **Ship Inn** (High Street, 01643 862507, www.shipinnporlock.co.uk, main courses £4.25-£9.95, double B&B £44-£58) in a room that had 'a decent pot de chambre and no fleas'. Nowadays it offers light, comfortable rooms that are refreshingly free of chintz. There's local produce on offer in the restaurant and a range of real ales on tap in the bar. Also on the High Street, the cosy **Countryman** (01643 862241, closed Mon-Fri in winter, main courses £8.50-£19.50) is another good bet for food, in particular steaks and seafood.

One of the most charming places to stay in Porlock is **The Oaks** (01643 862265, www.oakshotel.co.uk, closed Nov-Mar, set menu £27.50, double B&B £100), an Edwardian country house with views of the sea. Classic food is served in the dining room (non-residents should book in advance). Camping fans should try **Sparkhayes Farm Campsite** (01643 862470), near the centre of the village.

Right on the seafront at Porlock Weir, the **Anchor Hotel & Ship Inn** (01643 862753, set menu £16.75, double B&B £67.50-£127.50) is a quiet, comfortable option with hearty food on the menu. Also here is **Andrews on the Weir** (01643 863300, www.andrewsontheweir.co.uk, closed Jan, set menu £11.50-£32.50, double B&B £55-£100), a highly regarded restaurant with rooms. The menu positively groans with local produce, and although the decor's rather fussy, there are soothing views across the bay.

Finally, **Porlock Vale House** (01643 862338, www.porlockvale.co.uk, closed early Jan, double B&B £80-£120) is a relaxed country house hotel, full of log fires, comfy sofas, books, games and hunting memorabilia. It's also a renowned riding school, offering individual tuition and cross-country and hacking sorties.

Resources

Hospital
Minehead *The Avenue (01643 707251)*.

Internet
Minehead *Minehead Library, Banks Street (01643 702942)*. **Open** 9.30am-6pm Mon, Tue; 9.30am-6.30pm Thur; 9.30am-7pm Fri; 9.30am-4pm Sat. **Porlock** *Porlock Library, Old School Centre, High Street (01643 862763)*. **Open** 10.30am-12.30pm, 2-5pm Tue; 10.30am-12.30pm, 2-5pm, 5.30-7pm Fri.

Police station
Minehead *32 Townsend Road (01275 818181)*.

Post offices
Dunster *High Street (01643 821355)*. **Open** 9am-1pm, 2-5.30pm Mon-Thur; 9am-1pm Fri; 9am-12.30pm Sat.
Minehead *26 The Avenue (01643 702151)*. **Open** 8.30am-5.30pm Mon, Tue, Thur; 9am-5.30pm Wed, Fri; 9am-12.30pm Sat.
Porlock *High Street (01643 862429)*. **Open** 9am-1pm, 2-5.30pm Mon, Tue, Thur, Fri; 9am-1pm Wed; 9am-12.30pm Sat.

Tourist information
County Gate *Exmoor National Park Visitor Centre, A39, Countisbury (01598 741321)*. **Open** *Easter-Oct* 10am-5pm daily. Closed Nov-Easter.
Dunster *Exmoor National Park Visitor Centre, Dunster Steep (01643 821835)*. **Open** *Easter-Oct* 10am-5pm daily. *Late Oct-Dec* 11am-3pm Sat, Sun.
Minehead *17 Friday Street, The Parade (01643 702624)*. **Open** *Apr-June, Sept, Oct* 9.30am-5pm Mon-Sat. *July, Aug* 9.30am-5.30pm Mon-Sat; 10am-1pm Sun. *Nov-Mar* 10am-4pm Mon-Sat.
Porlock *The Old School, West End (01643 863150/www.porlock.co.uk)*. **Open** *Winter* 10am-1pm Mon-Fri; 10am-2pm Sat, Sun. *Summer* 10am-1pm, 2-5pm Mon-Fri; 10am-5pm Sat; 10am-1pm Sun.

From Countisbury to Combe Martin

The coastal village of **Countisbury** has an amazing piece of valour to its name. Beside the huge Iron Age bank of Countisbury Castle, up one of the most demanding of Exmoor's hills, a mission seemingly impossible was achieved on the night of 12 January 1899. Having failed to launch the lifeboat *Louisa* into mountainous seas, the crew decided to haul her up and over Countisbury Hill (widening corners of the road as necessary) to float her in quieter waters at Porlock Weir and go to the aid of the stricken *Forrest Hall*. The successful rescue remains one of the greatest feats in the annals of lifeboat service.

In the wooded glen to the south, Hoar Oak Water tumbles into the East Lyn River at **Watersmeet**. This beautiful wooded spot is the base station for exploring a great tract of National Trust land, and is close to the epicentre of the torrential rains that devastated Lynmouth in 1952 (*see p125* **Water, water everywhere**). Downstream at Bridge Pool, look down on the stumps of an ancient bridge destroyed in the flood and replaced to the west by the stone arch of Chiselcombe Bridge in 1957. The lush sessile oak woodland also includes Devon whitebeam, mountain ash and rare Irish spurge, beside luxuriant ferns and mosses in the damper zones. A number of gentle walks follow the rivers and valleys from here but there are also some strenuous alternatives signed up the slopes; those to the

Somerset

north reward the walker with fine views over the coast at Lynmouth. The only building in the area is **Watersmeet House**, built in 1830, opposite an old iron mine, as a summer fishing lodge. The house now incorporates a shop, seasonal restaurant and small exhibition devoted to the Lynmouth flood.

Lynton lies in an upper valley of the River Lyn, with the seaside village of **Lynmouth** on the coast below. Backed by the wooded gorges of the East and West Lyn rivers and hemmed in by gigantic cliffs, the twin villages enjoy a popularity out of all proportion to their size. During the Napoleonic Wars, tourists, artists and poets who were unable to reach popular continental destinations started to visit the area, finding in its craggy scenery an echo of the mountainous landscapes of Switzerland. Later in the 19th century, after the publication of RD Blackmore's *Lorna Doone*, a hotel boom took hold along Lee Road, which intensified with the belated arrival of the Lynton & Barnstaple Railway (long since defunct). The influx of seasonal visitors stimulated an architectural free-for-all in Lynton, resulting in an eclectic mix of styles and materials: Gothic and art nouveau, German and Swiss, terracotta and stone.

Victorian magazine magnate Sir George Newnes was typical of Lynton's new arrivals. He donated the town hall and the breathtaking water-powered **Cliff Railway** (01598 753486, www.cliffrailwaylynton.co.uk, closed late Nov-early Feb), whose Victorian cabins and cages still travel on chains up and down the precipitous cliff between the two settlements. The railway is commemorated in the **Lyn & Exmoor Museum**, which captures the feel of the moor with traditional agricultural artefacts and other displays.

In addition to the Cliff Railway, George Newnes also built a weekend home for himself on Hollerday Hill. The house sported state-of-the-art facilities, including its own electricity supply produced from private hydroelectric turbines. The system was revived in 1983 and now the town not only runs on its own power but also sells a surplus to the national grid.

The small hydroelectric station and a **Power of Water** exhibition are located in spectacular **Glen Lyn Gorge**, a steeply wooded valley that stretches inland behind Lynmouth. It is strewn with fern-laden trees and rocks, including huge boulders that tumbled down the River Lyn during the Lynmouth Flood Disaster. This event is remembered at the **Flood Memorial**

Country walk Doone Valley

Length 10 miles (16km)
Time approx 5hrs
Difficulty Some steep, exposed sections and rough terrain. Wet-weather gear, stout walking boots and a detailed map required.

Park and start from Exmoor National Park Visitor Centre at **County Gate** on the A39, at the Devon and Somerset boundary (OS map ref SS 793 486). Set off southwards through the gate opposite the walkers' shelter, inland, down to **Malmsmead** and the Doone Valley. Join another bridleway beside Oare Water. Turn right and then left over the footbridge. Walk up through the farmyard at Malmsmead.

Turn right along the lane and cross humped-backed, medieval Malmsmead Bridge. Turn left at the junction beside **Lorna Doone Farm**, alleged to be the home of John Ridd in the novel. You could pause to stoke up your calories here in the **Buttery Tearoom** (01598 741106), before following Post Lane upstream for 1,000 feet (320 metres); at the bend, go through a field gate and follow a bridleway southwards. **Cloud Farm & Riding Stables** (*see p120*) are on the Somerset side

of the water. Keep the boulder-strewn Badgworthy Water to your left as you walk through the deep-cut valley; it marks the county border.

After a third of a mile (500 metres), you will pass the **centenary stone** to author RD Blackmore, whose novel 'extols to all the world the joys of Exmoor'. It was erected by the Lorna Doone Centenary Committee in 1969. Follow the track through the mossy and stunted oaks of Yealscombe Wood and Badgworthy Wood before rising towards **Badgworthy Lees**. At the bend in the river cross a tributary that runs down from Great Black Hill. Continue for a third of a mile (500 metres) before crossing a lesser brook off Badgworthy Lees.

After a further third of a mile (500 metres) another stream and a path join from the right at Hoccombe Combe, beside the site of medieval **Badgworthy** (Lorna Doone's home) on the Devon side of the water. The cluster of cottages has now been reduced to lines and mounds in the bracken. Divert up the track for 750 feet (230 metres) to walk the grassy strip

Hall on the Esplanade. Nearby, the **Exmoor National Park Visitor Centre** (*see p126*) is housed in a 1930s pavilion. **Shelley's Cottage**, above the harbour, is one of two venues where the poet Percy Bysshe Shelley may have spent his honeymoon with bride Harriet in 1812.

A few hidden coves can be reached on foot in both directions from Lynmouth, and boat trips from the harbour (*see p125*) allow views of the less accessible parts of the coastline. The scenery beyond Lynton is spectacular inland as well as seawards, with the **Valley of Rocks** combining the best of both landscapes. Framed by craggy outcrops, it is arguably the most spectacular location on Exmoor. Castle Rock, towering above the coast road, is surrounded by a precipitous Tintagel-style curtain of rocks and looks just like a fortress. The Valley is reached on the coast path from Lynton, starting from Lee Road or North Walk.

Lee Abbey, a manor house above the crags of the Valley of the Rocks, served as a hotel and a preparatory school before becoming a monastic community at the end of World War II. On a promontory in the Abbey grounds, the clifftop folly of **Duty Point Tower** overlooks a popular rocky bathing beach at **Lee Bay**.

Further west, **Woody Bay** comprises a series of rounded headlands and rocky cliffs that dip into the sea. A ridiculously steep winding road climbs down through woodland to the lovely stony beach. It is certainly scenic but hardly the seaside spa that Colonel Benjamin Lake envisaged when he created hotels, guesthouses and a pier here in 1885. The project and the pier collapsed, both financially and physically. Woody Bay Hotel has since been gentrified as **Martinhoe Manor**, while the surrounding cliffs were bought by the National Trust in 1965. Access to the 790-foot (240-metre) **Martinhoe Beacon** is from a car park at Hunters Inn, on a five-mile (eight-kilometre) circular walk, via Highveer Point.

Above Woody Bay, the village of **Martinhoe**, surrounded by historic Martinhoe Common, is where Lorna Doone Ridd and three John Ridds have their gravestones. A few miles south, ancient **St Petrock's** church in the lovely village of **Parracombe** was saved from demolition by the intervention of John Ruskin and William Morris, despite being replaced by a Victorian church at the centre of the village. Not far from Parracombe are the perfectly preserved earthworks of **Holwell Castle**, a Norman motte-and-bailey fortress.

and have a look at the best of the two-roomed ruins, with paddocks on either side.

Then descend to the confluence of Hoccombe stream and Badgworthy Water. Continue to follow the main river southwards to a footbridge in half a mile (800 metres). Here, turn left, across the river, and set off on to the high moors, south-south-east towards Exford. Only proceed if the weather is good; conditions become elemental in fog, gales and snow; if in doubt, turn round and walk back to County Gate.

The onward course passes **Tom's Hill Barrows** and climbs **Great Tom's Hill**. Keep the stone wall to your right. The path gradually converges with it and goes through a gate. Bear left on the other side, heading south-east for just under half a mile (700 metres). Here you join a bridleway beside the fence and turn left along it. You are heading north and re-cross the wall in 1,300 feet (400 metres). Your course is now north-north-east, towards Oare, across **Manor Allotment**. (Allotments in these parts are exposed pastures rather than cabbage patches.)

Then go straight ahead across **Stowey Allotment** at 1,350 feet (411 metres) above sea level. Here, fork left, north-west, towards Oare (ignore the sign for Oareford). Keep straight on beside **Turf Allotment**, which is across the bank to your left.

After a little under half a mile (700 metres) go through the left-hand of the two gates above Withy Combe towards **Oare Common**, reaching **Cloud Allotment** after half a mile (800 metres). Stay on the west side of the bank, keeping it to your right, and proceed straight ahead for 900 feet (275 metres), through the gate near the corner.

You are now heading north; bear right to descend into **Oare**, emerging on the road, to the right of both the **Manor House** and **St Mary's Church**. This has a Blackmore memorial, complete with bearded caricature. After passing the church, turn right at the junction. Cross Oare Water at the medieval bridge and follow the lane uphill to the main road at **New Road Gate**. Turn left, walking westwards towards oncoming traffic, to return to **County Gate** in 1,200 feet (370 metres).

Watersmeet.
See p121.

The deep and wooded **Heddon Valley** stretches coastwards from Parracombe, past a National Trust Visitor Centre at scenic **Hunters Inn** (*see p126*), to a small, rocky beach at **Heddon's Mouth**. The old lime kiln on the beach is mentioned by Henry Williamson in *Tarka the Otter*.

Westwards is some of the most unspoilt coastline in the country, culminating at the **Hangman Hills** above Combe Martin. It's a tough hike to reach the summit of Great Hangman at 1,043 feet (318 metres), from where Girt Down extends north-east to a clifftop viewpoint at Blackstone Point, offering an awesome view across the Bristol Channel to the Gower peninsula. Continuing west, the coast path descends to Little Hangman (715 feet/218 metres) and Hangman Point, a rounded headland that shelters **Wild Pear Beach** at the western extreme of the National Park.

Lyn & Exmoor Museum

St Vincent's Cottage, Market Street, Lynton (01598 752225/www.devonmuseums.net/lynton). **Open** *Easter-Oct* 10am-12.30pm, 2-5pm Mon-Fri; 2-5pm Sun. Closed Nov-Mar. **Admission** phone for details.

Power of Water Exhibition

Glen Lyn Gorge, Lynmouth (01598 753207). **Open** *Easter-Oct* call for times. Closed Nov-Mar. **Admission** £3; £1.50 concessions.

Watersmeet House

Watersmeet Road, Lynmouth (01598 753348/ www.nationaltrust.org.uk). **Open** *Late Mar-Sept* 10.30am-5.30pm daily. *Oct-early Nov* 10.30am-4.30pm daily. Closed early Nov-late Mar. **Admission** free.

Activities

Boat trips

Exmoor Coast Boat Cruises (01598 752509) depart from Lynmouth harbour and are an excellent way of viewing the best of Exmoor's inaccessible, rugged coastline.

Riding

Explore the wide-open country beyond Lynton from **Outovercott Riding Stables** (New Mill Farm, Lynton, 01598 753341, www.outovercott.co.uk). More leisurely horse-drawn travel across the moor is provided by lovely, lumbering shire horses and wagons from **West Ilkerton Farm** (Barbrook, Lynton, 01598 752310).

Water, water everywhere

Thirty-four men, women and children died in the Lynmouth flood disaster on Friday, 15 August 1952. Exmoor had already received six inches (15 centimetres) of rain that month, saturating the ground; the death toll would have been higher but for the number of holidaymakers who cancelled their vacations and went home earlier in the week complaining about the atrocious weather. Incessant rain resumed at lunchtime, with some nine inches (23 centimetres) falling on the hills that funnel water into Lynmouth's narrow gorge. By 5pm both arms of the swollen River Lyn were threatening to burst their banks. An hour later, the Tors footbridge was swept away, followed by May Bridge as the debris reached the harbour. Utilities began to fail at 8pm when, despite the valiant efforts of engineers Reg Freeman and Charlie Postles, who were manning an emergency generator, the hydroelectric power station of Lynmouth Electric Light Company gave up the ghost. The power station was abandoned for ever at 9pm.

By this time, some 60 riverside properties in Barbrook and Lynmouth, including two Victorian hotels, had been destroyed, not just by the force of the water but by a battering surge of boulders, trees, telegraph poles, cars and the contents of houses further upstream.

Inland, people stood a better chance of escaping the worst of the floods, although bridges were ripped apart at Exford and Winsford. Even the great stones of Tarr Steps were swept away by the River Barle, with only one of its multiple sections remaining intact. Further downstream, two vans were washed seven miles (11 kilometres) down the valley as trees clogged Town Bridge at Dulverton, diverting the rapids through two cottages and the unsuspecting Golden Guernsey Milk Bar. To the west, the old railway embankment at Parracombe was breached, and the River Heddon gushed through the village, sweeping postman William Leaworthy to his death. The disaster was felt on a national scale too – the death toll included three Manchester scouts, who were swept from their tents beside Shallowford, on the River Bray at Filleigh. The body of another young holidaymaker was never identified.

Though much of the damage was repaired over the following years, Lynmouth would never look the same again. The old course of the river became a flood barrier at Riverside Road, with future waters redirected on a wider course through the town.

Where to eat, drink & stay

The National Trust has created superbly
situated refreshment rooms from the 19th-
century fishing lodge at **Watersmeet** (*see
p121*), but **Rocklyn Riverside Tea Garden**
(Tors Road, Lynmouth, 01598 753895, closed
late Dec) is perhaps even more alluring, set
in the gorge above the restored riverbank
of the River Lyn. Nearby **Shelley's Hotel**
(8 Watersmeet Road, Glen Lyn Gorge, 01598
753219, www.shelleyshotel.co.uk, double B&B
£59-£99) is another venue that claims to be
where the poet honeymooned in 1812. For the
best local seafood and game, try the **Rising
Sun Hotel** (01598 753223, www.risingsun
lynmouth.co.uk, main courses £16-£24, double
B&B £98-£148), a thatched smugglers' inn
on the harbourside that has been expanded
into a 16-bedroom complex, occupying several
adjoining cottages. Up the hill, **Lynton
Cottage Hotel** (North Walk, 01598 752342,
www.lynton-cottage.co.uk, closed late Dec-mid
Feb, set menus £20/£25, double B&B £79-
£140) is now much more than a cottage, with
16 ultra-frilly en suite rooms set in three acres.
The restaurant specialises in fresh Lynmouth
Bay lobsters.

At Martinhoe, the **Old Rectory Hotel**
(01598 763368, www.oldrectoryhotel.co.uk,
double B&B £90-£110) offers a relaxing stay
in traditional country-style rooms. The hotel
is set in extensive gardens, which are shared
with two self-catering cottages. Secluded self-
catering for groups is also provided by the
former **Heddon's Gate Hotel** near Hunters
Inn (01598 763313, www.hgate.co.uk, phone
for details).

Resources

Police station
Lynton *Lee Road (0870 577 7444).*

Post offices
Lynmouth *20 Lynmouth Street (01598 752333).*
Open 9am-5.30pm Mon-Thur; 9am-12.30pm Fri, Sat.
Lynton *Lee Road (01598 753313).* **Open** 8.15am-
5.30pm Mon-Fri; 8.15am-12.30pm Sat.

Tourist information
Hunters Inn *National Trust Visitor Centre,
Heddon Valley (01598 763402).* **Open** phone
for details.
Lynmouth *Exmoor National Park Visitor Centre,
The Esplanade (01598 752509/www.exmoor-
nationalpark.gov.uk).* **Open** phone for details.
Lynton *Lynton & Lynmouth Tourist Information
Centre, Town Hall, Lee Road (0845 660
3232/www.lyntourism.co.uk).* **Open** *Easter-Oct*
9.30am-5.30pm daily. *Nov-Easter* 10am-4pm Mon-
Sat; 10am-1pm Sun.

A riot of colour: **Countisbury Hill**. *See p121.*

Getting there & around

By bus
Southern National (01823 272033) runs services
(some seasonal) between Dunster, Minehead, Porlock,
Lynton and inland destinations. Buses can be flagged
down at any safe point on their journey.

By train
The most characterful way of arriving in Dunster
and Minehead is on the **West Somerset Railway**
from Bishops Lydeard (01643 707650, www.west-
somerset-railway.co.uk).

Inland Exmoor

The first thing you have to realise when
exploring Exmoor by car is that there are
few proper roads. Beyond the inadequate
skeleton of A and B routes, a third tier of
tortuous single-track lanes go up, down and
around, often bringing you back quite close
to where you started, while a fourth category
take you into a realm of scenic impossibilities
at deep fords, rutted bedrock or gates into
nowhere. Many serve a secondary purpose as
water-courses in a landscape where the annual
inland rainfall is almost twice that of the
adjoining coast.

Somerset

If you're setting out on foot, you should only hit the high moor after a favourable weather forecast. Better still, tune into the shipping forecast on Radio 4 (198 LW) and listen for Lundy, since going far into the hills is much like venturing out to sea. You need light winds (force 5 or below), no rain, and good visibility. If in doubt, don't venture out.

Exmoor Forest

Incorporating much of the highest and wildest terrain in the National Park, Exmoor Forest – a former royal hunting preserve – is reminiscent of the highlands of Scotland in places, with immense glens, the odd pine clump, and hardly a cosy cottage in sight. The rivers and streams are bubbly and sparkling; ravens croak, buzzards mew, dippers dart and deer rut. Man-made marks on the landscape are occasional and generally redundant, such as the once-palisaded entrenchment of **Cow Castle**, an Iron Age settlement on a conical hilltop between Simonsbath and Braddymoor.

At the very heart of the moor, the hamlet of **Simonsbath** has always been considered Somerset's wild west. Pronounced 'Simmuns-bath', the settlement was named after Sigmund, a legendary Danish leader, who aided Celtic resistance against the Saxons. Until the 19th century, the high moor surrounding Simonsbath was a barren no-man's land caught between parishes, and the village itself was not much more than Simonsbath House, built by James Boevey in 1654, and now a hotel (*see p128*). In 1808, 15,500 acres of the surrounding moor were sold to Midland ironmaker John Knight, who proceeded to create a mining community here to extract iron and copper from the headwaters of the River Barle. The Knights' legacy includes the former vicarage below the Victorian church of St Luke.

West towards Parracombe, adjoining look-alike moors and blanket bogs stretch either side of the **Chains** ridge, comprising the largest wilderness area south of Yorkshire. The focal point in this isolated landscape is **Pinkworthy Pond** (pronounced 'pinkery'), a desolate, half-empty lake behind a great embankment, which was created in 1830 to power John Knight's industrial enterprises. Across miles of deer sedge and the occasional heath spotted orchid, Bronze Age barrows and standing stones run along the ancient ridgeway, blending into the landscape and disappearing whenever hill-fog and clouds descend (which they do with alarming frequency). The best known is the **Longstone** north of Challacombe, which marks the source of the River Bray and is Exmoor's tallest standing stone. Further west is the

largest group of Bronze Age burial mounds on the moor at **Chapman Barrows**, while to the east, **Chains Barrow**, between Exe Head and Pinkworthy Pond, is the highest point in the area at 1,599 feet (487 metres), and offers far-reaching views on clear days.

East of Simonsbath on the B3223, **Exford** has long been an important crossing point on the River Exe, originally for packhorses transporting wool and cloth across the moor. Today the village is chiefly significant as the base for the **Devon & Somerset Staghounds**; like it or not, Exmoor was created as a medieval hunting ground, and there is still strong support for the hunt in this area. Red deer are Britain's largest native animal, and as herbivores, rather than predators, their hunting by dogs is particularly controversial. This became an issue for the National Trust in 1990, which subsequently banned stag-hunting on most of its land. The League Against Cruel Sports has also bought some 1,200 acres of Exmoor to establish hunt-free wildlife sanctuaries and there are now an estimated 4,750 red deer living in the National Park. Even so, hunting accounts for the death of nearly 100 stags a year during the autumn and spring seasons, with poaching, shooting and traffic accidents responsible for far larger numbers of fatalities.

Hunting aside, Exford makes a good starting point for ascents of **Dunkery Beacon**, the highest point on the moor. Having made much of Exmoor's inaccessibility, it has to be admitted that this superlative Somerset peak is relatively easy to reach. Four miles' (six and a half kilometres') walk north-east of Exford on the National Trust's Holnicote Estate, Dunkery Beacon rises from the heather-clad roof of Exmoor, with a cone-like cairn at 1,704 feet (519 metres). It rewards with a panoramic view that takes in the Bristol Channel and the coast of Wales to the north, the Quantock and Brendon Hills to the east, and the uplands of Somerset and Devon to south, extending as far as Dartmoor.

The northern slopes of Dunkery Beacon, two miles (three kilometres) south of the A39 and accessed by footpaths from a car park at Webber's Post, embrace **Horner Wood National Nature Reserve**, created by English Nature in 1995. The lush woods and moors here are the home range of the main red deer herds on Exmoor and also have the biggest and rarest lichen list in the British Isles. Bird life is also prolific in the nature reserve, from buzzards and ravens to pied flycatchers and wood warblers. On the edge of the wood, visit the pretty, Exmoor village of **Luccombe** and the traditional **Domesday Mill Pottery** at Wootton Courtenay (01643 841297).

Activities

Fishing

Nick Hart (01643 831101, www.hartflyfishing. demon.co.uk) is a fly-fishing expert who can transform even the most inept rod-handler into a casting king.

Landrover tours

Exmoor Safaris (01643 831229, www.exmoor-hospitality-inns.co.uk) offers off-road nature-spotting tours of the moor, departing from the Exmoor White Horse Inn in Exford (*see below*).

Riding

Catering for novices and children, **Burrowhayes Farm Riding Stables** (West Luccombe, 01643 862463, www.burrowhayes.co.uk) also has a caravan park and campsite.

Where to eat, drink & stay

Simonsbath House Hotel (01643 831259, www.simonsbathhouse.co.uk, closed late Dec, set menu £25, double B&B £75-£95) is a great choice for spacious accommodation and grand views. **Boevey's Tea Rooms** (01643 831622, closed Dec, Jan) in the barn next door does a good line in lunches and teas. It's also worth venturing south to Yarde Down, along the road between Simonsbath and South Molton, where you'll find the **Poltimore Arms** (01598 710381, closed Mon in winter, main courses £5.75-£9.25). This pub serves up real ales, decent home-cooked grub and is run entirely on a generator.

Stockleigh Lodge (Exford, 01643 831500, www.stockleighexford.freeserve.co.uk, double £45-£50) makes a good base for riding and exploring, with stabling for its equine guests and nine flouncy en suite bedrooms for their riders. For a dependable first-class dinner, try the **Crown Hotel** (Exford, 01643 831554, www.crownhotelexmoor.co.uk, set menu £29.50, double B&B £95-£110), which combines the relaxing air of a country club with a village setting. Also in Exford is the **Exmoor White Horse Inn** (01643 831229, www.exmoor-hospitality-inns.co.uk, main courses £11.25-£17.25, double B&B £80), which has expanded from a historic moorland hostelry into a comfortable hotel serving decent bar meals.

Exmoor's main **youth hostel** is near the centre of Exford (01643 831288, closed Wed-Sun from Nov to mid Feb, dorm bed £8.25-£11.50). For those who want to do it themselves, there's **Westermill Farm** (01643 831238), just outside the village, which has self-catering in log cabins (from £150 per week), plus a small campsite for tents (£4 per person per night).

The southern moor

Bridges are the strategic objectives on any progress across Exmoor. Many of the area's place names are simply for this or that river or stream crossed by a bridge or ford. In the village of **Withypool**, south of Exford, six medieval arches span the beautiful River Barle, while a couple of miles upstream the river is crossed by solitary **Landacre Bridge** (pronounced 'Lannaker') as it runs through Withypool Common. The bridge's picturesque setting and resident Exmoor ponies make this a somewhat over-popular picnic site on sunny days.

The most famous Exmoor bridge, though, is **Tarr Steps** south of Withypool. With 17 spans and a length of 180 feet (54 metres), this is the longest and best example of a primitive clapper bridge. A sophisticated form of stepping stones, Tarr Steps evolved into a series of stone piers held together by megalithic capstones weighing up to two tonnes apiece. During the flash-flood of August 1952 most of the stones were hurled downstream and had to be painstakingly replaced; they have now been numbered in case it happens again.

From Tarr Steps a number of lovely walks allow exploration of the area's ancient woodland, upstream to Withypool, east to Winsford Hill (*see below*) or downstream to **Dulverton**, on the southern edge of the moor. Claiming to be the 'Gateway to Exmoor', this small town is the site of the National Park Authority Headquarters (*see p117*) and of an **Exmoor National Park Visitor Centre** (*see p130*), which has a small permanent exhibition on Exmoor life. Behind the visitor centre, the **Guildhall Heritage Centre** (Monmouth Terrace, 01398 323841, closed Nov-Mar, free) houses the town museum with local exhibits from the turn of the 19th century and an art gallery of moorland images. In 1997 Dulverton was used as the setting for *Land Girls*, which told the story of the Women's Land Army during World War II.

Having drifted apart, the Exe and the Barle rivers from the high moor join up in the valley below Dulverton. Between March and September salmon run upstream, jumping weirs on the Exe to reach the spawning shingles high on the moor. For part of its length, their route is shadowed by the A396, which heads north towards Dunster. The village of **Winsford**, just west of the main road, is one of the prettiest settlements on Exmoor, with thatched cottages, a village green and several bridges crossing its numerous waterways. From here it's a pleasant hike west to the summit of **Winsford Hill** (1,400 feet/427 metres) and on to Tarr Steps, passing the ancient **Caratacus Stone** en route, which dates from the fifth or sixth century AD.

Activities

Landrover tours

Barle Valley Safaris (01643 851386) offers off-road nature-spotting tours of the moor, departing from the Exmoor House Hotel in Dulverton.

Where to eat, drink & stay

The former landlord of the **Royal Oak Inn** at Withypool (01643 831506, www.royaloak withypool.co.uk, main courses £7.50-£15.50) was an MI5 spy-master, who provided Ian Fleming with a model for James Bond. Despite this claim to fame, the pub remains warm and welcoming, with one of the best fish menus on the moor. Downstream, **Tarr Farm** (Liscombe, Dulverton, 01643 851507, main courses £8.95-£18.75) offers lunch and cream teas but makes its reputation with salmon and steaks for dinner.

Lewis's Tearooms in Dulverton (13 High Street, 01398 323850, main courses £3.50-£6) offers English breakfast, homemade lunches and cream teas. The **Lion Hotel** (Bank Square, 01398 323444, main courses £5.95-£10.25, double B&B £59) also does good pub grub and has a few beamed guest rooms. Excellent-value accommodation is provided at **Town Mills** off the High Street (01398 323124, www.town millsdulverton.co.uk, double B&B £48-£56), a Georgian millhouse with a laid-back atmosphere.

Pick of the places to stay in this area, though, is **Ashwick House** (01398 323868, www.ashwick house.co.uk, double B&B £84-£98), a large pile set in six acres of grounds above the River Barle, with comfy rooms and an upmarket menu.

At **Highercombe Farm**, (B3223, near Dulverton, 01398 323616, www.highercombe. demon.co.uk, closed Nov-Feb, double B&B £44-£54) you will wake up to deer, farm animals and delicious views. Both B&B and self-catering accommodation are available here, and evening meals can be provided. Further north, the cosy **Exton House Hotel** at Exton (01643 851365, set menu £18.75, double B&B £78-£97 incl dinner) is housed in a former rectory; local produce dominates the menu.

Self-catering options include the cottages at **West Hollowcombe** (Hawkridge, 01398 341400, www.exmoorselfcatering.co.uk), where the owners offer dinner followed by escorted deer-watching on the moor.

Resources

Internet

Winsford *Community Computer Centre, Old School (01643 851594/www.winsfordcentre.org.uk).* **Open** noon-8pm Mon; 9am-5pm Tue, Thur; 5-8pm Wed.

Post office

Withypool *Village Shop (01643 831178).* **Open** 8.30am-1pm Mon, Tue, Thur, Fri.

Somerset

Is anybody there? The wide-open spaces of **Exmoor Forest**. *See p127.*

Tourist information

Dulverton *Exmoor National Park Visitor Centre, 7-9 Fore Street, Dulverton (01398 323841/ www.exmoor-nationalpark.gov.uk).* **Open** *Apr-Oct* 10am-1.15pm, 1.45-5pm daily. *Nov-Mar* 10.30am-3.30pm daily.

Brendon Hills

From the Exe valley, the A396 heads north to **Wheddon Cross**, where it joins an older ridgeway, the B3224, which cuts west through the wilderness of Exmoor Forest and climbs east through the **Brendon Hills**.

From mine workings on the hills, iron ore was transported down the **West Somerset Mineral Railway**, which ran parallel to the present B3224 and then north to Watchet harbour and on to the blast furnaces of Ebbw Vale. The 12-mile (19-kilometre) line operated until 1898 with a partial revival in 1907 before its rails were lifted during World War I. A remarkable winch house lowered the trucks down a one-in-four incline (just west of Ralegh Cross) from the Brendon Hills to the hamlets of Comberow and Roadwater. One of the Cornish-style engine houses survives, just south of the B3224 near Burrow Farm.

Heading east to the junction of the B3190, a medieval wayside cross gives some character to the bland buildings of the corporate-style Ralegh's Cross Inn. Beyond are Iron Age remains at **Elworthy Burrows** and fantastic walking territory at **Combe Sydenham Country Park**. On the far eastern edge of the National Park, this is an area of beautiful woodland criss-crossed with ten miles (16 kilometres) of paths and nature trails. At the heart of the park is a 16th-century manor house that was home to Elizabeth Sydenham, second wife of Sir Francis Drake. Infrequent guided tours of the west wing of the house and of the medieval corn mill are offered in summer.

In the southern folds of the Brendon Hills is Exmoor's modern lakeland. **Wimbleball Lake** is a 375-acre reservoir supplied by the River Haddeo. South are the wooded slopes of Haddon Hill, while at the northern end a nature reserve surrounds Bessom Bridge, with paths extending for about ten miles (16 kilometres) around most of the shore. Further east, **Clatworthy Reservoir** has a fishing lodge and picnic site on its western shore; a formidable Iron Age hill-fort overlooks the lake from the other side.

Combe Sydenham Country Park

Monksilver, nr Taunton (01984 656284). **Open** *Park* Easter-Sept 9am-5pm daily. *House* phone for details. Closed Oct-Mar. **Admission** *Park* free; £5 vehicle charge. *House* £5; £2.50 concessions. **No credit cards.**

Activities

Fishing

Brown and rainbow trout can be caught on **Clatworthy Reservoir** from late March to mid October (01984 624658). **Wimbleball Lake** has a reputation for rainbow trout fishing, with permits and boats available from **Hill Farm** (01398 371372).

Riding

This is the easy end of Exmoor horse country, with the most comfortable base being **Knowle Manor Riding Centre** (Timbercombe, 01643 841342), a country house set in 100 acres. Facilities include a cross-country course with tuition for all abilities.

Sailing

Day visitors with their own dinghies are welcome at **Wimbleball Sailing Club** (01278 652146, www.users.zetnet.co.uk/wsc) on the west side of Wimbleball Lake. RYA instruction is also available.

Where to eat, drink & stay

Exmoor House (Wheddon Cross (01643 841432, www.exmoorhotel.co.uk, closed Dec & Jan, set menu £18, double B&B £55-£64) offers bright, comfy rooms and delicious home cooking. Outside the village, **Raleigh Manor** (01643 841484, www.raleighmanorhotel.co.uk, closed mid Dec-Jan, double B&B £62-£82.50) is a finely positioned Victorian villa with extensive views, providing local cuisine and fine wines. Fab B&B is offered at **West Mill** (Luckwell Bridge, 01643 841896, closed late Dec-early Jan, double B&B £50), a converted mill surrounded by glorious countryside.

In the Brendon Hills, the **Royal Oak** at Luxborough (01984 640319, double £65-£85) is an old-fashioned pub serving real ales and authentic country cooking. In the hills above the lakes of Wimbleball and Clatworthy, **Lowtrow Cross Inn** at Upton (01398 371220, www.lowtrowcross.co.uk, main courses £6.50-£13.95) does a mean fish pie. There's also a **campsite** (01398 371372, closed Oct-Apr) on the shores of Wimbleball Lake.

Resources

Post office

Wheddon Cross (01643 841235). **Open** 9am-5.30pm Mon, Wed-Fri; 9am-1pm Tue; 9am-12.30pm Sat.

Getting there & around

By bus

Southern National (01823 272033) provides a variety of local bus services (some seasonal) between Exford, Dulverton, Winsford and coastal destinations. Buses can be flagged down at any point on their journey.

Devon

Introduction

Devon, glorious Devon.

Since the early 19th century Devon has been the destination of choice for England's holidaying hordes, and its easy to see why. This large, diamond-shaped county has got pretty much everything the visitor could desire: instantly appealing countryside, fantastic beaches, well-established resorts, dramatic cliffs, cutesy villages, wild moorland – and even a couple of decent-sized cities, just to make sure you don't get too engrossed in the rural idyll. In **Plymouth** you'll find evidence of the county's illustrious seafaring heritage – not to mention an excellent aquarium, while in **Exeter** a Norman cathedral watches over a pleasing provincial city that eschews parochialism in favour of a lively arts scene and a laid-back student vibe.

Victorian resorts of varying size and appeal are strung along Devon's south coast, culminating at **Torquay**, the county's premier tourist destination. With its palm trees, prom and bucket spades, this Regency town is the archetype of the English seaside holiday, but there's more to Devon's coastal resorts than meets the eye: Torquay attracts young clubbers as well as ageing golfers, while **Sidmouth** hosts an international music festival in summer.

What's more, these tourist towns are far from being the whole story. In East Devon, fossil hunters and families will find plenty to entertain them on the unique sandstone **Jurassic Coast**, while west of Torbay rivers flow through the gorgeous countryside of the **South Hams** to the sea. Highlights in this area include the charming port of **Dartmouth**, the beach-fringed estuary at **Salcombe** and mile upon mile of heart-stopping scenery along the South West Coast Path.

The **North Devon** coast has a different appeal, with Exmoor's rocky coves giving way to expansive beaches that are pounded by the Atlantic ocean. A burgeoning surf scene animates the coastal villages of **Woolacombe** and **Croyde**, fisherman and tourists co-exist in steepling **Clovelly**, while the isolated outposts of **Morte Point**, **Hartland Point** and **Lundy Island** offer a uniquely elemental, back-to-nature experience.

Inland, Devon's rural heartland remains largely unruffled by the waves of tourism that surge towards the coast. In **East Devon** and **Mid Devon** you'll find a way of life determined by seasons rather than the demands of the visitor. Rolling hills create gentle, fertile landscapes where the grass seems greener and the skies bluer than anywhere else in the country. And finally, of course, there's **Dartmoor**, where prehistoric remains and shaggy ponies compete for your attention with acres of wild, unspoiled moorland.

Don't miss Devon

Croyde
The surfers' favourite: great beach, lively village, good pubs. *See p138.*

Grimspound
Dartmoor's most extensive and evocative Bronze Age site. *See p173.*

Hartland Point
Isolated and exhilarating. *See p143.*

Jurassic Coast
Fossick for fossils or just hang out on the beach. *See p158.*

Lundy
Escape from the 21st century to this wild granite island. *See p144.*

River trip on the Dart
It doesn't get much more idyllic than this. *See p194.*

Salcombe
A sugared-almond-coloured delight surrounded by the county's most beautiful coastal scenery. *See p197.*

North & Mid Devon

Top surfing spots, glorious walking country and charming market towns.

Heading west along the North Devon coast, the inaccessible rocky coves of the Bristol Channel give way to the wide sandy reaches of the Atlantic seaboard. Stunning beaches at **Woolacombe**, **Croyde**, **Saunton** and **Westward Ho!** attract visitors of all ages, who come to build castles in the sand, surf the rollers or explore the spectacular coast path. Although it's generally less touristy than South Devon, there are flurries of high-season activity around the surfing beaches, the Victorian resort of **Ilfracombe** and the picturesque coastal village of **Clovelly**.

The unassuming market town of **Barnstaple** is the area's transport hub and the focal point of the **Tarka Trail**, a long-distance walking and cycling route that takes in some of the region's most appealing scenery (*see below* **Tarka territory**), including the little-visited region of **Mid Devon** at the centre of the county. Characterised by rolling hills, fertile arable land and hidden hamlets, this pristine area is a prime example of quintessential English countryside.

Barnstaple & around

Situated at the head of the Taw estuary, **Barnstaple** is one of the oldest towns in the country, having been awarded its borough charter by King Athelstan over 1,000 years ago. By medieval times the town had developed into a prosperous port for the wool trade – the Long Bridge, which crosses the River Taw, dates from this time – a role that it continued to fulfil until the silting-up of the river in the 19th century. In the Victorian age the town became known for its red-clay pottery, known as Barum ware. It's still produced at the **Brannam Pottery** (01271 343035) on the outskirts of town, which offers guided tours for visitors as well as a pottery shop and small museum.

Close to the river, colonnaded **Queen Anne's Walk** is where 18th-century merchants conducted their business, shaking hands on a deal over the Tome Stone. The stone is now on display in front of the **Barnstaple Heritage Centre**, which has an interactive exhibition

Tarka territory

Just after the World War I the writer Henry Williamson abandoned London life in favour of a rented cottage near Georgeham in North Devon. Living almost like a hermit, he spent much of his time rambling through the countryside observing nature, and also looked after an otter cub whose mother had been shot. The otter thrived under his care until one day it caught its paw in a rabbit gin, almost severing three of its toes. Williamson managed to free the otter, but, driven by pain and fear, it escaped from its rescuer and disappeared.

Williamson tramped the river banks of the Torridge and the Taw in vain searching for the otter's distinctive tracks, and from his experiences, the story of *Tarka the Otter* (1927) was born. This evocative piece of nature writing has over the years become synonymous with North Devon.

The name Tarka has since been adopted for a railway line, a walking and cycling route, not to mention dozens of teashops

throughout the region. The **Tarka Line** between Exeter and Barnstaple follows the Taw river through countryside that has barely changed since Williamson's day, calling at rural stations with access to huge tracts of unspoiled Devon scenery.

Alight at Eggesford to join the 180-mile (290-kilometre) **Tarka Trail**, a recreational walking and cycling route that loops in a figure of eight from Barnstaple south to the rural heartland of the county, north to the beaches and cliffs of the North Devon coast and east into Exmoor. The waymarked trail is a great way to explore the varied scenery of North and Mid Devon, with easy access points along the route. For 32 miles (51 kilometres) between Braunton and Meeth the trail follows a disused railway line – a flat, traffic-free route that's perfect for cycling.

For further information contact the tourist offices in Barnstaple, Bideford or Great Torrington, or consult the website www.tarka.org.uk.

Devon

area detailing the town's history, including a reconstruction of a Saxon interior and a near life-size medieval market.

At the end of the Strand is the former site of Barnstaple's 11th-century castle. According to the Domesday Book, 23 houses were laid waste for its construction, but all there is to see now is a grassy mound and a modern library building. From here, flagstoned alleys lead to the town's main shopping area around the High Street, where the half-timbered storeys of the Tudor **Three Tuns** pub hang out over the road.

Butting on to the High Street is the **Pannier Market Hall**, an expansive vaulted building supported by graceful archways, where a markets has been held since 1855. Craft sales take place on Mondays and Thursdays from April to December, with general markets on Tuesdays, Fridays and Saturdays, and antiques markets on Wednesdays throughout the year. Opposite the pannier market is **Butchers Row**, a line of quaint open-fronted shops selling everything from traditional meats and laver (a local seaweed delicacy) to clotted cream and exotic breads.

South of Butchers Row, a cobbled, tree-lined area surrounds the parish church and **St Anne's Chapel**, which dates back to the 14th century, but was used as the town's grammar school from the 16th century until the 1920s.

Boutport Street is home to more shops, restaurants and inns, a multi-screen cinema and the **Queen's Theatre** (01271 324242), whose proud history as a significant regional venue stretches back to 1834. North Devon's reputation as a region for the arts has grown in recent years, with the **North Devon Festival** (01271 324242, www.northdevonfestival.org) combining intrinsically local events such as strawberry fairs with theatre performances by international names. The town is also noted for its over-the-top floral displays, which have achieved international recognition.

As the transport and commercial hub for North Devon, Barnstaple makes a good base from which to explore the surrounding countryside and coast. Just north of town, the **Broomhill Sculpture Gardens** encompass seven acres of wooded grounds dotted with figurative and abstract sculptures, ranging from a vast red stiletto by Greta Berlin to carved alder stumps by Giles Kent. Inside, the gallery hosts temporary exhibitions by local and national artists. There's also a restaurant and accommodation on site (*see p137*). Nearby, enjoy a ramble through rare trees and shrubs at **Marwood Hill Gardens**.

The A39 leads out of Barnstaple towards Exmoor, skirting the 3,500-acre National Trust-owned **Arlington Court Estate**, where Jacob sheep and Shetland ponies keep the grass in check, and herons and other waterbirds hang out around a lake.

At the heart of the estate is a neo-classical Victorian manor built in 1822 for the Chichester family. The gloriously cluttered interior has Regency and Victorian furniture, plus masses of intriguing *objets* collected by Rosalie Chichester (1865-1949) on her travels around the world. Elsewhere, check out Devon's largest colony of Lesser Horseshoe bats via the 'batcam' located in the basement.

Stiletto sculpture, **Broomhill Sculpture Gardens.**

Arlington Court

Arlington, nr Barnstaple (01271 850296). **Open**
House Apr-Oct 11am-5pm Mon, Wed-Sun. *Gardens
& carriages* Apr-June 10.30am-5pm Mon, Wed-Sun.
July, Aug 10.30am-4.30pm daily. Sept, Oct 10.30am-
5pm Mon, Wed-Sun. Closed Nov-Mar. **Admission**
House & garden £5.80; £2.90 concessions; £14.50
family. *Garden & carriages* £3.80; £1.90 concessions.
Credit MC, V.

Barnstaple Heritage Centre

*Queen Anne's Walk, The Strand, Barnstaple (01271
373003/www.devonmuseums.net).* **Open** *Apr-
Oct* 10am-5pm Mon-Sat. *Nov-Mar* 10am-4.30pm
Mon-Fri; 10am-3.30pm Sat. **Admission** £2.50; £2
concessions; £7.50 family. **Credit** AmEx, MC, V.

Broomhill Sculpture Gardens & Gallery

*B3230, nr Barnstaple (01271 850262/
www.broomhillart.co.uk).* **Open** *May, June, Sept,
Oct* 11am-4pm Wed-Sun. *July, Aug* 11am-6pm
Wed, Thur; 11am-4pm Fri-Sun. *Nov-Apr* noon-4pm
Thur-Sun. **Admission** £4.50; £3.50 concessions.
No credit cards.

Marwood Hill Gardens

*Marwood, nr Barnstaple (01271 342528/
www.marwoodhillgardens.co.uk).* **Open** dawn-
dusk daily. **Admission** £3. **Credit** MC, V.

Activities

Cycling

Bikes can be hired from **Tarka Trail Cycle Hire**
(Railway Station, Barnstaple, 01271 324202).

Where to eat, drink & stay

Barnstaple's dining scene remains largely
provincial and unambitious. Decent choices
include **Jalapeno Peppers** (Maiden Street,
Barnstaple, 01271 328877, main courses £5.95-
£13.95), which serves Mexican-style food,
while **62 The Bank** (62 Boutport Street,
01271 324446, main courses £7.95-£15.95) is
a good-quality bistro. It adjoins the bow-fronted
Royal & Fortescue Hotel (01271 342289,
www.brend-hotels.co.uk, double £52-£72),
a former coaching inn with traditional
accommodation and service.

North of town, **Broomhill Art Hotel
& Restaurant** (*see also p136*; set dinner
£14.95, double B&B £60) offers accommodation
in seven airy rooms. Guests have free access to
the gallery and sculpture gardens, and use of a
heated outdoor swimming pool. The restaurant
serves Mediterranean and Modern British food
and has jazz performances on some evenings.

South of Barnstaple, **Highbullen Hotel,
Golf & Country Club** (Chitlehamholt, 01769
540561, www.highbullen.co.uk, main courses
£25, double B&B £150-£190 incl dinner and

unlimited golf) is set in 200 acres of wooded
parkland and is all geared up for the active
visitor with its own 18-hole golf course, salmon
and trout fishing, swimming pools, tennis
courts, fitness suite and spa. The best rooms
are in the main building. At nearby Burrington
is **Northcote Manor Country House Hotel**
(01769 560501, set dinner £35, double B&B
£135-£180), an 18th-century country house
with local ingredients on the menu.

Resources

Hospital

North Devon District Hospital *Raleigh Park,
Barnstaple (01271 375000).*

Internet

Surfdotcom Café *4 Market Street, Barnstaple
(01271 378866).* **Open** 10am-5pm Mon-Sat.

Police station

North Walk, Barnstaple (0870 577 7444).

Post office

39-40 Boutport Street, Barnstaple (08457 223344).
Open 8.30am-5.30pm Mon, Tue; 9am-5.30pm Wed,
Fri; 8.45am-5.30pm Thur; 9am-12.30pm Sat.

Tourist information

Barnstaple Tourist Information Centre
The Square, Barnstaple (01271 375000).
Open 9.30am-5pm Mon-Sat.

From Braunton to Morthoe

From Barnstaple the A361 passes through
Braunton en route to the beaches and surf
of the Atlantic coast. Today the town is a
combination of cob-walled cottages, 1930s
villas, retirement bungalows and shops selling
wetsuits and surfboards, but for information
on its agricultural and maritime past, check
out the modest **Braunton Museum**.

On the edge of the town, the 340-acre **Great
Field** is one of only two surviving examples
of medieval strip farming in the country. The
most striking natural attraction, though, are
the eerily beautiful **Braunton Burrows**, the
largest area of sand dunes in the UK. Stretching
for about four miles (six kilometres) along the
shore, these high dunes of perfect golden sand
were designated a UNESCO Biosphere Reserve
in November 2002.

Near the estuary mouth, the dunes roll down
to the beach at **Broadsands** – a perfect spot
for a picnic, as long as you ignore the high-
speed jets from RAF Chivenor screaming
overhead. To the north the Burrows back on
to a huge expanse of privately owned beach at
Saunton Sands, with the coast path tracking
inland behind the dunes. You have to trek for

Devon

Braunton Burrows. *See p137.*

miles to reach the sea when the tide's out but the regular waves make it a good spot for novice surfers. Beach sports such as kite buggying and land yachting are banned, but you'll see plenty of kites making the most of stiff Atlantic breezes.

North of here narrow Devon lanes afford spectacular views out across Barnstaple (or Bideford) Bay and the Atlantic ocean. The road dips, weaves, curves and climbs between abundant hedgerows before reaching **Croyde**, an attractive village that successfully combines traditional charm with a youthful, surfing vibe. The thatched cottages are interspersed with vibrant pubs and a clutch of surf shops, ready to make the most of the waves that roll in at Croyde's golden beach (*see p140* **Surf check**). In summer there is a definite buzz to Croyde, with plenty of salty-haired boarders hanging around in peeled-off wetsuits. At the north end of the bay, precipitous **Baggy Point** affords astounding ocean views and challenging cliffs for rock climbing. If this all sounds far too energetic, you can also sample wicked Devon clotted cream ice-creams and fudge at the **Old Cream Shop** (01271 890425).

The wide embrace of Morte Bay offers the serious surfer, the holidaying family or the keen walker a superb two-mile (three-kilometre) stretch of fine, golden sand at **Woolacombe**. The beach has won awards for its cleanliness, water quality and facilities, and hosts an annual sand-castle competition in July.

Woolacombe Beach can get very crowded in high season, so for a quieter stretch of sand head to **Putsborough** at the south end of the bay or north to a brace of smaller sandy coves: **Barricane** is designated as a Site of Special Scientific Interest because of the colourful shells that are washed up here, while **Grunta Beach**

is named after a cargo of pigs that once ran aground offshore. The coves are backed by a tract of wild National Trust coastline that extends to **Morte Point** and beyond. Surrounded by treacherous offshore reefs at the interface of the Bristol Channel and the wide-open Atlantic, this imposing headland offers some of the most exhilarating coastal scenery in the county, including a lovely cove at **Rockham Bay**, reached via a long flight of steps.

Inland, the tiny village of **Mortehoe** clings limpet-like to the hog-backed hillside and makes a useful base from which to explore the coast path. For a break from nature's grandeur, check out the **Mortehoe Heritage Centre**, a small, family-friendly local history museum.

Braunton Museum
Bakehouse Centre, Caen Street, Braunton (01271 816688/www.devonmuseums.net). **Open** *Easter-Oct* 10am-5pm Mon-Sat. *Nov-Mar* 10am-4pm Mon-Sat. **Admission** free.

Mortehoe Heritage Centre
Mortehoe, Woolacombe (01271 870028/ www.devonmuseums.net). **Open** *Apr-June, Oct, Sept* 10am-3pm Mon-Thur, Sun. *July, Aug* 10am-6pm daily. **Admission** £1; 85p concessions; £2 family. **No credit cards**.

Activities

Golf
The two 18-hole championship links courses at **Saunton Golf Club** (01271 812436, www.saunton golf.co.uk) are open to visitors with the required handicap. Tee times should be booked in advance.

Surfing
Undoubtedly the best surf shop in the area is the **Little Pink Shop** (7 Moor Lane, Croyde, 01271 890453, www.littlepinkshop.com), which provides

daily web reports on local conditions as well as renting and selling everything a surfer could need. First-timers looking for lessons should get in touch with BSA-approved surf schools such as **Surf South West** (Croyde Bay, 01271 890400, www.surfsouthwest.com) or **Surfseekers Surf School** (Woolacombe, mobile 07977 924588, www.northdevon.co.uk/surfseekers). *See also p140* **Surf check**.

Where to eat, drink & stay

Saunton Sands Hotel (Saunton, 01271 890212, www.sauntonsands.com, double B&B £176-£238 incl dinner) has marvellous views over the bay and beaches, and a full range of leisure facilities including squash and tennis courts and indoor and outdoor pools. For food, **Squires Fish Restaurant** (Exeter Road, Braunton, 01271 815533, main courses £3-£6.25) is a decent seafood choice in Braunton.

Croyde has several eating and drinking options. The **Manor House Inn** (St Mary's Road, 01271 890241, www.themanorcroyde.com, main courses £5.50-£14.95) is a traditional village pub serving decent food, while **Hobbs Bistro** (6 Hobbs Hill, 01271 890256, closed Jan) is a well-regarded local restaurant. Nearby, the **Thatch Inn** (14 Hobbs Hill, 01271 890349, main courses £5.95-£12.95, double £45-£60) provides hearty pub meals (and copious booze) to the surfers who flock here in the evenings, plus accommodation for those who want to get an early start on the beach.

Further north, the **Woolacombe Bay Hotel** (01271 870388, www.woolacombe-bay-hotel.co.uk, closed Jan-early Feb, set meal £25, double B&B £120-£250 incl dinner) is set in its own grounds alongside the beach and has extensive facilities, including heated pools. An even more stunning setting is enjoyed by the traditional **Watersmeet Hotel** (Mortehoe, Woolacombe, 01271 870333, www.watersmeethotel.co.uk, set menu £29, double B&B £166-£262 incl dinner), which has panoramic views out to Lundy Island and private access to Combesgate Beach. There's fine cuisine in the restaurant here, but for a livelier atmosphere head to the **Red Barn** (Woolacombe Beach, 01271 870264), where you'll find plenty of surf-minded punters.

Resources

Internet
Braunton *Braunton Library, Chaloners Road (01271 388622).* **Open** 9.30am-7pm Mon; 9.30am-5pm Wed-Fri; 9.30am-1pm Tue, Sat.

Police station
Braunton *Station Road (0870 577 7444).*

Post office
Woolacombe *3 West Road (no phone).* **Open** 9am-5.30pm Mon, Tue, Thur, Fri; 9am-1pm Wed, Sat.

Tourist information
Braunton *Tourist Information Centre, The Bakehouse Centre (01271 816400).* **Open** *Apr-June, Sept, Oct* 10am-4pm Mon-Sat. *July, Aug* 10am-5pm daily. *Nov-Mar* 10am-3pm Mon-Sat.
Woolacombe *Tourist Information Centre, The Esplanade, Woolacombe (01271 870553/ www.woolacombe.tourism.com).* **Open** *Apr-Oct* 10am-6pm daily. *Nov-Mar* 10am-1pm Mon-Sat.

Ilfracombe & around

North Devon's premier resort, **Ilfracombe** enjoys a striking location cradled by steep-sided Devon hills. It was founded as a fortified Celtic settlement but grew to prominence as a maritime centre during the Middle Ages, when the town provided Edward III with ships and men for the invasion of France. By 1790 '100 sail of freighting ships and brigs fetching coal from Wales' were noted in the port records. The construction of a new pier in 1874 attracted paddle steamers with day trippers and in the same year the railway arrived, transforming Ilfracombe into a bona fide tourist destination.

For the rest of the Victorian era, Ilfracombe remained a hugely popular seaside resort – *Punch* declared it to be one of the 'loveliest English watering places'. The town's Victorian heritage is still very much in evidence today – particularly during **Victorian Week** in July, when residents dress up in period costume to celebrate the town's heyday with pageants, street fairs, Punch and Judy shows, a grand costume gala ball and a spectacular firework display. Throughout the 20th century the town was popular with elderly holidaymakers and families, but the growth of the surfing scene on the surrounding coast has recently injected the town with more youthful appeal.

From the elegant High Street, Ilfracombe spills down to a small east-facing harbour nestling between the mainland and a narrow protective promontory to the north. Nowadays the harbour is still quite busy with fishing boats and is the departure point for day trips on board the **Waverley Pleasure Steamers** (0845 130 4647, www.waverleyexcursions.co.uk) to Clevedon in Somerset (*see p96*). Ferry services to Lundy Island also depart from here (*see p144* **Pirates and puffins**).

Next to the harbour car park, the former lifeboat station now houses the **Ilfracombe Aquarium**, which offers an up-close look at all kinds of local watery wildlife, from an Exmoor stream to estuary, harbour and coastal habitats.

Devon

Those who want to enjoy the views above the surface should either set off west from the harbour along Capstone Parade, which winds its way up a steep hill to **Capstone Point**, or scale the grassy promontory of Lantern Hill at the tip of the harbour to reach **St Nicholas' Chapel**. The chapel was built c1321 as a resting place for pilgrims, and was also used as a lighthouse. On a clear day the views from here reach across to the south coast of Wales.

On the south-eastern edge of Ilfracombe, **Chambercombe Manor** was a Saxon manor that originally stood in its own grounds outside the town. Today the 11th-century buildings still cluster around a cobbled courtyard surrounded by four acres of lovely grounds incorporating an arboretum, rose and herb gardens, ponds and a bird sanctuary. The manor house is open to the public in summer and contains furniture from the Tudor to the Victorian eras.

Surf check North Devon

If you're heading down to this part of the country with surfing on your mind, then you couldn't choose a better base than **Croyde** (*see p138*). This is the honeypot of North Devon's surfing scene, attracting board-wise locals and visitors to its excellent surf shops and lively pubs. There are three options in the village itself – the beach, the reef and Downend Point – and, for those days when Croyde is blown out, there's a nicely sheltered beach at **Putsborough** (*see p138*), just a short drive away.

Croyde Beach can get impossibly crowded in summer, but when it's working, this sandy-bottomed break offers some of the best sport in the UK, with fast, hollow waves (particularly at low tide) that hold their shape in larger swells. Surfing the reef is only advisable if you're comfortable with pacy take-offs and rocks. The same goes for Downend Point. Check out www.croyde-surf-cam.com for a glimpse of what to expect.

A little further south, at **Saunton Sands** (*pictured*; *see p137*), you'll find a different wave altogether. Much slower than the sucky breaks at Croyde, Saunton's is a long wave that tends to appeal to longboarders and groms. Protection from northerly winds can also make Saunton a good bet on blowier days. North of Croyde, **Woolacombe** (*see p138*) also offers a kinder ride.

Heading west towards Hartland Point, **Westward Ho!** (*see p142*) is often rideable but rarely spectacular. However, neither does it suffer from the occasional flare-ups of 'localism' that can afflict Croyde and Woolacombe on really good days.

Finally, it's worth bearing in mind that, due to its position at the mouth of the Bristol Channel, the North Devon coast generally sees its biggest waves when the tide is rising – particularly in the last few hours before high tide. If the swell looks a bit puny at low tide, don't give up: a little patience may be all that's required.

Behind the striking Landmark Theatre is **Ilfracombe Museum**, which was described by Sir John Betjeman as the 'nicest and most old-fashioned provincial museum', and whose exhibits range from Victorian photos to a stuffed two-headed kitten.

At the western end of Wilder Road, Bath Place leads to Ilfracombe's unique **Tunnels Beaches**. The tunnels were originally carved out by Welsh miners in the early 19th century to provide easy access to Crewkthorne Cove. In subsequent years two tidal bathing pools (one for men; one for women) were constructed on the beach and an elegant Bath House offering hot and cold seawater baths was built at the entrance to the tunnels. The complex is now an attractive beach resort, with restaurant facilities, and lifeguards keeping watch over the tidal pool.

Further west, the coast path follows National Trust land across **Torrs Park** towards **Lee** village, fronted by a miniature cove of pebbles and rock pools. There is a feeling of seclusion here in spring and autumn but this is lost amid the ice-cream-quaffing summer crowds. Inland from Lee, walk back to Ilfracombe along the lovely wooded **Fuschia valley**.

A more strenuous walk will lead you east of town towards the grassy bulk of **Hillsborough**. There are incredible views from the summit and a series of dramatic rocky coves on the eastern side. For sand try **Watermouth Cove** (also accessible via the A399), a lovely spot for a picnic. Overlooking the shore here is **Watermouth Castle**, a faux 19th-century fortification adorned with Gothic arches and crenellations and surrounded by a theme park that will delight small children who are bored with their buckets and spades.

Right on the edge of Exmoor, **Combe Martin** is a famously long, spindly village that stretches along a pretty valley towards a pleasant bathing beach, with plenty of rock pools at low tide. The small town grew to prominence as a working harbour for the export of strawberries, hemp and silver from its mines, but is now chiefly significant for its location on the western fringe of Exmoor National Park with access to the imposing **Hangman Hills** (*see p125*).

On the main street, the **Pack of Cards Inn** was built by a local landowner in the 17th-century from his winnings in a card game, with four floors representing the different suits, 13 rooms (cards in each suit) and 52 windows (total cards in the pack). Each Spring Bank Holiday the village re-enacts the '**Hunting of the Earl of Rone**', an utterly bizarre festival in which the unfortunate 'Earl' is chased through the village by grenadiers and

drummers, before being mounted backwards on a donkey, led to the beach and dumped in the sea. The villagers then celebrate the Earl's demise with a hobby horse procession.

Just outside Combe Martin dinosaur models lurk in 25 acres of landscaped gardens at the **Combe Martin Wildlife Park**, roaring to command on the hour. There are also some real-life beasties here, including a snow leopard, monkeys, falcons and sea lions.

Chambercombe Manor

Chambercombe Lane, Ilfracombe (01271 862624/ www.chambercombemanor.co.uk). **Open** *Apr-Oct* 10.30am-5.30pm Mon-Fri; 2-5.30pm Sun. Closed Nov-Mar. **Admission** £4; £2.50 concessions. **No credit cards.**

Combe Martin Wildlife & Dinosaur Park

Combe Martin (01271 882486/www.dinosaur-uk.com). **Open** *Easter-Nov* 10am-4pm daily. Closed Dec-Mar. **Admission** £10; £7 concessions; £29 family. **Credit** AmEx, MC, V.

Ilfracombe Aquarium

Old Lifeboat House, The Pier, Ilfracombe (01271 864533/www.ilfracombeaquarium.co.uk). **Open** *Mar-June, Sept, Oct* 10am-4.30pm daily. *July, Aug* 10am-6pm daily. *Nov-Jan* phone for details. **Admission** £2.75; £2 concessions; £10 family. **Credit** MC, V.

Ilfracombe Museum

Wilder Road, Ilfracombe (01271 863541/www.devon museums.net). **Open** *Apr-Oct* 10am-5pm Mon-Sat. *Nov-Mar* 10am-1pm Mon-Sat. **Admission** £1.50; £1 concessions. **No credit cards.**

Tunnels Beaches

Bath Place, Ilfracombe (01271 879882/www.tunnels beaches.co.uk). **Open** *Apr, Oct, Nov* 10am-4pm daily. *May, June, Sept* 10am-6pm daily. *July, Aug* 9am-9pm daily. Closed Dec-Mar. **Admission** £1.95; £1.50; £6.50 family. **No credit cards.**

Watermouth Castle & Family Theme Park

nr Ilfracombe (01271 867474). **Open** *Apr-Nov* phone for details. Closed Dec-Mar. **Admission** £7.50; £5.50 concessions. **Credit** AmEx, MC, V.

Activities

Fishing

Boat charters and fishing trips are available from Ilfracombe harbour – call 01271 862363 for details.

Where to eat, drink & stay

Art groupies and food critics are waiting with baited breath for the much-delayed opening of Damien Hirst's new restaurant on the quay in Ilfracombe. In the meantime, visitors have an array of international cuisine to choose from in

Devon

town, including Caribbean at **Level Vibes** (63 Fore Street, 01271 863535) and Asian at **Emperor's Court** (111 High Street, 01271 866868, main courses £3.95-£6.50). **Atlantis** (29 St James Place, 01271 867835, main courses) offers funky fusion food against a backdrop of quirky water features and eclectic world music, while upstairs, friendly, good-quality hostel accommodation is provided by **Ocean Backpackers** (www.backpackers.co.uk/ ocean). A couple of doors along, at No.25, **Maddy's Chippy** (01271 863351) serves decent traditional fish and chips.

For somewhere to stay, the **Strathmore Hotel** (57 Brannock's Road, 01271 862248, www.strathmore.ukhotels.com, set dinner £24.50, double B&B £48-£70) is a cosy, friendly choice with comfy rooms, a pretty patio and ambitious international dinners. A more spacious option for families is the **Epchris Hotel** (Torrs Park, 01271 862751, www.epchrishotel.co.uk, double B&B £49-£55), which has an outdoor heated swimming pool, children's paddling pool and a games chalet.

Resources

Internet
Ilfracombe *Ilfracombe Library, The Candar (01271 862388).* **Open** 9.30am-5pm Mon, Fri; 9.30am-6.30pm Tue, Thur; 9.30am-1pm Wed, Sat.

Police station
Ilfracombe *Princess Avenue (0870 577 7444).*

Post office
Ilfracombe *26 High Street (01271 865234).* **Open** 8.30am-5.30pm Mon, Tue; 9am-5.30pm Wed-Fri; 9am-1pm Sat.

Tourist information
Combe Martin *Exmoor National Park Visitor Centre & Tourist Information Centre, Cross Street (tel/fax 01271 883319).* **Open** phone for details.
Ilfracombe *Tourist Information Centre, The Landmark, Seafront (01271 863001/ www.ilfracombe-tourism.co.uk).* **Open** *Apr-June, Oct* 10am-5.30pm daily. *July-Sept* 10am-6pm daily. *Nov-Mar* 10am-5pm Mon-Fri, 10am-4pm Sat.

Bideford & further west

West of Barnstaple at the mouth of the River Torridge, **Bideford** was dubbed the 'Little White Town' by Charles Kingsley. The phrase implies a spruce perkiness that this economically battered place can no longer quite sustain, but it's still a busy little town, where steep hills are indeed clad with white Victorian houses. Grandiose buildings around the quay are a reminder that Bideford was once a vital port, but now the town is characterised by high-

street chains and too much traffic. Forge up and away from the High Street, however, and you'll also come across some fine junk and antique shops, and a thriving Pannier Market.

Bideford's magnificent, medieval **Long Bridge** over the Torridge collapsed in 1968 but has been lovingly rebuilt; you can also view a brick-perfect scale model in the **Burton Art Gallery & Museum**, which is impressive on local crafts and history.

North of town, in **Appledore** is the place to buy fresh fish from Clovelly fishermen (get there early), or even to catch it yourself: ads for mackerel fishing expeditions line the quay, while lines and bait for crabbing can be bought from the local shops. When the tide is right a tiny passenger ferry runs from here across the Torridge estuary to **Instow**, where there's a fluffy beach and enough buckets and spades to dam the Yangtze.

Just inland, **Tapeley Park** is a 35-acre garden that's currently being overhauled by a member of the long-established local Christie family (of Glyndebourne fame). A great aura of peace hangs over the formal Italian terraces, the Permaculture garden and even, incredibly, the woodland children's play area. Rare breeds stalk the fields and rare trees are fringed with beautiful wild flowers.

Heading west out of Bideford on the A39 you'll pass signs urging you to visit **Westward Ho!** Proceed with caution. Sure, you'll find one of the area's finest sandy beaches, surfing, go-karting, a lovely seaside cricket pitch, the UK's oldest links golf course and, beyond, a sprawling, wind-blasted nature reserve called the **Burrows** (01237 479708). But this is still a rather depressing place, ruined by unfettered development.

Children will love it, of course, but then they'll also adore the area's theme parks – the slides and sheep at the **Big Sheep**; the scarier slides and hawks at the **Milky Way** (01237 431255, www.themilkyway.co.uk); and the, er, gnomes and flowers at the **Gnome Reserve & Wild Flower Garden** (08708 459012, www.gnomereserve.co.uk, closed Nov-Feb). The Big Sheep's the best – despite the awful puns – with a gently thrilling indoor play-ground ('Ewetopia'), genuinely interesting sheep-shearing demonstrations and plenty of puppies and piglets to coo over.

The coast beyond Westward Ho! is short on good beaches, but it is home to **Clovelly**, one of the world's most famous villages (with an admission charge and visitor centre to prove it). In high summer its cobbled, vertiginous streets are rammed with tourists, nosing into the whitewashed cottages, riding the donkeys and loading up on overpriced crafts. It's still worth a visit, however, and once the tourists have left, the ancient English aura of this working fishing village can still cast a spell. A little to the east, **Buck's Mill** is another rugged old village, with steep slopes and artists' huts, but has far fewer crowds to mar its rocky beach and great local walks.

Just past Clovelly the A39 swings south, draining tourists and traffic away from the beautiful backwater of **Hartland**. It's a remarkable area, centred on the idiosyncratic town, but encompassing a hinterland of working farms, self-sustaining hippies, holiday cottages, campsites and a grand old country seat – with its still very feudal family.

Hartland itself is home to the **Small School** – a lively experiment in progressive education – and a couple of fine potteries: the **Hartland** (012378 441693) and the **Springfield** (01237 441506). The postcards sold in the few shops that edge the narrow main street seem to date from the early '60s; but then so does the rest of the town. That said, it's a thriving place, with a regular schedule of fairs and fêtes, and when the last tourist departs you should be able to track down a blast of local music (folk, rock or even the male voice choir) in one of the pubs.

Follow the signs north from the town for the lighthouse at **Hartland Point**, where you can park the car and head in either direction for glorious walks along the coast. East is **Shipload Bay**, the area's most beautiful sandy beach, unfortunately inaccessible until further notice due to a landslide in 2002. South, meanwhile, the full blast of the Atlantic has contorted the exposed coast into some dramatic rock formations, including the 'Cow and Calf' rearing up from the ocean.

Hartland Abbey is sunk in its own damply romantic wooded valley to the west of Hartland town. It has been in the hands of the Stucley family for decades and the present scion still lives here with his brood, which lends the place a grand but homely atmosphere. There's been an abbey on the site since 1157 but the house mostly dates from the 18th and 19th centuries: inside is an evocative mishmash of family portraits and photos, antiques, exquisitely panelled rooms, abandoned suitcases, armour, stuffed birds, and a brigade of biddies serving peerless cakes and tea from an urn. Take your tea into the courtyard before heading for the grounds, which Gertrude Jekyll helped create in the early 20th century. They're fine, in a dank, fern-heavy kind of way, but the woodland walk to the coast is more appealing, with a rocky beach at the end that's swimmable at low tide.

The road past Hartland Abbey brings you to Stoke, home to the 13th-century **St Nectan's Church**, which is worth visiting for its airy

Hartland Point lighthouse, with great views.

interior, Stucley tombs and soaring tower. Beyond is **Hartland Quay** – something of a misnomer given that the last remnants of the quay were swept into the Atlantic more than 100 years ago. Walk south to **Speke's Mill Mouth** and you'll find a waterfall and a sandy beach (when the tide's right), while just inland from here is **Docton Mill & Gardens**, a sheltered series of stepped gardens set around an ancient water mill.

For a 'proper' beach, many visitors take the twisting, excitingly narrow road through the village of Welcombe to **Welcombe Mouth**, which has low-tide sand and high-season congestion. Walk south and you'll reach **Marsland Beach**, right on the Cornish border, which is emptier. For more expansive sand and surf, though, carry on south in to Cornwall.

Big Sheep

Abbotsham, nr Bideford (01237 472366/ www.thebigsheep.co.uk). **Open** *Easter-Oct* 10am-5.30pm daily. *Nov-Mar* 10am-5.30pm Sat, Sun. **Admission** £6.50; £5.50 concessions; £25 family. **Credit** MC, V.

Burton Art Gallery & Museum

Kingsley Road, Bideford (01237 471455/ www.burtonartgallery.co.uk). **Open** *Nov-Easter* 10am-4pm Tue-Sat; 2-4pm Sun. *Easter-Oct* 10am-5pm Tue-Sat; 2-5pm Sun. **Admission** free.

Clovelly Visitor Centre

Clovelly (01237 431781). **Open** *mid Feb-Easter* 9.30am-4.30pm daily. *Easter-Sept* 9am-5.30pm/6.30pm daily. *Oct-mid Feb* 10am-4pm daily. **Admission** £4; £2.75 concessions; £12 family. **Credit** AmEx, MC, V.

Devon

Pirates and puffins

Rising 400 feet (122 metres) out of the sea, 12 miles (19 kilometres) north of Hartland Point is the granite outcrop of Lundy Island. There is evidence that the island has been inhabited since at least Neolithic times, but for most visitors this remote wildlife haven remains a wonderfully isolated destination for escaping the rigours of the 21st century.

In 1166 the island was sold to the Marisco family, who gained a reputation for piracy around the Bristol Channel. Lundy's rocky coves and inlets were used as a base for their buccaneering activities until William de Marisco was hanged, drawn and quartered for treason in 1242. Following the demise of the family, Henry III constructed **Marisco Castle** on the south-eastern corner of the island. Its small sloping keep was rebuilt in the Civil War and is now a sought-after self-catering property.

Between 1748 and 1754 the island came under the jurisdiction of Barnstaple MP Thomas Benson, who used Lundy for smuggling illicit goods into England and also landed slaves here to work in the granite quarries on the eastern side of the island. It was not until the 19th century that Lundy finally approached respectability when it was sold to William Hudson Heaven, who legitimised the island's quarries and built **Millcombe House** as the family home.

Lundy was sold to the National Trust in the 1960s and is now managed by the Landmark Trust, an organisation that seeks to preserve the island's primitive atmosphere and varied wildlife. The coast ranges from gentle undulations on the eastern side to precipitous cliffs on its southern edge (including the sea-blown chasm of the Devil's Limekiln), while inland, the island is divided by dry stone walls, which provide a useful means of orientation. Exploring on foot you will encounter goats, ponies and Soay sheep, munching on the scrubby grass and heather; seals and basking sharks can often be seen around the coast.

Lundy is a breeding hotspot and migratory stopoff for over 280 different species of birdlife, including fulmars, kittiwakes, shearwaters and, famously, puffins ('*Lunde-ey*' is the Old Norse for 'puffin island'). The visits of other interesting species are detailed on a whiteboard in the well-known Marisco Tavern.

At least 200 ships have foundered on rocks and reefs around the island and ten of these wrecks can be visited on diving expeditions. Lundy's Marine Nature Reserve is one of the prime scuba sites in the British Isles, but anyone intending to dive must contact the warden in advance (*see below*).

WHERE TO EAT, DRINK AND STAY

Self-catering accommodation is available in highly individual properties on Lundy, including Marisco Castle, Millcombe House, the Admiralty Look Out, the Old Light Cottage, Government House and the Barn. Details are available from the warden at the **Lundy Shore Office** (The Quay, Bideford, 01237 470074, www.lundyisland.co.uk or the main Lundy number, 01237 431831) and bookings should be made months in advance.

GETTING THERE

MS *Oldenburg* (01237 470422, or book online at www.lundyisland.co.uk) sails from Bideford Quay to Lundy harbour twice a week throughout the year, with additional services from Ilfracombe during the summer. The crossing in each case usually takes about two hours but you should call to check sailing times as cancellations are common in bad weather. While most day trippers choose one of these routes, a far more exciting way of reaching the island is aboard the *Jessica Hettie*, which leaves from Clovelly in high season with only a dozen or so passengers. Contact **Clovelly Pottery** (01237 431042/431405) for further information. Alternatively, charter a helicopter from **Lomas Helicopters** (Abbotsham, Bideford, 01237 421054, www.lomashelicopters.co.uk).

Docton Mill & Gardens
Speke Valley, nr Hartland (01237 441369/ www.doctonmill.co.uk). **Open** Mar-Oct 10am-6pm daily. Closed Nov-Feb. **Admission** £3.50; £1-£3 concessions. **Credit** MC, V.

Hartland Abbey
Hartland (01237 441264/441234/www.hartland abbey.com). **Open** Apr-Oct 2-5.30pm Wed, Thur, Sun. Closed Nov-Mar. **Admission** £5; £4.30 concessions. **No credit cards.**

Tapeley Park Gardens
Instow, Bideford (01271 342371/860528). **Open** Mar-Oct 10am-5pm Mon-Fri, Sun. Closed Nov-Feb. **Admission** £3.50; £2.50 concessions. **Credit** MC, V.

Activities

Cycling
Bikes can be hired from **Bideford Cycle Hire** (Torrington Street, East-the-Water, Bideford, 01237 424123) and **Biketrail** (Fremington Quay, 01271 372586).

Surfing
Big Blue Surf School (Little Barn, Mead Barn Cottages, Welcombe, nr Bideford, 01288 331764) provides lessons for all abilities on the expansive beaches at Bude (*see p283*).

Watersport
Every kind of watersport is offered at the **Tamar Lakes** (01288 321712, www.swlakestrust.org.uk), nr Kilkhampton along the Devon–Cornwall border.

Where to eat, drink & stay

Don't expect to find too much in the way of refreshments around Bideford. If you want to eat well, head north for Appledore, where the **Quay Gallery & Coffee Shop** (01237 474801, closed most weekends except during school holidays) dishes out fry-ups, toasted sarnies, soup and monster milkshakes in a clutter of art and crafts. Another good choice in Appledore is the **Royal George** (Irsha Street, 01237 474335, main courses £8.50-£14), run by Barry, possibly North Devon's most flamboyant host. The pub overlooks the estuary and serves decent fresh fish.

Heading further east, Fremington Quay at Fremington is home to the **Quay Café** (01271 378783, www.fremingtonquaycafe. co.uk, closed Mon in winter, main courses £5.95-£13.95), a lovely, flower-strewn restaurant in an old railway station, complete with organic food, sensational ice-creams, exhibitions and a view over the estuary.

In Clovelly, the **Red Lion Hotel** (01237 431237, double £85-£150.50, main courses £2.95-£5.95) on the quay is a soothing spot in which to sample extra-fresh fish and sink

an evening pint (and there are 11 characterful rooms to stumble back to after dinner), while the **Hoops Inn** (Horns Cross, near Clovelly, 01237 451222, www.hoopsinn.co.uk, main courses £8.50-£16.50, double £100-£170) is a gem of a place serving superlative food and offering upscale accommodation in the main thatched 13th-century building and coach house. Also worth checking out are the ancient, low-slung **Coach & Horses** in pretty Buckland Brewer (01237 451395, main courses £5.95-£12.95) and the **Farmers Arms** in Woolfardisworthy (01237 431467, main courses £3.75-£9.95).

Clearly signposted on the edge of Hartland, **Fosfelle Hotel** (01237 441273, double £48-£60 per person) is a perfectly serviceable country hotel in spacious grounds. In the village itself, the **Happy Pear Café** (16 Fore Street, 01237 441286, www.happypear.co.uk, closed Oct-May, main courses £4.50-£6.50, set dinner £12.50-£16) specialises in organic vegetarian food.

On the coast is the **Hartland Quay Hotel** (01237 441218, main courses £4-£10), in a spectacular location, and with decent ale and chintzy rooms. Head to the **Stoke Barton Farmhouse** at nearby Stoke (01237 441238, closed Nov-Feb) for cream teas and table-trembling 'light lunches' in a dreamy setting.

Resources

Hospital
Bideford Hospital *Abbotsham Road, Bideford (01237 420200).*

Internet
Bideford Library *New Road, Bideford (01237 476075).* **Open** 9.30am-7pm Mon, Thur; 9.30am-5.30pm Tue, Fri; 9.30am-4pm Sat.

Police station
New Road, Bideford (0870 577 7444).

Post office
The Quay, Bideford (08457 223344). **Open** 8.30am-5.30pm Mon; 9am-5.30pm Tue-Fri; 9am-12.30pm Sat.

Tourist Information
Bideford Tourist Information Centre *Victoria Park, Kingsley Road, Bideford (01237 477676/ www.torridge.gov.uk).* **Open** Apr-Sept 10am-5pm Mon-Sat; 10am-4pm Sun. Oct-Mar 10am-4.30pm Mon, Tue, Thur, Fri; 10am-1pm Wed, Sat.

Mid Devon

The A386 from Bideford to Great Torrington follows the course of the River Torridge as it flows upstream, passing through the wooded valley where Tarka the Otter was supposedly born (*see p135* **Tarka territory**).

Devon

Upon reaching **Great Torrington** it's easy to miss the town's charms: the main road crashes down New Street – a drab strip of ailing pubs and traffic-cracked houses – skirting the centre entirely. Venture in to the town, though, and you will find the attractive town hall (which houses a free museum) and the 15th-century **Black Horse Inn**. Off the main square is yet another Victorian **Pannier Market** (open daily, though Thursday and Saturday are market days) and a clutch of decent shops. There's also the **Plough Arts Centre** (01805 624624, www.plough-arts.org.uk), which has a cinema, theatre, dance studio and café.

Great Torrington makes much of its Civil War connections: it was the site of a brutal battle in 1646, at which the Royalists were roundly slaughtered by the terrifying New Model Army led by Sir Thomas Fairfax. You can follow the Civil War Trail through the town to key sites (contact the tourist office for details) or join in with the various Civil War events held in Torrington throughout the year (usually involving fireworks on the common and a load of men dressed up in blouses, wielding firearms). At other times, visit the **Torrington 1646** museum, a kid-friendly attraction with costumed guides.

If you've ever wondered about the intricacies of glass blowing, **Dartington Crystal** is just outside town. But better by far, about a mile to the south, is the fabulous **RHS Rosemoor Garden**, an inspirational new 40-acre garden that's blossoming into one of the UK's most important horticultural sites. Highlights include the cottage garden, thousands of rare roses, some enviable fruit and veg and a glittering, fern-fringed lake. There's also a reliable café.

The best way to reach this idyll is to ditch the car and take to the **Tarka Trail** (*see p135* **Tarka territory**). Alternatively, take the A386 south out of Torrington, stopping off at the pretty villages of **Merton** and **Meeth**. Next is **Hatherleigh**, a picturesque small market town with the brooding tors of Dartmoor visible in the distance.

From here the Tarka Trail runs south as far as Okehampton before looping back north to **Eggesford** on the River Taw, where it joins up with the railway on the **Tarka Line** between Exeter and Barnstaple. Surrounding Eggesford is a tract of lovely forest and some gorgeously time-forgotten villages that repay exploration on foot. To the south, meanwhile, the main rail and road routes head west away from the river towards the ancient town of **Crediton**, the birthplace in 680 of Wynfirth (aka St Boniface).

Responsible for the Christian conversion of Germanic tribes in what is now the Netherlands and Germany, St Boniface also founded a monastery in his home town, which developed into an important religious centre. The abbey church became Devon's first cathedral in 909 and, although it was later supplanted by Exeter, Crediton continued to thrive as a prosperous wool town throughout the Middle Ages. Many of its medieval buildings were destroyed by fire in the 18th century, leaving the large, red **Church of Holy Cross** standing sentinel over the otherwise unremarkable town. Though it was first constructed in the mid 12th century, the present structure dates mostly from the 15th century but includes a fine 14th-century chapterhouse.

North-east of Crediton on the A396, **Tiverton**, known locally as 'Tivvi', is the largest town in Devon's heartland, built along the fast-flowing River Exe. In the medieval period this pre-Saxon settlement grew into a busy market town, and by the 16th century it had become a thriving centre for the wool industry, reaching its peak at the end of the 19th century. The town's wealth is reflected in the number of churches, most notably the elegant 18th-century **Church of St George** on St Andrew Street and the 16th-century **Church of St Peter**, with its fine Gothic carving.

The town's most significant building is the sandstone **Tiverton Castle** in St Peter's Street. Built in 1106 by the de Redvers family (the first Earls of Devon), it later passed to the Courtenays before falling to Parliamentarian forces during the Civil War. Still privately owned, the castle houses a collection of arms and armour that can seen on guided tours. There are also beautiful walled gardens.

Artefacts from the Civil War, the lace-making industry and the farming sector are on display at the impressive **Tiverton Museum**. This is one of the largest rural and social history collections in the South West, with exhibits ranging from pieces of armour to agricultural implements. The 'star' attraction is the Tivvy Bumper, a locomotive that once ran between Tiverton and Tiverton Junction.

As the trading centre for a large rural area, Tiverton's **Pannier Market** hosts a general market three times a week, with a craft and antiques market on Monday and an increasingly popular farmers' market on the third Wednesday of the month.

From the town, a road runs up Canal Hill to the **Grand Western Canal**. Work on the canal to Taunton started during the Napoleonic Wars, and was completed in the 1830s. From the canal basin a horse-drawn barge takes visitors on hour-long canal trips.

Devon

There are a number of historic houses in the area. To the north, **Knighthayes Court** is a Victorian Gothic mansion that retains many original interior features. Also notable are the gardens, with specimen trees, rare shrubs, terraces and herbaceous borders. Killerton was due to reopen by Easter 2003 following renovation work, but phone first to check if you're making a special trip.

Three miles (five kilometres) to the south of Tiverton, **Bickleigh Castle** dominates the pretty village of Bickleigh on the banks of the Exe. Originally a Norman moated castle, it was used as a Royalist stronghold in the Civil War. Visitors can wander round the chapel, armoury, guard room, Great Hall and spooky tower.

Further south, just off the B3181, **Killerton House** is an 18th-century National Trust mansion that was once home to the Acland family. The house contains a fascinating collection of period costumes, and the beautiful wooded grounds are perfect for an autumn stroll.

Bickleigh Castle

Bickleigh, nr Tiverton (01884 855363). **Open** *Easter-May* 2-5pm Wed, Sun. *June-early Oct* 2-5pm Mon-Fri, Sun. Closed mid Oct-Mar. **Admission** phone for details.

Dartington Crystal

Great Torrington (01805 626242/www.dartington. co.uk). **Open** 9am-5pm Mon-Fri; 10am-5pm Sat; 10am-4pm Sun. **Admission** £4.50; £3.50 concessions; free under-16s. **Credit** AmEx, MC, V.

Killerton House

Broadclyst, nr Exeter (01392 881345). **Open** *House* mid Apr-early Nov 11am-5pm Mon, Wed-Sun. *Garden* 10.30am-dusk daily. **Admission** *House & garden* £5.50; £2.70 concessions. *Garden only* £4; £2 concessions. Free under-4s. **Credit** MC, V.

Knightshayes Court

Bolham (01884 254665). **Open** *House* end Mar-early Nov 11am-5pm daily. *Gardens* early Mar-early Nov 11am-5.30pm daily. Closed mid Nov-Feb. **Admission** *House & gardens* £5; £2.80 concessions; £14.20 family. **Credit** MC, V.

RHS Rosemoor Garden

Great Torrington (01805 624067/www.rhs.org.uk). **Open** *Apr-Sept* 10am-6pm daily. *Oct-Mar* 10am-5pm daily. **Admission** £5; £1 concessions. **Credit** AmEx, MC, V.

Tiverton Castle

Park Hill, Tiverton (01884 253200/www.tiverton castle.com). **Open** *July, Aug* 2.30-5.30pm Mon-Thur, Sun. *Easter-June, Sept* 2.30-5.30pm Thur, Sun. **Admission** £4; £2 concessions; free under-7s. **No credit cards**.

Tiverton Museum

Beck's Square, Tiverton (01884 256295/ www.tivertonmuseum.org.uk). **Open** *Feb-Dec* 10.30am-4.30pm Mon-Fri; 10am-1pm Sat. Closed Jan. **Admission** £3.50; £2.50 concessions; £8 family. **No credit cards**.

Torrington 1646

Castle Hill, South Street, Great Torrington (01805 626146/www.great-torrington.com). **Open** *Apr-Oct* 11am-5pm Mon-Sat. *Nov-Mar* 11am-5pm Mon-Fri; 11am-1pm Sat. **Admission** £6.95; £4.75-£5.95 concessions; £19.50 family. **Credit** MC, V.

Activities

Canal boating

Horses dressed in traditional brasses draw canal barges along the Grand Western Canal (The Wharf, Canal Hill, 01884 253345) in Tiverton during the spring and summer. Rowing boats and day boats are also available for hire.

Cycling

Torridge Cycle Hire (Unit 1, Station Yard, Great Torrington, 01805 622633) can get you kitted out. In Tiverton, try **Maynard's Cycle Shop** (25 Gold Street, 01884 253979).

Horse riding

Rose & Crown Riding Stables (Palmers Lodge, Calverleigh, 01884 252060) provide lessons for beginners and hacks for more serious riders.

Where to eat, drink & stay

For an atmospheric pint, stop off at the fine old **Black Horse Inn** (Great Torrington, 01805 622121, main courses £4-£11.50). Applauded by top culinary critics, **Percy's Country Hotel & Restaurant** (Coombeshead Estate, Virginstow, 01409 211236, www.percys.co.uk, set menu £37.50, double £150-£195) is fast gaining a national reputation for its fine-quality organic cuisine. Luxurious accommodation is provided in light, modern rooms in a converted granary, and outside there are 130 acres to explore. For something small, pastoral and intimate, try **Blagdon Manor Hotel Restaurant** (Ashwater, near Beaworthy, 01409 211224, www.blagdon.com, closed early Jan, set menu £25, double B&B £90) in a quiet country setting, which dishes up good English cuisine. The **Eggesford Country Hotel** (Eggesford, 01769 580345, www.eggesfordhotel.co.uk, main courses £5-£16, double B&B £64-£80) offers permits for fly-fishing on the Taw, plus cycle rides and forest walks.

In Tiverton, **Four & Twenty Blackbirds** (43 Gold Street, 01884 257055, main courses £3-£5.95) serves hearty, home-made English food. Alternatively, try **Upstairs/Downstairs**

(1 Angel Terrace, 01884 254778, main courses £2.30-£5.25) for breakfast or a traditional English tea. Set on the banks of the River Exe at Bickleigh, the **Fisherman's Cot** (01884 855237, main courses £4-£12, double B&B £59) offers good-value food and accommodation.

Resources

Hospitals

Great Torrington *Torrington Cottage Hospital (01805 622208).*
Tiverton *Tiverton & District Hospital, William Street (01884 253251).*

Internet

Great Torrington *Thomas Fowler IT Centre, Castle Hill, South Street (01805 626120).* **Open** 9am-1pm Mon, Wed, Fri, Sat; 9am-9pm Tue, Thur.
Tiverton *Tiverton Library, Angel Hill (01884 252973).* **Open** 9.30am-5pm Mon, Thur; 9.30am-7pm Tue, Sat; 9.30am-1pm Sat.

Police station

Great Torrington *Pathfield (0870 577 7444).*
Tiverton *2 The Avenue (0870 577 7444).*

Post offices

Great Torrington *Torrington Post Office, 7 High Street (01805 622234).* **Open** 8.30am-5.30pm Mon, Tue, Thur; 9am-4.30pm Wed; 9am-5.30pm Fri; 9am-12.30pm Sat.
Tiverton *Market Walk (01884 256222).* **Open** 8.30am-6pm Mon-Fri; 8.30am-2pm Sat.

Tourist information

Great Torrington *Great Torrington Tourist Information, South Street Car Park (01805 626140).* **Open** 10am-4.30pm Mon-Fri; 10am-1pm Sat; closed Wed afternoons in the winter.
Tiverton *Tourist Information Centre, Phoenix Lane (01884 255827/tivertontic@middevon.gov.uk).* **Open** *Sept-June* 9.15am-5pm Mon-Fri; 9.15am-3.30pm Sat. *July, Aug* 9.15am-5pm Mon-Thur; 9.15am-5.30pm Fri; 9.15am-4pm Sat.

Getting there

By bus

Bus services are detailed in the North Devon guide published by Devonbus (01392 382800, www.devon.gov.uk/devonbus).

By train

First Great Western trains run from London Paddington to Tiverton Parkway, both direct and via Taunton. Return trains stop at Bristol and/or Exeter. Barnstaple is also served from Paddington, with a change at Bristol and/or Exeter (the latter goes to Barnstaple on the Tarka Line; *see p135* **Tarka territory**).

Tuck in Devonshire cream tea

Devon

The traditional county dish may be copied all over the world, but it is only authentic if thoroughly home-made in Devon from locally produced ingredients.

The search for the perfect Devonshire cream tea must start with a firm resolution neither to count calories nor to measure cholesterol: clotted cream, which is central to the whole experience, is the richest of all creams, containing 55% butterfat.

Miss breakfast and lunch if you must but, at four o'clock or thereabouts, find a teashop or a farmhouse where 'home-made' features widely on the menu. Once upon a time you would have come in from labouring in the fields for your afternoon tea, but sightseeing, coastal walking or hiking on the moors earns you the right to a holiday treat too.

Devonshire cream teas are easiest to define by stating what they are not. The jam is not served in a tiny impenetrable plastic box nor in a mini jar; the cream is neither white nor foamy; the scones are not perfectly symmetrical, shiny-topped cylinders. For the real thing, look for a generous bowl of lumpy,

home-made strawberry or raspberry jam, a seriously deep dollop of almost yellow clotted cream, with skeins of bubbled, golden crust on it, and warm scones, recently out of the oven, irregularly shaped and dusted with flour. Then there's the tea, which should be brewed in a china pot, poured into a china cup and served without sugar to counteract the sweetness of the scone.

Try to avoid getting into an argument with a local about the order in which to layer the filling of your horizontally split scone. Allegedly, the Cornish put butter, then jam and the cream on top. But in Devon it's usually lashings of cream first, followed by jam. A lifetime's research will help you decide which method suits you best: to butter or not to butter is indeed the question.

Of course, you may be offered cheese scones or scones with fruit in them, but the purists insist on two plain scones for a cream tea. Any mention of cider cake or whortleberry pie, however, and you've truly arrived – be sure to order these local delicacies even if you're full up.

Exeter & East Devon

Devon's rejuvenated county town is the gateway to a unique stretch of World Heritage coastline and some charming, unspoiled countryside.

Exeter

Holidaymakers steaming down the M5 usually bypass Exeter en route to the sandy seaside charms of the Devon and Cornish coasts. Discerning visitors, however, would do well to stop awhile in this historic city. Exeter makes an ideal centre for discovering the South West, and because of a constant influx of new blood – thanks to the university and the tourist trade – the city maintains a progressive and welcoming atmosphere.

HISTORY

Exeter's long history is still in evidence all around town, from the Roman city walls to the Gothic cathedral, the medieval houses to the modernised Phoenix Art Centre. The Roman army arrived in AD 50-55 and built a 42-acre fortress overlooking the River Exe, which became the base for a 5,000-strong legion and provided an ideal vantage point

The River Exe at **Exeter Quay**. See p153.

for Roman conquests of the South West. It was later abandoned, leaving the site to be converted into a civilian settlement known as Isca Dumnoniorum.

Alfred the Great refounded the city in the late ninth century, and it grew to become one of the most prominent Anglo-Saxon settlements in England, through the export of woollen cloth from its river port. Trade was further developed in the Norman and medieval eras, during which time the city's stunning Gothic cathedral was built. The construction of a weir in the 13th century meant that shipping was diverted to neighbouring Topsham, but in the 1560s a canal was constructed, linking the city to the estuary once more and restoring Exeter's status as a major port.

During the Civil War the city was taken first by the Royalists and then by the Parliamentarians, but remained one of the most prosperous towns in the country thanks to its wool and cloth trade. It was, in fact, not until the Napoleonic Wars signalled the decline of the Devon cloth industry, that Exeter experienced a significant slump in fortunes.

The city suffered considerable bomb damage in World War II, which destroyed part of the cathedral and wiped out many of the medieval streets. Several areas were subjected to inauspicious post-war makeovers in the second half of the 20th century, most notably the repugnant and thankfully small Princeshay area. Over the last few years, though, Exeter has enjoyed something of a renaissance; a blossoming café culture and thriving art scene has helped produce a laid-back yet lively provincial city, nestling against a backdrop of rolling hills and clear country skies.

TOURS

One of the best ways to discover Exeter is on one of the free **Red Coat Guided Walks** (01392 265203), which run throughout the year (except 25 and 26 December). There are various routes (most of which start outside the Royal Clarence Hotel in Cathedral Yard), incorporating different aspects and eras of Exeter's history. A particular favourite is the Catacomb Tour, which visits the architecturally fascinating Exeter catacombs, consecrated in 1837 and otherwise closed to visitors.

City walk The art of the city

Length 2 miles (3km).
Time 1hr (if you don't stop at all the galleries along the route).
Difficulty Easy. Pavements nearly all the way.

One of the strengths of Exeter's burgeoning art scene is its seemingly altruistic tendencies. Community art projects and street art are prominent and help to add a sparkle to the city.

For a decent stroll with a lot of art, a little history and a long drink at the end of it, start at the Exeter **Phoenix Art Centre** (*see p156*) on Bradninch Place, just off Gandy Street. The area around the Phoenix is enlivened by some fantastic street sculpture – including a unicorn created from an old engine. After pottering around the nearby shops, leave Gandy Street at its north end, crossing Queen Street into Paul Street. At the junction with North Street, the **Iron Bridge**, a lovely 800-foot (243-metre) ornate six-arched viaduct, will be on your right. A plaque at the city end of the bridge marks the position of the original North Gate into the city, which was demolished in the 18th century.

Continue from here into Bartholomew Street, left into Mary Arches Street, right into Fore Street and then second left into King Street. You can make a detour here down cobbled Stepcote Hill towards the medieval church of St Mary Steps or continue to the end of the road and into steep Preston Street. The **Spacex Gallery** at 45 Preston Street (01392 431786, www.spacex.co.uk) is a publicly funded venue that was established in 1978 by an artists' co-operative. It presents major contemporary visual art exhibitions featuring prominent and upcoming artists

from Britain and abroad, including Lois Weinberger, Bridget Riley and Yoko Ono.

At the bottom of Preston Street, at the junction with West Street, is the 'House that moved', a 15th-century building that, despite weighing over 21 tonnes, was strapped up and moved inch by inch for 450 feet (140 metres) from its original location on the corner of Edmund Street, in order for the new road to be built. It is now a bridalwear shop.

The nearby pedestrian crossing will take you over busy Western Way and onto a footpath that winds around towards the Quay area, coming out at the Custom House. From the Custom House head west along Commercial Road to **Mud Dock Cycleworks** (*see p154*) to marvel at the sculpture in the foyer. Created in the summer of 2002 by local artist, Alina Pripis, to celebrate National Bike Week, it is made entirely from bicycle parts and shows a man on, yes, a bike, with bending knees, moving fingers and swivelling head.

Heading up the hilly footpath next to the unashamedly cheesy **Hothouse Nightclub** (01392 211347) takes you back on to Western Way, from where a short right-hand walk along the pavement leads onto Holloway Road, where there's a faded but entertaining mural painted on the side of the **Globe Backpackers Hostel** (*see p157*). It depicts men at work on the building with scaffolding, buckets and cement, and chattering figures leaning from a faux window.

Back on the Quay, make for the **Prospect Inn** (01392 273152) on the left of the Custom House. This 17th-century imbibery was used in the filming of '70s series *The Onedin Line*, and is a great spot for a refreshing drink overlooking the Exe.

Sightseeing

The **Cathedral Church of St Peter** is at the heart of the city, looming over shoppers and strollers by day and dripping with amber lights by night. Evidence suggests Christian worship has taken place on this site since as early as AD 5. Most of the present cathedral was built in the 13th and 14th centuries, although the two towers date back to an earlier Norman building and were unusually incorporated into the transept of the Gothic structure. Local materials dominate the construction; much of it was built from limestone quarried in the East Devon village of Beer (*see p162*) and the 300-foot

(91-metre) arched and ribbed vault ceiling, which weighs a whopping 5,000 tonnes, stands on columns of Purbeck stone from Dorset. Dating from 1396, this is the longest unbroken Gothic vault in the world. Inside the cathedral, look out for the richly decorated ceiling bosses, the 14th-century minstrels' gallery, the 15th-century astronomical clock and the completely over-the-top carved oak Bishop's Throne from the early 14th century.

Surrounding the cathedral, spacious grassy **Cathedral Close** is a favourite spot for loafing about on a summer's day. Among the hotchpotch of Tudor, Restoration and Regency buildings is the Elizabethan **Mol's**

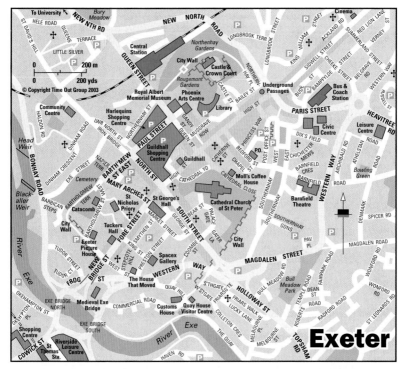

Coffee House. It's now a shop, but was once regularly patronised by the likes of Francis Drake and Walter Raleigh.

North of the Close on Queen Street, the **Royal Albert Memorial Museum & Art Gallery** is the city's other major sightseeing attraction. Housed in a striking neo-Gothic building, it is a quintessential example of high Victorian museology, with natural history, archaeology, ethnography, art and craft exhibits all demanding attention. Among the displays are a mural reconstruction of Exeter's Roman fortress and a model of the Roman bathhouse discovered near the cathedral in the 1970s. The natural history collection includes a stuffed giraffe, while the art gallery houses landscape paintings by local and national artists including Turner and Reynolds. Unusual clocks, early glass- and silverware, and local pottery round out the exhibits.

The museum is on the edge of **Rougemont Gardens**, a park created from the former moat of Rougemont Castle. The castle and its municipal yard were built under instruction from William the Conqueror in 1068, but although the red stone walls and gatehouse

loom large, nothing else of the original structure remains, and the walls now shelter the County Courts (which date from 1774). Footpaths run from here to adjoining Northenhay Gardens, believed to be the earliest public gardens in the country.

Accessed via Romangate Passage just south of the gardens are a network of **underground passages** that were once part of the town's medieval water system. Built in the 14th century, the narrow subterranean aqueducts can be visited on guided tours providing a unique view of underground Exeter – for non-claustrophobic visitors, at least.

The pedestrianised High Street cuts through the centre of the city to the south-east, with a number of interesting older buildings relieving the monotony of the usual shops and concrete. The **Guildhall** (01392 265500), thought to be the oldest municipal building still in use in the country, dates from 1330 and has a 15th-century timber roof and a colonnaded façade from 1592. (The ornate interior can be viewed from Monday to Friday as long as a civic function is not taking place.) A little further down is the medieval church of **St Petrock**

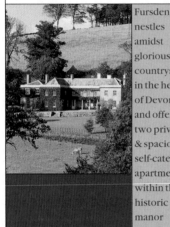

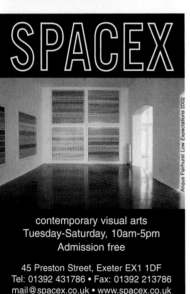

and tiny **Parliament Street**, which, at 25 inches (63.5 centimetres) wide in places, is thought to be the narrowest street in Europe.

High Street runs into Fore Street to the south, where you'll find another cluster of interesting historical buildings. On the Mint stands **St Nicholas Priory**, founded in 1087 as a Benedictine monastery, and Exeter's only surviving monastic building. Sections of the building open to visitors include the 900-year-old guest wing and Norman kitchen, an elaborate Tudor room and the grand guest hall. Another survivor is the **Tuckers Hall** at the bottom of Fore Street, the only remaining medieval guild in the city. Built for the city's weavers, fullers and shearmen, its imposing architecture and vaulted wooden roof are testament to the wealth these trades generated in the city during the Middle Ages. Beyond Fore Street, the remains of the original **medieval bridge** over the Exe are covered by swirling traffic on the Western Way. Head east from here to reach the Quay.

Once a thriving port exporting woollen cloth around the world, the **Quay** is now a great spot for laid-back loitering or waterside drinks and ice-creams. There are also antique and collectibles shops in this area, selling one-off pieces of furniture and jewellery from the warehouses and arches alongside the canal. Among the shops, cafés and bars is the historic brick **Customs House** (1681), which was used by HM Customs until 1989. Also here is the **Quay House Visitor Centre**, which houses displays on the development of the city, and the **Exeter Crafts Guild** (42-3 The Quay, 01392 214332, www.exetercraftsguild.com), which sells locally produced arts and crafts (with not a seed necklace or macrame pot-holder in sight). It also runs a small but well-stocked coffeeshop with a great line in irresistible cakes.

From the Quay, a pedestrian suspension bridge and a hand-pulled ferry provide access to the south bank of the Exe. (Follow the wide paved embankments on either side of the river north from the Quay for an interesting stroll.) The Quay is also the starting point for the **Exeter Canal**, opened in 1566 to improve trade access to the city. Running parallel to the river to the south-west, the five-mile (eight-kilometre) canal joins the Exe estuary just above Powderham Castle (*see p181*). There's a flat cycle trail along the towpath for the entire route. Alternatively, relax on a regular **canal cruise** on board *White Heather* (07831 108319) to the Double Locks and Turf Locks pubs (*see p154 and p155*).

On the east side of the estuary, just four miles (six kilometres) from the city, the scenic village of **Topsham** has a long and prosperous

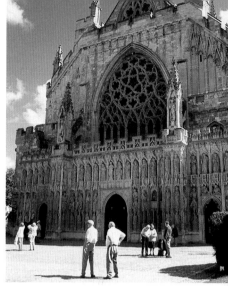

Cathedral Church of St Peter. *See p150.*

maritime and shipbuilding heritage that is explored in the **Topsham Museum**, housed in a 17th-century building with riverside gardens. Among the village's Dutch-style cottages are a number of good pubs, seafood restaurants and antique shops.

For something completely different – and to keep the kids happy – head for **Crealy Adventure Park** just outside Exeter at Clyst St Mary, where ponies, a selection of other strokable animals, go-karts, bumper boats and fairground rides provide an exhausting day's worth of entertainment for the young and the silly.

Cathedral Church of St Peter
Cathedral Close (01392 214219/www.exeter-cathedral.org.uk). **Open** 8am-6.30pm Mon-Fri; 8am-5pm Sat; 8.30am-7.30pm Sun. *Guided tours* daily; phone for details. **Admission** suggested donation £3. **Credit** (shop) AmEx, MC, V.

Crealy Adventure Park
Sidmouth Road, Clyst St Mary (01395 233200/ www.crealy.co.uk). **Open** *Apr-Oct* 10am-6pm daily. *Nov-Mar* 10am-5pm Wed-Sun. **Admission** *Indoor attractions* £4.50-£7.95; £3-£5.20 concessions; free under-3s. **Credit** AmEx, MC, V.

Quay House Visitor Centre
46 The Quay (01392 265213). **Open** *May-Oct* 10am-5pm daily. *Nov-Apr* 11am-4pm Sat, Sun. **Admission** free.

Royal Albert Memorial Museum & Art Gallery
Queen Street (01392 665858). **Open** 10am-5pm Mon-Sat. **Admission** free. **Credit** *Shop* MC, V.

Devon

St Nicholas Priory
The Mint, off Fore Street (01392 265858).
Open 2-5pm Wed, Fri, Sat. **Admission** free;
donations appreciated.

Topsham Museum
25 The Strand, Topsham (01392 873244/www.
topsham.org/museum). **Open** *Apr-Oct* 2-5pm Mon,
Wed, Sat, Sun. Closed Nov-Mar. **Admission** free.
Credit *Shop* MC, V.

Underground Passages
Romangate Passage, High Street (01392 265887).
Open *July-Sept* 10am-4.30pm Mon-Sat. *Oct-May*
noon-4.30pm Tue-Fri; 10am-4.30pm Sat.
Admission *July, Aug* £3.75; £2.75 concessions;
£11 family. *Sept-June* £3; £2 concessions; £8 family.
No credit cards.

Activities

Canoeing
Saddles & Paddles (4 Kings Wharf, the Quay
01392 424241, www.saddlepaddle.co.uk) hires bikes
and canoes for use on the canal. Canoeing weekends
and paddling parties can also be arranged.

Cycling
Bikes can be hired from **Mud Dock Cycleworks**
(Kennaway Warehouse, Commercial Road, 01392
270000, www.muddock.com) or from **Saddles &**
Paddles (*see above*), both located on the Quay. For
a map of cycle routes in and around the city, get a
free copy of the 'Exeter Cycle Guide & Map' from
the Tourist Information Centre.

Where to eat & drink

Boston Tea Party
84 Queen Street (01392 201181). **Open** 7am-6pm
Mon-Sat; 9am-6pm Sun. **Main courses** £4.50-£6.75.
Credit MC, V.
One of the city's original cool cafés. With its over-
stuffed sofas, inspired snack menu and bold decor,
it's the perfect antidote to the stresses of shopping.

Brazz Exeter
10-12 Palace Gate (01392 252525/www.brazz.co.uk).
Open noon-11pm Mon; 11am-11pm Tue-Fri; 10am-
11pm Sat; noon-10.30pm Sun. **Main courses** £8.95-
£14.95. **Credit** AmEx, MC, V.
South of the cathedral, Brazz is a popular and stylish brasserie, with tasty food, decent wines and slow
but friendly service. Check out the huge aquarium.

Café Paradiso
Hotel Barcelona, Magdalen Street (01392 281010/
www.hotelbarcelona-uk.com). **Open** noon-2pm,
7-10pm Mon-Sat; noon-2pm, 7-9pm Sun. **Main**
courses £6.50-£15.95. **Credit** AmEx, MC, V.
Designed like a circus big top with a glass wall overlooking the garden, Café Paradiso maintains Hotel
Barcelona's idiosyncratic style. The Mediterranean
menu of trad pizzas, grills, local fish and brasserie
favourites is big on flavour and gentle on the wallet.

Chaucer's Inn
223-6 High Street (01392 422365). **Open** 11am-
11pm Mon-Sat. **Main courses** £4.95-£13.95.
Credit AmEx, MC, V.
This historic pub does a particularly good line in
traditional hearty food and lovely unskimpy salads.
Its busy subterranean bar makes for a snug bolthole
on a winter's night.

Double Locks
Canal Banks, Alphington (01392 256947).
Open 11am-11pm Mon-Sat; noon-10.30pm Sun.
Main courses £5.45-£6.95. **Credit** MC, V.
On the canal to the south of the city, this pub is an
essential part of the Exeter experience, offering real
ale on tap (including the infamous Old Bastard), reg-
ular barbeques and a large canalside beer garden.
You can even camp here for free in summer, as long
as you eat and drink in the pub.

Galley Restaurant
41 Fore Street, Topsham (01392 876078/
www.galleyrestaurant.co.uk). **Open** noon-1.30pm,
7-11pm Tue-Sat. **Main courses** £16.95-£23.95.
Credit AmEx, MC, V.
A popular destination in Topsham, this renowned
fish restaurant is known for its accolade-winning
menu and kitschy interior – look out for the fish
swimming in the toilet cisterns.

Havana
The Quay (01392 498181/www.havanagoodtime.
co.uk). **Open** noon-11pm daily. **Main courses**
£8.95-£14.95. **Admission** *Comedy Club* £6; £5
concessions. *Salsa classes* £3. **Credit** MC, V.
Replacing the much-loved Mud Dock Café, Havana
offers a funky mix of food and live entertainment,
cocktails and cigars. The main menu is Mexican-
influenced, with Italian tapas served in the Blue
Room lounge. Head here on Sunday nights for
stand-up comedy, on Thursday nights for salsa
dancing (including classes), and Sunday lunchtimes
or Tuesday nights for jazz. Local bands perform on
Friday and Saturday nights.

Mad Meg's Restaurant
St Olaves Court, 162-3 Fore Street (01392 221225/
www.madmegs.co.uk). **Open** 6-10pm Mon-Wed;
11.30am-2.15pm, 6-10pm Thur, Fri; 6-10.30pm Sat;
11.30am-4pm Sun. **Main courses** £6.75-£17.85.
Credit AmEx, DC, MC, V.
For a unique dining 'experience', try Mad Meg's, a
tongue-in-cheek re-creation – complete with serving
wenches – of the legendary crazy cook who worked
for the Sheriff of Exeter in the mid 16th century.
Food is hearty and portions are generous.

Metzo Café Bar
153 Fore Street (01392 499666). **Open** 10.30am-
11pm Mon-Sat; 10.30am-10.30pm Sun. **Main**
courses £4.95-£5.95. **Credit** MC, V.
Bright bold colours, a decent lunch menu, and a
well-stocked bar, including dangerously high-proof
absinthe are the enticements at Metzo.

Bend it like Uri

With not much happening on the pitch – at the time of going to press, Exeter City Football Club (01392 255611, www.exetercityfc.co.uk), aka the Grecians, were languishing near the bottom of Division three – it's what's been happening in the boardroom that's been making local and national headlines.

In 2001, fresh from having led Swansea FC and Scarborough FC respectively into the financial doldrums, two entrepreneurs, John Russell and Mike Lewis, became part-owners of Exeter City. Their track records didn't exactly inspire confidence among Grecian supporters, who were further confounded in May 2002 by the appointment of spoon-bending supremo Uri Geller as co-chairman of the club.

Uri is no stranger to St James Park, having visited in 1997 with a view to improving Exeter's results by planting crystals in one of the goalmouths. Unfortunately, the Grecians went on to lose the following game against Chester City 5-1, and although Exeter avoided relegation that year, the unreliable crystals were removed.

Uri's interest in Exeter City seems originally to have been sparked by his son, Daniel (now co-vice chairman), whose support of ECFC

was explained by his father as being attributable to 'his involvement with Exeter in a previous life'.

The visit of Uri's pal, Michael Jackson, to St James Park in June 2002 added another surreal twist to the tale. To the incredulity of regular supporters, Mr Jackson, now an honorary director of the club, turned up on a specially chartered train from London and proceeded to address the people of Exeter, accompanied by the magician David Blaine and the singer Patti Boulaye. Most recently, on the TV show *I'm a Celebrity, Get Me Out of Here!*, Uri was filmed wearing an Exeter City shirt with 'Jackson' written on the back.

Predictably enough, such high-profile shenanigans have yet to translate themselves into anything approaching success on the pitch or financial well-being in the club coffers, and neither a couple of appearances by Lee Sharpe nor the threatened signing of Paul Gascoigne seem likely to help ECFC in the short or long term. In desperation, long-suffering supporters are pinning their hopes on a new club mascot instead. Athena, the Grecian Goddess, brings a softer, more voluptuous flavour to Grecian support; it can only be hoped that her fabled wisdom will prevail in the boardroom too.

Michael Caines

Royal Clarence Hotel, Cathedral Yard (01392 310031/www.michaelcaines.com). Open noon-2.30pm, 7-10pm daily. **Main courses** £16.25-£22.50. **Credit** AmEx, MC, V.

This is the top spot in town and one of the finest restaurants in the region. Michael Caines doesn't cook here himself – he's too busy at Gidleigh Park (*see p172*) – but his smart yet informal Exeter restaurant still manages to turn out superlative modern French food that delights the city's diners.

Puccinos

16 Catherine Street, off Cathedral Yard (01392 499333). Open 8am-6pm Mon-Wed; 8am-9pm Thur; 8am-11pm Fri, Sat; 10am-5pm Sun. **Main courses** £5.95-£10.95. **Credit** MC, V.

Ridiculously attractive waiting staff, witty scribblings on the wall and a café menu that matches the hype: delicious fruit smoothies, decent coffee and hunger-quashing food, from simple paninis and baguettes to pizzas, grills and salads.

St Olaves Hotel

Mary Arches Street (01392 217736/www.olaves.co.uk). Open noon-2pm, 7-9pm daily. **Main courses** £6.95-£12.95. **Credit** AmEx, MC, V.

This is a great spot for an intimate evening *à deux*. Well-executed classic modern British fare is served in cheerful, elegant surroundings.

Ship Inn

Martin's Lane (01392 272040). Open 11am-11pm Mon-Sat; noon-10.30pm Sun. **Main courses** £4.25-£10.95. **Credit** MC, V.

One of many pubs that claims to have been frequented by Sir Francis Drake, the friendly Ship features beams, nooks and crannies a-go-go.

Thai Orchid

5 Cathedral Yard (01392 214215). Open noon-2.15pm, 6.30-10.15pm Mon-Fri; 6.30-10.15pm Sat. **Main courses** £6.50-£9.50. **Credit** AmEx, MC, V.

A delicious oriental menu and a stunning view of the cathedral – what more could you want?

Turf Locks

private track off Lion's Rest, Exminster (01392 833128/www.turfpub.net). Open 10am-3pm, 6-11pm Mon-Fri; 11am-11pm Sat, Sun. **Main courses** £3-£8.50. **Credit** AmEx, MC, V.

The goes one further than the Double Locks (*see p154*) in that it's only accessible by foot, bike or boat. Just outside the city, in pretty Exminster, the Turf

Locks offers great home-made food, along with good wine and a tempting selection of beer and real ales. Accommodation is provided in summer (*see p157*).

Turks Head

202 High Street (01392 256680). **Open** 11am-11pm Mon-Sat; noon-10.30pm Sun. **Main courses** £2.85-£6.95. **Credit** (food only, over £5) MC, V.

This 15th-century inn next to the Guildhall is said to be where Dickens found the original inspiration for his Fat Boy character in *The Pickwick Papers*.

Arts & entertainment

For an up-to-date guide to what's on during your stay, get hold of a copy of *The List* (www.exeterlist.co.uk), the city's lively monthly listings magazine.

The **Exeter Festival** (01392 213161; first fortnight of July) is a cornerstone of Exeter life, and latterly has sprawled out beyond the city centre, encompassing the wider community with street theatre, jazz and blues events, classical concerts and cabaret. A particular highlight is the open-air Shakespeare production in the natural amphitheatre of Rougemont Gardens, staged by Northcott Theatre Company. The company's home is the **Northcott Theatre** in the university grounds (01392 493493), which, despite looking like a multi-storey car park, is an intrinsic and dynamic component of Exeter's cultural make-up, hosting touring companies and one-off specials in its 433-capacity auditorium and smaller studio theatre.

The **Phoenix Art Centre** (Bradninch Place, off Gandy Street, 01392 667080) has electrified the Exeter arts scene since its revamp in the late 1990s and now boasts a theatre (also used for films), music venue, several galleries, a media centre and a café-bar, plus dance, drama and art studios. Although it has long been a cornerstone of Exeter's cultural life, its impact has increased of late, partly due to the success of the **Fringe Festival**, a lively event held in summer that focuses on alternative shows and performers.

Beyond these two cultural mainstays, the **Barnfield Theatre** (Barnfield Road, 01392 270891) stages less avant-garde productions (Gilbert & Sullivan-style musicals and the like), while the **Exeter Picture House** (51 Bartholomew Street West, 01392 435 522) features some blockbuster movies but also notable arthouse and indie flicks. Check out the art exhibitions in its comfortable café-bar.

Nightlife

While there are several nightclubs in Exeter catering for the student crowd, most don't warrant a mention. The best of the bunch is **Timepiece**, tucked behind the High Street

on Little Castle Street (01392 493096, www.timepiecenightclub.co.uk). It's open throughout the week, with a mix of funk, samba, street music, swing, jazz, R&B, hip hop, indie nights and one-off specials, and the ground-floor wine bar is a great place to kick back. For an edgier experience try **The Cavern** (83-84 Queen Street, 01392 495370), a tiny little space seemingly stolen from the underground cellars of Queen Street, which runs dance, punk and indie nights and is favoured by upcoming live acts. For something different, regular Sunday stand-up comedy nights are held at **Havana** (*see p154*).

Shops & services

Though the high-street big boys have all set up shop in Exeter in recent years, it's the funky independent stores that make shopping in the city so enjoyable.

With cobbles underfoot, portraits on the walls and nearly as many bars as retailers, diminutive **Gandy Street** is a delightful introduction to the Exeter shopping experience. Seek out **Martian Records** (No.15, 01392 49653) and **Hen's Teeth** (No.18, 01392 413457) for CDs and vinyl, and don't miss the jewellers selling hand-made pieces, snuggled away in little alleys off the main drag.

Elsewhere, the **Fore Street Centre** (south from the High Street) attracts fashionistas and bargain-hunters in equal measure. Check out the long-reigning **Real McCoy** (Unit 21, 01392 410481), which sells vintage clothing, jewellery and accessories, and has a downstairs café that serves a mean cappuccino; you'll also find flyers and leaflets here for special events around town.

The **Harlequin Centre** just off Paul Street is a small and varied shopping arcade that leads into the more bog-standard Guildhall Shopping Centre. The **Cooks Shop** (Harlequin Centre, 01392 258576) is good for gastronomic gadgetry, while **Pumpkin** (Harlequin Centre, 01392 498961) offers striking gifts and stylish homewares. (There's another branch on Sidwell Street.) **Hawkins Bazaar** (6 High Street, 01392 421312) is another good bet for unique gifts, with a million and one trinkets and curios for sale.

For food visit **Guys** (5 Blackboy Road, 01392 259338), a tiny delicatessen and health shop on the edge of the city centre. It's worth a special trip for the range of vegetarian foods, organic produce and bread on offer. Exeter's **farmers' market** (01392 665757) is held in Fore Street and South Street on the last Wednesday morning of the month. There are also traditional markets, selling a bit of everything, on **Sidwell Street** and in **St George's Hall** (Fore Street); phone 01392 665480 for further information.

Where to stay

The **Turf Locks** (*see p155*) offers B&B accommodation (£30 per person) between April and September in comfortable double and twin rooms overlooking the canal and estuary. Booking is strongly advised.

Beach House

The Strand, Topsham, EX3 0BB (01392 876456). **Rates** £35 single occupancy; £60 double/twin. **No credit cards.**

This Georgian B&B has the River Exe lapping at the edges of its lovely mature garden. There are only two rooms, but they have both been thoughtfully decorated in soft, delicate fabrics.

Buckerell Lodge Hotel

Topsham Road, EX2 4SQ (01392 221111/ www.corushotels.com). **Rates** £99 single; £120 double. **Credit** MC, V.

If the countrified chocolate box style is to your taste, you'll like this place. It has floral duvets and landscaped gardens – and is within easy reach of the city centre. Enquire about triple/family room rates.

Galley Restaurant Cabins

41 Fore Street, Topsham, EX3 0HU (01392 876078/ www.galleyrestaurant.co.uk). **Rates** (B&B) £89.50 twin; £99.50-£125 double. **Credit** AmEx, MC, V.

One en suite double and two twin 'cabins' with shared bathroom are housed in a 17th-century cottage with cheerful yellow and blue decor, exposed brickwork, original beams and glimpses of the river. On the ground floor is a communal lounge and dining area with an open fire, where breakfast is served. Group bookings are available.

Globe Backpackers Hostel

71 Holloway Street, EX2 4JD (01392 215521/ www.exeterbackpackers.co.uk). **Rates** £10/£11 per person dorm; £30 double. **Credit** MC, V.

Housed in an 18th-century townhouse a stone's throw from the city walls and the trendy Quayside, this hostel is clean and cosy with good facilities, including internet access, bike hire and storage. Most accommodation is in single-sex dorms, but if you feel like splashing out, £30 will buy you a night in a four-poster.

Hotel Barcelona

Magdalen Street, EX2 4HY (01392 281000/ www.hotelbarcelona-uk.com). **Rates** £75 single; £85 double; £95/£105 suite. **Credit** AmEx, DC, MC, V.

The *Good Hotel Guide*'s Designer Hotel of the Year 2002, Hotel Barcelona sets a new standard in funky, stylish accommodation. Within strolling distance of the city centre, this 46-room hotel occupies a former eye hospital that cuts a striking shape on the skyline. Inside, it's all bright colours and humorous Gaudi-esque flourishes: psychedelic prints, '50s furniture and glistening chrome. Dine in the informal big-top restaurant (*see p154*) or check out the cabaret at the exclusive Kino nightclub. Fab.

Royal Clarence Hotel

Cathedral Yard, EX1 1HD (01392 319955/ www.regalhotels.co.uk). **Rates** £105 single; £130 double; £145/£155 suite. **Credit** AmEx, DC, MC, V.

The first inn in England to be named a 'hotel', the Royal Clarence is reserved for those on big budgets. Oozing luxury, the hotel has an unrivalled central location and fantastic food in the Michael Caines restaurant (*see p155*). Make sure you bag a room at the front for unbeatable views of the cathedral.

St Olaves Hotel

Mary Arches Street, EX4 3AZ (01392 217736/ www.olaves.co.uk). **Rates** £95 single; £115 double; £145 suite. **Credit** AmEx, MC, V.

Set in its own walled garden, this is a Georgian retreat in the heart of the city. The rustic-style decor is soothing rather than twee, with antiques, luxury fabrics, traditional prints and a stunning spiral staircase in the centre of the building. The restaurant's very good too (*see p155*).

Resources

Hospital

Royal Devon & Exeter Hospital *Barrack Road, Wonford, Exeter (01392 411611).*

Internet

Central Library *Castle Street, Exeter (01392 384200).* **Open** 9.30am-7pm Mon, Tue, Thur, Fri; 10am-5pm Wed; 9.30am-4pm Sat.

Police station

Heavitree Road, Exeter (0870 577 7444).

Post office

Bedford Street, Exeter (0845 7223344). **Open** 9am-5.30pm Mon-Sat.

Tourist information

Exeter Tourist Information Centre
Civic Centre, Paris Street, Exeter (01392 265700/ www.exeter.gov.uk). **Open** *June-Aug* 9am-5pm Mon-Sat; 10am-4pm Sun. *Sept-May* 9am-5pm Mon-Sat.

Getting there & around

By air

Exeter International Airport (01392 367433, www.exeter-airport.co.uk) is located off the A30, 7 miles (12km) outside the city. From the airport bus 56 runs Mon-Sat to Exeter bus station, Woodbury and Exmouth. The 379 bus serves Exeter bus station, Ottery St Mary, Honiton and Sidmouth on Sundays in summer. Taxis (01395 233 728) are available for hire at the taxi rank or by pre-booking. For further information, *see p292*.

By bus

The **bus station** is on Paris Street (01392 427711). **National Express** (0870 580 8080) runs frequent services to and from London Victoria (4hrs 30mins), Bristol (2hrs), Birmingham (approx 4hrs) and other

Devon

points in the UK. For local travel the city bus service is frequent and reliable; all-day passes cost £2.90. Call **Traveline** (0870 608 2608) for further details.

By train

Exeter has two main railway stations, **Central** (on Queen Street) and **St David's** (on Bonhay Road). Trains from London Waterloo via Salisbury, as well as local trains to and from Exmouth and Barnstaple, stop at both stations. Services from Birmingham New Street, London Paddington and Bristol Temple Meads stop at Exeter St David's only. For details call National Rail Enquiries on 08457 484950.

East Devon

Blessed with a varied coastline, lush valleys and resplendent russet woodlands, East Devon offers a wide scope of activity for families and de-stressing weekenders. Despite a reputation as a mecca for retirees, dignified resorts like **Sidmouth** – the St Tropez of its time – have maintained a chic regency charm that's now accessorised with modern cultural events. Moreover, the coastline – with its red sandstone cliffs, pebble beaches, unsual landslips and outstanding fossil remains – is recognised as one of the most important geological sites in the world. The so-called **Jurassic Coast** from

The beach at **Budleigh Salterton**.

Orcombe Rocks in Exmouth to Studland Bay in Dorset displays near-unbroken evidence of 185 million years of evolution and was designated a World Heritage Site by UNESCO in 2001.

Exmouth & around

South of Topsham, the Exe broadens into a wide marshy estuary, before emerging into the English Channel at **Exmouth**. With its expansive beach, soft grassy dunes, crazy golf and amusement arcades, this is a place for kitsch, candyfloss pleasure, but also makes a good base from which to explore the coast. From the old port at the western end of the town – now redeveloped as a marina and apartment complex – boat trips run up the estuary to Topsham or down the coast to Dawlish Point, while the surrounding countryside is perfect for a sun-dappled, tree-framed drive.

Marauding Vikings landed on the coast here in 1001 and by the Middle Ages Exmouth had become a significant port with a reputation as a smugglers' hideout. The town developed as a seaside resort during the Napoleonic Wars, resulting in some fine Georgian terraces, particularly in the exclusive residential area known as the **Beacon**. Today, the town's main point of interest remains its two miles (three kilometres) of golden sands, backed by a traditional seaside esplanade.

On the northern fringes of Exmouth, overlooking the estuary, **A La Ronde** is an eccentric folly built in 1798 and now owned by the National Trust. The 16-sided house was the brainchild of Jane and Mary Parminter and is filled with mementoes from their travels. The topmost gallery and stairway is entirely decorated with seashells.

Nearby **Woodbury Common** is an area of lowland heath that is popular with walkers and nature lovers; it is also the rural location of the anomolous **Nigel Mansell World of Racing** at the Woodbury Park Hotel, which serves as a homage to the former world champion's career.

Heading east from Exmouth, Sandy Bay has some decent beaches en route to the old-fashioned but charming town of **Budleigh Salterton**. Set at the mouth of the Otter estuary, the town takes its name from the salt marshes (salterns), from which salt was extracted during the Middle Ages. In contrast to Exmouth, Budleigh Salterton exudes a serene, one might almost say soporific, aura of respectability. In the 20th century the town was a favourite among literary bigwigs such as Noel Coward and PG Wodehouse, but these days it attracts hordes of retirees.

Ladram Bay.

Through the centre of town, a small open stream runs along much of the High Street towards a beautiful pebble beach whose clear waters are enclosed by striking tree-topped red cliffs. (If Budleigh's pebbles are too uncomfortable for you, a short trek west will bring you to a small stretch of foot-friendly sand at **Littleham Cove**.)

Overlooking the town beach on Marine Parade, the **Fairlynch Art Centre & Museum** is housed in a typical 19th-century thatched cottage, and houses worthwhile displays of local and natural history as well as entertaining collections of Victorian and Edwardian costumes and dolls. There's also a smugglers' cellar in the basement and a display of East Devon lacemaking in the top room. Adjacent to the museum, the **Octagon** is where Sir John Everett Millais painted *The Boyhood of Raleigh*, depicting the young Walter Raleigh and his cousin Humphrey Gilbert being told a story by a sailor on Budleigh beach. The painting is now in the Tate Britain in London.

Walter Raleigh (c.1552-1618) was, in fact, born two miles (three kilometres) inland in the hamlet of **Hayes Barton**, while his father was warden at All Saints church in **East Budleigh**. On the edge of the village, visit the splendid **Bicton Park Botanical Gardens**, consisting of over 60 acres of mature gardens, complete with graceful water features, fragrant borders and a 19th-century palm house that predates its counterpart at Kew by 20 years.

A short walk up the River Otter from the coast, **Otterton** is a beautiful village of archetypal thatched and timbered cottages. Daily flour-making demonstrations take place at the **Otterton Mill Centre & Working Museum** (01395 568521), and cultural events are held here throughout the year. The mill's organic flour is used to make delicious bread and cakes, which are sold in the café. From Otterton a lane leads to the stunning pebble beach at **Ladram Bay**. The East Devon coastline is distinguished by its striking sandstone cliffs but the examples here are particularly resplendent – despite the best efforts of the Ladram Bay caravan park (01395 568398, www.ladrambay.co.uk) to mar the scene.

A La Ronde

Summer Lane, nr Exmouth (01395 265514/ www.nationaltrust.org.uk). **Open** *mid Mar-Oct* 11am-5.30pm Mon-Thur, Sun. Closed Nov-mid Mar. **Admission** £3.50; £1.70 concessions. **No credit cards**.

Bicton Park Botanical Gardens

East Budleigh, nr Budleigh Salterton (01395 568465/www.bictongardens.co.uk). **Open** *Apr-Oct* 10am-6pm daily. *Nov-Mar* 10am-5pm daily. **Admission** £4.75; £2.75-£3.75 concessions; £12.75 family. **Credit** MC, V.

The multi-sided folly of **A La Ronde**. *See p158.*

Fairlynch Art Centre & Museum

27 Fore Street, Budleigh Salterton (01395 442666/ www.devonmuseums.net/fairlynch). **Open** *July, Aug* 11am-1pm Mon-Sat. *Easter-Oct* 2-4.30pm daily. Closed Nov-Mar. **Admission** £2; £1.50 concessions, £4 family. **No credit cards.**

Nigel Mansell World of Racing

Woodbury Park Hotel, Woodbury Castle, Woodbury (01395 233382/www.woodburypark. co.uk). **Open** 10am-6pm daily. *Tours* 11am daily. **Admission** £5; £3 concessions; £12 family. **Credit** AmEx, MC, V.

Activities

Boat trips

Stuart Line Cruises (cruises 01395 222144, fishing 01395 275882, www.stuartlinecruises.co.uk) runs all sorts of fishing trips, barbeque cruises and river cruises from its beach hut headquarters on Exmouth Marina.

Cycling

The 82-mile (140km) **Buzzard Cycle Route** takes in much of the coast and countryside of East Devon. Leaflets detailing this and other shorter routes are available from local tourist offices.

Golf

Nigel Mansell's **Woodbury Park** (Woodbury Castle, Woodbury, 01395 233382, www.woodbury park.co.uk) incorporates a country club with spa facilities, hotel (double B&B £136-£166) and 18-hole golf course.

Riding

Budleigh Salterton Riding School (Dalditch Lane, Budleigh Salterton, 01395 442035, www.devonriding. co.uk) is a BHS-approved school offering three- and four-day courses and cross-country lessons, plus pub rides across Woodbury Common to Otterton.

Sailing

Spinnakers Sailing Centre (The Harbour, Exmouth, 01395 222551, www.spinnakers.co.uk) is a RYA-registered, dedicated dinghy sailing school offering courses for both beginners and improvers on the Exe estuary.

Walking

The 62-mile (100km) **East Devon Way** starts in Exmouth (behind the bus and train stations) and runs inland, winding through some beautiful countryside before returning to the coast at Lyme Regis. Information is available from the Tourist Information Centre in Exmouth (*see p161*).

Where to eat, drink & stay

Although it's a bit wind-battered and scruffy, the **Deer Leap** pub (Esplanade, Exmouth, 01395 265030, main courses £3.95-£5.55) has an enviable position overlooking the sea and offers reasonable pub grub. For something a little more formal, also in Exmouth, try the **Seafood Restaurant** (Tower Street, 01395 269459, main courses £11-£14) for its hearty seafood platter.

Exmouth has no shortage of hotels – many of them housed in grand Regency terraces – but none of them particularly stand out from the crowd. For a traditional seaside stay the **Royal Beacon Hotel** (The Beacon, 01395 264886, www.royalbeaconhotel.co.uk, double B&B £85-£95) is one of the better choices with a great view and comfortable if rather fussy rooms. There's similarly old-fashioned, frilly decor at the **Devoncourt Hotel** (16 Douglas Avenue, Exmouth, 01395 272277, www.devoncourt.com, double B&B £95-£135), but this place benefits from subtropical gardens, sea views and indoor and outdoor pools. Slightly more unusual is the 11-bedroomed **Barn Hotel** on the edge of town (Foxholes Hill, 01395 224411, www.barnhotel.co.uk, closed 2wks Christmas, double B&B £55-£78), an Arts & Crafts house with its own private gardens and swimming pool. For pampering treats at a wallet-friendly price **Rosehill** (30 West Hill, Budleigh Salterton, 01395 444031, www.bnbrelaxed. demon.co.uk, double B&B £45-£70) is a real gem. The Grade II-listed Victorian house boasts spa facilities, massages, aromatherapy and beauty treatments, in addition to bed and breakfast facilities. Campers should try **Pooh Cottage Caravan & Camping Park** (Bear Lane, Budleigh Salterton, 01395 442354).

Resources

Hospital
Exmouth *Exmouth Health Centre, Claremont Grove (01395 226015).*

Police station
Exmouth *North Street (0870 577 7444).*

Post offices
Budleigh Salterton *23 High Street (01395 443272).* **Open** 9am-5.30pm Mon-Fri; 9am-12.30pm Sat.
Exmouth *4-6 Chapel Street (0845 722 3344).* **Open** 9am-5.30pm Mon-Fri; 9am-12.30pm Sat.

Tourist information
Budleigh Salterton *Tourist Information Centre, 14 Fore Street (01395 445275).* **Open** *Easter-June, Sept, Oct* 10am-5pm Mon-Sat. *July, Aug* 10am-5pm Mon-Sat; 11am-5pm Sun. *Nov-Easter* 10am-1pm Mon-Thur, Sat; 10am-3pm Fri.
Exmouth *Tourist Information Centre, Alexandra Terrace (01395 222299/www.exmouthguide.co.uk).* **Open** *Apr-June, Sept, Oct* 9.30am-5.30pm Mon-Sat. *July, Aug* 9.30am-5.30pm Mon-Sat; 10am-3pm Sun. *Nov-Mar* 10am-4pm Mon-Sat.

Sidmouth & further east

Sidmouth is the charming oddball of the East Devon coast. Nestled in a sheltered valley, hugged by wooded hills, it's a beautiful Regency town with kempt houses, splendid gardens and a sizeable geriatric population. However, there's also a bohemian hippy side to this otherwise prim resort, which draws a different style of visitor to the **Sidmouth International Festival** each August (*see p163* **Festival fever**).

Although Sidmouth featured in the Domesday Book as Sedemuda, it remained a minor fishing village until the 19th century, when the Duke of Kent retired here and the town blossomed into a desirable resort. Consequently, it is an architectural mixed bag, with many Georgian properties cosying up to thatched cob cottages. Sidmouth has around 500 listed buildings, most dating from the first half of the 19th century, interspersed with beautiful gardens that benefit from the mild climate. The number of blue plaques dotted around town is an indication of Sidmouth's popularity among the nobility and glitterati of the past. **Fortfield Terrace**, for example, proudly displays a double-headed eagle commemorating the stay of the Grand Duchess Helena, sister-in-law to the Tsar of Russia. She arrived in 1831 with an entourage of 100 gentlemen, ladies and servants – enough to rival Mariah Carey.

To gain an impression of Sidmouth in its heyday visit the **Sidmouth Museum** near the parish church, which has paintings of the town by the 19th-century watercolourist Peter Orlando Hutchinson, as well as lace-making demonstrations. The museum is also the start of guided strolls around the town, which will reveal 100-year-old jewellers, sedate tearooms and a wonderful time-warped grocers, **Trumps** (8 Fore Street, 01395 512446, www.trumpsofsidmouth.co.uk), purveyors of 'high class provisions' since 1813.

The gravelly town beach is backed by the Esplanade, decorated with some of Sidmouth's most extravagant and award-winning floral displays, while to the west is a pleasant sand and shingle beach at **Jacob's Ladder**.

On the other side of town, the coastpath runs east from Salcombe Hill along the cliffs, with access to secluded picnic sites and a good beach at **Weston Mouth**. Just inland, an area of protected heathland is the site of the **Norman Lockyer Observatory**. Built in 1912 by the eminent astronomer and astrophysicist, it is a working observatory and planetarium that makes the most of the clear Devon skies and allows visitors to view high-powered astronomical equipment in action.

Close by, and accessible via filmic country lanes, the **Sidmouth Donkey Sanctuary** is a haven for neglected and retired donkeys, and a must-visit for anyone with a soft spot for Eeyore. Inland, visitors can view the final

Devon

Beer.

stages of restoration of the **Sidbury Mill**, the last working watermill on the River Sid. The work of West Country artists is displayed in the **Kingfisher Gallery** here and cream teas are served in the coffeeshop.

Further east, the villages of Branscombe and Beer are picturesque delights. **Branscombe** is a winding settlement of thatched cottages that spread along a narrow valley. In the village, the **Old Bakery, Manor Mill & Forge** (01297 680333, www.nationaltrust.org.uk, closed early Nov-Easter) comprise a complex of buildings maintained by the National Trust. The stone-built, thatched bakery now serves as a tearoom, but the water-powered mill, which probably supplied the flour, has been restored to full working order, and the nearby forge is usually open for the sale of ironwork. From the village, a path leads to the National Trust-protected stony beach at **Branscombe Mouth**.

Beer Quarry Caves between Branscombe and Beer are a vast network of underground caverns created from the quarrying of Beer stone that took place from Roman times until 1900. The limestone was used in the construction of many famous buildings, including Exeter Cathedral (*see p150*), St Paul's Cathedral and parts of Westminster Abbey, and was much prized in masonry circles due to its malleability, which allowed fine detail to be carved. Guided tours of this fascinating complex take about an hour.

Beer still accommodates working fishing boats, but no longer the smugglers who once ran covert operations from the surrounding coves. An open stream, decorated with flowering tubs, runs through the centre of this charming village, emerging at a sheltered pebble beach, nestling between steep white cliffs. Apart from fishing and smuggling, lace-making was once the principal industry here, but now Beer relies on its picturesque location to lure the tourist pounds.

Scores of visitors descend on the village in August, for the highly enjoyable **Beer Regatta** (01297 21660), which features traditional street entertainment, water-based events and barrel rolling. Local pubs and hotels are usually bulging at the seams at this time, so book your accommodation well in advance.

On the hill overlooking the village, **Pecorama** is a low-key family attraction devoted to model railways. The highlight is the miniature Beer Heights Light Railway, which chugs its way through the gardens for a mile, offering passengers long-range views over Lyme Bay as far as Portland Bill in Dorset. More energetic visitors can enjoy the soaring views from **Beer Head**, an 128-metre (420-foot) headland, accessed along the steep cliffpath a mile (one and a half kilometres) south of the village.

Heading in the opposite direction, an easy stroll brings you to the fairly unexciting resort of **Seaton**, where beachside pubs, ice-cream vendors and deckchairs are far more prominent than anything of real cultural note. One attraction, though, is the **Seaton Tramway**, which runs inland along the Axe estuary as far as the ancient town of Colyton. Riding these narrow-gauge electric trams may not be a thrill-a-minute experience, but sitting on the top deck with the sun on your face can be a real treat. In summer the **Colyton Wagon Wanderer** (01297 553290, closed Oct-Apr) waits at the end of the line to take you into Colyton town centre on a wagon pulled by beautiful Suffolk Punch horses. Colyton's Norman church of **St Andrews** has an octagonal lantern tower,

believed to be one of only three in the country. It may have served as a navigation guide for sailors negotiating the River Axe.

Further north at the head of the valley, **Axminster** is a small market town, made famous by the carpets that have been made here since 1755. Not far away, tiny Devon lanes hide the **Lyme Bay Winery** (Shute, 01297 551355, www.lymebaywinery.co.uk), which sells award-winning ciders, wines and liqueurs made from locally grown fruits and flowers. One of the most popular varieties is Jack Ratt Cider, named after the notorious smuggler Jack Rattenbury.

Festival fever
Sidmouth International Festival

For one week each August, Sidmouth, the dignified elderly lady of the East Devon coast, slips into a little boho number, ties a daisy chain around her ankle and shakes loose to the sound of steel drums and funky world music.

The **Sidmouth International Festival** (01629 760123, www.sidmouthfestival.com), which celebrates its 50th anniversary in 2004, is widely regarded as one of the best folk music festivals in the country, attracting scores of official folk and world music acts, plus dozens of street performers, buskers,

stalls and revellers from around the globe. As well as events in the main arena – a large outdoor amphitheatre with a 5,000 capacity – unofficial entertainers fill the promenade and the town centre with colour, sound and activity throughout the week. Regular acts include the steel band who play for hours in the town square to rapturous applause and frenzied, infectious dancing. Day, weekend and week-long passes are available and should be bought well in advance. A dedicated campsite is provided for festival-goers, with shuttle buses to ferry them into town.

The coast path, meanwhile, heads east from Seaton through the fascinating **Undercliff National Nature Reserve** en route to Lyme Regis, just across the border in Dorset. The unique geology of the cliffs in this area – impermeable clay overlain by sands and chalk – has given rise to some of the largest landslides in Britain, creating acres of extra land known as 'undercliff' between the sea and the high cliffs. Over the years the undercliffs have been allowed to germinate naturally, resulting in one of the wildest and most unspoilt stretches of coastline in the county. The terrain is quite rough and overgrown in places, but intrepid walkers will be rewarded by beautiful scenery and rare flora and fauna.

Beer Quarry Caves

Quarry Lane (01297 680282/www.beerquarrycaves. fsnet.co.uk). **Open** *Easter-Sept* 10am-5pm daily. *Oct* 11am-4pm daily. Closed Nov-Mar. **Admission** (1hr tour) £4.75; £3.50 concessions; £15 family. **Credit** MC, V.

Norman Lockyer Observatory

Salcombe Hill, Sidmouth (01395 579941/512096/ www.ex.ac.uk/nlo). **Open** public programme varies; call for details. **Admission** £4; £2 children. **No credit cards**.

Pecorama

Underleys, Beer, nr Seaton (01297 20580/www. peco-uk.com). **Open** *Indoor exhibition* Oct-May 10am-5.30pm Mon-Fri; 10am-1pm Sat. June-Sept 10am-5.30pm Mon-Fri, Sun; 10am-1pm Sat. *Outdoor attractions* Apr-Sept 10am-5.30pm Mon-Fri, Sun; 10am-1pm Sat. Closed Oct-Mar. **Admission** £4.75; £3.20/£4.25 concessions; free under-4s. **Credit** MC, V.

Seaton Tramway

Harbour Road, Seaton (01297 20375/www.tram. co.uk). **Open** *Mar-July* 10am-5pm daily. *Aug* 10am-8.40pm daily. *Mid Oct, Nov* 10am-4pm Sat, Sun. Closed Dec-Feb. **Tickets** *Day Rover* £8.25; £5.50/£7 concessions; free under-4s. **Credit** MC, V.

Sidbury Mill & Kingfisher Gallery

Sidbury, nr Sidmouth (01395 597221/ www.kingfisher-gallery.fsnet.co.uk). **Open** *Apr-Sept* 2-5pm Fri-Sun. Closed Oct-Mar. **Admission** phone for details. **Credit** MC, V.

Sidmouth Donkey Sanctuary

Slade House Farm, Salcombe Regis, nr Sidmouth (01395 578222/www.thedonkeysanctuary.org.uk). **Open** 9am-dusk daily. **Admission** free. **Credit** *Shop* MC, V. *Shop* MC, V.

Sidmouth Museum

Hope Cottage, Church Street, Sidmouth (01395 516139/www.devonmuseums.net). **Open** *Easter-Oct* 2-4.30pm Mon; 10am-12.30pm, 2-4.30pm Tue-Sat. Closed Nov-Mar. **Admission** phone for details. **Credit** *Shop* MC, V.

Norman Lockyer Observatory. *See p161.*

Where to eat, drink & stay

As an established resort, Sidmouth offers a plentiful supply of hotels and B&Bs. Along the Esplanade, a reliable choice is the**Victoria Hotel** (The Esplanade, 01395 512651, www. victoriahotel.co.uk, set menus £17-£32, double B&B £79-£140 incl dinner), which stands in landscaped gardens, a stone's throw from the beach, and is stacked with facilities: indoor and outdoor pools, tennis courts, spa, games room and a smart restaurant. The nearby **Hotel Riviera** (The Esplanade, 01395 515201, www.hotelriviera.co.uk, main courses £16-£26.50, double £148-£208) is old-fashioned in the best sense, with attentive service, comfortable rooms, classic cuisine and a tinkling piano in the bar. The bow windows and long terrace overlook the sea. For a countrified treat at very affordable prices, **Pinn Barton Farm** (Pinn, Peak Hill, Sidmouth, 01395 514004, double B&B £46) offers cosy en suite rooms and proper farmhouse breakfasts.

Most of Sidmouth's hotels have their own dining facilities, so there's not a great choice of independent restaurants in the town. However, the sprawling Esplanade leaves ample space for pavement cafés and hotel terraces that are all perfect for a Pimm's pit stop. The **Marlborough** (01395 513320, closed late Dec-early Jan) is incredibly popular during the Festival and has a plentiful supply of outdoor seating, while a few doors down, the small **Marine** (01395 513145) is more youth-oriented than many Sidmouth imbiberies.

In nearby Sidford, the **Blue Ball Inn** (Stevens Cross, 01395 514062, from £19 two-course set meal, double £75-£88) offers good food and pleasant accommodation in centuries-old buildings. For a real treat, though, head to the 14th-century **Mason's Arms** in Branscombe (01297 680300, www. masonsarms.co.uk, main courses £8-£14.95, double £48-£150), where thatched roof, slate floors, ships beams and log fires create the perfect pub ambience. A good selection of ales is supplemented by an excellent menu of classic English and French dishes, which won the Devonshire Dining Pub of the Year Award in 2002. Accommodation is available in comfortable rooms and cottages, many of which have four-poster beds.

Away from the coast, **Kerrington House** in Axminster (Musbury Road, 01297 35333, www.kerringtonhouse.com, set menu £25, double B&B £118) is a bijou hotel with five en suite bedrooms, special breakfasts and an exquisitely prepared dinner menu available from Thursday to Sunday.

Resources

Hospitals

Axminster *Chard Street (01297 630400).*
Sidmouth *Victoria Cottage Hospital, May Terrace (01395 512482).*

Internet

Axminster *Axminster Library, South Street (01297 32693).* **Open** 9.30am-1pm, 2-5pm Mon, Tue; 9.30am-1pm Thur; 9.30am-1pm, 2-6.30pm Fri; 10am-noon Sat.

Police stations

Axminster *Lyme Close (0870 577 7444).*
Seaton *Queen Street (0870 577 7444).*
Sidmouth *40 Temple Street (0870 577 7444).*

Post offices

Axminster *West Street (01297 33244).*
Open 8.30am-5.30pm Mon-Fri; 8.30am-1pm Sat.
Seaton *22 Queen Street (01297 21772).*
Open 9am-5.30pm Mon-Fri; 9am-1pm Sat.
Sidmouth *132 High Street (01395 513950).*
Open 8.45am-5.30pm Mon-Fri; 8.45am-4.30pm Sat.

Tourist information

Seaton *Tourist Information Centre, The Underfleet (01297 21660/www.eastdevon.net/tourism/seaton).* **Open** *Apr-Oct* 10am-5pm Mon-Sat; 10am-2pm Sun. *Nov-Mar* 10am-2pm Mon-Sat.

Sidmouth *Tourist Information Centre, Ham Lane (01395 516441/www.visitsidmouth.co.uk).* **Open** *May-Oct* 10am-5pm Mon-Sat; 10am-4pm Sun. *Nov-Feb* 10am-1.30pm Mon-Sat. *Mar, Apr* 10am-4pm Mon-Thur; 10am-5pm Fri, Sat; 10am-1pm Sun.

Honiton & around

Nestling in the Otter Valley on the edge of the main A30 route to Exeter, the lively market town of **Honiton** was built on the success of its lace trade. However, nowadays this traditional craft has been superseded by the town's reputation as the antiques mecca of the South West – indeed, it's said to have more antiques shops and antiquarian bookstores than any other town in the country.

In the Middle Ages, Honiton was a centre for cloth. It was Flemish craftsmen who introduced the skilled production of lace to the town in the 16th century. In 1676 there were reportedly 5,299 lacemakers in East Devon of whom one third lived and worked in Honiton. The town's resulting prosperity is evidenced today in the fine Regency houses, which were built after devastating fires in the 18th century. By the 19th century, Honiton lace was so renowned that Queen Victoria commissioned local craftspeople to supply lace for her wedding dress, and later a christening robe for her eldest son Edward VII; the robe is still used for royal christenings today.

Housed in a 14th-century chapel (the town's oldest building), **Allhallow's Museum of Lace & Antiquities** holds the world's principal collection of Honiton lace and hosts regular demonstrations of lace-making throughout the year. There are also local history exhibits here, some of which date back 100,000 years.

The broad **High Street** is taken over by stalls at the twice-weekly markets (Tuesday and Saturday), while the **Honiton Show** in August is one of the best agricultural events in the region. More than a farming showcase, it also offers fresh produce and all sorts of organic scrumptiousness.

Many pretty villages and a couple of hidden attractions can be discovered close to Honiton by exploring the winding, high-hedged lanes of the Otter Valley and the Blackdown Hills. For an overview of this quintessential rolling Devon countryside, climb **Hembury Hill Fort**, the earliest Iron Age fort in Devon, located just off the A373.

Further south-west, **Ottery St Mary** is a small and unassuming Georgian town with a disproportionately rich history dating back over 1,000 years. Oliver Cromwell had his South West campaign headquarters here;

Devon

Combe House: a classic country-house hotel. *See p167.*

William Makepeace Thackeray set his novel *Pendennis* in the town and Samuel Taylor Coleridge was born in Ottery's old school house, while his father was headmaster of the local school.

Every 5th November the town eschews a traditional fireworks display in favour of a parade of flaming tar barrels. Believed to be a way of driving devils from the town, this bizarre – not to mention dangerous – ritual has taken place in Ottery since the 17th century. The barrels, sponsored by local pubs, are soaked with tar for several days in preparation for lighting on the night. Under the smoke-stung eyes of up to 20,000 onlookers, the fire-spewing barrels are then carried through the streets on the shoulders of local daredevils. As the event wears on, the size and weight of the barrels increase, peaking with the largest specimens (over 30 kilos/60 pounds) being carried at midnight. The atmosphere is one of camaraderie and machismo – and that's just among the spectators – but the mixture of danger and excitement sits well with warm gloves and a plastic cup of brandy. A huge cheek-warming bonfire is built on the banks of the River Otter, while a funfair provides some more conventional thrills. For further information have a look at the website: www.tarbarrels.co.uk.

You cannot fail to miss the imposing church of **St Mary** rising up in the centre of Ottery. It was the work of John de Grandisson, Bishop of Exeter, who in 1337 arranged for an extension and modification of the existing Saxon structure to create a miniature replica of Exeter's cathedral. The 500-year-old weathercock on the steeple is believed to be the oldest still in place in Europe, while the richly decorated interior houses a working astronomical clock thought to date from the 14th century.

North-west of the village is **Cadhay House**, a classic Tudor manor built by one of the governors of St Mary's church, and later embellished with Elizabethan and Georgian additions. The manor was restored in the early 20th century by the extravagantly named WC Dampier Wetham, and stands in an attractive herbaceous garden with original medieval fish ponds. It can be visited by guided tour on select days during the summer (phone 01404 812432 for details).

On the other side of the A30, **Escot Fantasy Gardens** are an entertaining blend of traditional gardens and wildlife park set within the grounds of the Kennaway family estate. The original gardens were laid out by Capability Brown in the 18th century but have been revamped to create a modern attraction.

Woodland paths lead through the beautiful flowers, shrubs and specimen trees to a bird of prey centre, a wetlands habitat, and an award-winning pet and aquatic centre. There's also a restaurant on site.

Allhallow's Museum of Lace & Antiquities

High Street, Honiton (01404 44966/www.cyberlink. co.uk/allhallows/honiton). **Open** *Apr-Sept* 10am-5pm Mon-Sat. *Oct* 10am-4pm Mon-Sat. Closed Nov-Mar. **Admission** call for details.

Escot Fantasy Gardens

Fairmile, nr Ottery St Mary (01404 822188/www. escot-devon.co.uk). **Open** 10am-5pm daily. Closed Christmas. **Admission** £3.50; £3.25 concessions; £12 family; free under-4s. **Credit** MC, V.

Where to eat, drink & stay

While you're in Honiton, don't miss an ice-cream pit stop at the **Honiton Dairy** (60 High Street, 01404 42075). For more substantial food, one of the best pubs in the area is the **Drewe Arms** in Broadhembury (01404 841267, closed 25 Dec, main courses £4.50-£16), which has a lovely garden for summer lunches and a cosy bar serving fresh fish dishes and local Otter beers. **Jack In The Green Inn** (Rockbeare, near Exeter, 01404 822240, www.jackinthegreen. uk.com, main courses £5.25-£14.50) is another foodie's delight. Winning accolades from all corners, including the Devon Pub of the Year Award in 2001, it serves a well-executed international menu that is great value for money. The **White Hart Inn** (A35, Wilmington, 01404 831764, main courses £5.25-£11.75) is an archetypal 16th-century thatched English pub full of misshapen corners, nooks and crannies Its classic pub menu is often accompanied by live music in the evenings.

If you've had your fill of chintz, stay at **West Colwell Farm** (Offwell, near Honiton, 01404 831130, www.westcolwell.co.uk), where contemporary and stylish bed and breakfast accommodation is provided in three en suite rooms with private decks and top-quality showers. Or you could sample the delicious English breakfasts at **Smallicombe Farm** (Northleigh, Colyton, 01404 831310, www.smallicombe.com, double B&B £50-£60), where rashers and bangers are produced from the farm's own rare-breed pigs. Self-catering is available here in a number of beautifully converted barns and outhouses.

More luxurious accommodation is provided at the former home of the Coleridge family in Ottery St Mary. **Salston Manor Hotel** (Ottery St Mary, 01404 815581, www.salston

hotel.co.uk, double B&B £99) has 27 en suite rooms, an indoor swimming pool and squash courts. Also in Ottery, **Tumbling Weir Hotel & Restaurant** (Canaan Way, 01404 812752, closed Christmas, main courses £7.95-£11.95, double B&B £74), with its pretty grounds, thatched roof and discreet waterside location, is tranquil and welcoming.

If you really want to spoil yourself, though, there's only one choice. **Combe House** (Gittisham, near Honiton, 01404 540400, www.thishotel.com, double B&B £138-£265) is one of the most romantic hotels in the country, and a justified favourite of the rich and famous. The classic, oak-panelled English country house has luxurious rooms looking out over glorious Devon countryside, and decorated with fine antiques and artworks. The gourmet restaurant (set menus £19.50-£32.50) serves fresh game, meat and locally caught fish accompanied by an impressive wine list.

Resources

Hospitals

Honiton *Marlpits Road (01404 540540).*
Ottery St Mary *Keegan Close (01404 816000).*

Police station

Honiton *High Street (0870 577 7444).*

Post offices

Honiton *64 High Street (0845 722 3344).* **Open** 9am-5.30pm Mon-Fri; 9am-12.30pm Sat.
Ottery St Mary *2 Mill Street (01404 812001).* **Open** 8.30am-5.30pm Mon-Fri; 9am-12.30pm Sat.

Tourist Information

Honiton *Tourist Information Centre, Lace Walk car park (01404 43716/www.eastdevon.gov.uk).* **Open** *Nov-Mar* 10am-2pm Mon-Sat. *Apr-Oct* 10am-4pm Mon-Sat.
Ottery St Mary *Tourist Information Centre, 10B Broad Street (01404 813964/www.eastdevon.gov.uk).* **Open** *Apr-early Nov* 9.30am-5pm Mon-Fri. *July-Sept* 9.30am-5pm Mon-Fri; 9.30am-2pm Sat. *Dec-Mar* 9.30am-2pm Mon-Fri.

Getting there

By bus

There are frequent buses from **Exeter** to Exmouth, Budleigh Salterton, Sidmouth, Beer, Seaton, Honiton, Ottery St Mary and Axminster, with interconnecting services to other towns and villages in the region. Call Stagecoach (01392 427711) or Traveline (0870 608 2608) for further information.

By train

South West Trains run frequent services from Exeter to **Exmouth** (30mins). The mainline London Waterloo–Paignton service stops at **Axminster** (2hrs 30mins) and **Honiton** (2hrs 45mins).

Dartmoor

Get back to nature in the wide, wild outdoors.

Designated as a National Park in 1951, Dartmoor is frequently referred to as the last great wilderness in southern England. Although the 367-square-mile (954-square-kilometre) former royal hunting ground is now largely devoid of woodland, the landscape is far more varied than its desolate reputation might suggest, encompassing grand vistas and empty spaces; gentle undulating misty hills and dramatic craggy tors – remainders of the 400-million-year-old volcanic plateau from which Dartmoor was formed. History is everywhere, in the shape of prehistoric hut circles, ancient field systems and Victorian mine workings, although sometimes it is difficult to distinguish between the hand of man and the hand of nature, as everything is made of granite and appears to have sprung from the earth.

Above all, Dartmoor is a place to enjoy the great outdoors, offering an earthy, back-to-nature experience that is almost primeval. Only the hardiest plants, animals and people survive here, so you'd be advised to invest in some sturdy boots and waterproof clothing if you want to 'off road'. You should also equip yourself with a good map and never underestimate the moor's harsh terrain and inclement weather.

You could always admire the scenery from the comfort of your car, of course, but this would be missing the point. Dartmoor is crossed by around 600 miles of paths, tracks and bridleways, which link up with long-distance walking routes including the **Two Moors Way** (*see p177*) and the 87-mile (140-kilometre) circular **Dartmoor Way**. For cyclists, the **Devon Coast to Coast Cycle Route** takes in part of the eastern moor, from Okehampton through Lydford to Tavistock and on to Plymouth. While exploring, note that livestock and wildlife roam freely across the moor, and although Dartmoor ponies look cute, it is illegal (not to mention dangerous) to feed them.

FURTHER INFORMATION

For detailed information about the National Park, contact the **Dartmoor National Park Authority** (Parke, Bovey Tracey, near Newton Abbot, Devon TQ13 9JQ, 01626 832093, www.dartmoor-npa.gov.uk). Visitor information is also available from the **Dartmoor Tourist Association** (High Moorland Business Centre, Princetown, Dartmoor, Devon, PL20 6QF,

01822 890567, www.discoverdartmoor.com). Drivers should note that the speed limit within the National Park is a strict 40 miles (64 kilometres) per hour.

Okehampton & north-western Dartmoor

West of Exeter, the main A30 to Cornwall runs through Devon countryside, with Dartmoor a constantly brooding presence to the south. Turn off the A30 to reach **Finch Foundry** at Sticklepath, a working forge dating from the 19th century and now under the care of the National Trust, with waterwheels powering an enormous hammer and grumbling grindstone. A little further west is **Belstone**, a pretty village offering easy access to the high moor around Belstone Tor.

Okehampton itself can appear a bit dismal as you approach it from the east, but the town centre is pleasant enough. The town has a long history as an Iron Age village, a Roman fort and a Saxon settlement. It was the coming of the Normans, however, that established it as a proper town, when Baron Baldwin de Brionne built **Okehampton Castle** shortly after the invasion of 1066. It is the only castle in Devon listed in the Domesday Book of 1086.

The present romantic granite remains are mostly of a later 14th-century building, which was largely destroyed by Henry VIII. There is graffiti in the keep left by French prisoners during the Napoleonic wars.

To get a feel for the hardships endured by those who have lived and worked on the moor through the ages, visit the understated but interesting **Museum of Dartmoor Life**, which has local exhibits devoted to domestic, agricultural and industrial activities. Across West Street is the 17th-century town hall, which was originally built as a private home; close by is a well-preserved Victorian shopping arcade and **Simmons Park**, an Edwardian pleasure garden laid out in 1906 and recently restored.

The three army firing ranges to the south of **Okehampton Camp** – indicated by a series of red and white posts with warning notices – incorporate some of the highest and wildest parts of the moor, including **Yes Tor** (2,028 feet/618 metres) and **High Willhays** (2,039 feet/

621 metres). Red flags by day and red lamps by night indicate when live firing is taking place; during these periods it is unsafe and unlawful to enter the range, but at other times, the public has free access to these areas. Most visitors, though, don't know that they're allowed on to the moor here, which means that you can enjoy whole swathes of dramatic moorland without another human being in sight. The firing programme for the following week is published in local newspapers every Friday, and updated daily on BBC Radio Devon. Information is also available on freephone 0800 458 4868 and on the internet at www.dartmoor-ranges.co.uk.

From Okehampton it is possible to catch the 'Dartmoor Pony' steam service (01837 55637, www.dartmoorrailway.co.uk) for two miles (three kilometres) through scenic countryside, terminating close to the stone quarry in **Meldon**. Fine views can be enjoyed right across Dartmoor from the former railway viaduct here, 120 feet (37 metres) above the West Okement valley. The refurbished viaduct is the largest of its kind in the UK and is open to walkers and cyclists.

Next stop is **Lydford**, an appealing village watched over by the brooding presence of **Lydford Castle** (admission free). The village was founded as a Saxon outpost and became one of Alfred the Great's defences against the Danes; the castle, however, dates from the 13th century and was used as court and prison for Dartmoor tinners who contravened the stannary laws, governing the weighing and stamping of tin. Next door is the **Castle Inn**,

(*see p170*) a contemporary of the castle, and the perfect base from which to explore the area.

Just outside Lydford, beautiful **Lydford Gorge** is the most popular attraction in the area. In the 17th century, this spectacular, densely wooded enclave formed by the River Lyd was a refuge for an outlaw band known as the Gubbinses, led by the 'Robin Hood of the West' Roger Bowle, who formed the basis for the hero in Charles Kingsley's *Westward Ho!*. Nowadays it is owned by the National Trust and shelters plentiful plant and birdlife, not to mention dozens of daytrippers. A fairly strenuous circular walk takes in the gorge's two main attractions: the 100-foot (30-metre) White Lady waterfall, and the Devil's Cauldron, a tumultuous pool, accessed via a narrow causeway, where you can watch the water pounding down from above; it's particularly impressive after heavy rain or a thaw. Check opening times as the gorge closes before sunset.

Museum of Dartmoor Life
West Street, Okehampton (01837 52295). **Open** *Easter-Oct* 10am-5pm daily. *Nov-Easter* 10am-4pm Mon-Fri. **Admission** free.

Activities

Golf
There are two visitor-friendly golf clubs near Okehampton: the good-value **Ashbury Golf Club** (Higher Maddaford Farm, Ashbury Road, 01837 55453), which has a hotel on site, and **Okehampton Golf Club** (Tors Road, 01837 52113).

Clapper bridge at Postbridge. *See p173.*

Devon

Riding

Day rides on the moor and riding holidays of up to a week are offered by **Skaigh Stables** (Belstone, 01837 840429, www.skaighstables.co.uk, closed Nov-Mar). For riding with accommodation, there's **Lydford House Hotel & Riding Stables** (*see below*) and **Dartmoor Horse Trails** (Little Budlake Farm, Bridestowe, 01837 861233).

Where to eat, drink & stay

In Sourton, south of Meldon, is the infamous and eccentric **Highwayman Inn** (01837 861243, www.thehighwaymaninn.net, main courses £2.50-£5, double B&B £55-£65). Entrance is through the body of the old Launceston to Tavistock coach, and once inside the sheer amount of ephemera and curios is mind-boggling. The pub serves organic wines and local ciders; food is standard pub-grub. Some bedrooms have four-poster beds.

Next to the A386 at Lydford, the **Dartmoor Inn** (Lydford, 01822 820221, closed Sun eve & Mon, main courses £3.75-£18) is a sprawling 16th-century coaching inn with a flower-filled, rustic interior. The kitchen uses locally sourced goodies to create flavoursome, unfussy dishes, served in huge portions. Special themed meals and jazz nights sometimes take place here.

Another great spot for food is the charming **Castle Inn** (01822 820241, closed late Dec, main courses £7.50-£14, double B&B £65-£90) in the centre of Lydford. It has all the classic country pub elements – oak beams, low ceilings and flagstones – combined with the authentic smells of woodsmoke and home-cooked food. Good bar food is supplemented by an ambitious restaurant menu in the evening, and there's a lovely beer garden at the back. Accommodation is provided in characterful, antique-strewn, rooms.

Alternatives in the area include **Moor View House** (Vale Down, Lydford, 01822 820220, set meal £20, double B&B £55-£65), a very English hotel with a traditional menu and an elegant Victorian atmosphere. Horsey types may prefer the **Lydford House Hotel & Riding Stables** (Lydford, 01822 820321, www.lydfordhouse.co.uk; phone for details), which offers riding tuition, moorland treks and traditional country-style accommodation. The hotel has corporate membership of the National Trust, so guests get free access to Lydford Gorge (*see p169*) and also reduced green fees at some nearby golf courses.

Resources

Hospital
Okehampton District Hospital *East Street (01837 52188).*

Internet
Okehampton Library *4 North Street (01837 52805).* **Open** 2-5pm Mon; 9.30am-7pm Tue, Fri; 9.30am-noon Wed; 9.30am-5pm Thur; 9.30am-1pm Sat.

Police station
Exeter Road, Okehampton (0870 577 7444).

Post office
8 George Street, Okehampton (01837 54666). **Open** 9am-5.30pm Mon, Tue, Thur, Fri; 9am-1pm Wed; 9am-12.30pm Sat.

Tourist information
Okehampton Tourist Information Centre, *Museum Courtyard, 3 West Street (01837 53020/ www.discoverdartmoor.com).* **Open** *Nov-Mar* 10am-4.30pm Mon, Fri, Sat. *Easter-June, Sept, Oct* 10am-5pm Mon-Sat. *July, Aug* 10am-5pm Mon-Sat; 10am-4.30pm Sun.

Moretonhampstead & north-eastern Dartmoor

Moretonhampstead, known as 'the gateway to the high moor', is a bustling little place with some interesting architecture. If you approach from Exeter, almost the first buildings you will see are the arcaded almshouses, dating from 1637. The town grew to prominence with the lucrative wool trade, and when this declined at the end of the 17th century, its position on the main route across the moor ensured it remained relatively prosperous. Nowadays, the town is

Castle Drogo. *See p171.*

best known as a centre for arts and crafts, with a large number of galleries for a place this size (consult the town website for details).

North of Moretonhampstead is **Chagford**, one of Devon's four medieval stannary towns, where the tin mined on the moors was weighed and valued. The town is characterised by its octagonal Gothic market house in the middle of the square, and still has a pleasantly timeless feel, with a cluster of thatched cottages and several pubs and hotels. There are some pleasant walks around the village and into the surrounding countryside, best topped off by a visit to the Three Crowns Hotel (*see p172*), which is said to be haunted by the ghost of Sydney Godolphin, a Cavalier poet killed by the Roundheads in 1642. Just outside Chagford, the **Mythic Garden Sculpture Exhibition** (Stoke Farm, 01647 231311) offers a New Age Dartmoor experience, with an arboretum, water gardens and sculpture exhibits.

Drewsteignton consists of low thatched houses – many dating from the 15th and 16th centuries – grouped round a square with the church at the centre. In the churchyard is a memorial to Julius Drewe, a wealthy tea merchant and founder of the Home & Colonial stores. Drewe wished to authenticate his station in life by having a castle built close to what he believed were his family's medieval roots. He chose a magnificent site above the Teign gorge, with far-reaching views in all directions, and commissioned the eminent Edwardian architect Sir Edwin Lutyens to design the building.

Begun in 1910 and never fully completed, **Castle Drogo** was the last castle to be built in Britain. Despite being less than a century old, the castle is medieval in feel, with austere granite walls, huge fireplaces, mullioned windows and decorative tapestries, but is also packed with modern conveniences, including elaborately appointed bathrooms and central heating. It is particularly interesting as an example of the Edwardian lifestyle of conspicuous consumption on a grand scale that was soon to die out. The number of electric servants' bells in the kitchen gives you an idea of how much work went on below stairs to keep the occupants and their guests happy. Outside, beautifully kept gardens, including a huge croquet lawn (where visitors can play), lead down to the wooded river valley.

Not far away, **Fingle Bridge** is a picturesque 16th-century packhorse bridge in the gorge below Drewsteignton that leads to open fields by the river, and delightful woodland walks in either direction.

South-west of Moretonhampstead is **North Bovey**, which must rate as one of the prettiest chocolate-box villages in the country, thanks to

its village green, surrounded by ancient trees. If you've got children to entertain, the **Miniature Pony & Animal Farm** here has enough cute animals and ponies to last you a lifetime, but also a very good craft centre and café.

South of North Bovey, near the village of Manaton, is **Bowerman's Nose**, one of the most dramatic tors on the moor. Centuries of weathering have lent it a sculptural quality and given rise to the legend that this is the petrified figure of a Norman bowman, caught on the moor by the phantom Evil Hunt, which turned him and his dog to stone; the dog, of course, is **Hound Tor** (1,360 feet/415 metres), a mile to the south. Just below Hound Tor are the remains of a medieval settlement inhabited from Saxon times to 1300, while to the west, on the road to Heatree Cross, is **Jay's Grave**, a small burial mound with a maudlin history. According to local lore, the grave contains the bones of Kitty Jay, an 18th-century workhouse girl who became pregnant by a local landowner's son and hanged herself in shame. In accordance with local custom, she was buried in an unmarked grave at a crossroads on the parish boundary. Touchingly, there are often fresh flowers on Kitty's grave, but no one knows who places them there.

Just south of Manaton, the **Becky Falls Woodland Park** (01647 221259, www.becky falls-dartmoor.com, closed Nov-Feb) is a privately owned tract of land, centred around a series of rock-strewn cascades. It's a little over-sanitised and over-visited, with a pets corner and some rescued birds of prey to look at, but the scenery is undoubtedly impressive. There are decent walks from here, but don't expect to enjoy them on your own: in summer the trails swarm with pac-a-mac'd tourists.

Just off the A382 between Moretonhampstead and Bovey Tracey is **Lustleigh**, another chocolate-box candidate, whose church may be one of the earliest ecclesiastical sites in Devon; an inscribed stone inside has been dated to the seventh century. Extending up from the village, the **Cleave** is a steep wooded escarpment that's very popular with rock climbers. There are great views from the top, but walkers will find it strenuous going.

Finally, on the far eastern edge of the moor, **Bovey Tracey** is a laid-back, appealing town, marred only by the coach parties that descend on its numerous teashops and pubs. There's easy access to Haytor and Widecombe from here along the B3387 (*see p174*).

Miniature Pony & Animal Farm

Wormhill Farm, North Bovey (01647 432400).
Open *Apr-Nov* phone for details. Closed Dec-Mar.
Admission £5.50; £4.50 concessions; free under-2s.
Credit AmEx, DC, MC, V.

Activities

Art

Courses in watercolours and pastels are offered by local artist **Ernie Godden**, based in North Bovey (01647 440434, www.erniegodden.co.uk).

Fishing

Phone 01647 277587 for information about fishing on the three scenic and well-stocked reservoirs east of the A382: **Tottiford** (brown trout); **Trenchford** (pike) and **Kennick** (rainbow trout).

Off-roading

The **South West Off-Road Driving Centre** (Ilsington, 01364 661557) has 250 acres of private land on which to play around in 4x4 vehicles, and also offers guided Dartmoor safaris.

Where to eat, drink & stay

West of Chagford lies the **Gidleigh Park Hotel** (Chagford, 01647 432367, www.gidleigh.com, closed 2wks Jan, set menus £26-£72.50, double B&B £425-£520 incl dinner), an oasis of unadulterated luxury set in 45 acres of the Teign valley. The mock-Tudor house incorporates 15 guestrooms, as well as plush but relaxing communal areas. The decor may be rather too traditional and floral for some tastes, but the standards of comfort and service are exemplary, particularly in the two-Michelin-starred restaurant, which serves exceptional, award-winning cuisine by the much-fêted Michael Caines.

If Gidleigh's out of your league, then **22 Mill Street** (01647 432244, closed 2wks Jan & June, set menu £29.50, double B&B £50) in the centre of Chagford may be the answer. Here you can enjoy well-executed modern European cuisine – including Dartmoor lamb – in understated, informal surroundings. There are a couple of bedrooms too. For a pint, the **Three Crowns Hotel** (High Street, Chagford, 01647 433444, main courses £10.75-£19.50, double B&B £60-£70) is a delightful 16th-century inn. Find yourself a spot outside by the stone portals and watch the world go by.

In Drewsteignton, the **Drewe Arms** (The Square, 01647 281224, phone for details) has a delicious selection of locally sourced food and real ales. It was formerly the home of Auntie Mabel, Britain's longest serving landlady (75 years). To get away from it all, try **Blackaller House** (North Bovey, 01647 440322, www.blackaller.co.uk, double B&B £68-£82), a 17th-century mill, peacefully located next to the River Bovey. In addition to bright, pretty bedrooms and a friendly atmosphere, the hotel provides excellent organic home cooking, always sourced from local suppliers. There's a lovely self-catering annex next door.

At the centre of the village, the **Ring o' Bells** in North Bovey (01647 440375, www.ringofbellsinn.com, main courses £4.50-£12, double B&B £78-£95) is an attractive 13th-century thatched inn part-owned by golfing enthusiasts. The pub serves excellent bar food (guaranteed free-range meat and fresh fish) and local ales, and can arrange tee times at the **Manor House Hotel** (Moretonhampstead, 01647 445000, www.lemeridien.com, closed early Jan, set menu £24.95, double B&B £140), which has its own 18-hole championship golf course. Built for the WH Smith newsagents' family in 1906, this neo-Jacobean manor featured as Baskerville Hall in the 1930s film of *The Hound of the Baskervilles*.

On sunny days, enjoy the gorgeous cottage beer garden at **The Cleave** in Lustleigh (01647 277223, www.thecleave.freeserve.co.uk, closed Mon in winter, main courses £4-£12). This is a classic village inn, with an inglenook fireplace, a collection of musical instruments on the walls, and a varied pub grub menu.

Resources

Internet

Moretonhampstead *Library, Fore Street (01647 440523)*. **Open** 10am-noon, 2.30-4.30pm Tue; 2.30-6pm Wed; 2.30-4.30pm Fri; 10am-noon Sat.

Post offices

Chagford *The Square (01647 433479)*. **Open** 9am-5pm Mon, Tue, Thur, Fri; 9am-1pm Wed, Sat.
Moretonhampstead *18A Court Street, Moretonhampstead (01647 440325)*. **Open** 9am-1pm, 2-5.30pm Mon, Tue, Thur, Fri; 9am-12.30pm Wed, Sat.

Tourist information

Bovey Tracey, *Lower Car Park, Station Road (01626 832047)*. **Open** 9am-5pm Mon-Sat.
Chagford *Tourist Information Centre, The Courtyard, 76 The Square (01647 432571)*. **Open** 9am-5pm Mon-Sat.
Moretonhampstead *Tourist Information Centre, 11 The Square (01647 440043)*. **Open** Oct-Easter 10am-5pm Fri-Sun. *Mar-Sept* 10am-5pm daily.

The high moorland

Leaving Moretonhampstead on the B3212, the road undulates and meanders up on to the high moor and the ancient drystone-wall field systems abruptly give way to the broad majestic sweep of open moorland. This is some of the most wildly dramatic scenery in the National Park, and if you stay on the B3212 you could be forgiven for thinking that there's nothing up here except acres of wilderness, but you'd be wrong. There are the remains of many early settlements on Dartmoor, and probably

Gidleigh Park Hotel.
See p172.

the most evocative (and happily, the most accessible) is **Grimspound**. (To reach it, turn off the B3212 at the top of a particularly steep hill, and head south towards Challacombe for just over a mile; Grimspound is situated on the left hand side). You can't see anything from the road, but a short climb up the hill from the layby will reward you with the remains of a circular village boundary enclosing a four-acre Bronze Age settlement containing 24 huts and various animal enclosures. The name is reputed to derive from the dwarf Grimgie, the mythical builder of the village, although 'Grim' may also mean death. *See also p175* **Country walk**.

Once you've soaked up the ancient atmosphere here, rejoin the B3212 to reach the **Warren House Inn** (*see p176*), an essential stop on any visit to the moor. At 1,545 feet (471 metres) it's the third highest pub in England, and boasts a fire that has allegedly been burning since 1845. Apparently, when the old inn burnt down, the landlord carried some burning peat across the road and built a fire around which to construct his new hostelry; it has never been allowed to go out since.

From the Warren House Inn you can strike out north across the moor for about two miles (three kilometres) to a large tract of woodland surrounding **Fernworthy Reservoir**. There are numerous hut circles in this area and some lovely scenic walks, with opportunities for

fishing and birdwatching. (Vehicle access is from Chagford.) West of Warren House, meanwhile, on the B3212, is where the dreaded 'Hairy Hands' are reputed to strike. This relatively recent phenomenon has resulted in several accidents, as drivers and motorbikers find the controls wrested from their grip by a pair of ghostly hands.

The **National Park Information Centre** (*see p176*) in **Postbridge** is worth a visit for detailed information on the area, but the real attraction in this village is the 13th-century **clapper bridge** just across the road. This simple structure of giant granite slabs across the East Dart river is the largest and best-preserved example on the moor and makes for a popular if somewhat crowded picnic spot. To avoid the daytrippers, take a turning south just outside Postbridge to **Bellever Forest**, an area of non-indigenous woodland that provides pleasant surroundings for gentle walks along the river.

Back on the B3212, two miles (three kilometres) from Postbridge are mills once used for the manufacture of gunpowder but now home to the **Powdermills Pottery** (01822 880263), which uses local clay and natural glazes. Beyond, at the intersection of roads and rivers, **Two Bridges** is little more than a crossroads and a hotel. However, it makes a good base from which to explore **Wistman's Wood**, a magical gathering of 300-year-old dwarf oaks, so bedecked with moss and lichen that they look like an illustration for *Lord of the Rings*.

From Two Bridges you can head east on the B3357 to **Dartmeet**, a popular beauty spot where the East and West Dart rivers converge in a steep valley. For a giggle en route, stop off at **Pixieland** (01364 631412, closed end Dec-mid Feb), purveyor of concrete garden gnomes, and top contender for kitschest shop in Britain. Dartmeet itself is rather marred by a large car park and hordes of picnickers in summer, but you can escape the crowds by climbing the surrounding hills.

Beyond Dartmeet, a network of lanes leads north-east to **Widecombe-in-the-Moor**, a picturesque village and genesis of the famous folk song, 'Widecombe Fair', which, incidentally, you'll probably hear at least 20 times before you regain the safety of your car/bicycle/grey mare. The song was written in 1880 by the Rev Sabine Baring Gould, whose other hit was 'Onward Christian Soldiers'. He is buried in the churchyard of **St Pancras**, a 14th-century parish church whose tower can be seen for miles across the moor. The churchyard is also the final resting place of the author Beatrice Chase (a descendant of William Parr, brother to the sixth wife of Henry VIII). Chase was a passionate Dartmoor enthusiast, largely responsible for the revival of Widecombe Fair in the 1930s. She is, therefore, in a way to blame for the china figures of 'Old Uncle Tom Cobley an' all' that litter the local shops. The fair is still held each year in the second week of September, but is now largely a tourist attraction rather than a cornerstone of local trade.

Haytor is another tourist honeypot, thanks to its proximity to the B3387. There are fantastic, all-encompassing views from the top of the tor, while the slope below the summit is a great spot for kite-flying. (For the more adventurous, climbing is very popular here and no permission is required.) A tramway was built on Haytor in 1820 to transport granite from the quarry here eight and a half miles (14 kilometres) to Ventiford Wharf, Teigngrace, where it was loaded onto barges and ships for the building of London Bridge, the British Museum and other important Victorian edifices.

Many people think of Dartmoor Prison at **Princetown** when they envisage Dartmoor, yet in reality the town (a couple of miles south-west of Two Bridges) is quite untypical of settlements on the moor. Despite trying to promote itself as a centre for walking, it doesn't manage to shake off the brooding institutional feeling engendered by the prison. Even sunshine and bright paint on the grey houses fail to dispel the slightly grim atmosphere.

The large grey granite mass of **HM Prison Dartmoor** was built in 1805 to house French, and later American, prisoners of war. There are poignant memorials in the cemeteries outside to the captives of both nations, who died in their hundreds during the 19th century. The **Prison Museum** has evocative displays on prison life, plus garden ornaments and other items made by present-day prisoners for sale in the shop.

Sir Arthur Conan Doyle stayed at the Duchy Hotel in Princetown to write *The Hound of the Baskervilles*. The building now houses the **High Moorland Visitor Centre** (*see p176*), a comprehensive source of information about Dartmoor and Conan Doyle. If you want to see for yourself what inspired the novel, take the unmarked road on the edge of Princetown south to **Whiteworks**, an abandoned village and tinworkings. Beyond here lies **Fox Tor Mires**, possibly the inspiration for Great Grimpen Mire in the book. Come here at dusk, particularly when a fog is descending, to savour the full Hammer Horror experience.

On the northern slopes of Fox Tor are the remains of **Childe's tomb**. Childe was the lord of the manor of Plymstock, who got lost in a blizzard while out hunting. To survive, he killed his horse and climbed into its belly, but not before bequeathing his lands in blood on a stone to whoever found his body. Thus, so the story goes, monks from Tavistock found him dead and inherited his manor. Further on is a road constructed by conscientious objectors ('conchies') who were imprisoned on Dartmoor during World War I.

HM Prison Dartmoor Museum

Princetown, Yelverton (01822 892130).
Open 9.30am-12.30pm, 1.30-4pm Mon-Thur, Sat; 9.30am-12.30pm, 1.30-3.30pm Fri, Sun. **Admission** £2; £1 concessions; £5 family; free under-5s. **No credit cards.**

Activities

Adventure sports

The well-established **Spirit of Adventure** (Powdermills, nr Princetown, 01822 880277, www.spirit-of-adventure.com) runs adventure weekends on the moor, encompassing climbing, abseiling, kayaking and orienteering, with specialist courses in these sports also available. Cheap hostel-style accommodation can also be provided.

Letterboxing

The High Moors are a centre for 'letterboxing', the practice of searching for (usually Tupperware) boxes hidden in remote places containing a rubber stamp, then collecting the stamp in your book to prove you've been there. Clues can be gleaned from other letterbox walkers, or by phoning 01364 73414. Further information is available on 01392 832768.

Country walk Grimspound circuit

Distance approx 5 miles (8km).
Time approx 3hrs.
Difficulty This is not a strenuous walk, being almost entirely on footpaths, but stout boots are advisable as it can be muddy and slippery.

Start at a layby on the left-hand side of the B3212 from Moretonhampstead (OS map 28 grid ref 675 809), about quarter of a mile (400 metres) before the **Warren House Inn** (*see p173*). Follow the trail, marked as the Two Moors Way, down into the valley, with Birch Tor on your left. At the foot of the valley is an intersection of paths; stay on the right-hand path. To your left up the hill you may be able to pick out the remains of Bronze Age hut circles and more recent old tin mine workings.

Just into **Soussons Down Forest**, the path forks; take the left-hand path, which climbs gently round the base of Challacombe Down, before reaching **Challacombe**, an unspoilt medieval hamlet nestling in the valley. The small plots of enclosed land you see here are known as 'lynchets' and date back 3,500 years to when the climate worsened and temperatures fell, and the high moor was abandoned in favour of the milder, more fertile valleys. The two elaborate stone constructions built into the walls to your left are vermin traps, which kept the farmed rabbits from the Headland Warren out of the fields, while allowing sheep through for grazing.

About three quarters of a mile beyond the cottages, but before you reach the farmhouse, take the footpath to the right, following the wall towards the road. There is a layby here with a sign for the Bronze Age settlement of **Grimspound** (*see p173*), which is a little way further up the hill. If you've got the energy, for a really impressive view, turn left just before you enter the compound and climb up **Hookney Tor** to look down. There's a small tumulus at the top, and you may spot a rare red grouse up here, although they are usually only active around dawn.

Once you've had your fill of the Bronze Age, head back down to the layby, and cross the road to regain the path past **Headland Warren Farm**. The farmhouse is a beautiful medieval building, which repays a closer look. The path swings left around the front of the farm and through the gap between Challacombe Down on your left and Birch Tor on your right. At the centre point of the two peaks, on the slope of Challacombe Down, are the **Challacombe Rows**, a prehistoric alignment of stones arranged on astral lines, and leading to a standing stone, whose significance is unknown. The rough ground in this area indicates the remains of mine workings. At the bottom of the valley rejoin the Two Moors Way, and head uphill back to the start. If you're desperate for a pint, a short yomp through the bracken and gorse will lead you towards the woodsmoke that signals the Warren House Inn.

Riding

Trot off on to the moor with **Shilstone Rock Riding & Trekking Centre** (Widecombe-in-the-Moor, 01364 621281). The local riding centre near Princetown is **Sherberton Stables** (Hexworthy, 01364 631023). Both cater for all abilities but have restricted opening times in winter.

Where to eat, drink & stay

High up on the moor, the **Warren House Inn** (near Postbridge, 01822 880208, main courses £2.50-£8.25) has a good selection of snacks and meals, plus local beers. Warreners Pie, a tasty rabbit and ale concoction is very popular.

The **Two Bridges Hotel** (Two Bridges, 01822 890358, www.twobridges.co.uk, set menu £25, double B&B £100-£150) combines traditional decor and ambience (four-poster beds, antiques) with contemporary amenities and stylish food. There's more country house comfort down the road at the **Prince Hall** (nr Two Bridges, 01822 890403, www.princehall.co.uk, double B&B £150-£185 incl dinner). In glorious seclusion and surrounded by fantastic scenery, the hotel offers spacious, varied rooms and highly accomplished cuisine.

Should you want to stay in Princetown, the **Plume of Feathers Inn** (The Square, 01822 890240, www.plumeoffeathers-dartmoor.co.uk, main courses £3.45-£7.95, double B&B £35) has simple guestrooms, a campsite, and a couple of high-quality bunkhouses for those who like the savour of other people's walking socks while they sleep. Nearby is the **Railway Inn** (Two Bridges Road, 01822 890232, main courses £4-£9), good for real ales and hearty food.

Near Dartmeet, **Brimpts Farm** (01364 631450, www.brimptsfarm.co.uk, closed Jan, double £37) offers innovative B&B and self-catering accommodation in converted granite barns. Rooms are furnished to a high standard, with additional amenities including a hot tub and sauna, and there's also a tearoom (closed Oct-Easter) serving oodles of clotted cream to passing visitors. For more substantial sustenance, try the **Old Inn** (01364 621207, main courses £3.25-£15.95) in Widecombe, though, like the rest of the village, it can be crowded.

Resources

Internet access

Princetown *Princetown Library, Claremont House, Tavistock Road (01822 890370).* **Open** 2.30-6.30pm Mon; 9.30am-noon Wed; 2.30-5pm Fri.

Post office

Widecombe-in-the-Moor *Manor Cottage (01364 621220).* **Open** *Winter* 8am-5.30pm Mon, Tue, Thur, Fri; 8am-5pm Wed, Sat; 8.30am-1pm Sun. *Summer* 8am-5.30pm daily.

Tourist information

Haytor *National Park Information Centre (01364 661520/www.dartmoor-npa.gov.uk).* **Open** *Easter-Oct* 10am-5pm Mon-Sat. Closed Nov-Mar.
Postbridge *National Park Information Centre (01822 880272/www.dartmoor-npa.gov.uk).* **Open** *Easter-Oct* 10am-5pm Mon-Sat. Closed Nov-Mar.
Princetown *High Moorland Visitor Centre, Tavistock Road (01822 890414/www.dartmoor-npa.gov.uk).* **Open** *Summer* 10am-5pm daily. *Winter* 10am-4pm daily. Closed 1st wk Mar.

Ashburton & south-eastern Dartmoor

Ashburton lies just off the A38, which roughly marks the southern border of Dartmoor. The former stannary town has slate-hung buildings, small courtyards and narrow lanes to explore. The 15th-century parish church has a typical barrel-vaulted roof. On North Street is the former Mermaid Inn, where General Fairfax the Roundhead leader stayed in 1642, while behind the town hall is a former gaming house with the different card suits carved into its frontage.

A visit to **Ashburton Museum** is recommended, not just for its local exhibits, but, incongruously enough, for its collection of Native American artefacts. Also, find time to pop into the 14th-century **Chapel of St Lawrence** (closed Oct-Apr), a private chapel for the Bishop of Exeter that was used as a school for 400 years. Each November the 'Court Leet', which dates back to Saxon times, meets here to vote in the portreeve and other town officials.

The scenery west of Ashburton is characterised by picturesque wooded valleys of ancient oak framing the River Dart, and encompassing the **Holne Chase Nature Reserve** and the **River Dart Country Park**. Head past Holne Chase towards Poundsgate and take a turning marked Spitchwick shortly after New Bridge to reach a favourite local spot for barbecues, ball games, swimming and cliff jumping on the banks of the river. On fine days there's a lively, almost seaside atmosphere here.

The nearby village of **Holne** was the birthplace in 1819 of Charles Kingsley, who wrote *The Water Babies* and *Westward Ho!*. Its 14th-century church has an hourglass carved into the pulpit. To the north, **Buckland in the Moor** is a showcase Dartmoor village of picturesque thatched cottages clustered in a wooded valley. Climb Buckland Beacon, a mile to the east, for fantastic views in all directions; the summit is marked with two granite slabs engraved with the Ten Commandments.

Further south, **Buckfast Abbey** (01364 645500, www.buckfast.org.uk) was founded in the early 11th century by Canute, refounded in the 12th century, dissolved by Henry VIII and finally rebuilt by French Benedictine monks between 1907 and 1938. The modern abbey is notable for its stained glass and peaceful gardens, although there's also an exhibition tracing its history and reconstruction. The abbey gift shop sells products made by the monks: mead, honey, and the notorious 'Bucky', aka Buckfast Tonic Wine, beloved of street drinkers throughout the land, while nearby, the **Mill Shops** (01364 643325) have a selection of craft goods from shoes to sheepskins, much of it locally produced.

The nondescript town of **Buckfastleigh**, a mile to the south, is the northern terminus of the **South Devon Steam Railway** (*see also p192*). You can catch a train to Totnes from here along the River Dart, or simply look round the museum and train collection. Right next door, **Buckfast Butterfly Farm & Otter Sanctuary** combines an amazing hothouse of free-flying exotic butterflies and moths with an outdoor reserve for the ultra-cute river creatures. Before leaving Buckfastleigh, check out the **Valiant Soldier**, a fascinating former pub that closed in the 1960s and was left entirely untouched until it was rediscovered in the '90s. All the furnishings, pub ephemera and even the money in the till have now been sensitively restored to create an engrossing time capsule of life in the 1940s and '50s.

At the southern tip of the moor, **Ivybridge** is largely notable as the starting point of the Two Moors Way, which follows a disused tramway through the wilds of the southern moorland, before joining the ancient Abbots Way towards Holne. Ivybridge is a good place to stock up on provisions before you head on to the moor, and the town tourist office can provided copious information about the route.

Ashburton Museum

1 West Street, Ashburton (01364 652648/ www.ashburtonmuseum.org). **Open** May-Sept 2.30-5pm Tue, Thur-Sat. Closed Oct-Apr. **Admission** £1; free under-16s.

Buckfast Butterfly Farm & Dartmoor Otter Sanctuary

Dart Bridge Road, Buckfastleigh (01364 642916/ www.ottersandbutterflies.co.uk). **Open** *Butterflies* mid Feb-mid Oct 10am-dusk daily. *Otters* Mid Feb-mid March 11am-3pm daily; mid March-mid Oct 10am-dusk daily. Closed mid Oct-mid Feb. **Admission** £4.95; £3.50-£4.50 concessions; £15 family. **Credit** phone for details.

Valiant Soldier

79 Fore Street, Buckfastleigh (01364 644522/ www.valiantsoldier.org.uk). **Open** Apr-Oct phone for details. Closed Nov-Mar. **Admission** £3; £7 family. **No credit cards**.

Activities

Adventure sports

River Dart Adventures (Holne Park, 01364 652511, www.riverdart.co.uk, closed Dec-Mar) incorporates a holiday village, campsite and adventure centre offering activities such as caving, climbing and watersports.

Cycling

Bikes can be bought or hired from the **Mountain Bike Centre** (Linhay Business Park, Ashburton, 01364 654080).

Fishing

In addition to the River Dart, try **Venford Reservoir** near Holne (permits 01837 871565).

Where to eat, drink & stay

Not far from Ashburton, the former hunting lodge of Buckfast Abbey has been turned into one of the most highly regarded hotels on Dartmoor. **Holne Chase** (Two Bridges Road, 01364 631471, www.holne-chase.co.uk, set menu £32.50, double B&B £130-£170) is a country house hotel set in 70 acres of woodland, with private walks along the River Dart and through the nature reserve. The hotel has comfortable rooms, a formal restaurant, a clutch of relaxed bar areas and a laid-back atmosphere. Riding, fishing and shooting can all be arranged.

Travellers on a tighter budget will find a very warm welcome at the **Church Inn** (Holne, 01364 631208, www.churchhouse-holne.co.uk, main courses £3.95-£15.50, double B&B £45-£60), where real ales are supplemented by wide-ranging bar snacks, unpretentious restaurant meals and unfussy rooms. In Buckfastleigh, the **Abbey Inn** (30 Buckfast Road, 01364 642343, main courses £6.95-£15.95, double B&B £60) enjoys a great spot on the river and offers traditional oak panelled cosiness and good food.

The top place to eat in Ashburton is **Agaric** (30 North Street, 01364 654478, main courses £13.95-£16.95), known for its ambitious cuisine. For tasty snacks in a more laidback atmosphere, try the **Moorish Licensed Café** (11 West Street, 01364 654011, main courses £8.50-£10.50).

Resources

Internet

Ashburton *Library, Old Town Hall, North Street (01364 652896).* **Open** 9.30am-noon, 2.30-4.30pm Wed; 9.30am-noon, 2.30-7pm Mon, Fri; 9.30am-12.30pm Sat.
Ivybridge *Library, 7A Keaton Road (01752 893140).* **Open** 9.30am-1pm, 2-7pm Mon, Fri; 2-5.30pm Tue, Thur; 9.30am-1pm, 2-5.30pm Wed; 9.30am-1pm Sat.

Devon

Police station

Ivybridge *Leonard's Road (0870 577 7444).*

Post offices

Ashburton *4 St Lawrence Lane (01364 652256).*
Open 9am-5.30pm Mon, Tue; 9am-12.30pm Wed-Sat.
Buckfastleigh *Buckfast Road (01364 643034).*
Open 9am-1pm, 2-5pm Mon, Tue, Thur, Fri; 9am-
1pm Wed; 10am-1pm Sat.
Ivybridge *Glanvilles Mill (01752 892623).*
Open 9am-5.30pm Mon-Fri; 9am-4pm Sat.

Tourist information

Ashburton *Tourist Information Centre, Town Hall,
North Street (01364 653426/www.ashburton.org).*
Open *Apr-Nov* 9.30am-4.30pm Mon-Sat. *Dec-Mar*
9.30am-4.30pm Mon-Fri; 9.30am-1pm Sat.
Ivybridge *Tourist Information Centre, Leonards
Road (01752 897035/www.ivybridge.info).* **Open**
Nov-Mar 9am-4pm Mon-Fri; 9am-2pm Sat. *Apr-June,
Sept, Oct* 9am-5pm Mon-Fri; 9am-2pm Sat. *July, Aug*
9am-5pm Mon-Fri; 9am-2pm Sat; 10am-2pm Sun.

Tavistock & western Dartmoor

Right on the western edge of Dartmoor is
Brent Tor, topped with the church of St
Michael of the Rocks. It is the fourth smallest
church in England, but can be seen for miles
due to its solitary position at 1,130 feet (344
metres). The climb to the top is well worth it for
amazing views in all directions, as far as the sea
at Plymouth. The tor was almost certainly a pre-
Christian site, and according to local mystics lies
on the 'Michael Line', a straight ley line that runs
through Glastonbury Tor, Avebury and any
number of other sites of ancient power. Don't
be surprised if you find bearded types in runic
sweaters when you get to the top.

East of the A386 is a trio of tiny villages
– **Horndon**, **Mary Tavy** and **Peter Tavy**
– that provide access to great walks through
Tavy Cleave (a steep valley cut through the
moor by the River Tavy). This area is densely
strewn with abandoned tin workings that are
more evocative than a hundred visitor centres
or industrial museums.

If all this wilderness has made you yearn for
civilisation, the next best thing is **Tavistock**,
an attractive place with tons of history. It was
a stannary town and from 974 to 1539 was
owned by Tavistock Abbey. At the dissolution
of the monasteries Henry VIII sold the abbey
and estates to the Duke of Bedford, whose
descendants completely remodelled the town,
re-routing the river and removing the abbey.
They remained the owners until 1911.

Tavistock's **Pannier Market** was built
in the 1850s as part of the Duke of Bedford's
urban regeneration programme, although there

had been a regular market on this site since
the 12th century. Today the market sells
produce on Fridays, with antiques, crafts and
bric-a-brac on Tuesdays. The **Goose Fair**
takes place on the second Wednesday in
October. Based on a medieval livestock market,
it's now characterised by stalls and fairground
rides, with goose served in many pubs and
restaurants. Around the Pannier Market, the
town hall, magistrates court, police station
and shops were all built at the same time and
survive as an unspoilt grouping that gives
the town centre around Bedford Square a
pleasant harmony of architecture and a
somewhat continental feel.

The Victorian building boom in Tavistock
was funded by the discovery of copper deposits
in the area, and a canal was constructed to
carry the ore to the port of Morwelham Quay
on the River Tamar (*see p206*). The canal is
subterranean for much of its length, but the early
stretch is pleasant for a short stroll, passing the
hamlet of Crowndale, where Sir Francis Drake
was born (*see p204* **Local heroes**). If you're
suffering from cultural withdrawal on the
moor, check out the **Wharf Gallery** (The
Wharf, Canal Road, 01822 611166, www.
tavistockwharf.com), a cinema, gallery and
performing arts venue with a decent café.

A few miles east of Tavistock on the B3357,
near the village of **Merrivale**, is an impressive
double row of ancient standing stones that
stretch for several hundred yards across the
weekend. Little known is about the date or
original purpose of this prehistoric site, but
during the 17th century it was used as a
dropping point for provisions for the plague
victims in exile on the moor and is hence
known locally as the **Plague Market**.

Located on the A386 towards Plymouth,
Horrabridge and **Yelverton** can be rather
clogged with traffic heading to the city. However,
from the latter you can head on to the high
moor via the B3212. There are scenic woodland
walks and fishing to be enjoyed at **Burrator
Reservoir**, while the dominant peak of **Sheep's
Tor** looks over acres of wild, open moorland.

Activities

Cycling

Mountain bikes and tandems can be hired from
Tavistock Cycles (Brook Street, Tavistock,
01822 617630).

Fishing

Anglers are well catered for, with fly-fishing (and
fresh trout for sale) at the **Tavistock Trout Farm
& Fishery** (Parkwood Road, Tavistock, 01822
615441) and on **Burrator Reservoir** (permits
01837 871565) near Yelverton.

Climbing **Hound Tor**.
See p171.

Dartmoor ponies.

Riding

Cholwell Farm & Riding Stables (Horndon, Mary Tavy, 01822 810526) and **Moorland Riding Stables** (Horndon, Mary Tavy, 01822 810293) each offer moorland rides for allcomers. Cholwell also provides tuition.

Where to eat, drink & stay

Browns Hotel (80 West Street, Tavistock, 01822 618686, www.brownsdevon.co.uk, main courses £9.95-£15.50, double B&B £90-£150) is a former coaching inn that has been beautifully refurbished, with a wine bar, brasserie, and simple yet elegant bedrooms. It's one of the few places to get a decent latte on Dartmoor, and there's even bottled water from a private well.

Elsewhere, the **Elephant's Nest Inn** (Horndon, near Mary Tavy, 01822 810273, main courses £3.50-£14.25) has to be worth a visit for its name alone, but is also a good place to enjoy unpretentious pub grub and real ale. It's very popular with 'hashers' – not the local dope fiends, but moorland runners. In the next village, the **Peter Tavy Inn** (Peter Tavy, 01822 810348, main courses £6.95-£12.95) has a tempting menu, real ales and 15th-century charm. Near Yelverton, the **Royal Oak Inn** (Meavy, 01822 852944, main courses £8-£15.50) has local farm produce on the menu. The pub dates back to 1510, so it was probably Sir Francis Drake's local. Finally, for stunning views of the southern moor, try the **White Thorn Inn** (Shaugh Prior, 01752 839245, main courses £5-£15), just inside the National Park.

Resources

Internet

Tavistock Library *The Quay, Plymouth Road (01822 612218).* **Open** 9.30am-7pm Mon, Fri; 9.30am-5pm Tue, Thur; 9.30am-4pm Wed, Sat.

Post office

4 Abbey Place, Tavistock (0845 722 3344). **Open** 8.30am-5.30pm Mon; 9.30am-5.30pm Tue-Fri; 9.30am-12.30pm Sat.

Tourist information

Tavistock Tourist Information Centre *Town Hall, Bedford Square (01822 612938/ tavistocktic@visit.org.uk).* **Open** *Summer* 9.30am-5pm Mon-Sat. *Winter* 10am-4.30pm Mon, Tue, Fri, Sat.

Getting there & around

By bus

The nearest **National Express** (0990 808080, www.gobycoach.com) termini are Exeter and Plymouth, connected by the **Transmoor Link** (No.82) buses that run across the moor roughly every 2hrs. There are also local services running on the moor, but forward planning is required to ensure you don't get stranded; call 0870 608 2608 for information.

By train

The private **Dartmoor Railway** (01837 55637, www.dartmoorrailway.co.uk) runs from Exeter via Crediton to Okehampton and Meldon in the north. Wessex trains run from Exeter to Ivybridge (55mins), with connections to Buckfastleigh at Totnes.

South Devon

England's answer to the Côte d'Azur boasts some of the country's most majestic coastline – and culture too.

South Devon encompasses the very essence of the English holiday experience. On the one hand there's **Torbay** – a conglomeration of tourist towns that vie for visitors with a heady mix of seaside attractions, golf courses and palm trees. On the other, there's the **South Hams**, an area of astounding natural beauty dotted with good-looking holiday hotspots, where classy seafood restaurants and art galleries outnumber the chip shops and amusement arcades.

Surrounding both these extremes is some of the most striking coastline in the country: golden beaches, rugged cliffs and heart-stopping ocean views that are guaranteed to put you in the holiday mood.

From the Exe to the Teign

There are two distinct routes heading towards Torbay from Exeter. The most direct is the A380, which climbs up and over the Haldon Hills to the market town of Newton Abbot. The more roundabout but much more scenic way is the A379, which skirts the Exe river estuary en route to Dawlish and Teignmouth. Running between the road and coast, the railway between Exeter and Newton Abbot makes for one of the most appealing train journeys in the country.

If you choose the A379, a few miles south of Exminster you may catch sight of the fallow deer that run wild in the grounds of **Powderham Castle**, the ancestral home of the Courtenay family. This historic house was built over 600 years ago and was used as a location for the 1993 film *The Remains of the Day*. There are regular guided tours of the magnificent staterooms, and visitors are free to roam the grounds, which include a rose garden and 18th-century woodlands.

A little further south, the estuary village of **Starcross** is a popular location for sailing and birdwatching, and is the embarkation point for ferries to Exmouth (*see p158*). Opposite the station is a red-brick pumphouse that was used on Brunel's 'atmospheric railway', constructed in 1845. This costly and short-lived piece of engineering used atmospheric pressure to propel trains along the line between Exeter and Newton Abbot.

A short drive from Starcross is the village of **Cockwood**, which has a picturesque harbour and one of the best pubs in the area (*see p183*). From here the A379 detours inland before rolling down into the seaside town of **Dawlish**.

Part Victorian and part Georgian, the town was once visited by Jane Austen and Charles Dickens. Nowadays, in summer at least, it is the preserve of the kiss-me-quick hat brigade, who hang out on the narrow sand and shingle beach. This is an OK spot for a dip as long as you don't mind mainline express trains thundering past your towel.

Gays Creamery in Brunswick Place (01626 863341) offers a huge variety of local produce, including honey, fudge and hefty pasties. To burn off those excess calories walk the pleasant coastal route to **Dawlish Warren** at the estuary mouth. Fronted by over a mile of golden sand dunes running on to a Blue Flag beach, Dawlish Warren is designed for families looking for a cheap 'n'cheerful car-free holiday. There are plenty of amusements, cafés, restaurants, pubs and shops here, plus nearby holiday parks offering caravan and chalet accommodation.

Stretching out into the estuary, a spit of land has been set aside as the **Dawlish Warren National Nature Reserve** (01626 863980, closed Mon-Fri in winter), supporting around 180 varieties of birds, plus dozens of native plants. Fascinating guided walks are offered in summer, but it's far less crowded and more appealing if you visit out of season.

The gentle scenery of the Exe estuary gives way to an altogether more dramatic landscape as you move south-west from Dawlish and the low-lying coast changes to jagged sandstone cliffs. Hemmed in by these red cliffs at the mouth of the Teign estuary is **Teignmouth**, a classic English seaside holiday town. Though it's bisected by possibly the ugliest bypass in Devon, the town retains an elegant sweep of Regency houses, which look out over the seafront promenade, formal gardens and a run-down Victorian pier.

An important fishing port since early times, Teignmouth was given a new lease of life by the building of the New Quay near the centre of town in 1821, which allowed the commercial export of granite from Dartmoor. Later in the 19th century the town's holiday reputation was

The glorious **Dart estuary** from Kingswear. *See p194.*

helped by the arrival of Brunel's railway from Exeter. The town attracted crowds of Victorian nouveaux riches, who took to the sea from bathing machines on the beach, while pleasure steamers set off from the pier for jaunts around the coast. Famous visitors included the poet John Keats, who is commemorated by a memorial on Northumberland Place.

Away from the seafront a maze of small streets houses interesting shops, a glut of pubs and the worthwhile **Teignmouth & Shaldon Museum**. Its local history exhibits include displays devoted to the South Devon Railway, a painting of Teignmouth by local maritime artist Thomas Luny (1759-1837) and a collection of artefacts taken from a 16th-century shipwreck (thought to be part of the Spanish Armada) that was recently discovered by a local boy out snorkelling off the coast.

Stop for cockles at the blue hut behind the jetty before taking the short ferry ride across the swift-flowing currents of the Teign to the charming village of **Shaldon**, where you'll find an appealing mix of thatched cottages and dinky Georgian houses along the narrow streets. The village comes alive in the summer with beach and sailing activity, and hosts an 18th-century market every Wednesday.

Stroll along Marine Parade to reach the **Ness**, a large sandstone headland at the river mouth with lovely sea views. Below the headland, sandy Shaldon Beach is accessed via an old smugglers' tunnel, while up the hill is the

Shaldon Wildlife Trust, a small award-winning zoo with mammals, reptiles and birds. Check out the squirrels in their tree-top runs.

At the head of the Teign estuary is the busy market town of **Newton Abbot**. Newton has been a hub of trading in this part of Devon for centuries – a livestock market is still held here – and received a significant boost with the arrival of the railways in Victorian times. You can discover more about the town's history at the **Newton Abbot Town & GWR Museum**. Elsewhere, **Tuckers Maltings** is the only working malthouse in Britain that is open to the public. The company has been based in the town for over 100 years and produces enough malt in one year to make 15 million pints of beer. Its in-house shop stocks over 200 bottled varieties.

Although the centre of Newton Abbot should be avoided in summer, when the roads become log-jammed with hordes of beach-bound tourists, the town is well placed for exploring the beautiful hidden countryside between Dartmoor and the coast. To the north, the imposing limestone cliffs of **Chudleigh Rock** form a natural playground for rock-climbing enthusiasts, while at the foot of the rock, **Ugbrooke House** – the ancestral home of Lord and Lady Clifford – lies amid quiet parkland and rolling hills. The original house was built c1200 but was replaced by a Tudor manor that was redesigned by Robert Adam in the 1760s. Rooms containing fine furniture, paintings, embroideries, porcelain and military memorabilia are open to the public during the summer, when tour guides recount tales of the Cliffords' long and colourful family history. Outside are beautiful grounds landscaped by Capability Brown, with lakes, majestic trees and views to Dartmoor.

Beyond the unremarkable town of Chudleigh, on the B3193, glorious ancient woodland conceals **Canonteign Falls** (01647 252434), England's highest waterfall, at 220 feet (67 metres). The natural appeal of the surrounding lakes and rock formations are supplemented by a wetland nature reserve, a children's assault course and cream teas in the Woodcutter's café, making for a somewhat overcrowded scene on summer weekends.

Newton Abbot Town & GWR Museum

2A St Pauls Road, Newton Abbot (01626 201121/ www.devonmuseums.net). **Open** *Feb, Mar* 10am-4pm Mon-Thur; 10am-noon Fri. *Apr-Oct* 10am-4pm Mon-Thur; 10am-noon Fri; 2-4pm Sat. **Admission** free. **No credit cards**.

Powderham Castle

Kenton (01626 890243/www.powderham.co.uk). **Open** *Apr-Oct* 10am-5.30pm Mon-Fri, Sun. Closed Nov-Mar. **Admission** £6.90; £3.90-£6.40 concessions; £17.50 family. **Credit** AmEx, MC, V.

Shaldon Wildlife Trust

Ness Drive, Shaldon (01626 872234/www.shaldon wildlifetrust.org.uk). **Open** 10am-4pm daily. **Admission** £3.50; £3 concessions; £10 family. **No credit cards**.

Teignmouth & Shaldon Museum

29 French Street, Teignmouth (01626 777041/ www.devonmuseums.net). **Open** *Easter, May-Sept* 10am-4.30pm Mon-Sat. Closed Oct-Mar. **Admission** £1. **No credit cards**.

Tuckers' Maltings

Teign Road, Osborne Park, Newton Abbot (01626 334734/www.tuckersmaltings.com). **Open** *Easter-Oct* 10am-5pm Mon-Sat. Closed Nov-Mar. **Admission** £4.95; £4.45 concessions; £13.85 family. **Credit** MC, V.

Ugbrooke House

Ugbrooke Park, Chudleigh (01626 852179). **Open** *mid July-early Sept* 1-5.30pm Tue-Thur, Sun. Closed mid Sept-early July. **Admission** £5.50; £5.20 concessions. **No credit cards**.

Activities

Adventure sports

Ashcombe Adventure Centre (Ashcombe, 01626 866766, www.ashcombeadventure.co.uk), between Chudleigh and Dawlish, offers quad-biking, archery, shooting and more.

Golf

Golf lovers can find 18-hole courses at **Dawlish Warren** (01626 862255), **Teignmouth** (01626 777070) and **Dainton Park** (Ipplepen, A381, 01803 813812); phone for further information, including details of green fees.

Watersports

Devon Windsurf & Canoe Centre (Decoy Lake, Decoy Country Park, nr Newton Abbot, 07971 051509) is run by former World Surf Canoe Champion Simon Discombe. Tuition is available in windsurfing and canoeing, with equipment also available for hire.

Where to eat, drink & stay

Rail enthusiasts may want to check out the Brunel displays at the **Atmospheric Railway Inn** (The Strand, 01626 890335, main courses £5.95-£14.95) in Starcross. Otherwise, a top choice is the **Anchor Inn** at Cockwood (01626 890203, main courses £9.95-£30), a 450-year-old smugglers' inn with a veranda overlooking the harbour.

In Teignmouth the former home of the maritime painter Thomas Luny has been converted into a very upmarket B&B: **Thomas Luny House** (Teign Street, 01626 772976, www.thomas-luny-house.co.uk, double B&B £60-£80). Pick of the pubs is the **Ship Inn** (Queen Street, 01626 772674) facing up the river; it's a great spot to watch the boats in the harbour. Another riverside pub is the revamped **Coombe Cellars** (Coombe, 01626 872423, main courses £5-£10),where the high-tide waters lap at the windows of the restaurant. Better still, head across the Teign to the **Wild Goose** (01626 872241, main courses £5-£16) at Coombeinteignhead, a trad country pub with open fires, real ales and a varied menu.

Close to Dartmoor, the award-winning **Nobody Inn** (Doddiscombleigh, 01647 252394, www.nobodyinn.co.uk, main courses £8.50-£11.50, double B&B £55-£70) is an inviting bolthole with low ceilings, an inglenook fireplace and antique furniture, not to mention a 700-strong wine cellar and impressive whisky list. Spacious, old-fashioned rooms are available above the pub or in a separate Georgian manor nearby.

Resources

Hospital

Newton Abbot *62 East Street (01626 354321).*

Internet

Teignmouth *Teignmouth Library, Fore Street (01626 774646).* **Open** 9.30am-7pm Mon, Wed; 9.30am-5pm Tue, Fri; 10am-1pm Thur; 9.30am-7pm Sat.

Police station
Teignmouth *Carlton Place (0870 577 7444).*

Post office
Teignmouth *Ashly Way (01626 773573).*
Open 9am-5.30pm Mon, Tue, Thur, Fri; 9am-
1pm Wed; 9am-12.30pm Sat.

Tourist information
Dawlish *Tourist Information Centre, The Lawn
(01626 215665).* **Open** 10am-1pm Fri,
Sat. *Mar-Nov* 9.30am-5pm Mon-Sat.
Newton Abbot *Tourist Information Centre,
6 Bridge House, Courtenay Street (01626 215667).*
Open 8.45am-4.45pm Mon-Sat.
Teignmouth *Tourist Information Centre,
The Den (01626 215666/www.southdevon.org.uk).*
Open *Nov-Mar* 10am-4pm Mon-Sat. *Apr-Oct*
9.30am-5pm Mon-Sat.

Torbay

Torbay is the collective name for the three very
different but closely linked holiday towns of
Torquay, **Paignton** and **Brixham**, which
line the ten-mile (16-kilometre) arc of Tor Bay.
Together they form the most popular holiday
destination in the UK: a mecca for retirees,
families and, increasingly, young party
animals, all seeking their own version of
the traditional English seaside holiday.

Thanks to a famously mild climate that
allows tropical vegetation to thrive, Torbay
has been harnessed with the aspirational label
of the 'English Riviera'. On a warm August
afternoon there is certainly a continental feel
to Torquay's palm-fringed promenade, but
you may find the Mediterranean vibe harder
to detect among Paignton's amusement arcades
on a wet day in February. Nevertheless, in
among the holiday parks, campsites, hotels,
guesthouses and golf courses are areas of
rare natural beauty. The beaches around
Babbacombe are backed by steep, tree-clad
cliffs, while the headlands of **Hope's Nose**
and **Berry Head** offer breathtaking views
across the majestic sweep of the bay.

Torquay & around

From humble beginnings as a small medieval
fishing village **Torquay** has grown to become
the self-styled 'capital' of the English Riviera.
The town's setting on seven hills is impressive,
and at night – if you half close your eyes –
the lights and palm trees can make it appear
truly magical.

Torquay only really took off as a holiday
destination during the Napoleonic Wars, when
the natural anchorage of Tor Bay turned the
town into an important naval base. Officers'

families moved to the area, followed by
moneyed tourists, who had been prevented
by the war from visiting foreign shores. By
the time the railway reached Newton Abbot
in the 1840s word had spread about Torquay's
climate and beneficial sea air; the resort soon
became popular with consumptives and those
seeking to escape the grime of London.

Agatha Christie was born in Barton Road,
Torquay in 1890 and spent most of her life in
the area. In World War I she worked in the
Red Cross dispensary at the town hall, where
she gained a knowledge of poisons – central
to the plot of her first published novel, *The
Mysterious Affair at Styles*, which introduced
Hercule Poirot to an unsuspecting world.

More recently, Torquay was fictionalised in
the cult comedy *Fawlty Towers*, which poked
fun at the town's petty provincialism and
geriatric visitors. Torquay's tourist officials
still battle with this stereotype today: the town
is full of small hotels of limited ambitions and is
often referred to locally as 'God's waiting room'
due to the numbers of elderly folk it attracts.

However, there's an undeniable appeal to
the town's seafront prom, elegant terraces
and garden villas, particularly in the hilly
residential areas of Meadfoot and Babbacombe,
and although Torquay's origins as a Victorian
resort are still clearly visible, a continued
programme of redevelopment has dragged
the town subtly into the 21st century. With
increasing numbers of young people now
holidaying in the town, in August Torquay
can seem more like the brash Costa del Sol
than the staid English Riviera.

Say what?

Travelling round Devon ('*Dem*' or '*Deb'm*')
today you could be forgiven for wondering
if there are any true Devonians left in the
county, particularly in the holiday hotspots.
You'll no doubt hear the dulcet tones
of London, Birmingham, Liverpool and
Newcastle on your travels, but a true
Devon accent can be pretty hard to detect.
There are, however, some telltale signs.
Devonians are naturally curious people,
and many of their remarks are in fact
questions: the most common form of
greeting is '*orright?*', while a new arrival
to a pub may enquire '*wosson then?*'.
To discover someone's whereabouts,
Devonians usually ask '*wearsunto?*' –
or '*wearserto?*' in the case of a woman
or '*maid*'. (The latter is actually

THE CENTRE

The focal point of the town is the bustling **Old Harbour** where, on balmy summer evenings, tourists throng the seafront and pleasure cruisers fill the marina. Boat trips leave from here to the bay's main beaches and to more distant destinations, including Exmouth and the Dart.

The harbour is also the site of a multi-million-pound regeneration programme that aims to inject some sophistication into Torquay's waterfront. Tides have been controlled to make sure the sludgy mud is always hidden by water and a glittering pedestrian bridge across the inner harbour mouth allows access on foot to the north and south piers. In addition to modernised facilities, a visitor attraction has been built to replace the derelict Torquay marine spa at Coral Island. Run by Paignton Zoo, **Living Coasts** (opening July 2003) aims to recreate a naturalistic coastal environment for sea otters, seals, penguins and seabirds. The attraction claims to focus on the conservation of the world's marine habitats, but has incurred the wrath of local environmentalists, who say it is nothing more than a large aviary.

To the east of the harbour, **Torquay Museum** has also recently undergone a major revamp. Exhibits at this absorbing local museum range from prehistoric artefacts found at Kents Cavern (*see p186*) to extensive displays relating to the life of local crime queen Agatha Christie. Natural science collections are now housed in the new Time Ark Gallery, while the Devon Farmhouse recreates a Victorian farm kitchen.

West of the harbour are the town's two main beaches, **Livermead Beach** and **Abbey Sands**. The latter takes its name from **Torre Abbey**, founded as a monastery in 1196 but converted into a private residence following the dissolution in 1539. Remains of the original abbey buildings include the castellated 14th-century gatehouse, the ruined abbey church, a medieval 'Spanish' barn – once used to hold prisoners from the Armada – and the former Abbot's hall, which was converted into a chapel by the Catholic Cary family in the 18th century.

Since 1930 Torre Abbey has served as the mayor's office and the municipal art gallery, with an impressive selection of artwork dating from the 18th to the mid 20th century, plus sculpture, silverware and antiquities housed in several historic rooms. There is also a small collection of manuscripts and personal effects associated with Agatha Christie. Outside, the attractive gardens are planted with rare species and enclose a balmy tropical palm house.

AROUND TORQUAY

Torquay's plushest hotel, the **Imperial** (*see p188*), occupies a commanding position on the cliffs east of the marina. From here a tourist leaflet will guide you along the 'Agatha Christie Mile', a route that takes in buildings and sights associated with the author. Alternatively, you can strike out on the coast path just beyond the Imperial towards the natural cliff arch known as **London Bridge**. The coast rises to a jagged jumble of cliffs at **Daddyhole Plain** – a panoramic viewpoint from which you can gain a sense of the geography of

Devon

Devonshire

pronounced '*merde*' but be careful with this one, particularly near the cross-channel ferry port in Plymouth.)

While we're in this neck of the woods, it's worth noting that Plymothians, or '*Janners*', are proud of being completely unintelligible to the rest of Devon (and, of course, Cornwall). Plymothians have little respect for their close neighbours, as evidenced in the expression '*Carnish campliment*', which refers to a gift that has no value.

To ensure a trouble-free visit to Devon it is imperative to understand '*dreckly*'. This is a cross-border expression roughly equating to '*mañana*' in Spain, and is deeply imbued with a cultural significance that sums up the essence of life in the South West. Although a literal translation is

'directly', this does *not* equate to 'straight away'. More likely, it means 'in a bit', 'maybe tomorrow' and 'possibly never'.

Another common phrase is '*ere!*', used to signal anything from pleasant surprise – as in 'I say, that's a particularly fine combine harvester' – to anger or hostility: 'get off my land'. If you fail to understand the nuances of '*ere!*', you may be referred to as '*mairzed*' or '*mazed*', meaning 'mad'.

Finally, remember that Devonians are acutely aware of the straw-chewing stereotype associated with them and will often play up the yokel aspect, particularly for '*vurriners*' (foreigners) and '*grockles*' (tourists), so be careful not to take all you hear at face value. Only the Wurzels ever said 'oo aar' and meant it.

the bay – before descending to the sandy, pebbly strip of **Meadfoot Beach**, backed by cafés and shops.

From here the coast path winds out to **Hope's Nose**, at the most westerly tip of Tor Bay, before continuing north along Ilsham Marine Drive towards the sheltered shingle of **Anstey's Cove** and **Redgate Beach**, where on a fine day you really could be on the Mediterranean.

Inland from here, the network of caves at **Kents Cavern** is one of the most important Palaeolithic sites in Europe. The prehistoric finds here date back over 700,000 years, making this the oldest recognisable human dwelling place in Britain. Full details of the archaeology and geology of the caves are given on regular guided tours. Look out for the unusual sandstone rock formations – including one appropriately called 'the Face'.

North of Redgate Beach, the coast path crosses a high limestone plateau at **Wall's Hill**, where Iron Age field systems are still visible among the wild flowers. Beyond, steep tree-clad cliffs shelter the shallow sandy strands of **Babbacombe** and **Oddicombe**.

During the summer, a cliff railway makes the steep ascent from the beaches to the long, grassy esplanade of Babbacombe Down, perched high on level ground, with grand views out to sea. Behind it are the village suburbs of **Babbacombe** and **St Marychurch**, where you'll find **Babbacombe Model Village**, set in four acres of beautiful gardens. Over 400 models are on display here, from villages to towns, hydroelectric stations and even a mini Stonehenge. Nearby, St Marychurch's busy shopping precinct houses the popular **Bygones** attraction, a life-sized Victorian street, with shops and period rooms brought to life with authentic smells and sounds.

On the other side of town, **Cockington** seems to have been transported straight from the front of a chocolate box into the incongruous setting of suburban Torquay. The heart of the village has been artificially held in a time warp to preserve its cluster of impossibly picturesque thatched cottages, working smithy, waterwheel and millpond. Hordes of slack-jawed tourists pore over trinkets in the gift shops or jaunt around the village in horse-drawn carriages. If this all gets rather tiresome, find some peace in the lovely wooded parkland and lakes at 17th-century **Cockington Court** (01803 606035, www.countryside-trust.org.uk). There's a craft centre, glass-blowing workshop and café in the house, and a 14th-century church in the grounds.

Babbacombe Model Village
Hampstan Avenue, Babbacombe (01803 315315/ www.babbacombemodelvillage.com). **Open** *Apr-June, Sept* 10am-5pm daily. *July, Aug* 10am-10pm daily. *Oct-Mar* 10am-4pm daily. **Admission** phone for details. **Credit** MC, V.

Bygones
Fore Street, St Mary's Church (01803 326108/ www.bygones.co.uk). **Open** *Mar-June, Sept, Oct* 10am-6pm daily. *July, Aug* 10am-9.30pm Mon-Thur; 10am-6pm Fri-Sun. *Nov-Feb* 10am-4pm daily. **Admission** £4.50; £3.50 concessions; £13 family. **No credit cards**.

Kents Cavern
91 Ilsham Road (01803 215136/www.kents-cavern.co.uk). **Open** *Apr-June, Sept, Oct* 10am-5pm daily. *July, Aug* 10am-10pm daily. *Nov-Mar* 10am-4pm Tue-Sun. **Admission** *Guided tours* £6; £3.80-£4.90 concessions; £17.60 family. **Credit** MC, V.

Torquay Museum
529 Babbacombe Road (01803 293975/ www.devonmuseums.net). **Open** *Apr-Oct* 10am-5pm Mon-Fri; 10am-4pm Sat, 1.30-5pm Sun. *Nov-Mar* 10am-5pm Mon-Fri; 10am-4pm Sat. **Admission** phone for details. **No credit cards**.

Torre Abbey Historic House & Art Gallery
The Kings Drive (01803 293593/www.torre-abbey.co.uk). **Open** *Apr-Oct* 9.30am-6pm daily. *Nov-Mar* by appointment only. **Admission** £3; £2.50 concessions; £7.50 family. **No credit cards**.

Activities

Golf
Torquay Golf Club (Petitor Road, 01803 314591, www.torquaygolfclub.com) is an 18-hole cliff-top course with great sea views. Non-members are permitted with a handicap certificate. To practise your swing, try **Torbay Golf Centre** (Grange Road, 01803 528728), an all-weather floodlit driving range with a nine-hole pitch and putt course.

Sailing
International Sailing School on Beacon Quay (tel/fax 01803 297800) offers RYA tuition in dinghy sailing for all levels, plus jetski training.

Scuba diving
Sub-aqua skills are taught by **Riviera Sports** (The Watersports Centre, Meadfoot Sea Road, 01803 214966) and **Divers Down** (139 Babbacombe Road, 01803 327111, www.diversdown.co.uk). Babbacombe Beach is the most popular spot for beginners.

Windsurfing
Torquay Windsurf Centre (Victoria Road, 01803 212411, www.kitesurfing-torquaywindsurfing.co.uk) offers lessons in windsurfing and kitesurfing, and has equipment available for hire.

Brixham: boats, fish and cheeky seagulls. *See p189.*

Where to eat & drink

Of Torquay's vast range of eateries, one of the best is **Mulberry House** (1 Scarborough Road, 01803 213639, main courses £9.50-£12.50), a neighbourhood restaurant offering well-executed Modern British cuisine in welcoming surroundings (*see also p188*). Superbly fresh fish is served in simple style at **No.7 Fish Bistro** (7 Beacon Terrace, 01803 295055, main courses £12.95-£17.50), or there's a Mediterranean-inspired menu at **Vaults Cellar Bistro & Tapas Bar** (23 Victoria Parade, 01803 380288, main courses £6.95-£16.95) – plus a three-course French dinner on Friday nights.

Torquay also boasts an excellent Indian restaurant, the **Balti Garden** (23 Abbey Road, 01803 290087, main courses £5.50-£8.95) and a traditional Thai eaterie: **Annie's** (16 The Terrace, 01803 295746, main courses £6.95-£10.95). The oldest pub in town is the **Hole in the Wall** (6 Park Lane, 01803 200755, main courses £10-£18), which has a cobbled courtyard and a decent pub-grub menu.

A visit to this part of Devon wouldn't be complete without sampling the local fish and chips. **Hanbury's** in Babbacombe (Princes Street, 01803 314616, main courses £3.49-£13)

has won the South West Fish & Chip Shop of the Year award four times and offers table service as well as takeaway meals.

Arts & entertainment

Torquay is the setting for numerous summer events. In July, the **Kick up the Arts** festival features open-air concerts, street theatre, comedy and workshops, while August is **regatta** season throughout Torbay, with boaty action on the water, air displays in the sky, and plenty of onshore entertainment for the landlubbers. For details, consult www.englishrivierafestivals.co.uk.

Surprising as it may seem, Torquay has become a clubbing hotspot in the South West, with a large number of venues serving up a popular mix of dance, house and R&B – although you shouldn't expect anything remotely cutting-edge. Also, be aware that Torquay's party reputation attracts stag and hen groups, who turn the town centre into something of a booze-fuelled assault course on weekend nights.

One of the most popular clubs is **Claire's** (Torwood Street, 01803 211097, www.claires nightclub.com), a house and R&B venue that features big name DJs on the decks. Young

Devon

party animals flock to the **Venue** (Torwood Street, 01803 213903) for retro pop, commercial house and – ooh – foam parties, while their glammed-up elders hang out at **Valbonne's** (161 Higher Union Street, 01803 290458, www.thevalbonne.com). **The Coco Lounge** (50-54 Union Street, 01803 212414) draws in a glitzy crowd (over-25s only) for guest DJs and theme nights. There's also eating, drinking and dancing at **Café Mambo** (Harbourside, 01803 291112, www.hiota.com).

If clubbing's not really your scene, more sedate entertainment – West End musicals, Gilbert and Sullivan operettas and the like – is provided by the **Princess Theatre** (Torbay Road, 08702 414120), while **Babbacombe Theatre** (Babbacombe Downs Road, 01803 328385, closed Jan) hosts variety acts and stand-up comics whose TV careers hit the rocks long ago: Cannon and Ball, anyone?

Where to stay

At the top of Torquay's long accommodation list is the **Imperial** (Park Hill Road, 01803 294301, www.paramount-hotels.co.uk, double B&B £75-£110 incl dinner), the only five-star hotel in the area. Built in the 1860s, this grand pile is perched on a cliff top overlooking the bay (many bedrooms have huge private balconies) and has a colourful history, entertaining such notable guests as Emperor Napoleon III, King Edward VII and the Beatles. Sip cocktails in the Piano Bar; stuff yourself with a cream tea in the Palm Court or save your appetite for a top-notch dinner – either in the Regatta Restaurant (main courses £16.50-£39.50) or the more informal TQ1 Brasserie (main courses £5.95-£17.95).

Pretenders to the Imperial's crown include the four-star **Grand Hotel** (Seafront, 0808 100 2529, www.grandtorquay.co.uk, double B&B £87-£117 incl dinner), an elegant seafront choice where Agatha Christie spent her honeymoon, and the comfortable **Corbyn Head Hotel** (Torbay Road, 01803 213611, double B&B £100-£148 incl dinner), which overlooks Livermead Beach. High-quality contemporary English cuisine is served in the Corbyn's Orchid Restaurant (main courses £17.50-£20.95).

For accommodation with a more personal feel, **Mulberry House** (*see p187*) is one of Torquay's most attractive guesthouses, with three lovingly furnished rooms. Beyond the hurly-burly of the resort, visitors can find a quiet spot at **Orestone Manor** (Rock House Lane, Maidencombe, 01803 328008, closed early Jan, main courses £14-£22, double B&B £104-£180). The hotel is surrounded by trees but still has views of the sea and its 12 bedrooms are decorated in comfortable, colonial style.

Resources

Hospital
Torbay Hospital *Lawes Bridge, Torquay (01803 614567).*

Internet
Net Zone *6 Newton Road, Torquay (01803 291215/www.net-zone.co.uk).* **Open** 9.30am-6pm Mon-Fri, 9am-5pm Sat.
Torquay Library *Lymington Road, Torquay (01803 208300).* **Open** 9.30am-7pm Mon, Wed, Fri; 9.30am-5pm Tue; 9.30am-1pm Thur; 9.30am-4pm Sat.

Police station
South Street, Torquay (0870 577 7444).

Post office
Castle Circus, Fleet Street, Torquay (01803 209670). **Open** 9am-5.30pm Mon-Fri; 9am-12.30pm Sat.

Tourist information
Tourist Information Centre, Vaughan Parade, Torquay (01803 297428/www.theenglish riviera.co.uk). **Open** *May-Nov* 9.30am-5pm daily. *Dec-Apr* 9.30am-5pm Mon-Sat.

Paignton, Brixham & around

At the centre of the Torbay conglomeration, **Paignton** lacks the cosmopolitan atmosphere of its larger neighbour, but also harbours none of its pretensions – with Paignton what you see is what you get. This is a cheap 'n' cheerful 'family' resort of gaudy amusement arcades and tacky gift shops, centred around a spacious pink sandy beach and Victorian pier. The harbour bustles with activity in the summer, and Paignton Green comes alive with funfairs, parades and candyfloss for the **Torbay Carnival** in July.

A pleasant stroll past the sandstone cliffs of Roundham Head takes you south to **Goodrington Sands**, a decent spot for a swim. Here you'll find the **Quay West Beach Resort**, which incorporates a water park, pub and shopping complex. To the south, **Broadsands Beach** and **Elbury Cove** offer quieter, bucket-and-spade entertainment for those wishing to escape the hordes.

The town's main attraction is **Paignton Zoo**, an imaginative 75-acre site representing some of the world's most threatened natural habitats – savannah, forest, wetland, tropical forest and desert – and providing a home for elephants, giraffe, flamingos, big cats, reptiles and more. Recent developments include a purpose-built Ape Centre, housing several species of primate in naturalistic surroundings.

Elsewhere, **Oldway Mansion** was built for the American sewing-machine tycoon Isaac Singer, and restored in grand style by his son, Paris, in 1904. There's memorabilia on the ground floor – including some early Singer sewing machines – but the rest of the council-owned mansion is used only for civic events. However, members of the public are free to roam around the ornate gardens and lush parkland.

In summer and over Christmas the **Paignton & Dartmouth Steam Railway** (01803 555872) runs from the centre of town (next to the main railway station) to Kingswear at the mouth of the River Dart. Accompanied by guards in Victorian costume, trains travel along the coast with dramatic glimpses of the bay, before giving way to the gentle scenery of the Dart valley. A 'round robin' ticket (£12, £11 concessions, £32 family) allows you to continue by ferry to Dartmouth and riverboat to Totnes, before bussing it back to Paignton.

Brixham is just a 15-minute drive from Paignton, but the contrast between the two towns couldn't be greater. For centuries fishing has been the lifeblood of this picturesque little port and remains so, despite a gradual decline in the industry. Nestled around the harbour are rows of fishermen's cottages linked by stepped alleyways and steep streets. Despite a proliferation of tacky tourist shops and flocks of unbelievably audacious seagulls, Brixham enjoys an intimacy that's hard to find anywhere else in Torbay.

Brixham established itself as a fishing port in the Middle Ages and by the mid 1800s was one of the largest fisheries in England. The **Brixham Museum** in New Road traces the maritime history of the town through photos and seafaring artefacts. In the harbour a full-scale replica of Sir Francis Drake's **Golden Hind** commands attention – although the 16th-century seafarer only visited Brixham once in 1588 aboard the captured galleon *Capitana*. Nearby is an imposing statue of William of Orange, who landed in Brixham in 1688 to end the reign of the Stuarts.

A walkway links Oxen Cove to the breakwater, which circumvents both the inner and outer harbours. Adjacent to the breakwater is the town's main beach, while a little further east, there's free access to **Shoalstone Pool**, an open-air, seawater swimming pool in a lovely location. The town's only sandy beach is on the other side of town at **St Mary's Bay**.

In fact, if it's sand that you're after then Paignton's probably a better bet, but Brixham's coastline makes up for any shortfall. Enclosed at either end by rugged cliffs, the town makes a great base for walking. To the north-west a path links the small pebbly beaches of **Fishcombe** and **Churston Quay**, backed by a large area of delightful woodland, while to the east, the imposing limestone promontory of **Berry Head** juts out 200 feet (61 metres)

Take the scenic route to Buckfastleigh on the **South Devon Railway**. *See p192.*

above the sea. The headland has played a part in the defence of the nation for hundreds of years and has extensive Napoleonic and Iron Age remains. It also attracts flocks of nesting seabirds and is a great spot to enjoy the views back across the bay. South of Berry Head nine miles (14 kilometres) of uninterrupted – and at times challengingly steep – coast path lead to Kingswear and the River Dart via **Man Sands**, a quiet and unspoilt little bay.

Brixham Museum

Bolton Cross, Brixham (01803 856267/www.brixhamheritage.org.uk). **Open** *Easter-Oct* 10am-5pm Mon-Fri; 10am-1pm Sat. Closed Nov-Mar. **Admission** £1.50; £1 concessions; £3.50 family. **No credit cards.**

Golden Hind

The Quay, Brixham (01803 856223/www.golden hind.co.uk). **Open** *Mar-June, Sept, Oct* 9am-4pm daily. *July, Aug* 9am-10pm daily. Closed Nov-Feb. **Admission** £2; £1.50 concessions. **No credit cards.**

Oldway Mansion

Torquay Road, Paignton (01803 207930). **Open** *Nov-Mar* 9am-5pm Mon-Fri. *Apr-Oct* 9am-5pm Mon-Fri; 2-5pm Sun. **Admission** free. *Guided tours* £1; 75p concessions. **No credit cards.**

Paignton Zoo

Totnes Road, Paignton (01803 697500/www.paigntonzoo.org.uk). **Open** *Summer* 10am-6pm daily. *Winter* 10am-dusk daily. **Admission** £6.50; £5.30 concessions; £20.40 family. **Credit** AmEx, MC, V.

Quay West Beach Resort

Goodrington Sands, Paignton (01803 555550/www.quaywest.co.uk). **Open** *late May-early Sept* dawn-dusk daily. Closed mid Sept-mid May. **Admission** £7.95; £6.95 concessions; £25 family. **Credit** MC, V.

Activities

Kite surfing

Mission Adventure (Bank Street, Brixham, 01803 855796) is the place to go for anything to do with adrenaline activities, especially power kiting and kite surfing. Kite surfing courses can be arranged.

Sailing

Trinity Sailing (01803 883355, www.trinity sailing.co.uk) offers residential sailing trips on board a traditional gaff-rigged Brixham trawler. No experience is necessary.

Where to eat, drink & stay

The **Palace Hotel** (Esplanade Road, 01803 555121, www.palacepaignton.com, double B&B £76-£105) used to be the home of the Singer

sewing-machine family, and retains a modicum of faded bygone grandeur. For modern facilities, though, you're better off at the **Redcliffe Hotel** (Marine Drive, 01803 526397, www.redcliffehotel.co.uk, double B&B £118-£128 incl dinner), a colonial building on the seafront, with indoor and outdoor pools, a spa, putting green and children's play area.

The restaurant scene in Paignton is very limited. A handful of large pubs, like the **Inn on the Green** (Esplanade Road, 01803 557841, main courses £6.95 £12.95), offer a decent selection at affordable prices, but those looking for a more discerning dining experience should travel to Torquay, Brixham or Totnes.

In Brixham the **Quayside Hotel** (King Street, 01803 855751, www.quaysidehotel.co.uk, double B&B £80-£96) has cosy en suite rooms overlooking the harbour, a restaurant specialising in fresh fish, and a busy, friendly bar. You can also sample Brixham fish, seafood and other delicacies at **Pilgrims** (64B Fore Street, 01803 853983, set meals £18.50/£21), a nautically themed restaurant with a good local reputation. The **Poop Deck** (15 The Quay, 01803 858681, closed Dec-Mar, main courses £9-£15) is another decent choice, serving international dishes, plus a roast on Sundays.

Inland, the **Church House Inn** in Marldon (Village Road, 01803 558279, main courses £8.50-£16, double B&B £50) has a welcoming atmosphere, excellent bar food, real ales and open log fires in winter, while the **Churston Court Inn** (Churston, 01803 842186, www.churstoncourt.com, main courses £9.95-£16.95, double B&B £60-£90) offers creaking staircases, mullioned windows and snug rooms with four posters.

Resources

Hospitals

Brixham *Greenswood Road (01803 882153).*
Paignton *Church Street (01803 557425).*

Police stations

Brixham *Rea Barn Road (0870 577 7444).*
Paignton *Southfield Road (0870 577 7444).*

Post offices

Brixham *Fore Street (01803 882226).* **Open** 9am-5.30pm Mon-Sat.
Paignton *Torquay Road (0845 722 3344).* **Open** 9am-5.30pm Mon-Wed, Fri, Sat; 8.45am-5.30pm Thur.

Tourist information

Brixham *Tourist Information Centre, Old Market House, The Quay (01803 852861/www.theenglish riviera.co.uk).* **Open** *May-Sept* 9.30am-6pm daily. *Oct-Apr* 9.30am-5pm Mon-Fri.
Paignton *Tourist Information Centre, Esplanade Road (01803 558383/0906 680 1268/*

www.theenglishriviera.co.uk). **Open** *Apr-June*
9am-5pm Mon-Sat. *July-Oct* 9.30am-6pm Mon-Sat;
10am-6pm Sun. *Nov-Mar* 9.30am-5pm Mon-Sat.

Getting there & around

By bus

National Express (08705 808080, www.gobycoach.
com) coaches run to Torquay coach station at
Lymington Road. Nearly all local buses in the
Torbay area run from Victoria Parade in
Torquay, adjacent to the harbour. For details
consult www.devon.gov.uk/devonbus.

By train

Torquay and Paignton are served by **Virgin
Trains** (www.virgin.com) from Exeter St David's,
Bristol Temple Meads and the north of England.
Wessex Trains (www.wessextrains.co.uk)
operates local services to and from the Exe
estuary (via Exeter Central).

Open-air market
at **Totnes**.

The South Hams

West of Torbay, the South Hams' lush valleys
and snaking rivers stretch from Dartmoor's
rocky foot to the English Channel, criss-crossed
by a maze of high-banked lanes bound to show
up your driving inadequacies. The area is a
magnet for tourists, who adore the chocolate-
box villages and stunning coastal scenery.

As a result, property prices have tripled and
high season sees more cars than ever pack the
primitive roads – until the 20th century the main
route in was by boat. However, those braving
the crush are unlikely to be disappointed. When
the sun shines, the coastal towns of Salcombe
and Dartmouth really sparkle, while the
windswept cliffs and glorious beaches offer
plenty of opportunities to escape for the day.

Totnes & around

The ancient market town of **Totnes** is only a
few miles inland from Torbay but couldn't be
further away in terms of atmosphere. Its long
history stretches back to Saxon times when it
was a fortified settlement built to protect the
upper Dart from Viking raids, and reached its
zenith in the 16th century as a river port for
the wine and cloth trades.

In the 20th century the cultural influence of
nearby Dartington Hall (*see p192*) seeped into
Totnes, transforming the unpretentious town
into an appealing centre for the creative, the
alternative and the plain unusual. Writers,
musicians, therapists, herbalists and others
have settled here in large numbers to create
a unique community vibe. Every Friday the
open-air market sells everything from organic
vegetables to didgeridoos, and with buskers on
every corner, this is a chance to see Totnes at
its most diverse. A rather different scene is
presented at the Elizabethan market, on
Tuesday mornings in summer, when local
people and traders dress in period costume.

At other times, the best way to get a flavour
of the town is to take a stroll up **Fore Street**,
the steep main thoroughfare that leads from
the River Dart up to the castle. Totnes's ancient
heritage quickly becomes apparent in the fine
16th- and 17th-century buildings that blend
seamlessly with health food shops, crystal
emporiums, New Age bookstores and vegan
cafés. The **Elizabethan Museum** on Fore
Street is housed in one of the finest period
buildings in Totnes. It has an engaging array
of exhibits charting the town's history, and
one room detailing the achievements of former
resident Charles Babbage (1791-1871), who
invented an early precursor of the computer.

Devon

Check out the high art at **High Cross House** in the grounds of **Dartington Hall**.

As you wander up Fore Street towards the arch of the medieval **East Gate**, be careful not to miss the famous **Brutus Stone**, set into the pavement on the right-hand side (outside No.51). According to legend, Brutus (grandson of Aeneas) landed in Totnes in 1170 BC as the founding king of Britain, using this piece of granite as a stepping stone to reach the shore.

From the East Gate the old town walls lead round to the church of **St Mary** (c1460) and to the colonnaded **Guildhall**, built in 1533 on the site of an 11th-century priory. The Council Chamber, former magistrates' court and town gaol are all open to the public; you'll also see the table where Oliver Cromwell planned his South West campaigns in 1646.

Totnes Castle sits imposingly above the town with fine views over the surrounding countryside. Built shortly after the Norman Conquest, the castle was one of the first stone fortifications to be constructed in Devon and is an excellent example of a motte-and-bailey design. During the summer it forms the backdrop for open-air theatre, medieval pageants and other special events.

At the bottom of town, **Steamer Quay** is the departure point for river trips down the Dart to Dartmouth. Contact **Riverlink** (01803 834488, www.riverlink.co.uk) for details of

sailing times. To travel upstream, take the **South Devon Railway** (0845 345 1427, www.southdevonrailway.org, closed Nov-Feb), whose steam locomotives puff their way along the beautiful Dart valley to Buckfastleigh on the edge of Dartmoor (*see p176*).

The line runs close to the grounds of **Dartington Hall** (01803 866688), an arts and education centre that is recognised as one of the most important cultural institutions in the South West. At its heart is the spectacular medieval Great Hall, built by the Earl of Huntingdon in the late 14th century and saved from dereliction in the 20th century by Dorothy and Leonard Elmhirst.

The Elmhirsts bought Dartington in 1925 and turned it into a progressive school, run on anti-authoritarian, creative lines. Although the school closed in 1987, the estate continues to promote education and the arts through a wide variety of cultural events, including concerts, plays and film screenings, plus courses at the Dartington College of Arts. For details contact **DartingtonARTS** (01803 847070, www.dartingtonarts.co.uk).

The public are free to wander around the beautiful grounds, which are littered with sculptures and ancient trees. Amid the parkland, **High Cross House** strikes a daring modernist pose. Originally built for the headmaster Bill Curry in the 1930s, it now serves as a fabulous gallery for the Elmhirsts' art collection. On the edge of the estate, examples of contemporary arts and crafts – including Dartington Glass – are on view and on sale at the **Dartington Cider Press Centre** (Shinners Bridge, 01803 847500, www.dartingtonciderpress.co.uk).

On the other side of Totnes, **Berry Pomeroy Castle** commands a romantic setting in a wood on a cliff edge. Reputedly one of the most haunted sites in England, the castle exudes an eerily brooding atmosphere. The original medieval castle here was substantially rebuilt in the 15th century. Its outer walls encircle the remains of an elaborate Renaissance mansion that was started by the Duke of Somerset but never completed.

Berry Pomeroy Castle

nr Totnes (01803 866618/wwwenglish-heritage.org.uk). **Open** *Apr-Sept* 10am-6pm daily. *Oct* 10am-5pm daily. Closed Nov-Mar. **Admission** £2.80; £1.40-£2.10 concessions. **No credit cards.**

Elizabethan Museum

70 Fore Street, Totnes (01803 863821/ www.devonmuseums.com). **Open** *Easter-Oct* 10.30am-5pm Mon-Fri. Closed Nov-Mar. **Admission** £1.50; £1 concessions. **No credit cards.**

Guildhall

Ramparts Walk, Totnes (01803 862147). **Open** *Apr-Oct* 10.30am-4.30pm Mon-Fri. Closed Nov-Mar. **Admission** £1; 25p-50p concessions. **No credit cards.**

Totnes Castle

Totnes (01803 864406/wwwenglish-heritage.org.uk). **Open** *Apr-Sept* 10am-6pm daily. *Oct* 10am-6pm Wed-Sun. Closed Nov-Mar. **Admission** £1.80; 90p-£1.40 concessions. **No credit cards.**

Where to eat, drink & stay

One of the top spots for food in Totnes is **Effings** (50 Fore Street, 01803 863435, main courses £6.95-£14.95), where excellent Modern European lunches with all the trimmings are served on a handful of tables at the back of a fine food deli. **Rumour** (30 High Street, 01803 864682, main courses £8.50-£15) is a lively place to enjoy anything from a beer to a full-scale meal, while its sister establishment **Wills Restaurant** (3 The Plains, 0800 056 3006, closed Jan, main courses £14.95-£18.95) offers imaginative gourmet dishes in idiosyncratic Regency surroundings. **Willow Vegetarian Garden Restaurant** (87 High Street, 01803 862605, main courses £5.70-£7.50) has a huge range of vegetarian

and vegan food, plus organic wines and beers, and live music on Friday nights.

Downstream from Totnes, the **Maltsters Arms** (Bow Creek, Tuckenhay, 01803 732350, www.tuckenhay.com, main courses £7.75-£18.95, double B&B £50-£125) enjoys an idyllic setting near the River Dart. Once owned by TV chef Keith Floyd, it has reinvented itself in recent years with log fires and a restaurant overlooking the creek. Towards Paignton, **Parliament House** (Longcombe, near Totnes, 01803 840288, double B&B £55-£65) is a low-slung thatched property where William of Orange is supposed to have held his first parliament, while back in town, the **Old Forge** (Seymour Place, Totnes, 01803 862174, double B&B £52-£58) offers a variety of accommodation in a 600-year-old building.

Resources

Internet

Totnes Library *27A High Street, Totnes (01803 862210).* **Open** 9.30am-5pm Mon, Wed; 9.30am-7pm Tue, Fri; 9.30am-1pm Thur, Sat.

Police station

Ashburton Road, Totnes (0870 577 7444).

Post office

39 Fore Street, Totnes (01803 867542). **Open** 8.30am-4.30pm Mon-Fri; 8.30am-noon Sat.

Tourist information

Tourist Information Centre, The Town Mill, Coronation Road, Totnes (01803 863168/ www.totnesinfo.org.uk). **Open** 9.30am-5pm Mon-Sat.

Dartmouth & around

Reached only by boat or ear-popping road descent, Dartmouth and sister village Kingswear form an impressive first sight. Properties of every size, colour and era cling haphazardly over the sleek River Dart: a town planner's nightmare but a visitor's delight. Despite summer parking chaos and the cheekiest seagulls around, seafarers and land-lovers alike flock here for good food, stunning views, not to mention some quirky shops and galleries. The influx hits crisis point in late August each year with a glorious week of boating and boozing at the **Royal Regatta** (www.dartmouthregatta.co.uk).

Dartmouth has been a mariner's haven since Anglo-Saxon times, thanks to its natural deep-water anchorage. During the Middle Ages it was a hub of sea trade, exporting corn and wool in return for wine and other exotic goods. In the 12th century Dartmouth residents waved off ships on the second and third crusades; three centuries later, they cheered Elizabethan seafarers setting out on voyages of discovery.

Devon

The Pilgrim Fathers rested here on their first sailing to the New World in 1620; and in 1944, 480 US navy ships departed from Dartmouth for the D-Day landings in Normandy. Since the 19th century the town has also been home to the **Britannia Royal Naval College**.

At the centre of town is the **boat float**, a harbour for small craft that is overlooked by the venerable **Royal Castle Hotel** (*see p197*). On nearby Duke Street, the **Butterwalk** is a 17th-century former merchant's house with a ground-level granite colonnade supporting elaborately carved upper storeys. Charles II held court in a magnificent panelled room here in 1671, but now its creaking floors are home to the Sloping Deck Restaurant and **Dartmouth Museum**. Maritime curios, including an extensive model ship collection, are joined by artefacts relating to Thomas Newcomen (1663-1729), the Dartmouth-born blacksmith who invented an early version of the steam engine – you can see one in action in the **Newcomen Engine House**, next to the tourist office in the Royal Avenue Gardens.

Beyond the Butterwalk, Foss Street is a pretty pedestrianised street of multicoloured shops, including the celebrated **Simon Drew Gallery** (No.13, 01803 832832). On the other side of Duke Street, Anzac Street leads to the medieval church of **St Saviour**. It's worth popping inside to see its finely carved choir screen and the 14th-century wrought-iron work on the oak door in the south porch.

Beyond the church, the town's narrow streets are characterised by an appealing, higgledy-piggledy assortment of historic buildings, including the **Cherub Inn** on Higher Street. This rickety, timber-framed pub dates from 1380 and is the oldest building in Dartmouth. **Agincourt House** is another 14th-century survivor down the hill on Lower Street, where you'll also find the browsable **D'Art Gallery** (01803 834923, www.dart-gallery.com). Nearby, No.1 Fairfax Place is a 17th-century house with fine wood carving and oriel windows.

The streets and alleys emerge on to the waterfront at **Bayard's Cove**, a delightful cobbled quay lined with elegant 18th-century houses. The small fort at the far end was built by Henry VIII in 1510 to serve as a second line of defence for the town, while a stone outside the Dartmouth Arms pub records the sailing of the Pilgrim Fathers from this spot in 1620.

A mile south of town, beyond the wooded inlet of Warfleet creek and the much-missed Gunfield Hotel (now a private residence), is **Dartmouth Castle**. It's best reached during the summer by boat from the Embankment – a short, breezy trip that will have you dreaming of a life on the ocean waves. The castle perches on the cliffs at the estuary mouth, mirrored by a smaller fortification on the Kingswear side. If the harbour was threatened by attack from the sea, a large chain would be hoisted across the estuary between the two fortifications.

Commissioned by Edward IV and completed in 1403, Dartmouth Castle was the first in Britain to be designed specifically for artillery warfare, although from the water the most dominant feature is the tower of **St Petrox**, a 17th-century church used by the soldiers.

From the castle, follow the coast path through woodland towards Sugary and Compass coves, where the flat rocks make a perfect picnic spot. The steep, grassy field above is topped by former coastguard cottages and has unrivalled views out to sea.

AROUND THE ESTUARY

Across the river from Dartmouth, the Paignton & Dartmouth Steam Railway (*see p189*) terminates at **Kingswear**. Thin, colourful cottages crowd up the hill from the station, while paths lead out of the village to Kingswear Castle and the estuary mouth.

In a spectacular position on a headland to the east is National Trust-owned **Coleton Fishacre House & Gardens**, created in the 1920s by Rupert and Dorothy D'Oyley Carte. Their Arts and Crafts-style mansion still retains its original fittings, but the real highlight is the gardens, which incorporate dense woodland, camellias, rhododendrons and rare rainforest species. A network of steep paths stretches as far as the cliff edge.

To reach the Kingswear side of the estuary, pedestrians can catch the passenger ferry from Dartmouth pontoon, but it's just as fun to squeeze on to the Lower Car Ferry, which is hauled across the river by tugs from a landing stage near Bayard's Cove. Or there's the Higher Car Ferry, which departs from Dartmouth's North Embankment to join up with the A379 towards Torbay.

For longer, more leisurely excursions, take a boat trip up the Dart towards Totnes with **Riverlink** (*see p192*), stopping off at the lovely riverside village of **Dittisham**. In the middle of the river here is the anchorstone, where unfaithful wives were allegedly once tied up as punishment. Nowadays the village is a rather more easygoing place of artists and sailors. **Coombe Farm** (01803 722352, www.rileyarts.com, www.coombegallery.com) offers a range of residential art courses and has a lovely gallery featuring quality local work.

Opposite Dittisham is 17th-century **Greenway House**, former home of Agatha Christie and now owned by the National Trust. The house is privately occupied but the

Start Point Lighthouse: guiding ships since 1836. *See p196.*

subtropical grounds are open all summer. Passenger ferries (01803 833206) run from Dittisham and Dartmouth to the estate between March and November, and visitors arriving by boat receive discounts on admission.

TOWARDS START POINT

Start Bay's sweeping arc of high cliffs and shingle beaches stretches some 20 miles (32 kilometres) from Dartmouth to Start Point. Void of tourist traps, it is a place for hearty walks and fresh air, rounded off by a good pub lunch. Just driving along the A379 coast road is a joy, but note that stunning views make for slow traffic in summer.

Alternatively, take one of the back roads. The Blackpool valley is particularly pretty, stretching several lush miles inland from the pine-backed embrace of **Blackpool Sands**, a lovely dog-free Blue Flag beach with a café and watersports facilities.

From Blackpool Sands, perilous hairpin bends lead to the quiet cliff-top village of **Strete**, once inhabited by smugglers. The road out offers spectacular views over the long sweep of **Slapton Sands** and the **Slapton Ley National Nature Reserve** (www.slnnr.org.uk). The large freshwater lake of Slapton Ley is a geo-morphological gem, separated from the sea by a narrow shingle bar and surrounded by a variety of wetland habitats that are rich in wildlife. Scarily, Slapton's shingle ridge is now being eaten by the sea at an alarming rate, hitting the national headlines in January 2001 when part of the main road was destroyed and a war memorial toppled.

During World War II US forces took over Slapton Sands to prepare for the D-Day invasions. About 3,500 people were evacuated from the area, returning after a year to find buildings damaged, fields cratered and overgrown, wildlife decimated and stray mines still littering the area. In **Torcross**, at the end of the Ley, there's a memorial to the 749 Allied soldiers killed during a live-ammunition rehearsal for the invasion. Many were victims of an ambush by German torpedoes, but to the shame of the Allied commanders, others were killed by so-called friendly fire. An original Sherman tank, recovered from the sea in 1984, is a stark reminder of the tragedy.

Delightful **Slapton** village is tucked behind hills about a mile inland. In 1372 Sir Guy de Brien founded a chantry here, of which only a rook-infested, highly atmospheric tower remains, fronted by the lovely Tower Inn (*see p197*). **Slapton Ley Field Centre** (01548 580466) is also based in the village.

Abandoned **Hallsands**.

It issues fishing licences for the Ley and runs regular guided walks.

Further south, **Beesands** is a mini version of Slapton Sands but without the traffic. The uncompromising fishing village has hardly changed for centuries – though many old cottages are now holiday homes. Stock up on fresh lobster at **Britannia Shellfish** (The Viviers, 01548 581186), before striking out along the coast path to 'new' **Hallsands**, a singularly bleak hamlet at one end of a shingle beach, with several derelict buildings teetering at the mercy of the encroaching waves.

The southern end of the village used to be a thriving fishing community, but controversial dredging along the beach at the turn of the 19th century undermined its natural shingle breakwater, leaving the village vulnerable to the sea. A heavy storm in 1917 destroyed the centuries-old settlement leaving a few desolate ruins, clinging to the crumbling cliffs.

Beyond the ruined village, the coast path swoops through thick bracken, heather and gorse towards the jagged arm of **Start Point**, whose treacherous waters are littered with shipwrecks, including four German U-boats from World War II. A mile offshore, the shifting sand bar of Skerries Bank is capped by white horses even on calm days, and becomes a raging torrent when

the turning tides make water race around the point. **Start Point Lighthouse** was built in 1836 in an effort to minimise wreckage in the area. It's now operated remotely via computer, but guided tours are still available in summer (call 01803 770606 for details).

Around the point, **Mattiscombe Beach** is a secluded, sandy cove with rockpools at low tide and beginners' surf. If you are lucky you may even see some seals, which live around the rocks here. It makes a lovely spot for a swim, en route to Prawle Point (*see p198*), Devon's most southerly headland.

Coleton Fishacre House & Gardens
Broen Stone Road, Kingswear (01803 752466/ www.nationaltrust.org.uk). **Open** *Garden* Mar 11am-5pm Sat, Sun. Apr-Nov 10.30am-5.30pm Wed-Sun. *House* Apr-Nov 11am-4.30pm Wed-Sun. Closed Dec-Feb. **Admission** *House & gardens* £5; £2.10 concessions; £12.50 family. *House only* £3.90; £1.90 concessions. **Credit** (shop) MC, V.

Dartmouth Castle
Castle Road, Dartmouth (01803 833588/ www.english-heritage.org.uk.). **Open** *Apr-Sept* 10am-6pm daily. *Oct* 10am-5pm daily. *Nov-Mar* 10am-4pm Wed Sat. **Admission** £3.20; £2.40 concessions. **Credit** MC, V.

Dartmouth Museum
The Butterwalk, Dartmouth (01803 832923/ www.devonmuseums.net/dartmouth). **Open** *Apr-Oct* 10am-4.30pm Mon-Sat. *Nov-Mar* noon-3pm Mon-Sat. **Admission** £1.50; 50p-£1 concessions. **No credit cards**.

Greenway Gardens
Greenway Road, Galmpton (01803 842382/ www.nationaltrust.org.uk). **Open** Mar-Oct 10.30am-5pm Wed-Sat. Closed Nov-Feb. **Admission** £3.70; £1.40-£2.90 concessions. **Credit** MC, V.

Activities

Canoeing
Canoe Adventures (1 Church Court, Harberton, 01803 865301) offers canoe trips up the Dart.

Fishing
For fishing trips try **Picnic Boat** (07968 785650), which also runs more leisurely sunset cruises.

Watersports
Venus Company (01803 770209) runs the beach shop and café, and hires watersports equipment on Blackpool Sands.

Where to eat, drink & stay

The jewel in the crown of Dartmouth's impressive dining scene is the riverside **Carved Angel Restaurant** (2 South Embankment, 01803 832465, www.thecarvedangel.com, set meals £25-£42), an elegant, half-timbered establishment with a nationwide reputation. Innovative Modern British cuisine is the order of the day here. For a more down-to-earth version, visit the **Carved Angel Café** (7 Foss Street, 01803 834842, main courses £4.95-£8), which serves stuffed baguettes at lunchtime and well-prepared fish dishes in the evening. Other good choices include the light and airy **Anzac Street Bistro** (2 Anzac Street, 01803 8355155, closed Jan, main courses £10-£13.50, double B&B £60), where local ingredients are cooked to perfection, and accommodation is provided in two pleasant, bright bedrooms.

The 17th-century **Royal Castle Hotel** (The Quay, 01803 833033, www.royalcastle.co.uk, main courses £12.95-£16.95, double B&B £49.95-£84.95 per person) is a cosy central base with many original features and some four-poster beds. Choose between the glitzy harbour bar or the Galleon Lounge for decent food and drink. Also in town, the **Little Admiral Hotel** (27-9 Victoria Road, 01803 832572, www.little-admiral.co.uk, closed Jan, set meals £16.50/£18.50, double B&B £60-£130) is a bijou hotel with stylish traditional rooms, an adventurous dinner menu and hearty breakfasts. Moored in the middle of the Dart, **Res Nova** (07770 628 967, closed Jan-Mar, main courses £9-£15, double B&B £45) is a fun floating barge with comfy, basic cabins and an on-board restaurant. It runs its own boat taxi service to and from the town.

Among Dartmouth's numerous atmospheric pubs, try the **Cherub Inn** (Higher Street, 01803 832571, main courses £6-£13.50) or cross the Dart to the **Ship Inn** at Kingswear (01803 752348, main courses £3.50-£10) for potent scrumpy and the last of the evening sun. In the morning, the fab **Café Alf Resco** (Lower Street, 01803 835880, closed late Jan-early Feb) serves the best hangover-curing brunch selection, including full fry-ups.

Away from the hubbub, **Fingals Hotel & Restaurant** at Dittisham (01803 722398, www.fingals.co.uk, closed Jan & Feb, set dinner £27.50, double B&B £85-£140) is a gorgeous, rambling retreat offering patchwork quilts, roaring fires, plenty of original art and lively conversation round the communal dinner table. It also boasts a heated pool, lawn tennis, a fleet of wooden boats, a family of friendly ducks and a beautifully converted self-catering barn for those who want to do-it-themselves.

South of Dartmouth, the **Laughing Monk Restaurant** (Totnes Road, Strete, 01803 770639, main courses £13.50-£15) offers good food using local ingredients, while the 14th-century **Tower Inn** (Slapton, 01548 580216,

www.slapton.org, main courses £8.95-£15, double B&B £50) serves upmarket pub grub in a candlelit bar-restaurant (book in advance). Hidden up a narrow side road, overlooked by the ruined chantry tower, the latter is a delightful find, with a flower-filled beer garden and cosy en suite rooms. Near Slapton, **Start House** (01548 580254, double B&B £25) is a comfortable Georgian home with views over the Start valley. Finally, in Torcross, the beachside **Start Bay Inn** (01548 580553, main courses £4.20-£9) is renowned for its fish and chips.

Resources

Internet
Dartmouth Library *Newcomen Road, Dartmouth (01803 832502)*. **Open** 9.30am-7pm Mon, Thur; 9.30am-5pm Tue, Fri; 9.30am-1pm Sat.

Police station
Flavel Street, Dartmouth (0870 577 7444).

Post office
Plymco *Mayor's Avenue, Dartmouth (01803 832730)*. **Open** 8.30am-5.30pm Mon-Fri; 8.30am-1pm Sat.

Tourist information
Visitor Information Centre *The Engine House, Mayor's Avenue, Dartmouth (01803 834224/www.dartmouth-information.co.uk).* **Open** *Apr-Sept* 9.30am-5.30pm daily. *Oct-Mar* 9.30am-4.30pm Mon-Sat.

Salcombe & around

Until the 1950s **Salcombe** was an unpretentious village of fishermen and ship builders quietly getting on with their lives. Now, second-home owners and miffed locals are noisily trying to get on with each other. While yachties dub it England's answer to St Tropez, others are getting très stroppy about the extortionate house prices and yuppie atmosphere. Some say the chocolate-box town will melt in its own heat, while others thank goodness for a thriving tourist industry in this former backwater. Most visitors, however, will just delight at the town's stunning setting and pastel-coloured charm.

The snug town centre nestles in a steep incline at the mouth of the Kingsbridge and Salcombe estuary – actually a flooded valley affording views of turquoise water, wooded creeks and imposing cliffs. Dolphins, porpoises and rare birds are attracted to this gorgeous National Nature Reserve, where yellow beaches fringe the shores and boats pepper the water, particularly during the Yacht Club and Town Regattas.

The town's topography makes for narrow, twisting streets, so ditch the car as soon as possible and explore on foot. Island Street has plenty of interesting shops, including **Cove's Quay Gallery** (01548 842666, www.covesquay.co.uk), while elsewhere, boat builders and chandlers jostle for room with stylish sailing boutiques. Gourmands can visit **Salcombe Dairy** (Shadycombe Road, 01548 843228) for cartons of scrumptious ice-cream. For something a little more edifying, **Salcombe Maritime Museum** has informative displays describing Salcombe's role as a trading centre and smugglers' haven.

Just out of town children wielding buckets and spades flock to the attractive beaches at **North** and **South Sands**, reached in summer only by boats from Ferry Steps on Whitestrand Quay (01548 561035). A little further on, in the village of Sharpitor, is cliff-top **Overbecks Museum & Garden**, an imposing Edwardian house owned until 1937 by the eccentric scientist Otto Overbeck. The upper floors are given over to a youth hostel, but downstairs you'll find a fascinating display of taxidermy, ship-building exhibits and a number of bizarre Overbeck inventions – look out for the 'Rejuvenator', a machine intended to extend human life expectancy. The subtropical, terraced gardens cover six acres, and boast incredible views towards Salcombe.

South of Sharpitor, the coast path winds south to the rocky promontory of **Bolt Head** guarding the estuary mouth. Continue for five miles (eight kilometres) west of here across Bolberry Down, with its towering cliffs, to enjoy some of the most spectacular coastal scenery in the area, including a lovely small beach at **Soar Mill Cove**. The walk culminates at **Bolt Tail**, overlooking the sheltered arc of Bigbury Bay (*see below*).

There's equally stunning scenery on the other side of the estuary. From Salcombe's Ferry Steps, regular boats (01548 842364) ply the crossing to **East Portlemouth**, once a thriving village but now a scenic suburb with access to sandy **Mill Bay**. From here cliff walks lead towards Gara Rock and **Prawle Point**, a shipwreck hotspot, crowned by a coastguard lookout. En route the coast path takes in rugged cliffs once occupied by Iron Age settlers – the remains of a hill fort can be seen near the **Gara Rock Hotel** (East Prawle, 01548 842342) – and skirts sheltered beaches such as beautiful **Elender Cove**. Many of the rocky outcrops follow a distinctly piggy theme: look out for Pig's Nose, Gammon Head and the Ham Stone.

For a more tranquil excursion, take a boat up the estuary to explore its myriad inlets and hidden valleys, including **Frogmore** and **South**

Pool creeks, or continue to **Kingsbridge** at the head of the estuary. This is the main town and transport hub in the area, but doesn't quite live up to its waterside setting, thanks to the presence of a sprawling car park along the south quay, and the busy A379 on the other side. However, the **Cookworthy Museum of Rural Life** on the town's steep main drag is worth a rainy-day visit. It's housed in a former 17th-century grammar school and contains an authentic schoolroom and the reconstruction of an Edwardian apothecary store.

Kingsbridge also provides easy access to the villages and beaches along Bigbury Bay, a wide arc of golden sands and tricky tides that attracts a holiday crowd of families, golfers and windsurfers. At the southern tip of the bay, the twin villages of Inner and Outer Hope – a mix of pretty thatch, boxy bungalows and several outdated hotels – cluster around **Hope Cove** in the shelter of Bolt Tail. Further north the thatched village of **Thurlestone** is fronted by a golf course and a series of glistening white, top-quality beaches at **Thurlestone Sands**.

At the mouth of the River Avon, **Bantham** has a west-facing surf beach that at low tide stretches some quarter of a mile across the estuary to **Bigbury-on-Sea**. This is a fairly unattractive, 20th-century holiday and retirement settlement, compensated by incredible sea views and an expansive shallow beach that's perfect for windsurfing. A ferry crosses the estuary twice daily in summer, but it's also possible to walk an eight-mile (13-kilometre) circuit inland along both banks of the river via the 15th-century bridge at **Aveton Gifford**.

At low tide you can stroll – or take the bizarre sea tractor – from Bigbury-on-Sea across the tidal sandbar to **Burgh Island**, famed for its art deco hotel (*see p200* **Island retreat**). The hotel grounds are strictly off limits to day trippers, but you can have a pint at the Pilchard Inn (*see p201*) or walk to the ruined picnic hut at the top of the island for panoramic sea views.

West of Bigbury is **Challaborough Beach** – hard to miss for screaming kids and 500-odd static caravans – and beautifully secluded **Ayrmer Cove**, while inland along the Avon valley there are blissful woodland walks to be enjoyed around Woodleigh and Loddiswell along the abandoned Primrose Line track, which once ran between South Brent and Kingsbridge. North again are the **Blackdown Rings**, the remains of an Iron Age hill fort built around 400 BC. Hardly anyone heads out here, so you're guaranteed some peace and quiet.

Further west on the A379, **Modbury** is a fiercely proud little market town that was once a hub of the wool trade. It's a great

How about that for a view? **Overbecks Museum & Garden**. *See p198.*

place to spend an hour or two, browsing for antiques – check out **Collector's Choice**, 27 Church Street, 01548 831111) – or deli goodies – **Mackgill's Delicatessen** (4 Church Street, 01546 830860) is recommended.

West of town the River Erme is flanked by the private and heavily forested **Flete Estate** (Mothercombe, Holbenton, 01752 830308, www.flete.co.uk). The imposing Tudor house was used as a maternity hospital and evacuee home during the World War II bombing of Plymouth, and has now been converted into retirement homes. Desirable holiday cottages are dotted around the estate, but you should phone in advance for permission to explore its 1,000 acres of beautiful unspoilt countryside.

Wildlife on the pretty Erme estuary was threatened in May 1990 by a massive crude oil slick from the tanker *Rose May*. Booms across the river mouth staved off the worst effects but it was still a big clean-up job to restore **Mothecombe Beach** to its sandy glory. This private beach can be reached via Holbeton and is popular with surfers who catch rollers on incoming tides. Beyond, the coast path weaves a pleasant route past **Stoke Beach** towards **Stoke Point** and Wembury Bay (*see p205*).

Cookworthy Museum of Rural Life
108 Fore Street, Kingsbridge (01548 853235/ www.devonmuseums.co.uk). **Open** *late Mar-Oct* 10.30am-5pm Mon-Sat. Closed Nov-mid Mar. **Admission** £2; £1.50 concessions; £4.50 family. **No credit cards**.

Overbecks Museum & Garden
Sharpitor, Salcombe (01548 842893/ www.nationaltrust.org.uk). **Open** 10am-8pm daily. **Admission** *Museum & garden* £4.20; £2.10 concessions. *Garden only* £3.30; £1.65 concessions; £11.50 family. **Credit** MC, V.

Salcombe Maritime Museum
Market Street (no phone). **Open** *Apr-Oct* 10.30am-12.30pm, 2.30-4.30pm daily. Closed Nov-Mar. **Admission** £1. **No credit cards**.

Activities

Diving
Diventure Salcombe (Tucker's Marine, Brewery Quay, Island Street, Salcombe, 01548 843663, www.diventure.net) arranges dive trips and provides PADI training. Scuba gear and mountain bikes can also be hired.

Golf
Thurlestone Golf Club (Thurlestone, 01548 560405) is an 18-hole golf course. For fantastic views, also try the hill-top **Bigbury Golf Club** (01548 810412).

Sailing
Moored in the estuary above Salcombe, a former Mersey ferry serves as the renowned **Island Cruising Club** (01548 531176, www.icc-salcombe.co.uk), offering RYA dinghy sailing with on-board accommodation. A friendly alternative is **South Sands Sailing** (South Sands Beach, 01548 843451, www.salcombewatersports.co.uk), which provides RYA tuition and also hires out dinghies, catamarans and kayaks for use on the beach.

Devon

Where to eat, drink & stay

In summer, finding a quiet Salcombe restaurant is nigh on impossible, so be prepared to book ahead. **The Galley** (5 Fore Street, 01548 842828, closed winter) is probably the town's best-known eaterie and has an excellent reputation for fresh fish. Other good options include **Clare's** (01548 842646, closed Jan, main courses £10-£14.95) and the **Boatswain's Brasserie** (01548 842189, closed winter), which has an upmarket menu and modish interior. The ever-popular **Ferry Inn** (Fore Street, Salcombe, 01548 844000, main courses £4.50-£9.95) is a good bet for good food, real ale and a lively atmosphere.

High tides will lead you up the estuary to the appealing **Millbrook Inn** (South Pool, 01548 531581, main courses £4.95-£13.50), an attractive creekside hostelry serving good pub grub. In Kingsbridge the top choice is plain-fronted **Ship-to-Shore** (45 Church Street, 01548 854076, www.ship-to-shore.co.uk), a high-quality, Modern British restaurant, offering fine fish dishes and French wines. Also here is the bright and funky **Pig Finca Café** (The Promenade, 01548 855777, main courses £8-£10), where tasty food is served to Latino beats.

On the east side of the estuary, a mile's walk inland from Prawle Point, the **Pig's Nose Inn** (East Prawle, near Kingsbridge, 01548 511209, main courses £2.50-£7) is an eccentric pub with hearty food, a lively music scene and saggy old sofas to collapse in.

Good-quality accommodation in Salcombe itself comes with a very high price tag – especially in high season. A luxurious central choice is the **Marine Hotel** (Cliff Road, 01548 844444, www.bookmenzies.com, set meal £32.50, double B&B £100-£200 incl dinner), where estuary views are complemented by a waterside leisure complex. Up the hill, visitors on a more limited budget can still enjoy glorious views from the

Island retreat

Although it's easily reached – by sand or sea tractor, depending on the tide – ten-acre Burgh Island exudes a sense of romantic remoteness that's rare on the South Devon coast. Pilchard fishermen and pirates once made a lonely living here and, according to some the ghost of legendary Tom Crocker, shot by customs men outside the 14th-century Pilchard Inn (*see p201*), still roams the island in search of hidden booty.

In 1895 music hall singer George Chirgwin bought the island and built a hotel, turning the place into a high-society bolthole, where big names and hangers-on could escape the limelight. In 1927 he sold the lot to Archibald Nettlefold, a wealthy industrialist and then owner of London's Comedy Theatre. 'Uncle Archie' built the present 'country house by the sea', complete with copper-green turret, leaning Ganges Bar (part of former naval ship HMS *Ganges*), ballroom and sea-fed mermaids' pool.

The Jazz Age jet set couldn't get enough of it, flocking to Burgh Island for wild parties and to seek inspiration for their various arts: Noel Coward planned to spend three days and ended up staying for three weeks; Edward Windsor brought Wallis Simpson here; and Agatha Christie regularly ensconced herself in the Beach Hut to pen both *Evil under the Sun* and *And Then There Were None*.

World War II brought the fun to a halt. Barbed wire surrounded the island and it is thought Eisenhower and Churchill occasionally met at the redundant hotel. With peacetime, however, the glamour returned, bringing a new wave of star guests, including the Beatles, who stayed during a tour to escape adoring fans.

During the 1970s the building became run-down and its future looked pretty bleak, but the arrival of new owners the following decade signalled an upturn in the hotel's fortunes and the painstaking restoration of its former art deco glory.

The current owners took over in 2002 and are continuing the renovations. Now defined as a 'retreat of discreet and rather English glamour', the **Burgh Island Hotel** (01548 810514, www.burghisland.com, double £260-£360) offers a taste of rare, unadulterated luxury. Televisions are out, but helicopters are most definitely in, with at least one a week landing here to a champagne greeting. In the evening guests are urged to dress up and enjoy it – the more glitz the better. Dances are held in the restored ballroom, cocktails can be sipped in the Palm Court or Peacock Bar, and excellent meals using local produce are offered each evening in the exclusive restaurant. All it needs is for Poirot to turn up to complete the scene.

Overbecks Youth Hostel (Sharpitor, 01548 842856, closed Nov-Mar, double £27), which also offers no-frills meal options.

About a mile's stroll from North Sands, **Yeoman's Country House** (Collaton, Salcombe, 01548 560085, www.yeomans house.co.uk, double B&B £80-£120) is a 16th-century longhouse located at the head of a lush valley. Its rural setting is reflected inside by immaculate country-cottage decor.

West of Salcombe, the **Thurlestone Hotel** (Thurlestone, near Kingsbridge, 01548 560382, www.thurlestone.co.uk, closed Jan, double B&B £100-£200) is a high-quality family option just a stone's throw from sandy beaches, with its own golf course, tennis courts and pool. The **Royal Oak** (Higher Town, Malborough, 01548 561481, £4.50-£8.95) hosts lively folk music sessions every Wednesday and forms the focus for the village's Music and Arts Festival each summer.

On Burgh Island the atmospheric, weather-beaten **Pilchard Inn** (01548 810514, main courses £4-£8.50) has a wonderful terrace where you can sample the traditional pub food. If you can't afford to stay in the Burgh Island Hotel (*see p200* **Island retreat**), there's another very good option on the mainland. Edwardian-style decor, comfortable bedrooms, stunning views and a quality menu have won the **Henley Hotel** (Folly Hill, Bigbury-on-Sea, 01548 810240, closed Nov-Mar, double B&B £80-£88) a glowing reputation. In the next village, don't be alarmed by a sign that reads 'Please Drive Slowly through the Pub'. The charming, low-beamed **Dolphin Inn** (Kingston, 01548 810314, main courses £7-£14.50, double B&B £55) sits on either side of the road, with punters wandering back and forth. There's cottagey, en suite B&B here, plus good food.

About ten miles (16 kilometres) from Salcombe in the heart of the countryside is the **Buckland-Tout-Saints Hotel & Restaurant** (Goveton, 01548 853055, www.tout-saints.co.uk, closed Jan, main courses £15-£17, double B&B £150-£340). This 16th-century manor house is elegance uncut, with wood panelling, gourmet French cuisine and vast, romantic rooms.

Equally off the beaten track is **Hazelwood House** (Loddiswell, 01548 821232, double B&B £25-£50 per person), a rambling property owned by three artists. Its shabby, much-loved interior is characterised by big cushions, cats and log fires – the setting for cultural evenings and art courses, as well as basic bed and breakfast.

For a little more elegance try **Plantation House Hotel** (Totnes Road, Ermington, 01548 831100), a former Georgian rectory set in lovely countryside. The rooms are stylish, spacious and utterly chintz-free, and the hotel's acclaimed Matisse Restaurant serves delectable Modern British cuisine with a colonial Caribbean twist.

Resources

Hospital
South Hams Hospital *Plymouth Road, Kingsbridge (01548 852349).*

Internet
Kingsbridge *Kingsbridge Library, Ilbert Road (01548 852315).* **Open** 9.30am-7pm Mon, Fri; 9.30am-5pm Tue, Wed; 9.30am-1pm Thur, Sat.
Salcombe *Salcombe Library, Cliff House, Cliff Road (01548 843423).* **Open** 9.30am-7pm Mon, Fri; 9.30am-5pm Tue, Wed; 9.30am-1pm Thur, Sat.

Police stations
Kingsbridge *Fore Street (0870 577 7444).*
Salcombe *Onslow Road (0870 577 7444).*

Post offices
Modbury *14 Broad Street.* **Open** 9am-5.30pm Mon, Tue, Thur, Fri; 9am-1pm Wed, Sat.
Kingsbridge *Ilbert Road, The Quay (01548 852348).* **Open** 8.45am-5.30pm Mon-Fri; 8.45am-12.30pm Sat.
Salcombe *The Old Shipwright's Arms, Fore Street (01548 842536).* **Open** 9am-5.30pm Mon-Fri; 9am-12.30pm Sat.

Tourist information
Kingsbridge *Information Centre, The Quay (01548 853195/www.kingsbridgeinfo.co.uk).* **Open** *Apr-Sept* 9am-5.30pm Mon-Sat; 10am-4pm Sun. *Oct-Mar* 9am-5pm Mon-Sat.
Modbury *Tourist Information Centre, 5 Modbury Court (01548 830159/www.modburydevon.co.uk).* **Open** *Apr-Oct* 10am-5pm Mon-Sat. Closed Nov-Mar.
Salcombe *Tourist Information Centre, Market Street (01548 843927/www.salcombeinformation. co.uk).* **Open** *Apr-Oct* 10am-5pm Mon-Sat; 10am-4pm Sun. *Nov-Mar* 10am-3pm Mon-Thur; 10am-5pm Fri, Sat.

Getting there & around

By train
Mainline services between Exeter St David's and Plymouth stop regularly at Totnes station (Station Road, Totnes).

By bus
First Western National (Plymouth, 01752 402060) runs frequent daily services between Totnes and Kingsbridge, and between Plymouth and Dartmouth (via Kingsbridge). **Tally Ho** (Kingsbridge, 01548 853081) runs Mon-Sat between Kingsbridge Quay and Salcombe, with **Stagecoach Devon** (Torbay, 01803 664500) covering the same route on Sun.

Devon

Plymouth & Around

Sailors, sharks and some of the South West's grandest country houses.

Plymouth's prime location, on a deep-water, sheltered harbour at the mouth of the rivers Plym, Tavy and Tamar, was first used to advantage during the Hundred Years War with France (1337-1453), and in the centuries that followed the port was at the forefront of Britain's rise from insignificant island kingdom to dominant imperial power.

During the 16th and 17th centuries pilgrims, pirates, merchants and adventurers all set sail from the city to find wealth and land overseas. Among them was the city's most famous naval hero, Sir Francis Drake, whose ship, the *Golden Hind*, embarked on her epic global voyage from Plymouth in 1577. Drake was followed by Captain James Cook in the 18th century on voyages of discovery to the Pacific; by Charles Darwin in the 19th century, whose pioneering expeditions revolutionised our understanding of natural history, and by Sir Francis Chichester in the 20th century, who became the first English man to sail solo around the globe.

With the building of the **Royal Naval Dockyard** at Devonport in the 17th century, Plymouth's stature as a naval base of national importance was sealed. (Today the working docks are generally closed to the public, but visitors can get a behind-the-scenes glimpse of the action during the hugely popular annual **Plymouth Navy Days** in August.) However, Plymouth's naval prowess made it a major target for German bombs in World War II, which devastated the Victorian city centre. Post-war redevelopments were bold but unkind, lending the city a grim, concrete countenance that sits ill with its rich seafaring heritage.

Subject to continuing regeneration, the city can nevertheless appear as an ugly sprawl, dominated by heavy traffic and uninspiring architecture; delve a bit deeper, though, and there are some delights on offer. The wide estuary of **Plymouth Sound** is undoubtedly one of the finest natural harbours in the country; huddled, half-timbered houses of the **Barbican** district shelter an increasingly eclectic array of shops, studios, bars and restaurants, while the redeveloped harbour brings new waterfront attractions to the heart of the old city. What's more, Plymouth makes an accessible base from which to explore the historic houses and beautiful scenery of the **Tamar valley**, along the border between Devon and Cornwall.

Sightseeing

The city

Approaching Plymouth from the east, high-rise blocks, shops and university buildings provide a backdrop for the burnt-out Gothic shell of **Charles Church** on Charles Cross roundabout – a poignant reminder of the destruction wreaked on the city by the Luftwaffe. North-west of here, at Drake Circus, is **Plymouth City Museum & Art Gallery**, which houses an appealing collection of natural and social history exhibits, plus fine and decorative arts dating from the 16th to the 20th centuries. There are paintings by prominent local artists, such as Sir Joshua Reynolds, plus a number of works by the Newlyn and St Ives schools.

Compared with the bustling centre of town, the nearby **Hoe** – meaning 'High Place' – is literally a breath of fresh air. With superb views over Plymouth Sound, Drake's Island (once used as a prison) and the breakwater beyond, this broad, grassy esplanade is an ideal spot to get your bearings and watch the comings and goings of warships and other vessels. Several monuments line the Hoe – including a huge, white naval cenotaph and an imperious statue of Sir Francis Drake, coolly staring out to sea. The statue stands appropriately close to the green where Drake is supposed to have finished a bowls match before launching his withering attack on the Spanish Armada (*see p204* **Local heroes**).

In front of the statue is **Smeaton's Tower** (now open to the public again following extensive refurbishment). It's worth making the climb up its 93 steps for breathtaking views of the city, the Sound and north to Dartmoor. Originally built as a lighthouse in 1759 and sited 14 miles (22 kilometres) out to sea on Eddystone Rocks, the red-and-white striped tower was replaced in 1882 and brought ashore stone by stone to be reassembled on its present site. Nearby, **Plymouth Dome** tells the story of the city – tragedies as well as triumphs – through a range of high-tech interactive displays, reconstructions and models.

The imposing walls of the **Royal Citadel** dominate the eastern end of the Hoe. Built during the reign of Charles II, it was ostensibly

Plymouth & Around

designed to defend the city from foreign attack, but was more likely intended to prevent an uprising among Plymouth's anti-Royalist citizens – a theory supported by the fact that many of the cannons point menacingly towards the city. The ramparts, 17th-century Governor's House and 19th-century Royal Chapel of St Katharine can all be visited as part of a guided tour (contact the tourist office for details), but this is still a working military site and access is often limited.

Just to the north of the citadel, the **Barbican** was one of the few areas of Plymouth to escape the wartime bombing and is the jewel in the city's crown. Built on the edge of **Sutton Harbour**, the area is a maze of medieval streets, dotted with some fine Tudor buildings. The narrow lanes have become home to an intriguing array of shops, restaurants, cafés, galleries and art studios. One of Plymouth's most treasured artists, Robert O Lenkiewicz (*see p29*), lived and worked in the Barbican until his death in 2002, and although his former studio is closed to the public, some of his vast body of work can still be viewed at the **Annexe Gallery** (19 The Parade, Barbican,

01752 263208, www.robertlenkiewicz.co.uk). There's also a mural by the artist on Southside Street, depicting local faces and characters.

Until the end of 2002, the best place to start an exploration of the Barbican was the purpose-built **Mayflower Centre**, a well-designed modern visitor attraction detailing Plymouth's maritime heritage. However, in early 2003, the future of the centre was uncertain; contact the tourist office for updated information (*see p209*).

The building sits just a stone's throw from the **Mayflower Steps**, which commemorate the departure of the Pilgrim Fathers from this spot in 1620; a plaque lists the names of all of the 100-odd passengers, who set sail aboard the *Mayflower* to begin a new life in Massachusetts. You, too, can take to the water here, by joining one of the regular harbour cruises or fishing trips (*see p207*). Nearby, the former fishmarket is now the site of the **Barbican Glassworks** (The Old Fishmarket, Barbican, 01752 224777), where you can watch Dartington glassblowers at work and buy items in the shop.

One of the Barbican's finest buildings is the 17th-century **Elizabethan House** in New Street, once home to a local sea captain.

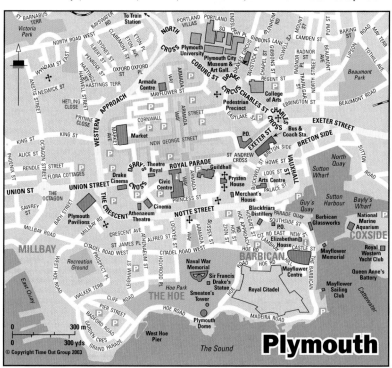

© Copyright Time Out Group 2003

Plymouth

The house retains much of its original architecture and its interior is sumptuously decorated with period furniture and textiles.

Another well-preserved gem is the **Merchant's House**, located just beyond the Barbican on St Andrew's Street. Originally inhabited by a 17th-century merchant and mayor of Plymouth, this timber-framed building now houses an absorbing museum, with three floors devoted to different periods in the city's history. North of the museum,

St Andrew's is a post-war reconstruction of the city's original 15th-century parish church, and features six vibrant, modern stained-glass windows by John Piper.

Plymouth's large fishing fleet unloads its catch at a modern fishmarket at **Coxside**, on the other side of Sutton Harbour (reached by footbridge from the Barbican). Also here, on an area of former wasteland, is one of the city's triumphs. The **National Marine Aquarium** houses Britain's biggest collection of marine

Local heroes Sir Francis Drake

Plymouth, 20 July 1588: the day dawns bright and breezy. Sir Francis Drake, unsure when the mighty Spanish Armada will show up, fancies a spot of friendly rivalry before the bloodshed – bowls on the Hoe, perhaps?

He meets Lord Admiral Charles Howard, the commander of the English fleet, on the smooth turfed ridge that stretched at the time from Millbay in the west to the Barbican. But as the game begins, a fellow officer rushes up to announce that the enemy has been sighted off Cornwall in a crescent of 130 vessels so huge that the sea appears to groan.

To everyone's surprise, Francis Drake, the naval second-in-command, insists there is no hurry. 'We have time enough to finish the game and beat the Spaniards too,' he says, and calmly beats his companion at bowls.

Drake's sang froid wasn't as ridiculous as it sounds – the great mariner was well aware that no boat could sail from Plymouth against the rising tide and south-west wind. His foresight saved the English sailors exhausting hours battling against the elements.

It was late in the day when 60 English warships finally slipped quietly to sea, anchoring at Rame Head. The following afternoon they spotted the enemy and moved into position, a few ships remaining at the headland, while others, unseen, sailed behind the Spanish. By moonlight they let the first cannonball fly, while their comrades attacked from behind.

The English fleet was far outnumbered, yet its small ships were so fast they could dart between the Spanish, wreaking havoc with fire. After three hours, realising they could not board the mighty foreign vessels, they returned to port, where Plymouth's citizens had crammed the Hoe to witness a great explosion as the Spanish ship *San Salvador* blew up.

The Spanish must have been wondering why the English had fled. But Howard had another trick up his sleeve. He asked Drake to lead a fleet of ships behind the Armada, gradually herding them towards Dover, where further English vessels lay in wait.

En route, Drake, with his famous nose for treasure, seized the crippled Spanish *Rosario*, taking 50,000 escudos, plus prisoners and ammunition. Moving down the Channel, the English separated into four squadrons, enjoying skirmishes with the enemy at the Isle of Wight. Eventually, the flagging Spaniards were beaten near Calais in a final assault led by Drake.

Even now, Plymouth still oozes pride for Drake's part in the Armada defeat, which helped save Elizabethan Britain from Spanish invasion. A statue crowns the Hoe and St Nicholas Island opposite was renamed Drake's Island in honour of the great seadog. Drake's former home at Buckland Abbey (*see p205*) is open to the public, and Plymouth Dome (*see p202*) has a multimedia exhibition detailing his exploits.

animals, with over 4,000 on display in a variety of recreated habitats. Although the emphasis throughout remains squarely on conservation and education, major redevelopment work has added some superb new features: a simulated Atlantic reef can be viewed through a giant window, while the Mediterranean exhibit provides a 2.5-million-litre warm seawater home for the aquarium's sand tiger sharks and other creatures.

Elizabethan House
New Street, Barbican, (01752 304380/304774). **Open** *Apr-Sept* 10am-5pm Wed-Sun. **Admission** £1.10; 60p concessions; free under-5s. **No credit cards.**

Merchant's House Museum
St Andrew's Street (information 01752 304774). **Open** *Apr-Oct* 10am-5.30pm Tue-Fri; 10am-5pm Sat. Closed Nov-Mar. **Admission** phone for details.

National Marine Aquarium
Rope Walk, Coxside (01752 220084/600301/ www.national-aquarium.co.uk). **Open** *Apr-Oct* 10am-6pm daily. *Nov-Mar* 10am-5pm daily. **Admission** £8; £4.50-£6.50 concessions; free under-3s; £22 family. **Credit** AmEx, MC, V.

Plymouth City Museum & Art Gallery
Drake Circus, City centre (01752 304774/ www.plymouthmuseum.gov.uk). **Open** 10am-5.30pm Tue-Fri; 10am-5pm Sat. **Admission** free.

Plymouth Dome
The Hoe (01752 600608). **Open** *Apr-Oct* 10am-5pm daily. *Nov-Mar* 9am-4pm Tue-Sat. **Admission** £4.50, £3-£3.50 concessions; £12 family. **Credit** AmEx, MC, V.

Smeaton's Tower
The Hoe (01752 603300). **Open** *Apr-Oct* 10am-4pm daily. *Nov-Mar* 10am-3pm Tue-Sat. **Admission** £2; £1 concessions. **No credit cards.**

Heading east

East of Plymouth off the A38, **Saltram House** is a sumptuous neo-classical feast. Originally a Tudor manor, it was rebuilt in the 18th century by the wealthy Parker family, with interiors by Robert Adam. Among the ultra-elegant rooms is the Saloon, a Regency orgy of ornate plaster and glittering chandeliers. Elsewhere admire period furniture, chinoiserie and several fine works of art by Joshua Reynolds. Saltram's popularity was boosted a few years ago when it featured as Norland House in the film version of Jane Austen's *Sense and Sensibility*. Around the house is a landscaped park, spoiled only by traffic noise from the nearby A38.

Further east, near Sparkwell, the 30 acres of **Dartmoor Wildlife Park** incorporate one

of the largest collections of big cats in the South West, including jaguars, pumas and lynx, plus various deer herds and a falconry centre. One of the highlights for children is the daily hands-on 'Close Encounters' session, during which they can get up-close-and-personal with the park's inmates, including hand-reared lion cubs.

South of here back lanes lead over the hills and the dual carriageway to the Yealm estuary on the edge of the South Hams. The beautiful fishing villages of **Newton Ferrers** and **Noss Mayo** are tucked in a side shoot of the wooded, Y-shaped river and are best explored on foot, or by boat. Yachting and tourism have replaced crab and pilchard fishing as the mainstay of the economy here, and the cute, higgledy-piggledy cottages are increasingly becoming second homes or retirement pads.

When the tide is out, walkers can stroll between the villages, but at high water catch a ferry (01752 880079, no service Oct-Feb), or make the short walk via Bridgend. The ferry also runs to **Warren Point** at the estuary mouth, from where a gentle walk will lead you round to **Wembury Bay**, where there's a good beach café selling cream teas.

Dartmoor Wildlife Park
Sparkwell (01752 837645/www.dartmoor wildlife.co.uk). **Open** 10am-6pm daily. **Admission** *Oct-Mar* £6.95; £4.45-£5.45 concessions; £20 family. *Apr-Sept* £7.45; £5-£6 concessions; £22 family. **Credit** MC, V.

Saltram House
off A38, nr Plympton, (01752 333500). **Open** *House* Apr-Sept noon-4.30pm daily; Oct 11.30am-3.30pm daily. *Garden* Apr-Oct 11am-5pm daily; Nov-Mar 11am-4pm daily. **Admission** £6.30; £3.10 concessions; £15.70 family. *Garden only* £3.30; £1.60 concessions. **Credit** MC, V.

Heading north

In Plymouth's northern suburbs is **Crownhill Fort**, built in the 19th century as a state-of-the-art defence against potential French invasion. Decommissioned in the 1980s and fully restored, it's a great place to explore, with Victorian barracks and World War II gun emplacements linked by a network of passageways. For the full-on military experience, visit on an artillery day, when the fort's cannons are put to use.

Further north, follow the A386 towards Dartmoor to reach **Buckland Abbey**, the former home of Sir Francis Drake. The abbey was founded by Cistercian monks in the 13th century and was later converted into a country house by Sir Richard Grenville (a seafaring cousin of Walter Raleigh). Drake was Grenville's arch-rival at court and bought the property by devious means.

Devon

Mount Edgcumbe Park: glorious gardens on the edge of the Sound. *See p207.*

The building is full of artefacts associated with Drake and Grenville, including 'Drake's Drum', a legendary percussion instrument that is supposed to sound whenever England is in danger. Architecturally, the most interesting room is the Great Hall, which was converted from the nave of the original abbey church in the 16th century. Outside is a huge monastic barn, an Elizabethan garden, craft workshops, and pleasant walks through the grounds and along the wooded valley of the River Tavy.

Further west, there are more excellent walking opportunities along the River Tamar, which marks the boundary between Devon and Cornwall. During the 19th century this was one of the busiest waterways in the country, with ships constantly plying the route from **Morwellham Quay** to the sea at Plymouth and beyond. The Quay first developed in the 12th century as an export site for Devon's mineral riches, but its glory days came in the early Victorian era, when it became the most important copper port in the country. Today the restored site, with its warehouses, copper mine, smithy and waterwheel is a mecca for primary school groups 'doing' the Victorians, but it remains authentic and entertaining enough to justify a half day's visit.

Across the Tamar from Morwellham, the Cornish village of **Calstock** clings to the steeply wooded valley side above the river. There was once a thriving shipyard here, but now jumbles of slate and granite cottages hug

the river edge under a magnificent railway viaduct. A scenic walk downstream leads to **Cotehele Manor**, a beautifully preserved Tudor manor set in lovely walled gardens. Acquired by the Edgcumbe family in 1353, the house was largely rebuilt in the early 1500s and has altered very little since then. Arranged around three courtyards, the buildings contain a truly impressive array of Flemish tapestries, exquisite embroidery, richly carved furniture and Tudor armour. Stroll through the parkland to reach a folly, where you can climb the dingy, stone staircase for fantastic views of the Tamar valley. Also, seek out the perfectly preserved mill and blacksmith's forge, or chill out at the restaurant and gallery by the river on Cotehele quay (01579 352711).

Buckland Abbey

Yelverton (01822 853607/www.nationaltrust.org.uk). **Open** *Apr-Oct* 10.30am-4.45pm Mon-Wed, Fri-Sun. *Nov, Dec* 10.30am-4.45pm Sat, Sun. *Jan-Mar* phone for details. **Admission** *House & grounds* £5; £2.50 concessions; £12.50 family. *Grounds only* £2.70; £1.30 concessions. **Credit** AmEx, MC, V.

Cotehele Manor

St Dominick, nr Saltash (01579 351346/ www.nationaltrust.org.uk). **Open** *Gardens* dawn-dusk daily. *Manor* Apr-Oct 11am-4.30pm daily. *Mill* Apr-Oct 1-5pm Mon-Thur, Sat, Sun. **Admission** *Manor, gardens & mill* £6.60; £3.30 concessions; free under-5s. *Gardens & mill* £3.80; £1.90 concessions; free under-5s. **Credit** AmEx, MC, V.

Crownhill Fort
Crownhill Fort Road, Crownhill, Plymouth (01752 793754/www.crownhillfort.co.uk). Open Apr-Oct 10am-5pm Mon-Fri, Sun. *Nov-Mar* pre-booked groups only. **Admission** £4.50; £2.50-£3.50 concessions; £10 family. **Credit** MC, V.

Morwellham Quay
nr Tavistock (01822 832766/833808/ www.morwellham-quay.co.uk). Open Mar-Oct 10am-5.30pm daily. Closed Nov-Feb. **Admission** £8.90; £3.70-£7.80 concessions; free under-5s; family £26. **Credit** MC, V.

Heading west

The **Rame Peninsula** juts into Plymouth Sound on the Cornwall side of the Tamar. Reached by car ferry on the A374 or by regular passenger ferries from the city (*see p209*), the peninsula is dominated on its eastern side by **Mount Edgcumbe Park**, 865 acres of glorious landscaped gardens and parkland edged by a section of the South West Coast Path. At its heart is the former home of the Edgcumbe family, a reconstructed Tudor manor, restored in 1958 with beautiful 18th-century furnishings and family treasures.

The peninsula offers a blissful escape from city life. To make a day of it, explore the former smuggling villages of **Kingsand** and **Cawsand**, on the coast to the south of the park, or head straight for **Whitsand Bay**, a magnificent four-mile beach, where rolling waves sweep across the sands.

Mount Edgcumbe Park
Cremyll, Torpoint (01752 822236). Open Country park dawn-dusk daily. *House & Earl's Garden* Apr-Sept 11am-4.30pm Wed-Sun. **Admission** £4.50; £2.25-£3.50 concessions; £10 family. **Credit** MC, V.

Activities

Boating
Boat trips from Sutton Harbour are a great way to view the Sound as well as the warships docked at Devonport. For details contact **Plymouth Boat Cruises** (01752 671166) or **Tamar Cruising** (01752 822105). Boats for exploring the Yealm estuary can be hired from Noss Mayo (01752 872189).

Riding
Wembury Riding School & Livery Centre (Wembury, 01752 862676/862312) organises treks for all abilities around the area.

Watersports
Sailing and watersports are offered by the **Mount Batten Centre** (70 Lawrence Road, 01752 404567, www.mount-batten-centre.com), minutes from the Barbican by water-taxi. **Plymouth Sailing School** (Queen Annes Battery, Coxside, 01752 667170, www.plymsail.co.uk) runs a range of RYA courses,

while **Reactive Watersports** (Queen Anne's Battery, Coxside, 01752 255999, www.reactive watersports.co.uk) is a wind- and kitesurfing shop and school, offering friendly advice and tuition.

Walking
The **Tamar Valley Discovery Trail** is a waymarked 30-mile route along the varied Tamar valley from Plymouth to Launceston. For details of this and other, shorter trails, contact the Tourist Information Centre.

Where to eat & drink

There's no shortage of drinking and eating spots around the Barbican and Sutton Harbour, with characterful pubs, stylish restaurants and cafés dishing up a wide array of cuisine. The waterfront area has a particularly continental ambience, with al fresco dining in summer.

Worth checking out is **Zucca!** (Discovery Wharf, 01752 224225, main courses £4.95-£12.25), an Italian bar-brasserie with great pizzas and pastas; and **Bistro Bene** (Dolphin House, Sutton Harbour, 01752 254879), a cosy little French-style restaurant with views over the marina. For Indian cuisine try **Baba's** (134 Vauxhall Street, 01752 256488, main courses £7.50-£22.50).

No round-up of food in the Barbican area would be complete without a mention of **Cap'n Jaspers** (Whitehouse Pier, 01752 262444). This highly individual eating emporium began life as a small shack at the old fishmarket, supplying the fishermen with hot drinks and cheap, filling food. When the land was redeveloped Jaspers moved to new premises near the Barbican Glassworks (*see p203*) but the low-priced food and bizarre humour remain. Check out the half-yard hotdogs if you dare.

Further inland, **Restaurant des Amis** (2 St Andrew's Street, 01752 667880, main courses £10.95-£15.50) is known for its French specialities and quality wine list, while **Les Jardins de Bagatelle** (11 Old Town Street, 01752 257786, main courses £2.60-£3.65) is a delightful café serving pastries, baguettes and great coffee. The best eaterie in the city, though, is **Chez Nous** (13 Frankfort Gate, 01752 266793, closed Feb & Sept, set meal £35 3 courses), a bijou Gallic bistro serving excellent French cuisine.

Outside Plymouth, the **Ship Inn** (01752 872387, main courses £7.75-£16.50) at Noss Mayo has an upmarket menu, decent wine list and friendly staff, plus the added attraction of a terrace with gorgeous river views. A good alternative is the **Dolphin Inn** at Newton Ferrers (01752 872007, main courses £5.60-£11), which serves traditional food in an equally satisfying setting.

Devon

Plymouth Pavilions (Millbay Road, 01752 229922, www.plymouthpavilions.com) stages a diverse range of shows, from rock concerts to opera to all-night raves. For jazz aficionados the much-loved **Jazz Café** (11 The Parade, Barbican, 01752 672127, www.barbican jazzcafe.com) is a must, with a year-round programme of music every night of the week. For rock and pop the **Cooperage** (Tin Lane & 134 Vauxhall Street, 01752 229275) hosts decent local and national bands.

Theatre-goers in Plymouth can enjoy performances by distinguished repertory companies at the **Theatre Royal** (Royal Parade, 01752 267222, www.theatreroyal.com) or experimental dance and drama by national and regional touring groups at the **Barbican Theatre** (Castle Street, 01752 267131, www.barbicantheatre.co.uk). The **Plymouth Arts Centre** (38 Looe Street, 01752 206114, www.plymouthac.org.uk) has a thriving independent cinema, exhibition space and a vegetarian restaurant.

The main focus of Plymouth's nightlife has traditionally been the less-than-salubrious Union Street, home to plenty of clubs and pubs.

The new **Barbican Leisure Park** (Shapters Road, Coxside) adds a multiplex cinema (01752 222241) and the large-scale, commercial dance club **Destiny** (01752 255057) into the mix.

Right on the Hoe, the **Bowling Green Hotel** (9-10 Osborne Place, Lockyer Street, 01752 209090, www.bowlinggreenhotel.com, double B&B £56) offers decent accommodation in a rebuilt Victorian building. A slightly more upmarket choice is the elegant **Admiral Wiltun Hotel** (39 Grand Parade, 01752 667072, www.wiltunhotel.co.uk, double B&B £50-£125), whose waterfront patio offers stunning views over Plymouth Sound and Drake's Island. The **New Continental Hotel** (Millbay Road, 01752 220782, www.new continental.co.uk, double B&B £85-£103) is Plymouth's largest independent hotel, set in a Victorian building right in the heart of the city. The **Hotel Mount Batten** (Lawrence Road, Mount Batten, 01752 405500, double £44-£55) is a promising new venture in an excellent location overlooking the Sound.

East of the city, there's quality farmhouse B&B at the 400-year-old **Broadmoor Farm**

Drink up Plymouth Gin

Housed in historic buildings in Plymouth's Barbican district is England's oldest gin distillery. Since 1793 Black Friars has been making Plymouth Gin to a unique recipe, using an unchanged distilling process that combines a unique blend of botanicals with soft Dartmoor water.

Plymouth Gin is documented in 1896 as the original base for the first Dry Martini, and over the years has been enjoyed by the likes of Winston Churchill, Franklin D Roosevelt, Ian Fleming and Alfred Hitchcock. But it's not just famous faces who enjoy a tipple; thanks in no small part to the Royal Navy, Plymouth Gin is now in demand all over the world.

For almost 200 years every British warship that has left port has had its own supply of Plymouth Gin; for most of the last century 800 'barrows' of the stuff were supplied to Her Majesty's Fleet each year. In World War II a bottle of Plymouth Gin was presented to any British gunner in Malta who managed to sink an enemy ship. This practice was revived during the Falklands War when a case of gin was presented to each of the

five British warships responsible for the sinking of Argentine vessels.

But the history of Plymouth Gin is not confined to a long-running rendition of 'what shall we do with the drunken sailor?'. The Black Friars distillery is housed in a former Dominican monastery that dates back to 1431, and provided lodging for the Pilgrim Fathers on their last night on English soil.

A tour of the complex begins with an audio-visual presentation on the history of gin and the Barbican, and then moves on to the distillery itself, where visitors can see the 155-year-old copper pot in which the gin is still made. Finally, in the weighing room visitors can touch and smell the botanicals that are used in the recipe, as well as having a taste of the delicious finished product. Cheers.

Black Friars Distillery

60 Southside Street (01752 665292/ www.plymouthgin.com). **Open** (by guided tour only) *Jan-Feb* 10.30am-3.30pm Sat. *Mar-Dec* 10.30am-3.30pm Mon-Sat; 11.30am-3.30pm Sun. **Admission** £2.75; £2.25 concessions; free under-16s. **Credit** MC, V.

Whitsand Bay.
See p207.

at Newton Ferrers (01752 880407, double B&B £45), which has tasteful rooms and generous breakfasts. In Yealmpton **Kitley House Hotel & Restaurant** (01752 881555, www.kitley househotel.com, set dinner £23-£32, double B&B £99) is a palace of a house set in parkland. Huge rooms and top-notch cuisine are among its draws, though you'll pay for the quality.

Near Wembury the beautiful **Langdon Court Hotel & Restaurant** (Langdon Court, Down Thomas, 01752 862358, www.langdon court.co.uk, set dinner £16.50, double B&B £75-£85) was originally built for Katherine Parr, sixth wife of Henry VIII. The tasteful, spacious rooms all have stunning views, and the menu incorporates local seafood and organic meat and vegetables.

Resources

Hospital
Derriford Hospital *Derriford Road, Plymouth (01752 777111).*

Internet
Learning Ware *15-17 Union Street, Plymouth (01752 201830).* **Open** 9am-5pm Mon-Thur; 9am-4pm Fri.

Police station
Charles Cross, Plymouth (0870 577 7444).

Tourist information
Barbican Tourist Information Centre *Island House, 9 The Barbican, Plymouth (01752 265105/ barbicantic@plymouth.gov.uk).* **Open** *Summer* 9am-5pm Mon-Sat; 10am-4pm Sun. *Winter* 9am-5pm Mon-Fri; 10am-4pm Sat.
Plymouth Tourist Information *Discovery Centre, A38/A374 jct, Crabtree, Plymouth PL3 6RN (01752 266030).* **Open** *Summer* 9am-5pm Mon-Sat; 10am-4pm Sun. *Winter* 9am-5pm Mon-Fri; 10am-4pm Sat.

Getting there & around

By air
Plymouth City Airport (0845 773 3377, www.sutton-harbour.co.uk/plymair.cfm) is located 4 miles (6.5km) north of the city, off Derriford Road, signposted from the A386. CityBus and First Western National (*see below*) both run bus services to the city centre, and taxis (01752 222222) can be hired from the terminal building. *See also p292.*

By bus
National Express (08705 808080, www.GoBy Coach.com) buses run from the bus station in Bretonside to Heathrow Airport (4hrs) and Victoria Coach Station, London (5hrs).

Local bus services are run by **Citybus** (01752 662271/222221) and **First Western National** (01752 402060/222666), both of which also operate from the bus station.

By train
Plymouth station is located in the city centre and is served by mainline trains from London Paddington (3-4hrs), Bristol (2hrs), Birmingham (3-4hrs) and other destinations throughout the UK.

The Tamar Valley Line runs north along the Tamar from Plymouth to the pretty villages of Calstock and Gunnislake (1hr).

By boat
Brittany Ferries (08703 665333/www.brittany-ferries.co.uk) run from the Millbay Docks in Plymouth to Roscoff in northern France and Santander in northern Spain.

A car ferry operates 24hrs between Devonport and Torpoint (foot passengers travel free). **Tamar Cruising** (01752 822105) runs a passenger ferry from Stonehouse in Plymouth to Cremyll on the Rame Peninsula, and there are also fair-weather launches in summer from Mayflower Steps to Cawsand. Upriver, the Tamar Passenger Ferry runs from Calstock to Cotehele.

Devon

Cornwall

Introduction

Daring to be different.

The Tamar is more than a river: it's a symbol of Celtic separateness. Cross Brunel's Albert Bridge between Plymouth and Saltash and you leave England behind – or so the Cornish would have you believe. The local celebration of Celtic culture and identity sometimes reveals a loose grip of fact for the sake of romanticism, but the number of 'Kernow' car stickers and the rich canon of songs still heard in Cornish pubs will remind you that this county is, indeed, a distinct part of the South West.

What's more, Cornwall has some classy tourist sights to set against its ancient heritage. First up is the all-conquering **Eden Project**, a revolutionary environmental attraction that needs no introduction. The **Tate St Ives** heads up a vibrant contemporary art scene in the far west, while the brand, spanking new **National Maritime Museum Cornwall** at Falmouth at last provides a state-of-the-art setting for an exploration of the county's maritime history.

Yet these man-made attractions have to be pretty spectacular to compete with the show put on by nature. Inland, there are few parts of Cornwall that equal the charm of Devon, but the mini wilderness of **Bodmin Moor** deserves special mention for its ancient remains and rock formations, as do the extraordinary subtropical gardens that flourish in the south of the county.

It's the coast, however, that's the real draw. Rivers flow through lush valleys and estuaries, emerging in the south at old fishing ports such as **Looe**, **Fowey** and **Falmouth**. Further west, the **Lizard** and **Penwith** peninsulas attempt to outdo each other in striking coastal scenery and jaw-dropping beaches: swarms of summer sun-seekers do little to detract from the splendour of **Kynance Cove**, and even a theme park can't spoil the thrill of **Land's End**.

From **Perranporth** to **Bude**, the Atlantic coast is surfing territory, with impressive swells that will have even the most determined landlubber itching to ride the waves. **Newquay** is the centre of the scene, but you'll also find plenty of quieter stretches of sand. And should you tire of the beach, check out the restaurants in **Padstow**, the ruins at **Tintagel** or strike out along the wonderful South West Coast Path.

Finally, beyond the western extremity of the peninsula are the **Isles of Scilly**, a cluster of dreamy, low-lying islands characterised by sunshine, flowers and gleaming white sands.

Don't miss Cornwall

B3306
Top contender for most scenic road in the country. *See p255.*

Eden Project
Cornwall's most famous tourist attraction grows better by the year. *See p233.*

Isles of Scilly
Sunshine, beaches, flowers and birds. *See p286.*

Lost Gardens of Heligan
Gardeners will be green with envy. *See p235.*

Minack Theatre
One of the few places where you can take a dip in the sea during the interval. *See p255.*

National Maritime Museum Cornwall
Loads of boats and funky gadgets put Falmouth on the map. *See p240.*

Seafood
Its at its best in Fowey (*see p227*), Penzance (*see p250*), St Ives (*see p259*) and Padstow (*see p276*).

Surfing
Everyone should try it at least once. *See p253 and p268.*

Cornwall

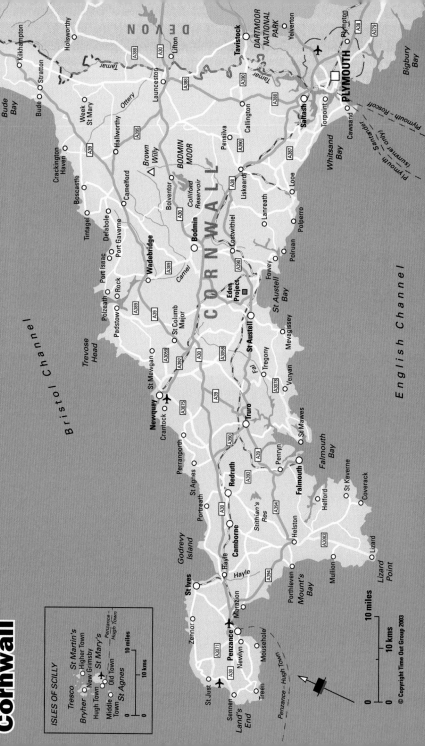

East Cornwall

This underrated part of the county is a nature-lover's paradise.

Moorland sheep seem unbothered by the bizarre granite **Cheesewring**. *See p222.*

Each year, thousands of cars packed nose to tail on the A30 from Devon, heaving with surfboards and beach gear, pass through this lovely part of Cornwall in a rush to the sea. But by doing so they miss out on one of the most beautiful and unspoiled parts of the county.

Just over the border from Devon, the medieval town of **Launceston**, with its castle ruins and impressive architecture, provides easy access to the wilds of **Bodmin Moor**. This is the smallest of the South West's three moorlands but its peaks, rocky tors and extensive heathland give an impression of wild remoteness way beyond its size. Harsh and bleak in the coldest months, Bodmin Moor comes alive in spring with a myriad of rivulets and streams, wild flowers and birds. Herds of hardy ponies roam free, grazing alongside sheep and cattle. The peaks and the ridges that run across the moor are topped with huge stones layered one upon another, sculpted into extraordinary shapes by the winds.

Walkers should equip themselves with a good map (OS Explorer 109 is highly recommended), and exercise caution to avoid

the occasional bog, especially after heavy rain or in thick fog. Careful driving is essential, too, as livestock have a habit of wandering aimlessly across the roads.

Running south from the moor are gloriously lush river valleys, the product of millions of years of rainfall flushed down from the higher ground. On the coast, the ports of **Looe** and **Polperro** are a wonderful introduction to the fishing villages of South Cornwall and afford access to lovely scenery along the South West Coast Path.

Launceston to Camelford

Launceston, the ancient capital of Cornwall, is a busy, charming market town that acts as the traditional gateway between Dartmoor and Bodmin Moor. Although not much of the 12th-century town wall remains, evidence of Launceston's medieval fortifications is provided by **Southgate Arch** (which was originally one of three entries to the town) and by the impressive 11th-century castle, the seat of the first Earl of Cornwall.

Set high above the town on a mound, **Launceston Castle** must have been an imposing sight to enemy forces. A large part of the original construction has disappeared over time, but enough remains to make the steep trip up to the keep worthwhile. On a clear day the views in every direction are spectacular: immediately surrounding the town are deeply undulating valleys and on the horizons to the east and west respectively are the dramatic profiles of Dartmoor and Bodmin Moor.

Lawrence House Museum on Castle Street has a diverse range of exhibits and a full history of the town and surrounding area. Elsewhere are examples of every type of architecture since the Norman Conquest. Two churches worth visiting are **St Mary Magdalene** (completed in 1542), which is famous for its ornate carved exterior, and **St Thomas's** (dating from 1152), built on the edge of the Kensey river. Beside the latter are the remains of the town's 12th-century Augustinian priory. The traditional town centre still supports an array of independent shops, including **Warrens**, an award-winning butcher, whose counters display local, traditionally reared meat.

Locomotives from the late 19th century chug along the **Launceston Steam Railway** (01566 775665) from a small transport museum at St Thomas Road, Launceston to Newmills. The five-mile (eight-kilometre) round trip follows the route of the old Waterloo to Padstow line through the Kensey valley.

Fifteen minutes north of town at North Petherwin is the **Tamar Otter Sanctuary** (01566 785646, www.ottertrust.org.uk, closed Nov-Mar), which rescues orphaned and injured otters and breeds cubs with a view to returning them to the wild. Try to get here for feeding time – noon and 3pm. There is also a wildfowl pond here and a woodland walk with deer.

There are some charming villages all around Launceston. One of the loveliest is **Alturnan**, where John Wesley often stayed on his frequent preaching trips around Cornwall. In the village a pretty 15th-century packhorse bridge straddles the River Inney, overlooked by the stunning church of **St Nonna**, known as the 'cathedral of the moor' and built on the site of a sixth-century Celtic church. Inside are decoratively carved pew ends and immense stone pillars carved from single pieces of moorland granite.

Around Altarnun are gentle, leafy lanes that can safely be explored on foot. Take a walk to the Rising Sun Inn (*see p217*), or strike out towards the bleak expanse of high moor seen on the horizon.

The A395 skirts the northern fringes of Bodmin Moor between the towns of Launceston and Camelford. En route, a left turn before the village of Hallworthy leads to **St Clether**, where there's a riverside shrine to the saint, complete with chapel stone, altar and holy well. Further on, turn right at **Hallworthy** (which still has a bustling livestock market on Fridays) to visit **Warbstow Bury**, an impressive prehistoric defensive earthwork and one of a dozen contenders for King Arthur's burial site.

In the moor's north-eastern corner, the riverside market town of **Camelford** is a compact place, often clogged with slow-moving traffic. Apart from its proximity to the high moor, reasons to stop include the groovy **Indian King Arts Centre** (Fore Street, 01840 212111, www.indianking.co.uk) for poetry, painting and theatre by international performers, and the **North Cornwall Museum**, which incorporates a 19th-century Cornish kitchen with slab range, oven and boiler.

Although the word Camel actually derives from a conflation of 'cam' meaning crooked and 'hayle' meaning estuary, Camelford has become associated over the years with Camelot, legendary court of King Arthur (*see p10* **Local heroes**). The myth has been perpetuated by the presence of a carved seventh-century stone at nearby **Slaughterbridge**, which supposedly marks the king's final battle at Camlann. What's certain is that a battle did take place here in the ninth century between the Saxons and the Celts, but Arthurian enthusiasts insist the stone is evidence of Arthur's fatal wound at the hand of Mordred. The myths and countermyths are explored in full at the **Arthurian Centre**.

Camelford is a good place from which to explore the moor. **Crowdy Reservoir** is popular with wildlife enthusiasts, and there's also access from the town to the moor's highest peaks: **Rough Tor** (1,311 feet/400 metres) and **Brown Willy** (1,375 feet/419 metres). The latter's name is enough to induce adolescent giggles in all but the most strait-laced visitor, but in fact is a corruption of 'bronewhella' or 'highest hill'. Both peaks can be seen for miles around, and offer wonderful views over all of Cornwall, and neither are particularly strenuous to climb, as long as you are equipped with suitable clothing, sturdy footwear and a decent map.

Rough Tor, three miles (4.8 kilometres) south-east of Camelford, is the more accessible of the two as there is a small car park close to its base. As you start the ascent, look out for the ghost of Charlotte Dymond, who was

Cornwall

murdered on the moor in 1844 – allegedly by her lover, Matthew Weekes, who was later hanged for the crime (*see p218*). There are the ruins of a medieval chapel on the summit, and the southern slopes are dotted with Bronze Age hut circles. Serious walkers can continue south-east from here to the summit of Brown Willy before descending for a little over three miles (five kilometres) to Jamaica Inn at the heart of the moor (*see p220*).

Arthurian Centre

Slaughterbridge, Camelford (01840 212450/ www.arthur-online.com). **Open** *Easter-Oct* 10am-6pm daily. Closed Nov-Mar. **Admission** £2.50; £1.50 concessions. **Credit** MC, V.

Launceston Castle

Launceston (01566 772365). **Open** *Apr-Sept* 10am-6pm daily. *Oct* 10am-5pm daily. *Nov-Mar* 10am-1pm, 2-4pm Fri-Sun. **Admission** £2; £1-£1.50 concessions; free under-5s. **No credit cards**.

Lawrence House Museum

Castle Street, Launceston (01566 773277). **Open** phone for details. **Admission** free; donations welcome.

North Cornwall Museum

The Clease, Camelford (01840 212954). **Open** *Apr-Sept* 10am-5pm Mon-Sat. Closed Oct-Mar. **Admission** £2; £1-£1.50 concessions. **Credit** phone for details.

Where to eat, drink & stay

The **Westgate Inn** (Westgate Street, Launceston, 01566 772493, main courses £2-£6.95) serves up a range of good pub grub including Sunday roasts. Around the corner on Church Street, **VG Deli** (01566 779494) will make up crusty baguettes of your choice and has an excellent range of local cheese.

South of town, the **Springer Spaniel** (near Lezant, 01579 370424, main courses £5-£13) serves local beef, lamb, game and fresh fish. The resident spaniels give an especially friendly welcome to any canine customers. On the edge of the moor, the **Rising Sun** (01566 86332) is a 16th-century building that has been run as a pub for over 150 years. Judging the simple interior, flagstones and wooden benches, nothing much has been changed in the meantime.

Launceston has few places to stay but excellent bed and breakfast is provided at **11 Castle Street** (01566 773873, double B&B £45), where good-looking rooms are supplemented by an exemplary chef-cooked brekkie. Three miles east of Launceston at Lifton, the **Arundell Arms** (01566 784666, www.arundellarms.com, set dinner £33, double B&B £60-£75 per person) is a top-rate

country house hotel, with 20 miles (32 kilometres) of private fishing on the River Tamar and its tributaries. The dining room menu is first-rate, featuring seasonal dishes including local seafood and meat. There's also good-quality bar food (main courses £9.75-£14.75).

Another good choice is the **Barton** (Laneast, near Launceston, 01548 550312, double B&B £40-£60), a comfortable, friendly B&B in a Grade II-listed Georgian farmhouse, with 30 acres of peaceful grounds and fishing on the River Avon. From summer 2003, self-catering accommodation will be provided in converted farm buildings. For the moment, self-caterers should consider **Cullacott** (Yeolmbridge, near Launceston, 01566 772631), one of the most important medieval houses to survive in Cornwall. Built during the 15th century, the building has been split into two properties that retain many of their original features and authentic furnishings.

Resources

Hospital

Launceston Hospital, *Launceston (01566 765653).*

Internet

Copytech *2 Exeter Street, Launceston (01566 777407/www.copytechsouthwest.co.uk).* **Open** 9am-5pm Mon-Fri; 10am-2pm Sat.

Police station

Moorland Road, Launceston (0870 577444).

Post office

5 Westgate Street, Launceston (01566 776856). **Open** 9am-5.30pm Mon-Fri; 9am-12.30pm Sat.

Tourist information

Launceston Tourist Information Centre, *Market House Arcade, Market Street, Launceston (01566 772321/772333/www.launcestonlive.com).* **Open** phone for details.

Bodmin & around

On the western edge of the moor, **Blisland** is an enchanting village of granite cottages set around a pretty green. Its striking Norman church, with its brightly coloured rood screen, is dedicated to the little-known saints Protus and Hyacinth and has a beautiful interior.

From Blisland there are walks out on to the moor in every direction. A short stroll will bring you to **Jubilee Rock**, a giant volcanic rock that is perhaps the oldest on the moor, and which was carved by Lieutenant John Rogers to commemorate the coronation of George III in 1821.

Cornwall

Three miles (five kilometres) north-east of Blisland is **Hawk's Tor**, on whose slopes is a circle of Neolithic standing stones known as the **Stripple Stones** – only four remain upright. Close to another standing stone at Ryedown is the **Delphi Bridge** (or the De Lank Ford Bridge), one of the most popular beauty spots on Bodmin Moor.

By car the narrow and at times very steep country lanes to the west of the moor take in some idyllic countryside covered in ancient deciduous woodland, with nearby villages, such as **St Mabyn** and **St Tudy** particularly worth a look. South of St Mabyn on the road to Washaway is **Pencarrow House**, an impressive Georgian manor still privately owned. It was built in 1771 by one of the founders of Lloyds Bank and contains an eclectic but very fine selection of furniture and paintings. After exploring the house, take some time to stroll around the 50 acres of park and woodland, where jazz concerts are held during the summer.

The largest of the settlements in this area is **Bodmin**, on the western fringes of the moor. It's a no-frills place that was an important religious centre in the Dark Ages thanks to the foundation of a priory by **St Petroc** in the sixth century. The town's mainly 15th-century granite church is dedicated to the saint and is the largest parish church in Cornwall. Inside, admire the fine wagon roof, and look out for St Petroc's Casket (c1170), which once held the holy man's bones.

On the other side of Fore Street **Bodmin Museum** has a well-laid-out display of local and social history, but the **Court Room Experience** next door is more fun. Here, moving and talking models re-enact the trail of Matthew Weekes, who was controversially hanged for the murder of his lover Charlotte Dymmond on the moor in 1844 (*see p217*). Visitors get to decide for themselves whether he was guilty or not.

Until 1862 public executions took place at the infamous **Bodmin Gaol** on Berrycombe Road, with crowds flocking from all over the county to witness its grisly events. The 18th-century gaol is still a forbidding place to visit, with a grim display of dungeons, pillories, execution blocks and stocks.

Dominating the skyline above the town is **Gilbert's Monument**, a 144-foot (44-metre) obelisk that crowns Bodmin Beacon. The monument was built in 1857 in honour of the distinguished military general Walter Raleigh Gilbert, a descendant of Sir Walter Raleigh. It's well worth making the climb up here for the excellent views of the surrounding countryside.

West of Bodmin at **Nanstallon**, the mild climate and fertile land encourage viticulture. (Before you snigger at the concept of Cornish wine, note that the 'crisp, grass-streaked' Seyval Blanc made it into the *Daily Telegraph's* top ten international wines for under £10.) The **Camel Valley Vineyard** offers guided tours and tastings.

Close by, Boscarne Junction is the start of a 13-mile (21-kilometre) steam train journey on the **Bodmin & Wenford Railway** (01208 73666, www.bodminandwenfordrailway.co.uk, no service Nov-Feb), which passes through lovely countryside as far as Bodmin General Station just south-east of town. The station was formerly on the Great Western train route, but is now used for the restoration of steam locomotives. North of the station, **Cardinham Woods** are an excellent place for a stroll.

Just two and a half miles (four kilometres) south-east of Bodmin is one of Cornwall's grandest houses, superbly situated over the Fowey valley by Respryn Bridge. **Lanhydrock House** was first constructed in the 17th century but was rebuilt after a fire in the late 1800s, resulting in the high Victoriana of the decor. The house is now owned by the National Trust, with 50 or so rooms open to the public. One of the few remaining 17th-century interiors is the picture gallery, which has a stunning barrel-vaulted ceiling depicting scenes from the Old Testament. Wonderful gardens surround the house and are the setting for summer jazz and blues concerts. In spring the bloom of camelias, azaleas, magnolias and rhododendrons is breathtaking. Footpaths lead from the gardens to 1,000 acres of park and woodland beyond.

Bodmin Gaol
Berrycombe Road, Bodmin (01208 76292). **Open** *Mid Apr-early Nov* 10am-6pm Mon-Fri; 11am-6pm Sat. **Admission** £3.90; £2 concessions. **No credit cards.**

Bodmin Museum
Shire House, Mount Folly Square, Bodmin (01208 77067). **Open** *Apr-Sept* 10.30am-4.30pm Mon-Sat. *Oct* 11.30am-3.30pm Mon-Sat. Closed Nov-Mar. **Admission** free.

Camel Valley Vineyard
Little Denby, Nanstallon, nr Bodmin (01208 77959/ www.camelvalley.com). **Open** *Tours* Easter-Sept 2-5pm Mon-Thur; 2-6pm Fri; 10am-1pm, 2-4pm Sat. No tours Oct-Mar. *Wine shop* 10am-5pm Mon-Fri. **Admission** *Grand tour & tasting* £5. **Credit** MC, V.

Lanhydrock House
Lanhydrock House, nr Bodmin (01208 73320/ www.nationaltrust.org.uk). **Open** *Apr-Oct* 11am-5pm Tue-Sun. Closed Nov-Mar. **Admission** £7; £3.50 concessions. **Credit** AmEx, MC, V.

Pencarrow House & Grounds

Pencarrow (01298 841369/www.pencarrow.co.uk).
Open *Apr-Oct* 11am-5pm Mon-Thur, Sun. Closed Nov-Mar. **Admission** *House & grounds* £6; £3 concessions. *Grounds only* £3; free under-16s. **Credit** MC, V.

Courtoom Experience

Shire Hall, Mount Folly Square, Bodmin (01208 76616). **Open** *Easter-Oct* 10am-5pm Mon-Sat. *Nov-Mar* 10am-5pm Mon-Fri. **Admission** £3; £1.50-£2 concessions; £7.50 family. **Credit** MC, V.

Activities

Cycling

The eastern end of the **Camel Trail** (*see p279*) lies a mile or so west of Blisland at Poley Bridge. From here 17 miles (27km) of beautiful old railway track will take you through the stunning Camel valley towards Bodmin, Wadebridge and the Camel estuary. Bikes can be hired from **East Rose Farm**, St Breward (01208 850674).

Tuck in Cornish pasty

A trip to Cornwall would not be complete without sampling a traditional Cornish pasty. Although the origins of the pasty are lost in the mists of time, these sturdy, pocket-shaped pastries first came to prominence in the 19th century as a convenient, all-in-one meal for miners, with a savoury filling at one end and jam at the other. In the filthy underground conditions, the miner could hold the pasty's crimped edge while he ate, discarding it at the end without soiling the rest of his meal. It seems sadly ironic that this ingenious, self-contained miner's food should have proved more enduring than the industry itself.

So, what separates the sumptuous delights of a real Cornish pasty from the tasteless, bland, mass-produced imitations found all over the UK? Simply being the Cornish side of the Tamar will greatly improve the quality and, of course, steering clear of any pre-packaged versions helps. Another crucial factor is the mix of ingredients: for a perfect pasty you need a good balance of beef (cut, never minced), potato, onion, turnip (or swede), generous seasoning and golden pastry (either flaky or shortcrust).

One of the best places to get hold of a pasty of such quality is at the award-winning **Ann's Famous Pasty Shop** (Beacon Terrace, The Lizard, 01326 290889). Clearly signposted and painted a garish yellow, this bakery provides huge, cheap, tasty pasties of such calibre that they're even delicious cold. The owner, Ann Muller, hit the headlines in 2002 when she burned the Stars and Stripes outside her shop in response to a scathing comment by *New York Times* food critic William Grimes, who claimed that 'Cornwall, England probably offers more bad food per square mile than anywhere else in the civilised world.'

Thankfully, the county's best restaurants and pasty shops prove that Mr Grimes' opinion is very wide of the mark: in Truro,

try **WC Rowe** (22 Victoria Square, 01872 261281) or **Blewetts Bakery** (Cathedral Chambers, 13 High Cross, 01872 222856), where eagerly queuing locals are a common sight all year round.

Vegetarians visiting Cornwall need not despair since most bakeries now provide a selection of equally tasty non-meat pasties. **St Agnes Bakery** (Churchtown, St Agnes, 01872 552308), for instance, serves stilton and cheddar versions that make fine alternatives to the original. More adventurous variations – such as cod with tarragon, and pork with apple – may also be found, particularly in upmarket hotspots such as St Ives and Padstow. However, while it's good to try these chi-chi wannabes, it's worth remembering that the traditional Cornish pasty remains the bestseller for a very good reason.

Where to eat, drink & stay

The award-winning **Blisland Inn** (01208
850739, main courses £4.75-£10.95) on the
village green at Blisland makes a perfect
refreshment stop. Run by an impressively
proportioned and friendly publican, it has
stocked over 1,750 different ales in the past
eight years, including the highly rated King
Buddha, made exclusively for the publican
by Cornish Sharps Brewery. Jukeboxes and
fruit machines are banned here, but it all gets
very merry on Wednesday evenings when
locals and visitors pack out the place for
quiz night. Decent alternatives in the area
include the **Cornish Arms** at St Tudy
(01208 850656, main courses £6.50-£9) or
the **Old Inn** at St Breward (01208 850711,
main courses £5.95-£16). The **St Mabyn Inn**
(01208 841266, main courses £7.95-£12.75)
is a slightly more upmarket choice, offering
good local fish dishes.

To stay, 16th-century **Levethan** (near
Blisland, 01208 850487, www.levethan.co.uk,
set dinner £25, double £70-£80) is set in a
secret valley, with 30 acres of wooded gardens,
a stream and a swimming pool. It offers very
luxurious B&B in comfortable antique-
decorated rooms, or self-catering in the
stable and barn conversions.

Another lovely choice is **Tredethy Country
House Hotel** (Helland Bridge, 01208 841262,
www.tredethyhouse.co.uk, closed late Dec-
mid Jan, set dinner £22, double B&B £80-
£180), which is furnished with artefacts,
many of them African, from the owners'
travels. An accomplished restaurant menu
is supplemented by a particularly good wine
selection, and outside there's a heated pool
and nine acres of gardens.

In St Tudy, the **Old Rectory** (01208 850027,
double B&B £60-£70) is an attractive stone
building with antique furniture and a croquet
lawn, while **Polrode Mill Cottage** (01208
850203, www.polrodemillcottage.co.uk, set
meal £22.50, double £68-£80), also in the
village, is a pretty 17th-century guesthouse
with a large streamside garden and an
impressive menu of local produce.

Resources

Hospital
*Bodmin Hospital, Boundary Lane, Bodmin
(01208 251577).*

Internet
*Bodmin Library, Lower Bore Street, Bodmin
(01208 72286).* **Open** 9.30am-6pm Mon-Wed;
9.30am-6pm Fri; 9.30am-12.30pm Sat.

Post office
St Nicholas Street, Bodmin (01208 72845).
Open 9am-5.30pm Mon-Fri; 9am-noon Sat.

Tourist Information
Bodmin Tourist Information Centre, *Shire
Hall, Mount Folly, Bodmin (01208 76616/
www.bodmin-live.com).* **Open** *Apr-Oct* 10am-
5pm Mon-Sat. *Nov-Mar* 10am-5pm Mon-Fri.

South & east Bodmin Moor

South of the A30, Bodmin Moor is characterised
by wide open spaces of heath, softened by
tracts of thick deciduous woodland, deep river
valleys and gorges. Viciously prickly, vivid
yellow gorse bushes proliferate, competing
by midsummer with the subtler purple of
moorland heather.

Prehistoric stone circles and burial sites
are concentrated on the south-eastern edge of
the moor, and are the source of a host of local
legends. After a few pints of the local Doom
Bar ale it may be possible to see the Piskies,
kindly imps bewigged in grey-green lichen,
or the capricious and vengeful Spriggans,
scraggy dwarfs that haunt the burial sites and
dolmens, and are said to steal babies and whip
up hailstorms to frighten solitary travellers.
More recently, these mythical creatures have
been joined by the slightly more substantial
Beast of Bodmin, a puma, panther or wild
cat that is widely blamed for the unexplained
slaughter of ponies and sheep all over the moor.

Set midway along the A30 between
Launceston and Bodmin, **Jamaica Inn** is the
geographical and spiritual heart of Bodmin
Moor. The inn was an important staging post
on the turnpike road across the moor for several
centuries and also a smuggling centre, but only
came to prominence as a tourist attraction when
Daphne du Maurier set her bestselling novel
here after frequent visits to the inn in the 1930s.

The inn has now expanded into a hotel,
restaurant and tourist complex with a number
of attractions. A perfectly good restorative
pub lunch can be had at the buffet bar before
a visit to the Daphne du Maurier room or
the adjoining **Mr Potter's Museum of
Curiosities**, a mad-cap collection of Victorian
taxidermy and other weird and wonderful
exhibits. Also here is the **Smugglers at
Jamaica Inn** exhibition, which recreates some
of the scenes and characters from du Maurier's
novel in a series of audio-visual tableaux. Far
more interesting, however, is the collection of
smuggling artefacts, including the traditional
gadgets used to conceal contraband goods.

From the Inn it's a three-mile (five-kilometre)
walk north to Brown Willy (*see p216*) or a mile
or so's stroll south to **Dozmary Pool**, which on

Cornwall

Fast-flowing River Fowey at **Golitha Falls**.

sunny days is visible as a bright blue diamond from miles around. Arthurian legend claims that this atmospheric spot is the lair of the Lady of the Lake and the final resting place of King Arthur's sword Excalibur (*see p10* **Local heroes**). Another local story tells of John Tregeagle, the cruel steward of Lanhydrock, who was cursed to endlessly empty the pool with a broken limpet shell while being tormented by a swarm of devils.

Close to Dozmary are two much larger recreational lakes providing birdwatching, fishing and beautiful walks year round: **Colliford Lake** in the west is an important site for over-wintering wildfowl and is regarded as a top spot for natural brown trout fishing, while **Siblyback Lake** has sandy beaches and an excellent watersports centre (*see p222*) that hires windsurfers, sailing boats and canoes and offers RYA-approved tuition.

South of Siblyback, Dranesbridge is the starting point for a stunning riverside walk to **Golitha Falls**. The walk follows the rapid waters of the River Fowey as they hurtle along a deep gorge and over a series of cascades. Surrounding the river are ancient lichen-clad woodlands that blossom with a profusion of wild flowers in spring.

Further west the villages of Warleggan, Cardinham and St Neot are good starting points for exploring the lush, wooded fringes of the moor. **St Neot** is a delightful place and is worth visiting for its church alone, which boasts a beautiful 15th-century interior and some of the most stunning stained glass in the country, depicting scenes from the Old Testament, saints' lives and local personalities. Near the village are the **Carnglaze Slate Caverns**, which have been worked since ancient times. The true extent of the caverns is unknown, but guided tours take visitors deep underground to a great blue-green lake.

The south-eastern corner of the moor, meanwhile, has some great scenery around the desolate peaks of **Kilmar Tor**, **Hawk's Tor** and **Trewartha Tor**, as well as a concentration of Bronze Age remains clustered around **Minions**, the highest village in Cornwall.

The most impressive of all the prehistoric sites is the **Hurlers**, located just outside the village, which consists of three circles of massive standing stones. Although their original purpose is unknown, local lore suggests they are men turned to stone for playing the Cornish game of hurling on a Sunday. South of Minions, near the village

Stained glass in **St Neot** church. *See p221.*

of Darite, is a huge Stone Age burial chamber known as **Trevethy Quoit**, while to the north, the entirely natural **Cheesewring** is an extraordinary pillar of granite slabs that has been eroded by the moorland winds.

On the eastern fringes of the moor, at Upton Cross, the **Sterts Open Air Theatre & Arts Centre** (01579 362382, www.sterts.co.uk) stages performances ranging from Shakespeare to musical comedies. Conditions are fairly basic – timber seats for the audience – but there's an all-weather canopy to keep off the rain. The centre also exhibits and sells the work of over 30 artists and sculptors, and organises one-day workshops in a wide range of arts and crafts.

Close by, on the banks of the Lynher, **Netherton Farm** is where the popular Cornish yarg cheese is produced. Visitors can witness the process first hand, from milking the cows to cutting the curds. The cheese is wrapped in nettles and left to develop in a special ripening room, resulting in a delicious, delicate flavour.

Just beyond the moor's southern fringes, perched high above the Looe river valley, is the ancient stannary and market town of **Liskeard**. It's largely unremarkable except as a useful transport hub, but a visit to the **Liskeard Museum** gives an insight into the surrounding area and its roots in mining.

Carnglaze Slate Caverns

St Neot, nr Liskeard (01579 320251/ www.carnglaze.com). **Open** 10am-5pm Mon-Sat. **Admission** £5; £3.50 concessions; £15 family. **Credit** MC, V.

Liskeard Museum

Forrester's Hall, Pike Street, Liskeard (01579 346087). **Open** 11am-4pm Mon-Fri; 11am-1.30pm Sat. **Admission** free.

Mr Potter's Museum of Curiosities & Smugglers at Jamaica Inn

Jamaica Inn, Bolventor, nr Launceston (01566 86838/86025/www.dumaurier.org/jamaica/ inn.html). **Open** *Nov-Mar* 11am-4pm daily. *Apr-July, Sept, Oct* 10am-5pm daily. *Aug* 10am-7pm daily. **Admission** *1 museum* £2.50; £2 concessions; £6.95 family. *Both museums* £4; £3 concessions; £8.95 family. **Credit** MC, V.

Yarg Cheese Farm

Netherton Farm, Upton Cross, nr Liskeard (01579 362244/www.cornishyarg.co.uk). **Open** *Mar-Oct* 10am-5pm Mon-Fri (last tour 2.45pm). Closed Nov-Feb. **Admission** *Tours* £3; £1.50-£2 concessions. **Credit** MC, V.

Activities

Fishing

Fishing permits for the stocked rainbow trout on **Siblyback Lake** are available from a self-service kiosk (£16.75) or from the ranger (01579 342366). Permits for natural brown trout fishing on **Colliford Lake** are available from Colliford Tavern. Contact the ranger (01579 342366) or check the South West Lakes trust website at www.swlakestrust.org.uk.

Watersports

For windsurfing, sailing or canoeing at **Siblyback Lake**, call the watersports office on 01579 346522.

Where to eat, drink & stay

Pubs form the main eating and accommodation options in this area. The much-extended **Jamaica Inn** (Bolventor, 01566 86250) is no longer the evocative place it once was, but has en suite rooms from £55 and serves hearty country food. Further south, the **Cheesewring Hotel** (Minions, 01579 362321, main courses £3.50-£12.50) is the highest inn in Cornwall at 995 feet (303 metres) and offers traditional pub fare. Outside the village, **Crows Nest** (01579 345930, main courses £6.95-£11.95) is a 17th-century pub with low beamed ceilings, open fires and decent bar meals, while further west at St Neot, the **London Inn** (01579 320263, main courses £5.95-£12.95) does a great traditional Sunday lunch. At Upton Cross the **Caradon Inn** (01579 362391, main courses £4.95-£7.95) is an atmospheric spot serving excellent

Cornwall

Sunday roasts, while the **Sterts Theatre Bar & Café** (*see p222*; main courses £6-£10) has a very good modern menu.

Just outside the charming village of North Hill, **Berrio Bridge House** (01566 782714, double £50-£58) is an excellent B&B, where breakfast is served in a conservatory overlooking the pretty garden. The owners have fishing rights on the River Lynher, which flows through the property.

For a treat, though, try **Cabilla Manor** (near Mount, 01208 821224, www.cabilla.co.uk, double B&B £70), a stunning Georgian house set in acres of woods and moorland. The home of explorer Robin Hanbury-Tennison and his wife, the house is full of fascinating artefacts and beautiful furniture from their travels.

Resources

Hospital
Passmore Edwards Hospital, *Liskeard (01579 335277).*

Internet
Liskeard Library *Barras Street, Liskeard (01579 343285).* **Open** 9.30am-6pm Mon, Tue, Thur, Fri; 9.30am-4pm Sat.

Police station
Greenbank Road, Liskeard (0870 577 7444).

Post office
The Parade, Liskeard (no phone). **Open** 8.30am-5.30pm Mon, Tue; 9am-5.30pm Wed-Fri; 9am-12.30pm Sat.

Tourist information
Liskeard Tourist Information Centre *Forrester's Hall, Pike Street, Liskeard (01579 349148/www.liskeard.gov.uk).* **Open** 10.30am-4pm Mon-Fri; 10.30am-1.30pm Sat.

Towards the coast

From Liskeard it is possible to take a train along the beautiful, scenic Looe valley to the south coast. The track makes a steep curving descent to its first stop at **Coombe**, which is just half a mile away from the town, but 200 feet (60 metres) closer to sea level. There are further stops at five or six villages en route, all of which are the starting point for great walks.

At **Sandplace** the river becomes tidal and the estuary is scattered with the rotting hulls of old wrecks, no doubt due to the local belief that anyone who dismantles them will have a run of bad luck. Here the railway is forced on to a causeway, giving passengers the strange impression that they are travelling on the water.

Choosing to drive or cycle in the same direction will take you along narrow, winding, blissfully sylvan lanes southward towards Looe. Outside the village of St Keyne is the beautifully preserved well of **St Cuby's**, where newlywed couples traditionally rush to have the first sip of water, believing the winner will then rule the household. Further down the valley at **Duloe** is a prehistoric circle of eight massive standing stones and an excellent pub, the Plough (*see p226*).

The bustling port of **Looe** occupies both sides of the valley at the mouth of the river, with narrow streets of compact old fishermen's cottages twisting and turning steeply up on either side. Once distinct settlements, East and West Looe are connected by a 15th-century seven arched bridge, from where Fore Street runs south on the eastern side of the estuary as far as Buller Quay and the harbour. Tourists began arriving in Looe in the early 19th century to bathe from the surrounding beaches but the town didn't really begin to draw the crowds until the building of the railway in 1879. Much of the history of the town is recorded in the **Old Guildhall Museum**, one of Looe's oldest buildings, which dates back to about 1500.

A busy fish market is still held on the east side of the harbour, supplying excellent seafood to the fishmongers behind the market and to most of the town's pubs and restaurants. If you're keen to make your own catch, fishing trips are advertised on blackboards along the quay. Looe is the centre for shark-fishing in the UK, but less adventurous mackerel-fishing expeditions and pleasure trips are also on offer.

One of the most popular excursions takes visitors to **Looe Island** (aka St George's), a large green blob lying a mile offshore. Once the site of a Celtic monastery, the island was bought by two sisters in the 1970s, who lived there alone for over 20 years. The island is now a bird sanctuary managed by the Wildlife Trust.

Beyond the harbour the protective arm of **Banjo Pier** extends out into the bay, marking the western end of popular **East Looe Beach**. Further east, and accessible via the coast path, are **Sanders Beach** and **Millendreath**, not to mention endless little coves and rock pools. The coast path continues east from here to a sandy beach at **Seaton** and to the linear cliff-top villages of **Downderry** and **Portwrinkle** on the edge of Whitsand Bay (*see p207*). Both villages offer breathtaking views out to sea on a clear day. Inland is the charming village of **St Germans**, with its 16th-century almshouses and 12th-century church. A walk along the River Tiddy from St Germans quay affords lovely glimpses upstream through the splendid arches of the railway viaduct.

Cornwall

On the west side of the Looe estuary, meanwhile, visit 14th-century **St Nicholas** church before heading either to the expansive sandy bay at **Hannafore Beach** or up the cliff for great views of Looe Bay. Just four miles (2.5 kilometres) further on is undeniably quaint **Polperro**. The village has become something of a tourist honeypot in recent years, but still supports over a dozen fishing vessels, which unload a wonderful selection of local fish, mussels, cockles, squid, lobsters and crabs on to the quay. As a result you can enjoy delicious seafood in any number of pubs and restaurants jostling for space along the village's narrow streets.

During the 19th century Polperro was a prosperous smuggling port, with many fishermen benefiting from this illegal trade by stashing contraband among the hauls of pilchards. You can explore the town's fascinating history at the **Polperro Heritage Museum of Smuggling & Fishing**, which is housed in a former pilchard factory near the quay.

Out of season, Polperro is a pleasant place for a quiet wander, but by midsummer it tends to be overrun with tourists. To avoid the bustle, head off to the sleepy village of **Porthallow** or enjoy the pink-grey rocks and beach at **Talland Bay**. Inland is the pretty village of **Lanreath**, where you'll find an entertaining mix of local contraptions housed in a tithe barn at the **Lanreath Folk & Farm Museum**.

For most people, however, the major attraction in this area is the stretch of the jagged coastline between Polperro and Polruan. Owned almost entirely by the National Trust, it provides opportunities for some exhilarating and invigorating walks around the cliff tops and headlands, while the secluded coves below are great for a refreshing swim or a picnic.

Polruan is a very old fishing village of closely packed whitewashed cottages overlooking the estuary to the busier town of Fowey (*see p227*). All kinds of watersports can be arranged at the quay or you can chug up the river to **Lerryn**, whose tidal creek is

Say what? Cornish

Dolly Pentreath of Mousehole, who died in 1777, was reportedly the last monoglot speaker of Cornish. However, this ancient Celtic language has just about survived into the 21st century, with the rudiments taught in some Cornish schools, and the local BBC radio station broadcasting a weekly news roundup in the indigenous tongue. Cornish is defined by the European Union as a 'minority language' – a mark of official recognition that has bolstered renewed enthusiasm for the language at grass roots level.

Although you are very unlikely to come across conversations in Cornish during a visit to the county, what you will hear is a musical, softly weatherbeaten English, with its own distinct intonation and rich local vocabulary. Even 50 years ago the regional Cornish accent varied between different social groups and from town to town – someone from Camborne (*Camburn*) might have had a different delivery from someone from St Austell (*Snozzle*), for example. These days the accent – '*proper Cornish*', as it is '*knawn*' – is much more homogenised.

Locals, especially in West Cornwall, use 'thee' in the reduced form '*ee*', thus 'How are you?' becomes '*Alrigh', are 'ee*?'. '*Un*' (and occasionally '*a*') is used to mean 'it', so 'have you done it?' becomes '*dunnun avee?*';

'have you seen it?' – '*seenun avee?*'; 'did it cost much?' – '*Costee much dida?*' and so on. Interestingly, this tendency to reverse the word order is thought to be inherited from Cornish grammar.

Expect to be addressed frequently as '*me 'ansome*' (don't get overexcited, it's generally unrelated to looks); '*me lover*' (no romantic engagement is sought), or '*me bird*' (mainly for women): all casual terms of endearment. Then, less endearingly, there's the noun '*emmet*' meaning tourists. This word is particularly prevalent during the summer months and is more often than not preceded by '*bledy*'.

A couple of impressively unequivocal similes also warrant a mention: '*ruffazrats*' denotes someone of uncultured upbringing; stay away from someone who is '*teasy asn adder*'; and find the lightswitch if it's '*darksaashaft*'.

Finally, the Cornish do things '*dreckly*' – the mother of all West Country expressions (*see also p184*). If someone tells you that they are doing something '*dreckly*', they are talking about an indeterminate period of time that generally falls between minutes and months. Relax. When the task is finally completed, you can guarantee the result will be '*proper job!*'

Fishing and boating are the order of the day at pretty **Polruan**. *See p224.*

distinguished by a pretty 16th-century bridge. The riverside walks here are said to have inspired Kenneth Graham to write *The Wind in the Willows*. Head north out of the village on the wooded footpath to reach the windswept and lonely church of **St Winnow**, with its intricately carved Tudor benches and the oldest rood screen in Cornwall. Alternatively, from Polruan follow signs for the **Hall Walk** to **Bodinnick**, from where the ferry makes regular crossings to Fowey.

Lanreath Folk & Farm Museum

Lanreath, nr Looe (01503 220321). **Open** *Easter-Oct* 10am-6pm daily. Closed Nov-Mar. **Admission** £2.50; £1.50 concessions. **No credit cards**.

Old Guildhall Museum

Higher Market Street, East Looe (01503 263709). **Open** *Easter, May-Sept* 11.30am-4.30pm Mon-Fri, Sun. Closed Oct-Mar. **Admission** £1.50; 50p concessions. **No credit cards**.

Polperro Heritage Museum of Smuggling & Fishing

Mawdsley Rooms, The Warren, Polperro (01503 273005). **Open** phone for details. **Admission** phone for details.

Activities

Canoeing

Floating Leaf Canoes (01503 240566, www.floatingleafcanoes.co.uk) organises guided canoe trips along the sheltered Looe valley.

Diving

Looe Divers (Marine Drive, Hannafore, Looe, 01503 262727, www.looedivers.com) offers equipment and instruction in snorkelling and scuba diving.

Fishing

For game fishing, contact **Looe Chandlery** (West Quay, Looe, 01503 264355), which can arrange trips to catch shark, conger and mackerel. To hire or buy fishing tackle in Polperro, try **Rod & Line** (01503 272361).

Riding

St Veep Riding School (Lerryn, 01208 873521) runs day courses and summer camps for all levels.

Where to eat, drink & stay

Every kind of cuisine is available in Looe. The 500-year-old **Jolly Sailor** (Princes Square, 01503 263387, main courses £4.45-£8.45) is reliable for a decent lunch and a variety of ales,

Cornwall

Trout fishing on **Colliford Lake**. *See p221.*

while **Trawlers** (Buller Quay, 01503 263593, main courses £14-£20) specialises in quality fresh fish straight off the boat. For a wicked cream tea, don't miss **Millie's Tea Shop** (01503 265966) near the west quay.

A mile from the sea and with fantastic coastal views of Looe Island is **Bucklawren Farm** (St Martin, Looe, 01503 240738, www.bucklawren.co.uk, main courses £10.50-£15.50, double B&B £48-£52), whose Granary Restaurant has an excellent menu of traditional English recipes. More expensive is the quiet and comfortable **Klymiarven Hotel** (Barbican Hill, East Looe, 01503 262333, www.klymiarven.co.uk, closed Jan, main courses £4.95-£15.95, double B&B £58-£110), positioned high up on the hillside.

Inland, try the **Old Plough House** in Duloe (01503 262050, main courses £6.95-£11.50) for an excellent local menu, and the **Well House** (St Keyne, near Liskeard, 01579 342001, www.wellhouse.co.uk, set menu £32.50, double £115-£170) for intimate country house accommodation and a sophisticated, Modern European restaurant.

On the coast between Looe and Polperro, **Talland Bay Hotel** (Talland-by-Looe, 01503 272667, set menu £27.50, double £90-£180) has a heated swimming pool and lovely clifftop terraced gardens. It's expensive but worth it for real luxury and a very good restaurant. The best eaterie in Polperro itself is reckoned by many to be **The Kitchen** (Fishna Bridge, 01503 272780, closed Oct-Mar, main courses £9.50-£15), which dishes up fresh local fish in funky fusion styles. Also check out the **Cottage Restaurant** (01503 272217, closed Nov-Mar, double £55-£59, main courses

£10.50-£17), which serves upmarket seafood and provides B&B accommodation, and the **Blue Peter Inn** (01503 272743), which has a particularly good selection of West Country real ales.

Inland at Pelynt, 14th-century **Penellick** (01503 272372, set dinner £15-£21.50, double £50-£64) offers exceptional bed and breakfast, with evening meals by arrangement. Also here is the 16th-century **Jubilee Inn** (01503 220312, main courses £6.90-£12, double £60-£104), which has a quintessential village pub feel, with flagstones, big log fires, a flower-filled courtyard and a decent all-round menu. The **Punch Bowl Inn** in Lanreath (01503 220218, main courses £5-£13) is also full of history, having once been a courthouse, a coaching inn and a smugglers' meeting house.

Further west, the **Lugger Inn** (01726 870007, main courses £3.95-£10.95) on the quay at Polruan is a friendly local with views over the little harbour, while the **Old Ferry Inn** (01726 870237, main courses £4-£14, double £65-£100) at nearby Bodinnick has a decent restaurant menu plus accommodation.

In the riverside village of Lerryn, enjoy a garden lunch, a pint of Sharps Doom Bar or some local cider at the **Ship Inn** (01208 872374, main courses £6.50-£14) before retiring to **Collon** (01208 872908, double £60), an excellent farmhouse B&B with lovely rooms overlooking the Fowey valley.

Resources

Post office

Fore Street, East Looe (01503 262110).
Open 9am-5.30pm Mon-Fri; 9am-1pm Sat.

Tourist Information

South East Cornwall Discovery Centre
Millpool, West Looe (01503 262777/www.southeast cornwall.co.uk). **Open** *Easter-Oct* 10am-6pm Mon-Sat. *Nov-Mar* 10am-4pm Mon-Sat. Closed late Dec-mid Jan.

Getting there & around

By bus

National Express (08705 808080, www.gobycoach. com) runs daily coach services from London, Exeter and other UK destinations to Launceston, Bodmin and Liskeard. **First Western National** (0870 6082608, www.firstwesternnational.co.uk) operates local services including routes from Launceston and Liskeard to Plymouth.

By train

First Great Western (08457 000125) runs direct services along the main Exeter–Penzance route, calling at Liskeard (for connections to the scenic Looe Valley line) and Bodmin.

South Cornwall

Boats, beaches and gardens galore.

Cornwall's southern seaboard encompasses some of the county's most picturesque scenery. A far cry from the pounding surf of the Atlantic, this coastline is characterised by myriad rivers flowing through many-fingered estuaries to the sea. It's a place for pottering around in boats and sunbathing on sandy beaches, but also has its fair share of rugged, dramatic cliffs accessible via the South West Coast Path. What's more, South Cornwall revels in an abundance of superlative gardens (the **Lost Gardens of Heligan** top the list), which add a touch of tropical intrigue to this holiday region.

The coastal villages and towns here have all succumbed to tourism to a certain degree, but the most appealing retain a sense of their fishing and smuggling heritage. **Fowey** is an attractive, upwardly mobile port that has mended its buccaneering ways to become a mecca for yachties. Further west the Pimms and blazers give way to a much more gritty scene around St Austell Bay, where tankers still export china clay from the huge harbour at Par. The centre of the clay industry is **St Austell**, a rather unprepossessing place saved from anonymity by its proximity to the hugely successful **Eden Project**.

Mevagissey, to the south, is one of the most popular destinations in the area and can become overrun with tourists in high season. Visit in winter to rediscover the charm of this historic fishing and smuggling port, or head further south to explore the stunning scenery around **Veryan Bay** and **Gerrans Bay**. South again, and the gorgeously undeveloped **Roseland Peninsula** butts on to the **Carrick Roads** estuary, a complex network of creeks and rivers to which the twin charms of boating and beaches attract plenty of visitors. The untouristy and self-sufficient 'city' of **Truro** commands the head of the estuary, while the mouth is dominated by bustling, arty **Falmouth**, a focus for tourism in the area and the location of the spectacular new **National Maritime Museum Cornwall**.

Fowey & Lostwithiel

Fowey, originally a fishing village close to the open sea, did not come into its own as a port until the 14th century, when it sent ships to assist in the ongoing wars with France. However, what began as legitimate naval skirmishes soon degenerated into out-and-out buccaneering by the Cornish boats. The

Cornwall

Beach babes at **Porthluney Cove**. See p235.

self-styled 'Fowey Gallants' raided the French and Spanish coasts and plundered foreign vessels in a binge of illegal privateering that continued for an embarrassingly long time after peace had been established, ending only in the 1470s when Edward IV stripped the town of its military capability.

Today Fowey's broad deep-water estuary more prosaically supports a thriving commercial port, not to mention innumerable yachts and pleasure crafts. Every August the town's increasingly affluent inhabitants and visitors turn out in force for the **Fowey Royal Regatta & Carnival** (01726 832133), when pubs and restaurants set out tables on the street, market stalls stay open late and parties go on into the early hours.

Despite being dedicated to the tourist industry, Fowey's undeniably stunning setting and its diverse historical and literary associations raise its profile considerably. The streets have changed little over time, and are crammed with architecture from the Elizabethan through to the Georgian eras. Flanking the harbour are the ruins of twin 14th-century forts, which were originally erected after a Spanish raid in 1380. Nevertheless, continental incursions continued, most devastatingly in 1456, when French forces burned down half the town.

One near-victim of the fire was the 15th-century church of **St Fimbarrus**, which marks the traditional end of the Saints' Way from Padstow (*see p279*). The restored church contains many references to the prominent local Treffry family, whose extravagantly fortified private manor has dominated the heart of the town since the 13th century.

Next door to St Fimbarrus, the **Literary Centre** has a small display on the writers associated with Fowey, most notably Daphne du Maurier (*see p229* **Local heroes**), but also Kenneth Graham, who was married in St Fimbarrus church, and Sir Arthur Quiller-Couch, whose Fowey-inspired novel *Troy Town* was written at the Haven, a house on the esplanade. Literary groupies descend on the town in early May for the **Daphne du Maurier Festival of Arts & Literature** (01726 223535, www.restormel.gov.uk/daphne), a ten-day cultural feast of talks, author-readings and concerts.

Opposite the tourist office, pop into the **Fowey River Gallery** (38 Fore Street, 01726 8333828), which showcases work by some of Cornwall's finest contemporary artists.

Heading south of town towards the mouth of the harbour brings you to **Readymoney Cove**, which is small, sandy and good for swimming. From here a footpath leads to **St Catherine's Point**, where the minimal remains of a fort built by Thomas Treffry for Henry VIII stand on the site of a medieval chapel. A stroll around the ruins offers wonderful sea and estuary views.

A little further west lies secluded **Polridmouth**, where du Maurier's Rebecca met her untimely end. Backed by a small lake, it is accessible only on foot from the coast path or from Menabilly Barton Farm (a short walk inland). Du Maurier fans may catch a glimpse of the author's home, Menabilly, up in the trees behind the beach. *See also p234* **Coastal walk**.

At the head of the Fowey estuary is **Lostwithiel**. In the early 13th century, this riverside township was a major port used for the export of tin from Bodmin. In the Duchy Palace, the metal was smelted and 'coigned' before being shipped out to the Continent. The palace, on Quay Street, was largely destroyed during the Civil War, but the impressive ruins of the 12th-century motte-and-bailey **Restormel Castle** still overlook the valley and provide an atmospheric setting for a picnic.

On Church Lane, off Fore Street, the 13th-century parish church of **St Bartholomew** was desecrated during the Civil War when Parliamentarian forces christened a horse (yes, really) in the font. Heavily besieged by the opposing Royalists throughout August of 1644, the townsfolk emerged shattered and starving from the experience. During the siege Charles I and his more refined retinue were housed at beautiful **Boconnoc House**, a private estate just outside the town, which can be visited only very occasionally during the year (phone 01208 872507 for details).

Though the port has long since disappeared and there are few remaining clues to its eventful past, Lostwithiel survives as a pleasant market town, with a fine 15th-century five-arched bridge spanning the River Fowey. Centuries of local domestic history can be explored in the **Lostwithiel Museum**, housed in the old Corn Exchange.

Daphne du Maurier Literary Centre

5 South Street, Fowey (01726 833619/ www.fowey.co.uk). **Open** 10am-5pm daily. **Admission** free. **Credit** *Shop* MC, V.

Lostwithiel Museum

Corn Exchange, 16 Fore Street, Lostwithiel (01208 872079). **Open** *Easter-Sept* 10.30am-12.30pm, 2.30-4.30pm Mon-Sat. Closed Oct-Mar. **Admission** free. **No credit cards**.

Restormel Castle

off the A390, nr Lostwithiel (01208 872687). **Open** *Apr-Sept* 10am-6pm daily. *Oct* 10am-5pm daily. Closed Nov-Mar. **Admission** £2; £1-£1.50 concessions; free under-5s. **No credit cards**.

Activities

Boating

The best way to explore the beautiful Fowey estuary is by pottering around in a boat. Small motorboats can be rented Easter-Sept from **Fowey River Boat Hire** (01726 832874, www.fowey-river-boat-hire.co.uk). If you prefer someone else at the helm, **Fowey River Steamers** (01726 833278) offer regular estuary and coastal cruises in the summer starting from the Town Quay.

Golf

The **Lostwithiel Golf & Country Club** (Lostwithiel, 01208 873550) has an 18-hole course, not to mention hotel accommodation and extensive leisure facilities – everything, in fact, that a visiting golfer could need.

Sailing

For sailing buffs, temporary membership is available at the **Royal Fowey Yacht Club** (01726 832245, www.rfyc-fowey.org.uk).

Where to eat, drink & stay

Seafood in Fowey can be sublime. Family-run **Sam's** (20 Fore Street, 01726 832273, main courses £5.95-£11.95) is a hip hangout in the town serving excellent food to a funky jazz accompaniment; specialities include authentic bouillabaisse.

Decent fish can also be found on the menu at many of Fowey's pubs, most of which also offer reasonably priced rooms. The **Ship Inn** (Trafalgar Square, 01726 834931, main courses

Local heroes Daphne du Maurier

Born on 13 May 1907 into a hugely artistic and talented family, Daphne du Maurier would seem to have been predestined for literary success. Her grandfather was George du Maurier, a *Punch* cartoonist and author of *Trilby* and *Peter Ibbetson*; her adoring father Gerald was an actor-manager and matinée idol, who encouraged her to write.

Daphne completed her first novel, *The Loving Spirit*, at the family's home in Bodinnick when she was just 19. It was published in 1931, and – in the best traditions of romantic fiction – so affected a handsome young Grenadier Guard, Major Tommy Browning, that he sailed his yacht to Fowey to meet the author. They fell in love and were married within a year.

The following decade saw du Maurier produce a candid biography of her father, followed by three hugely successful novels: *Jamaica Inn* (1936), a tale of smuggling set at the eponymous inn on Bodmin Moor; *Rebecca* (1938), which won fame as a romantic novel although the author intended it as a psychological study in jealousy; and *Frenchman's Creek* (1941), a Restoration tale of a woman fleeing with her children to Cornwall, leaving her dull husband in town. The subsequent filming of these novels and of short stories *The Birds* and *Don't Look Now* compounded Daphne du Maurier's global reputation.

Life seemed to imitate art in the summer of 1942, when du Maurier, like the heroine of *Frenchman's Creek*, took her children to live in Cornwall at a rented house on Readymoney Cove near Fowey. Then, in 1943, du Maurier

leased a house called Menabilly on the Rashleigh Estate near Fowey. Daphne and her sisters had stumbled upon the property years before, while trespassing in the woods on the estate, and though it was neglected and unlived in, the house made a huge impression on the young writer. From this early encounter, du Maurier kept Menabilly in her mind, later using it as the inspiration for Rebecca's Manderley.

Menabilly was always the perfect home for Daphne du Maurier. It was the embodiment of everything she loved about Cornwall as well as being a refuge from the sometimes unwelcome publicity surrounding her success. Rarely socialising away from the estate, du Maurier preferred the company of her dogs and children, and was never happier than when tramping through the parklands and woods around the house or trekking down through the trees and over the cliffs to the beach at Polridmouth.

World War II took Tommy Browning to the Far East, where he stayed until 1946. Du Maurier completed *The King's General* (dedicated to her husband) in the same year and steadfastly remained at Menabilly, even refusing to budge when, at the end of the war, Browning's new job required him to live in London.

Browning died in 1965, and the idyll at Menabilly came to an end in 1969, when the lease on the house expired. From then until her death in 1989 du Maurier, still writing, lived at Kilmarth, another property on the Rashleigh Estate, overlooking Par and St Austell Bay.

Cornwall

An earthly paradise: the **Eden Project**. See p233.

£5.95-£8.50, double B&B £40-£60) is one of the town's oldest buildings, and serves generous portions of good grub, though its popularity with young locals can make it crowded and noisy. Well-kept St Austell ales are served here and at the **King of Prussia** (Town Quay, 01726 833694, main courses £4.50-£7, double B&B £50-£65). Another good spot for food and drink is the **Galleon** on Fore Street (01726 833014, main courses £4.30-£9.50, double B&B £58-£68), which has a terrace overlooking the harbour and Sunday jazz sessions. Also try the **Royal Oak** (01208 872552, main courses £5.50-£11.95, double B&B £70) at Lostwithiel for a good helping of steak and kidney pie.

Housed in an elegant 19th-century manor house, **Fowey Hall Hotel** (Hanson Drive, 01726 833866, www.foweyhall.com, set menu £24.50/£29.50, double B&B £155) is a seriously upmarket hotel that is not sniffy about kids. Luxury on a smaller scale, swimming pool included, can be enjoyed at the **Cormorant on the River** in Golant (01726 833426, www.cormoranthotels.co.uk, main courses £12-£16, double £100), which enjoys fantastic views of the estuary.

Resources

Hospital
Fowey *Fowey & District Hospital, Green Lane (01726 832241).*

Internet
Fowey *Fowey Library, Caffa Mill House, 2 Passage Lane (01726 832332).* **Open** 10am-6pm Tue; 10am-5.30pm Wed-Fri; 10am-12.30pm Sat.

Post offices

Fowey *4 Custom House Hill (01726 832398).* **Open** 9am-5.30pm Mon-Fri; 9am-12.30pm Sat. **Lostwithiel** *3 Queen Street (01208 872535).* **Open** 9am-1pm, 2-5.30pm Mon-Fri; 9am-12.30pm Sat.

Tourist information

Fowey *Ticket Shop, 4 Custom House Hill (01726 833616/www.fowey.co.uk).* **Open** *Apr-Oct* 9am-5.30pm Mon-Fri; 9am-5pm Sat; 10am-5pm Sun. *Nov-Mar* 9am-5.30pm Mon-Fri; 9am-12.30pm Sat. **Lostwithiel** *Community Centre, Liddicoat Road (01208 872207).* **Open** *Easter-Oct* 10am-5pm daily. *Nov-Easter* 10am-5pm Mon-Sat.

St Austell & the bay

Unlike the ancient towns of Fowey or Lostwithiel, St Austell has a strictly industrial heritage. It was here, in the mid 18th century, that William Cookworthy struck metaphorical gold when he discovered massive deposits of kaolin surrounding the town. Ever since, St Austell has been at the heart of the region's all-important (though now declining) china clay industry, which replaced copper and tin mining as the lifeblood of the region. For an informed history of the subject visit **Wheal Martyn China Clay Museum**, which includes a 19th-century clay works.

Venture on to the moors above and behind St Austell to find a bleak industrial landscape of chasmic pits and cut-off waste tips. This is clay country – no quaint white cottages here, only severe grey granite villages under a wide sky, and a landscape ravaged by centuries of mining. The cavernous pits, surreal as a lunar landscape, have formed the backdrop to numerous film and TV productions, from *Dr Who* to *James Bond*.

By the late 1990s, with china clay in decline, tin mining long played out and its remaining engine houses now decoratively derelict, St Austell was teetering on the brink of suburban non-entity. In the nick of time, though, the town was delivered from such a fate by the construction of the much-fêted **Eden Project** (*see p233*) a few miles away.

As a direct and timely result of Eden's exponential growth, St Austell is taking a deep breath and embarking on a £40-million three-year rebuilding programme. Not before time. Although there are some fine Georgian and Victorian buildings, the town centre is largely a shabby combination of crumbling '60s tenements and poorly realised stabs at modernisation. Opposite the 15th-century **Holy Trinity Church**, the old **Market House**, which dates from the 1840s, is disappointingly underused. Winston Churchill in his liberal youth once climbed its granite staircase to electioneer from the balcony.

At the highest point of the town stands **St Austell Brewery**, still owned and run by the Hicks family after almost 150 years. The brewery has a visitor centre and runs, by appointment only, a guided tasting tour of the original 1893 brewhouse.

St Austell Bay is a sweep of coves between two headlands, the **Gribbin** to the east, topped by a red-and-white striped day mark, and **Black Head** to the west, where tiny smugglers' beaches, unmarked and precarious, cluster at the foot of scrubby cliffs. Between the two headlands lingers the slightly shabby essence of the 1950s family holiday: sandy beaches and rock pools, shrimping nets and deckchairs. Though seasonally busy, this is a far cry from the in-yer-face resorts on the north coast: no pounding Atlantic breakers or surf culture here.

The crescent-shaped beach at **Polkerris**, tucked neatly into a cove under the Gribbin, is safe, clean and busy, but is reduced to a tiny strip when the tide comes in. For a more accommodating stretch of sand, try **Par**, to the west. This is a lovely dune-backed beach with a large car park, although its proximity to the docks can be offputting. Beyond Par, **Crinnis Beach** is a manmade, mile-long stretch of gritty but clean sand.

The impressive harbour complex at Par, including the massive granite breakwater, was built in the early 1800s by industrialist and entrepreneur Joseph Treffry, the so-called 'King of Mid Cornwall', in order to facilitate transportation to and from his mines. Today, due entirely to his vision, tankers still pootle in and out of the port.

An unusually broad, straight road, designed to take horse-drawn clay wagons three abreast, runs down the hill from St Austell to the sea at **Charlestown**, an elegant Regency harbour that has survived more or less in its original state. Once a fishing port called Polmear, Charlestown became the major site for the export of china clay when Charles Rashleigh created the harbour here in the late 18th century. Nowadays, Fowey and Par have taken over as the centres of clay export for the region leaving Charlestown to dwell in its own idyll, free of modern development.

Its well-preserved looks owe more than a little to that acme of cash and trash, the film industry. Stars of the show are undoubtedly the square riggers in Charlestown harbour – impressive tall ships that are regularly done up in all sorts of guises for film sets and corporate beanos. Guided tours of the ships are available from **Square Sail Shipyard**, which owns the entire seafront, including access to the small surrounding beaches. These are adequate at low tide and safe for small children, although uncharacteristic large, white pebbles – the remains of ballast from 18th-century cargo ships – make them somewhat uncomfortable.

Charlestown Regatta in August is a fun-filled week of land- and water-based shenanigans, with a good dose of community spirit. At other times rainy-day diversion is provided by the **Shipwreck & Heritage Centre**, an entertaining maritime museum with an attached café.

Charleston makes a good base for extended hikes along the coastal footpath, and for trips further afield. **Porthpean**, to the south-west, is regarded as St Austell's town beach and is a local favourite, with great stretches of rocks and pools at low tide. The cliff edge crumbles and falls here on a regular basis, so heed the warning signs.

St Austell Brewery
Trevarthian Road, St Austell (01726 66022/ www.staustellbrewery.co.uk). **Open** *Guided tours* 11am, 2.30pm Mon-Fri. **Admission** (over-8s only) £4; £3 concessions. **Credit** MC, V.

Shipwreck & Heritage Centre
Quay Road, Charlestown (01726 69897/ www.shipwreckcharlestown.com). 10am-5.30pm daily. Closed Nov-Feb. **Admission** £4.45, £2.50-£3.45 concessions; free under-10s. **Credit** MC, V.

Square Sail Shipyard
Charlestown Harbour (01726 70241/67526). **Open** *Easter-Oct* 11am-5pm daily. Closed Nov-Mar. **Admission** £3; £2 concessions. **No credit cards**.

Wheal Martyn China Clay Museum
Carthew, St Austell (01726 850362). **Open** *Mar-Oct* 10am-6pm daily. *Nov-Feb* 10am-4pm Wed-Sun. **Admission** £5; £3 concessions. **Credit** MC, V.

Activities

Golf
Golfers have the choice of three 18-hole courses in the area: **St Austell** (Tregongeeves, 01726 74756), **Carlyon Bay** (Sea Road, 01726 814228), and **Porthpean** (Porthpean Road, 01726 64613). The last of these has the cheapest green fees (£14 per round).

Where to eat, drink & stay

St Austell itself is far from foodie heaven, although the **Thin End** (41A Fore Street, 01726 75805, main courses £1.50-£8.50) is a local favourite for generous sandwiches and gorgeous cakes.

For a better eating and drinking experience, head out of town to the excellent **Polgooth Inn** (Ricketts Lane, Polgooth, 01726 74089,

main courses £5-£16) or to the whitewashed **Rashleigh Inn** at Polkerris (near Par, 01726 813991, main courses £5-£15). Known locally as the 'Inn on the Beach', the latter is idyllically sited only feet from the sand and, in summer, makes a perfect (if absurdly busy) spot for a large gin and tonic.

Serious diners should head for **Boscundle Manor** (Tregrehan, St Austell, 01726 813557, www.boscundlemanor.co.uk, closed Jan-mid Feb, set menu £30, double B&B £130-£180), a gorgeous pink granite country house hotel with indoor and outdoor pools. Impeccably fresh local produce is served in the formal dining room here. On the coast, the grand **Carlyon Bay Hotel** (Sea Road, Carlyon Bay, 01726 811001, www.carlyonbay.com, set menu £28, double B&B £164-£258) is an ultra-exclusive resort with more facilities than you can shake a stick at – including a helipad. The restaurant is a very swish jacket-and-tie affair, with bay views and wonderful food.

In Charlestown, the **Pier House Hotel** (Charlestown Road, 01726 67955, www.pier househotel.com, main courses £8.95-£19.70, double B&B £80-£95), right on the front, has sea views, and also serves splendid seafood (the lobster is especially good). If a cream tea appeals, try the **T'Gallant Guest House** (6 Charlestown Road, 01726 70203, closed late Dec, double B&B £45-£48), which also does light lunches and reasonably priced B&B. Inland, **Eastern Promise** (1 Moor View, Grampound, 01726 883033, main dishes £6.20-£10) serves surprisingly good Chinese cuisine in a tiny dining room.

Resources

Hospital
St Austell *Community Hospital, Porthpean Road (01726 291100).*

Internet
St Austell *Leisure Drome Cyber Café, 2 Biddicks Court (01726 67398).* **Open** 9.30am-5pm daily.

Police station
St Austell *1 Palace Road (0870 577 7444).*

Post offices
Charlestown *Village Store, 79 Charlestown Road (01726 68877).* **Open** 9am-1pm, 2-5.30pm Mon, Tue, Thur, Fri; 9am-1pm Wed, Sat.
St Austell *10 High Cross Street (08457 223344).* **Open** 9am-5.30pm Mon-Fri; 9am-12.30pm Sat.

Tourist information
St Austell *Tourist Information Centre, Southbourne Road (01726 879500/www.cornish-riviera.co.uk).* **Open** *Easter-Oct* 9am-6pm daily. *Nov-Mar* 9am-5pm Mon-Sat.

Cornwall

Eden Project

If anything has put Cornwall back on the tourist map in recent years it is the construction, at the long worked-out Bodelva clay pit, of the astoundingly successful Eden Project.

From conception (back in 1994) to realisation (ongoing), the driving force behind the project has been Tim Smit, fresh from successfully resurrecting the Lost Gardens of Heligan (*see p235*). His vision for Eden was to communicate to the general public the importance of plants to the future of mankind. The undertaking required a vast site and the development of unique giant greenhouses, known as biomes, that could recreate the earth's different climatic zones. Smit's unfazed enthusiasm in the face of huge logistical problems, together with the dedication of the team he built around him, has brought to life a monster success story that has outgrown everyone's expectations.

Starting at the visitors' centre on the lip of the crater, visitors descend into the pit for a first sight of the gigantic geodesic domes. Crouched against a south-facing wall, the vast unsupported span of the **Humid Tropics Biome** – all breathless jungle and crashing waterfall – houses habitats ranging from Amazonia through West Africa and Malaysia to Oceania, with bananas, rubber, cocoa, coffee, teak and mahogany. To get an idea of the scale of the world's largest greenhouse, consider that it is the height of 11 double-decker buses and could contain the Tower of London.

The smaller, slower-growing **Warm Temperate Biome** is almost apologetic by comparison. It contains plant species from South Africa, California and the Mediterranean, while outside in the 'roofless biome' of the temperate regions the mild Cornish climate allows sunflowers, hemp, tea and native species to thrive. Inventively planted terraces climb energetically skywards up the edge of the pit, past quirky sculptures and ranks of fluttering prayer-flags.

The message, forcefully conveyed throughout the site, is of the on-going symbiotic relationship between man and the environment. If this all sounds a little earnest, the reality is a lot more fun – the Eden Project gets its message across with style and imagination.

Despite the resounding praise the project has already received, the work doesn't end there. In addition to a varied programme of events – including talks, workshops and summer performances in the open-air arena – plans are under way for the construction of a semi-arid biome and education facilities, and for the creation of the Eden Foundation, which aims to 'fuse science and art, technology and communication'.

PRACTICALITIES

Allow at least half a day to do the Eden Project justice. A visit to this predominantly open site can take hours and is best made in dry weather. It's also worth avoiding the middle of the day and bank holidays, when traffic queues lasting several hours are commonplace. Sometimes the sheer volume of visitors means that the site is shut to prevent overcrowding. And remember – this is a work in progress, so don't expect everything to be in bloom when you visit. Guided tours of the site run throughout the day but should be booked in advance.

Eden is signposted from the A30, the A390 and the A391, and is also on the National Cycle Network. The nearest railway station is at St Austell and there are daily buses to Eden from St Austell and Newquay. You can now purchase a ticket to Eden from any railway station in the UK, covering your entrance fee and a bus transfer service to and from the project.

Eden Project

Bodelva, nr St Austell (01726 811911/ www.edenproject.com). **Open** *Apr-Oct* 9am-6pm daily. *Nov-Mar* 10am-4.30pm daily. **Admission** £10; £4-£7.50 concessions; free under-5s. **Credit** MC, V.

Cornwall

It's a shame about **Mevagissey**. This honest working port seems to have sold out for the quick thrill and the easy buck. The narrow streets and cobbled alleyways, little changed since Napoleonic times, are undeniably charming but many of them have been taken over by a depressing mess of tacky shops brazenly targeting holiday souvenir-hunters. The harbour – built in the 15th century and enlarged in the 18th century – still has some dignity, but the best way to see the village in the summer is from the sea.

Alternatively, escape to the **Mevagissey Museum**, which gives a comprehensive historical overview of the town and its inseparable themes of fishing and smuggling. The museum is housed in an 18th-century boathouse that was originally used for the construction and repair of smuggling boats, that were specially designed to outrun the customs men (*see p12* **Bootylicious**).

Polstreath beach, a lovely stretch of sand, lies below the cliffs on the north edge of town, accessible only by 200 precarious-looking steps, but the main beach in the area is at **Pentewan**, to the north. Approached via a vertiginous hill, the far left-hand side of the beach is public domain, but the lion's share belongs to the long-established Pentewan Sands Caravan Park. The village is the start of the **Pentewan Valley Cycle Trail**, an off-road cycle track that winds through a wooded river valley for two and a half miles towards St Austell.

Further north are the **Watering Lane Nurseries**, where plants destined for the Eden Project are grown. Head east to reach the hamlet of **Trenarren**, located on the west side of Black Head in the dip of a steep valley. The hamlet is now a mere scatter of cottages still owned for the most part by the Hext family, but the broad headland is a perfect place for a picnic, with a grand view of the bay. Follow the steep road down through the village to **Hallane**, a magical little beach (at low tide)

Coastal walk Par to Polridmouth

Length 3 miles (4.8km).
Time 2hrs 30mins (including a stop for lunch).
Difficulty moderate. Do not attempt the coast path after prolonged rainfall, when wet mud can make the cliff edges hazardous.

The path starts at **Par Sands**, to the left of the car park, over a small bridge. It's easy to miss but worth finding in order to avoid an undignified scramble up the rocks.

Narrow in places, this first stretch (45mins) runs along the low cliff above Par Sands, continuing through pastureland before degenerating into a rather steep scramble down into **Polkerris**, emerging behind the **Rashleigh Inn** (*see p232*). Plan to leave Par Sands at around noon so that you arrive at the inn in time for a light lunch.

Leaving Polkerris, the sign for the footpath points vaguely in the direction of the beach and then loses interest; you should make a sharp left turn before reaching the sand to lead you to where the path climbs up sharply through a pretty wood on to the **Gribbin**. This is the steepest section of the walk by far, but the views from the top, across the whole of St Austell Bay, make it worthwhile: the western boundary of the bay is marked by distant Black Head, under which sits the inaccessible house and harbour at Rope Hawne; the beaches of

Silvermine and King Joey lead round to Porthpean, and on to private Duporth, followed by Charlestown's sheltering harbour and the great swathe of Crinnis, leading in turn to Spit Beach and the industrial excess of Par.

It's an easy stroll from now on, accompanied by butterflies and the scent of honeysuckle in season. Above the slate cliffs of the Gribbin hunting kestrels sometimes ride the wind, while below cormorants spread their wings to catch the sun. You may also see a lone fisherman trying his luck off the rocks. Looking back from here, about a mile out of Polkerris, should give you a sight of **Menabilly**, the home of Daphne du Maurier (*see p229* **Local heroes**). Finally, from the candy-striped day mark on the headland, it is a blissful downhill walk to reach **Polridmouth**, with its lake-backed beach.

To avoid backtracking, which can be boring however inspiring the scenery, you could start by taking two cars to the finish point at Polridmouth, leaving one as a guaranteed ride home. There's a car park in the field above Menabilly Barton Farm, ten minutes' walk up a track from Polridmouth beach; you'll also find an honesty milk churn for the 40p parking fee.

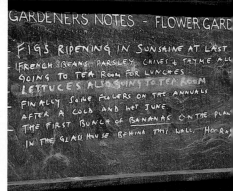

Find plenty of green-fingered delights in the **Lost Gardens of Heligan**.

with a waterfall and a lone holiday let. Opposite the car park, barely visible behind its high granite wall, is the house where local-boy-turned-eminent-historian AL Rowse lived until his death in 1993.

The chief attraction in this area, though, lies just two miles west of Mevagissey on the B3273. The award-winning **Lost Gardens of Heligan** were originally part of a historic estate owned by the Squires Tremayne but fell into decline in the early 1800s and lay neglected for nearly two centuries. They were rescued from complete obliteration in the mid 1990s, when Tim Smit (later the brains behind the Eden Project) and John Nelson set about restoring the gardens as a tribute to their original creators, and as an inclusive attraction for the public to enjoy. This is a stunningly conceived project that not only gives a sense of the drive and dedication of the great 18th- and 19th-century plant-hunters, but also conveys a wider message of conservation and ecological sustainability through a diversity of habitats. There are exhilarating jungle boardwalks, tranquil woodland hikes and, at the heart of the project, the garden itself – not just a showpiece but a busy, productive enterprise. Guided tours of the gardens are conducted twice a day in summer.

While in the area, it's worth popping over to **Polmassick Vineyard**, just two miles away, near St Ewe. Planted in 1978, this tiny, idyllic vineyard produced its first commercial crop in 1993 and now provides a range of good white and rosé estate-bottled wines. Take a glass on the pretty canopied terrace before strolling around the vineyard. You can snack here, but evening meals are by appointment only.

Heading south from Mevagissey, you'll find a curiously suburban but safe stretch of sandy beach at **Gorran Haven**, but for a little more seclusion with a bit more effort try **Vault** beach to the south, accessed from a National Trust

car park at the top of Lamledra Hill. It's a good ten-minute walk down the cliff to the beach, but your reward is a stunning stretch of rarely crowded sand. (Note that an unwritten rule seems to group naturists at the far end.)

Dramatic **Dodman Point** marks the eastern extreme of **Veryan Bay**, a wide arc of largely unexploited coastline that stretches for five miles as far as Nare Head. Beaches around the bay include delightfully quiet **Hemmick** and nearby **Porthluney Cove**, backed by the spectacular fantasy-Gothic **Caerhays Castle**. Opening times to the castle are very limited, but the gardens, which keep longer hours, are well worth a look, with acres of glorious exotica.

Others gardens worth visiting near Mevagissey include **Trewithen**, just off the A390 between St Austell and Truro, and the excellent **Probus Gardens**, a little further down the road. Trewithen is a grand Georgian estate with 28-acre gardens, which – like Caerhays and Heligan – owes much of its glory to the great plant-hunters of the 19th century. In contrast, the Probus gardens were established 30 years ago as a testing ground for horticultural practices and a source of information for local gardeners. They host regular art and craft exhibitions, plus horticultural courses and plant surgeries.

Caerhays Castle

Gorran, nr St Austell (01872 501310/ www.caerhays.co.uk). **Open** *Castle* mid Mar-early May 1-4pm Mon-Fri. *Gardens* Mar-June 10am-4.30pm daily. Closed July-Feb. **Admission** *Gardens only* £4.50; £2 concessions; free under-16s. *Castle & gardens* £8; £3.50 concessions; free under-16s. *Guided tour* £4.50. **Credit** MV, V.

Lost Gardens of Heligan

Pentewan, St Austell (01726 845100/ www.heligan.com). **Open** *Oct-Mar* 10am-3.30pm daily. *Apr-Sept* 10am-4.30pm daily. **Admission** £6; £3-£5.50 concessions. *Guided tours* £1.50. **Credit** MC, V.

Mevagissey Museum

East Wharf, Inner Harbour, Mevagissey (01726 843568). **Open** Easter-Sept 11am-5pm daily. Closed Oct-Mar. **Admission** £1; 50p concessions. **No credit cards.**

Polmassick Vineyard

Polmassick, St Ewe (01726 842239). **Open** May-Sept 11am-5pm daily. **Admission** 50p; free under 16s. **No credit cards.**

Probus Gardens

Probus (01726 882597/www.probusgardens.org.uk). **Open** Mar-Oct 10am-5pm. Closed Nov-Feb. **Admission** £4; £3 concessions; free under-16s. **Credit** MC, V.

Trewithen Gardens

Grampound Road, nr Truro (01726 883647/ www.trewithengardens.co.uk). **Open** Mar, June-Sept 10am-4.30pm Mon-Sat. Apr, May 10am-4.30pm daily. **Admission** £4.25; £4 concessions; free under-15s. **Credit** MC, V.

Activities

Fishing

Sea-fishing trips, ranging from spinning for mackerel with a handline to deep-sea expeditions, are touted on blackboards along the harbour wall. To charter a boat in advance, contact **Mevagissey Shark & Angling Centre** (West Quay, 01726 843430).

Where to eat, drink & stay

Mevagissey has a number of very good fish restaurants: try **Haven Restaurant** (16 Fore Street, 01726 844888, main courses from £12), **Salamander** (4 Tregony Hill, 01726 842254, main courses £9.50-£14.75) and the Portuguese-owned **Alvorado** (2 Polkirt Hill, 01726 842055, closed mid Dec-Jan, main courses £11.50-£15).

Friendly, family-run accommodation is provided by the **Spa Hotel** (Polkirt Hill, Mevagissey, 01726 842244, www.spahotel. freeserve.co.uk, double B&B £35) and the **Headlands Hotel** (Polkirt Hill, Mevagissey, 01726 843453, closed Dec & Jan, double B&B £62-£68), while the **Trevalsa Court Hotel** (Polstreath Hill, Mevagissey, 01726 842468, closed Dec-Feb, double B&B £74-£150) has an excellent restaurant (also open to non-residents, set dinner £23).

North up the coast, seriously good eating can be enjoyed at the **Old School House** (West End, Pentewan, 01726 842474, closed Jan, phone for details), where the modern English cooking focuses on seafood, while south of town, the **Rising Sun Inn** (Portmellon Cove, 01726 843235, closed Nov-Feb, main courses £9.95-£19.95) is just across the road from the beach and offers amazing ocean views.

Resources

Internet

Tele Cottage 14 Church Street, Mevagissey (01726 842266). **Open** 9am-5pm Mon-Sat; 9am-12.30pm Sat.

Post office

Mevagissey Post Office 3 St George's Square, Mevagissey (01726 843488). **Open** 9am-5.30pm Mon-Fri; 9am-12.30pm Sat.

Tourist information

Mevagissey Tourist Information Centre St George's Square, Mevagissey (01726 844857/ www.mevagissey-cornwall.co.uk). **Open** Easter-Oct 10am-5pm Mon-Fri; 11am-5pm Sat, Sun. Nov-Mar 11am-3pm Mon-Fri.

Truro

Located at the head of the Carrick Roads estuary, the 'capital' of Cornwall has an air of cultural and financial self-sufficiency that sets it somewhat apart from the rest of the county. As a comforting microcosm of urban life, Truro tends to attract those big-city refugees wishing tentatively to live the aga-saga without getting their feet muddy.

Approaching the outskirts of Truro on the A390 from St Austell, the tone is set by **Tresillian**, a well-heeled suburban stretch overlooking the tidal river. Here, in 1646, at

Probus Gardens put on a show. See p235.

the existing thatch-roofed Wheel Inn, Sir Ralph Hopton and his Royalists surrendered to Sir Thomas Fairfax, thereby putting an end to the Civil War in the west.

Truro, however, was historically and commercially significant long before the 17th century. Richard Lucy, then Chief Justice of England, first built a castle here in the 12th century on the current site of the admirably stark new **Courts of Justice** on Edward Street. Set between the rivers Truro, Kenwyn and Allen, Truro was soon a major port for the export of copper and tin, and in 1305 became a stannary town, one of only five in the county where the biannual testing of smelted tin could be carried out (see p14). Ultimately, though, the city lost much of its shipping trade to the more convenient deep-water harbour downriver at Falmouth.

The 18th and 19th centuries marked the city's real growth period, when prosperous landowners and mining entrepreneurs chose to build their grand townhouses in 'the London of Cornwall', resulting in much of the city's Georgian architecture, including the former **Assembly Rooms** on High Cross. Truro was granted city status by Queen Victoria in 1877 and the triple-spired **cathedral** was finally completed in 1910.

Sprouting up from the surrounding houses at the centre of town, this Gothic revival building remains Truro's most obvious landmark. It was the first new-build cathedral in England since Salisbury cathedral in 1220 and was built on the site of a 16th-century parish church, which was partly incorporated into the new structure. The new cathedral had somehow to be squeezed in among the city's existing buildings, forcing the architect, John Loughborough Pearson, to build a clearly visible bend into the nave.

As well as some of the world's finest Victorian stained glass, look out for the heavily carved Bishop's throne, the font and the Father Willis organ, set in its unusual stone vaulted chamber. Works of art include Penwith artist John Miller's huge canvas *Cornubia – Land of the Saints* and the late 20th-century *Calvary* by Craigie Aitchison.

Outside the cathedral, the cobbled square and pedestrianised Pydar Street give this part of the town a bustling, almost medieval air, heightened by the presence of 'kennels' or water channels in many of the older lanes. Behind the war memorial in Boscawen Street is the **Coinage Hall**, a Victorian structure on the site of the original 14th-century building. The stannary court met outside the hall to referee disputes between the tinners. It now houses a pizza restaurant and tea shop.

Nearby, the Victorian City Hall houses the impressive **Hall for Cornwall** (Back Quay, 01872 262466, www.hallforcornwall.co.uk), the brainchild of entrepreneur Chris Warner. Having worked with Sam Wanamaker on the rebuilding of London's Globe Theatre, Warner campaigned vigorously during the 1990s for the establishment of a venue west of Plymouth in which to stage commercial productions of any size. There is little in City Hall's grand Italianate façade to hint at its brave new interior, but inside you'll find a new 950-seat auditorium, plus a coffee shop, bars and a restaurant. Entertainment here ranges from Abba singalongs to Brecht/Weil operas. City Hall also hosts frequent flea and craft markets, and, Tardis-like, still has room for council offices, the Mayor's Parlour and the Tourist Information Centre (see p238).

There is hardly a trace now of the working quays that once interfaced the town with its rivers, but a rather grand new piazza, known as Lemon Quay Square, fills the gap in front of City Hall. On a sunny day it's packed with insouciant crowds and café tables, lending the centre a distinctly continental vibe.

Round the corner on **Lemon Street** Georgian houses rise elegantly out of the city towards the pretty cupola of **St John's Church**. There's a memorial here to the Truro-born explorers Richard and John Lander, who were the first Europeans to canoe down the River Niger to the sea. The real architectural gem, though, is exquisite **Walsingham Place**, just off Victoria Square, a complete Georgian terrace trapped in its own time-warp in the heart of the city. At No.14 is the office for the **Kneehigh Theatre Company** (01872 223159, www.kneehigh.co.uk), an adventurous and increasingly acclaimed Cornish drama group that performs experimental new works in unusual places: down quarries, in disused factories, barns and open fields. Seize any opportunity to get hold of tickets for one of the performances.

On the other side of Victoria Square, River Street is where you'll find the **Royal Cornwall Museum**, the best exhibition space in the county and a must-visit for anyone interested in Cornwall's history and culture. Besides a permanent display on the history of Cornwall from the Stone Age to the present, the museum has an excellent selection of paintings by the Newlyn School of artists (see p26), including the recently acquired *China Clay Pit, Leswidden* by Harold Harvey.

Would-be geologists will appreciate the renowned 18th-century collection of rare minerals, the most important part of which was put together by Phillip Rashleigh

Cornwall

(1729-1811) of Menabilly, while budding artists can drool over the old master drawings in the De Pass Gallery. Attached to the museum is the Courtney Library, which specialises in local history resources, and a popular coffee shop.

Royal Cornwall Museum
River Street (01872 272205/www.royalcornwall museum.org.uk). **Open** 10am-5pm Mon-Sat. **Admission** £4; £2.50 concessions. **No credit cards.**

Truro Cathedral
14 St Mary Street (01872 276782/www.truro cathedral.org.uk). **Open** 8.30am-6pm daily. **Admission** free; suggested donation £3. **Credit** *Shop* MC, V.

Where to eat, drink & stay

Catering to the city's well-heeled and discerning diners, **Bustopher Jones** (62 Lemon Street, 01872 279029, main courses £4.95-£13.50) is a popular, self-styled bistro-wine bar, with a good Mediterranean-biased menu. It's currently holding its own against stiff competition from nearby newcomer **Café Citron** (76 Lemon Street, 01872 274144, main courses £6-£15), a smart café-bar with an ambitious international menu. **Baba** (32 Lemon Street, 01872 26269, main courses £5.50-£15) has a well-deserved reputation for imaginative Indian cuisine, and for good Italian food the supremely trendy **Piero's Ristorante** (Kenwyn Street, 01872 222279, main courses £5.60-£13.80) is usually booked to the hilt. The friendly **Numberten** (10 Kenwyn Street, 01872 272363, main courses £9.50-£12.80) also has a deliciously tasty, reasonably priced menu.

Good town-centre pubs include the **Old Ale House** (7 Quay Street, 01872 271122, main courses £2.70-£6.25), which serves hand-pumped beers (no spirits) and good grub, though live music nights can be very busy. The **Wig and Pen** (Francis Street, Truro 01872 273028, main courses £5.50-£9.95) is also a decent bet with a quiet, comfortable atmosphere. Worth leaving town for is the **Heron Inn** at Malpas (01872 272773), idyllically fronting on to the River Fal. The food can be exceptional here, though high-season demand means there's little chance of dawdling over a meal.

Truro's accommodation list no way lives up to its dining options, so you're far better staying somewhere on the coast and exploring the town on a day trip. Among the limited choices is **Alverton Manor** (Tregolls Road, 01872 276633, www.alvertonmanor. demon.co.uk, main courses £15, double B&B £115-£165), a sturdy 19th-century manor

house with all the trimmings. The grounds of the hotel are lovely and it's only a 15-minute walk from the town centre.

Resources

Hospital
Duchy Hospital *Penventinnie Lane, Treliske, Truro (01872 226100).*

Internet
Internet Connection *5 Quay Mews, Truro (01872 264567).* **Open** 10am-6pm Mon-Fri.

Police station
Tregolls Road, Truro (0870 577 7444).

Post office
High Cross, Truro (08457 223344). **Open** 9am-5.30pm Mon-Sat.

Tourist information
Truro Tourist Information Centre *Municipal Buildings, Boscawen Street, Truro (01872 274555/ www.truro.gov.uk).* **Open** *Apr, May, Sept, Oct* 9am-5.30pm Mon-Fri; 9am-1pm Sat. *June-Aug* 9am-5.30pm Mon-Sat. *Nov-Mar* 9am-5pm Mon-Fri.

The Roseland Peninsula

Bounded to the west by the many-fingered Carrick Roads estuary and to the east by the bays of Veryan and Gerrans is the Roseland Peninsula (named after the Cornish word 'ros', meaning promontory). With none of the edginess of more economically depressed areas to the north and west, the peninsula has long been colonised by the wealthy and the retired, This is holidayland with a soft centre: a place where glorious countryside gives way to magnificent coastal views at every turn.

It's a straight run down the A3078 from Tregony to **St Mawes**, at the southern end of the peninsula. On a headland tucked neatly inside the Fal estuary, this charming spot has been a swanky holiday destination since fashionable Edwardians promenaded the waterfront. Today it remains a boating enthusiast's dream, with miles of inland waterways to explore.

Along with Pendennis Castle at Falmouth (*see p241*), the trefoil-shaped **St Mawes Castle** was built under Henry VIII as a defence against the threat of French and Spanish invasion, but saw no action until the Civil War, when the castle was quickly surrendered to Parliamentarian forces – hence its current pristine state. Though sturdily functional, the castle is quite elaborately embellished with gargoyles and carved detail, and survives as one of the most complete of Henry VIII's chain forts. The low profile and round contours of the massively thick-walled building would have made it a difficult and dangerous target for enemy ships; in Tudor times even the roof was used as a gun platform with the small domed turret acting as a lookout point. Guided tours of areas of the castle usually closed to visitors take place on Wednesday afternoons in June and September.

In summer, ferries cross the Percuil river from St Mawes harbour to the picturesque village of **St Anthony-in-Roseland**, which has an attractive 13th-century church. At the very south-western tip of the peninsula, strategically important **St Anthony's Head** is marked by a lighthouse and a number of abandoned fortifications, including a World War II battery.

Rounding the headland, the south coast is a haven for seabirds, which nest among its rocky outcrops. There are also glorious sandy beaches around **Gerrans Bay**, particularly at Carne and Pendower. Backed by dunes, these stretches of sand are beautifully clean and have stunning views of Nare Head to the east and Greeb Point to the west. A little way inland the tree-covered mound of **Carne Beacon** is one of the largest Bronze Age barrows in the whole country.

Just to the north, faintly twee **Veryan** is defined by its curious crucifix-topped roundhouses, which were built in the 19th century by a local minister for his five daughters. The houses were constructed without corners so that the devil would have nowhere to hide.

On the eastern side of Nare Head, the tiny, atmospheric harbour at **Portloe** is squeezed into a steep, rocky ravine. The village supports a small fishing fleet and an excellent hotel, but many of its cottages have been snapped up by aspirant second-homers and are empty during the winter.

An easy three-mile (4.8-kilometre) walk north from St Mawes along the estuary, meanwhile, leads to tiny creekside **St Just-in-Roseland**, where the 13th-century church of St Just is exquisitely upstaged by the subtropical landscaping of its steep, lushly planted churchyard, eulogised by Betjeman as being 'to many people the most beautiful on earth'.

Further north, the B3289 arrives at **King Harry Ferry** – the Fal's only vehicular crossing point (*see p242*) – from where it's a short walk to the 500-year-old **Smugglers Cottage** (01872 580309) near Tolverne. Requisitioned by the Admiralty in the build-up to the D-Day landings, the cottage is now the departure point for passenger ferries to Falmouth and Truro (*see p242*) and serves a mean cream tea.

St Mawes Castle

St Mawes (01326 270526). **Open** *Apr-Sept* 10am-6pm daily. *Oct* 10am-5pm daily. *Nov-Mar* 10am-1pm, 2-4pm Wed-Sun. **Admission** £3; £1.60-£2.40 concessions. **Credit** MC, V.

Activities

Sailing

Classic Sailing (Mermaids, St Mawes, 01326 270027) offers RYA courses and sailing holidays aboard traditional yachts and tall ships.

Where to eat, drink & stay

There is no shortage of accommodation at the top end of the market in this area. St Mawes boasts the internationally acclaimed **Hotel Tresanton** (St Mawes, 01326 270055, www.tresanton.com, double B&B £195-£265), *le dernier cri* in the sort of studied simplicity that comes very, very expensive. Designer Olga Polizzi's cleverly pitched homage to understated chic makes this an oasis of luxury for A-listers. Dinner on the terrace offers a more affordable slice of the dream for non-residents (set menu £33). Putting up some pretty stiff opposition is the 17th-century **Lugger Hotel** at Portloe (01872 501322, www.luggerhotel.com, set menu £35, double B&B £80-£120 per

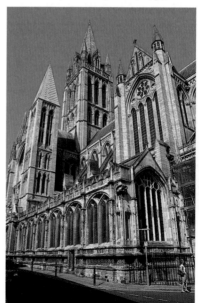

Truro Cathedral. *See p237.*

person). Sophisticated yet far from snooty, this haven of good taste has the sea on its doorstep and local artwork on its walls. Top-notch contemporary dishes, including hard-to-beat fresh seafood, are immaculately served in the beautiful restaurant.

There's also the **Nare Hotel** (Carne Beach, Veryan-in-Roseland, 01872 501111) in a fabulous position overlooking Gerrans Bay, which goes full-throttle for the English country house experience and pulls it off in some style. Its nautically themed Quarterdeck Restaurant serves stunningly presented dishes, with an emphasis on seafood.

Thankfully, travellers on a budget have choices, too: the **Rising Sun Hotel** at St Mawes (The Square, 01326 270233, set menu £29) serves up superior pub grub, while **Broom Parc** (Veryan, 01872 501803, double B&B £25-£35 per person) offers very reasonable B&B in a stunning cliff-top setting. (The house was used as a location for TV drama *The Camomile Lawn*.) A rural option is **Bohurrow Farmhouse** (Bohortha, St Anthony-in-Roseland, Portscatho, 01872 580966, double B&B £23.50 per person) where breakfast comes with sea views.

Resources

Tourist information

Roseland Visitor Centre *Millenium Rooms, St Mawes (01326 270440/www.roseland.org.uk).* **Open** *Mar-Oct* 10am-5pm daily. *Nov-Feb* phone for details.

Falmouth & around

Formed from the Fal and numerous tributary rivers, the Carrick Roads estuary is one of Britain's finest deep-water anchorages. Its name comes from the Cornish word 'carrek', meaning rock, and refers to Black Rock, a significant shipping hazard at the mouth of the estuary.

Henry Tudor recognised the importance of protecting this deep incursion into the heart of the peninsula, and in 1540 built Pendennis Castle high on a promontory guarding the entrance to the estuary. However, it was not until the late 16th century that **Falmouth** town began to grow up around the fishing harbour of Falmouth Haven. Until then ships had to run upriver to anchor at Penryn, Tresillian or Truro.

Following the Civil War Falmouth's prestige was advanced by the Killigrew family, local merchants who masterminded the construction of the deep-water harbour. Further prosperity came in 1688, when Falmouth became a Packet Station with fast brigantines carrying mail and bullion from Custom House Quay to the

Mediterranean and the colonies. From 1860 the docks were developed for ship-building and repair, still an important part of the town's industry, although in the 20th century the focus of the town shifted markedly towards tourism. More recently, Falmouth has developed a thriving arts scene, partly thanks to the presence of the College of Art, which also gives the town a lively student vibe.

Falmouth's topography can be confusing, as there are two distinct waterfronts – one on the river and one on the sea. The river frontage is the oldest part of town and includes the main shopping street, which runs from **Prince of Wales Pier** (where the ferry departs for St Mawes) to **Custom House Quay**, changing name three times on the way and affording tantalising glimpses of the river between the buildings. Most points of interest in the town are along this stretch.

Just off the High Street is the Moor, the old town's main square. The bus station is here, along with **Falmouth Art Gallery** (01326 313863, www.falmouthartgallery.com), which houses a permanent collection of works by the likes of Edward Burne-Jones and Alfred Munnings, in addition to exhibitions of contemporary art. If you're interested in exploring more of the local art scene, visit the **Falmouth Arts Centre** (24 Church Street, 01326 317090). Established in 1835 as the town's main venue for theatre productions, concerts and film screenings, it also hosts exhibitions in its three art galleries, including work by students from **Falmouth College of Art**. There are numerous other private galleries scattered around town.

From the Moor, climb **Jacob's Ladder**, a flight of 111 steps, for a view of the old town and the harbour. Nearby is Falmouth's parish church dedicated to **King Charles the Martyr** in 1662 in demonstration of the town's Royalist sympathies.

Further along Arwenack Street is pretty **Custom House Quay**, which was built in the 1670s by the Killigrew family and instrumental in Falmouth's subsequent development. (The family's mansion, **Arwenack House**, is further down the street towards the docks.)

The opening of the much-vaunted **National Maritime Museum Cornwall** finally took place at the end of 2002. This awesome new attraction occupies a brand new site on the harbour and incorporates 12 galleries, each focusing on a different aspect of maritime life, with plenty of entertaining human interest stories instead of the usual dry facts and figures. At the heart of the exhibition space is a vast three-storey hall, where boats of all shapes and sizes hang suspended. Visitors can explore the

Cornwall

gallery by means of walkways and touch-screens. Other highlights include the Lookout, a 95-foot (29-metre) observation tower offering panoramic views of the town and estuary. At its foot, the unique Tidal Zone sits on the sea bed with two large windows looking directly out into the submarine world of Falmouth harbour. High-tech gadgetry is put to best use throughout the museum: impressive audio-visual displays, state-of-the-art navigational equipment, interactive exhibits, a boat-building workshop and even simulated winds on the mini boating lake all help to bring the seafaring world to life in astonishing and entertaining detail.

All in all, it's put Falmouth's other attraction firmly in the shade. **Pendennis Castle** lies east of the town centre at the mouth of the estuary. It's a more workaday contemporary of the castle at St Mawes (*see p238*), but its position makes for a much more memorable visit. Pendennis is also far larger, having been expanded by Elizabeth I at the end of the 16th century. During the Civil War, the young Prince Charles (later Charles II) sheltered here before escaping to the Continent, narrowly avoiding a siege of the castle by Parliamentary forces. The Keep houses displays of cannons and artillery, and battle re-enactments take place on the gun deck in summer.

In contrast to the everyday bustle of the old town, Falmouth's seafront is a 'real' holiday resort. Plush hotels back on to the beaches of **Gyllyngase** and **Swanpool**, while a little further west, **Maenporth** retains some exclusivity, with less tourist paraphernalia and fine cliff walks.

No visit to Falmouth would be complete without a trip on the water. Inland the estuary breaks up into a myriad rivers and creeks that are perfect for lazy summertime exploration by boat. Facing Falmouth across the Penryn river, **Flushing** is named after the Dutch engineers from Flessinghe who first drained the area's marshland and built the seawall and quays. This suburb is dominated by the fine houses of wealthy packet captains who lived a life of fashionable excess.

Further north towards Truro you'll come to blissful and upmarket **Feock**, which offers easy access to the National Trust gardens at **Trelissick**. This riverside estate contains an extensive park and woodland, plus a sheltered garden featuring many delicate and exotic plants. The house is not open to the public, but there is a craft gallery, a shop, two restaurants and fine Georgian stable block on site. King Harry Ferry runs from here to the Roseland Peninsula (*see p242*).

Cornwall

St Mawes Castle survived the Civil War unscathed. *See p238.*

National Maritime Museum Cornwall

Discovery Quay, Falmouth, (01326 313388/ www.nmmc.co.uk) **Open** 10am-5pm daily. **Admission** £5.90; £3.90 concessions; £15.50 family. **Credit** MC, V.

Pendennis Castle

Castle Drive, Falmouth (01326 316594). **Open** *Apr-Oct* 10am-6pm daily. *Nov-Mar* 10am-4pm daily. **Admission** £4.20; £2.10-£3.50 concessions; free under-5s. **Credit** MC, V.

Trelissick Gardens

Feock, nr Truro (01872 862090/www.national trust.org.uk). **Open** *Estate* dawn-dusk daily. *Gardens* mid Feb-Oct 10.30am-5.30pm daily. **Admission** £4.60; £2.30 concessions; £11.50 family. **Credit** AmEx, MC, V.

Where to eat, drink & stay

Falmouth has plenty of good seafood restaurants. The tiny **Seafood Bar** (Quay Street, 01326 315129, closed mid Nov-mid Dec, main courses £13.50-£14.25) is a reliable spot with a good local reputation, while the award-winning **Three Mackerel** (Swanpool Beach, 01326 311886, main courses £9.95-£14.95) complements a stunning location with a lively clientele.

Alternatives include the über-trendy **Hunkydory** (46 Arwenack Street, 01326 212997, main courses £11.75-£16.95), which backs up friendly service with reasonably priced top-notch food, or there's **Steppes Restaurant** (57 Church Street, 01326 210353, closed early Jan, main courses £8.99-£13.99), which serves tasty, all-you-can-eat stir-fries.

The Flushing ferry will take you to the **Sticky Prawn** (Flushing Quay, Flushing, 01326 373734, phone for details), where a quayside setting provides the ideal backdrop for fresh ingredients, expertly cooked. Further afield, the **Pandora Inn** at Restronguet (Mylor Bridge, 01326 372678, main courses £6.75-£13.95) is located in a stunning 13th-century thatched building, and is one of the area's best-known pubs. It was once owned by Captain Edwards, who famously captured the *Bounty* mutineers then ran his ship aground on the Great Barrier Reef. Arrive at the Pandora by yacht for a bit of nautical credibility; it's an idyllic setting, especially in summer when you can eat on the jetty.

Seafront accommodation in the town includes the grand Victorian **Falmouth Hotel** (Castle Beach, 01326 312671, www.falmouthhotel.com, double £60-£70) and the **Membly Hall Hotel** (Cliff Road, 01326 312869, www.memblyhall hotel.co.uk, double B&B £52-£66). Harbourside, visitors can enjoy the discreet Georgian

elegance of the **Grove Hotel** (Grove Place, 01326 319577, www.thegrovehotel.net, double B&B £55).

Resources

Hospital

Falmouth Hospital *Trescobeas Road, Falmouth (01326 434700).*

Internet

Quench Juice Café *The Moor, Falmouth (01326 210294).* **Open** 9.30am-6.30pm Mon-Sat; 11am-4pm Sun.
Falmouth Library *Municipal Buildings, The Moor, Falmouth (01326 314901).* **Open** 9.30am-6pm Mon, Tue, Thur, Fri; 9.30am-4pm Sat.

Police station

Dracaena Avenue, Falmouth (0870 577 7444).

Post office

The Moor, Falmouth (08457 223344). **Open** 8.45am-5.30pm Mon, Tue; 9am-5.30pm Wed-Fri; 9am-12.30pm Sat.

Tourist information

Falmouth Tourist Information Centre *28 Killigrew Street, Falmouth (01326 312300).* **Open** *Apr-July* 9.30am-5.30pm Mon-Sat. *Aug, Sept* 9.30am-5.30pm Mon-Fri; 10am-2pm Sun. *Oct-Mar* 9.30am-4.30pm Mon-Fri; 10am-4pm Sat.

Getting there & around

By ferry

From Fowey, a car and passenger ferry runs throughout the day to Bodinnick (£1.80). There's also a regular passenger service to Polruan (70p) and a less-frequent service (weather permitting) to Mevagissey (www.mevagissey-ferries.co.uk, £6). Tickets are sold aboard or on the quay.

A passenger ferry departs from Truro quayside for Falmouth four times a day, and the King Harry Ferry (01872 862312, www.kingharryferry.co.uk) runs from Trelissick Gardens to the Roseland Peninsula. Regular passenger ferries (01872 580309, www.tolverneriverfal.co.uk, £3 per stage) ply the Carrick Roads estuary between Truro, Smugglers Cottage, Falmouth and St Mawes, and there's also a summer ferry (01326 313234) from St Mawes to St Anthony (£1.70 return).

By train

The mainline Plymouth–Penzance service stops at Lostwithiel, St Austell and Truro. A branchline runs from Truro to Falmouth. For further information contact **Wessex Trains** (www.wessextrains.co.uk).

By bus

First Western National (www.firstwestern national.co.uk) runs regular bus services from St Austell to Fowey, Mevagissey, Goran Haven and Truro. Onward buses from Truro serve Tregony, St Mawes and Falmouth.

From the Lizard to Land's End

Travel all the way to the tip of the country for golden sands, picturesque fishing villages, high-class seafood and a thriving art scene.

Going for the slow burn on **Porthminster Beach**. *See p259.*

The Lizard (from the Cornish 'lys ardh', or high point) and Land's End are the most southerly and the most westerly points on the UK mainland respectively. They are both wild, beautiful, ancient places dominated by granite and blessed with extraordinarily clear light. The coast path here offers spectacular walks that take in the imposing drama of the Penwith Peninsula, the unspoiled rawness of the Lizard Peninsula and a large quota of stunning beaches, including **Kynance Cove** and **Whitesand Bay**. Amid all this natural splendour, manmade highlights include the cliff-top, open-air **Minack Theatre** near Porthcurno and the fairy-tale vision of **St Michael's Mount** near Penzance.

Remote yet cultured, these western outposts have drawn scores of artists over the years, resulting in several high-quality galleries. Top of the list is the **Tate**, a high-profile visitor attraction that draws culture vultures

to the seaside town of St Ives. The region's increasingly excellent restaurants are also causing a stir, offering unexpectedly stylish settings for fresh fish and seafood from the fishing ports at **Newlyn** and **St Ives**.

To top it all, special events like **Flora Day** in Helston and the **Golowan Festival** in Penzance provide an extra incentive for people to travel that little bit further to west Cornwall.

Lizard Peninsula

Helston & around

The only town on the Lizard of any size is **Helston**, famous for its annual celebrations around 8 May, when the town is decorated with bluebells and gorse, and schoolchildren dress in white and wear garlands in their hair. Festivities include the theatrically based ritual the Hal-an-Tow, in which St Michael slays the devil and St George slays the dragon, and culminate with the processional 'Furry Dance', in which townsfolk dress up and dance in and out of the houses in a Christian echo of a possibly more robust pagan ritual.

Helston lost its role as a river port in the 13th century due to the silting up of the Cober estuary. However, it remained an important stannary and market town at the heart of one of Cornwall's key mining districts. Today it boasts several attractive buildings, many of them in Coinagehall Street (look out, too, for the 'kennels' – open streams running along the gutters). The Monument at the end of the street was built in 1834 in memory of Humphry Millet Grylls, a Helston banker and solicitor, who had helped to keep the local tin mine open, thus safeguarding 1,200 jobs.

Also on Coinagehall Street is the grand Victorian **Guildhall**, which houses the town hall and council chambers, with the ground-floor Corn Exchange used for craft markets and jumble sales. A farmers' market is held here every Monday (01736 365336).

At the back of the building in the old Butter Market is **Helston Folk Museum**, which displays an eclectic array of domestic artefacts and cottage industrial equipment of the 19th and 20th centuries, plus a cannon taken from the HMS *Anson*, which ran aground in 1807 on the Loe Bar at the head of the Cober estuary. The disaster prompted Helston man Henry Trengrouse (1772-1854), in sight of the wreck but helplessly shorebound, to devise his Rocket Apparatus and Bosun's Chair. Although this invention was ignored by successive British governments during Trengrouse's lifetime, it later evolved into the Breeches Buoy, a winch now used all over the world for rescuing people from the sea. Trengrouse's original apparatus is on display, along with his portrait in oils, in the museum, and there's a monument to him in the parish church of **St Michael**, in belated recognition of his great service to humanity.

A plaque on Wendron Street marks the birthplace of another famous son of the town, Bob Fitzsimmons (1862-1917), a bare-knuckle fighter who became heavyweight boxing champion of the world at the turn of the 19th century and whose name lives on in the busy **Fitzsimmons Arms** (36 Coinagehall Street, 01326 574897).

On the outskirts of Helston, **Flambards Village Theme Park** will not be everyone's cup of tea, but is nonetheless a good-value diversion from nature's bounty. Originally conceived as an aviation museum, it now

A calm day in the pretty fishing village of **Porthleven**. *See p245.*

boasts white-knuckle rides, an astoundingly authentic re-creation of Victorian England and an unsettling Britain in the Blitz exhibit, complete with sandbags and sirens. Close by, the Royal Navy Air Station at Culdrose hosts an Air Day (01326 552461) in July that proves hugely popular with aviation enthusiasts.

South-west of Helston woodland paths take you through the National Trust's Penrose Estate to **Loe Pool**, the largest freshwater lake in Cornwall, cut off from the sea by a shingle and sand bank, known as the Loe Bar. The lake is supposedly the mythic home of the Lady of the Lake and the final resting place of King Arthur's sword, Excalibur, although Dozmary Pool on Bodmin Moor also vies for this distinction.

On the coast, the prevailing winds whip straight into south-west-facing **Porthleven**, restricting its development into anything larger than a fishing village (although it has by no means escaped the inevitable suburban sprawl from Helston and RNAS Culdrose). Massive sea defences are evidence of the village's vulnerability to gale-driven winter waves, and entry into the harbour from the sea remains a perennially hazardous undertaking. Bathing off the attractive beach, especially near the Loe Bar, is dangerous due to freak waves and strong currents, although experienced surfers will relish the challenge (*see p253* **Surf check**).

At the eastern end of the beach, the peaceful atmosphere of **Gunwalloe**, with its farm, beach and precariously sited church, belies its long history of smuggling and shipwreck. The forbidding mass of 200-foot (61-metre) **Halzephron Cliff** (from the old Cornish 'als yfarn', meaning hell's cliff) has claimed many ships along this unforgiving coastline. The bodies of sailors washed ashore here were refused burial in hallowed ground, and until the early 18th century were unceremoniously dumped in a cliff-top pit. Enduring tales of buried treasure have led centuries of fortune-seekers to dive for the two tons of Spanish coins reputedly lying off Dollar Cove, and dig for the fabulous wealth of pirate John Avery buried, legend has it, in the Gunwalloe sands.

Inland a must-visit is beautiful **Godolphin House**, an exquisite part-Tudor, part-Stuart manor built by the powerful Godolphin family on the wealth of the surrounding mines. The second Earl of Godolphin also owned the famous Godolphin Barb horse, one of only three Arab stallions from which all British thoroughbreds are descended.

Although Godolphin House is undergoing extensive renovation, it remains a stunning evocation of the period, with mullioned windows, original Elizabethan stables and a glorious colonnade leading through the screen wall into a courtyard. Beyond, magical gardens are surrounded by pretty woodlands, and incorporate old carp ponds. The estate has been used as a location for many films and TV programmes including the popular BBC *Poldark* series.

For an insight into how the Goldophins made their money, visit **Poldark Mine**, north of Helston. The mine dates from 1725, making it one of the oldest complete mine workings open to the public in Europe. Relying on just man and animal power, it was a major source of employment for the local community until its closure in 1810. Fascinating subterranean guided tours (definitely not for the claustrophobic) detail the life and work of the miners, while the surrounding gardens display pieces of mining equipment, with attendant amusements for younger visitors.

Flambards Village Theme Park

Culdrose Manor, Helston (01326 573404/ www.flambards.co.uk). Open Apr-Oct 10am-6pm daily. Closed Nov-Mar. **Admission** £11.95; £5.75 concessions. **Credit** MC, V.

Godolphin House

Breage, nr Godolphin (01736 763194/762409). **Open** *Apr-Sept* 11am-5pm Tue-Fri; 2-5pm Sun. Closed Oct-Mar. **Admission** *House & gardens* £5. *Gardens only* £2. **Credit** MC, V.

Helston Folk Museum

Church Street, Helston (01326 564027/ www.helstonmuseum.org.uk). **Open** 10am-5pm Mon-Sat. **Admission** £2. **No credit cards.**

Poldark Mine

Wendron, nr Helston (01326 573173). **Open** *Easter-Oct* 10am-6pm daily; last tour 4pm. *Nov-Mar* phone for details. **Admission** free. *Mine tours* £5.75; £3.75 concessions; £15.50 family. **Credit** MC, V.

Activities

Boat trips

Fishing and sightseeing trips along the Lizard's coast are offered by **Porthleven Angling Centre** (Harbourside, Porthleven, 01326 561885) and by **Cornish Spirit** (Mullion, 01326 241556).

Cycling

Cycling is a great way to explore the predominantly flat landscape of the Lizard. Bikes can be hired in Helston from **Family Cycles** (7 Church Street, 01326 573719).

Where to eat, drink & stay

The thatched 15th-century **Blue Anchor Inn** (50 Coinagehall Street, Helston, 01326 562821, main courses £3.50-£7.50) is the oldest continuously operating brew-pub in the country

Cornwall

and notorious for the strength of its range of Spingo ales (the specials are particularly potent). Flagstoned floors and small, beamed rooms form a great setting for tasty pub food. Persuasive punters may also get a tour of the brewhouse and cellars. Another historic drinking hole is the 450-year-old **Angel Hotel** (16 Coinagehall Street, Helston, 01326 572701, main courses £5.50-£10.50, double B&B £60). It has an intriguing 40-foot (12-metre) well set into the floor of the main bar, and a medieval dining room, complete with minstrels' gallery. B&B guests may catch a glimpse of resident ghost 'Nellie'.

In Porthleven, try locals' favourite **Critchards** (Harbourside, 01326 562407, closed mid Dec, Jan, main courses £9.95-£15, double B&B £55-£65), a converted millhouse serving seafood with a pan-Asian twist. The **Halzephron Inn** (Gunwalloe, 01326 240406, main courses £5-£17, double B&B £39 per person) is another good coastal choice, combining cosy rooms and heart-warming food with the atmospheric surroundings of an old smugglers' haunt – a shaft at the back of the pub connects to an underground passage.

Resources

Police station
Godolphin Road, Helston (0870 577 7444).

Post office
8-30 Coinagehall Street, Helston (01326 572659). **Open** 9am-5.30pm Mon-Fri; 9am-12.30pm Sat.

Tourist information
Helston Tourist Office *79 Meneage Street, Helston (01326 565431/info@helstontic.demon. co.uk).* **Open** 10am-4pm Mon-Fri; 10am-1pm Sat.

The Lizard & around

Heading south from Helston, the peninsula takes on an altogether more untamed character. Underlying serpentine rock (a greenish magnesium silicate) is covered by a dour and dramatic sweep of heathland that is home to 15 of Britain's rarest plants, while on the coast, dramatic cliffs shelter unspoilt fishing villages and tempting sandy coves.

Goonhilly Downs (from the old Cornish *gun helghy*, meaning 'the hunting downs') at the heart of the peninsula are agriculturally barren, but have nonetheless grown an impressive crop of hardware. At Bonythorne the huge turbines of a windfarm do their bit to supplement the national grid, while further south is **Goonhilly Satellite Earth Station**, whose impressive satellite dishes dominate the scrubby interior. A high-tech multimedia visitor

centre and guided tour of the site provide a marketing-led insight into satellite technology, including details of the first intercontinental satellite picture, which was transmitted from here to the USA in 1962.

An earlier major technological breakthrough took place on the coast to the west of Goonhilly in 1901, when the first transatlantic Morse signal was sent from **Poldhu Cove** to Guglielmo Marconi in Newfoundland. In 2001 the **Marconi Centre** (call 01326 241656 for information) was constructed on the headland to mark the centenary of this historic transmission. It houses displays on Marconi and other aspects of Cornwall's communication history, and provides a permanent home for the local amateur radio club. There's a granite obelisk commemorating Marconi on the cliffs to the south of the sandy beach.

Follow the coast path south to reach the popular surfing beach at **Polurrian**, and tiny, dramatic **Mullion Cove**, where a handful of cottages cluster around a lovely rocky harbour. Inland, **Mullion** is the largest village on the peninsula and makes a useful base for exploration of the area. The richly carved pews in the 16th-century church of St Mellanus are worth a look, as is the **Mullion Gallery** (Nansmellyon Road, 01326 241170, closed Jan, Feb), which features the work of local Lizard artists and craftspeople.

Between Mullion and the Lizard lies rugged and beautiful **Kynance Cove**, the most popular beach on the peninsula. Best seen at low tide, this glorious white-sand cove is distinguished by spectacular rock formations and islets that stand to attention just offshore. The rocky stacks glow with green, red and blue serpentine and bristle with wild flowers in summer. A toll road leads from the A3083 to a National Trust car park at the top of the cliffs, from where there's a steepish climb down to a seasonal café and shop on the edge of the sand.

At the tip of the peninsula, the charms of **Lizard** village are somewhat subsumed by dull cafés and gift shops groaning with serpentine knick-knacks, but from here it's a short walk to mainland Britain's most southerly headland. **Lizard Point** has escaped the tourist excesses of Land's End and is marked only by the twin towers of the Lizard Lighthouse and a couple of attendant shops and cafés. There are tours of the Lighthouse throughout the summer (phone 01326 290065 for details), but the surrounding coastline is the main draw: a dramatic jumble of cliffs, caves and coves pounded by relentless waves. The cottage where Marconi carried out his pioneering radio experiments overlooks a sandy beach just to the east of the point, while beyond, the coast path leads north-east towards the exhilarating **Devil's Frying Pan**, a 200-foot (61-metre) deep blowhole.

Delightful **Cadgwith** for once gloriously lives up to the hype. Fishing boats line up on the sheltered pebble beach, surrounded by picture-postcard cottages of serpentine and thatch. (Park at the top of the village to avoid becoming entangled in its steep, narrow lanes.) In Cadgwith, check out the seasonal **Crows Nest Gallery** (01326 290246, closed winter) right down by the beach. Continuing north, the coast path passes Carleon Cove and the overgrown remains of a serpentine-cutting plant, at its peak in the Victorian era but now reduced to a cottage industry.

The B3293 heads south-east from Helston across the expanse of Goonhilly Downs to the coast at **Coverack**. This unspoilt fishing village was once a centre of smuggling, but is now favoured for its unspoilt coastal setting, with traditional granite cottages lining up along an arc of sand and shingle. There's a working harbour at the southern end of the bay and glorious views out to sea.

Further north, **Porthoustock** presents an interesting contrast to the comfy perfection of Cadgwith. This defiantly non-touristic fishing village has an uncompromising grey shingle beach and is flanked by the dour workings of a roadstone quarry to the right and the grey hulk of a loading bay to the left. Despite its harsh appearance, Porthoustock has become something of a diving mecca thanks to the proximity of the notorious **Manacles**, a jagged, mostly submerged two-mile offshore reef, upon which many ships and men have come to grief.

About a mile inland from Manacle Point, **St Keverne** churchyard is full of the victims of the reef, including most of the 113-strong crew of the steamship *Mohegan*, lost in just 20 minutes in October 1898. The church itself has a ribbed, octagonal spire, used as an important landmark by centuries of sailors. A memorial plaque on the wall remembers the village blacksmith Michael Joseph, who was executed for his part in the failed 1497 Cornish Rebellion. Joseph led rebels to London to protest against punitive taxes, but was captured after defeat at the Battle of Deptford Bridge; a statue just outside the village commemorates the 500th anniversary of the event.

On the coast north of St Keverne is the hamlet of **Porthallow**, largely unremarkable except for the presence of the **Porthallow Vineyard** (01326 280050), which sells locally produced ciders, wines and liqueurs – and hosts free tastings.

The prettily wooded inlets of the Helford river form the northern boundary of the Lizard Peninsula, encroaching deep inland and trailing clusters of bosky villages and lush gardens. One such inlet is the lovely (and reputedly haunted) **Frenchman's Creek**, famously romanticised by Daphne du Maurier. It's a short walk from here to the charming and salubrious hamlet of **Helford**, an old smugglers' haunt surrounded by picturesque woodland, from where ferries cross the river to **Helford Passage** on the north shore. Nearby **Port Navas** is one of the prettiest of the creekside villages – and also one of the most gastronomically rewarding, thanks to the **Royal Duchy Oyster Farm** (01326 340210; phone in advance), which does a nice line in shellfish. A pleasant walk east will bring you to the lush vegetation of **Trebah Garden**, situated in a steep, wooded ravine. The garden is characterised by waterfalls, hydrangeas and 100-year-old ferns, and is surrounded by ancient trees. Adjoining Trebah, the National Trust **Glendurgan Garden** has a famous 19th-century laurel maze to complement its riot of subtropical planting. Both gardens drop down through wooded valleys to sandy beaches on the Helford river.

Gweek, at the head of the estuary, was until the 1930s a thriving port and the point of departure for many local emigrants seeking a better life in the colonies. Nowadays the **National Seal Sanctuary** is the main attraction. Opened in 1958, the sanctuary is devoted to the rescue and care of a range of marine unfortunates.

Occupying 1,000 acres between the Helford river and Goonhilly Downs, the grand estate of **Trelowarren** (Mawgan, 01326 221224, www.trelowarren.com) is still owned by the Vyvyan family after 600 years. The Jacobean house has been converted into luxury self-catering apartments, while the outbuildings house a restaurant, pottery and weaving workshops (01326 221583), a plant nursery and a smart gallery run by the Cornwall Crafts Association (01326 221567). There are plenty of desirable *objets* for sale here, and not a raffia tablemat in sight. Surrounding the house, restoration continues on the 18th-century landscape gardens, while woodland tracks lead through the estate to the banks of the river.

Goonhilly Satellite Earth Station

B3293, nr Helston (0800 679593/www.goonhilly. bt.com). **Open** *mid Feb-Mar, Nov, Dec* phone for details. *Apr, May, Oct* 10am-5pm daily. *June-Sept* 10am-6pm daily. Closed Jan-mid Feb. **Admission** £5; £3.50/£4 concessions; £15 family. **Credit** MC, V.

Glendurgan Gardens
Mawnan Smith, nr Falmouth (01326 250906).
Open 10.30am-5.30pm Tue-Sat. Closed Nov-mid
Feb. **Admission** £3.90; £9.75 family. **Credit**
phone for details.

National Seal Sanctuary
Gweek, nr Helston (01326 221361/
www.sealsanctuary.co.uk). **Open** 9am-
dusk daily; phone for details. **Admission**
£7.50; £5.50 concessions. **Credit** AmEx,
MC, V.

Trebah Gardens
Mawnan Smith, nr Falmouth (01326 250448/
www.trebah-gardens.co.uk). **Open** 10.30am-5pm
daily. **Admission** £5; £4.50 concessions.
Credit AmEx, MC, V.

Activities

Boating
Helford River Boats (Helford Passage, 01326
250770, closed Nov-Mar) hires sailing and motor

St Michael's Mount

Lying just off the coast at Marazion, St
Michael's Mount is the stuff of fairytales,
an island castle at its most magical when
peeping through a low-lying sea mist.

Legend claims the mount was originally
the lair of the giant Cormoran, who tyrannised
the local population but was defeated in true
David and Goliath fashion by a little Cornish
boy. Early records from the fourth century,
however, show that the mount began life
as a bustling, busy port for the fishermen of
Marazion. Its religious status was conferred
when a vision of St Michael appeared to a
group of local sailors in the fifth century. A
church was built on the spot and by the eighth
century a monastery had been founded there.

Edward the Confessor built a chapel on the
mount in the 11th century, and donated it to
the Benedictine monks of Mont St Michel,
the island monastery in Brittany on which St
Michael's Mount had been modelled. Links
with the monastery's Breton counterpart
were later severed by Henry V during the
Hundred Years War (1337-1453), and after
the dissolution of the monasteries, the mount
was converted into a fortress. It was used
as a store for Royalist arms during the Civil
War, before becoming the residence of the
St Aubyn family. St Michael's Mount was
donated to the National Trust in 1954 by
Lord St Levan, although his son, the fourth
baron, still lives on the site.

Cornwall

boats for exploring the river's hidden inlets. Prices for a six-seater motorboat are £21 for an hr, £43 for 3hrs or £73 for a day.

Diving
Lizard Diver (01326 221446, www.lizarddiver. co.uk) offers PADI instruction for all abilities, plus diving trips to the peninsula's reefs and wrecks.

Golf
Mullion Golf Club (Cury, nr Helston, 01326 240685) has a glorious cliff-top 18-hole course.

For the modern visitor it's an exciting trip over to the Mount either by causeway or boat (£1 each way). The harbour below the castle is surrounded by a cluster of cottages now housing shops, restaurants and a dairy. It's a steep climb from here up the Pilgrims' Steps to the castle entrance, but you can pause to admire the giant's stone heart in the cobbles on the way.

Inside, the castle is disarmingly cosy and compact, with paintings, weapons and military trophies dominating the displays. The two most striking rooms are the deliciously feminine Blue Drawing Room, with its fussy rococo details, and the former monks' refectory, which was updated in the 17th century as the Chevy Chase Room (named after the hunting frieze around the walls based on the 'Ballad of Chevy Chase', not the actor).

The importance of the castle as a fortress is highlighted in the Garrison Room, from where the Armada was first sighted on 30 July 1588. Today the view from the battlements takes in the fabulous gardens and the dramatic coast beyond.

Returning to the harbour for lunch, try Hobbler's Choice, a local fish dish, at the **Sail Loft Restaurant** (01736 710507, closed Nov-Mar, main courses £4-£13).

St Michael's Mount
(01736 710507/tide & ferry information 01736 710265/www.stmichaelsmount. co.uk). **Open** *Castle & gardens* Apr, May, Oct 10.30am-5.30pm Mon-Fri. June-Sept also 10.30am-5.30pm most Sat, Sun. Last entry 4.45pm. Nov-Mar by guided tour Mon, Wed, Fri only; phone for details. *Gardens only* Apr, May Mon-Fri. June-Sept most Sat, Sun. **Admission** *Castle & gardens* £4.80; £2.40 children; £13 family. *Gardens only* £2.50. **Credit** MC, V.

Riding
Cury Riding Stables (Church Road, Cury, nr Helston, 01326 240591) caters for both experienced riders and beginners.

Windsurfing
From March to November budding windsurfers can get tuition at **Coverack Windsurfing Centre** (Coverack, 01326 280939).

Where to eat, drink & stay
For stunning views look no further than the relaxed **Mullion Cove Hotel** (Mullion, 01326 240328, www.mullioncove.com, main courses £5-£15, set meal £23.50, double B&B £30-£140), which stands on a headland overlooking miles of sea and coastline. The 16th-century **Old Inn** (Churchtown, Mullion, 01326 240240, main courses £5.95-£11.95), near the centre of the village, was reputedly patronised by Marconi and has good pub grub, but for the last word in freshly made crab sandwiches try the **Colroger Delicatessen** (Mullion, 01326 240833), which also has home-baked goods and Cornish cheeses.

Just east of Lizard Point, **Landewednack House** (Church Cove, 01326 290909, double B&B from £42 per person) is an intimate home with incredible views across its beautiful gardens to the sea. An outdoor pool and luxurious bedrooms, combined with a no-children policy, ensure a relaxing stay. Self-catering can be arranged.

Just to the south of St Keverne, stop off at **Roskilly's** (Tregellast Barton, 01326 280479, main courses £3-£8) to watch over 50 varieties of scrumptious ice-cream being made from the farm's own Jersey milk and cream. An informal restaurant serves tasty organic produce, and there are barbecues in summer.

For something a bit more upmarket try the modern and sophisticated **Tregildry Hotel** (Gillan, Manaccan, 01326 231378, closed Nov-Feb, double B&B £75-£95 incl dinner). Superbly situated, overlooking Gillan Creek, the Helford river and Falmouth Bay, the hotel boasts a menu featuring fresh local produce. At Trelowarren Estate, the French chef at the **New Yard Restaurant** (01326 221595, closed Jan, set meal £18-£25) translates the best of local produce into the culinary delights of South West France. For details of self-catering accommodation and camping on the estate, phone 01326 221224.

On the other side of the estuary an inlet leads to the hamlet of Nancenoy, where you'll find the award-winning **Trengilly Wartha Inn** (01326 340332, set meals £21.50/£27.50, double B&B £78), which is well known for its top-notch food and cosy bedrooms.

Cornwall

Resources

Post office
Coverack *The Cove (01326 280210)*. **Open** 9am-5pm Mon, Wed-Fri; 9am-12.30pm Tue, Sat.

Tourist information
St Keverne *Lizard Peninsula Tourism Association, Trenoweth Farm (01326 281079/ www.thelizard.co.uk)*. **Open** 10am-6pm daily.

Getting there & around

By bus
Truronian (01872 273453) runs bus no.T1 between Truro and Helston (1hr), continuing through Mullion to the Lizard. T2 buses run from Truro to St Keverne and Coverack, while frequent T3s connect the Lizard villages with each other. **First Western National** (01872 261111) buses nos.2 and 2A run alternate hourly services from Penzance to Flambards and Helston. Further information is available from www.buses.org.uk.

Penwith Peninsula

Penzance & around

Heading along the A394 from Helston, a series of sandy beaches tempts you towards the sea. The expanse of **Praa Sands** (a surfer's favourite) is particularly appealing if you avoid the bungalow-ville, caravan park element and head for the eastern side towards Rinsey Head, where there are the remains of cliff-edge tin mines. Beyond, there's another lovely beach at **Perranuthnoe**, leading down from low cliffs.

Mount's Bay is a great place for sailing and windsurfing. The main town here is the popular holiday resort of **Marazion**, one of Cornwall's oldest chartered towns, whose peculiar name refers to the traditional markets (*marghas*) that were held here as far back as the 11th century. The traffic-locked main street is the site of the unremarkable **Marazion Museum**, but most visitors prefer the large sandy beach with clusters of rock pools, backed by an RSPB wetland reserve.

Despite these seaside attractions, it is the irresistible lure of **St Michael's Mount** (*see p248*) that pulls in the crowds. At low tide it is possible to walk the cobbled causeway to the isle; otherwise, frequent boats ferry visitors across for £1 each way.

Penzance is an unpretentious, workaday place with a smattering of seaside irreverence, down on its promenade. To experience the town at its most lively, visit during the ten-day **Golowan Festival** (Feast of St John;

www.golowan.com) in June. This pagan midsummer ritual was revived in 1991 and now attracts thousands of onlookers. The grand finale is at the weekend: on Mazey Eve, anarchy rules with the election of the Mayor of the Quay and a spectacular fireworks display, while on Mazey Day itself, processions lead towards the harbour, where boats gather for the traditional sea and sail.

At other times explore the town's winding back streets, which offer an alternative, arty vibe, particularly around the Georgian quarter, near the subtropical **Morrab Gardens**.

Penzance's main shopping drag is **Market Jew Street**, which extends uphill from the Wharfside Shopping Centre to the 19th-century market house (now a bank). Turn left here into historic **Chapel Street**. Once bustling with mule trains laden with copper ore on their way to the harbour, it is now full of good pubs, cafés and shops. **Fishboy**, for example, at no.64 (01736 331846), sells individual, funky clothes using a diverse range of fabrics.

Victory in the Battle of Trafalgar was first announced from the minstrels' gallery at the old **Union Hotel**, but the most striking building on Chapel Street is the **Egyptian House**, built in 1830 as a museum and geological repository. It is decorated with extraordinary colours and lotus-bud capitals and has a fantastic jewellery shop, **Amalgam** (No.6, 01736 361354), on the ground floor, showcasing pieces from some of the country's leading designers.

On nearby Parade Street, concerts and theatre productions are staged at the **Acorn Theatre** (01736 365520, www.acorntheatre. co.uk), a converted chapel with a funky café in the basement, while at the bottom of the street, **Trinity House National Lighthouse Centre** is a hands-on museum that includes the reconstructed living quarters of a lighthouse keeper.

Beyond Chapel Street, the harbour is a mix of pleasure craft, fishing boats and the occasional visiting tall ship. It is also the docking home for the *Scillonian III* ferry to the Isles of Scilly. As harbour gives way to promenade, you'll spot the art deco-styled lido of the **Jubilee Pool** (01736 350490, www.jubileepool.co.uk, closed Oct-Apr) jutting out into the bay. This tidal, saltwater (though chlorinated) open-air swimming pool was built to mark George V's silver jubilee. Also on the harbourside is **Round the Bend**, a hands-on exhibition of kooky mechanical automata.

Head west along the Promenade and then north up Morrab Road to reach the **Penlee House Gallery & Museum**. This Italianate Victorian villa, set in parkland, has the largest collection of paintings by the Newlyn School,

There's something fishy about **Newlyn**.

which dominated the art scene in Penwith at the turn of the 19th century (*see p26*). Look out for the atmospheric *The Rain It Raineth Every Day*, painted in 1889 by Norman Garstin, and contrast the earliest work in the collection, *Mount's Bay* (1794) by William Brooks, with the gallery's most recent acquisition, *Mount's Bay Impression* (1992), by the late John Miller. The gallery's collection of art metalwork, known as Newlyn Copper, is another attraction, and there's also a database of local painting and photographs from the 1860s to the present day.

The museum, meanwhile, which was founded in 1839, covers 6,000 years of Cornish history, with exhibits ranging from Stone Age tools to the mining safety lamp invented by Penzance's famous son Humphrey Davy (1778-1829). The Orangery café is good value and the exotically planted gardens are a lovely spot for an afternoon stroll.

On the outskirts of Penzance is 16th-century **Trereife House** (01736 362750, closed Oct-May; phone for details) with its fine Queen Anne façade and beautiful 18th-century formal gardens. The Le Grice family have lived here since 1798 and the present owner conducts fascinating tours of the house. Cream teas are served in the Willow Pattern Tearooms in the courtyard.

Almost joined to Penzance to the south and protected by the long arms of its two piers, **Newlyn** nevertheless retains its own individual edge, thriving on a conjunction of art and fishing. This is the county's biggest fishing port and the site of a fabulous fish festival over the August bank holiday. For the rest of the year the town's fishing heritage is thoroughly explored, with the use of boats, nets, drawings and other paraphernalia, at the stylish and award-winning **Pilchard Works**, a museum that incorporates a working pilchards factory.

Artists were originally attracted to Newlyn by the exceptionally clear light, and formed an artists' colony here from the 1880s, which came to be known as the Newlyn School. Newlyn continues to attract artists today, and some of their work is displayed in the small **Newlyn Gallery** (New Road, 01736 363715, www.newlynartgallery.co.uk). It also has a great shop selling original artworks, prints, jewellery, cards and books.

Mousehole (pronounced 'Mowzel'), a little further west, is a tourist's dream, with its tiny, sheltered harbour and winding lanes. Dylan Thomas, who honeymooned here in 1937, thought it the prettiest village in England. Inevitably, Mousehole is overrun with tourists in high season, so try to visit at other times to enjoy its flower-clad cottages and narrow streets at their best.

Every 23 December the village makes Star-Gazey pie in memory of Tom Bawcock, a local fisherman who is said to have saved Mousehole from starvation in the early 20th century by setting sail in a storm to land a large catch of fish. The unusual pie consists of whole pilchard heads poking through a pastry case.

Just above Mousehole and Newlyn is the compact and attractive village of **Paul**, with its impressive church of St Pol de Leon. Inside the church, a plaque commemorates Dolly Pentreath, the last recorded monoglot speaker of Cornish, who died in 1777.

A great coastal walk takes you from Mousehole to **Lamorna**, a cove backed by a luscious green valley. The curvaceous quay and nearby cottages were built by Captain Owen, who came to quarry granite here in the 1850s. Chunks of quarried stone and tumbling cliffs form a dramatic backdrop that has

Cornwall

attracted many artists and writers, like Derek Tangye. **Lamorna Pottery** (01736 810330) is famous for its colourful glazes, but also stocks other gifts, and serves great cream teas in the café.

Just beyond the junction, where the coast road from Lamorna meets the B3315, are the **Merry Maidens**, an ancient circle of 19 standing stones. Legend has it that the stones are a group of women who were petrified for dancing on a Sunday. The two **Pipers** who played for the women were also turned to stone; they stand about half a mile away on the other side of the road.

Another important ancient site in the region is the Iron Age hill settlement at **Chysauster** (near Gulval), signposted off the B3311 towards St Ives. This wild, exposed site dates from the first century BC and features the best-preserved beehive hut circles in the UK. Eight stone buildings can be identified, of which three have discernible hearths, corn grinders and drains.

For beautiful gardens, head to **Trengwainton** just off the A3071. At its best in springtime, this sheltered estate incorporates magnificent wooded walks through the stream-fed valley and a ha-ha lawn with stunning views to the south coast. Thanks to the Gulf Stream, the walled gardens contain many plants that cannot be grown anywhere else in the UK. There's a shop at the entrance and a well-designed timber café for lunches and teas.

Penlee House Gallery & Museum
off Morrab Road (01736 363625/www.penlee house.org.uk). **Open** *Oct-Apr* 10am-4.30pm Mon-Sat. *May-Sept* 10am-5pm Mon-Sat. **Admission** £2; £1 concessions. **Credit** MC, V.

Pilchard Works
Newlyn (01736 332112/www.pilchardworks.co.uk). **Open** *Easter-Oct* 10am-6pm Mon-Fri. Closed Nov-Mar. **Admission** £3.25; £2.95 concessions; £10 family. **No credit cards.**

Round the Bend
The Harbourside, Barbican, Penzance (01736 332211/www.golowan.com). **Open** *Easter, June-Oct* 11am-5pm daily. Closed Nov-Mar, May. **Admission** £2.50. **No credit cards.**

Trengwainton Gardens
off the A3071, nr Penzance (01736 362297). **Open** *mid Feb-Oct* 10am-5pm Mon-Thur, Sun. Closed Nov-mid Feb. **Admission** £3.90; £9.75 family. **Credit** phone for details.

Trinity House National Lighthouse Museum
Chapel Street, Penzance (01736 360077/ www.trinityhouse.co.uk). **Open** *Easter-Oct* 10.30am-4.30pm daily. **Admission** £3; £1-£2 concessions; £6 family. **No credit cards.**

Activities

Boat trips
Dunn Marine runs a variety of trips aboard MVS *Mermaid* and *Viking*, ranging from coastal cruises to Lamorna Cove to all-day deep-sea angling excursions and shark fishing trips. There's a good chance of spotting some dolphins. For further information, contact the Dockers' Rest Café (Wharf Road, Penzance, 01736 362405) or phone 01736 368565.

Cycling
Bikes can be hired in Penzance from **Pedals Bike Hire** at the Wharfside Shopping Centre (Wharf Road, 01736 360600, www.pedalsbikes.co.uk) and from the **Cycle Centre** (Knights Warehouse, Bread Street, 01736 351671).

Kitesurfing
X-treem-Air Kitesurfing School (Old Station car park, Marazion, 0787 606 8278, 01209 822141, www.x-treem-air.com) will introduce you to the crazy world of kitesurfing.

Landrover tours
Harry Safari in the Land of Legend (01736 711427, www.harrysafari.co.uk) runs quirky, personal history tours of the peninsula and further afield, with pick-up points in Penzance and St Ives.

Where to eat, drink & stay

There's been a marked improvement in the quality of dining in Penzance of late, with a number of hotels and restaurants now offering well-executed local specialities in contemporary settings. Self-caterers, meanwhile, should head straight for **The Deli** (27 Market Place, 01736 350223) to stock up on gourmet goodies.

Exemplifying the newfound style is **Abbey Restaurant** (Abbey Street, off Chapel Street, 01736 330680, main courses £14-£18), which offers a confident Modern European menu, snazzy bar area and views over Mount's Bay. Next door, the 17th-century **Abbey Hotel** (01736 366906, www.abbey-hotel.co.uk, double B&B £100-£150) casts a spell of away-from-it-all indulgence. Owned by former '60s model Jean Shrimpton, the hotel's sumptuous bedrooms are complemented by delicious food in the restaurant.

Close by are another clutch of good eateries and two of Penzance's best hostelries: the **Turk's Head** (49 Chapel Street, 01736 363093), reputed to be the oldest pub in town, and the **Admiral Benbow** (46 Chapel Street, 01736 363448), which is shaped like a ship's galley. The **Bakehouse Restaurant** (Old Bakehouse Lane, Chapel Street, 01736 331331, main courses £10-£15) is set around a Mediterranean-style courtyard and serves generous Modern European dishes with a few Asian touches,

Surf check Lizard to Land's En

With everything from a reef break considered by many to be the best in the country to more accessible, consistent beach breaks, the stretch of coast from the Lizard to St Ives has a range of waves to suit all-comers.

The most challenging spot is **Porthleven** (*see p245*) with its superb and (for the less experienced) hazardous reef break, which draws large crowds of experienced, no-nonsense locals when it's working in a big swell. More fun, less edgy and definitely safer is the relatively deserted beach break.

Further west towards Penzance is **Praa Sands** (*see p250*), a long and picturesque bay that offers holidaymakers and funboarders reasonable protection from the wind, while serving up decent peaks to more experienced riders. And if things get too big here, you can always head a little further up the A394 to **Perranuthnoe** (*see p250*), where there's a smaller beach with more manageable waves.

Rounding Land's End brings you to some of England's most reliable beach breaks. First – and best known – is **Sennen Cove** (*see p255*), which, due to its position as Britain's most westerly beach, tends to pick up even the weakest Atlantic swells. Basically, if it's not working here, you may as well pack up your stuff and head back home. For this reason, Sennen (and the shifting peaks of Gwenvor Point at its northerly tip) tend to get crowded in the summer months, especially during flat spells.

Compared to the livelier surfing hubs further up the coast towards Newquay, this area of Cornwall is relatively sleepy. Prime spots such as Porthleven can be superb places in which to chill out and soak up fishing village charm by the bucketload – just don't expect to find the kind of salty surf-dog scene that you might encounter around Newquay or Croyde.

---

while nearby **Cocos** (12-13 Chapel Street, 01736 350222, main courses £8-£12) hosts live bands and is usually buzzing with regulars, tucking into the good-value tapas (£3.50-£7) and daily specials.

Another funky spot is the **Penzance Arts Club** (Chapel House, Chapel Street, 01736 363761, www.penzanceartsclub.co.uk, double B&B £70-£100). Housed in an 18th-century building that was once the Portuguese embassy, this is now the avant-garde domain of artists and their followers, and features jazz nights, poetry readings and games in the bar. The in-house restaurant, **Passion** (01736 332555, main courses £9.95-£16.95), serves contemporary English food with a twist.

Away from the Chapel Street strip, Penzance has plenty of good-value B&Bs and small hotels like **Camilla House** (Regent Terrace, 01736 363771, double B&B £50-£60), whose top rooms have great ocean views. For the big seaside hotel experience, try the **Queen's Hotel** (The Promenade, 01736 362371, double B&B £94-£120), slap-bang on the seafront. **Bay Restaurant, Café & Gallery** (Mount Prospect Hotel, Britons Hill, 01736 366890, main courses £14-£16) is a swanky place to eat, drink and enjoy art, with fine views over Penzance. The attached hotel is rather traditional but does boast the only pool in town. Pick of the places to eat and stay, though, is the award-winning **Summer House Restaurant with Rooms** (Cornwall Terrace, 01736 363744,

www.summerhouse-cornwall.com, set menu £23.50, double B&B £75-£95) set in a beautiful Regency house, just behind the seafront. Here, owner/chef Ciro Zaino works wonders with fresh ingredients to create delicious Mediterranean-style dishes, and the five immaculate bedrooms demonstrate seaside chic with a touch of French rustic style.

Heading east, the **Godolphin Arms** (Marazion, 01736 710202, www.godolphinarms. co.uk, main courses £6.95-£14.95, double B&B £70-£120) has an unrivalled view of St Michael's Mount. The best rooms have private terraces and the large bar terrace is perfect for a snack in the sun. Not far away in Perranuthnoe, the 12th-century **Victoria Inn** (01736 710309, main courses £7.25-£13.95) is the oldest inn in Cornwall and offers decent pub grub in a delightful patio garden.

In Newlyn, **Jelbert's Ices** (9 New Road, Newlyn, 01736 366634, closed Nov-Mar) sells vanilla ice-cream to die for, and the **Strand Café** (36A The Strand, 01736 333846, main courses £3.50-£7) is a laid-back spot for breakfast, with second-hand CDs for sale. For lunch on the run, try the excellent fish and chips from **Quirky's** (3 Commercial Road, Mousehole, 01736 732211), but for a romantic candlelit vibe opt it has to be the **Cornish Range Restaurant** (6 Chapel Street, Mousehole, 01736 731488, main courses £12.50-£17.50). It's committed to the use of local produce, including excellent fish, and has

Cornwall

accommodation in four smart, contemporary rooms (double B&B £65-£75). An alternative is provided by the **Old Coastguard Hotel** (The Parade, Mousehole, 01736 731222, www.oldcoastguardhotel.co.uk, main courses £8-£16, double B&B £70-£95), a relaxed haven set in lovely gardens by the sea.

Resources

Hospital
Penzance *West Cornwall Hospital, St Clare Street (01736 874000).*

Internet
Penzance *Penzance Library, Morrab Road (01736 363954).* **Open** 9.30am-6pm Mon-Fri; 9.30am-4pm Sat.

Police station
Penzance *Penalvern Drive (0870 577 7444).*

Post office
Penzance *Market Jew Street (01736 362464).* **Open** 9am-5.30pm Mon-Fri; 9am-12.30pm Sat.

Tourist information
Penzance *Tourist Information Centre, Station Approach (01736 362207/www.go-cornwall.com).* **Open** *June-Sept* 9am-5.30pm Mon-Sat; 10am-1pm Sun. *Oct-May* 9am-5pm Mon-Fri; 10am-1pm Sat.

Land's End & around

West Penwith could be another country – wild, remote and bounded by so much sea it's almost an island in itself. It stays light here for 40 minutes after darkness hits London. The weather is milder too – thanks to the North Atlantic Drift – but often unpredictable, with sun, cloud and rain to be found at the same time just a few miles apart. There are stunning beaches to discover on the south coast, such as Porth Chapel near St Levan and Pednevounder beach below Treen, while the north coast offers dramatic, cinematic views punctuated by the ruins of tin mines and engine houses. Fantastic walking is to be had here on the coast path and also along parts of the Tinner's Way, a centuries-old route between St Just and St Ives (*see p256* **Country walk**).

West from the hidden and cultivated Lamorna valley a gutsy, more exposed landscape takes hold, interspersed with small settlements such as the unspoilt fishing hamlet of **Penberth Cove**, just off the B3315. Further west is the attractive village of **Treen**, where a short walk across the cliffs reveals Logan's Rock weighing 70 tonnes, and once so precisely poised that a mere push would set it rocking or 'logging'. A scandal was caused in 1824, when Oliver Goldsmith's nephew knocked

Blast from the past: a ruined **tin mine**.

the huge boulder off its granite pillar; although he managed to replace it, Logan's Rock has remained immobile ever since.

At low tide the beautiful sand bar and beach at **Pednevounder** (reached from Porthcurno or Treen) is reminiscent of tropical shores with its turquoise sea and white sands, while inland on the B3283 the village of **St Buryan** has a 15th-century church that was used in Sam Peckinpah's controversial '70s film *Straw Dogs*.

Continuing west, the B3315 brings you to **Porthcurno**, a popular holiday spot with a broad, sandy beach sheltered by Gwennap Head to the west and Cribba Head to the east. It is home to the **Museum of Submarine Telegraphy**, which tells the story behind the 14 undersea cables laid here in 1870 to keep Britain in touch with the Empire. Porthcurno was also Cornwall's secret underground communications centre during World War II.

The big draw, though, is the **Minack Theatre**, a Greek-inspired amphitheatre cut into the cliffs 200 feet (61 metres) above the beach. The theatre was founded by the remarkable Rowena Cade, and its first production in 1932, aptly, was *The Tempest*. Although the site has been modernised and extended, the magic of Cade's original vision remains. The visitor centre tells the story of the theatre, with photographs, old costumes and a video, but the best way to experience the Minack is to pack jumpers, waterproofs and a picnic and see a performance there. Book well in advance if you want to secure tickets.

Further west the no-through road ends at **St Levan**, a pretty, sheltered hamlet with a pathway down to secluded Porth Chapel beach. Nearby, a turning winds towards the small fishing hamlet of **Porthgwarra** (also known as 'Sweetheart's Cove'), whose shoreline is accessed via a manmade tunnel through the rock. The glorious B3315, meanwhile, heads further up the coast, eventually joining the last leg of the A30 as it hurries towards Land's End.

Not only is **Land's End** (in Cornish '*pen-von-las*', meaning end of the earth) the beginning and end of mainland Britain (a concept exploited on everything from postcards to pub signs), but it is surrounded by some of the most spectacular coastline in the country, with imposing granite outcrops standing sentinel over far-reaching ocean views. It is all the more astounding, then, that developers got permission to build the naff **Land's End Experience** right on the edge of the headland.

The 'experience' capitalises on Land's End's unique tourist status, with displays, multimedia exhibits and plenty of merchandise. Factual details about air-sea rescues, wrecks (including the *Torrey Canyon* oil tanker in 1967) and loopy journeys to and from John o' Groats are combined with King Arthur myths and smuggling stories to create a commercial blurring of fact and fiction. There's a sad irony in the fact that coachloads of tourists are prepared to pay for the simulated sound and light shows, when the real thing is to be found just steps outside. Having said that, there's pleasure to be had from scrambling around the lifeboat and trawler exhibits or exploring the refreshingly understated farm, the Land of Greeb, set apart from the main buildings on the cliff top. And away from the gimmicks and the crowds, the coast path reveals an area of evocative natural beauty, where you may just spot Atlantic grey seals, basking sharks and dolphins.

Heading north from Land's End, a turning off the A30 leads towards **Sennen**. The cliff-top area known as Churchtown is a nondescript

residential mish-mash, but the steep road down to the buzzy holiday spot at **Sennen Cove** offers much more, with a harbour, a smattering of shops, the Old Success Inn and the Round House Gallery (originally used as a winch house and net store). The main attraction, though, is famous **Whitesand Bay**, a west-facing arc of golden sand that is a popular surfing spot, with the secluded Gwynver beach beyond.

Inland, a left turning off the A30 at Croes-an-Wra (Witch's Cross) climbs towards the hill of **Chapel Carn Brea**, reputed to have the widest sea view of any place on mainland Britain; the Isles of Scilly stand out on a clear day just 28 miles (45 kilometres) off the coast. The road then runs downhill to link up with the beautiful coastal B3306, heading north towards St Just. En route it passes the basic and rather quirky **Land's End Aerodrome** (01736 788771), open for scenic flights (£25-£55) and trips to the Isles of Scilly.

St Just is the only significant town in this area, approached from the scenic B3306 coast road or directly from Penzance on the A3071. It is a no-frills, no-fuss place of granite terraces and ex-miners' cottages, surrounding a busy market square. Behind the clock tower is the *plain-an-gwarry*, an open-air theatre used for miracle plays in the Middle Ages and Methodist meetings in the 18th century. The normally workaday village livens up considerably for the Festival Lafrowda (01736 788669), held in July, which features music, exhibitions and performances by local theatre groups. If you've got some time to kill, it's worth checking out **Just Cornish** (Fore Street, 01736 787877, www.justcornish.com), a shop selling anything associated with the county, including Cornish language material from beginner courses to place name guides.

Two miles (three kilometres) west of the town, it's well worth descending the hill to see the dramatic beauty of **Cape Cornwall** laid out below. England's only 'cape' is topped by a minestack (closed in 1870), which overlooks the rockpools of Priest's Cove. To the south, the sheltered micro-climate of the **Cot valley** leads from St Just to the lovely cove at Porth Nanvern, which is packed with huge, rounded stones.

Heading inland, visit the hidden village of **Sancreed** to view the fine wheel-shaped Celtic cross in its churchyard, and stop off at **Carn Euny**, an Iron Age village incorporating a remarkably well-preserved 60-foot (18-metre) 'fougou' or underground passage, whose original purpose remains a mystery.

North from St Just along the B3306 are the ruins of a hardcore mining territory, with settlements that run into one another towards

Cornwall

Country walk Among the ancients

Length 7-8 miles (11-13 km).
Time required 3hrs 30mins.
Difficulty Some steep sections; the paths can get very waterlogged.

The walk begins at Morvah, five miles (eight kilometres) from St Just on the B3306 with parking by the **Morvah School House & Gallery** (01736 787808, closed Mon-Wed), a good spot for coffee or a light lunch. Walk past the church to the B3306 junction where 50 yards south at the sharp bend there's a granite stile signed 'public footpath'.

The path follows field boundaries in a south-easterly direction and meets a small road to the right of **Carne Farm**. Turn right and follow the road until it turns into a track signed 'Chun Downs', climbing uphill in a south-westerly direction. At the top of the track is the house used in Sam Peckinpah's 1971 film *Straw Dogs*, starring Dustin Hoffman and Susan George, re-released in 2002 after a lengthy ban.

Follow the track north-west from the house and take the left-hand fork, which eventually turns south, up towards the commanding stone structure of **Chun Quoit**, a capstone burial chamber dating from the Stone Age. Uphill to the east is **Chun Castle**, an Iron Age fort with the ruins of two stone circular walls and glorious views of the Atlantic coast to the north and Mount's Bay to the south-east. Take the path from the fort over ruined walls and outer ditches to find a north-easterly path (often overgrown) through the gorse and

heather, running down towards the fields below. Here the onward path is marked with yellow arrows and skirts the height of **Morvah Carn** before emerging on to the minor Morvah–Madron road opposite Dakota Farm.

Turn right south-east downhill for about 600 yards to the **Men-an-Tol Studio** (01736 368282, closed Jan, Feb, Dec), worth a stop to view the work of Ian Cooke, printmaker, artist and writer, whose book *The Tinner's Way & Nearby Ancient Sites* is a great guide to the area.

Opposite the studio the path, once a major part of the Tinner's Way, continues up the farm track north-east until it levels out close to some derelict buildings on the left. A signpost on the right directs you over a granite stile to **Men-an-Tol** ('stone of the hole'; *pictured*), an ancient stone hoop that is steeped in myth. Known locally as the 'Devil's Eye', it is rumoured to have the power to heal anyone that crawls through it. Sir Norman Lockyer thought it was an astronomical instrument but similar stone rings found elsewhere are believed to be entrances to burial chambers. There is a smattering of standing stones around the stone ring itself. Take the path south-east from the most northerly standing stone across the white downs of Morvah. Cross a stream and then climb up towards the restored **Ding-Dong Tin Mine** standing out on the horizon. The views across to St Michael's Mount, the Lizard and the north coast are outstanding.

Pendeen. One of the most spectacularly sited mines perches on the rocky coast a short distance from St Just at **Botallack** and can be clearly seen from the coast path.

Geevor Tin Mine, the last operating mine in Penwith, closed down in 1990, and is now an outstanding heritage centre telling the story of Cornish coastal mining. Tours lead visitors through the old tunnels, while a guide brings to life the claustrophobic, dangerous conditions in which the miners worked. The highlight is the descent through the 18th-century horizontal shaft.

Half a mile from Geevor are the remains of the Levant Mine, which closed in 1930. Undersea tunnels, once rich with tin and copper, are topped by cliff-edge brick buildings housing the operational **Levant Beam Engine**, the oldest in the country, which was

originally used for winding men and materials up from the shaft. A mechanical breakdown caused the death of 31 miners here in 1919.

The promontory at Pendeen Watch is home to the **Pendeen Lighthouse**, which has been in operation since 1900. The lighthouse is open for tours during the summer, though the promontory offers spectacular views at all times of year; watch out for seals, dolphins, kestrels and buzzards.

After Pendeen the villages spread out again until you reach **Morvah**. Head inland from here to discover some fascinating ancient remains, accessible either by road or along the **Tinner's Way**, an 18-mile (29-kilometre) walking route that retraces the ancient paths along which tin and copper were transported from St Just to the sheltered anchorage of St Ives Bay (*see above* **Country walk**).

the large standing stone known as **Men Scryfa**, which commemorates 'Rialobran, the son of Cunoval', possibly a sixth-century Celtic king. The path descends to a point where it joins several routes. Take the narrow track that climbs up in a north-westerly direction, following the boundary of a field to the left between the granite heights of Watch Croft and Carn Galver.

Coming over the crest of the hill, the Atlantic suddenly spills into view to the west, with the remains of the **Carn Galver Tin Mine** below. Here the path drops down towards the B3306 coast road for the quick route back to Morvah.

To continue, turn right 200 yards to the north-east. The private climbing centre on the right is where Lord John Hunt and Sherpa Tensing Norgay celebrated the tenth anniversary of the ascent of Everest in 1963; it was the first time Tensing had seen the sea. Follow the path west-north-west down from the mine for 400 yards through a granite stile and gate towards the coast path.

Follow the coast path to the south-west, first crossing over a small stone bridge before climbing uphill with a good view to **Pendeen Lighthouse**. The path hugs the coastline in a general westerly direction and at points like **Trevean Cliff** comes awesomely close to the edge. It's about two miles (three kilometres) of coast walking to reach Morvah; follow the diagonal yellow arrow on the outskirts of the village to emerge just east of the church.

Rejoin the track 75 yards from the mine and turn left, heading north-east. Pick out a path 30 yards on the left winding across the surrounding hillocks and head north-east on to the moor again towards the rocky outcrop called Carn Galver. Once on to the moor, head uphill until the land levels out and the small path joins a main bridleway. Turn left and 30 yards ahead are the seven remaining stones of the **Nine Maidens** circle, yet another set of naughty girls who danced on the sabbath.

Continuing north-west, about 150 yards on the left is the **Four Parish Stone**, which marks the junction between Zennor, Gulval, Madron and Morvah. Continue downhill in a north-westerly direction and look west across to

Geevor Tin Mine

off B3306 nr Pendeen (01736 788662/www. geevor.com). **Open** *Late Mar-mid Nov* 10am-5pm daily. *Mid Nov-late Mar* 10am-4pm daily. **Admission** £6.50; £6 concessions; £17.50 family. **Credit** MC, V.

Land's End Experience

Land's End (01736 871220/hotline 0870 4580 044/www.landsend-landmark.co.uk). **Open** from 10am daily. **Admission** *Individual attractions* £2.50-£4. *Inclusive ticket* £10; £6-£8 concessions; £28 family. **Credit** MC, V.

Levant Beam Engine

Trewellard, nr Pendeen (National Trust 01736 786156). **Open** *May, Oct* 11am-5pm Tue, Fri. *June* 11am-5pm Wed-Fri, Sun. *July-Sept* 11am-5pm Mon-Fri, Sun. *Nov-Apr* phone for details. **Admission** £4; £2-£3.50 concessions; £10 family. **No credit cards**.

Minack Theatre

Porthcurno (01736 810181/www.minack.com). **Open** *Exhibition Centre* Apr-Sept 9.30am-5.30pm daily except during matinée performances; Oct-Mar 10am-4pm daily. *Performances* May-Sept phone for details. **Admission** *Centre* £2.50; £1.80 concessions. **Tickets** £5.50-£7. **Credit** MC, V.

Museum of Submarine Telegraphy

Porthcurno (01736 810966/810478/www. porthcurno.org.uk). **Open** *July, Aug* 10am-5pm daily. *Mar-Oct* 10am-5pm Mon-Fri, Sun. *Nov-Feb* 10am-4pm Mon, Sun. **Admission** phone for details.

Pendeen Watch Lighthouse

off B3306, nr Pendeen (01736 788418). **Open** *Easter-Oct* 10am-5pm Mon-Fri. Closed Nov-Mar. **Admission** £2.50; £1.50 concessions; £5 family. **No credit cards**.

Cornwall

The setting steals the show at the **Minack Theatre**. *See p255.*

Activities

Golf

In a stunning location, the **Cape Cornwall Golf & Country Club** (St Just, 01736 788611, www.capecornwall.com) is the most westerly 18-hole golf course in England (£20 for 18 holes). Other facilities include an indoor pool and a fitness centre.

Riding

Land's End Riding School (Trevescan Farm, Trevescan, Sennen, 01736 871989) is open all year and offers 5 rides per day, with evening rides available on request.

Surfing

Sennen Surf Centre (Sennen Cove, 01736 871458/ 871404) offers friendly, BSA-approved lessons – anything from 2hrs to 5 days – for beginners and improvers. **Freetime Holidays Learn to Surf** (Stone Cottages, St Levan, 01736 871302) offers BSA-approved surf tuition at Sennen Cove, plus introductory rock-climbing lessons and bicycle hire.

Where to eat, drink & stay

In the pretty village of Treen visit the **Logan Rock Inn** (01736 810495, main courses £4-£15), a quintessential Cornish pub oozing character and olde worlde charm. Cricket memorabilia dominates the decor and there's local Tinner's Bitter on tap at the bar. Campers will find it hard to beat the low-key, cliff-top **Treen Camp Site** (01736 810526, closed Oct-Mar).

Just down from the Minack Theatre in Porthcurno is the **Mariners' Lodge** (01736 810236, www.marinerslodgehotel.co.uk, double £50-£70), where the best guestrooms have a terrace boasting some of the finest sea views in West Penwith.

Around the coast, off the A30 at Sennen, the **Whitesands Lodge** (01736 871776, www.whitesandslodge.co.uk, main courses £5.95-£9.50, double B&B £49-£59, dorm £12) in Sennen is a funky, quietly psychedelic hangout that offers dorm accommodation as well as en suite B&B. The excellent café-restaurant serves good-value snacks, lunches and cream teas. There's also an exclusive ten-place campsite with access to the facilities. Two great daytime cafés to try down at Sennen Cove are **Billyz** (01736 871611) and the handy **Sennen Beach Café** (01736 871404), which offers good-quality fast food.

On the outskirts of St Just, off the Cape Cornwall road, is the **Boscean Country Hotel** (01736 788748, www.bosceancountry hotel.co.uk, double £23-£27), an old doctor's house with oak panelling and a quirky atmosphere. Dinner, if required, is at 7pm on the dot and showcases inventive cooking using local produce.

To the north is the superbly located **Botallack Manor** (St Just, 01736 788525, double B&B £26-£28 per person), an atmospheric 17th-century home above the coast path. The bedrooms, some of which have four-poster or half-tester beds, drip with exquisite antiques and there's a dreamy walled front garden. Nearby, an upmarket yet good-value B&B in Trewellard is the **Field House** (01736 788097, closed Oct-Mar, main courses £6.50-£7.50, double B&B £22-£25 per person), whose uncluttered rustic style incorporates sea views and a garden room café for light lunches and evening meals.

Resources

Internet
Access is provided by St Just Tourist Office & Library (*see below*).

Post offices
St Just *Market Street (01736 788432).* **Open** 9am-5pm Mon-Sat.
Sennen *(01736 871700).* **Open** 8.30am-7pm Mon-Sat; 9am-1.30pm Sun.

Tourist information
St Just *Tourist Office & Library, Market Street (01736 788669).* **Open** 10am-5pm Mon-Wed; 10am-6pm Fri; 10am-1pm Sat.

St Ives & around

West Penwith has a particular quality of light that has attracted artists for years. St Ives remains at the heart of this artistic community and a perfect setting for a branch of the Tate.

The town is a holiday favourite, with its award-winning beaches and enticing higgledy-piggledy streets. It is set on the wide scoop of St Ives Bay, which includes an impressive five-mile (eight-kilometre) stretch of sands from Hayle up to Godrevy Head. In the opposite direction, the scenic B3306 road heads away from the holidaying hordes, west towards St Just, taking in heart-stopping coastal scenery and the charming village of Zennor.

St Ives is named after St Ia, who according to legend was the first to come to this coast, having sailed across from Ireland on an ivy leaf. Arriving into St Ives today, by more conventional means, it is easy to see why he was attracted to this spot. For many people, St Ives is the best seaside town in the country, with sandy beaches at every touch and turn – surfers' favourite **Porthmeor Beach**; the more hidden **Porthgwidden Beach** on the other side of the Island outcrop; the handy **Harbour** beach; and the wide, sandy stretch at **Porthminster Beach**, with its neat row of beach-huts. In high season St Ives is reminiscent of Mediterranean shores, while in winter it offers the perfect, atmospheric weekend break.

St Ives' main shopping area is on Fore Street, behind the harbour, but there's good browsing to be had in the twisting 'downlong' alleys (where the fishermen used to live) and 'uplong' (where the miners once lived). Parking is the real bugbear, so in high season arrive by train along the delightful branch line from St Erth. The railway hugs the coast through Lelant and Carbis Bay, rolling into town just above Porthminster Beach.

St Ives Festival of Music and the Arts (01736 798888, www.st-ives-events.org) in September features international performers and a showcase for everything from classical music to jazz and folk, comedy, theatre and poetry. The other big annual event is New Year's Eve when around 40,000 people crowd the narrow streets and broad sands for fancy dress and fireworks.

In the 1850s St Ives was a centre of the fishing industry, but by the 1900s pilchard stocks had declined and the town was

Cornwall

attracting shoals of artists instead. The old pilchard cellars and sail lofts were converted into studios, particularly along Back Road West, which were opened once a year for public viewing. St Ives' popularity and artistic reputation increased in the following decades, but it was the arrival of Barbara Hepworth, Ben Nicholson, Russian sculptor Naum Gabo and the potter Bernard Leach in the 1930s that really put the town on the international art map. These abstract pioneers were followed in the '60s by another wave of artists, including Patrick Heron, Terry Frost and Peter Lanyon, who further developed the style and reputation of the so-called St Ives School (*see p27*).

Today artists continue to come to West Penwith, for the light, the land- and seascapes, the space and pace of life, and the company of other artists (*see p264* **Ones to watch**). The town's artistic heritage has spawned many galleries (*see below* **Straight to the art**), most notably the **Tate St Ives**, which opened in 1993. This heavyweight public gallery attracts art lovers from far and wide, and has established the town as a year-round visitor destination. The building itself is a cracker, with a striking curvy design that doesn't trumpet its status but rather rubs shoulders with the surrounding granite architecture. Although it is the undisputed flagship of Cornwall art, the gallery has an

Straight to the art

Check out the following galleries for a chance to pick up some local treasures.

Badcock's Gallery

Strand, Newlyn (01736 366159/ www.badcocksgallery.co.uk). **Open** *Jan-Mar phone for details. Easter-Dec 10.30am-5.30pm Mon-Sat.*
A contemporary gallery that's home to well-known and up-and-coming artists, Badcock's is right on Newlyn harbour, with a sister gallery on Chywoone Hill (01736 874850). Also sells innovative jewellery and other handmade crafts.

Belgrave Gallery

22 Fore Street, St Ives (01736 794888/ www.belgravegallery.com). **Open** *10am-1pm, 2-6pm Mon-Sat.*
This branch of the London gallery specialises in major artists associated with St Ives, such as Sir Terry Frost (whose *Blue, Yellow & Red for Newlyn Blue*, 1996, is pictured right) and Wilhelmina Barns-Graham. Also look out for up-and-coming stars like Henrietta Dubrey.

Great Atlantic Map Works Gallery

West Place, St Just (01736 788911/ www.greatatlantic.co.uk). **Open** *10am-5pm Mon-Sat; 2-5pm Sun.*
A very successful gallery showcasing local artists garnering an international reputation, like Neil Pinkett and Kurt Jackson (*see p264* **Ones to watch**).

Navigator Contemporary Arts

41 Fore Street, St Just (01736 787052/ www.navigatorgallery.co.uk). **Open** *11am-5pm Tue-Fri; 10.30am-5pm Sat; 2-5pm Sun.*

This bright and airy gallery displays a diverse range of affordable arts, crafts and sculpture by Crafts Council members and others.

New Millennium Gallery

Street-an-pol, St Ives (01736 793121/ www.stives.dircon.co.uk). **Open** *Mar-Dec 10.30am-4.30pm Mon-Sat. Closed Jan, Feb.*
A stylish and sharp gallery space on three storeys, showing high-quality abstract and figurative work, with regular solo shows.

intimate feel that is in danger of being upstaged by its beautiful beachside location. In fact, it can sometimes be difficult to concentrate on the art when the views are so stunning – most notably from the top-floor open terrace by the excellent café.

The Tate is a showcase for 20th-century painters and sculptors, particularly those associated with St Ives. On arrival, visitors are greeted by the huge, lead-free, stained-glass window by Patrick Heron, whose vibrant colours exploit St Ives' famous luminosity. Elsewhere look out for the naïve art of fisherman-turned-artist Alfred Wallis (*see p27*); the pottery of Bernard Leach and Shoji Hamada (for both *see p27*); elemental sculptures by

Penwith Galleries

Back Road West, St Ives (01736 795579). **Open** 10am-1pm, 2.30-5pm Tue-Sat.
Founded in 1949 by a group of artists including Barbara Hepworth and Ben Nicholson, this extensive gallery complex occupies a former Mariners' Church. The unique building incorporates public galleries, a bookshop and artists' studios.

St Ives Ceramics

1 Lower Fish Street, St Ives (01736 794930/www.st-ives-ceramics.co.uk). **Open** 10am-5pm Mon-Sat.
Contemporary ceramics by up to 50 potters are sold alongside a large range of domestic wares.

Wills Lane Gallery

1 Wills Lane, St Ives (01736 795723). **Open** Summer 10.30am-5pm Mon-Sat. Winter phone for details.
This is the longest-established private contemporary gallery in Cornwall. Major painters of the St Ives School are shown here alongside other artists, including, er, David Bowie.

Yew Tree Gallery

Keigwin, nr Morvah (01736 786425/ www.yewtreegallery.com). **Open** 10.30am-5pm Tue-Sat; 2-5pm Sun during exhibitions only.
Located on the inspirational north coast, this stone-built gallery and glasshouse is surrounded by sculpture gardens and shows contemporary fine and applied arts.

Barbara Hepworth; and striking paintings from the 1950s and '60 by the likes of Lanyon, Frost and Heron. In addition to the Tate collection, the gallery also hosts special exhibitions by local and international artists.

From the gallery, wind your way through the alleys and streets towards the harbour, where fishermen still land their catch at Smeaton's Pier. Nearby, the absorbing **St Ives Museum** brings to life the history of this Cornish port, with displays on pilchards, art, mining and the railways, supplemented by an eccentric collection of ephemera. Beyond the museum, the beaches of Porthgwidden and Porthmeor are divided by the **Island**, a blustery headland with St Nicholas Chapel at its tip. Climb up here for expansive views of the bay.

On the other side of the harbour, the **Barbara Hepworth Museum & Sculpture Garden** is a must for any visitor. This highly enjoyable small museum was Hepworth's home from 1949 until her death in a fire here in 1975. It is now owned by the Tate and offers an inspiring real glimpse into the sculptor's life, with her studio preserved just as she left it. Beautiful pieces of sculpture, including *Fallen Images* (which was completed only a few months before her death), are complemented by extensive background material on the artist, while the wonderful garden displays many of her larger pieces in a glorious subtropical setting. Many demonstrate her fascination with Cornwall's ancient menhirs and dolmens.

Situated just down the hill, off Bedford Road, another tranquil haven is provided by the **Trewyn Subtropical Gardens**, where wooden sculptures hide out among the grass and banana trees.

WEST OF TOWN

Before you set off along the coast, take time to visit the **Leach Pottery** on the north-western outskirts of St Ives. Established by Bernard Leach in 1920, the working pottery now houses a permanent exhibition of ceramics by Leach, Shoji Hamada and their numerous disciples, demonstrating Leach's pioneering work with Far Eastern glazes and techniques.

After this, though, there's nothing to keep you from the exceptional scenery of Penwith's north coast. In summer open-topped buses run along the B3306 from St Ives to St Just, allowing visitors to take in the full glory of the landscape, but you'll get an even better idea of its rugged beauty on foot by setting out along the coast path.

Zennor is the signature village along this stretch, with a nest of granite cottages, cosying up to the Tinner's Arms pub (01736 796927). DH Lawrence lived in the village during World

Cornwall

Porthminster Beach Café. *See p264.*

War I and used it as a setting for *Women in Love*; it was also the home of Patrick Heron, whose house, Eagle's Nest, is dramatically sited just off the B3306.

Not to be missed in the village is the kooky **Wayside Folk Museum**, which houses over 5,000 artefacts – everything from prehistoric seed grinders to literary memorabilia – together with photographs of Zennor life and a reconstruction of a traditional Cornish kitchen. Also visit the church of **St Senara** to see the famous 'Mermaid Chair' created from two 16th-century bench ends. The carving on the chair refers to a legend in which a local choirboy was lured into the sea by a mermaid, never to return. Apparently, his singing can still occasionally be heard from **Pendour Cove**, a small beach overlooked by the stunning cliffs of **Zennor Head**. There are fabulous walks along the coast on either

side of Zennor, with the looming drama of **Gurnard's Head** pushing out into the Atlantic, a mile or so to the west.

EAST OF TOWN

Almost joined to St Ives to the east, **Carbis Bay** has a stunner of a beach with amazing views, but the village is a rather characterless jumble of B&Bs and hotels. **Lelant** is altogether more attractive, with a pretty church and a nature reserve overlooking the Hayle estuary.

The town of **Hayle** is workaday and a touch faded but regeneration plans are afoot, and it's worth visiting just to sample a pasty from the famous **Philps** bakery (East Quay, 01736 755661). Apart from that, the beaches are the thing here. Backed by *towans* (dunes), they offer acres of family-friendly sand between swathes of holiday camps and caravan parks.

At the head of St Ives Bay, **Godrevy Head** is a superb spot, with sand dunes, gigantic rock pools that are large enough to swim in, and good surf. **Godrevy Lighthouse** is immortalised in Virginia Woolf's *To the Lighthouse*, in which the author fondly remembers her childhood holidays in St Ives.

Barbara Hepworth Museum & Sculpture Garden

Barnoon Hill, St Ives (01736 796226/www. tate.org.uk). **Open** *Nov-Feb* 10am-4.30pm Tue-Sun. *Mar-Oct* 10am-5.30pm daily. **Admission** £3.95; £2.25 concessions. **Credit** MC, V.

Leach Pottery

Higher Stennack, St Ives (01736 796398/ www.leachpottery.com). **Open** 10am-5pm Mon-Sat. **Admission** £2.50; £1.50 concessions. **Credit** MC, V.

St Ives Museum

Wheal Dream (nr Smeaton's Pier), St Ives (01736 796005). **Open** *Easter-Oct* 10am-5pm Mon-Fri; 10am-4pm Sat. Closed Nov-Mar. **Admission** £1.50. **No credit cards**.

Tate Gallery

Porthmeor Beach, St Ives (01736 796226/www. tate.org.uk). **Open** *Mar-Oct* 10am-5.30pm daily. *Nov-Feb* 10am-4.30pm Tue-Sun. **Admission** £4.25; £2.50 concessions. **Credit** MC, V.

Wayside Folk Museum

Zennor (01736 796945). **Open** *Apr* 11am-5pm daily. *May-Sept* 10am-6pm daily. *Oct* 11am-5pm Mon-Fri, Sun. Closed Nov-Mar. **Admission** free.

Activities

Art

The **St Ives School of Painting** (Back Road West, 01736 797180, www.stivesartschool.co.uk) offers art courses for beginners and more experienced painters. Lessons are held in one of the original studios.

Oh we do like to be beside the seaside...
St Ives. *See p259*.

Ones to watch

In addition to the venerable Sir Terry Frost and Wilhelmina Barns-Graham (*see p28*) there are plenty of successful younger artists working in studios around the Penwith Peninsula. Their creations can be found in the local galleries but are also making a splash at prestigious art venues around the world. For further information, read *Behind the Canvas, 40 Artists Working in West Cornwall* by Sarah Brittain and Simon Cook.

Sandra Blow

Born in London in 1925, Sandra Blow studied at St Martins College and the Royal Academy. In 1957 she stayed at Zennor, where she became friends with local artists including Bryan Wynter and Peter Lanyon, and eventually moved to St Ives in 1994. Her strong, abstract paintings have a raw, vital quality about them, and demonstrate instinctive use of colour.

Kurt Jackson

Jackson took art classes at Ruskin College in Oxford while studying zoology at the university. He now lives in St Just and likes to paint and draw out in the field, often incorporating mud, grass and written notes into his work. His pieces display the edge and essence of the Penwith landscape and are garnering an increasing amount of international recognition.

Rachael Kantaris

Rachael was born in Australia in 1967, but lives in St Ives. She worked for Wilhelmina Barns-Graham and now runs her own print workshops (details on www.kantaris.com/rachael/rachael.htm). Kantaris specialises in etching, which allows her to explore her fascination with the interaction of colours. She also paints.

Maggie Matthews

Welsh-born Matthews came to Penwith in 1988 after studying art at Newport and Exeter. She has a studio in Newlyn, where she produces colourful, abstract paintings inspired by the land, sea, sky and the interplay of the weather and the seasons.

Neil Pinkett

A local boy from St Just, Neil Pinkett worked as a designer in London before returning to Cornwall to realise his dreams of being a painter. From his studio in Zennor he uses the local land, sea and townscapes as inspiration for his oil paintings, which are dramatic and passionate.

Cycling

Bikes can be hired from **Hayle Cycles** (36 Penpol Terrace, Hayle, 01736 753825).

Surfing

Ride the waves of St Ives Bay with the help of the **St Ives Surf School** (Penbeagle House, Penbeagle Way, St Ives, 07765 571334), which is based on Porthmeor Beach, or **Shore Surf School** (46 Mount Pleasant, Hayle, 01736 755556, www.shoresurf.com).

Where to eat & drink

For a small town, St Ives has an amazing selection of places for eating and drinking, from grab-and-run pasty joints to top-notch fish restaurants. One of the latter is the specialist **Seafood Café** (45 Fore Street, 01736 794004, www.seafoodcafe.co.uk, main courses £6.95-£15.95), which combines Conranesque decor with a very welcoming vibe. Choose your catch from the iced display and then pick a sauce to go with it: dill and honey, fresh hollandaise, ginger and spring onion, etc. There's also excellent fish and chips for £6.95.

On sunny days the relaxing **Porthminster Beach Café** (Porthminster Beach, 01736 795352, closed Jan-Mar, main courses £10.75-£16.50) could be on the Mediterranean. It's right on the beach, with views over the bay, and its large terrace is the perfect spot for a lazy coffee – or a fantastic cream tea. The stylish interior is the setting for regular arts exhibitions as well as an excellent fishy menu, including the likes of crispy skinned wild sea bass with sea scallops. Its sister café at Porthgwidden Beach is smaller but offers similar food in another top location.

Right by the busy harbour, **OnShore** (01736 796000, main courses £5.45-£12.95) has a varied Mediterranean menu including authentic pizzas from a wood-burning stove. Nearby, **Alba** (The Old Lifeboat House, The Wharf, 01736 797222, main courses £12-£17) has been beautifully converted from the skeleton of the old lifeboat station. This sleek eaterie serves top-class Modern European cuisine with a dash of the Far East (there's a sushi chef on site). Make sure you save some room for the home-made ice-cream.

Blue Fish Restaurant (Norway Lane, 01736 794204, closed Nov-Feb, main courses £9-£14) is another deft conversion, this time from a narrow net loft into a simple but groovy blue and white restaurant, with a fantastic terrace overlooking the harbour. The long Mediterranean menu includes great tapas.

If you're fed up with fish, visit the **Jarmini Café & Restaurant** (The Warren, 01736 797975, www.jarmini.com, closed winter, phone for details), a relaxed, purple-hued eaterie that serves fab breakfasts, tasty paninis and modern Anglo-Indian fusion dishes. It is great for veggies or vegans.

Heading out of town, try the **Gurnard's Head Hotel** (B3306, Treen, near Zennor, 01736 796928, www.cornwall-online.co.uk/gurnards-head, main courses £9-£12.50), where the best tables overlook the dramatic north coast. Enjoy a pint of Knocker beer and a half-pint of Atlantic prawns or the scrumptious Cornish seafood broth. There's regular live music here, and B&B in basic but comfortable en suite rooms (double £50-£70).

Where to stay

The hotels and B&Bs in St Ives don't match the high quality of its restaurants, with many stuck in a terminally tired rut. Worth mentioning for its facilities, however, is **Tregenna Castle Hotel** (01736 795254, www.tregenna-castle.demon.co.uk, double B&B £55 per person incl dinner), which enjoys a commanding setting over the bay and offers badminton, tennis, indoor and outdoor pools, golf and subtropical gardens; the self-catering units are a better option than the uninspiring rooms. Also at the top of town is **Garrack Hotel & Restaurant** (Burthallan Lane, 01736 796199, www.garrack.com, main courses £9-£16, double B&B £114-£162), a family-run hotel with full-on ocean views and clean, comfy rooms in a modern annexe. The commendable restaurant uses local produce, including fresh lobster, and has an impressively extensive wine list. The indoor pool is a bonus.

Closer to the action, **Grey Mullet** (2 Bunkers Hill, 01736 796635, double B&B £22-£26 per person) is a quintessential 'downlong' cottage just 20 yards from the harbour. The granite rooms are full of art and old oak beams, while terrific breakfasts are served in the atmospheric cellar dining room. On the other side of the town centre, the **Pedn-Olva Hotel** (West Porthminster Beach, 01736 796222, www.thewalterhickshotel.co.uk, set meals £18/£23.50, double B&B £65-£84 incl dinner) makes the most of its top location by Porthminster Beach. It's been successively

refurbished in a refreshingly modern, Mediterranean style, with lovely sun terraces and a small pool outside. Fresh, local fare is put to good use in the Lookout Restaurant.

West of St Ives backpackers stop off at the **Old Chapel** (Zennor, 01736 798307, www.zennorbackpackers.co.uk, rates £9-£10 per person), which offers simple rooms plus a café serving good-value food, while couples will find **Cove Cottage** (Gurnards Head, near Zennor, 01736 798317, www.cornwall-online.co.uk/cove-cottage, closed Nov-Feb, double B&B £70) ideal for a romantic escape. Its beautifully decorated guestrooms are perched above a secluded sandy cove that's perfect for swimming and dolphin spotting. Breakfast is served on the terrace in warm weather, and for dinner, the **Gurnard's Head Hotel** (*see above*) is a short climb up the hill. Or there's **Tregeraint House** (B3306, near Zennor, 01736 797061, double B&B £50), a classic Cornish cottage bursting with good taste. Run with verve by a local potter, its cosy, rustic-chic rooms are supplemented by gardens with views to Gurnard's Head. Superb breakfasts.

Resources

Internet
St Ives *Library, Gabriel Street (01736 795377).*
Open 9.30am-6pm Tue-Fri; 9.30am-12.30pm Sat.

Post office
St Ives *Tregenna Place (01736 795004).*
Open 9am-5.30pm Mon-Fri; 9am-12.30pm Sat.

Tourist Information
St Ives *Tourist Information Centre, The Guildhall, Street-an-pol (01736 796297).* **Open** *Summer* 9am-6pm Mon-Sat; 10am-4pm Sun. *Winter* 9am-5pm Mon-Sat.

Getting there

By bus
National Express (08705 808080) coaches arrive in Penzance from Truro and further afield. From here, local buses head north to St Ives, and west to Newlyn, Paul and Mousehole, with a few continuing as far as Land's End. There are also a few services from Penzance to St Just. An open-top bus (01736 69469) runs along the scenic route between Land's End and St Ives from May Bank Holiday to end Sept.

By train
First Great Western (08457 000125) operates daily services from London Paddington to Penzance (the journey takes at least 5hrs); change at St Erth for the branch line to St Ives. It is also possible to travel by Motorail (08456 010847) from London to Penzance for £94 return (car and driver).

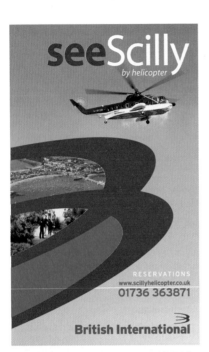

The North Coast

Top surfing beaches, culinary treats and a ruined Arthurian castle.

Cornwall's Atlantic coast is more rugged than its counterpart on the English Channel, characterised by dramatic cliffs, fabulous beaches and some of the biggest waves in the country. Historically, this area has been defined by the twin industries of fishing and mining: derelict engine houses still dot the landscape around **Camborne**, **Redruth** and **St Agnes**, providing a fascinating counterpoint to the leisure-driven activities of today. The largest resort is **Newquay**, a mecca for British surfers and their hangers-on. If you're not one of them, then its numerous beaches are certainly worth a visit, but the town's chip-shop gaudiness and its attendant tourist hordes may soon have you fleeing for other locales. These might include **Padstow**, famed for its fish restaurants and lovely estuary; **Tintagel** with its stunning ruined castle; the surfing centre of **Bude**; or the atmospheric coastal villages of **Port Isaac**, **Boscastle** and **Morwenstow**.

Redruth & around

'There's been a terrible earthquake in Redruth,' a local joke announces, adding gravely, 'It caused two million pounds worth of improvements.' Slanderous one-liners aside, it's true that Redruth and its sister town Camborne are not the most appealing tourist destinations in the county. However, as centres of the Cornish mining industry in the 19th century, they deserve a second glance.

During the 1850s this part of Cornwall was one of the largest mining areas on the planet, producing two-thirds of the world's copper. However, the discovery of cheaper deposits of ore overseas at the end of the 19th century heralded the decline of Cornish mining and a slump in the area's fortunes. While evidence of their industrial heritage is everywhere to be seen, Camborne and Redruth have struggled to find a role in the modern era.

The glorious beach at **Bedruthan Steps**. *See p273.*

Cornwall

Surf check North Cornwall

Laid bare to the muscular swells of the North Atlantic, the stretch of Cornwall's northern coastline from St Agnes to Morwenstow harbours some truly world-class surfing breaks. On the downside, many of these spots are for experienced surfers only and are closely guarded by local crews, so beginners are better off exploring the two main hubs of the north Cornish scene: **Newquay** (see p272) and **Bude** (see p283). But be warned: even off-season, expect crowds when the surf is working.

The best surfing around Newquay is to be had at **Fistral Beach**, which is divided into three main breaks – Little Fistral, North Fistral and South Fistral. It's a sandy-bottomed beach break, which offers everything from fast, hollow waves to slow and manageable rides for groms and weekend splashers. For the lazy or uninitiated, **Towan** has less consistent, generally mushy waves, popular with fun-boarders who are just finding their feet.

The options around Bude fall into three main categories. First is **Widemouth Bay**, the indicator for the region and a good spot for beginners since it works at all stages of the tide. In Bude itself, there's **Crooklets** (a decent beach break shared with holidaymakers and swimmers) and **Summerleaze** (a good bet when the others are blown out). Beyond these hubs, seasoned riders who don't have favourite nooks of their own should head for the reef- and beach-breaks at **Constantine** (see p276).

The biggest waves come in the autumn and winter, when Atlantic storms stir up some fat ground swells. Flat spells in summer are a constant source of frustration to locals and of crushing disappointment to those who've covered hundreds of miles of motorway for a weekend's surfing. So, before you head off, consult www.6ftoffshore.com to check the swell and wind direction (anything in the eastern quadrant is good) and to make sure you won't be wasting your time.

That said, **Redruth** – from 'rhyd' meaning ford and 'ruth' meaning red – boasts some dignified civic architecture and a lovely old Cornish thoroughfare in the form of Fore Street. Moreover, the town was recently made the recipient of government funding, with a view to restoring its more rundown areas. In the centre, the unglamorous but thorough **Old Cornwall Society Museum** displays minerals, mining artefacts and neolithic tools found nearby.

Camborne (meaning 'crooked hill') is a more intimate place, whose bargain and charity shops are interspersed with shows of civic swagger such as **Camborne Library** on Cross Street. Outside stands a statue of local inventor Richard Trevithick (1771-1833), who created the first true beam engine, which allowed the mining of much deeper shafts. He was born in the village of Penponds near Camborne in a thatched cottage now administered by the **Trevithick Trust** (01209 612154, www.trevithicktrust.com; phone for details of the irregular opening hours) and is remembered at the annual **Trevithick Day** festival (www.trevithick-day.org.uk) in Camborne on the last Saturday in April. This event celebrates the area's mining history with concerts, Cornish dancing and a steam engine parade.

The Camborne School of Mines, located midway between Camborne and Redruth, has displays of glittering underworld minerals in its

Geological Museum, plus information on the regional industry and a gallery of local art. On a far bigger scale, the **Mineral Tramways Discovery Centre** lays out the history of Cornish mining with a permanent indoor exhibition of maps, diagrams and tools. Outside is a restored pumping house (Taylor's Shaft) and an operational winding engine, while surrounding the centre are waymarked trails that reveal Cornwall's 'Copper Kingdom' in its multiple aspects (see p269).

Beyond the towns the moorland is bracing, with masses of wrecked engine houses – many choked in greenery – creating a scene of unique desolation. Dominating the whole region is the ragged, boulder-strewn summit of **Carn Brea**, crowned by an imposing cross and a folly castle. There are vestiges of a neolithic hill fort here, as well as ancient copper workings.

Cornish miners worked long and hard, often for a pittance. Illness and accident were daily hazards, and most miners were lucky if they reached their 40th birthday. What's more, during the boom years, the area's population quickly outgrew its social facilities, resulting in widespread poverty and appalling living conditions. Many found consolation in Methodism, as preached by John Wesley (1703-91) on his frequent visits to Devon and Cornwall. An open-air venue for such exhortations was the acoustically sensitive natural amphitheatre of **Gwennap Pit**, near St Day, just outside of Redruth, which is still used for Methodist meetings on Whit Monday.

On the coast at the mouth of the Red River (named after the iron oxide that stained the water) is **Portreath**, or 'Sandy Cove', a fishing port developed in Georgian times by the mining tycoon Sir Francis Bassett. The port's industrial past is still visible in the imposing granite quays of the cliff-enclosed harbour, and in the old Poldice–Portreath tramroad, which joined the mines of Gwennap and St Day. As elsewhere, when the copper lodes became exhausted, Portreath gradually altered from a hard-edged industrial community to one clutching at the fragile straws of tourism. Amid the healed scars of industry are chalets, bungalows and transitory tourist shops fronting a north-facing sandy beach that draws hundreds in summer. To get away from the crowds, strike out south along the coast path as far as **Hell's Mouth**, where vast black cliffs descend into the boiling sea.

Geological Museum

Camborne School of Mines, Pool (01209 714866/ www.ex.ac.uk/CSM/). **Open** 10am-4pm Mon-Fri. **Admission** free.

Mineral Tramways Discovery Centre

Old Cowlin's Mill, Penhallick, Carn Brea, nr Redruth (01209 612917). **Open** phone for details. **Admission** phone for details.

Old Cornwall Society Museum

Council Chambers, 1 Penryn Street, Redruth (01209 215084/www.redruth.org). **Open** 10am-4pm Wed-Fri. **Admission** free; donations welcome.

Activities

Walking & cycling

The **Mineral Tramways** walking and cycling routes are the best way to explore Cornwall's 'Copper Kingdom'. The Coast to Coast Trail (11 miles/17.5 km) links the historic mining harbours of Portreath and Devoran, retracing the route of two early horse-drawn tramroads. The Great Flat Lode Trail (6.5 miles/10.5km) circumnavigates Carn Brea, while the short Tresavean Trail (2 miles/1.5km) near Lanner has good views of St Austell's china clay pits.

Where to eat, drink & stay

For a decent bite to eat, there's the **Brea Inn & Restaurant** (Higher Brea, near Camborne, 01209 713706, closed Mon lunch, main courses £7-£13), originally an 18th-century alehouse. Rather plusher is the light-fronted **Penventon Hotel** (West Road, Redruth, 01209 203000, double £78-£110), which provides three-star accommodation and a restaurant that flaunts Venetian chandeliers and French tapestries. In the middle of Portreath, tucked in beside the old viaduct, **Tabb's** (Railway Terrace, Tregea, 01209 842488, closed Tue, main courses £11.50-£19) is the area's most commendable eaterie, with a conservatory front converted from a granite forge. Everything from the bread to the ice-cream is made on the premises. Inland, the **Old Vicarage** (Church Road, Stithians, 01209 860396, main courses £5-£12, double £60-£65) has cosy rooms and a beer garden.

Resources

Internet

Redruth *Redruth Library, Clinton Road (01209 219111).* **Open** 10am-6pm Mon-Fri; 10am-1pm Sat.

Police station

Camborne *South Terrace (0870 577 7444).* **Redruth** *Drump Road (0870 577 7444).*

Post office

Portreath *Penberthy Road (01209 215774).* **Open** 9am-5.30pm Mon-Fri; 9am-12.30pm Sat. **Redruth** *61 Fore Street (08457 223344).* **Open** 9am-5.30pm Mon-Fri; 9am-12.30pm Sat.

St Agnes & around

No longer the heartbeat of the community, ruined engine houses rise up around St Agnes like ruinous exclamation marks, recalling the old saying, *'Sten Sen Agnes an gwella sten yn Kernor'* or 'St Agnes is the best tin in Cornwall'.

Originally a fishing settlement, St Agnes grew in significance in the late 18th century when a harbour was built at steep, storm-lashed **Trevaunance Cove** to allow the export of copper and tin. Today, barely a brick of the harbour remains, but a superb model of it in **St Agnes Museum** shows how goods were hauled up the cliffside. The museum also houses photos and diagrams about the history of the area, from neolithic farming to post-industrial reclamation, plus an expressive self-portrait by John Opie (*see p26*).

Today's straggling town is centred around the Victorian parish church and a chummy squeeze of galleries, shops and brownstone cottages. A little further down is **Stippy Stappy** hill, beloved of photographers and lined with a row of wisteria-clad cottages. Artists and craftspeople sell their wares – everything from watercolours to metalwork, and tartan to fudge – in galleries around Quay, Vicarage and Churchtown streets. Grab a 'Craft Trail' leaflet from the tourist office (*see p272*) to lead you around. There's more craft action at the creative complex of

Cornwall

Setting out for the surf at **Newquay**. *See p272.*

Presingoll Barns (01872 553007) on the B3277, just outside town. Rather more rough and ready are **Blue Hills Tin Streams** at Wheal Kitty above Trevaunance Cove, where the traditional early methods of Cornish tin mining are re-created for visitors. Inland, meanwhile, are the legless pleasures of the **Cornish Cyder Farm**, with its farm animals, tractor rides and distillery.

To get an idea of the impressive terrain in this area, with ranks of wrecked engine houses set against the bracing prospect of sea and shore, stagger up the heathery summit of **St Agnes Beacon** (629 feet/192 metres), one of Cornwall's best vantage points, with views extending to St Ives and Trevose Head. The surrounding coast is dotted with popular surfing beaches, notably **Porthtowan** and **Chapel Porth** to the south.

The next sizeable resort up the coast, **Perranporth**, is a riotous ramble of chalets, bungalows and older terraces. Once a hard-pressed fishing and mining settlement, today it has a golf course, palm-fringed streets and a plethora of beach shops. Architectural decor is a little gimcrack: plenty of inns, pastel-fronted guesthouses and instant eateries. Significantly, though, Perranporth has one of the oldest surfing clubs in the country, and

its beach is understandably the town's chief attraction. The long, smooth stretch of **Perran** (or **Ligger**) **Bay** is hammered by Atlantic rollers and backed by a variegated selection of caves, rocky arches and traces of old mineworkings. Surfing is pretty good here at all times, particularly at **Penhale Sands** at the north end of the bay.

For some spirituality amid so much waterborne fun, take a walk across Penhale sand dunes, which preserve one of the oldest foundations in the county. The **Oratory of St Piran**, patron saint of tinners, was abandoned in the 11th century and lost for hundreds of years. It was dug up in 1835 and later encased in a concrete shell, but has since succumbed to the sands once more (controversial plans to uncover the ruins are ongoing).

The history of the oratory is explored in **Perranzabuloe Folk Museum**, which also has local agriculture and mining exhibits, and material relating to **Piran Round**, a massive Iron Age site beside the B3285 that was adapted for use as a *plain-an-gwarry* (open-air theatre) during the Middle Ages.

Blue Hills Tin Streams

Wheal Kitty, St Agnes (01872 553341/www.blue hills.com). **Open** 10.30am-5pm Mon-Sat. **Admission** £3.50; £1.50 concessions. **Credit** MC, V.

Cornish Cyder Farm

A3075, nr Penhallow (01872 573356). **Open** 9am-5pm Mon-Fri. **Admission** free.

Perranzabuloe Folk Museum

Oddfellows Hall, Ponsmere Road, Perranporth (01872 573431). **Open** 10.30am-4.30pm Mon-Fri; 11am-1pm Sat. **Admission** free.

St Agnes Museum

Penwinnick Road, St Agnes (01872 553228). **Open** *Easter-Oct* 10.30am-5pm daily. Closed Nov-Easter. **Admission** free.

Activities

Golf

Perranporth Golf Club (Budnick Hill, 01872 572454) is an 18-hole seaside course with unrestricted access for visiting players.

Riding

Goonbell Riding Centre (Goonbell, St Agnes, 01872 552063) provides lessons and hacks for children and adults.

Surfing

Lessons in wave-riding are offered by **St Agnes Surfing School** (35 Saint Trevaunance Road, 01872 553094); wetsuits and boards can be hired or bought from **Aggie Surf Shop** (4 Peterville Square, St Agnes, 01872 553818, www.aggiesurfshop.com).

Where to eat, drink & stay

In hermetic seclusion is the three-star **Rose-In-Vale Country House Hotel** (Mithian, St Agnes, 01872 552202, www.rose-in-vale-hotel.co.uk, closed Jan, Feb, main courses £11.95-£14.95, double B&B £54.50-£84.50), an 18th-century country house with formal, flowery bedrooms, a cocktail bar and a restaurant, all set in 11 acres of wooded grounds. Massages are available on request.

In the centre of town, try the good-value **St Agnes Hotel** (Churchtown, 01872 552307, www.st-agnes-hotel.co.uk, main courses £8.75-£12.25, double B&B £30-£55), a relaxed village hostelry, with six floral-free en suite rooms, an airy bar and an à la carte restaurant. Don't miss the dusky, convivial atmosphere of the **Railway Inn** (Vicarage Road, St Agnes, 01872 552310, main courses £4.50-£16.95), an unprettified Cornish pub, with a resident ghost, good food and real ales.

Rather more kitsch is the **Driftwood Spars Hotel** (Trevaunance Cove, 01872 55248, www.driftwoodspars.com, main courses £4.50-£15, double B&B £36-£40), a former sail loft and warehouse that hosts popular live music evenings. Perching on the edge of the beach nearby, **Schooners Bistro** (01872 553149, main courses £8.95-£15.75) is perfect for those who like a sunset beaming over their seafood.

In Perranporth, the **Tide's Reach Hotel** (Ponsmere Road, 01872 572188, closed Jan-Mar, double £25) has cheerful budget rooms and also incorporates **Tidy's Vegetarian Restaurant** (set meal £11.95). The modernised **Seiners Arms** (Beach Road, 01872 573024, main courses £8.95-£12.95, double £31) occupies the site of former pilchard-curing cellars and has an oceanside sun terrace, while **Rafter's** (St George's Hill, 01872 572878, closed Jan, Feb, main courses £7-£14) serves fairly priced fish dishes. Located right on the beach, the **Watering Hole** (Bathsheba Surf, 01872 572888, closed Jan, main courses £4.50-£12.95) is the liveliest spot in the area, with a bustling bar, summer barbecues and live music.

Resources

Internet

St Agnes *St Agnes Library (01872 553245).* **Open** 10am-7pm Tue; 10am-5pm Wed, Thur; 10am-1pm Sat.

Post office

St Agnes *24 Churchtown (01872 552348).* **Open** 9am-5.30pm Mon-Fri; 9am-12.30pm Sat.

Cornwall

Tourist information

Perranporth *Tourist Information Centre, Cliff
Road (01872 573368/www.perraninfo.co.uk).*
Open *Summer* 10am-12.30pm, 2-5pm Mon-Fri;
10am-1pm Sat. *Winter* 10am-12.30pm, 2-5pm
Mon-Thur.
St Agnes *Tourist Information Centre, 20
Churchtown (01872 554150/www.stagnes.com).*
Open 9am-9pm Mon-Sat; 11.30am-8.30pm Sun.

Newquay & around

As Cornwall's centre of fun, **Newquay** is
racier and tackier than, say, Fowey or St
Mawes, but has none of the peephole hilarities
– or dismalities – of, say, Blackpool. That's
because it's a Cornish rather than an English
resort – vivid, wild and bracing, with a gold-
rush euphoria in the jostle of over-dressed
Victorian hotels, holiday chalets, bars, clubs,
surf shops and ice-cream parlours.

Newquay is by no means as new as its name
implies, having first developed in the 15th
century as a secure harbourage from the heavy
seas. During the 19th century the town waxed
on the pilchard trade, with a fleet of 40 'seining'
boats unloading vast hauls to be cured and
stored in the town's cellars. From the **Huer's
Hut** at the western end of the bay, the
watchman or 'huer' kept a look-out for shoals
of pilchards, alerting the fisherman by yelling
'heva' through a long horn. From the 1840s
the harbour was used to export copper and
china clay, but the arrival of the GWR marked
the decline of Newquay's maritime trade.
No matter; by then its seaside character had
taken hold and was rapidly expanding.

Today, although criticised for unashamedly
selling out to the tourist market, Newquay
retains an undeniable appeal thanks to its
glorious sandy beaches and Atlantic breakers,
which have turned it into the undisputed
surfing capital of the UK. National and
international wave-riding championships
provide the excuse for some of the biggest
summer events in the South West, including
Run to the Sun (www.runtothesun.co.uk) on
the last weekend in May. Based at Trevelgue
Holiday Park, this is the country's largest
custom car and VW festival, when Beetle-
enthusiasts and dance music fans throng the
town for a weekend of camping, cars, dancing
and, erm, waterpistol fights.

NEWQUAY'S BEACHES

From the beachside Island Crescent, a
miniature, privately owned suspension bridge
makes a daring leap across to an outcrop on
Towan Beach. Nestling next to the harbour,
this is the most central of Newquay's beaches
and consequently the busiest during the

summer silly season, with numerous
watersports-hire outfits and the undersea safari
of the **Blue Reef Aquarium** keeping the
crowds entertained. Beyond the harbour,
the houses and roads soon run out, and a
path continues past the Huer's Hut to the
undeveloped cliff top at **Towan Head** for
great ocean views. On the west side of the
headland is the cove of **Little Fistral**, followed
by **Fistral Beach** proper, a west-facing strand
that bears the full brunt of the Atlantic. It's
Newquay's premier surfing venue and the
setting for national and international surfing
competitions (*see p268* **Surf check**). At the
far end of Fistral Beach, East Pentire Head
overlooks the Gannel estuary as it noses out to
sea. On the south side of the estuary – reached
by ferry from Pentire hamlet – the village
of **Crantock** is a secluded suburb, with a
window-box charm that appeals to the retired,
and a north-west-facing beach backed by
grass-topped dunes. Beyond Kelsey Head,
Holywell Bay is another popular dune-
surrounded beach with parking, toilets and
snacking facilities.

Heading in the opposite direction from
the centre of town, the ragged curves of the
hotel-fronted cliffs shelter **Great Western**,
Tolcarne and the wonderfully named **Lusty
Glaze** beaches. Controversial plans are afoot to
create a £6-million artificial surf reef off-shore
at Tolcarne, but for the moment these sheltered
stretches of sand remain the preserve of
beginners with body boards.

Next up is road-level **Porth Beach** with
Porth Island at its eastern end. This was the
site of an Iron Age settlement and is linked
to the mainland by a footbridge. Beyond are
the wind-honed sandy reaches of **Watergate
Beach** – a two-mile (three-kilometre) stretch
that's big enough to pick up any surf going,
but seems to work best at half-high tide.

OTHER ATTRACTIONS

Amid the surf-talk and the nightlife, visitors
don't tend to get overexcited about Newquay's
buildings, although the Edwardian parish
church of **St Michael's** deserves a respectful
glance. For something older and far grander,
look up **Trerice Manor** in the rural lanes to
the south of town. Now owned by the National
Trust, this was the former seat of the Catholic
Arundells and is one of Cornwall's outstanding
Elizabethan manors. Beyond the Dutch-gabled
façade are period rooms displaying Brussels
tapestries and Stuart portraits. For students of
herbaceous spruceness, there's also a strangely
appealing lawnmower museum in the grounds.
Nearby, take a nostalgic ride on the **Lappa
Valley Steam Railway**.

In Newquay itself, ridiculous rainy-day diversion is provided by **Tunnels Through Time**, an attraction recreating some of the myths of Cornwall's past, 'starring' models of the Giant Bolster, King Arthur, magicians, pirates and smugglers. More worthwhile are the free-ranging, furred and fanged inmates at **Newquay Zoo**, situated in Trenance Park, which also incorporates a leisure centre, boating lake and miniature railway, as well as 26 acres of subtropical greenery and flowers.

AROUND NEWQUAY

East of Newquay, **St Columb Major** has the durable qualities of an ancient market town with its own ways, means and gala days. It's best viewed from the north end, where half-slated, rickety cottages snuggle up to the 15th-century church, which holds tombs to the ubiquitous Arundells. Around Shrove Tuesday each year, an ancient hurling match takes place in St Columb, using the far ends of the town as goalposts. The streets are boarded up as two rival teams scrum for a silver ball representing the sun. A less injurious event is the music festival in late August, when seasoned conductors combine with talented young performers from all over the country for a series of classical concerts.

The Iron Age hillfort of **Castle Dinas** presides over the landscape east of St Columb, with triple ditches, tumuli and ramparts rising over 700 feet (213 metres), while to the west, the secretive Vale of Lanherne shelters the lovely village of **St Mawgan in Pydar**, where a church surrounded by dozing slate-and-granite cottages draws you into a time slip. Since 1794 the old Arundell manor in St Mawgan has accommodated a Carmelite convent. The village also has a **Japanese Garden & Bonsai Nursery**, which somehow fits discreetly into this Celtic enclave.

The seaboard extension of this tranquil spot is **Mawgan Porth**, an open-jawed bay that, despite being well-equipped with hotels, cafés and surfing facilities, has a dark, brooding feel. A short cliff walk along the southern headland will take you to the more secluded **Beacon Cove**, while a two-mile (three-kilometre) drive north leads to **Bedruthan Steps**, one of the most spectacular beaches on this coastline. A steep stone staircase drops down to the sand, allowing a close-up view of the dramatic towering volcanic stacks; according to legend, they are the stepping stones of local giant Bedruthan.

Before Trevose Lighthouse went up in 1847, Bedruthan Steps was notorious for shipwrecks. The brig *Samaritan*, laden with cotton and silks, ran aground here in 1846, and

for months afterwards, locals were seen clad in the salvaged finery. Today the swaggering precipices, topped with grass and heather, remain as perilous as ever. Sharp rocks and ferocious waves make bathing impossible, and even shorebound visitors should beware the dangerous tides. Better perhaps to enjoy the magnificent scenery on a cliff-top walk towards Park Head. Above the beach is a car park, tea shop and information centre, adapted from the counting house of the Carnewas Mine.

Blue Reef Aquarium

Towan Promenade, Newquay (01637 878134/ www.bluereefaquarium.co.uk). **Open** 10am-5pm daily. **Admission** £5.50; £4.75 concessions; £16.95 family. **Credit** MC, V.

Japanese Garden & Bonsai Nursery

St Mawgan, nr Newquay (01637 860116/ www.thebonsainursery.com). **Open** 10am-6pm daily. **Admission** £2.50; £1 concessions. **Credit** AmEx, MC, V.

Lappa Valley Steam Railway

St Newlyn East, nr Newquay (01872 510317/ www.lappavalley.co.uk). **Open** *Easter-Oct* 10am-5.20pm daily. Closed Nov-Easter. **Admission** £6.50; £5.50 concessions; £19.80 family. **Credit** MC, V.

Newquay Zoo

Trenance Gardens, Newquay (01637 873342/ www.newquayzoo.co.uk). **Open** *Apr-Nov* 9.30am-6pm daily. *Nov-Mar* 10am-5pm daily. **Admission** £6.75; £4.95 concessions. **Credit** AmEx, DC, MC, V.

Trerice Manor

Kestle, nr Newquay (01637 875404/ www.nationaltrust.org.uk). **Open** *Late Mar-early Nov* 11am-5.30pm Mon, Wed-Fri; phone 1st to check. Closed mid Nov-mid Mar. **Admission** £4.50; £3.70 concessions; £11.30 family. **Credit** MC, V.

Tunnels Through Time

St Michael's Road, Newquay (01637 873379/ www.tunnelsthroughtime.co.uk). **Open** *Easter-Oct* from 10am daily. Closed Nov-Mar. **Admission** phone for details. **Credit** phone for details.

Activities

Beach sports

Surfing too boring for you? The **Extreme Academy** (01637 860840, www.watergatebay.co.uk) on Watergate Bay offers lessons in kite-buggying, kite-boarding, kite-surfing, wave-skiing, land-yachting and other extreme sports.

Cycling

Bikes can be hired from **Newquay Bike Hire** (Unit 1, Wesley Yard, Newquay, 01637 874040), a long-established cycle shop that will deliver and collect from your hotel.

Cornwall

Fishing

Boards on Newquay harbour advertise shark, wreck and reef fishing trips from May to October.

Golf

Holywell Bay Golf Park (Holywell Bay, 01637 830095, www.holywellbay.co.uk/golf) has an 18-hole course, and no membership or dress code.

Sailing

Courses in **Cornish Day Sailing** are offered by Dick Tuscon (Langorrock, 28 Gustory Road, Crantock, 01637 830956).

Surfing

Newquay is awash with surf shops, surf schools and even the odd surf-obsessed lodging. To help you join the wave-chasing dudes, lessons are offered by numerous outfits, including **Newquay Surfing Centre** (01637 850737, www.nationalsurfing centre.com, closed Nov-Mar), which is run by the British Surfing Association (01736 360250, www.britsurf.co.uk). Other schools include **Seven Bays Surf School** (12 Steps, Trenance, Mawgan Porth, 01637 860959); **West Coast Surfari** (27 Trebarwith Crescent, 01637 876083); **Dolphin Surf School** (Rewinda Lodge, 17 Eliot Gardens, 01637 873707, www.surfschool.co.uk); the **Winter Brothers** (32 Headland Road, 01637 879696, www. winterbrothers.com, closed Jan & Feb), and **Reef Surf School** (0707 123 4455, www.reefsurf school.com), all of which can also arrange simple accommodation for those who want to eat, drink and sleep the surfing lifestyle. For hiring or buying gear, one of the best shops is **Fistral Surf Company** (1 Beacon Road, 01637 850520).

Contact the British Surfing Association for details of surfing competitions and events around Newquay. Further information is provided online at www.surfnewquay.co.uk and on local radio at Malibu Surf (105.5FM).

Where to eat & drink

Finns Restaurant (Old Boathouse, South Quay Hill, 01637 874062, closed Jan) serves up burgers and sandwiches at lunchtime and more ambitious fare in the evening. There are open sarnies, salads, pasta and fish at **Chy-An-Mor Café Bar** (12 Beach Road, 01637 873415, closed Nov-Mar) overlooking Towan Island and flaming cocktails to accompany the Mexican food at party venue **Señor Dicks** (East Street, 01637 851601). Also try **Ed's Restaurant** in the Edwardian Hotel (*see p275*).

Popular pubs include **Central** (Central Square, 01637 873810), which has outdoor tables, and the **Red Lion** (North Quay Hill, main courses £4.75-£12), with its decent pub grub. For great homemade cakes, seek out the award-winning **Trenance Cottage Tea Room & Garden** (Trenance Lane, 01637 872034, closed Nov-Mar), and for classic fish and chips, try **Truscotts** (19 Fore Street, 01637 877562).

Away from the centre, the surfing fraternity congregate at the hip, California-style **Beach Hut Bistro** (Watergate Bay, 01637 860840, main courses £5-£15) for evening cocktails, Cornish tapas and impressive global cuisine. **Lewinnick Lodge Bar & Restaurant** (Pentire, 01637 878117, main courses £6-£15) has stunning views of Fistral Beach to set off its fresh fish. Anyone wanting an inland jaunt might try the **Smuggler's Den** (Trebellan, Cubert, 01637 830209, main courses £6.95-£14.95), a thatched 17th-century farmhouse serving delicious fish pie.

Nightlife

Newquay's clubs play a crowd-pleasing but predictable variety of retro pop, house, garage and hip hop. If you're not too fussy about your beats, you should have a good time – just watch out for the inevitable stag and hen parties, larging it on an excess of Stella and sunstroke.

Chart fare and old favourites from the '70s and '80s set the tone at **Berties** (East Street, 01637 872255), the largest club in town. There's more of the same at pub-club **Fosters** (Narrow Cliff, 01637 872255), while Australia-themed party venue **Walkabout** (The Crescent, 01637 853000) has a School Disco on Wednesday and live acts at the weekend. **Sailors** (111-117 Fore Street, 01637 872838) packs 'em in with a mixture of dance and disco faves from Thursday to Sunday, while **Tall Trees** (Tolcarne Road, 01637 850313) dishes up everything from dance to grunge. On Beach Road, check out **The Beach** (01637 872194), one of the most popular clubs in town, or the stylish **Koola Bar** (016376 873415), for drum and bass, UK garage and hip hop.

Where to stay

Good-value dorm beds and other facilities are provided at **Tubes Surf Lodge** (86 Tower Road, 01637 859179, www.tubessurflodge.co.uk, £18.50 per person), **Matt's Surf Lodge** (110 Mount Wise, 01637 874651, www.matts-surf-lodge.co.uk, £12.50-£15 per person) and **Home Surf Lodge** (18 Tower Road, 01637 873387, www.homesurflodge.co.uk, closed Sept-Mar, £18.50-£20 per person). There are also several campsites in the area; contact the tourist office for details (*see p276*).

Bedruthan Steps Hotel

Mawgan Porth (01637 860555/reservations 01637 860860/www.bedruthan.com). **Rates** £48-£82 double. **Credit** MC, V.

Spacious, bright rooms – including good-value suites for families – have sliding glass doors opening out towards palm-fringed grounds and a swimming pool overlooking the beach. The large dining area serves fresh seafood, beef and venison, and there's a Balinese-style bar for cocktails. Spa treatments add a touch of luxury.

Crantock Bay Hotel

West Pentire, Crantock (01637 830229/ www.crantockbayhotel.co.uk). Closed 2wks early Nov. **Rates** *£49.50-£83.50 double.* **Credit** *AmEx, DC, MC, V.*
This popular family hotel is recommended for its superb setting and easy access to the nearby coastal footpath. It also has extra facilities for rainy days: an indoor pool, gym and sauna, plus plenty of books and toys. Local specialities feature on the menu.

Edwardian Hotel

3-7 Island Crescent, Newquay (01637 874087/ www.edwardian-hotel.com). Rates £35-£50 double. **Credit** *MC, V.*
Overlooking Towan Beach, this friendly hotel has modern en suite rooms, most with lovely views. Ed's Restaurant is a bright, relaxing spot, with a progressive vegetarian and seafood selection.

Harbour Hotel

North Quay Hill, Newquay (01637 873040/ www.harbourhotel.co.uk). **Rates** *(B&B) £40-£50 per person.* **Credit** *MC, V.*
Five en suite rooms with balconies make the most of this hotel's supreme location, perched right above the harbour. Decor combines antiques and pine, but you'll be too busy looking at the view to notice.

Headland Hotel

Headland Road, Newquay (01637 872211/ www.headlandhotel.co.uk). **Rates** *£43-£103 single; £75-£280 double; £120-£320 suite.* **Credit** *AmEx, DC, MC, V.*
Superbly placed in 10 acres of grounds and bedecked with pediments and pinnacles, the Headland Hotel was the setting for the 1989 TV version of Roald Dahl's *The Witches*. It entices with 100 en suite rooms, a terrace, bar and restaurant, all with views over Fistral Beach. Self-catering accommodation is provided in nearby cottages.

Resources

Hospital

Newquay & District Hospital, St Thomas' Road, Newquay (01637 893600).

Internet

Cyber Surf, 2 Broad Street, Newquay (01637 875497). **Open** *May-Oct 10am-10pm daily. Nov-Apr 11am-6pm daily.*

Police station

Tolcarne Road, Newquay (0870 577 7444). **Open** *8am-6pm daily.*

Post office

31-3 East Street, Newquay (08457 223344). **Open** *9am-5.30pm Mon-Fri; 9am-12.30pm Sat.*

The coast path between Rock and Polzeath: a walker's paradise. *See p277.*

Cornwall

Tourist information

Newquay Tourist Information Centre
*Municipal Building, Marcus Hill (01637 854020/
www.newquay.co.uk).* **Open** *May-Sept* 9am-5.30pm
Mon-Sat; 9am-4pm Sun. *Oct-Apr* 10am-4.30pm Mon-
Fri; 10am-noon Sat.

The Camel Estuary & around

Once a bare, inhospitable region, where men
eked out a living from agriculture, fishing and
mining, the craggy bays and tortuous inlets
that held back development around the Camel
Estuary are now attractions in themselves. The
looming slate cliffs are buckled and compacted
by thundering Atlantic waves that break on to
some of the finest beaches in the UK.

The approach to **Padstow** along the A389
is soothing. You wind through low hills and
sloping fields, after which the road plunges
and takes a looping detour, exposing a swipe of
yellow sand. Next you are gaping at the blazing
blue of the Camel Estuary, and before you know
it you have arrived at the harbour: an animated
marine shambles of crabbers, netters, yachts
and pleasure cruisers. (Ferries to Rock – *see
p277* – depart from here throughout the year).
Surrounding the harbour, slate-hung, red-brick
and grey cottages accommodate pasty parlours,
boutiques, chip shops and dark cavernous bars.

The town's patron saint, Petroc, is supposed
to have first come bobbing up the estuary in
the sixth century. Since then, Padstow has been
invaded by Danes, angry miners and – once
fishing and shipbuilding declined – hordes of
artistic tourists, eager to write, paint and grow
beards. Today, modern visitors take pleasure
trips around the estuary on board the *Jubilee
Queen* cruiser, in the hope of glimpsing a seal,
a dolphin, or one of the celebs hanging out in
nearby Rock.

World-famous are Padstow's May Day
celebrations, when the **Obby Oss**, a monstrous
effigy made out of hoopwork, tarpaulin and
sprays of horsehair, is paraded through the
streets to the accompaniment of singing and
a crashing Breton drum. The Oss is attended
by teams of white-dressed men and women
led by the Teazer, who thrusts a phallic club
around the beast's body. The ritual is generally
believed to be some kind fertility rite or a
celebration of the onset of summer; its insistent,
pulsing rhythms go on until midnight, when the
carnage of cans, litter and alcoholic prostration
is a tourist feature in itself. If you can't attend
the event, you can see an 'Oss' in the rather dull
Padstow Museum on Market Strand.

Padstow's dark slate parish church houses
the tombs of the Prideaux family whose manor,
Prideaux Place, sits imperiously in its own
deer park above the port. The building dates
from 1592 and is stuffed full of porcelain,
antique glass, memorabilia and portraits by
John Opie. There are other more unusual details
too, including an art nouveau light switch,
an ingenious early hi-fi system and a glorious
16th-century ceiling in the Great Chamber.

As an utter contrast, visit the town's
fascinating **National Lobster Hatchery**,
where you'll learn that lobsters taste with their
feet; that they have three stomachs and can live
to be about a hundred. Elsewhere in town, have
a browse in the **Padstow Contemporary
Art Gallery** (3A Parnell Court, 01841 532242,
www.padstowgallery.com), which features art
and ceramics from art nouveau to the 1960s,
as well as contemporary work.

Heading west out of Padstow, the estuary
is lined with lovely dune-backed beaches and
guarded at its mouth by the fatal sandbanks
of **Doom Bar**, where countless ships have
foundered. Beyond the massive headland of
Stepper Point, the coast path leads west to the
Edwardian holiday suburb of **Trevone**, shaded
by tamarisk and pine, and fronted by a superb
spread of sand and rockpools (*see p277*
Coastal walk). A little further on is sheltered
Harlyn Bay, a crescent of golden sand
shielded by Trevose Head and Cataclews Point.

Beyond Trevose Head, blustery and bracing,
Constantine Bay is named after the chapel
of St Constantine, now standing in ruins in
Trevose Golf Course. Big breakers come
bulldozing in here, making it a surfers'
favourite, but beginners and bathers should
watch out for the hazardous riptides. Connected
to Constantine to the south, **Treyarnon Bay**
is another good spot for surfing, although
caravans, an open-air swimming pool and
ample car parking mean it gets very crowded.

Continuing down the coast are a number of
other scenic beaches and coves, each with their
own characteristics and appeal. The sandy
funnel of **Porthcothan** is a favourite due to
its dramatic cliffs, caves and blowholes;
Booby's Bay has the skeletal remnants of
a World War I German ship preserved in the
sand, while **Polventor** – or Mother Ivey's Bay–
takes its name from a farmer's widow who
claimed the rights to all the shipwreck pickings
along this part of the coast.

Inland from Padstow, and accessible via the
Camel Trail (*see p279*), is the medieval wool-
town of **Wadebridge**, whose 17-arch bridge
was built over a dangerous river crossing in
the Middle Ages. The silting of the river and
the opening of the railway to Padstow in
1899 marked the end of the town's waterborne
prosperity, but traces remain in the old quays
by the river's edge. Today the town is chiefly

Coastal walk Trevone Bay

Distance 7 miles (11 km).
Time 3hrs 30mins.
Level Moderately demanding walk, with some steep, exposed sections. Strong shoes or boots are advised.

Facing the sea, a footpath leads up the right-hand side of Trevone Bay to the **Round Hole**, a collapsed coastal cave and ominous funnel through which the sea surges. In summer the surrounding sheer cliffs are dotted by a froth of sea pinks and sprigs of heather. Follow the path for a third of a mile (half a kilometre) to the spectacular natural arch of **Porthmissen Bridge** and on to the gulf of **Tregudda Gorge**, a chasm with an eerie, otherworld atmosphere, where, years ago, an old man is said to have heard mermaids singing to him. Offshore, Gulland Rock and the jagged grouping called King Phillip can be seen.

Carry on for less than a mile to **Gunver Head** and beyond, along a exhilarating level stretch that follows the contours until it reaches **Butter Hole**, a huge hollow dropping 100 feet (30 metres) to a stony base where a cavern lets in the sea. Nearby, the steep inlet of **Pepper Hole** takes its name from the cargo washed in from shipwrecked vessels.

You are now approaching an area of disused slate quarries and the **Daymark** or tower of the old lighthouse at Stepper Point.

This guarded the entrance to the Camel Estuary and warned sailors of **Doom Bar**, a rocky ridge where 300 ships foundered between 1760 and 1920. The Daymark is fenced off as dangerous but you can follow the coastal path along either the upper or lower routes, the first passing the coastguard lookout, the second leading down into quiet **Hawker's Cove**, where a deserted lifeboat station moulders. Hawker's is a marvellous place for swimming, backed by dunes in which rare plants and insects thrive.

The upper path winds along the estuary for two miles (three kilometres) to **St George's Cove** and the war memorial. From here you can continue into Padstow for a snack, or push on with the walk, taking a turning to the right around the edge of the fields and culminating at the wall of the deer park of **Prideaux Place**. Take the lane that heads northwards from here towards **Tregirls** across gently sloping fields, then veer left and continue for just over a mile to the attractive hamlet of **Crugmeer**. In high summer poppies hide among the fields of gold, creating the perfect impressionist landscape. Go through the cluster of buildings and then turn off the lane to the right; the track leads downhill for nearly a mile to **Porthmissen Farm** and back to Trevone Bay.

---

notable for hosting the Royal Cornwall Show in June (01208 812183) and an annual folk festival in mid August (01208 816193).

Wadebridge acts as a stepping stone to **Rock** and **Polzeath**, twin resorts on the north side of the estuary. Slightly less accessible than the Padstow side, this is swimming, surfing and sailing country par excellence, fêted by celebrities of TV and film. Anyone glancing at the tidy bungalows and scatter of small craft will not instantly grasp the connection, but Rock is presently blushing under the nicknames 'Little Chelsea' and 'Kensington-on-Sea'. Tara-Tamara-Hervey wannabes, with more pearls than sense, flock to this area in the hope of rubbing shoulders with such acclaimed fugitives as Princes William and Harry, who learned to water-ski here.

The flat sands and dunes of **Daymer Bay**, between the two resorts, are beloved of kids, sun-worshippers and windsurfers, and backed by St Enodoc Golf Course and the dome of Brea Hill. A stroll will lead you to the 13th-century church of **St Enodoc**, where the late laureate Sir John Betjeman is buried. The church was once known as 'Sinking Neddy' as it was all but buried in sand, but now it sits serenely amid the grass-bound dunes. Betjeman spent many holidays in this area, in the hamlet of **Trebetherick** on the edge of Polzeath, and his attachment to Cornwall is explored at the **John Betjeman Centre** in Wadebridge.

Polzeath has another alluring beach of fine sand and gentle surf that's perfect for beginners, while beyond, the estuary culminates in **Pentire Point** and the **Rumps**, two looming National Trust headlands, scarred with the remains of an Iron Age fort.

Surrounded by glorious coastal scenery five miles (eight kilometres) north-east of Polzeath, the fishing village of **Port Isaac** provides a dramatic prospect of white slate-hung cottages clinging to a steep incline above a 700-year-old harbour and shingle beach. Explore the compact wedge of buildings and 'drangways' (one of which is called Squeeze-ee-belly Alley),

Cornwall

St Enodoc church, where Sir John Betjeman is buried. *See p277.*

bright with fuchsias and hollyhocks. Although Port Isaac does not attract the holidaying hordes in quite the same way as Padstow and Polzeath, it epitomises the plight of picturesque villages throughout Cornwall, where property prices have skyrocketed and every other home belongs to someone from outside the area.

Adjacent **Port Gaverne** has a sheltered pebbly beach that's good for swimming. The harbour here was built as an outlet for the quarries at Delabole (*see p282*), with wagons of slate being packed and loaded into schooners by chains of local men and women. The third in this trio of coastal settlements is desolate **Port Quin**, 'the village that died', now owned by the National Trust. Consisting of a strip of cottages on a lonely promontory, and linked to the other villages only by the South West Coast Path, Port Quin is said to have lost its population during a storm in the 17th century; a more likely explanation is that the village was gradually abandoned as pilchard stocks shrank and occupants died or moved out.

Inland, visit the **Portreath Bee Centre** at St Minver, a living exhibition of working bees, and the restored **Long Cross Victorian Gardens** at Trelights. There's statuary, a maze, water features and a pets' corner here, but even the presence of a hotel and a pub can't dispel the gardens' slightly eerie atmosphere.

A summer music festival draws people from all over Cornwall to the nearby 15th-century church of **St Endellion** to hear some of the best young musicians in the country, while a few miles south, a contented cluster of cottages, well-preserved church (esteemed for its 15th-century stained glass windows and wagon roof), and the old slate-floored **St Kew Inn** (01208 841259, main courses £5.95-£11.95), create a pastoral idyll at **St Kew**.

John Betjeman Centre
1 Southern Way, Wadebridge (01208 12392).
Open 10am-4.30pm Mon-Sat. **Admission** free.

Long Cross Victorian Gardens
(01208 880243). **Open** 10.30am-dusk daily.
Admission £2. **Credit** MC, V.

National Lobster Hatchery
South Quay, Padstow (01841 533877/www.national lobsterhatchery.com). **Open** May-Sept 10am-6pm daily. Oct-Apr 10am-4pm Mon-Sat. **Admission** £2.50; £1.50 concessions. **No credit cards**.

Padstow Museum
Market Strand, Padstow (01841 532470).
Open 10.30am-4.30pm Mon-Fri; 10.30am-1pm Sat. **Admission** 50p; 30p concessions. **Credit** MC, V.

Portreath Bee Centre
(01208 862192). **Open** Apr-Oct 10am-6pm daily.
Nov-Mar 10.30am-4.30pm Tue-Sat. **Admission** £1.50; 75p concessions. **Credit** MC, V.

Prideaux Place
Padstow (01841 532411). **Open** Easter, May-Oct 12.30-5pm Mon, Thur-Sun. Closed Nov-Mar. **Admission** House & gardens £6; £2 concessions. Gardens only £2; £1 concessions. **No credit cards**.

Cornwall

Activities

Golf

St Enodoc Golf Club in Rock (01208 863216) incorporates two beautifully sited courses on the edge of the estuary, one of which allows unrestricted access for visiting players. Enjoying a spectacular position over Constantine Bay is **Trevose Golf Club** (01841 520208, www.trevose-gc.co.uk), which has extensive country club facilities.

Sailing

The **Camel School of Seamanship** (The Pontoon, Rock, 01208 862881) offers two-hour lessons in dinghy sailing. Equipment is also available for hire.

Surfing

Rebound Surf (Constantine Bay, 01841 520208, closed Oct-Easter) offers one-to-one tuition for £25 per person, while **Harlyn Surf School** (16 Boyd Avenue, Padstow, 01841 533076, closed Nov-Apr) can combine tuition with accommodation and full board. On the other side of the estuary, **Surf's Up!** (Polzeath Beach, 01208 862003) offers short or full-day surfing lessons, plus wetsuit and board hire.

Walking & cycling

The **Camel Trail** (01208 813050) follows a disused railway line along the estuary from Padstow to Wadebridge (6 miles/9.5km); another 8 miles (12.5km) takes you through wooded river valleys to Bodmin and the western fringe of the moor. Bikes can be hired at **Padstow Cycle Hire** (01841 533533), and there are pubs and teashops en route for refuelling. The Camel Trail coincides with start of the **Saints' Way**, a walking route that stretches for 30 miles (48km) to the south-coast port of Fowey (*see p227*), taking in woodland, moorland and the 'White Alps' of the china clay district around St Austell. The trail was used by Christian missionaries in the Dark Ages, and by Irish and Welsh traders who wanted to avoid the treacherous waters around Land's End.

Where to eat & drink

Piscatorial magnate Rick Stein has left his mark everywhere, his Padstow business having grown from a single harbourside bistro to incorporate three restaurants, a seafood delicatessen (South Quay, 01841 533868, closed Jan & Dec), a gift shop (8 Middle Street, 01841 532221), accommodation (*see p280*) and a master chef school. Under his tutelage, Padstow has shed its ragged fishing jersey for a natty white dinner jacket to become one of the most popular dining destinations in the South West.

In addition to the restaurants and hotels reviewed below, cafés, pasty shops and pubs abound in Padstow and around; harbourside venues in Port Isaac are a good bet for uncomplicated seafood.

Alwyn's Pavillion

Rock Road, Rock (01208 862622). **Open** *Easter-Oct* 7-9.30pm daily. *Nov-Mar* 7-9pm daily. **Main courses** £10.95-£19.50. **Credit** MC, V.
An ooh-là-là French menu of classic and provincial dishes is served in the bistro-style surroundings of this converted shop, where artwork covers the walls.

Margot's

11 Duke Street, Padstow (01841 533441/ www.margots.co.uk). **Open** noon-2pm, 7-9.30pm daily. **Set meals** £19.95 2 courses; £24.95 3 courses. **Credit** AmEx, MC, V.
A friendly eaterie that doesn't stand on ceremony, Margot's is big on fish and seafood, but has tempting meat and veggie choices too, prepared with flair.

No.6 Café & Rooms

6 Middle Street, Padstow (01841 532093). **Open** *May-Oct* 7-10pm daily. *Nov-Apr* 7-10pm Mon, Thur-Sun. **Main courses** £12-£15. **Credit** MC, V.
Karen Scott serves up exquisite seafood at her small but buzzy restaurant; try seared scallops with chilli dressing or parmesan-encrusted whiting with thyme-roasted vegetables. *See also p280.*

Pescadou

South Quay, Padstow (01841 532915/www.walter hickshotel.co.uk). **Open** noon-2.30pm, 7-9.30pm daily. **Main courses** £12-£25. **Credit** AmEx, MC, V.
Set beside the harbour, Pescadou is shiny, sleek and contemporary, offering Mexican-style crab salads, monkfish, char-grilled salmon and the like.

Rick Stein's Café

10 Middle Street, Padstow (01841 532700/ www.rickstein.com). **Open** 9am-3pm, 7-9.30pm daily. **Main courses** £8.50-£14.95. **Credit** MC, V.
The most informal (and cheapest) of the Stein eateries is airy and laid-back, with a menu to match: Thai fishcakes, moules marinière and Atlantic prawns are typical. It's also a great spot for breakfast.

St Petroc's Bistro

4 New Street, Padstow (01841 532700/ www.rickstein.com). **Open** noon-1.30pm, 7-9.30pm daily. **Main courses** £13.50-£16.50. **Rates** (B&B) £105-£170 double. **Credit** MC, V.
Rick Stein's modern bistro is housed in one of the oldest houses in Padstow and offers classy dining in a relaxed atmosphere. Main dishes range from whole lobster salad to steak frites, and are accompanied by a well-chosen international wine list.

Seafood Restaurant

Riverside, Padstow (01841 532485/www.rick stein.com). **Open** noon-2pm, 7-10pm daily. **Main courses** £16.50-£44. **Rates** (B&B) £105-£190 double. **Credit** MC, V.
This much-fêted restaurant delivers what many consider the finest seafood and fish cooking in the UK. Ingredients are carefully sourced, and innovation in the kitchen is balanced with simplicity to allow flavours to shine through. An impeccable wine list rounds out the experience. Book well in advance.

Cornwall

Where to stay

Guesthouses, hotels, holiday chalets and self-catering cottages jostle and compete in this area, with prices ranging from the apologetic to the pocket-searing. Although there are some atmospheric rooms above the Seafood Restaurant and at St Petroc's (for both, *see p279*), the best accommodation in the Stein empire is at **Edmund's House** (10 Middle Street, Padstow, 01841 532485, closed late Dec, double B&B £220), set in private gardens overlooking the Camel Estuary. The six minimalist yet luxurious rooms are kitted out with en suite marble bathrooms, oak flooring and French doors; those on the ground floor also have a private deck area for sunbathing. Guests get an automatic reservation at the Seafood Restaurant. A less extravagant choice is **No.6** (*see p279*; double £85), whose lovely rooms are bright and cosy with a Mediterranean vibe.

For good-value B&B in special surroundings, try **Treverbyn House** (Station Road, 01841 532855, double £30-£45), with glorious views, open fires and a fab turretted bedroom, or the former 17th-century rectory at **Molesworth Manor** (Little Petherick, 01841 540292, www.molesworthmanor.co.uk, closed Nov-Feb, double £60-£80), where you can enjoy breakfast in the conservatory and evening drinks in one of the elegant lounges. There's also self-catering accommodation in a beautifully converted barn.

Adjoining the golf course at Rock, family-friendly **St Enodoc** (Rock, 01208 863394, www.enodoc-hotel.co.uk, closed Dec-Feb, main courses £15.25-£19.75, double £85-£180) has chic interiors by Emily Todhunter. Modern New World cuisine, accompanied by wonderful fresh bread, is served in the stylish but unpretentious surroundings of the Porthilly Bar & Grill. Outside is a heated swimming pool and superb views of the Camel Estuary.

In Port Isaac, choose between the **Slipway Hotel** (0870 0110189, www.portisaac.com closed Jan, main courses £9-£25, B&B £24-£60 per person), right on the harbourfront, or the **Castle Rock Hotel** (4 New Road, 01208 880300, www.castlerockhotel.co.uk, closed Jan, main courses £9-£15, double £24-£40), perched high on the cliff with amazing views of rock, sea and sky. The former provides reliable fish dishes, ales and wines in a beamy, slate-pillared setting, while the latter serves fresh seafood in a surprisingly classy restaurant.

Just over the hill, the 17th-century **Port Gaverne Hotel** (01208 880244, closed Jan-mid Feb, set meal £22, double £35-£45) huddles in a funnel-shaped cove. In the old part of the hotel the bedrooms are rugged and beamed; in the modern part they're light and inspiring. The restaurant emphasises local fish and seafood.

For something completely different, try camping in a tipi in a secluded lakeside setting at **Tregeare** (Pendoggett, near St Kew, 01208 880781, www.cornish-tipi-holidays.co.uk, closed Oct-mid Apr, rates £295-£450 per week). For details of more conventional campsites in the area, contact the local tourist information centres (*see below*).

Resources

Internet

Internet access for visitors is provided by Padstow TIC (*see below*).

Post offices

Padstow *Duke Street (01841 532297).* **Open** 9am-5.30pm Mon-Sat.
Port Isaac *19 Fore Street (01208 880306).* **Open** *Apr-Nov* 9am-5.30pm Mon, Tue, Thur, Fri; 9am-1pm Wed; 9am-12.30pm Sat. *Nov-Mar* 9am-4.30pm Mon, Tue, Thur, Fri; 9am-1pm Wed; 9am-12.30pm Sat.
Wadebridge *The Platt (01208 812813).* **Open** 8.30am-5.30pm Mon, Thur; 9am-5.30pm Tue, Wed, Fri; 9am-12.30pm Sat.

Tourist information

Padstow *Tourist Information Centre, North Quay (01841 533449/www.padstow.uk.com).* **Open** *Mar-Oct* 9.30am-5pm daily. *Nov-Mar* 9.30am-4.30pm Mon-Sat.
Wadebridge *Tourist Information Centre, Eddystone Road (01208 813725/www.wadebridge live.com).* **Open** 9.30am-5pm Mon-Sat.

Tintagel & around

It's best to visit Tintagel on a stormy day. Not only will you see vast blooms of spray flowering from the beach as the breakers hammer the rock, but the bleak, straggling village seems of a piece with its setting. Bad weather suits the treeless moorland and the hard-faced, slate-dressed cottages rather better than bright sunlight which, if anything, serves only to highlight the boisterous commercialism that has attached itself to the town thanks to its much-vaunted status as the possible birthplace of King Arthur (*see p10* **Local heroes**).

And, yes, it has to be said, the main street oozes tourist tat. It seems the Knights of the Round Table have gathered here with the intent of knocking the visitor senseless with souvenirs: glass baubles, rubber tarantulas, huge prickly shells and mystic oils to revive you when the banquet of plenty gets too much. The apotheosis of this experience is to be had in **King Arthur's Great Halls**, a pseudo-medieval attraction created in the 1930s by a

Tuck in to serious shellfish at Rick Stein's **Seafood Restaurant**. *See p279.*

London grocer. Here a laser lightshow illuminates 73 pre-Raphaelite stained-glass windows depicting knights clobbering baddies and rescuing damsels for all they're worth. Still, among all this Arthur-mania are some worthwhile buildings, including the slate-flagged **Old Post Office**, formerly a 15th-century manor with wide fireplaces and tiny windows, now owned by the National Trust. And, if some aspects of Tintagel seem ridiculous, **Tintagel Castle** is sublime and should on no account be missed. Cast out on its lonely island, this wild rock-girt fortress terrifies and amazes by its scale and harshness.

During the Dark Ages, Tintagel Island is the focus of a monastic settlement linked to the mainland by a natural causeway, which was gradually worn away by the elements. Over the centuries, the nucleus of huts and religious buildings was abandoned until, in the middle of the 12th century, Earl Reginald of Cornwall started to build a castle on the island. Reginald's brother was a patron of Geoffrey of Monmouth, the Welsh scholar whose influential *History of the British Kings* first promoted King Arthur as a great hero, and it is thought that Reginald, in erecting his grandiose stronghold, was seeking a little legendary lustre. The castle was further developed in the 1230s by Richard, younger brother of Henry III, but was neglected and finally abandoned by future Earls of Cornwall, resulting in the blackened fragments that survive today.

Since medieval times, much scholarly effort has been put into establishing a stronger basis for Tintagel's heroic past than Geoffrey's stirring, fantastical chronicle, and every so often a substantial relic is uncovered. In 1998 much excitement was generated when a broken piece of sixth-century slate, the so-called 'Arthur Stone', was found while excavating traces of the island's Dark Age community. The slate (now housed in the Royal Cornwall Museum in Truro; *see p237*) is inscribed 'Artognov', the Latin form of the Celtic name Arthnou. Whether Arthnou was King Arthur is far from proven, but the slate at least hints that a high-ranking noble resided in this stronghold in the sixth century.

Approach to the castle is via a signposted path from the village – landrovers are on hand in summer to transport the lazy or infirm – or via the South West Coast Path at Glebe Cliff. The coast around here is particularly wild and impressive, with steep windswept cliffs interrupted by glorious unspoilt beaches. South of Tintagel, **Trebarwith** is a mile-long stretch of sand backed by cliffs and caves, with the powerful hump of Gull Rock looming offshore. The wild seas test the skills of young surfers, but the beach is only accessible at low tide.

The inland scene also has its dramas and declivities. From the coast near Bossiney Cove, paths lead upstream along the River Trevillet as it cuts through beautiful Rocky Valley and

Cornwall

St Nectan's Glen towards **St Nectan's Kieve** (www.stnectan.currantbun.com), where a 60-foot (18-metre) waterfall plunges into a deep rock basin. Described as one of the most spiritual places in the country, the Kieve has been a place of reverence and healing since pre-Christian times and is reputed to be the site of St Nectan's holy cell, now hidden underneath a privately owned hermitage (which charges admission to the site). The rocky gorge is also touted as Cornwall's most haunted place, subject to eerie chanting and the apparition of a hooded figure.

Between Tintagel and Camelford is **Delabole**, where slate has been worked for over 450 years. **Delabole Quarry** (01840 212242, www.delaboleslate.com; phone for details of seasonal tours) is an awesome 500-foot (152-metre) gash of ashy slate. A winding track hairpins down the quarry-face to the bottom of the vast chasm, where beetle-sized lorries grind and throb; fork-lifts haul blocks like motorised ants, and pumping engines slurp up water from a dim, dust-filled pool.

The hill above the village is dominated by **Delabole Windfarm**, a platoon of high-masted, triple-bladed propellers that loom eerily out of the mist like abstracts of the legendary Cornish giants. Members of the public can get a close-up look at the turbines by visiting the impressive **Gaia Energy Centre**, which demonstrates renewable water, wind and solar power through interactive exhibits and an audio guide.

Boscastle, to the north-east of Tintagel, is often described as charming or quaint, but it is actually an awesome little place, wedged along a winding fjord with slopes broken by jagged rocks and patches of rough bracken. From the harbour the **Devil's Bellows** blowhole can be seen frothing and fuming for about an hour on either side of low tide. The cliffs are barnacle-dark and alarming to look at, but for grandeur and moodiness the scene is unbeatable.

In the village, the **Museum of Witchcraft** is avowedly the largest collection of its kind, drawing inspiration from Cornwall's pagan roots but displaying an international array of devil dolls, animal deformities and ritual curses. For more on the history, geography and geology of the region, visit **Boscastle Visitors' Centre** (*see p283*).

Thomas Hardy came to Boscastle in 1870 as a young architect, commissioned to restore the church of **St Juliot** (signposted off the B3263). Here he met and courted the curate's red-haired sister-in-law, Emma Gifford, and his impressions of the area are vividly preserved in *A Pair of Blue Eyes*.

North of Boscastle, the coastal road winds and climbs to a topographical crescendo at spectacular **High Cliff** (731 feet/223 metres) overlooking Strangles Beach, before descending steeply to **Crackington Haven**, whose beach is another popular surfers' haunt.

Gaia Energy Centre

Delabole, (01840 213321/www.gaiaenergy.co.uk). **Open** *Apr-Oct* 10am-6pm daily. *Nov-Mar* 11am-3pm Tue-Sun. **Admission** £4.95; £4.50 concessions; £14.50 family. **Credit** AmEx, MC, V.

King Arthur's Great Halls

Fore Street, Tintagel (01840 770526). **Open** *Summer* 10am-5pm daily. *Winter* 11am-3pm daily. **Admission** phone for details.

Museum of Witchcraft

The Harbour, Boscastle (01840 250111/ www.museumofwitchcraft.com). **Open** *Easter-Hallowe'en* 10.30am-5.30pm Mon-Sat; noon-5.30pm Sun. Closed Nov-Mar. **Admission** £2; £1 concessions. **No credit cards.**

Old Post Office

Tintagel (01840 770024). **Open** *Apr-Oct* 11am-5.30pm. Closed Nov-Mar. **Admission** £2.30; phone to check. **Credit** MC, V.

Tintagel Castle

Tintagel (01840 770328/www.english-heritage.org.uk). **Open** *Apr-Sept* 10am-6pm daily. *Oct* 10am-5pm daily. *Nov-Mar* 10am-4pm daily. **Admission** £3.20; £1.60-£2.40 concessions; free under-5s. **Credit** MC, V.

Where to eat, drink & stay

Tintagel's combination of fractured coastline and sheltered valleys provides a romantic backdrop for holiday lets – such as the four cottages at **Halgabron Mill** (St Nectan's Glen, 01840 770661, www.halgabronmill.co.uk) – and characterful guesthouses. The **Mill House Inn** (01840 770200, www.themillhouse-inn.co.uk, main courses £6.95-£13, double £60-£80) braves the breezes of storm-tossed Trebarwith Strand. Its dining room is next to an old mill stream, and the chic, light interiors retain a touch of elemental integrity through old floorboards and dark wood furniture. Higher up, on a superb clifftop perch, the **Port William Inn** (01840 770230, closed 25 Dec, main courses £7.45-£11.95, double £36.50-£43.50) is a popular hostelry serving seafood and vegetarian dishes at bar menu prices. It also has en suite rooms with sea views.

Up the coast at Bossiney, **Old Borough House** (01840 770475, set meals £25, double £74) was reputedly once owned by Sir Francis Drake, and was also home to the author and

Local heroes Reverend Hawker

Reverend Stephen Hawker (1803-75) was one of the great squarsons (squire and parson) of the 19th century, a noted poet, scholar and reformer, who is credited with the introduction of the Harvest Festival into English churches. He was a magnetic mix of passion, compassion and stark resoluteness, whose natural eccentricities were heightened by a prediliction for opium.

Stories about Hawker's incumbency at Morwenstow (1834-75) are legion: how he preached to his dogs and took a pet pig with him on parish visits; how, dressed as a mermaid, he sprawled on the rocks at Bude and serenaded the sailors; how he conversed with angels in an opium haze; how he wrote *The Quest of the Sangraal* and beat Tennyson at his own game, and how he revived the spirit of St Morwenna, the parish's Celtic saint.

Aside from his colourful behaviour, Hawker was known for his excessive generosity and scrupulousness. This coast had long been one of the most treacherous in England, and many parishioners made a living from the rich pickings of shipwrecked vessels, yet Hawker demanded that every sailor driven ashore by the pitiless westerlies should have a Christian burial. He acquired the title 'the vicar in seaboots' because of his diligence in retrieving drowned bodies. Right into old age and whatever the time of night, if a ship was driven shoreward in a storm, Hawker would rouse his helpers and proceed down the steep cliffs to give assistance to anyone who had survived the wreckage. The *Caledonia of Arboath* foundered on Vicarage Rocks in 1842. Its figurehead marks the final resting place of the ship's captain in the graveyard of **Morwenstow church**, and is one of the more poignant relics of the parish's stormy past.

Where the reputations of other great Victorians have soured, Hawker's survives. His presence looms in the stepped mock-Tudor gables and Gothic windows of **Morwenstow Vicarage**, where each chimneypot mimics the spire of a church, and in the tiny **Hawker's Hut** perched high above the yawning rocks on Vicarage Cliff. No more than a sturdy driftwood shed, this hut is where the Reverend would sit smoking opium in his cassock, gazing at the ocean and composing poetry.

playwright JB Priestley during World War II. The emphasis here is on log-fired, Dickensian comforts and quality food.

In Boscastle, the 16th-century **Wellington Hotel** (The Old Road, 01840 250202, main courses £8.50-£14.50, double £58-£152) is a respectable hideout set in ten acres of wooded grounds, with log fires, real ales and an Anglo-French seafood restaurant. More rumbustious, the **Napoleon Inn** (High Street, 01840 250204, main courses £4.50-£8.75) dates from 1549, making it the oldest pub in the village. Slate floors, oak beams, log fires and lots of Nelson, Napoleon and Wellington memorabilia are brought to life by regular live music. By the harbour, former stables house an atmospheric **youth hostel** (01840 250287, closed Nov-Mar, £10.25 per person) with dorm accommodation in the hay loft.

Finally, Hardy-lovers may not be able to resist the lovely **Old Rectory** at St Juliot (01840 250225, www.stjuliot.com, closed Dec-Feb, double B&B £50), where the novelist first met his wife. Set in three acres of south-facing gardens, it's a welcoming, intimate spot, with a self-catering apartment in the converted stables.

Resources

Post office
Tintagel *Bossiney Road (01840 770899)*. **Open** 9am-5.30pm Mon, Tue, Thur, Fri; 9am-noon Wed; 9am-12.30pm Sat.

Tourist information
Boscastle *Boscastle Visitors' Centre, Cobweb car park (01840 250010/www.bocastle-live.com)*. **Open** *Summer* 10am-5pm daily. *Winter* 11am-4pm daily. Tintagel *Visitors Centre, Bossiney Road car park (01840 779084/www.tintagel-live.com)*. **Open** *Mar-Oct* 10am-5pm daily. *Nov-Feb* 10.30am-4pm daily.

Bude & around

High up in the north-west corner of the county, **Bude** is not as pugnaciously Cornish as, say, Padstow. But it's less stand-offish and keener to please. A bright, gusty, open-planned place, the town values its industrial past, while developing its prospects as a lively, multi-faceted resort. The last two decades have seen cycling, sailing, a golf course and a jazz festival jostle for prominence with the natural assets of glorious beaches and the South West Coast Path.

Cornwall

Originally called 'Bude Haven', this is the spot where the tiny River Neet twists across a flat valley to a broad belt of sand shadowed by a line of dark, ragged cliffs. A hermitage once stood on Chapel Rock, whose light guided ships into the bay. Later a small port grew up, taking in coal, ironware and timber, and exporting agricultural produce. A transformation occurred in 1820 when the foundations for **Bude Canal** were laid, with one arm reaching 30 miles (48 kilometres) inland to Launceston, the other to Holsworthy in Devon. Barges carried the calcium-rich sand of the coast to the infertile uplands of Exmoor and beyond. The grand plan was to link with the upper Tamar, thus joining the Bristol and English Channels, but the railway arrived long before that ambition could be realised, and the canal rapidly declined. Nowadays the canal is visited by fishermen, boaters, walkers and naturalists, the latter attracted by the towpaths' fascinating hinterland of scrub and wetland, where rare birdlife thrives.

The history of the canal is explored in more detail at the **Bude & Stratton Museum**, alongside exhibits tracing the town's maritime and trading heritage. Behind the museum is the neo-Gothic castellated home of Cornish inventor Sir Goldsworthy Gurney (1793-1875). Famous as the first man to make the long journey from London to Bath in a steam carriage, he also revolutionised lighthouses by combining oxygen with revolving mirrors to intensify illumination and create a flashing beam. Goldsworthy's genius is honoured by a stark illuminated spike, known as the **Bude Light**, in the grounds of his former home, which uses fibre optics to create a nightly zodiacal pageant.

During the last week of August crowds flock to Bude for the **Jazz Festival** (01288 356360, www.budejazzfestival.co.uk), involving over 150 events and four street parades. At other times, most visitors come for the remarkable expansive beaches, where Atlantic breakers create a splendid swathe of surf as the highest tides in the county streak over the sands.

The most central of Bude's beaches is the vast strand at **Summerleaze**, with its own seawater swimming pool. Just to the north, **Crooklets** is the site of numerous surfing and lifesaving competitions, while beyond, **Sandy Mouth** lives up to its name with a sweep of sand and rock pools (at least at low tide). Offshore reefs create some good surf at the narrow sandy cove of **Duckpool**, a little further on. To the south is **Widemouth Bay**, whose golden sand and reliable waves attract hordes of beachbums. The coast here is a geologist's wonderland, with fractures, tilts and slatey inclines, gouged by steep-sided valleys that end in waterfalls at Speke's Mill Mouth and Marsland.

Ducking out of the bullying Atlantic gales, between Bude and Hartland Point to the north, **Morwenstow** fits tidily into a small wooded combe close to the Devon border. Despite magnificent coastal scenery and a fine beach, the village is most famous for its connection to the eccentric Victorian vicar Reverend Stephen Hawker (*see p283* **Local heroes**), who served at the parish church.

Bude & Stratton Museum

The Wharf, Bude (01288 353576/ www.budemuseum.org.uk). **Open** *Easter-Oct* noon-6pm daily. Closed Nov-Easter. **Admission** 50p. **No credit cards**.

Another tough day at **Polzeath**. *See p277.*

Activities

Adventure sports

Bude is well known as a centre for outdoor pursuits, with a number of accredited organisations offering lessons in a vast array of activities, including surfing, kayaking, archery, rock climbing and canoeing. Try **Atlantic Pursuits** (20 Priestacott Park, Kilkhamton, 01288 321765); **Shoreline Outdoor Pursuits** (11A Crooklets Beach, 01288 354039, www.bude.co.uk/shoreline); or **Bude Surfing Experience** (08707 775111, www.bude surfingexperience.co.uk).

Surfing

Boards and wetsuits can be hired from **Life's a Beach** (Summerleaze Beach, 01288 361856), while everything a surfer could need is sold at the long-running **Surf Spot** (6 Belle Vue, 01288 352875) and at **Zuma Jay's Surf Shop** (20 Belle Vue Lane, 01288 354956, www.zumajay.co.uk).

Where to eat, drink & stay

Bude is not a top dining destination. The **Villa Restaurant** (16 The Strand, 01288 354799, main courses £8.95-£23) is probably the town's best eaterie, with good fish and wine selections. Two places claim to crimp the best pasties in town: **Pengella Pasties** (Bell Vue Lane, 01840 770223) and **Morwenna's** (2 Morwenna Terrace, 01288 356600, main courses £2.95-£9), which also has a simple menu of curries, veggie bakes and the like. A good chippie is **Mermaid** (Prince Street, 01288 354769), which does a decent line in locally caught fish. As homage to the famous vicar, try the **Rectory Tearooms** (Morwenstow, 01288 331251), which date from the 13th century.

Centrally located beside Bude Canal, the turretted **Falcon Hotel** (Breakwater Road, 01288 352005, www.falconhotel.com, double B&B £90-£94) has walled gardens and easy access to the beach. Decor is flouncy but comfortable, with a seductive candlelit restaurant. **Camelot Hotel** (Downs View, 01288 352361, www.camelot-hotel.co.uk, closed mid Dec-early Jan, set meals £19, double B&B £54.50-£60 incl dinner) looks out over the North Cornwall Golf Course to the sea. It's a sprawling, gabled building with light, airy decor, palm-shaded lawns and a popular restaurant.

Inland at Stratton, the small **Stratton Gardens Hotel** (Cot Hill, 01288 352500, www.cornwallonline.co.uk, set meals £15, double £60) offers great-value, pretty rooms and tasty local cuisine, while **Cann Orchard** (Howard Lane, 01288 352098, double B&B £34-£50) is a rambling farmhouse set in attractive gardens and encircled by woodland. There are two self-catering cottages here too, which are rented out to families.

South down the coast, **St Genny's House** (St Genny's, 01840 230384, double £44-£60) is a former vicarage in a wooded valley with sea views. An uncomplicated homely atmosphere is accentuated by pretty fabrics and paintings in the four guest rooms. Self-caterers, meanwhile, may enjoy the purpose-built **Forda Lodges** (Kilkhampton, near Bude, 01288 321413, www.fordalodges.co.uk), located in a wooded river valley with private fishing, swimming pool and games facilities.

Resources

Internet

Bude *Library, The Wharf (01288 352527)*.
Open 9.30am-6pm Mon-Wed, Fri; 9.30am-12.30pm Sat.

Police station

Bude *Landsdown Close (0870 577 7444)*.

Post offices

Bude *The Crescent (01288 352048)*. **Open** 9am-5pm Mon-Fri.
Morwenstow *Morwenna Road (01288 331428)*. **Open** 7am-5.30pm Mon-Fri.

Tourist Information

Bude *Tourist Information Centre, The Crescent (01288 354240/www.bude.co.uk)*. **Open** *Nov-Mar* 10am-4pm Mon-Fri; 10am-1pm Sat. *Apr-Oct* 9.30am-5pm Mon-Sat; 10am-4pm Sun.

Getting there & around

By air

Newquay Cornwall Airport is 5 miles (8km) north-east of Newquay town centre (signposted off the A3059). **Summer Court Travel** (01726 861108) runs a bus service to the town centre that meets Ryanair flights (£3.50 single); the same company will take you by taxi for £10 (£20 to Truro). The No.556 from **Western Greyhound** (01637 871871) also runs every 2hrs Mon-Sat.

By bus

Camborne, Redruth, Newquay and Wadebridge are all served by **National Express** coaches from around the country (08705 808080, www.gobycoach.com). Local buses are provided by **Truronian** (01872 273453) and **Western Greyhound** (01637 871871), although services to isolated areas can be infrequent.

By train

Stations at **Camborne** (South Terrace Road) and **Redruth** (Station Road) are served by direct trains on the London Paddington–Penzance and Birmingham New Street–Penzance routes. The journey in each case takes nearly 5hrs. **Newquay** station (Cliff Road) is served by a branch line from Par, near St Austell.

The Isles of Scilly

Do believe the hype – the Scillies are a world apart.

Located 28 miles (45 kilometres) off Land's End, the Isles of Scilly (only say 'Scilly Isles' if you want to annoy the locals) comprise five inhabited islands – St Mary's, Tresco, Bryher, St Martin's and St Agnes – and over 100 uninhabited ones, some little more than lumps of rock in the sea. Although the exposed, rugged cliff tops can take a battering during storms, the islands' position, in the middle of the Gulf Stream, gives them a climate that's kinder than the rest of the country and allows subtropical vegetation to flourish. The islands were designated an Area of Outstanding Natural Beauty in 1975 and it's easy to see why. There are no theme parks or raucous nightclubs here, just clear blue waters, golden sands, rugged heathland, wild flowers and dramatic rock formations. If it's isolation and inspiration you're after, you've come to the right place.

According to legend, the Scillies are the remains of the Lost Land of Lyonesse, to which King Arthur's men retreated after their leader's last fatal battle. The reality is rather more mundane – the islands are part of the same granite mass as Land's End, and were probably joined to the mainland long ago. Archaeological evidence, in the form of ancient burial mounds, show that the islands have been inhabited for at least 4,000 years. The Phoenicians and the Romans are known to have settled here – it was the latter who gave the Scillies their name – from the Latin *Sillinae Insulae*, or Sun Isles.

In the early 12th century Henry I granted the islands to the Benedictine order of Tavistock, who established the famous abbey on Tresco. Constantly bothered by pirates, the monks found life here tough, and after centuries of turbulence the islands were leased in 1571 to the Cornish Godolphin family, who built defences to protect against invasion. The islands enjoyed a period of stability until the outbreak of the Civil War, when they bravely resisted the parliamentarian onslaught until 1651. The Godolphins resumed control of the islands during the Restoration, but as absentee landlords, leaving the inhabitants to supplement their hand-to-mouth existence by looting the frequent shipwrecks off the coast and smuggling contraband goods.

A new landowner, Augustus Smith, arrived on the islands in 1834, bringing much-needed educational and agricultural reforms. Smith also constructed roads and cracked down on smuggling, and in 1872 his nephew, Lieutenant Dorrien-Smith, introduced commercial flower-growing, an industry that remains important today. Since the 1960s tourism has been the mainstay of the Scillies' economy, but development has been deliberately low-key in an attempt to preserve the islands' character, and farming and fishing remain important occupations for their 2,000 inhabitants.

The islands are a haven for a variety of wildlife, including rare migratory birds that are not found in other parts of the United Kingdom (refer to www.scillybirding.co.uk for further information). Glorious sandy beaches can be found at every turn, while crystal clear waters make for some of the best scuba conditions in the country. Although the islands' appeal is apparent at any time of year, perhaps the best time to visit is in the spring, when a profusion of flowers (in particular on Bryher and St Agnes) create a riot of colour against a backdrop of sea and sky.

Exploring the islands

St Mary's

Though it's only two and a half miles (four kilometres) across at its widest point, St Mary's is the largest of the Isles (all the others are known as 'off-islands'). Its main centre, **Hugh Town**, is located on a narrow isthmus on the island's south-western side, flanked to the south by **Porthcressa Beach**, a pretty, sheltered bay, and to the north by the less appealing town beach where boat trips, launches and the *Scillonian III* passenger ferry (*see p290*) come and go from the sweeping stone pier.

Useful cultural and historical background to life on the islands is provided by the **Isles of Scilly Museum**, whose centrepiece is the *Klondyke*, a fully rigged pilot gig. Racing these traditional wooden rowing boats is the main sport in the Scillies, with races taking place every Wednesday and Friday in summer from the uninhabited island of Samson to the quay at Hugh Town. The Scillies also host the annual World Pilot Gig Championships (www.pilotgigs.co.uk) each May, when you can cheer the crews on from passenger boats that follow each race.

Garrison Hill rises up at the end of the promontory west of Hugh Town, offering a perfect vantage point from which to view the archipelago. The hill is named after the fortifications built here in the 18th century, but the dominant structure is the 16th-century, eight-pointed **Star Castle**, built as a defence against the Spanish Armada, but now a hotel (*see p289*).

In the other direction, Telegraph Road leads from Hugh Town towards the island's interior; passing **Carreg Dhu** (pronounced 'Crake Dew', meaning Black Rocks; 01720 422404), a volunteer-run community garden whose 1.5 acres house subtropical plants, shrubs and trees. A little further on is the **Longstone Heritage Centre**, a local history museum, with a restaurant and gift shop.

Heading east from Porthcressa Beach, a path loops south round the jagged rocks of **Peninnis Head**, passing intriguing rock formations such as the 'Kettle and Pans' close to **Peninnis Lighthouse**. Beyond is a sheltered beach at **Old Town Bay**; the straggling settlement here was the island's main port until the 17th century.

East of Old Town, near the airport, the small bay at **Porth Hellick** is overlooked by a monument to Rear-Admiral Sir Cloudesley Shovell, who accidentally steered his fleet into the rocks off the island during a storm in 1707, resulting in the deaths of 2,000 men. A hoard of Spanish treasure was recovered from the wreck in the 1960s. Shovell's body was washed ashore the following day, and later buried at Westminster Abbey in London. A mile to the north, **Pelistry Bay** is one of the island's most secluded and picturesque beaches, with beautiful sands that at low tide form a sandbar to **Toll's Island**. This is an idyllic spot, but on no account be tempted to swim here at high tide, when the sandbar is liable to cause dangerous rip tides.

Heading north-west round the coast you'll come to the most impressive prehistoric remains on the archipelago at **Halangy Down**, with stone huts, a burial chamber and a standing stone that is thought to date back to 2,000 BC.

Isles of Scilly Museum

Church Street, Hugh Town (01720 422337). **Open** *Summer* 10am-4.30pm Mon-Sat. *Winter* 10am-noon Mon-Sat. **Admission** £2; 50p-£1 concessions. **No credit cards**.

Longstone Heritage Centre

Longstone (01720 423770). **Open** *Mid Mar-early Nov* 9.30am-5.30pm daily. Closed mid Nov-early Mar. **Admission** £2; 50p concessions; £4.50 family. **No credit cards**.

Tresco

Car-free Tresco is the biggest off-island, at a whopping two miles by one mile. Located in the waters between St Martin's and Bryher, it is largely sheltered from the blustery winds that tend to assault the rest of the archipelago, though exposed areas can take a battering, particularly on the wilder northern coast.

Tresco is particularly popular with day trippers: although a couple of decent accommodation options can be found here, some seasoned visitors dismiss the island as too pricey and exclusive, a reputation that's not helped by the fact that Tresco is still in private hands, leased from the Duchy of Cornwall by the Dorrien-Smith family.

The highlight of the island is the subtropical **Abbey Gardens**, the Isles of Scilly's biggest attraction. Surrounding the ruins of the 12th-century Benedictine priory, the gardens were laid out in 1834 by Augustus Smith and are home to some 20,000 exotic plants from 80 countries around the world, including date palms, flame trees and cacti. Among the lush, dense vegetation are ornaments, sculptures and the Abbey Pool (a great spot for bird-watching), while near the entrance, the **Valhalla** exhibition has a collection of figureheads and memorabilia salvaged from local shipwrecks (entry is free when you pay admission to the Abbey Gardens).

The gardens dominate the southern half of Tresco, with stunning beaches lining the coast on either side at **Appletree Bay** and **Pentle Bay**, where enthusiasts search for shells among the sands. To the north, the twin settlements of **New Grimsby** (on the west side) and **Old Grimsby** (on the east) straddle the centre of the island. The former is the location of **Gallery Tresco** (01720 424925, closed late Nov-early Feb), which is housed in an old boathouse and displays an interesting collection of work by contemporary Cornish artists.

A short walk around the coast north from New Grimsby leads to the ruins of the late 16th-century **King Charles' Castle**, built to protect the waters between Tresco and Bryher, but replaced by the more imposing **Cromwell's Castle** in 1651. The latter looks out over the sandy cove of Castle Porth to Hangman's Island, a large rock where 500 Royalists are said to have been executed on a single day during the Civil War.

Abbey Gardens

01720 424105. **Open** 10am-4pm daily. **Admission** *incl Valhalla exhibition* £8.50; free under-16s. **Credit** MC, V.

Cornwall

The view out to sea from the **Island Hotel** on Tresco. *See p290.*

Bryher

Bryher (a Celtic word meaning 'place of hills')
has the lowest population of the inhabited
islands and is one of the least-visited
destinations in the Scillies. But it's a place
of raw, rugged beauty, ranging from serrated
cliffs to tufty moorland and granite outcrops,
with unrivalled views from the headlands.

Bryher Town, near the main quay, is a
small sheltered settlement looking out to New
Grimsby Channel. There's not too much to
occupy visitors here, once you've had a gander
at the oldest church on the Scillies, **All Saints**,
built in the mid 18th century. After that, climb
up **Watch Hill** for views of the whole
archipelago. More amazing vistas – over the
western isles and the Atlantic – are to be had
from **Shipman Head** at the island's northern
tip. Gales frequently lash the western side of
the island, making aptly named **Hell Bay**,
below the headland, an awe-inspiring sight.

By contrast, the east coast has safe, clear
waters that in summer become a playground for
divers and snorkellers. South-facing **Rushy
Bay** is a sheltered sandy crescent overlooking
uninhabited Samson. With its crystal-clear
waters, this is regarded as one of the best
beaches on the Isles of Scilly, but the sea here
(as throughout the Scillies) can be extremely
cold, even at the height of summer.

St Martin's

North-east of Tresco, uncrowded St Martin's is
considered by many to be the most beautiful
island in the archipelago. Flower growing is the
main industry here, but in addition to colourful
fields you'll also find some stunning beaches
and jaw-dropping views, in particular from
St Martin's Head on the north-east coast.
The island is sparsely inhabited and virtually
pollution free, making its waters among the
best in the Scillies for scuba-diving.

St Martin's main quay lies on **Par Beach**, a
slice of pure white sand and translucent waters.
Just inland are **Higher Town** (which has
the only shop on the island) and **St Martin's
Vineyard**, where you can stock up on souvenir
wine after one of the lively tours.

On St Martin's southern coast, **Lawrence's
Bay** is a long, sandy beach that's a perfect
spot for collecting shells or chilling out. Further
west is **Lower Town**, from where you can
enjoy terrific views across to the uninhabited
islands of Teän and St Helen's (*see p289*).

On the north coast, the imaginatively named
Great Bay and **Little Bay** are secluded
spots worth seeking out. Climb across the
boulders from the latter at low tide to wild
White Island (pronounced 'Wit') in order
to explore **Underland Girt**, a huge
underground cave.

St Martin's Vineyard

nr Higher Town (07712 295330/www.stmartins vineyard.co.uk). **Open** *Tours* Apr-Sept 10am-4pm Mon-Fri. **Admission** *Tour & tasting £3.* **No credit cards.**

St Agnes

The craggy island of St Agnes is set apart from the trio of Bryher, Tresco and St Martin's, and is the most south-westerly community in the British Isles. The simple lifestyle is fully embraced here: bird- and butterfly-watching are about as energetic as it gets, and when the weather is fine most visitors are happy simply to admire the beautiful flowers and clear seas.

Boats land and leave from Porth Conger, on the north-west of the island, where you'll also find St Agnes' most attractive beach, **Covean**. When the tide is right you can walk across the sandbar from here to the tiny island of **Gugh**, where you'll find rocky outcrops and a Bronze Age standing stone and burial chamber.

Inland, St Agnes is dominated by the squat, white form of the **Old Lighthouse**, which dates from 1680, making it one of the oldest in England. Near to picturesque **Periglis Cove** on the western side of the island is a miniature stone maze, known as **Troy Town Maze**, which is said to have been laid out by the lighthouse keeper's bored son in 1729.

The wild heathland of the wonderfully named **Wingletang Down** takes up much of the south of St Agnes, edged on its western side by impressive coastal scenery and on its eastern side by **Beady Pool**. This inlet takes its name from a haul of beads from a wrecked 17th-century Venetian trader that was washed up on the shores here. Above the cove, two enormous boulders indented with a three-foot deep basin form the **Giant's Punchbowl**, the most extraordinary rock formation on the Scillies.

The uninhabited islands

Samson, the largest of the Scillies' uninhabited islands, was populated until the 1850s, when poverty and the threat of eviction by Augustus Smith forced the islanders to resettle elsewhere. A particularly beautiful beach lies at the foot of **North Hill**, while significant prehistoric remains dot the slopes above. At low tide look out for the **Samson Flats**, the remains of ancient field systems that show up in the sands between Samson and Tresco.

Teän, just off St Martin's, has large, crescent-shaped sandy beaches, while, behind it, **St Helen's** has the ruins of a church that are worth exploring. On the other side of St

Martin's, the milder **Eastern Isles** are home to puffins and grey seals, with fantastic beaches on **Great Arthur** and **Great Ganilly**.

The best place to spot grey seals, puffins and shags, however, is the **Western Rocks** beyond St Agnes, which bear the brunt of the Atlantic storms and have seen many shipwrecks.

Activities

Boat trips

In addition to the **St Mary's Boatmen's Association** (*see p290*), private launches offer a variety of boat trips around the islands: the *Spirit of St Agnes*, for example, runs daily from St Agnes to St Mary's and also follows the weekly gig race (*see p286*). Wildlife-spotting excursions to Bishop Rock lighthouse, via the Western Rocks, and to the Eastern Isles can also be arranged.

Diving

St Martin's Diving Services (Higher Town, St Martin's, 01720 422848) provides scuba and snorkelling equipment and tuition for all levels.

Walking & wildlife tours

Wildlife tours (01720 422212) led by a local ornithologist take place Mar-Oct, leaving at 9.45am from the Old Quay, St Mary's. You can also explore the island on a half-day archaeological walk; phone 01720 423326 for details. Information on bird-watching tours of the other islands are available from the tourist board in St Mary's.

Watersports

The **Rat Island Sailboat Company** (01720 422060) operates from Porthmellon on St Mary's and from Pentle Bay on Tresco, offering lessons in many different watersports, including kayaking, sailing, windsurfing and power-boating.

Where to stay, eat & drink

Although there are a variety of hotels, B&Bs, guesthouses, self-catering cottages and campsites dotted around the islands (check with the tourist office for details), the choice is limited. It's always wise to book ahead, especially if you're visiting in peak season or in winter, when some places are closed altogether. It's also worth noting that there are few stand-alone restaurants on the islands, and many hotels may insist that guests stay on a half- or even full-board basis.

On St Mary's, the historic **Star Castle Hotel** (01720 422317, www.starcastlescilly. demon.co.uk, set menu £28, double B&B £55-£120 incl dinner) is located in the eponymous castle and has two restaurants, an indoor pool and a café. (Try to get a room in the main hotel rather than in one of the less than atmospheric modern chalets.) Nearby is **Garrison House** (01720 422972, double £60-£70), a decent B&B

Cornwall

in a Grade II-listed house. A fab little licensed café and tea gardens can be found at **Carn Vean** (Pelistry, 01720 422462, closed some days in winter), while in Hugh Town, the **Mermaid** (01720 422701) is a popular drinking hole, ideal for soaking up the Scillonian atmosphere.

On Tresco, the 'cheaper' option is the **New Inn** (New Grimsby, 01720 422844, www.tresco.co.uk, set dinner £27, double B&B £138-£230 incl dinner), the island's only pub. The rooms here are upmarket, and are supplemented by a heated outdoor pool, a relaxed bar and a garden. The even more expensive (and better known) alternative is the **Island Hotel** (Old Grimsby, 01720 422883, www.tresco.co.uk, double B&B £228-£420 incl dinner). Situated right by the beach with breathtaking views, the hotel definitely has a five-star location and excellent food, but the accommodation is perhaps at odds with the hefty price tag.

The **Hell Bay Hotel** (01720 422947, double B&B £170-£360 incl dinner) is the only hotel on Bryher. Despite the name and location, it's a low-key place, although extensive renovations have added an outdoor pool, health club, and four modern suites in an adjoining cottage. The restaurant serves a well-priced Modern British and Mediterranean menu, and excellent breakfasts. Otherwise, Bryher's general shop sells delicious fresh pies, breads and pasties.

On St Martin's the posh choice is the friendly **St Martin's on the Isle Hotel** (01720 422090, www.stmartinshotel.co.uk, double B&B £210-£410 incl dinner), where the rooms all have enviable views but are otherwise pretty characterless. The hotel's main draws are its indoor swimming pool and award-winning restaurant food. A good place for fresh bread and buns is **St Martin's Bakery** in Higher Town (01720 423444).

On St Agnes a lovely B&B is **Covean Cottage** (01720 422620, £52-£64 B&B per person), located a short walk through fields to the sea. For an extra £15 you get a great home-cooked dinner using local produce. A fine spot to enjoy a beer and local pasties is the garden of the **Turk's Head** (01720 422434), which overlooks the bay back towards St Mary's. It's the most south-westerly pub in the British Isles.

Resources

St Mary's is the only island with a bank and cashpoint, though a couple of places offer cash-back services on debit cards and others charge (through the roof) to cash cheques. Note that many shops close early on a Wednesday, except in peak season.

Post offices

Bryher *General store, White House (01720 422010).* **Open** 9am-5.30pm Mon-Fri; 9am-1pm Sat. **St Agnes** *General store (01720 422364).* **Open** *Apr-Oct* 9am-6pm Mon-Sat; 10am-noon Sun. *Nov-Mar* 9.30-11.30am, 3-5pm Mon-Fri; 3-5pm Sat. **St Martin's** *Higher Town (01720 422801).* **Open** *Apr-Oct* 8.30am-5pm Mon, Tue, Thur, Fri; 8.30am-12.30pm Wed, Sat. *Nov-Mar* 9am-12.30pm, 1.30-4.30pm Mon, Tue, Thur, Fri; 9am-12.30pm Wed, Sat. **St Mary's** *Hugh Town (01720 422454).* **Open** *May-Oct* 8.15am-5pm Mon-Fri; 8.15am-12.15pm Sat. *Nov-Apr* 8.15am-4.30pm Mon-Fri; 8.15am-12.15pm Sat. **Tresco** *Estate Office (01720 424113).* **Open** 9.30am-1pm, 2-4pm Mon, Tue, Thur, Fri; 9.30am-12.30pm Wed.

Tourist information

St Mary's *Isles of Scilly Tourist Information Centre, Hugh Street, Hugh Town (01720 422536/ tic@scilly.gov.uk).* **Open** *Jan-May* 8.30am-5pm Mon-Fri; 8.30am-noon Sat. *June-Sept* 8.30am-6pm Mon-Fri; 8.30am-5pm Sat; 9am-noon Sun. *Oct-Dec* 8.30am-5pm Mon-Fri.

Getting there & around

By air

If you fancy arriving in style, **British International Helicopters** (01736 363871, www.scillyhelicopter.co.uk) make the 20min hop from Eastern Green in Penzance (just off the A30) to either St Mary's or Tresco (no service Sun). Alternatively, **Isles of Scilly Travel** (0845 710 5555, www.ios-travel.co.uk) runs flights to St Mary's airport from Bristol, Exeter, Newquay and Land's End. There are also flights from Bournemouth and Southampton. Bear in mind that flight frequencies vary with the season, and reservations should be made well in advance. *See also p292.*

By boat

The *Scillonian III*, operated by **Isles of Scilly Travel** (*see above*) runs once daily from Penzance to St Mary's (Mon-Sat from late Apr to late Oct; Mon, Wed, Fri, Sat only from Oct to mid Nov and in early Apr). The crossing takes 2hrs 40mins and can be very rough. There are no services late Nov-Mar. **St Mary's Boatmen's Association** (01720 422078) runs a connecting boat service from St Mary's Quay to the off-islands at 10.15am every day (at 10am for Tresco). You'll also find plenty of private launches to take you between the islands – enquire at the tourist office for information.

By road

Two cab companies operate on St Mary's – **Richard Hand** (01720 423007) and **Island Carriers** (01720 422662) – and a scheduled bus service runs in the holiday season, starting from outside the Town Hall in Hugh Town. On the other inhabited islands make the most of the opportunity to cycle or walk. Bikes can be hired from **Buccabu Hire** (Porthcressa, St Mary's, 01720 422289) or from the **Estate Office** on Tresco (*see above*).

Directory

Directory

Getting There & Around

Airlines

The following airlines operate scheduled UK and Ireland services to/from airports in the South West; for details of specific routes served by these airlines, refer to the relevant airport below.

Aer Arann Express
UK reservations 0800 587 2324/ www.aerarann.ie.

Air Wales *UK reservations 0870 777 3131/www.airwales.co.uk.*

Aurigny Airlines *01481 822886/ www.aurigny.com.*

British Airways *UK reservations 0845 773 3377/flight information 0870 551 1155/www.british airways.com.*

British European Airways *0990 676676/www.flybe.com.*

Easyjet *0870 6000 000/ www.easyjet.com.*

Isles of Scilly Skybus *0845 7105555/www.islesofscilly-travel.co.uk.*

Ryanair *UK reservations 0905 102 0500/UK flight information 0871 246 0000/www.ryanair.ie.*

South West airports

Bristol International
0870 1212 747/www.bristol airport.co.uk. Located 8 miles (13km) south of the city centre.
Bristol airport is served by scheduled flights to/from 27 European destinations, plus numerous seasonal charter flights. There are currently no direct services to/from London terminals, but there are daily flights to/from the following UK and Ireland destinations: Belfast (British European and Easyjet), Cork (Aer Arann Express), Dublin (British Airways and Ryanair), Edinburgh (British Airways and Easyjet), Glasgow (British Airways and Easyjet), Guernsey (Aurigny Airlines), Isle of Man (British European), Isles of Scilly (Isles of Scilly Skybus), Jersey (British Airways), Newcastle (British Airways), Newquay (British

Airways) and Plymouth (British Airways). For details of onward transport from the airport, *see p72*.

Exeter International
01392 367433/flight information 08705 676676/www.exeter-airport.co.uk. Located west of the city, just off the A30.
Exeter currently offers no direct flights to/from London and other UK mainland airports but British European Airways operates scheduled services to/from Dublin, Guernsey and Jersey. There are also summer flights to the Scillies with Isles of Scilly Skybus and seasonal charter flights to selected European destinations. For details of onward transport from the airport, *see p157*.

Newquay Cornwall
01637 860600/860950/ www.sutton-harbour.co.uk/ newquay.cfm. Located 5 miles (8km) north of Newquay on the A3059.
Now managed by Plymouth City Airport, this regional airport is served by four daily British Airways flights to/from London Gatwick (two are via Plymouth) and a daily Ryanair service to/from London Stansted (*see below*). Isles of Scilly Skybus operates twice daily flights to/from the Isles of Scilly, with additional services in summer. For details of onward transport from the airport, *see p285*.

Plymouth City
01752 204090/flight information 0845 773 3377/www.sutton-harbour.co.uk/plymair.cfm. Located in the north of the city, just off the A386.
British Airways runs direct scheduled services to/from Bristol, Newquay and London Gatwick (4 times a day; *see below*), while Air Wales operates services to Cork and Dublin. For details of onward transport from the airport, *see p209*.

London airports

London's airports remain the chief transport hubs for air travellers to the UK. Onward flights to South West airports are limited but there are extensive rail and bus links.

Gatwick
0870 000 2468/www.baa.co.uk/ gatwick. Located 30 miles (50km) south of central London, off M23.
BA currently runs four daily flights from Gatwick to Plymouth; two of these continue to Newquay, which is also served by two direct flights. In addition, regular National Express coach services (*see p293*) run from Gatwick bus station to destinations throughout the South West.
Rail services link Gatwick with London Victoria station, from where travellers to the South West will need to use underground, bus or taxi services to reach Paddington or Waterloo stations (*see p293*) for rail connections to the region.

Heathrow
0870 000 0123/www.baa.co.uk/ heathrow. Located 15 miles (24km) west of central London, off M4.
There are no flights to the South West from LHR, but the Heathrow Express rail service (0845 600 1515, www.heathrowexpress.co.uk) runs to London Paddington (*see p293*) between 5am and midnight daily (journey time 15-20mins) for rail connections to the region.
National Express (*see p293*) runs daily coach services from Heathrow Central bus terminal to most destinations in the South West.

Stansted
0870 000 0303/www.baa.co.uk/ stansted. Located 35 miles (60km) north-east of central London.
Ryanair operates a daily flight to Newquay. There are also frequent train services to London's Liverpool Street station, from where travellers to the South West will need to use underground, bus or taxi services to reach Paddington or Waterloo stations (*see p293*) for rail connections to the region.

Bristol Temple Meads (*see p72*) is a major station on the national rail network receiving frequent mainline services from London (via Bath Spa), the Midlands, the North of England and Wales. Beyond

Bristol, mainline services run south via Weston-Super-Mare and Taunton to **Exeter St David's** (*see p158*). This is another significant hub, from which mainline services continue south and west towards Newton Abbot, Plymouth, Bodmin Parkway, Truro and Penzance at the end of the line. Additional services from London Waterloo and the South East run to Exeter St David's and beyond (via Salisbury and Honiton) and to Bristol Temple Meads (via Basingstoke, Salisbury, Westbury and Bath Spa).

For up-to-date information on rail services throughout the UK, contact **National Rail Enquiries** (08457 484950/ www.nationalrail.co.uk). The website has live departure boards, journey-planning facilities and links to all UK operators. To book tickets, contact the relevant rail operator (*see below*) or log on to www.thetrainline.com.

In-depth information on the rail network in Devon and Cornwall is provided online at www.carfreedaysout.com, which gives regional rail links and contact details for individual stations.

Operators

International **Eurostar** services (08705 186186/ www.eurostar.com) arrive into London Waterloo.

First Great Western
tickets & reservations 08457 000125/www.firstgreatwestern.co.uk. First Great Western runs fast, frequent services from London Paddington to Bath Spa (1hr 30mins), Bristol Temple Meads (1hr 45mins), Exeter St David's (3hrs), Plymouth (3-4hrs), Penzance (5-6hrs) and intermediate stations.

South West Trains
tickets & reservations 0845 600 0650/www.southwesttrains.co.uk. South West Trains run from London Waterloo (via Basingstoke, Salisbury and Honiton) to Exeter St David's (3hrs 15mins), Plymouth, Penzance and intermediate stations.

Virgin Cross Country
tickets & reservations 08457 222333/www.virgin.com/trains. Virgin operates long-distance rail services to the South West from Scotland, the North of England and the Midlands. All services are via Birmingham New Street, calling at Bristol Temple Meads, Exeter St David's, Plymouth, Penzance and intermediate stations.

Wessex Trains
tickets & reservations 0870 900 2320/www.wessextrains.co.uk. Wessex Trains operate regional services to Bristol Temple Meads from south Wales, the Cotswolds (via Bristol Parkway) and the south coast (via Castle Cary, Frome and Bath Spa; change at Castle Cary for connections to Taunton). Trains from Bristol run along the main south-west route through Exeter St David's and Plymouth to Penzance.

The company also operates many local services in the region, including the Tarka Line between Exeter and Barnstaple (*see p135*), the Tamar Valley Line from Plymouth to Gunnislake (*see p209*), the Looe Valley line from Liskeard to Looe (*see p226*), and the following branch lines: Exeter Central–Exmouth; Par–Newquay; Truro–Falmouth; St Erth–St Ives.

Fares & tickets

Rail fares vary depending on how far in advance you book your ticket and on any restrictions that may apply, with open returns (no restrictions) being the most expensive option and **Apex** (limited availability; book in advance) the cheapest. Single fares are rarely significantly cheaper than returns and may even be the same price.

For details of regional rail passes, enquire at any staffed railway station.

By bus

National Express (08705 808080/www.gobycoach.com) operates a comprehensive long-distance bus network around the country. Major centres in the South West, including Bath, Bristol, Exeter, Plymouth, Truro and Penzance are served by frequent services

from London's Victoria Coach Station, Birmingham and other UK cities, with more limited services running to smaller towns in the region. Ticket prices tend to be lower than the corresponding rail fare but the journey is usually longer.

Within the region services are provided by a number of local companies. Coverage and reliability varies greatly from place to place, so do not rely on local buses as your sole means of transport if you want to explore remoter corners.

Traveline (0870 608 2608, www.traveline.org.uk) deals with public transport enquiries throughout the South West region. Information is also provided on the official county council websites: www.bathnes.gov.uk; www.somerset.gov.uk; www.devon.gov.uks; www.cornwall.gov.uk. For detailed timetable information, contact the appropriate service provider:

Bristol: *First Cityline (0117 955 8211/www.firstcityline.co.uk).*

North Somerset & Bath: *First Badgerline (01934 620122/ www.firstbadgerline.co.uk).*

South Somerset: *First Southern National (01823 272033/ www.firstsouthernnational.co.uk).*

North Devon & Exmoor: *First Red Bus (01271 345444/ www.firstgroup.com).*

Exeter & East Devon: *Stagecoach Devon (01392 427711/www.stage coachbus.com) or First Western National (01823 272033/ www.firstgroup.com).*

South & West Devon: *Stagecoach Devon (01803 664500, www.stagecoachbus.com) or First Western National (01752 402060/ www.firstgroup.com).*

Plymouth: *Citybus (01752 222221).*

East Cornwall: *First Western National (01752 402060/ www.firstgroup.com).*

Mid Cornwall: *First Western National (01208 79898/ www.firstgroup.com).*

West Cornwall: *First Western National (01209 719988/ www.firstgroup.com).*

Lizard & North Cornwall: *Truronian (01872 273453/ www.truronian.co.uk).*

By car or motorbike

The main road route into the South West is the **M5**, which runs south from Birmingham to Bristol, Taunton and Exeter. The **M4** from London or Wales intersects with the M5 just north of Bristol. Holidaymakers from south-east England can avoid the motorway by taking the **A303** through the heart of Somerset, or the **A35** along the south coast. Both roads join the main **A30** near Honiton, Devon.

Beyond Exeter, the region is motorway-free, although dual carriageways provide quick access between the major centres. The **A30** from Exeter crosses the top of Dartmoor and continues through Bodmin moor to Penzance, while the **A38** runs south of Dartmoor and on to Plymouth and Bodmin. The **A39** is the main route along the North Cornwall coast as far as Barnstaple, while the **A361** provides a relatively fast link to North Devon from the M5.

In high summer, remember that all these routes are likely to be very crowded, with slow-moving caravans causing significant delays, so allow plenty of time for your journey.

Caravans are also an annoyance on the region's minor roads, though you're just as likely to find yourself behind a muddy tractor, a flock of sheep or a large group of walkers. In all these cases, excellent reversing skills, limitless patience and a laid-back attitude are essential, as the South West's narrow, winding high-hedged lanes can disorientate even the most experienced driver.

Nevertheless, having your own set of wheels – whether four or two – is a definite bonus if you're venturing beyond the main cities and tourist centres.

Breakdown services

If you're a member of a motoring organisation in another country, check to see if it has a reciprocal agreement with a British organisation. Each of the following offers a 24-hour breakdown service.

AA (Automobile Association)
Information 08705 500600/ breakdown 0800 887766/members 0800 444999/www.theaa.co.uk.

ETA (Environmental Transport Association) *68 High Street, Weybridge, Surrey KT13 8RS (01932 828882/www.eta.co.uk).*

RAC (Royal Automobile Club)
RAC House, 1 Forest Road, Feltham, Middx TW13 7RR (breakdown 0800 828282/office & membership 08705 722722/www.rac.co.uk).

Legal requirements

● The minimum legal age for driving a car or motorbike in the UK is 17.
● You must have a valid, signed driving licence for the category of vehicle you are driving.
● Seatbelts must be worn at all times unless you are exempt. The driver must ensure all children under 14 years wear seatbelts or sit in an approved child restraint.
● Unless otherwise indicated the speed limits for cars and motorcycles are 30mph (in built-up areas), 60mph (single carriageways), 70mph (dual carriageways), 70mph (motorways). Maximum fine for speeding is £1,000 (£2,500 for motorway offences).
● You must not drive if alcohol in your body exceeds the following levels: 35µg per 100ml of breath; 80mg per 100ml of blood; 107mg per 100ml of urine
● Proper control of your vehicle must be exercised at all times; use of a handheld mobile phone is forbidden, and you should avoid eating or drinking at the wheel.

Parking

In addition to central car parks, larger towns and cities often have a Park 'n' Ride scheme, which can take the hassle out of parking. Even in rural areas there tends to be a designated car park near major attractions and sights. If you have to leave your car far from your destination, take the necessary security precautions.

Stopping in rural areas in order to explore on foot (or study a map) is a question of common sense – before stopping, ensure your vehicle will not prove an obstruction or hazard to other road users or pedestrians.

Vehicle hire

To hire a car, you must have at least one year's driving experience and a full current driving licence; in addition, many car hire firms refuse to hire vehicles out to people under the age of 23. If you're an overseas visitor, your driving licence is valid in Britain for a year. Prices for car hire vary wildly; always ring several competitors for a quote (see the *Yellow Pages* or www.yell.com).

Alamo *0870 400 4508/www.alamo. com.* **Open** 8am-7pm Mon-Fri; 8am-6pm Sat; 9am-4pm Sun. **Credit** AmEx, MC, V.

Avis *08705 900500/www.avis.co.uk.* **Open** 24hrs daily. **Credit** AmEx, DC, MC, V.

Budget *0800 181181/ www.gobudget.com).* **Open** 9am-5.30pm Mon-Fri; 8am-4pm Sat. **Credit** AmEx, DC, MC, V.

Enterprise *01252 353620/ www.enterprise.com.* **Open** 8am-6pm Mon-Fri; 8am-noon Sat. **Credit** AmEx, MC, V.

Europcar *0870 607 5000/ www.europcar.com.* **Open** 24hrs daily. **Credit** AmEx, DC, MC, V.

Hertz *0870 599 6699/ www.hertz.com.* **Open** 24hrs daily. **Credit** AmEx, MC, V.

By boat

For details of ferries to the Isles of Scilly, *see p290.*

Brittany Ferries
08703 665333/www.brittany-ferries.co.uk.
Brittany Ferries operates day and night between Plymouth and Roscoff in France, with less frequent sailings to/from Santander in Spain.

By bicycle

For details of cycling routes around the region, *see p39.*

Resources A-Z

Accommodation

The massive tourist influx to the South West each year demands an extensive range of accommodation that caters for all budgets.

In each area chapter of this guide we've given our pick of accommodation in the region. For a wider selection, get in touch with the local tourist office when planning your trip and ask them to send you details of hotels, B&Bs, campsites and self-catering properties in the area.

Peak season varies from place to place, but most hoteliers will put their prices up just before Easter, and lower them at the end of September or in early October. Bank holiday weekends often attract the biggest crowds, so if you're planning to visit a tourist destination during this time, book your accommodation well in advance. Also take note of local events such as carnivals, surfing championships, festivals and so on (the main ones are listed throughout this guide), as they may result in accommodation being fully booked several weeks ahead of time.

Conversely, remember that away from the major cities, small hotels, guesthouses and B&Bs often close entirely in the winter, although you'll still likely to find a room in the larger hotels or local pubs.

Accommodation rates in the UK are usually inclusive of VAT, but you should always check to avoid any unpleasant surprises when you get your bill. Equally, find out about single supplements, bed-and-breakfast deals, special offers and weekend breaks. City hotels often charge a cheaper rate at weekends for non-business customers, and resort destinations may offer great deals for off-season breaks. Note that B&Bs and rural campsites may not accept credit cards.

Hotels, guesthouses & B&Bs

The AA, RAC and English Tourism Council (ETC) have joined forces to standardise their accommodation rating system. Stars are used for hotels, with five stars reserved for those world-class properties that excel in every field, from accommodation to service and facilities to food.

Diamonds are used to grade 'Guest Accommodation' (guesthouses, B&Bs, inns and farmhouses), with the rating (from one to five) usually based on the quality of guest care rather than the provision of facilities. Cleanliness, service, comfort and the standard of food are all taken into account.

This type of accommodation is plentiful in the South West and is generally of a good standard, although you should watch out for outdated decor and rather lackadaisical service. Prices start from around £20 per person per night, but can reach much higher levels in stylish, independent joints. For many visitors the intimate atmosphere of a guesthouse is preferable to the anonymity of a larger hotel.

For further information on the rating system consult www.englishtourism.org.uk.

Hostels

Hostels often represent the cheapest accommodation option, with low prices helping to stretch backpackers' around-the-world-budget. Private twin rooms are usually available, although it's cheaper to share a dorm, with prices starting from as little as £8 per person per night. Whenever possible, book ahead.

You can join the **International Youth Hostel Federation** (IYHF) for £13 (£6.50 for under-18s) at any participating hostel, or through www.yha.org.uk, which also allows you to book a bed in advance. If you're not a member you'll pay an extra £2 a night. YHA hostels usually have good facilities including internet access and some are housed in unusual or historic buildings. However, they often operate a curfew and may be closed in the winter.

Independent hostels tend to have a less institutional feel and demonstrate a more relaxed attitude. They are good places to meet single travellers and may organise special social events, although they can also become noisy and overcrowded, particularly in popular tourist destinations.

Self-catering

There are hundreds of self-catering options in the South West, with some truly beautiful properties available for hire, particularly from organisations like the **National Trust** (0870 458 4411, www.national trust.org.uk) and **Landmark Trust** (01628 825925, www.landmarktrust.co.uk).

Self-catering allows you to organise your holiday according to your own schedule. Moreover the cost can be very reasonable, especially if you rent a larger property with a group of friends – prices start from around £300 per week in high season for a property sleeping four people.

Directory

Note that most properties are rented out on a weekly basis, and added extras such as laundry, maid service and food provisions can vary hugely; check with the agency before you book.

Agencies

Blue Chip Vacations *3 Brixham Marina Walk, Brixham, Devon (01803 855282/www.bluechip vacations.com).*

Cornish Farm Holidays *01872 510050/www.cornish-farms.co.uk.*

Cornish Home Holidays *Dept 6, 12 Parade Street, Penzance, Cornwall (01736 368575/www.chh.co.uk).*

Cornish Riviera Holidays *Westcotts Quay, St Ives, Cornwall (01736 797891/ www.cornishrivieraholidays.co.uk).*

Cornish Traditional Cottages *Blisland, Bodmin, Cornwall (01208 821666/www.corncott.com).*

Helpful Holidays *Mill Street, Chagford, Devon (01647 433593/ www.helpfulholidays.com.*

Toad Hall Cottages *Eliot House, Church Street, Kingsbridge, Devon (01548 843089/843089/ www.toadhallcottages.com).*

Campsites & camping barns

There are campsites all over the South West. Although there are always those that will brave a night under canvas at any time of year, the tent and caravan season only really takes off when temperatures pick up. Camping is the perfect choice for travellers who want to get close to nature and avoid the expense of a B&B or hotel. Prices for a single-tent pitch start from around £8. Official campsites are graded on a star system and vary hugely, ranging from a spare half-acre of land in a farmer's field to a full-on holiday park with static caravans, extensive facilities and on-site entertainment.

It is usually possible to turn up with your tent without a reservation, though you'd be wise to book in peak season. Also note that some campsites may cater specifically for

families and so may not welcome large mixed groups, while those on the north coasts of Devon and Cornwall may be overrun with surfers.

Outside designated campsites be aware that most land is owned privately or by the National Trust, and pitching up may be illegal. If in doubt, ask nearby first. For the rules and regulations governing free camping on Exmoor or Dartmoor, contact the relevant National Park Authority (*see p117 and p168*).

A handy alternative in bad weather is a camping barn, a very basic hostel providing simple, self-catering accommodation sheltered from the elements. Most are run by the YHA (*see p295*) but you don't need to be a member to bed down for the night.

For details of campsites in a certain area, contact the local tourist office or consult www.ukcampsite.com.

Age restrictions

You must be 16 or older to buy cigarettes in the UK; 17 or older to drive and 18 to buy alcohol. Carry a valid form of identification with you if you look younger than these minimum ages. For both hetero- and homosexuals, the age of consent in Britain is 16.

Attitude & etiquette

The pace of life in the West Country is generally slower than in much of the UK, and urban defensiveness and aggression is less evident, even in big cities like Bristol and Plymouth (although there are certain areas of these cities that it's wise to avoid). Do yourself and everyone around you a favour by easing down a gear or two before arrival. The sense of community, particularly in rural areas,

remains strong, with people usually showing friendly respect for those around them. West Country folk are generally welcoming to those visiting the region, but you should be aware of a lingering resentment towards ignorant tourists (known as 'grockles' in Devon and 'emmits' in Cornwall), who leave gates open, ignore tides, allow their dogs to worry sheep, or behave in other thoughtless ways. Acting in a particularly flash manner is also unlikely to do you any favours, especially in some of the economically depressed areas.

Consumer

Most shops in the UK will happily offer a full refund for faulty or defective goods, as long as you retain the receipt. If you experience any difficulty in obtaining a refund, contact the local council's Trading Standards department for help and legal advice.

Customs

When entering the UK, non-EU citizens and anyone buying duty-free goods should note the following import limits:

● 200 cigarettes or 100 cigarillos or 50 cigars or 250g (8.82 oz) of tobacco.
● 2 litres of still table wine plus either 1 litre of spirits/strong liqueurs (more than 22% alcohol by volume) or 2 litres of fortified wine (under 22% abv), sparkling wine or other liqueurs;
● 60cc/ml of perfume;
● 250cc/ml of toilet water;
● other goods to the value of £145 for non-commercial use;
● the import of meat products, fruit, plants, flowers and protected animals is restricted or forbidden.

Since the Single European Market agreement came into force at the beginning of 1993, people over the age of 17 arriving from an EU country have been able to import large quantities of goods for their own personal use, but Customs officials may need convincing that you do not intend to sell any of the goods.

Disabled

Disabled visitors are likely to find that newly built attractions and hotels are designed with accessibility in mind, for example the Eden Project, @tBristol, the National Maritime Museum Cornwall in Falmouth and Bath's Thermae Bath Spa. In contrast historic sites, older hotels and small guesthouses are often less accessible. In all cases it is wise to phone ahead to check the provision of facilities.

The ETC's National Accessible Scheme for self-catering and serviced accommodation includes standards for hearing- and visually-impaired guests, as well as those with mobility impairment. Approved NAS accommodation in the South West is listed on **www.westcountrynow.com**. If you have any special requirements, check with your chosen establishment before you book.

Useful contacts

Can Be Done
7-11 Kensington High Street, Kensington, London W8 5NP (020 8907 2400/www.canbedone.co.uk). **Open** *Phone enquiries 9am-5.30pm Mon-Fri.*
Specifically tailored holidays and tours around the UK for the disabled.

DIAL UK
01302 310123/www.dialuk.org.uk. **Open** 9am-5pm Mon-Thur; 9am-4pm Fri.
Provides details of local groups in the UK that can offer free advice on all aspects of disability.

Holiday Care
Sunley House, 4 Bedford Park, Croydon, Surrey CR0 2AP (0845 124 9971/www.holidaycare.org.uk). **Open** *Helpline* 9am-5pm Mon, Tue; 9am-1pm Wed-Fri.
An advisory service specialising in disabled holiday accommodation.

Smooth Ride Guides
Duck Street Barns, Furneux Pelham, Herts SG9 0LA (01279 777966/ www.smoothrideguides.com). **Open** 9am-5pm Mon-Sat.
Travel guides listing activities, attractions, accommodation and leisure facilities for people with mobility difficulties.

Tripscope
Vassall Centre, Gill Avenue, Fishponds, Bristol BS16 2QQ (tel/textphone 08457 585641/ www.tripscope.org.uk). **Open** *Phone enquiries 9am-5pm Mon-Thur; 9am-4.30pm Fri.*
A phone-based travel advisory service for the elderly and disabled,.

Electricity

The United Kingdom electricity supply is the standard European 220-240V, 50-cycle AC. British plugs use three pins rather than two, so travellers with appliances from mainland Europe should bring an adaptor, as should anyone using US appliances, which run off 110-120V, 60-cycle AC.

Embassies & consulates

Individual departmental opening times are given on the websites.

American Embassy *24 Grosvenor Square, London W1 (020 7499 9000/www.usembassy.org.uk).* **Open** 9am-5pm Mon-Fri.
Australian High Commission *Australia House, Strand, London WC2 (020 7379 4334/ www.australia.org.uk).* **Open** 9.30am-3.30pm Mon-Fri.
Canadian High Commission *38 Grosvenor Street, London W1 (020 7258 6600/www.canada.org.uk).* **Open** 8-11am Mon-Fri.
Irish Embassy *17 Grosvenor Place, London SW1 (020 7235 2171).* **Open** 9.30am-1pm, 2.30-5.30pm Mon-Fri.
New Zealand High Commission *New Zealand House, 80 Haymarket, London SW1 (020 7930 8422/ www.nzembassy.com).* **Open** 9am-5pm Mon-Fri.
South African High Commission *South Africa House, Trafalgar Square, London WC2 (020 7451 7299/www.southafricahouse.com).* **Open** 8.30am-1pm, 2-5pm Mon-Fri.

Emergencies

In the event of a serious accident, fire or incident, call **999** – free from any phone in the UK, including payphones – and specify whether you require ambulance, police or the fire service.

For the addresses of Accident & Emergency (or minor injuries) departments and regional police stations, please refer to the 'Resources' section in each area chapter of this guide. For helplines, *see p299.*

Gay & lesbian

Attitudes towards gay and lesbian visitors in the South West differ widely from place to place.

As you might expect, you are more likely to come across liberal attitudes in urban centres than in rural backwaters. Bristol, in particular, is welcoming to same-sex couples, with a decent selection of venues catering for different tastes; Exeter's gay scene is more limited, although a handful of city venues host weekly gay nights.

Outside the cities it's a bit more hit and miss: many hoteliers, publicans and other hosts will not bat an eyelid at same-sex couples, but managers of more 'traditional' establishments (particularly those catering for an ageing, conservative clientele) may succeed in making homosexual visitors feel unwelcome. Despite a reputation as a laid-back destination, much of the South West remains a heartland for traditional 'values' and prejudices.

Gay & Lesbian Switchboard (South West)
01392 422016/www.switchboard southwest.org.uk. Information and advice on many aspects of the gay and lesbian scene in the region.

Health

Free emergency medical treatment under the National Health Service (NHS) is available to the following:

● European Union nationals, plus those of Iceland, Norway and Liechtenstein. These groups are also entitled to specific treatment for a non-emergency condition on production of form E112 or E128.
● Nationals (on production of a passport) of Bulgaria, the Czech and Slovak Republics, Gibraltar, Hungary, Malta, New Zealand, Russia, former Soviet Union states (not Latvia, Lithuania and Estonia) and the former Yugoslavia.
● Residents, irrespective of nationality, of Anguilla, Australia, Barbados, British Virgin Islands, Channel Islands, Falkland Islands, Iceland, Isle of Man, Montserrat, Poland, Romania, St Helena, Sweden, Turks & Caicos Islands.
● Anyone who has been in the UK for the previous 12 months.
● Anyone who has come to the UK to take up permanent residence.
● Students and trainees whose courses require more than 12 weeks employment in the UK during the first year. Others living in the UK for a settled purpose for more than six months may also not be liable to charges.
● Refugees and others who have sought refuge in the UK.
● Anyone formally detained by the immigration authorities.
● People with HIV/AIDS at a special clinic for the treatment of sexually transmitted diseases, although treatment is limited to a diagnostic test and counselling associated with that test.

There are no NHS charges for the following services:

● Treatment in Accident & Emergency departments.
● Certain district nursing, midwifery or health visiting services.
● Emergency ambulance transport.
● Diagnosis and treatment of certain communicable diseases, including STDs.
● Family planning services.
● Compulsory psychiatric treatment.

Accident & emergency

For the address of an A&E or minor injuries department in a particular region, refer to the relevant area chapter.

Complementary medicine

British Homeopathic Association

15 Clerkenwell Close, London EC1R OAA (020 7566 7800/ www.trusthomeopathy.org). **Open** *Phone enquiries* 9am-5pm Mon-Fri. The BHA will indicate your nearest homeopathic chemist and/or doctor.

Institute for Complementary Medicine

PO Box 194, London SE16 7QZ (020 7237 5165/www.icmedicine.co.uk). Send an SAE and two loose first-class stamps for a list of registered practitioners or training advice.

Contraception & abortion

Family planning advice, contraceptive supplies and abortions on the NHS are free to British citizens, EU residents and foreign nationals living, working and studying in Britain. If you decide to go private, contact one of the organisations listed below. You can also call the Contraception Helpline on 020 7837 4044 for your nearest branch of the **Family Planning Association**. The 'morning after' pill, effective up to 72 hours after intercourse, is now available over the counter, but will cost you a hefty £20.

British Pregnancy Advisory Service

08457 304030/www.bpas.org. Callers are referred to their nearest clinic. Advice, contraceptives and pregnancy testing.

Brook Advisory Centre

0800 018 5023/www.brook.org.uk. **Open** *Helpline* 9am-5pm Mon-Fri. Advice and referrals on sexual health, contraception and abortion, plus free pregnancy tests for under-25s. Call for your nearest clinic.

Dentists

Dental care is free under the National Health Service to the following British residents:

● Under-18s.
● Under-19s in full-time education.
● Pregnant women and those with a baby under the age of one when treatment begins.
● People receiving Income Support, Jobseeker's Allowance, Family Credit or Disability Working Allowance.

All other patients must pay NHS charges, which start from around £4 for a check-up. To find an NHS dentist, get in touch with the local Health Authority or a Citizens' Advice Bureau (*see p299*).

Doctors

If you're a British citizen or working in the United Kingdom, you can go to any general practitioner (GP). If you're not visiting your usual GP, you'll be asked for details of the doctor with whom you are registered, in order that your records can be updated. People ordinarily resident in the UK, including overseas students, are also permitted to register with an NHS doctor.

Hospitals

To find a local hospital with an A&E or minor injuries department, refer to the 'Resources' section in each area chapter of this guide; for other hospitals, refer to the *Yellow Pages*. For details of what to do in an emergency, *see p297*.

Prescriptions

Many drugs in the UK are only available on prescription. A pharmacist will dispense medicines on receipt of a prescription from a registered GP. NHS prescriptions cost £6.10, but under-16s and over-60s are exempt, and contraception is free to all. If you're not eligible to see an NHS doctor, you'll be charged cost price for medicines prescribed by a private doctor. Pharmacists, who must be qualified, can advise on the appropriate treatment for

Directory

minor ailments. Most pharmacies keep regular shop hours (9am-6pm; closed Sun).

STDs, HIV & AIDS

NHS Genito-Urinary Clinics are affiliated to major hospitals. They provide free, confidential treatment of STDs and other problems, such as thrush and cystitis; offer counselling about HIV and other STDs; and conduct blood tests to determine HIV status.

The 24-hour **National AIDS Helpline** (English 0800 567123/textphone 0800 521361/other languages 0800 917227) is free and confidential. For details of other helplines, *see below*; for abortion and contraception services, *see p298*.

Helplines

See also above **STDs, HIV & AIDS**. For gay and lesbian helplines, *see p297*.

Alcoholics Anonymous
020 7833 0022/www.alcoholics-anonymous.org.uk. **Open** *Phone line* 10am-10pm daily.
Operators will put you in touch with a member in your area.

Childline
Freepost 1111, London N1 OBR (0800 1111/textphone 0800 400 222/www.childline.org.uk). **Open** *Phone lines* 24hrs daily.
Free helpline for children and young people in trouble or danger.

Citizens' Advice Bureaux
Council-run CABs offer free legal, financial and personal advice. Check the phone book for your local branch.

NHS Direct
0845 4647/www.nhsdirect.nhs.uk. **Open** 24hrs daily.
NHS Direct is a first-stop service for medical advice on all subjects.

MIND
Granta House, 15-19 Broadway, London E15 4BQ (0845 766 0163/www.mind.org.uk). **Open** *Information* 9.15am-5.15pm Mon-Fri.
MIND can offer help for mental distress, and provides factsheets on all facets of mental health.

Narcotics Anonymous
020 7730 0009/www.ukna.org. **Open** 10am-10pm daily.
NA offers advice and informs callers of their nearest meeting.

National Missing Persons Helpline
0500 700 700/www.missing persons.org. **Open** 24hrs daily.
NMPH publicises information on anyone reported missing. It can artificially age photographs and offers a 'Message Home' freephone service (0800 700 740).

Refuge Helpline
08705 995443. **Open** 24hrs daily.
Refuge referral for women suffering domestic violence.

Samaritans
08457 909090/www.samaritans. org.uk. **Open** 24hrs daily.
The Samaritans listen to anyone with emotional problems. It's a popular service, so persevere when phoning.

Victim Support
National Office, Cranmer House, 39 Brixton Road, London SW9 6DZ (0845 303 0900/www.victim support.com). **Open** *Support line* 9am-9pm Mon-Fri; 9am-7pm Sat, Sun.
Victims of crime are given emotional and practical support, including advice on legal procedures.

Insurance

Foreign visitors are strongly advised to take out personal insurance to cover trip cancellation, emergency medical costs and loss or theft of personal belongings, money or travellers' cheques. It's difficult to arrange travel insurance once you've arrived in the UK, so do so before you leave your home country.

Even if your country has a reciprocal medical treatment arrangement with Britain (*see p298*), it's important to check that your insurance includes adequate health cover. If you plan on taking part in outdoor pursuits such as horse-riding, sailing or diving, you should also consider additional 'dangerous sports' cover.

Keep a record of your policy number and the emergency telephone number with you at all times.

Internet

More and more internet cafés are springing up across the region, and most central libraries now offer some kind of facility, often on a free but limited basis. Larger hotels tend to provide access from within the comfort of your own room, and even smaller establishments are likely to have their own web page and email address for easy contact.

Massive competition in the ISP sector has meant that prices have plummeted, and there are now a great many ISPs that do not charge a subscription fee, only billing for calls. If you want to get set up online in the UK, check one of the many internet publications for details of current deals; the best is *Internet* magazine. For the most useful South West websites, *see p308*.

Left luggage

Airports

Call the following numbers for details of left luggage facilities:
Exeter Airport *01392 367433.*
Gatwick Airport *South Terminal 01293 502014; North Terminal 01293 502013.*
Heathrow Airport *Terminal 1 020 8745 5301; Terminal 2 020 8745 4599; Terminal 3 020 8749 3344; Terminal 4 020 8897 6874.*
London City Airport *020 7646 0162.*
Luton Airport *01582 395212.*
Stansted Airport *01279 663213.*

Train stations

To find out whether a train station offers a left luggage facility, call 08457 484950.

Legal help

Those in legal difficulties should visit a Citizens' Advice Bureau (*see above*) or contact the groups below for information and advice.

Directory

For details of legal aid provision, contact the **Legal Services Commission** in London (020 7759 0000/ www.legalservices.gov.uk).

Community Legal Services Directory

0845 608 1122/www.justask.org.uk. **Open** 9am-10pm daily.
A free telephone service will put you in touch with government agencies and law firms.

Law Centres Federation

Duchess House, 18-19 Warren Street, London W1 (020 7387 8570/www.lawcentres.org.uk). **Open** Phone enquiries 10am-6pm Mon-Fri. Free legal help for people who can't afford a lawyer. This central office connects you with a local centre.

Bath Central Library

19 The Podium, Northgate Street, Bath (01225 787400). **Open** 10am-6pm Mon; 9.30am-7pm Tue-Thur; 9.30am-5pm Fri, Sat; 1-4pm Sun.

Bristol Central Library

College Green, Bristol (0117 903 7200/www.bristol-city.gov.uk). **Open** 9.30am-7.30pm Mon, Tue, Thur; 9.30am-5pm Wed, Fri, Sat; 1-4pm Sun.

Exeter Central Library

Castle Street, Exeter, Devon (01392 384225). **Open** 9.30am-7pm Mon, Tue, Thur, Fri; 10am-5pm Wed; 9.30am-4pm Sat.

Plymouth Central Library

Central Library, Drake Circus, Plymouth, Devon (01752 305912/ www.plymouthlibraries.info). **Open** 9.30am-7pm Mon, Fri; 9.30am-5.30pm Tue-Thur; 9.30am-4pm Sat.

Taunton Library

Paul Street, Taunton, Somerset (01823 336334). **Open** 9.30am-5.30pm Mon, Tue, Thur; 9.30am-7pm Wed, Fri; 9.30am-4pm Sat.

Truro Library

Union Place, Truro, Cornwall (01872 279205). **Open** 9am-6pm Mon-Fri; 9am-4pm Sat.

Always inform the police if you lose anything, if only to validate insurance claims. For details of the nearest police station, refer to the 'Resources' section in each area chapter of this guide; only dial 999 if violence has occurred. Report lost passports to the police and to your embassy (*see p297*).

Airports

For property lost on the plane, contact the relevant airline or handling agents; for items lost in a particular airport, contact the following:

Bristol Airport *British Airways 01275 473435; Service Air (for all other carriers) 01275 473543.*
Exeter Airport *01392 367433.*
Gatwick Airport *01293 503162.*
Heathrow Airport *020 8745 7727.*
Newquay Airport *01637 860600.*
Stansted Airport *01279 663293.*

Public transport

If you've lost property in a station or on a train, call 08700 005151; an operator will connect you to the appropriate station. To enquire about items lost on buses, contact the service provider.

Magazines

After years of boom, the new millenium saw a heavy downturn in the UK magazine industry. Having said that, *Loaded, FHM* and *Maxim* are remain the biggest men's titles, while women still flock to *Cosmopolitan, Vogue, Marie Claire* and *Elle.* Celebrity magazines thrive, with the glossy *Heat* doing particularly well, and style mags like *i-D* and *Dazed and Confused* have found a profitable niche. *The Spectator*, the *New Statesman*, *Prospect* and the *Economist* are about as good as it gets at the serious end of the market, while the satirical fortnightly *Private Eye* adds a little levity.

In the South West regional publications worthy of note include *Venue*, a *Time Out*-style weekly listings mag for Bristol and Bath featuring up-to-date information and decent journalism. *The List* does the same job on a monthly basis for Exeter, while Plymouth-based *Twenty4Seven* is a youthful monthly lifestyle mag with listings information for music and nightlife venues throughout Devon and Cornwall. South West editions of the *Big Issue*, which are sold on the streets of Bristol, Bath and Exeter by homeless people, are also worth a look.

Keep an eye out, too, for *Decode*, a well-designed, visually attractive bi-monthly arts mag for Bristol and Bath, and *Exeter Flying Post*, an alternative, left-of-centre monthly that is one of the oldest titles in country, pre-dating *The Times*.

Finally, a handful of glossy monthlies (*Somerset Life, Devon Life, Cornwall Today* and others) offer mainstream articles about each county, with lots of colour photos and informative – though unchallenging – editorial.

Newspapers

At the serious end of the scale is the broadsheet. The right-wing *Daily Telegraph* and *The Times* (which is best for sport) are balanced by the *Independent* and the *Guardian* (best for arts). All have bulging Sunday equivalents bar the *Guardian*, which has a sister Sunday paper, the *Observer*. The pink *Financial Times* (daily) is the best for business facts and figures. In the middle of the market, the leader has long been the right-wing *Daily Mail* (and *Mail on Sunday*); its rival, the *Daily Express* (and *Sunday Express*), continues to struggle. The most popular kind of newspaper in the UK is still the tabloid, with the *Sun* (and Sunday's *News of the World*) the undisputed leader; the *Daily Star* and *Mirror* are its main rivals, while the *People*, the *Sunday Mirror* and a new *Sunday Star* provide weekend sleaze.

The following regional papers provide the (often uneventful) news for their respective areas, and give a good idea of local flavour: *Bristol Evening Post; Bath Chronicle; Western Daily Press* (Somerset); *Weston & Someset Mercury; Express & Echo* (Exeter); *Mid Devon Gazette; North Devon Journal; Evening Herald* (Plymouth); *Herald Express* (South Devon); *Western Morning News* (Devon and Cornwall); *West Briton* (Cornwall); *The Cornishman* and *Cornish Guardian*.

Radio

National stations

BBC Radio 1 *98.8 FM*. Youth-oriented pop, indie and dance music.
BBC Radio 2 *89.1 FM*. Bland during the day, but good after dark.
BBC Radio 3 *91.3 FM*. Classical music dominates, but there's also discussion, world music and other arts (try Andy Kershaw, 10.15-11.30pm Fri, or Late Junction, 10.15pm-midnight Mon-Thur).
BBC Radio 4 *93.5 FM, 198 LW*. The BBC's main speech station. Today (6-9am Mon-Fri) bristles with self-importance.
BBC Radio 5 Live *693, 909 AM*. Rolling news and sport. Avoid the phone-ins, but Up All Night (1-5am nightly) is terrific.
Classic FM *100.9 FM*. Classical music for people who don't like it.
Jazz FM *102.2 FM*. Smooth jazz (aka elevator music) now dominates.
TalkSport *1053 & 1089 AM*. TalkSport puts its focus on phone-ins. Best to stick with 5 Live.
Virgin *105.8 FM, 1215 AM*. Music with attitude – but not too much.

Local radio

Bath GWR *103 FM*.
Bristol GWR *96.3 FM*.
Gemini FM (Exeter) *96.4, 97.0, 103 FM*.
Lantern FM (North Devon) *96.2/97.3 FM*.
Orchard FM (Somerset) *96.5/97.1/102.6 FM*.
Plymouth Sound *97 FM*.
All of the above are part of the same chain giving you 'today's best mix' – contemporary hit radio, with plenty of adverts, unchallenging pop music and smug presenters.

BBC Radio Devon *103.4 FM*. Good West Country chat, with a little more substance than some of its commercial counterparts.
BBC Radio Cornwall *103.9, 95.2 FM*. A thick slice of Kernow with some proper accents to boot.
BBC Radio Bristol *95.5, 94.9 FM 1548AM*. Phone-ins, news, sport and a little bit of music.
BBC Somerset Sound *1566 AM*. More of the above. A new frequency has put an end to interference from a Russian radio station.

Television

The next generation of TV in the UK is now here, so the non-network sector is now crammed with stations on a variety of formats (satellite, cable and digital). We've listed the pick of the channels.

Network channels

BBC1 The Corporation's mass-market station. There's a smattering of soaps and game shows, and the odd quality programme. Daytime programming, however, stinks. As with all BBC radio and TV stations, there are no commercials.
BBC2 In general, BBC2 is free of crass programmes. That doesn't mean the output's riveting, but it's not insulting, offering a cultural cross-section and plenty of documentaries.
ITV1 Carlton West Country (Cornwall, Devon, and parts of Somerset and Dorset) and ITV1 West of England (Bristol, Bath, parts of Somerset and Wales) bring the ITV network schedule to viewers in the South West, as well as broadcasting regular regional news bulletins and local programmes. ITV2 is on digital.
Channel 4 C4's output includes extremely successful US imports (*Friends, ER, The Sopranos*), but it still comes up with some gems, particularly films.
Five Since launching Britain's newest terrestrial channel has offered sex, US TV movies, sex, rubbish comedy, sex, more sex and US sport, but has shown signs of moving upmarket of late with some nice docs.

Satellite, digital & cable channels

BBC News 24 The Beeb's rolling news network.
CNN News and current affairs.
Discovery Channel Science and nature documentaries.
FilmFour Channel 4's movie outlet, with 12 hours of programming daily.
MTV Rock/pop channel that borrows from its US counterpart.

Performance Dance, theatre and opera, plus interviews with the stars.
Sky News Rolling news.
Sky One Sky's version of ITV.
Sky Sports Sports. There are also Sky Sports 2 and Sky Sports 3.
UK Gold Reruns of BBC and ITV successes of yesteryear.
UK Horizon Science documentaries.
VH-1 MTV for grown-ups.

Money

Britain's currency is the pound sterling (£). One pound equals 100 pence (p). Coins are copper (1p, 2p), silver (round: 5p, 10p; seven-sided: 20p, 50p), yellowy-gold (£1) or silver in the centre with a yellowy-gold edge (£2). Paper notes are blue (£5), orange (£10), purple (£20) or red (£50). The Marks & Spencer chain is unusual in that it also accepts payment in Euros (€).

Western Union

0800 833833/www.westernunion.com. The old standby for bailing cash-challenged travellers out of trouble. Beware: it can be pricey.

ATMs

As well as inside and outside banks, cash machines can be found in some supermarkets and other shops, and in larger rail stations. The vast majority accept withdrawals on major credit cards, and most also allow withdrawals using the Maestro/Cirrus debit system.

Visitors to the Isles of Scilly should note that the only ATM is on St Mary's (*see p290*).

Banks

You can exchange foreign currency at banks and bureaux de change (*see p302*). Exchange and commission rates on currency vary hugely, so it pays to shop around. Commission is sometimes charged for cashing travellers' cheques in foreign currencies, but not for sterling travellers' cheques, provided you cash the cheques at a bank affiliated to the issuing bank (get a list when you buy your cheques); commission is also charged if you change cash into another currency. You always need ID, such as a passport, to exchange travellers' cheques. If you want to open a bank or building society account, you'll need a passport for identification and probably a reference from your home bank. Standard banking hours are 9.30am to 3.30pm Monday to Friday, with some banks closing on Wednesday afternoons and opening on Saturday mornings.

Bureaux de change

You'll be charged for cashing travellers' cheques or buying and selling foreign currency at a bureau de change. Commission rates, which should be clearly displayed, vary. **Thomas Cook** (www.thomascook.co.uk) has branches in major towns and cities. Major rail stations also have bureaux de change.

Credit cards

Although many places accept credit cards, you shouldn't rely solely on this form of payment to make purchases in rural areas or to settle your bill in small B&Bs. Visa and Mastercard are the most widely accepted, Diners Club and American Express less so.

Report **lost/stolen credit cards** immediately to both the police and the 24-hour services below, and inform your bank by phone and in writing.

American Express
01273 696933.
Diners Club *01252 513500.*
MasterCard/Eurocard
0800 964767.
Switch *08706 000459.*
Visa/Connect *0800 895082.*

Tax

With the exception of food, books, newspapers, children's clothing and a few other choice items, UK purchases are subject to VAT – value-added tax, aka sales tax – of 17.5 per cent. Unlike in the US, this is included in prices quoted in shops. Beware: some hotels naughtily quote room rates exclusive of VAT. Be sure to ask whether the rate quoted includes tax.

Natural hazards

● Despite the Environment Agency's efforts, flooding affects many areas of the South West on an annual basis, resulting in road blockages, property damage, injury and worse. For updated information, phone 0845 988 1188 or see www.environment-agency.co.uk.
● Exposure is a particular danger on the South West's moors, so clothing and footwear suited to the conditions should always be worn. Before you set out, inform someone where you are going and roughly what time you expect to be back. Carry adequate water and food.
● Overexposure to the sun is a risk in the summer heat. On particularly hot days, avoid sitting in the sun between 11am and 3pm, and always wear adequate sun protection: SPF15 sun-cream and a hat.
● Strong tides and rip currents can catch out unsuspecting surfers and swimmers, carrying them out to sea with alarming speed. Always stay within the designated areas on the beach (between the red/yellow horizontal striped flags) and never swim when red flags are on display.
● Exploring the coves, caves and rocks of the region's coastline, although fun, can be dangerous, with swift incoming tides cutting off return routes to the mainland. Always check local high/low tide times and make sure you inform someone of your whereabouts before you set off.

Opening hours

As a rule of thumb, businesses are generally open from 9am to 5pm Monday to Friday, while shops normally operate from 10am to 6pm Monday to Saturday (some also open for up to six hours on a Sunday). Pubs and bars are open 11am-11pm Monday to Saturday and noon-10.30pm Sunday. For banking hours *see above*; for post office hours, *see p303.*

Note that opening times for sights, attractions, restaurants and independent shops in the South West can be erratic, particularly in low season, so always phone first to check before making a special journey to a specific venue. Also be aware that many establishments, including all banks, close on public holidays (*see p306*).

Police stations

If you've been robbed, assaulted or involved in an infringement of the law, contact your nearest police station. (We've listed them under 'Resources' in each chapter of this guide; you can also look under 'Police' in the phone book or call Directory Enquiries on 118180.) If you have a complaint about the police, ensure that you take the offending police officer's identifying number (it should be displayed on his or her epaulette). You can then register a complaint with the **Police Complaints Authority** (10 Great George Street, London SW1P 3AE, 020 7273 6450), at any police station or by visiting a solicitor or Law Centre.

Postal services

You can buy stamps at post offices and in many shops and newsagents. Current prices are 20p for second-class letters,

28p for first-class letters and 37p for letters to EU countries. Postcards cost 37p to send within Europe and 40p to countries outside Europe. Rates for other letters and parcels vary according to weight and destination.

DHL (08701 100 300, www.dhl.co.uk) and **FedEx** (0800 123800, www.fedex.com) offer local and international courier services.

Post offices

Post offices are usually open 9am-5.30pm Monday to Friday and 9am-noon Saturday. We've listed post offices for each area under 'Resources' in the relevant chapter. For general post office enquiries, call the central information line on 08457 223344 or consult www.postoffice.co.uk.

Poste restante

If you want to receive mail while you are away, you can have it sent to any major post office counter, where it will be kept at the enquiry desk for a month. Your name and 'Poste Restante' must be clearly marked on the letter, followed by the address of the post office. You'll need ID (such as a passport) to collect it.

Religion

The South West offers the facility for worship for all the major religions and, through places like Glastonbury and Totnes, also has provision for little-practised, obscure faiths. Methodism still has a significant following in parts of Cornwall.

Having said that, non-Anglicans may have to travel out of their way to get to a suitable place of worship; local Tourist Information Centres and council offices should be able to provide the relevant information.

Safety & security

Compared with the rest of the UK, the South West has relatively low crime rates; Devon and Cornwall are two of the safest counties in the country. Suspicion and mistrust are not the watchwords of the day and walking through the streets by yourself can be done in relative security. However, the urban sprawls of Bristol and Plymouth have the usual inner-city problems, with drug-related crimes and street gangs being a particularly problem in parts of Bristol. Rural locations are also not immune from law-breakers, so use common sense and follow these basic rules.

● Keep wallets and purses out of sight, and handbags securely closed.
● Don't leave your belongings unattended, especially in pubs, on public transport, or on the beach.
● Don't wear expensive jewellery that can be easily snatched.
● Don't keep your passport, money, credit cards, etc, together. If you lose one, you'll lose them all.
● Don't carry a wallet in your back pocket, and don't flash money or credit cards around.
● Don't walk alone in badly lit or unpopulated areas at night.

Smoking

Smoking is permitted in almost all pubs and bars, though some may have no-smoking areas. In restaurants you should specify whether you'd like a smoking or no-smoking table. Smoking in hotels is at the establishment's discretion: many hotels will stipulate no smoking in the bedrooms, but will have designated smoking areas in the bar or restaurant. Smoking is forbidden in shops and on public transport.

Study

Higher education

Bath Spa University
Newton Park Campus, Newton St Loe, Bath BA2 9BN (01225 875875/www.bathspa.ac.uk).

Bristol University

Senate House, Tyndall Avenue, Bristol BS8 1TH (0117 928 9000/www.bristol.ac.uk).

Exeter University

Northcote House, The Queen's Drive, Exeter, Devon EX4 4QJ (01392 661000/www.exeter.ac.uk).

Falmouth College of Arts

Woodlane Campus, Falmouth, Cornwall TR11 4RH (01326 211077/www.falmouth.ac.uk).

University of Plymouth

Drake Circus, Plymouth, Devon PL4 8AA (01752 600600/www.plymouth.ac.uk).

University of Bath

Claverton Down, Bath BA2 7AY (01225 388388/www.bath.ac.uk).

University of the West of England

Coldharbour Lane, Bristol BS16 1QY (0117 965 6261/www.uwe.ac.uk).

Useful organisations

BUNAC

16 Bowling Green Lane, London EC1 (020 7251 3472/www.bunac.org.uk). Open 9.30am-5.30pm Mon-Thur; 9.30am-5pm Fri.
Visiting students from the US, Canada, Australia or Jamaica can get a blue BUNAC card, enabling them to work in the UK for up to six months. BUNAC students should obtain an application form OSS1 from BUNAC, which is then submitted to the nearest Jobcentre to obtain permission to work.

Council on International Educational Exchange

Work in Britain Department, 20th floor, 633 3rd Avenue, New York, NY 10017, USA (00 1 212 822 7244/www.ciee.org). Open 9.30am-5.30pm Mon-Fri.
The Council on International Educational Exchange helps young people study, work and travel abroad. It's divided into international study programmes and exchanges.

National Bureau for Students with Disabilities

Chapter House, 18-20 Crucifix Lane, London SE1 (0800 328 5050/textphone 0800 068 2422/www.skill.org.uk). Open Phone enquiries 1.30-4.30pm Mon-Thur.

Directory

Telephones

Throughout this guide, we have listed telephone numbers with their appropriate area code. If you're calling from outside the UK, dial the international access code of the country from where you're calling, then the UK code (44), then the full number, omitting the first 0. For example, to make a call to 0117 954 2426 from the USA, dial 011 44 117 954 2426.

To dial abroad from the UK, first dial 00, then the relevant country code from the list below:

Australia 61; **Austria** 43; **Belgium** 32; **Brazil** 55; **Canada** 1; **Czech Republic** 420; **Denmark** 45; **France** 33; **Germany** 49; **Greece** 30; **Hong Kong** 852; **Iceland** 354; **India** 91; **Ireland** 353; **Israel** 972; **Italy** 39; **Japan** 81; **Netherlands** 31; **New Zealand** 64; **Norway** 47; **Portugal** 351; **South Africa** 27; **Spain** 34; **Sweden** 46; **Switzerland** 41; **USA** 1.

Public phones

Public payphones take coins, credit cards or prepaid phone-cards (sometimes all three). The minimum cost is 20p: this buys a 110-second local call (11p per minute), although some payphones, such as the counter-top ones found in many pubs, charge more.

Operator services

Operator

Call **100** for the operator if you have difficulty in dialling; for an early-morning alarm call; to make a credit card call; for information about the cost of a call; and for help with international person-to-person calls.

Dial **155** if you need to reverse the charges (call collect) or if you can't dial direct, but be warned that this service is very expensive.

Directory enquiries

Dial **118180** to find out any registered phone number in Britain, or **153** for international numbers. Phoning the service from a private line is expensive, and only two enquiries are allowed per call, but the service is free from public call boxes.

Talking Pages

This 24-hour free service lists the numbers of thousands of businesses in the UK. Dial **0800 600900** and say what type of business you require, and in what area.

Telephone directories

Phone directories are available at post offices and libraries, and are issued free to all UK households; hotels should also provide them. The *Yellow Pages* (also accessible online at www.yell.com) gives a list of businesses and services in each area.

Mobile phones

Mobile phones in the UK work on either the 900 or 1800 GSM system. As this is used through much of Europe, it's worth checking whether your service provider has a reciprocal arrangement with a UK-based company. The situation is more complex for travellers from the US, where the GSM system usually runs on the 1900 band. This being the case, US visitors need a reciprocal arrangement with a UK-based provider *and* a tri-band handset in order to make calls in the UK.

The simplest option may be to buy a 'pay as you go' phone when you get to the UK instead (about £40-£200). There's no monthly fee and calls are charged not by billing but by buying (widely available) cards that slot into your phone in denominations of £10 and up. Check before you buy whether the phone is capable of making and receiving international calls.

Telegrams

There is no longer a domestic telegram service, but you can still send telegrams abroad: call 0800 190190. This is also the number to call to send an international telemessage: phone in your message and it will be delivered by post the next day (at a cost of 92p a word, including the recipient's name and address).

Time

The UK operates on Greenwich Mean Time, which is five hours ahead of Eastern Standard time. In spring the UK puts its clocks forward by one hour to British Summer Time (BST). In autumn the clocks go back to GMT.

Tipping

In Britain it's accepted that you tip in taxis, restaurants (some waiting staff rely heavily on tips), top-end hotels, hairdressers and some bars (but never in pubs). Ten per cent is normal, although some restaurants will claim as much as 15 per cent. Always check if service has been included in your bill: some restaurants include service, then leave the space for an additional gratuity on your credit card slip.

Toilets

Public toilets are few and far between, and those that exist may be appallingly scruffy or charge a small fee for the privilege of using them. Pubs and restaurants generally reserve their toilets for customers only.

Tourist information

Tourist Information Centres are located throughout the South West and provide a wealth of information on all aspects of visiting the region. Tourism is a major source of income, and as a result, the flow of information is usually reliable and detailed.

For the address, phone number and website of a particular centre, refer to 'Resources' in the relevant

Directory

area chapter of this guide; for more general tourist information, contact South West Tourism.

UK information
Britain Visitor Centre *1 Regent Street, Piccadilly Circus, London W1 (no phone/www.visitbritain.com).* **Open** *Oct-May* 9.30am-6.30pm Mon; 9am-6.30pm Tue-Fri; 10am-4pm Sat, Sun. *June-Sept* 9.30am-6.30pm Mon; 9am-6.30pm Tue-Fri; 9am-5pm Sat; 10am-4pm Sun.
Heathrow Airport *Terminals 1, 2 & 3 tube station, Heathrow Airport, TW6.* **Open** 8am-6pm daily.

Regional information
South West Tourism
01392 360050/0870 442 0880/ www.westcountrynow.com
The regional tourist board for the South West of England can provide copious information on Bristol, Bath, Somerset, Devon and Cornwall (plus Dorset, Gloucestershire and Wiltshire) including full details of accommodation options and sightseeing attractions. Overseas visitors have their own website (www.visitsouthwestengland.com).

Visas & immigration

Citizens of EU countries don't require a visa to visit the UK; citizens of other countries, including the USA, Canada and New Zealand, require a valid passport for visits of up to six months' duration. The immigration department of

the Home Office deals with queries on immigration, visas and work permits from Commonwealth countries.

To apply for a UK visa, allowing you entry for a maximum of six months, or to check your visa status **before you travel**, contact the British embassy, consulate or high commission in your own country. For information about work permits, *see p306*.

Home Office
Immigration & Nationality Bureau, Lunar House, 40 Wellesley Road, Croydon, Surrey CR9 1AT (0870 606 7766/application forms 0870 241 0645/www.homeoffice.gov.uk). **Open** *Phone enquiries* 9am-4.45pm Mon-Thur; 9am-4.30pm Fri.

Weights & measures

The United Kingdom is gradually moving towards full metrication. Distances are still measured in miles but recent legislation means that all goods are now officially sold in metric quantities, with no legal requirement for the imperial equivalent to be given. The following are some useful conversions.

1 centimetre (cm) = 0.39 inches (in)
1 inch (in) = 2.54 centimetres (cm)
1 yard (yd) = 0.91 metres (m)
1 metre (m) = 1.094 yards (yd)

1 mile = 1.6 kilometres (km)
1 kilometre (km) = 0.62 miles
1 ounce (oz) = 28.35 grammes (g)
1 gramme (g) = 0.035 ounces (oz)
1 pound (lb) = 0.45 kilogrammes (kg)
1 kilogramme (kg) = 2.2 pounds (lb)
1 pint (US) = 0.8 pints (UK)
1 pint (UK) = 0.55 litres (l)
1 litre (l) = 1.75 pints (UK)

When to go

Tourist season in the South West runs from April until the end of October, and is at its peak during the school summer holidays in July and August. At this time expect some incredible increases in price, as everyone clamours to take their holidays when the chances of hot weather are higher. However, plan a trip for autumn or winter and you may well be rewarded with some crisp, sunny days. And although you may not be able to swim in the sea, the coast is likely to be at its most exhilarating when devoid of the summer crowds.

It's inevitable that virtually everywhere is busier in summer, with well-known tourist-pullers like Bath, Torquay, Newquay and Padstow all becoming a little manic at this time. You're unlikely to notice the influx of visitors in Bristol, Exeter and Plymouth, although even these cities are subject to seasonal demand.

Travel advice

For up-to-date information on travelling to a specific country – including the latest news on safety and security, health issues, local laws and customs – contact your home country government's department of foreign affairs. Most have websites packed with useful advice for would-be travellers.

Australia
www.dfat.gov.au/travel

Canada
www.voyage.gc.ca

New Zealand
www.mft.govt.nz/travel

Republic of Ireland
www.irlgov.ie/iveagh

UK
www.fco.gov.uk/travel

USA
www.state.gov/travel

Climate
The British climate is notoriously unpredictable, and the South West, in particular, is well known for its changeable weather. The variety of weather systems and the speed at which they can arrive and depart is likely to catch out all but the most well prepared visitor. Inland and coastal variations do occur, with Dartmoor, Exmoor and Bodmin Moor often subject to more severe winds and heavier rainfall due to their height above sea level.

Directory

Temperature check

Daily temperatures (minimum/maximum) in °C

	Bristol	Exeter	Plymouth	Penzance
Jan	3/8	3/8	3/8	4/10
Feb	3/7	3/8	3/8	5/11
Mar	5/10	3/10	4/9	6/12
Apr	6/12	4/12	5/12	6/14
May	9/17	7/16	8/14	9/16
June	12/19	11/19	11/17	11/18
July	14/22	12/21	13/19	13/20
Aug	14/21	12/21	13/19	14/21
Sept	12/18	10/18	11/17	12/22
Oct	9/14	8/14	9/14	11/17
Nov	6/11	5/11	6/11	11/13
Dec	4/8	4/9	4/9	4/11

Depending on wind direction, one coastline may experience warm weather while the other is subject to much lower temperatures. What's more, many coastal areas enjoy their own microclimate, which can be completely at odds with general weather patterns. Bearing this in mind, you should pack wet-weather gear and some warm clothing at all times of year, and keep an eye on the local weather forecast. For further information, phone Weathercall on 09003 444 900 (60p per min) or consult www.met-office.gov.uk.

Spring extends approximately from March to May, though winter often seems to last well beyond the end of February. May is often very pleasant.

Summer (June, July and August) can be unpredictable, with searing heat one day followed by sultry greyness and thunderstorms the next. High temperatures, humidity and pollution can create problems for anyone with hayfever or breathing difficulties, but you also shouldn't rule out biting winds and heavy rain.

Autumn starts in September, although the weather can still have a mild, summery feel. Real autumn comes with October, when the leaves start to fall. When the November cold sets in, you'll be reminded that the UK is situated on a fairly northerly latitude. Flooding is a particular hazard at this time of year, especially in low-lying parts of Somerset.

Winter may contain the odd mild day, but don't bank on it. December, January and February are usually pretty chilly, although snow is rare except on the most exposed parts of Dartmoor and Exmoor.

Public holidays

On public holidays (widely known as bank holidays), many shops remain open, but public transport services generally run to a Sunday timetable. The exception is Christmas Day, when almost everything shuts.

New Year's Day 1 Jan.
Good Friday Fri 18 Apr 2003; Fri 9 Apr 2004; Fri 25 Mar 2005.
Easter Monday Mon 21 Apr 2003; Mon 12 Apr 2004; Mon 28 Mar 2005.
May Day Holiday Mon 5 May 2003; Mon 3 May 2004; Mon 2 May 2005
Spring Bank Holiday Mon 26 May 2003; Mon 31 May 2004; Mon 30 May 2005.
Summer Bank Holiday Mon 25 Aug 2003; Mon 30 Aug 2004; Mon 29 Aug 2005.
Christmas Day 25 Dec.
Boxing Day 26 Dec.

Working in the South West

Finding temporary work in the South West can be a full-time job in itself. Those with a reasonable level of English who are EU citizens or have work permits may find work in catering, labouring, bars, or shops. Much of the work is seasonal by nature, and comes and goes with the tourist trade and harvest time. Graduates with an English or foreign-language degree could try teaching. Other ideas can be found in publications by the Council on Educational Exchange (*see p303*).

Locally, check newspapers, newsagents' windows and Jobcentre noticeboards; the nearest Jobcentre can be found under 'Employment Agencies' in the *Yellow Pages*.

Work permits

With a few exceptions, citizens of non-European Economic Area (EEA) countries have to have a work permit before they can legally work in the United Kingdom. Employers who are unable to fill particular vacancies with a resident or EEA national must apply for a permit to the Department for Education & Employment (*see below*). Students from the US, Canada, Australia or Jamaica should contact BUNAC (*see p303*).

Working holidaymakers

Citizens of Commonwealth countries aged 17-27 may apply to come to the UK as a working holidaymaker without a DfEE permit by contacting their nearest British Diplomatic Post in advance.

Department for Education & Employment *Work Permits UK helpline (0114 259 4074/ www.workpermits.gov.uk)*. **Open** *Phone enquiries* 9am-5pm Mon-Fri.

Home Office *Immigration & Nationality Directorate, Lunar House, 40 Wellesley Road, Croydon, Surrey CR9 2BY (0870 606 7766/ www.ind.homeoffice.gov.uk)*. **Open** *Phone enquiries* 9am-4.45pm Mon-Thur; 9am-4.30pm Fri.

Overseas Visitors Records Office *180 Borough High Street, London SE1 (020 7230 1208)*. **Open** 9am-4.30pm Mon-Fri.

Directory

Further Reference

Fiction

Ackroyd, Peter *Chatterton*
Tragi-comic satire based on
the short life of the young
Bristol poet and forger
Thomas Chatterton.

Austen, Jane *Northanger
Abbey* Catherine Morland
learns about life, love and
novels in Georgian Bath.

Austen, Jane *Persuasion*
Austen's last complete novel
combines a gentle, almost
melancholy, love story with
well-observed social satire, with
several chapters set in Bath.

Barker, Nicola *Five Miles
from Outer Hope* Quirky
appealing novel about a
16-year-old misfit growing
up in the Burgh Island Hotel.

Beer, Patricia *Moon's
Ottery* Romance and intrigue
in an East Devon village at the
time of the Spanish Armada.

Blackmore, RD *Lorna
Doone* A romantic,
melodramatic tale of 17th-
century brigands on Exmoor.

Doyle, Arthur Conan
The Hound of the Baskervilles
A chilling Sherlock Holmes
mystery set on Dartmoor.

Du Maurier, Daphne
Frenchman's Creek
Restoration love story set on
the Helford River, with plenty
of swashbuckling action.

Du Maurier, Daphne
Jamaica Inn Pacy smuggling
tale set on Bodmin Moor.

Du Maurier, Daphne
Rebecca Gripping tale of a
timid second wife living in
the shadow of her formidable
predecessor – the mysterious
'first Mrs de Winter'.

Fielding, Henry *Tom Jones*
An 18th-century romp,
following the eponymous
hero on adventures from
Somerset to London.

Graham, Winston *Poldark*
A family saga in ten novels
set around Perranporth and St
Agnes in the late 18th century.
Filmed as a hugely successful
TV series in the 1970s.

Gregory, Philippa
A Respectable Trade Bristol's
18th-century slave trade
provides the context for a love
story between the wife of an
English slave trader and an
African in domestic service.

Hardy, Thomas *A Pair
of Blue Eyes* A tragic tale of
love and class conflict, partly
based on Hardy's courtship of
his first wife in Cornwall.

Kipling, Rudyard
Stalkey & Co Kipling's
experiences of public school
in North Devon come to life
in nine tales.

Lawrence, DH *Kangaroo*
Semi-autobiographical story of
how the Lawrences were forced
to flee Cornwall in World War I
on suspicion of spying.

Masefield, John *Jim Davis*
A smuggling tale set in 19th-
century Devon.

Pilcher, Rosamund *The
Shell Seekers* Hugely popular
novel about three generations
of the Keeling family in
Cornwall and London.

Powys, John Cowper
A Glastonbury Romance
Sweeping epic set in the
mystical Somerset town.

Quiller-Couch, Arthur
The Delectable Duchy Short
stories set in Fowey (loosely
disguised as Troy Town) at
the end of the 19th century.

Waugh, Evelyn *Brideshead
Revisited* Waugh mourns the
passing of the English
aristocratic way of life.

Wesley, Mary *The
Camomile Lawn* Set on the
Roseland peninsula, this
novel interweaves the lives
of three families during and
after World War II.

Williamson, Henry *Tarka
the Otter* One of the most
evocative pieces of nature
writing in the English language.

Woolf, Virginia *To the
Lighthouse* Set on a Hebridean
island, this novel is shot
through with Woolf's memories
of family holidays in St Ives
and has Godrevy Lighthouse
as its central symbol.

Non-fiction

Betjeman, John *Betjeman's
Cornwall* Prose and poetry
musings on the life, landscape
and architecture of the poet
laureate's favourite county.

Burton, SH *The West
Country* A powerful, personal
overview of the area by a well-
regarded local history writer.

Cross, Tom *Catching
the Wave: Art & Artists in
Contemporary Cornwall*
A great introduction to the
Cornish art scene.

Du Maurier, Daphne
Vanishing Cornwall An
overview of Cornish life by the
popular 20th-century novelist.

**Robinson, Derek and
Wiltshire, Vic** *Krek Waiter
Speke Bristle/A Load of Ole
Bristle* Illustrated guide to the
hilarity of the Bristol accent.

Rowse, AL *A Cornish
Childhood* An autobiography
covering the eminent
historian's early life in
Cornwall in the early 1900s.

Sager, Peter *The West
Country* Entertaining, wide-
ranging and idiosyncratic
guide to the region (including
Wiltshire and Dorset), with
plenty of historical and
cultural anecdotes.

Seal, Jeremy *The Wreck at
Sharpnose Point* Engrossing
piece of historical detective
work, as the author attempts to
trace the crew of the *Caledonia,*
wrecked on the coast near
Morwenstow in the 1800s.

Directory

Poetry

Beer, Patricia *Collected Poems* Straightforward poems by the Devon-born writer that conceal an edge of humour.

Betjeman, John *Collected Poems* The laureate's poetry includes many references to and his beloved Cornwall.

Causley, Charles *Collected Poems* Contemporary Cornish ballads.

Chaucer, Geoffrey 'Prologue to the Wife of Bath's Tale' Chaucer's polygamous pilgrim is one of the raunchiest creations in the *Canterbury Tales*.

Coleridge, Samuel Taylor *Selected Poems* Some of the Devon-born poet's most enduring work (including 'Kubla Khan', 'Rime of the Ancient Mariner' and 'Frost at Midnight') was written in and inspired by the Quantock Hills and Exmoor.

Eliot, TS 'East Coker' The second of *The Four Quartets* evokes the Somerset village where the poet's ancestors lived before emigrating to America.

Hardy, Thomas *Poems 1912-1913* An ageing Hardy reflects on youth and love in Cornwall.

Tennyson, Alfred *In Memoriam* Written in memory of his friend Arthur Hallam, this elegy is one of the greatest poetic explorations of the nature of faith and religious doubt.

Film

The Belstone Fox (1973) A sort of foxy *Black Beauty* set on Dartmoor, starring a young Dennis Waterman and Bill Travers in a tale about what happens when you mess with the natural order of things.

Blue Juice (1995) Sean Pertwee, Catherine Zeta Jones and Ewan McGregor live the surfing life in North Cornwall.

Chicken Run (2001) Feature-length animation from the makers of Wallace and Gromit.

The Hound of the Baskervilles (1939) Basil Rathbone super-sleuths his way around Dartmoor in this classic Holmes mystery.

Land Girls (1997) The West Somerset Railway is just one of several South West locations used in this film of three girls working on farms in the West Country during World War II.

Rebecca (1940) Daphne Du Maurier's tale becomes a masterly Hitchcock movie with Laurence Olivier and Joan Fontaine.

The Remains of the Day (1993) Shot at Powderham Castle in Devon, this film shows Anthony Hopkins in fine form as the repressed butler struggling to deal with his master's Nazi sympathies and his own emotions.

Saving Grace (2000) Gently humourous film set in Cornwall about a widow who tries to clear her debts by growing marijuana.

Sense & Sensibility (1995) Filmed on location at Saltram House in Devon, this hugely successful adaptation of the Austen classic features Emma Thompson and Kate Winslet as the Dashwood sisters.

Straw Dogs (1971) Recently re-released controversial film about a mild American university researcher who erupts into violence in a Cornish village.

Swept from the Sea (1996) Based on a Joseph Conrad short story, the film tells the tale of a Russian vessel shipwrecked near an isolated Cornish village in the 19th century. Filmed on location around Cornwall.

The War Zone (1999) Harrowing film based on the novel by Alexander Stuart about incest and family breakdown in rural Devon.

www.carfreedaysout.com Comprehensive online guide to public transport, cycling routes and walking trails in Somerset, Devon and Cornwall.

www.cornishfish.co.uk Cornish Fish Direct's website – freshly caught Newlyn fish delivered straight to your door.

www.dartmoor-npa.gov.uk Official National Park website.

www.english-heritage. org.uk Information about historic sites run by English Heritage.

www.englishtourism.co.uk Official tourist board website with links to other useful online resources, including the comprehensive www.travelengland.co.uk

www.exmoor-nationalpark.gov.uk All you need to know about the National Park.

www.goodbeachguide. co.uk Marine Conservation Society's guide to the best beaches in the UK, based on strict water-quality testing standards.

www.nationaltrust.org.uk Information on all the National Trust's properties.

www.sieved.co.uk/bristol/ Youth-oriented site with listings and articles about Bristol.

www.6ftoffshore.com Regularly updated surf reports provided by 'scouts' at surfing sites around the country.

www.sw-watersports.com All about sailing, surfing, waterskiing and windsurfing in the South West.

www.surfwax.co.uk Devoted to beach-based sports in Devon and Cornwall.

www.venue.co.uk Online version of the Bristol and Bath listings magazine.

www.westcountrynow. com The official South West Tourism website.

Directory

Index

Index

Advertisers' Index

Please refer to relevant pages for full details